ONE-HIT WONDERS

EDITED BY BILL NOWLIN

ASSOCIATE EDITORS LEN LEVIN AND CARL RIECHERS

Society for American Baseball Research, Inc.
Phoenix, AZ

One-Hit Wonders

Edited by Bill Nowlin
Associate editors Len Levin and Carl Riechers

Society for American Baseball Research, Inc.
Phoenix, AZ

Copyright page copy:
One-Hit Wonders
Edited by Bill Nowlin
Associate editors Len Levin and Carl Riechers

Copyright © 2021 Society for American Baseball Research, Inc.
All rights reserved. Reproduction in whole or in part without permission is prohibited.
978-1-970159-56-1 One-Hit Wonders ebook
978-1-970159-57-8 One-Hit Wonders paper
Library of Congress Control Number: 2021915561
Front cover image by Dreamstime
Back cover images depict the actual baseballs hit for base hits by Larry Ray, Cory Aldridge, and Dana Williams.

Book design: Rachael E. Sullivan
All baseball card images courtesy of the Topps Company, unless otherwise noted. Thanks to Michael and Linda Hanks, and to Bruce Erricson for images supplied.
Copyright © 2021 Society for American Baseball Research, Inc.
All rights reserved. Reproduction in whole or in part without permission is prohibited.
Cronkite School at ASU
555 N. Central Ave. #416
Phoenix, AZ 85004
Phone: (602) 496-1460
Web: www.sabr.org
Facebook: Society for American Baseball Research
Twitter: @SABR

CONTENTS

1. ONE-HIT WONDERS 5
   By Bill Nowlin

2. CORY ALDRIDGE 10
   By Tony S. Oliver

3. HUGH ALEXANDER 15
   By Brian Flaspohler

4. DAN ARDELL 21
   By Bill Nowlin

5. JEFF BANISTER 26
   By Benjamin Sabin

6. VINCE BELNOME 29
   By Darren Gibson

7. TIM BIRTSAS 32
   By Steve Friedman

8. JEFF BITTIGER 36
   By Joel Rippel

9. FRANK BOYD 40
   By Chad Moody

10. MATT BROWN 45
    By Joel Rippel

11. CRAIG CACEK 48
    By Max Effgen

12. CARLOS CASIMIRO 53
    By Malcolm Allen

13. GUSTAVO CHACIN 58
    By Tony S. Oliver

14. DOUG CLAREY 62
    By Joe Schuster

15. VIBERT CLARKE 65
    By Mitch Lutzke

16. KEN CROSBY 68
    By Tom Hawthorn

17. JASON DAVIS 71
    By Max Effgen

18. RAOUL "ROD" DEDEAUX 76
    By Richard Cuicchi

19. JIM DERRINGTON 81
    By Don Zminda

20. ALEX GEORGE 85
    By Joel Rippel

21. EDDIE GERNER 88
    By Jack V. Morris

22. FRED GLADDING 92
    By Paul Hofmann

23. ROY GLEASON 97
    By Charlie Bevis

24. ED GLENN 103
    By Mike Cooney

25. KEITH GORDON 109
    By Tim Deale

26. BOBBY GUINDON 113
    By Bill Nowlin

27. JOHN LOUIS HAIRSTON SR. 119
    By Richard Cuicchi

28. BILL HARMAN 123
    By Niall Adler

29. AARON HEILMAN 129
    By Peter Seidel

30. CHRIS JELIC 133
    By Tara Krieger

31. STAN JOHNSON 141
    By Alan Cohen

32. ED KENNA 145
    By Phil Williams

33. JOHN LEOVICH 151
    By Eric Vickrey

34. DAVE LIDDELL 155
    By Alan Raylesberg

35. ERNIE LINDEMANN 159
    By Phil Williams

36. CHUCK LINDSTROM 165
    By Richard Bogovich

37. RED LUTZ 172
    By Bob Webster

38. EMIL MAILHO 175
    By Dan Schoenholz

39. DAVID MATRANGA 180
    By Joel Rippel

40. SPARROW MCCAFFREY 183
    By Bob LeMoine

41. ROGER HORNSBY MCKEE 185
    By Jack Zerby

42. BILL MILLS 190
    By John Heeg

43. FRANK MILLS 193
    By Mike Cooney

44. GUY MORRISON 200
    By Bob LeMoine

45. AL NAPLES 203
    By Bill Nowlin

46. TITO NAVARRO 208
    By Rory Costello

47. CURLY ONIS 212
    by Mike Huber

48. STEVE ONTIVEROS 216
    By Clayton Trutor

49. BILL PETERMAN 219
    By Chris Rainey

50. DAN PLESAC 223
    By Paul Hofmann

51. BOB POSER 228
    By Henry Berman, MD

52. AL RAFFO 234
    By Brian C. Engelhardt

53. LARRY RAY 240
    By Mike Cooney

54. ARTHUR RHODES 246
    By Ryan Brecker

55. EDDY RODRIGUEZ 250
    By Gerard Kwilecki

56. ROBERTO RODRIGUEZ 254
    (A/K/A ROBERTO MUÑOZ)
    By Tony S. Oliver

57. FRANK SAUCIER 258
    By Jim Ball

58. SCOTT SERVICE 264
    By Len Pasculli

59. ROE SKIDMORE 269
    By Rory Costello

60. CHARLIE SNOW 275
    By Mike Cooney

61. JOE STAPLES 277
    By Bill Staples Jr.

62. TOM SULLIVAN 283
    By Mike Mattsey

63. CLAY TOUCHSTONE 287
    By Joe Schuster

64. MATT TUPMAN 294
    By Bill Nowlin

65. FRED WATERS 299
    By Jeff English

66. DANA WILLIAMS 305
    By Tony S. Oliver

67. LES WILLIS 310
    By Joel Rippel

68. KID WILLSON 314
    By Bob Webster

69. GEORGE YANTZ 318
    By Tim Hagerty

70. JOE ZAPUSTAS 323
    By Mike Mattsey

71. ED ZMICH 326
    By Gregory H. Wolf

72. CONTRIBUTORS 330

ONE-HIT WONDERS

By Bill Nowlin

The idea for this book came from an interview I conducted with Bobby Guindon on February 23, 2018. His one hit was a double for the Boston Red Sox on September 27, 1964. With eight career at-bats, Guindon holds a .125 career batting average. In the course of the interview, he mentioned that he had been featured in a book titled *One-Hit Wonders*. I looked it up online and bought a copy. It was written (and I believe self-published) by George Rose in 2004.[1] The book noted a website and provided an email address. Fourteen years later, neither of them worked.

Rose said there had been "approximately 200 players in the one hit wonder club" and his book provided capsule stories on 75 of them. He said there were an additional 104 listed at the end of the book – but he must have forgotten to include the promised list. It isn't there. I have a 2009 edition of the book; perhaps it was included in the 2004 edition but omitted in the later one.

In any event, when I asked Tom Ruane of Retrosheet if he could prepare a list for me, he came up with 1,389 names. His list embraced the years 1875 through 2017. The resulting list ran from Fernando Abad to Ed Zmich. Abad, a relief pitcher, appeared in 363 major-league games from 2010 with Houston to 2017 with the Red Sox; his record was 8-27. He batted only nine times, with one hit in 2012. He did pitch for the San Francisco Giants again, in 2019, and got into 21 games but never had even one plate appearance.[2] Zmich, a left-handed pitcher like Abad, had a career that had started exactly 100 years earlier than Abad's, in 1910 for the St. Louis Cardinals. He relieved in seven games and started in six; his record was 1-5 (though he was undefeated 1-0 in 1911 after an 0-5 first year). He eked out one base hit in 17 at-bats. Zmich also drove in a run, but in a different game.

Rose's book didn't include any players prior to 1930. It's not clear why.

Looking only at the list Tom sent, there were exactly 500 "one-hit wonder" players before 1930. But many of them were pitchers. If Rose's mission was only to look at position players, and only for the years 1930 through, say, 2004, one comes up with a figure that is indeed around 200.

All in all, there are no small number of major leaguers who produced one hit – and only one hit – in the course of their major-league careers. Some had very brief careers. Some had longer ones. There were 69 players who had only one plate appearance. And produced a base hit in that one opportunity. There are 90 players through 2018 who appear to have retired with a lifetime 1.000 batting average.[3]

Of course, that means that of the 1,389 one-hit wonders, some 1,320 players had more than one opportunity. Fred Gladding had 68 plate appearances (and 63 at-bats) but had only the one base hit. It's probably not surprising that Gladding was a pitcher, and that he played in the days before the DH, but he had a long career, pitching in 13 seasons from 1961 through 1973. His one hit came in his ninth year. It was a single for the Astros in the first game of a July 30, 1969, doubleheader against the Mets, an RBI single in the top of the ninth inning. It seems he caught the Mets bullpen at just the right time. His run batted in was the fifth of 11 runs scored that inning.

The nonpitcher with the most plate appearances was center fielder Skeeter Shelton of the 1915 New York Yankees. He played in 10 games, stepped into the batter's box 43 times, and got a single in the sixth of his 10 games, the second game of an August 28 doubleheader in Detroit. He was 1-for-7 that day (and 1-for-40 in his career.)

Second least-productive for a position player was third baseman Bill McNulty, who played for Oakland in 1969 (17 plate appearances – 10 of them resulting in strikeouts – and no hits) and again in 1973 in the final game of his career, a single off Nolan Ryan. He had 12 plate appearances in 1973, for a total of 29.

Others (all of them pitchers) who had 50 or more plate appearances: Wei-Yin Chen (64), Aaron Heilman (54), Rick van den Hurk (54), and Will Sawyer (50).

ONE-HIT WONDERS

We have to knock Chen off our list, however. He collected six base hits in 2018.

Some of the one-hit wonders had a home run as their one hit. In fact, 22 of them did. Of the 22, 13 of them were pitchers. Not all of them had careers that ended in 2017. Nolan Fontana, for instance, was a second baseman with the Angels who homered in the ninth inning of the May 26 game in Miami; the Angels lost, 8-5. He continued to play in 2018 and had the misfortune (?) of getting one more base hit. He's now a two-hit wonder and will not be mentioned again in this book.

Let's look at a few other stats:

Tripled for their only base hit: There were 22 such players. Fourteen were pitchers.

Doubled for their only base hit: There were more, as one would expect, than those who tripled for their only hit. In fact, 179 players counted a double as their only hit. Bobby Guindon and 178 others. Of the 179, 108 of them were pitchers.

Runs batted in: There are obviously numerous ways to drive in a run without a base hit. Walk (or get hit by a pitch) with the bases loaded. Hit a sacrifice fly. Hit into a fielder's choice. A pitcher, Gene Woodburn of the 1911-12 Detroit Tigers, collected four RBIs, but had only one base hit (it was not a grand slam.) There were 13 different players who each had three RBIs but also only one base hit. Only one of them – Mark Worrell – hit a homer and drove in three. It's perhaps of some marginal interest that there were also two brothers named Worrell who were both pitchers. Todd had two base hits in his career; his brother Tim had eight. Some 69 batters drove in two runs (not necessarily all with their one base hit, of course.)

Other players with three RBIs are Frank Boyd, Matthew Brown, Carlos Casimiro, Webbo Clarke, Ensign Cottrell, Ed Gerner, Fred Gladding, Steve Ontiveros, Pat Paige, Al Raffo, Tony Tonneman, and Fred Waters.

Runs scored: One could score hundreds of runs without even getting one base hit. Just keep walking, getting hit by pitches, reaching on errors, etc., and then get driven in. Don Hopkins of the 1975 and 1976 Oakland A's scored 25 runs but had just one hit. He was, perhaps not surprisingly, often a pinch-runner. Hopkins appeared in 85 games, but played a position (outfielder) in only 21 of them. He had only eight plate appearances, and just the one base hit. The hit came in his 60th game – a single to lead off the eighth inning in a July 22, 1975, game at Detroit. He was forced at second base on a subsequent at-bat. It was not a great loss; the A's held a 16-4 lead at the time.

MULTIPLE TEAMS

Many of the players in question played for only one team and were not of lengthy tenure with their team. There were 29 position players who saw duty with more than one team. Only one of them – Ed Glenn, a shortstop – played for three teams. There were 29 who played with two teams. Of those, eight (including Mr. Glenn) played all or some of the time in the nineteenth century.

Three pitchers played for an astonishing 11 different teams: Roberto Hernandez, Scott Service, and Trever Miller. Five others played for 10 teams: Dana Eveland, Doug Jones, Gregg Olson, Jim Poole, and Arthur Rhodes. All in all, there were 15 pitchers who worked for eight or more teams and collected only one base hit. (Oddly, both Olson and Poole were on the 1995 Cleveland Indians team – though Olson's base hit came for the 1998 Diamondbacks while Poole's was for the San Francisco Giants, also in 1998.)

FREQUENCY OF THE OCCURRENCE

By decade, looking at the year the player in question began his career, we find the following number of one-hit wonders

- 1871-1880: 31 (but we counted only players who played in the years 1876 through 1880)
- 1881-1890: 89
- 1891-1900: 60
- 1901-1910: 103
- 1911-1920: 122
- 1921-1930: 99
- 1931-1940: 62
- 1941-1950: 84
- 1951-1960: 78
- 1961-1970: 72
- 1971-1980: 84
- 1981-1990: 96
- 1991-2000: 138
- 2001-2010: 160

One sees increases during the decade when the American League began and during the years 1911-1920 when the Federal League made its appearance in two of those years, but when there was again an increase in the sheer number of players. And once the designated hitter came in and American League

ONE-HIT WONDERS

pitchers did not need to bat, we see another increase. We can see that teams simply turned over players on the 25-man roster more quickly in the latter two decades.

GETTING A HIT, OR GETTING HIT, IN YOUR FIRST AT-BAT

Dave Liddell seems to have spent a total of maybe 20 seconds in a major-league batter's box. On June 3, 1990, he was playing for the New York Mets. The Mets were at Veterans Stadium playing the Phillies that Sunday afternoon. The Phillies held an 8-1 lead after seven innings. So manager Bud Harrelson decided to give the kid a shot; Liddell was 12 days short of turning 24. Harrelson had him pinch-hit for catcher Mackey Sasser, leading off the top of the eighth. Liddell was to face the starter, lefty Pat Combs. He stepped into the box and swung at the first pitch. It was a groundball that skipped between shortstop and second and into center field. A walk pushed Liddell to second. He tagged and took third base on a fly ball to right, and then he ran home and scored on a wild pitch. He caught in the bottom of the eighth and when Mets pitcher Julio Machado struck out Tom Herr, Liddell recorded a putout in the only chance he had. He was in the on-deck circle when the third out was recorded in the top of the ninth. He never appeared in another major-league game. He'd seen only one pitch, but collected a base hit (and scored), and he can boast a 1.000 fielding percentage to go with his 1.000 batting average, 1.000 on-base percentage, and 1.000 slugging percentage.

It's one thing to get into one game only and collect a base hit. But we've also seen Fred Gladding, who similarly had one base hit but in 63 at-bats, giving him a career batting average of .016.

Clearly, not everyone gets a base hit in his first at-bat. For Gladding, it was actually his 50th plate appearance. Forty-nine previous times he'd stepped into the batter's box and failed to get a hit. He'd never walked, either. There were only two times he'd reached base, on a sacrifice hit in 1965 and another in 1967. When he did get his hit, it came with the bases loaded. He drove in one run.

Dana Williams came up to bat for the very first time – and got hit by a pitch. It was the top of the ninth on June 19, 1989, the Red Sox playing in Chicago. The White Sox were winning, 8-2. There was one out and nobody on base. Donn Pall was pitching for Chicago. Williams pinch-hit for Randy Kutcher. And Pall hit him with his first pitch. The next batter lined the ball into short right field, and it was fielded swiftly enough that Williams was forced at second base. It was his first time at bat – in the fifth game in which he appeared – that he collected his one and only hit, a double to left field at Fenway Park. In all, he appeared in eight games, with six plate appearances.

COLLECTING ONE HIT IN ONE AND ONLY ONE PLATE APPEARANCE

There are 69 players whose career at the plate consisted of only one plate appearance – and they got a base hit. Because these plate appearances resulted in a base hit, each of the plate appearances was by definition also an at-bat. Some 49 of them were pitchers, eight were catchers, two were second basemen, two were third basemen, and two were right fielders. Six of them have no designated position. They appeared as pinch-hitters but played no position.

Roy Gleason of the Dodgers had a unique experience. He came to the plate only once, but scored three runs. Gleason appeared in eight games in 1963. The first seven times, he was inserted as a pinch-runner. Only in his eighth appearance did he come to bat. He doubled, and later scored.

THE SPAN OF CAREER YEARS FOR ONE-HIT WONDERS

It's one thing to get a base hit in your first at-bat. It's another thing to serve as a major-league ballplayer for years and only once get a hit. Arthur Rhodes, for instance, had a big-league career spanning 21 seasons, from 1991 to 2011. He was, of course, a pitcher, and an American League pitcher at that. Rhodes didn't pitch in every one of those 21 seasons. He was out during 2007. But he did pitch in 20 of them, appearing in 900 games. One hit in 900 games. Over all those years, he came to bat only six times. He had seven seasons under his belt, and then came 1998. In an interleague game against the Phillies, Rhodes came to bat in the top of the sixth and struck out. He stayed in the game and came up again in the top of the seventh and singled up the middle into center field. And then he played in 12 more seasons, without another hit.

Doug Jones played in 16 seasons – with one hit. Dan Plesac and Clay Touchstone each played over a span of 18 seasons; they each had one hit. In Touchstone's case, though, he played in only three seasons, 1928, 1929, and 1945. Roberto Hernandez, Scott Service, and Bobby Tiefenauer pitched for, respectively, 17 seasons, 12 seasons, and 10 seasons with one base hit apiece.

ONE-HIT WONDERS

In all, there are 65 players – all pitchers – who played in a span of 11 or more seasons with just one base hit. Another 15 played over the course of 10 or more seasons. There were two non-pitchers. Kid Willson was one such player. He first played in 1918 for the Chicago White Sox, with three plate appearances and no hits. He spent years in the minors and out of baseball, reappearing in the majors in 1927 (again with the White Sox). This time, having gone all those years, he collected a base hit in his first game. On May 20, he pinch-hit in a game the White Sox were losing 11-1. He lined out to left field. Willson stayed in the game, playing left field himself. Second time up, he reached on a fielder's choice, and later scored. He lined out to first base his third time up, and then he singled to left field in the bottom of the ninth.

The other nonpitcher whose career spanned 10 years was Cory Aldridge. He also saw big-league duty in just two seasons, with eight years in between. Aldridge broke in during the 2001 season with the Atlanta Braves. By the time he was elevated to the majors in September 2001, Aldridge had already accumulated 432 base hits in the minor leagues. With the Braves, he had five at-bats but no base hits. It was back to the minors in 2002. In the years 2002 through 2009, he added 800 more base hits in minor-league ball. That's a total of 1,232 base hits in the minors, but he was still hoping to return to the majors. He was brought up to the big leagues again in July 2010 – this time with the Angels – for a little more than a week. He got his one hit in the fourth of the five games in which he appeared. He had 95 hits for Salt Lake in 2010, so add those in, too. In his professional career, which also included the Mexican League, Venezuelan League, and Korean baseball, he had 1,980 base hits – one of which was his hit in the major leagues.

AGE OF THE BATTER

Jerry Hurley, catcher with the 1901 Cincinnati Reds, born in 1875.

Lon Ury, first baseman for the 1903 St. Louis Cardinals, born in 1877.

Blaine Thomas, right-handed pitcher for the 1911 Boston Red Sox, born in 1888.

Hurley was thus 25 or 26 years old at the time of his base hit. Ury was the same – 25 or 26. And Thomas was 23 or 24. They are far from the youngest, though. There are 33 players our list who were teenagers at the time of their hit. The six youngest are:

Jim Derrington (1956) – 16 years and 305 days
Alex George (1955) – 16 years and 358 days
Roger McKee (1943, 1944) – 17 years and 18 days
Ed Fuller (1886) – 17 years and 117 days
Vern Freiburger (1941) – 17 years and 269 days
Mike Loan (1912) – 17 years and 356 days

There were seven players who were 18 years old, and 20 who were 19. Fourteen of the 33 were pitchers, but the other 19 were not.

Who was the oldest?

Oddly, there are two players tied for the honor. Improbably, they both played for the same team and could have served as a battery.

Les Willis (1947), a pitcher for the Cleveland Indians, was 39 years and 136 days old.

Quincy Trouppe (1952), a catcher for the Indians, was also 39 years and 136 days old.

During World War II, Phillies outfielder Lee Riley was 37 years and 252 days old. There were four players (all pitchers) who were 36: from oldest to youngest, they are: Otho Nitcholas (1944), Dan Quisenberry (1989), Doug Jones (1994), and Tim Harikkala (2007). Everyone else on the list was aged 20 through 35.

DINING OUT ON THEIR DAY OF GLORY

Messrs. George and Derrington intrigued us, which is the reason we have included both in this book.

Alex George got his base hit on September 20, 1955. As of Opening Day of the 2021 season, it had been more than 65 years that he's been dining out on his day of glory. Jim Derrington's hit came almost exactly a year later – September 30, 1956.

Imagine being a local celebrity treated to a drink at a local tavern on the strength of your hit in the big leagues. If Alex George had been treated once a day since September 1955, that would be more than 23,000 drinks on the house.

If each drink were a 12-ounce drink, that would be 276,000 ounces of beverage, or 2,156 gallons.

Roger McKee is included in this book, too.

The "one-hit wonder" who lived the longest after recording his one hit was Bill Otis. The center fielder played in four games in a three-day stretch for the 1912 Yankees (still officially named the Highlanders at the time). On July 5 in Washington, Otis singled. He had his major-league base hit. And he hit it off Walter Johnson, no less! New York finished in last place that year, and won none of the four games in which Otis appeared. He was 1-for-17. He'd been born the day before Christmas in 1889; he died just nine days before his 101st birthday. From the date of his base hit

ONE-HIT WONDERS

to the date he died, he had enjoyed the memory for 78 years and 163 days.

Bill Mills gave Otis a run for his money. Another Bay State-born ballplayer (Mills was born in Boston on November 2, 1919), Mills got his lone hit for the Philadelphia Athletics in his first plate appearance, on May 19, 1944. He stepped to the plate four other times, hitless, but he did work a walk on May 28. As of his death on August 9, 2019, Mr. Mills had lived 75 years and 83 days.

WHERE WERE THE ONE-HIT WONDERS BORN?

Most of them were born in the United States, which should come as no surprise. A listing of one-hit players from 1871 through 2018 totals 1,372 names. Of these, 82 played in 2018 – but none of the foreign-born ones got a hit in either 2019 or 2020. Leaving that aside for now, all but 151 of the players listed were born in the USA. Puerto Rico was listed separately; there are also 18 Puerto Rican natives who are one-hit wonders.

The other countries represented by one-hit wonders are, in descending order:

Dominican Republic	49	(Enny Romero was on the 2017 list but got a hit in 2018, however. Dennis Santana got one in 2019, and Freddy Peralta got two in 2019)
Venezuela	28	(Ranger Suarez got a hit in 2019)
Canada	17	(Mike Soroka got four hits in 2019)
Cuba	15	
Mexico	9	
Panama	6	
Japan	5	
England	4	
Germany	4	
Australia	2	
Ireland	2	
South Korea	2	

...and then one each from the following countries:

Aruba	(pitcher Calvin Maduro,, 1997)
Austria-Hungary	(pitcher Joe Hovlik, 1911)
Czechoslovakia	(third baseman John Stedronsky, 1879)
France	(pitcher Duke Markell, 1951)
Italy	(pitcher Lou Polli, 1932)
Latvia	(outfielder Joe Zapustas, 1933)
Netherlands	(pitcher Rick van den Hurk, 2007)
Nicaragua	(pitcher Porfi Altamirano, 1982)
Northern Ireland	(pitcher P. J. Conlon, 2018)
Philippines	(pitcher Bobby Chouinard, 2008)
Russia	(pitcher Jake Livingston, 1901)
Sweden	(pitcher Axel Lindstrom, 1916)

There are 13 names of players that do not show a country of birth; all are from the nineteenth century. There is one Smith and one Jones, two named Quinn and one named Quinlan. Seven of them are known only by their last name; we don't know their first name. If someone is sufficiently inspired and able to learn a few of them, that would be nice for baseball history.

There comes a point when it's time to stop. I don't think we need to know the shortest player, or the tallest player, with just one hit. Or work off the listed weight of players.

As indicated, this book was first conceived in February 2018. Tom Ruane's first listing was prepared in April. By June 2018, we started signing up authors. And in April 2019, Anthony Castrovince of MLB.com picked up on one aspect of the story with an article, "They had 1 career AB, 1 career hit. Nothing else."[4] In a way, it's surprising not more attention has been accorded these players. We hope this SABR book will help give some of them a little more attention and respect. They did, after all, accomplish something almost every reader of this book (if only in an idle moment) likely once dreamed of doing.

NOTES

1. https://www.amazon.com/One-Hit-Wonders-Baseball-Stories/dp/059531807X/ref=sr_1_fkmrnull_1?keywords=one+hit+wonders+-George+Rose&qid=1555082577&s=books&sr=1-1-fkmrnull

2. As this book goes to the designer, Abad is in spring training in 2021 with the Baltimore Orioles. There still might come a time in which he bats, and gets a second base hit.

3. One keeps open the possibility that one of these may yet return in 2021 or later and make an out.

4. https://www.mlb.com/news/mlb-ultimate-one-hit-wonders

CORY ALDRIDGE

By Tony S. Oliver

Explorer Juan Ponce de León was way off. More than five centuries before Global Positioning Systems became commonplace, his obsession with the mythical fountain of youth took him from the Spanish Caribbean colonies to the still unexplored Floridian peninsula, where he met his demise when the natives did not take kindly to his quest. In hindsight, perhaps he should have looked higher up the North American continent, especially in the Northeast. Maybe water did not hold the secret to eternal youth, but rather the green grass of a freshly mown outfield and the crisp dirt of a manicured infield. Dozens of players, from Cooperstown immortals Tim Raines and Rickey Henderson to veterans eager for one last shot like Carlos Baerga and José Offerman have made returns to the majors after spending time in the Atlantic League.[1] For another group, the mere mortals, the circuit provided a way to prove their skills were still sharp enough to reach or return to the grandest of stages, after toiling for years in the minors.

Cory Jerome Aldridge was firmly in this latter group as he set the league on fire in 2008. Patrolling the outfield for the Newark Bears, he slashed .365/.440/.565,

The baseball Cory Aldridge hit for his one base hit.

committed no errors on the field, and even pitched two scoreless innings. His former employer, the Kansas City Royals, were impressed enough to re-sign him to a minor-league contract that eventually brought him back to the major leagues. His story, however, began what seemed like a long time ago, on a baseball diamond hundreds of miles away.

Aldridge was born in San Angelo, Texas, on June 13, 1979. His mother, Jean, was a nurse in the school district he attended; his father, Jerry, played in the NFL and USFL and upon retirement, embarked on a career with the Texas Department of Corrections. Hall of Famer Greg Maddux was born in same hospital as Aldridge, a bond that would become strong once the latter reached the majors. Growing up, Cory played soccer, basketball, and football in addition to baseball, idolizing Fred McGriff and Cecil Fielder. Though the Rangers were the closest big-league team, Aldridge followed the Cubs and the Braves thanks to the nationwide reach of WGN and WTBS.

He was chosen by the Braves in the fourth round of the 1997 amateur draft, an experience he found surprising. "I remember not knowing anything. I did not know anyone who had been drafted. My high-school coach told me I might get chosen. … I remember sitting at home and hoping for a call. I didn't know I'd go as high as I did." The class of 1997 featured Troy Glaus, J.D. Drew, Jon Garland, and Lance Berkman (first round), Randy Wolf and Scott Linebrink (second round), Jeremy Affeldt (third round), and Chone Figgins (fourth round).[2] Michael Young and Tim Hudson were both picked after Aldridge. The Braves selected 69 players, four of whom made it to the majors.[3] Five days after the draft, on June 8, he signed on the dotted line and began his professional career.

Atlanta assigned Aldridge to the rookie Florida Gulf Coast League, where he hit a respectable .278 in 46 games but displayed little power (.391 slugging). It was enough for the Braves to promote him to Danville (Appalachian League), led by phenom Rafael Furcal. In 1998 Aldridge was third on the team in batting

ONE-HIT WONDERS

(.294), prompting the franchise to send him to Macon of the Class-A South Atlantic League for 1999. Hurlers were more developed and Aldridge was overmatched; he struck out almost four times as often as he walked and hit a pedestrian .251. Undeterred, he attained similar results with Class-A (advanced) Myrtle Beach in 2000. Having been drafted out of high school, he was younger than most of his peers. "I thought I saw the world, coming from Texas and playing in all these places. Wilson Betemit was the first person from the Dominican Republic I met; I didn't know he couldn't speak English. I didn't know what was out there." In hindsight, he realized he lacked "world awareness," adding, "Back then I didn't know any better, so that's part of what I do now with kids, help them understand what's out there." He jokes that his school Spanish was terrible, but he picked it up quickly when reaching base and talking to the opponents while reaching second: "Sometimes I was Puerto Rican, Sometimes I was Dominican."

Aldridge opened 2001 with Double-A Greenville, collecting 508 plate appearances and reaching base at a .323 clip. While his numbers were respectable, they did not scream "blue-chip prospect." Atlanta, however, had other plans. Aldridge had almost made the team out of spring training but was deemed not quite ready, which he came to acknowledge was due to immaturity that often accompanies youth. Prior to a game against the Orlando Rays, manager Paul Runge tapped him on the shoulder to tell him, "You're going to Montréal. John Schuerholz and Bobby Cox want to see you."

The 2001 edition of the Braves dynasty took command of first place in mid-July. Once rosters expanded in early September, Atlanta had a small lead it did not relinquish the rest of the way. The major leagues were an eye-opening experience: "I was nervous, having never been in a stage that big. I had never been out of the country." Chipper Jones, himself a wunderkind when he arrived in Atlanta at a young age, provided guidance, and Maddux showed him the ropes. They knew "the baseball player in me needed to figure things out. … All those guys were nice guys. I didn't like B.J. Surhoff, I thought he was mean to me, but he wasn't. Years later, I said, 'Man, you were an a**hole to me.' He said, 'No, you were a young dumba**.' We shook hands and laughed. He was like Kirk Gibson, he was that guy, never laughed. He would come out prepared for the game."

On September 5, 2001, Aldridge debuted during a 10-4 loss against the Expos. Reliever José Cabrera was lifted to begin the eighth inning; his spot in the batting order was given to Aldridge, who took over for Brian Jordan in right field while Tim Spooneybarger took the mound. Aldridge fielded a single to right field by Geoff Blum, but Montréal did not score and neither did Atlanta in the top of the ninth. Aldridge made his way to the box score as an afterthought.

Four days later in Chicago, he was summoned to pinch-run for Bernard Gilkey, who had led off the ninth with a walk and had advanced to second on Marcus Giles's single. A fly ball to center field by Julio Franco and a strikeout by Wes Helms kept the runners glued to their stations before Jordan took first base on six pitches. But pitcher Ron Mahay got Surhoff to fly out, stranding Atlanta. The true highlight for Aldridge was meeting former Brave McGriff, who now donned the Cubs uniform. "Maddux took me under his wing as a young guy, since we were both from a small town. I'd shared something about liking McGriff. … Maddux told me to go to the batting cage and there was McGriff taking batting practice. He had signed a bat for me and we chatted; that was one of the coolest experiences I've ever had."

The 9/11 attacks paused baseball activity as the nation struggled to comprehend the scale of the monstrosity. After play resumed, the Braves traveled to New York to meet the Mets in an emotionally charged series for both franchises. In a game on September 21, Atlanta took the lead in the eighth frame. Julio Franco walked with two outs, triggering Aldridge into the game as a pinch-runner. Jones singled, moving Aldridge to second, and Jordan doubled to the left-center-field gap. Though he had yet to have an official plate appearance, Aldridge was now credited with a run scored. The contest was decided in the bottom of the inning as Mike Piazza hammered a Steve Karsay offering for a two-run home run. Aldridge played in the other games of the series, striking out on September 22 in his sole at-bat and pinch-running in the finale.

The two franchises met again in Atlanta, with the Braves winning, 8-5, on September 29. Aldridge replaced Jones, this time in left field, but no ball was hit in his direction. Mark DeRosa pinch-hit for him in the bottom of the eighth. The Braves overcame a four-run deficit in the night to beat the Mets as Jordan hit a game-ending grand slam off John Franco.

Aldridge got his sole start in the team's 161st game; facing young flamethrower Josh Beckett, he struck out twice and grounded to the pitcher, then struck out in a three-pitch at-bat against Vladimir Nuñez. He took the field as a defensive substitution the next day but did not enjoy either any fielding chances or plate

ONE-HIT WONDERS

appearances. The team did not include him in the postseason roster.

Despite the sudden end to his season, Aldridge beamed with excitement. The Braves "gave an opportunity for me to go to the big leagues, kind of feel it out and try to kind of find my place. I got to be around Chipper, Gilkey, and Jordan."[4] But spring, with its natural connotation of rebirth and renewal, was cruel to Aldridge: "I was supposed to be the fourth outfielder. I came up in the infield one day, I threw, and then I couldn't throw anymore."[5]

Aldridge returned to the Gulf Coast League to rehabilitate his injury. Back in 1997, as a wide-eyed 18-year old, he was one year younger than his peers. In 2002, he was almost 3½ years older; he played in 17 games before being shut down for the year. He returned to Greenville in 2003 but hit .234/.298/.395 and the franchise parted ways with the outfielder on May 24, 2004.

Eight days later, the Kansas City Royals offered Aldridge a minor-league deal. He remained in Double A but switched to the Wichita Wranglers of the Texas League. Patrolling the outfield for 79 games, he hit .239 but slugged .511, impressing the front office with his power. He began 2005 in Wichita but his .874 OPS prompted a call-up to Triple-A Omaha. The Pacific Coast League pitching proved tough, and Aldridge struggled to a .195 average, which the Royals found unacceptable. On October 15, 2005, he was granted free agency. Two moths later the Mets offered him a spot with the International League's Norfolk Tides. His start to the 2006 season was inauspicious – 13-for-83 – and merited a release. The White Sox took a chance and he responded with a solid .287 average for Double-A Birmingham for the remainder of 2006. He again donned the Barons uniform in 2007 and hit .259 in 124 games, not good enough for the White Sox, with whom he parted ways after the season.

Prompted by former teammate Josh Pressley, Aldridge decided to try the independent Atlantic League. "I got a ticket to Newark, and I actually had the most fun I think I had in a long time playing baseball," he said. "I went out there hit like .400 ... I didn't have to worry about any front-office things."[6] His batting line was .365 with a 1.005 OPS, proving he had plenty left in his tank. Though the love for the game loomed large in his decision to keep playing, Aldridge was cognizant of the financial reward. "Your average minor-league player probably makes five grand a year, and your average first (major-league) paycheck is probably 10 to 15 grand."[7] Looking back at this time in the minors, he shrugged. "I didn't have anything better to do. I didn't have a backup plan. The best thing I did was play independent ball. I was tired of the business, I was tired of being hurt, a lot of negatives in my life. I figured out I loved baseball and changed my mindset, not caring about the front office, going back to where I was."

The Royals re-signed Aldridge and he returned to the Double-A Texas League for the remainder of 2008. He hit .269 in 49 games for Northwest Arkansas, earning a promotion to Triple-A Omaha in 2009. He hit well (.316/.361/.582) but surprisingly, Kansas City did not offer him a 2010 contract. The California Angels, who had seen him in the circuit against their Salt Lake City affiliate, signed him on December 3, 2009, and he quickly paid off with the 2010 Salt Lake City Bees: he hit a solid .318 in 83 games before receiving the call from the parent club.

Almost nine years after his debut, Aldridge returned to the major leagues. At first glance, few things had changed in the game: Bud Selig was still commissioner, 30 franchises participated in the regular season, and Mike Scioscia managed the Angels. However, most of his 2001 Braves teammates had retired, the iPhone and Facebook had been invented, and Anaheim had changed its name to the clunky "Los Angeles Angels of Anaheim."

Wearing home whites on July 4, Aldridge enjoyed two plate appearances in an 11-0 win over the Royals. Taking over for Hideki Matsui in left field, he caught a fly ball from his former teammate Betemit in his only defensive chance. At bat, he grounded out to second base against Victor Marte and lined out weakly to shortstop against Dusty Hughes. Despite his 0-for-2 line, he was ecstatic. He started the next day against the White Sox in Chicago, grounding out in his first two at-bats. He struck out swinging in the seventh before grounding out in the ninth, ending the day hitless in four plate appearances. On July 8 he hit ninth in the batting order but neither he nor his teammates could solve John Danks, who allowed only two hits in a 1-0 Chicago victory. Aldridge reached on an error and struck out twice.

The Angels next visited Oakland for a three-game set. On July 10 the Athletics jumped to an eight-run lead by the third inning which grew to a 13-run advantage by the fifth. Scioscia had lifted Erick Aybar and Bobby Abreu in the sixth, plugging Kevin Branden at third base and Aldridge in right field, moving Brandon Wood from third base to shortstop. In the eighth, Aldridge faced Ross Wolf with two out. (Paul

ONE-HIT WONDERS

McAnulty and Bobby Wilson had struck out.) With Wood at third, Aldridge turned on a Wolf offering to deep left field for a triple. Wood scored while Aldridge caught his breath, a scant 90 feet from his starting point. Howie Kendrick then went down swinging, but Aldridge had attained his first base hit with the rarest of them all: a triple.[8] "I remember nothing at all about that game! I was not getting into the games I thought I would. ... I am just going to try to do what I do naturally. ... He had two strikes on me. ... I just said, 'I'm going with this pitch right here.' I was tired of being nervous."

Scioscia granted Aldridge another start the next day, but he went 0-for-3 (two strikeouts) as Oakland beat Los Angeles, 5-2. Though he returned to the minors, Aldridge had now tasted success on the big stage. His career line (1-for-18, with one run, one run batted in) could not properly capture the roller-coaster emotions he had experienced. He still had a lot of baseball left in him; at his age (31), he was still in his prime and he was unwilling to hang up his spikes. Aldridge decided to pursue international ball during the winter; he joined the Águilas (Eagles) of Mexicali for the 2010-2011 Mexican Pacific League. The team finished in seventh place (out of eight) though Aldridge contributed a .299 average with a .922 OPS. He continued his foreign exposure in the 2011 Korean Baseball League, signing with the Nexen Heroes, though he was unable to replicate his recent magic: he hit .237 in 117 games. Returning to Mexico, he suited up for six games with the pennant-winning Tomateros (Tomato-pickers) of Culiacán during the 2011-2012 campaign.

He remained south of the border, working for the Diablos Rojos (Red Devils) of Mexico City. He smoked the league to a .363 clip in 2012, raising the interest of the Angels, who inked him to a Triple-A deal with Salt Lake City. Pitchers there baffled him, limiting him to a .215 average and 91 strikeouts in 251 at-bats. He returned to Mexico for another winter, rejoining Culiacán for 61 games and slashing .268/.385/.567 in 2012-2013.

Aldridge split time between two teams during the 2013 Mexican (Summer) League, playing for both the Quintana Roo Tigres and the Acereros (Steelworkers) of Monclova, though he failed to make a dent with either club. Returning to the Atlantic League, Aldridge hit .284 for Somerset in 89 games. He enjoyed a banner year with the Caribes (Caribs) of Anzoategui of the Venezuelan Winter League, hitting .378 with an OPS of 1.129. He played in 19 additional contests during the postseason, garnering 24 hits, though his team lost the final series against Magallanes.[9] "I loved playing in Venezuela, Mexico, and Korea. ... The fans were awesome and loved the players. I wish I'd gone when I was younger; I had so many injuries I wish would have played winter ball. Winter league is great with so many cultures. ... But Venezuela, the country is beautiful but it was in a terrible state. ... Sometimes we had electricity blackouts; there was a lot of greatness spoiled with bad leadership."

Aldridge began 2014 in the Mexican League for the Monterrey Sultanes (Sultans), clubbing .345 with a 1.122 OPS. The Blue Jays signed him, assigning him to Double-A New Hampshire, where he hit .271 and earned a promotion to Triple-A Buffalo but he hit .226 in 16 games. He returned to Latin America, playing played 15 games in the Mexican Pacific League with Culiacán before Venezuela summoned him back, and he played 38 games with the Caribes with a .246 average.[10] He wrapped up his career with Monterrey in the summer of 2015, batting .273 in 18 games.

At age 36 and far removed from his high-school exploits, Aldridge retired from professional baseball. As of 2019 he lived in Katy, Texas and spent his time as a hitting instructor, seeking to mentor more players to understand the game. He was active on social media via his Twitter handle @aldridge32 and Instagram @coryaldridge, answering questions from parents and young athletes alike: "There's a lot to be learned from someone's successes and struggles, and I don't mind using mine to help someone else."

ACKNOWLEDGMENTS

To Cory Aldridge for graciously discussing his career via a phone interview. Unless otherwise specified, quotations stem from the author's interview with Aldridge on August 29, 2019.

SOURCES

In addition to the sources cited in the Notes, the author also consulted game information on Retrosheet.org

NOTES

1. Atlantic League Professional Baseball Notable Alumni, atlanticleague.com/players/notable-alumni/.
2. Major-league amateur draft of 1997 selections, baseball-almanac.com/draft/baseball-draft.php?yr=1997.
3. Major-league amateur draft of 1997, Atlanta Braves selections baseball-reference.com/draft/?team_ID=ATL&year_ID=1997&draft_type=junreg&query_type=franch_year&from_type_jc=0&from_type_hs=0&from_type_4y=0&from_type_unk=0.
4. Nick Diunte, "Why Wilkin Castillo's Decade-Long Major League Return Is All Too Familiar for One Former Ballplayer," *Forbes*, June 28, 2019. forbes.

ONE-HIT WONDERS

5   com/sites/nickdiunte/2019/06/28/why-wilkin-castillos-decade-long-major-league-return-is-all-too-familiar-for-one-former-ballplayer/#3e02bf0e4d89.

5   Diunte.

6   Diunte.

7   Diunte.

8   As of the start of the 2019 season, of the 1,306 retired major leaguers with only one hit, 19 did so with a home run, 21 swatted a triple, 167 connected for a double, and the remainder singled. (baseball-reference.com/tiny/NUBHk) However, since 1876, the major-league historical record shows triples being the least likely, with 3.43 percent of all historical hits. (baseball-reference.com/leagues/).

9   pelotabinaria.com.ve/beisbol/mostrar.php?ID=aldrcor001.

10   pelotabinaria.com.ve/beisbol/mostrar.php?ID=aldrcor001.

HUGH ALEXANDER

By Brian Flaspohler

Hugh "Red" Alexander was a promising 20-year-old, having just hit 57 home runs with a high batting average in two minor-league seasons, and tasting his first cup of coffee in the big leagues. He managed one single in 11 at-bats during his late-season callup and was looking forward to a long career as a player. Then he lost his hand in an offseason accident at the family farm, and his career as a player was ended. He overcame the injury, became a scout, and went on to a long and successful career in baseball, scouting players in eight different decades and signing more players who made the major leagues than any other scout.[1]

Hugh Alexander was born on July 10, 1917, near Lead Mine, a small unincorporated community in south central Missouri.[2] He was the second of three sons (Henry and Claude) his father, Harry, and mother, Mae, were raising while trying to scratch out a living farming the unproductive ground.

When Hugh was 5, the farming family was lured by the siren call of the Oklahoma oil boom. They moved to the oil fields near Cromwell, Oklahoma, where Harry became a roughneck working for the oil companies in the area while Mae did laundry for the oil workers, took care of her boys, and had another baby (daughter Edith).

Growing up in the oil fields was a very difficult life. The family made do with a very basic level of shelter, living in field tents the first couple of years in Oklahoma, and moving around as Harry worked in different oil fields. Harry was a hard worker, smart and ambitious, and he was promoted to a field supervisor in the late 1920s. The main change for the family was that they were able to move to a wood-frame house. But they still lived in the oil fields, which were their kids' playground. The boys played ball in their spare time using wells as bases and sliding on the polluted ground, ruined from exposure to spilled oil. But Harry and Mae expected them to work. That was the guiding principle of the family. As soon as they were old enough, they were given chores to instill that work ethic.

Alexander went to a one-room schoolhouse in Cromwell for his elementary school education. Most oil-field kids attended school only through the eighth grade because at that point they were able to get a paying job and start contributing to the family finances. Hugh was athletic from a young age and Harry encouraged him to be tough. He taught him boxing and began matching Hugh against older athletes to make a few dollars when carnivals came to town. Hugh also played against older children in baseball and football and caught the eyes of the Seminole high school coaches.

With his parents' and the coaches' encouragement, Alexander attended Seminole High School. It took longer than 30 minutes to get to and from Seminole, if a ride was available. Typically his father would drop him off in the morning and he would hitch a ride home in the afternoon. The trip took too much time, leaving no free time for sports participation. So Harry negotiated a deal with the local fire chief. Hugh would live at the Seminole firehouse during the week, cleaning and doing odd jobs to pay for his keep. He also got a job cleaning the local movie theater for $1 a day. This left Hugh time to for sports but also meant he had very little supervision. He learned to hustle at the local pool hall and play a mean game of poker. Around this same time, Harry was promoted to a job where he was in charge of negotiating mineral rights from local farmers. Hugh picked up deal-making tips from his father that he had no idea he would need in the future.

Alexander was an amazing all-around athlete. He played football, baseball, and basketball, and ran track. By his junior year, he was elected the captain of all four teams. He had great speed, running the 100-yard dash in under 10 seconds. By comparison, Jesse Owens' world record was 9.6 seconds. As a tailback on the football team, he led Seminole to an unofficial Oklahoma high-school championship. In one game he ran for 505 yards and six touchdowns, averaging 25 yards per carry. He also played semipro baseball (under an assumed name) in Oklahoma City during the

ONE-HIT WONDERS

summers to make a few bucks.³ He was a broad-shouldered, cocky, and aggressive young man with an extremely high opinion of himself.

During those semipro games, Alexander was first noticed by baseball scouts, including Cy Slapnicka, a legendary baseball lifer working as a scout for the Cleveland Indians. Slapnicka had recently signed Bob Feller and was beating the bushes looking for more talent for the Indians. Alexander had been approached by Hank Iba, famed basketball and baseball coach at Oklahoma State, who offered him a chance to play baseball and run track for the university. Iba noted that Alexander potentially could represent the United States in the 1936 Olympics in track. But Alexander wanted money, not an education, and there was no money in track and field. Slapnicka offered him $250 to sign with the Indians but he cagily asked for more. Slapnicka then promised him a $1,000 bonus when he made the major leagues. That was a given, the arrogant Alexander figured, so he signed the deal. Slapnicka noted that the broad-shouldered youth had all the tools except for a weak throwing arm. But four tools out of five could mean a baseball star.

The Indians assigned the 6-foot, 190-pound 18-year-old to the Fargo-Moorhead Twins of the Class-D Northern League. Homesickness didn't impact Alexander's play. The long bus rides and bad hotels must have seemed luxurious compared to his situation growing up. As the youngest player on the roster, he played in all 122 games in 1936 and led the team with 28 home runs, a .348 batting average, and 101 RBIs. Alexander was named by the league's writers and managers as the center fielder on the all-star team, while finishing fourth in the circuit in home runs and batting average.⁴ The Twins ended up fifth in the eight-team league, missing the playoffs. At the end of the season Cy Slapnicka showed up in Fargo and paid Alexander $600, "to tide you over this winter because you are some kind of ball player."⁵

The Indians obviously liked what they saw in the young man. Alexander was promoted to the Springfield (Ohio) team in the Class-C Middle Atlantic League. Nine of his teammates were destined to appear in the major leagues, including Phil Masi and Chuck Workman. He started the season hot, batting .438 through the first two weeks, but was struck down by a respiratory infection that caused him to miss a few games.⁶ There were no lasting negative effects, because for the season he displayed excellent power, with 29 home runs in 305 at-bats, 88 RBIs, 22 stolen bases, and a .344 batting average. One season highlight was a 13th-inning walk-off grand slam against Dayton on June 15.⁷ The aggressive young man had a bad moment too. On July 1 his temper got the better of him. He vehemently argued a called third strike, earning a suspension, a $5 fine from the umpire, and a $25 fine from his manager.⁸

The Cleveland Indians wanted to see their hot prospect for an extended period so on August 12 they put Alexander on the major-league roster. On August 15 he debuted in right field in the second game of a doubleheader against the Chicago White Sox at home. On his second at-bat, he hit a Texas Leaguer to center field, stole second, and took third on a long fly ball. He was thrown out at home on a groundball to complete the eventful trip around the bases. He committed an error allowing a runner to take an extra base which did not contribute to any White Sox runs.⁹ Alexander made his second and last big-league start five days later against the White Sox in Chicago, going 0-for-4 and striking out twice. His remaining big-league appearances consisted of three unsuccessful pinch-hit opportunities, one time pinch-running, one defensive substitution, and a month and a half of watching from the bench. Eleven at-bats, one bloop single, five strikeouts, and one steal summed up his cup of coffee. He also recorded two putouts in right field against the solitary error. Clearly he needed more seasoning but there was no reason to think the young man wouldn't continue to improve.

Alexander went home in the offseason and went back to work. On December 5, 1937, he was working on a water pump on the family farm. The pump was difficult to start, but he had handled it before. This time he got the pump started but his shirt sleeve got tangled in the gears. He tried to rip the sleeve off but it was a double-stitched work shirt and he couldn't pull the sleeve loose. His left hand was pulled into the gears and mangled. Mother Mae was nearby and heard his cries for help. She helped free him and drove him to the hospital in Seminole but they could do nothing to save the hand. The doctor at the hospital completed the amputation.¹⁰

Alexander was undeniably a top-notch prospect. Si Burick, a *Dayton Daily News* scribe, summed it up when he reported on Hugh's accident. "The most colorful ball player and probably the most promising in the Mid-Atlantic League last summer was Springfield's Hugh Alexander. A white-haired Adonis, whom the fans called 'Cotton' and his fellow players knew as 'Red,' Alexander laughed and fought his way through the league. Fans everywhere booed him but

ONE-HIT WONDERS

loved him for his colorful antics. Like a wrestler, he used to make wry faces and shake his fists at his tormentors, then burst into laughter in the privacy of the dugout. He was Alexander the Great."[11]

Harry and Mae had simple advice for their son. The accident has happened and thinking about it doesn't do any good. They would not allow him to do nothing, lounge around, drink beer, and sponge off the family. Very shortly after he got home, he took a job pouring drinks at a saloon in Seminole.

Cy Slapnicka and the Indians had not forgot about their player. Slapnicka must have seen some characteristics he liked in Alexander. Or at the least, the Indians felt they owed him a chance at a job after the accident. Slapnicka called just before Christmas and told him, "Hughie, you're about to become a baseball scout, and if you agree the $1,000 bonus is yours."[12] Alexander didn't know anything about scouting but thought that sounded better than a life serving beer in a saloon.

The Cleveland Indians trained in New Orleans in 1938. Alexander met Slapnicka there and started his training. The 20-year-old was about to become the youngest scout in baseball history. Slapnicka asked him to grade players they saw during spring training and they compared notes. Hugh's experience seeing some of the best players in baseball while riding the Indians bench helped give him a frame of reference for the skill level required in a major-league player. Slapnicka gave him hints on what to look for, like a pitcher's mechanics and a fielder's first step when the ball is hit. He especially focused on pitching because he admittedly knew nothing about the pitcher's craft. Also, Slapnicka told him to find out as much as possible about the player's character. The scout needed to project a youngster from what he is today to what he could be. And somehow, they needed to figure out if the player had the character, work ethic, etc. to turn into that future big leaguer. Slapnicka also insisted that Alexander develop a strong network of contacts to be used to find prospects.

At the end of spring training, Alexander went on the road. His territory was expansive: Texas, Oklahoma, New Mexico, and the upper Plains states. He really had no idea how to find and sign players. He met other scouts on the road, but in the times before the amateur draft, scouts kept their information very close. One of his guiding principles was that if he wasn't sure about a player, he would walk away. He didn't want to waste the owner's money on a nonprospect. Because his territory was so large, he felt he needed a plan to direct his scouting. He wrote several commandments that he would follow:

- *I shall make plans. Be bold, be daring. After all, a young scout lacks only the experience of making bad decisions.*
- *I shall travel the dirt roads, gravel roads, and blacktops to see new players.*
- *I shall not whine. It is a time waster and won't win me any friends or sign me any new players.*
- *I shall be lucky once in a while, but most of my successes will be plain old hard work, making personal contacts.*
- *I shall have a pair of well-trained eyes to spot the true mechanics of the game.*
- *I shall know the difference in a player who thinks "I shoulda made that last play" and "I woulda not gotten that last play."*[13]

No matter how many games Alexander could get to, he found that scouts had a lot of time on their hands. The older men who traveled in the same territory were a hard-living lot and he spent plenty of time with them but he didn't let it distract him from his duties. He kept a diary of his travels and the players he saw and sent in reports to Slapnicka. He would not permit anyone to call him handicapped. How could someone drive thousands of miles and live independently with a handicap? In fact, in order to make some extra cash, he would frequently bet someone he could tie his shoes faster than they could. Once the unsuspecting mark saw he had one hand, the bet was on. Hugh claimed he never lost this bet.

After Alexander's first year on the road (with Slapnicka checking in on him occasionally), he had signed exactly zero players. It was a year of training and developing sources of information. He attended games throughout Texas and Oklahoma, the National semipro tournament in Wichita, the American Legion All-Star tournament in St. Joseph, Missouri, college games, and high-school games. He did take enough time off from traveling to marry Thelma Jewell McBride of Seminole on June 12, 1938. Slapnicka was pleased with Alexander's progress and asked him to continue scouting.

In March 1939, Oklahoma A&M's Hank Iba called Alexander with a hot tip. There was a young Indian-American on campus who was a hot prospect recruited by football scouts. Baseball scouts hadn't heard of him because he had only started pitching his senior season. What Alexander saw was a hard-throwing big man who wasn't afraid to pitch inside. He sent his scouting

ONE-HIT WONDERS

report on Allie Reynolds to Slapnicka, who told him to keep watching. After Reynolds threw a no-hitter, Hugh called Slapnicka and told him he had a fastball nearly as fast as Feller's and that they needed $1,000 to sign him. Cy didn't want to spend that much money but Hugh followed his first commandment. Taking a tip from how his father did business with poor landowners when negotiating mineral rights, Alexander borrowed $1,000 from the bank and brought the cash over to Reynolds's home. Allie had a wife and young baby in the humble dwelling and as soon as he saw the cash fanned out on the kitchen table, he immediately signed the deal. Reynolds was Alexander's first signing and it turned out to be a great one.[14]

Alexander's years scouting with the Indians were fruitful but he learned by hard experience. In that time, players were not allowed to sign a contract until their class graduated from high school. Many rural youngsters either had no birth certificate or had quit school after eighth grade, so it could be difficult to know if a scout was complying with the rule. Commissioner Kenesaw Mountain Landis summoned Alexander to his office early in his scouting career over a possible breach of this rule. Neither he nor the Indians were penalized but Landis left him with a stern warning that he would run Hugh out of baseball if he was caught cheating.

In 1941 Alexander's mentor Cy Slapnicka was fired from the Indians but this didn't affect Alexander's position with the Indians. By then, he had already scouted and signed Dale Mitchell, Pat Seerey, and others and he was being recognized among some baseball men as a person with an eye for talent. In midsummer of 1941, he met Branch Rickey at a game in Pueblo, Colorado. Rickey, then the general manager of the St. Louis Cardinals, had heard of him and they talked for a time. Rickey gave him some advice about searching for talent and Alexander noted it.

During the war years, scouting was very difficult. Gas rationing meant that getting to games was difficult; also, many players were serving in the armed forces. Alexander scouted some military bases, only able to sign players when they were discharged. He also helped a colonel at a base, feeding him names of good ballplayers in the military. The officer arranged to have the best transferred to his base so he could dominate the military tournaments.

Hugh and Thelma had a daughter in 1942 but all the time on the road makes for a difficult relationship. By 1952 he was divorced. He was scouting a huge territory and some of his players (Dale Mitchell and Gene Bearden) helped the Indians win the World Series in 1948, but he didn't get everyone right. He scouted Mickey Mantle and wrote in his book "No prospect" after watching him strike out 14 times over a week. He also noted Mantle for a return visit but the Yankees beat him to it.[15]

In 1952 Paul Richards, manager of the White Sox, and Frank Lane, general manager, impressed by Alexander's reputation, recruited him to scout for them. Alexander never discussed his reasons for leaving the Indians, so it would only be speculation. But he had known Richards from scouting and was impressed with his baseball smarts. Alexander's territory didn't change but his focus did. Richards wanted speed, defense, and (like everyone) good pitching. However, with Trader Frank Lane in house, most of the organization focus was on trading for players, not in scouting new talent.

Alexander started using his contacts to find a new job. Fresco Thompson, the director of the Dodgers farm system, knew Alexander from scouting meetings in the early 1950s. With a couple of quick conversations, he found himself as a field scout for the Brooklyn Dodgers starting in the 1956 season. Again, he had the same territory as before, roads and towns he was very familiar with.

The minor leagues were undergoing a major contraction at this time. When Alexander started with the Dodgers, they had 14 farm teams. They were on the verge of moving to Los Angeles (which they would do in 1958). By 1961 the Dodgers farm system was depleted because of trades of prospects. Farm director Buzzie Bavasi wanted to restock the system. He held a meeting with his scouts, laid out a goal of signing 100 players, and provided the financial resources to do so. This was an unprecedented number of players but Bavasi told the scouts that if they had any issues negotiating with players, they should call either Alexander or Bert Wells for help because they were the two best scouts the Dodgers had. Also, by 1962 the Dodgers were down to 10 farm teams but with expansion there were more major-league teams looking for talent. It would be a challenging time for Alexander.

Two of Alexander's early signings with the Dodgers were Carl Warwick and Frank Howard. With Warwick, he followed one of his precepts for signing a player: Meet with the parents, especially the mother, and recruit them. He always felt the mother typically made the final decision. During a meeting with Warwick's parents, he offered a $20,000 bonus, an additional $5,000 a year for three years, plus $5,000 if he made the majors. At the moment of the offer, his parents fell in love with Alexander![16] Howard had already decided he wanted to play for the Dodgers, and had received higher offers from other organizations. His unusual request was for a $108,000 bonus, the $8,000 for his parents to make a down payment on a house. The organization was happy to comply.

When the Dodgers initially scouted Don Sutton, scout Leon Hamilton (and to be fair, pretty much all the other scouts) call him a nonprospect. However, after Alexander got a look at him, he believed he could be a major-league pitcher and wanted to offer a deal. But the organization had already turned him down, and didn't want to reverse course. This irritated Alexander and he jumped up the chain of command. In due course, Hamilton was ordered to sign the paperwork committing Sutton to the Dodgers, giving the proper appearance to the deal. Sutton's father wouldn't let Hamilton back in the house because of the earlier disrespect, so the Dodgers had to send another scout in to get Sutton's signature.

In 1965, the major leagues instituted the amateur draft system. This changed the scouting game tremendously. No longer would scouts be involved with signing players. No more secret scouting reports or keeping your information close to the vest. Alexander was disappointed in the changes but as a baseball lifer, he changed with the times.

In 1972 Alexander's friend Paul Owens, soon to be general manager of the Philadelphia Phillies, offered him a new challenge. He would be a special-assignment scout and would have much more input in the effort to try to build a winning team from the rubble of the current organization. His salary was $15,000, which made him the highest paid scout in baseball.[17] He helped improve Philadelphia's focus on building from within, noting that the Dodgers reserved $1 million for signing bonuses while the Phillies spent $400,000.

Owens soon hired Dallas Green to run the farm system and the trio became the architects of the Phillies' winning teams. Alexander would go scout any situation the team needed him in and would provide his take on potential trades and the draft. The first big deal he had a hand in was to push the Phillies to trade for Steve Carlton. Now known as Uncle Hughie throughout baseball for his knowledge and years in the game, he learned from his extensive network of Carlton's salary disagreement with the Cardinals and how the team was willing to move him. So the Phillies were able to take advantage. Other key trade acquisitions in the next few years included Garry Maddox, Bake McBride, and Tug McGraw. Key drafts included Lonnie Smith, Alan Bannister, and Dick Ruthven. Alexander's influence was suggested by Bill Conlin in a *Philadelphia Daily News* article: "When Hughie Alexander talks in a mellow baritone that suggests sour mash bourbon and unfiltered cigarettes, you can hear a pin drop in the Phillies' boardroom."[18]

Alexander also paid close attention to the rules. At this time, there were two major league drafts, held in January and in June. Marty Bystrom, a pitcher for Miami-Dade Community College, was skipped over in the June, 1976 draft. There was a little-known clause in the draft rules which said a player who wasn't drafted was a free agent until two weeks before the next draft. Hugh jumped on this, signing him for $50,000 in December, thereby not risking losing him to another team in January. Baseball executives were so upset by the move that the rule was changed for the following year.[19]

No great situation lasts forever. In 1981 Dallas Green became general manager of the Chicago Cubs. In 1982 the Phillies traded for Joe Morgan and Tony Perez. That helped them in 1983, but the trades of prospects for major leaguers took its toll. One particularly damaging trade was sending Ryne Sandberg to the Cubs as an extra player to acquire Ivan de Jesus. Maybe karma for the Carlton steal was in play. The aging Phillies sank back to a second-division team.

Sometime in the late 1970s or early '80s, Alexander married a woman named Lois and lived in Palm Harbor, Florida. He much preferred the climate there to Oklahoma's. With the Phillies, he spent at least 200 days a year away from home, which continued to contribute to his fluid home life. A Jayson Stark article implied that Lois was his sixth wife, but this researcher couldn't find any marriage records to confirm any marriages other than to his first wife.[20]

Dallas Green encouraged Alexander to join him in Chicago in 1987. This would be Alexander's final employer. Green left soon after but Jim Frey took over and of course Uncle Hughie knew him and was comfortable with the situation. In 1989 the team celebrated his 50th year in scouting. His time with Chicago was filled with any special assignment the team would send him on, along with trying to share his wisdom with other people in the organization. In 1998 he finally retired, but continued to occasionally scout spring-training games for the organization. In 2000, he scouted one last game during spring training.

ONE-HIT WONDERS

Alexander had an entire book written about him, largely focused on his work as a baseball scout.

This completed his career, scouting in eight different decades.

Over the years, Alexander signed 63 players who eventually made the major leagues.[21] In 1984 he founded the Scout of the Year program to honor baseball scouts. In 1996 he finally agreed to receive the award. There is no way to count the number of games he watched or players he scouted. In 1994 he moved to a 16-acre horse ranch near Brooksville, Florida. He bought the property because Lois always liked it when they drove by, but she died before they could move in. In 1999, suffering from lung cancer, he moved to Spring Hill, Florida, then relocated to Oklahoma City after spring training in 2000 to be near his sister, Edith. The lifelong smoker died of lung cancer on November 25, 2000. His remains were cremated and interred in Maple Grove Cemetery in Seminole, Oklahoma.[22]

SOURCES

In addition to the sources cited in the Notes, the author accessed Baseball-Reference.com, Ancestry.com, and Newspapers.com.

NOTES

1. Dan Austin, *Baseball's Last Great Scout* (Lincoln: University of Nebraska Press, 2013), 3.
2. Austin, 6.
3. Austin, 15.
4. "The Northern League," *The Sporting News*, September 10, 1936: 6.
5. Austin, 20.
6. "The Mid-Atlantic League," *The Sporting News*, May 20, 1937: 6.
7. "The Mid-Atlantic League," *The Sporting News*, June 24, 1937: 10.
8. "The Mid-Atlantic League," *The Sporting News*, July 8, 1937: 8.
9. "White Sox Win Double Header from Indians," *Chicago Tribune*, August 16, 1937: 23.
10. There are various versions of the accident. What type of pump Alexander was working on, who was with him, and how he gots to the hospital vary. This story is from Dan Austin's book and seems to be the most likely.
11. Si Burick, "Si-Ings," *Dayton* (Ohio) *Daily News,* December 7, 1937: 23.
12. Austin, 23.
13. Austin, 33.
14. Austin, 38.
15. Austin, 64.
16. Austin, 84.
17. Austin, 117.
18. Bill Conlin, "Uncle Hughie," *Philadelphia Daily News,* November 15, 1983: 84.
19. Austin, 137.
20. Jayson Stark, "He Is the Phillies Unknown Soldier," *Philadelphia Inquirer*, June 15, 1983: 1D.
21. Austin, 163.
22. Greg Auman, "Baseball Scout in Eight Decades Dies," *Tampa Bay Times*, November 29, 2000: 89.

DAN ARDELL

By Bill Nowlin

For the Los Angeles Angels, 1961 was the first year in franchise history. For first baseman Dan Ardell, it was his first year in the big leagues, too. Though he'd been born in Seattle, he'd been raised in the LA area, graduating from University High in Los Angeles and then going to the University of Southern California, also in LA. It was also, as it happened, his only year in the big leagues.

Daniel Miers Ardell was indeed born in Seattle, on May 27, 1941. In a January 2019 interview, he explained, "My mother's name was Miriam and my father's name was Barclay. Miers is my mom's maiden name. My father was in the theater and church and school equipment business. He bid on the seats going into Dodger Stadium, that kind of thing. He did that

for most of his life. He went to Manual Arts High School, so you can guess that was not the high academic school of LA. He did not graduate from college. My mom did not graduate from college. But my great-grandfather was the second president of Indiana University. There was quite a wide range in our family.

"My twin brother, Dave, went to UCLA. We both grew up UCLA fans. We grew up about a mile from UCLA. Hated SC. Hated the Los Angeles Angels (of the old Pacific Coast League), because I was a Hollywood Stars fan. And I ended up within a relatively short period of time playing for both."[1]

Barclay Ardell was a native of Vancouver, British Columbia, a Canadian citizen. The family moved to the Los Angeles area when Dan and Dave were around 4 years old. His father encouraged them to play baseball from a very early age. "He got us started at the age of 4. It was early. We were very lucky. He definitely pushed us on it, but it was not in a bad way. We both enjoyed doing it. We both played varsity basketball, too. I remember when we were in the 12th grade and he asked, 'How did you guys ever learn to play basketball without me?' It wasn't braggadocious. He just didn't understand how we learned to play basketball."

The year they turned 10, their father became one of the founders of the West LA Little League in 1951 and remained active with it for quite some time.

In both 1957 and 1958, Dan was named All-City first baseman. Brother Dave was also All-City.

After graduating from high school, Dan spent a little more than six months in the US Army, from February to August 1959. He had graduated in January and wasn't due to start at USC until September. "I figured I'd just do the six-month program," he said. "Get it out of the way. So I went in a week out of high school. All US basic training and then I was in the artillery. I was in the Fire Direction Center, where we would determine where the guns would shoot. I was a math-type guy and so I got to do that instead of the real stuff. I was in the Reserve for seven years. I should have been called up during the Berlin Crisis,

ONE-HIT WONDERS

but Dedeaux, I think, got ahold of the colonel or something and said, 'He's playing baseball' and they gave me a deferment. I stayed in the Reserves but I was never called up."

Dan played at USC under legendary coach Rod Dedeaux. Coaching the Trojans in his 20th season, Dedeaux had seen his teams win their 11th consecutive California Intercollegiate Baseball Association title in 1961. On June 3 Tom Satriano doubled and Ardell tripled to break a 4-4 eighth-inning tie and beat Washington State for the NCAA district title. Dedeaux then saw his team go all the way to the College World Series, win all five games there, and by beating Oklahoma State in the championship game, triumph as the College World Series champions.

Dan's twin, Dave, played for UCLA, infield and outfield but a little more outfield. Dedeaux had had only one scholarship to give to USC and it went to Dan. Dan was a little larger than Dave, by two to three inches in height. Dave was right-handed and Dan was left-handed. They were definitely not identical twins. "He played at UCLA for three years and was the captain," Dan said. "At one point, he laughingly said, 'I think I had more at-bats than anybody in UCLA history.' He was a good ballplayer. He was All-City. Nothing great, but very, very solid."

After Dan Ardell's sophomore year, he was signed by the Angels for a bonus of $37,500. Tom Satriano was signed on the same day. At Dan's request, his signing bonus was paid out over five years. Roland Hemond was the scouting director for the fledgling ballclub. Hemond told Dan that if he did well, he'd be called up to the big leagues after the minor-league season was over.

Ardell was sent to the Artesia (New Mexico) Dodgers of the Class-D Sophomore League, a Dodgers farm club. The Angels had only two farm teams at this point, and neither needed a first baseman. Ardell spent about a month with Artesia, managed by Spider Jorgensen. The team finished 48-78, in last place in the six-team league, 29½ games out of first place. Ardell, 20 years old, played in 33 games, batting .240. There were 13 players on the team with a higher batting average. He likewise ranked 14th in on-base percentage. He drove in 25 runs, ranking ninth. He made nine errors in the 33 games, though as a first baseman he saw a lot of action. His fielding percentage was .971. "The Sophomore League was so bad," Ardell once wrote, "that it folded at season's end."[2] The team reported an attendance of 9,724 – for the whole season. Why did Dan Ardell get the call to the major leagues?

Obviously, the Angels needed players. As of August 30, they were 29½ games out of first place, and seventh in the standings of the 10-team American League.

Ardell was 6-feet-2 and listed at 190 pounds. He batted and threw left-handed. And somehow full of self-confidence. "I was thoroughly convinced I belonged in the major leagues. My fielding was suspect, and I did not hit left-handers well, but I was sure I could work through these problems. My optimism outran my talent."[3]

Ardell was added to the roster on September 1. Called up at the same time were "Jim Fregosi, Tom Satriano, Buck Rodgers, Dean Chance, and me. And a guy named Bob   ut. He threw bullets, but he threw his arm out. Out of the five they called up, three were pretty good."[4]

After he sat on the bench for about a couple of weeks, Ardell's debut game came at Metropolitan Stadium in Minneapolis on September 14. Due to rain the days before, the Angels and Twins played two on that date. In the first game, the Angels held a 3-1 lead after eight innings. In the top of the ninth, two singles and a walk loaded the bases. Earl Averill pinch-hit and singled, driving in one more run. Manager Bill Rigney sent in Ardell as a pinch-runner for Averill. Joe Koppe walked, forcing in a fifth run. Ardell moved up to second base, but a 9-2 double play ended the inning. The Angels won, 5-1.

Two days later, he pinch-ran again, this time at Comiskey Park in Chicago. With a 6-3 lead, he ran for Steve Bilko in the top of the seventh. He advanced to second on a groundout and to third on another groundout, but a third groundout ended the inning. Once again, he was running in the pitcher's spot in the order and so left the game in favor of a reliever.

Ardell's third appearance was also as a pinch-runner. This time, he scored. After seven innings the White Sox held a 2-1 lead. Averill led off, pinch-hitting for the pitcher. He singled and Ardell entered to run for him. A single and a sacrifice moved him to third base. George Thomas singled, driving in two runs. It became 3-2, Angels, but the White Sox tied it in the ninth and won it in the 10th.

On Wednesday, September 20, the Angels were at Tiger Stadium and this time, Ardell got a chance to hit, his first at-bat in the big leagues. It was the top of the ninth and the Tigers had a 6-2 lead as the inning began. George Thomas reached on an error, and made his way to second base, though there were then two outs. Ted Kluszewski singled to center and scored Thomas, making it 6-3. "The day I got the base

ONE-HIT WONDERS

hit, Bill Rigney didn't know me from squat. I was sitting at the end with Satriano or Fregosi or whoever it was, and he says, 'Rook! Rook, get up here and hit.' We looked at each other, not knowing who he was referring to and he points to his left arm. I was the only left-hander there, so I knew he wanted me to hit. No advance notice. Nothing."

Ardell was to face Detroit's Ron Kline. He tells the story: "I saw myself as a power hitter, and did not think Kline looked overpowering. It was clear to me that I could hit a home run and make it a 6-5 ballgame. It was probably also clear to Kline that I was a big young rookie thinking about hitting a home run. He threw me pitches that were around the plate, ones that were not overpowering. Finally, he threw one that looked very hittable. I swung and almost broke my knuckles, but the ball had enough on it to get over the second baseman's head for a single. The pinch-runner on first rounded second too aggressively. The right fielder gunned the ball to second and the runner was tagged out. The game was over. And I was standing on first base, batting 1.000."[5]

Ardell added, "I was unhappy that we had lost, but ecstatic about getting on base in my first at-bat. I was confident that many more at-bats and hits lay ahead."

There were three at-bats ahead, but no more hits.

Playing for the first time in front of the home crowd, at Los Angeles' Wrigley Field, Ardell pinch-hit in the September 23 game. In the bottom of the ninth, with one out, nobody on, and the Angels down by two runs, he batted for Jim Fregosi and struck out.

On the 24th, he pinch-ran in the seventh inning and got as far as third base but the inning then ended. Again, he'd been running in the pitcher's spot and so did not play in the field.

On September 27, it was Trojans Day and Ardell took the field for the first time, playing first base and batting eighth against the Washington Senators. The game in Los Angeles drew 1,717 spectators. First time up, Claude Osteen struck him out. Second time up, in the fourth, he drew a walk. In the sixth, he grounded back to the pitcher to end the inning. In the eighth, with the Angels down by one run, Ardell was asked to sacrifice and did, successfully moving up two baserunners into scoring position. The first one scored on a wild pitch; had he not been advanced to third base, he would not have been able to score. And then pinch-hitter Buck Rodgers doubled, driving in the go-ahead run. The Angels won the game, and Ardell's sacrifice had truly paid off.

Though he had no way to know it at the time, his major-league career was over. He had the one base hit to show for it (one more than many). He had scored one run and – with the sacrifice – helped win a ballgame.

Ardell's career batting average was .250, with an on-base percentage of .400. He'd played the complete game on the 27th and handled 13 chances without an error, a lifetime fielding percentage of 1.000.

The question was asked: If you'd had two hits in the major leagues, it wouldn't really have been as interesting, right?

Ardell replied, "I think that's exactly true. There's no way I should have played in the major leagues. I hit the perfect timing. Everything was perfect. At USC I had an All-American in front of me so I wasn't going to play. Willie Ryan. 5'8". 140 pounds. Nobody would sign him because he was too small. But he was exceptional. He was All-American and had another year to go."

Speaking in early 1962, however, he might yet have had a bright career in front of him. Coach Dedeaux was very high on Ardell's prospects, declaring, "Dan Ardell will be the Angels' first baseman eventually. Dan has size, real good power, and can run. He's intelligent and he has good desire."[6] Dedeaux noted that he'd even stolen home more than once.

In December, Ardell married Pam Allen. The marriage lasted some years and produced two children.

Over the wintertime, it was reported that Dan, his brother, Dave, and their father worked importing clothes from Hong Kong.[7] This venture was nowhere near as grand as it may have seemed to the reporter at the time. More than 50 years later, Dan recalled, "We thought we'd turn it into a business; I think we sold two suits."

In 1962 Ardell joined the Angels for spring training at Palm Springs, California, but at the end of camp was assigned to the San Jose Bees of the Class-C California League. He played in 105 games that year, but it was a season interrupted by a very bad beaning in the first inning of a June 17 home game against Stockton. His season stats were not impressive, either before or after the incident. "I started the season slowly," he wrote, "and then, in June, facing another of those dreaded left-handed pitchers, I took a fastball in the forehead. It happened at twilight, when it was difficult to see the ball. … I literally did not see the pitch. … The ball bounced off my forehead and went past third base. I was unconscious but not paralyzed as they took me from the field."[8] He had a concussion and a broken

ONE-HIT WONDERS

right orbital bone. After consultation, doctors decided it might be more dangerous to operate than to see if the injury would heal.

It did heal, and Ardell was back on the field about six weeks later. He finished with a .239 batting average (.366 OBP), drove in 46 runs, and scored 70 times. He struck out 101 times and hit 11 home runs. There was one good feeling he was left with at the end of the season: "Although I finished the season as poorly as I have begun it, I did have the winning RBI in the final game to win the league championship."[9]

Ardell transferred from USC to San Jose State. He also invested part of his signing bonus in real estate and began to work part-time for a realtor.

In 1963 spring training was with the minor-league clubs, in a growing Angels system. From the two teams in 1961, the system had grown to five in 1962. Ardell began the 1963 season with the Nashville Volunteers of the Double-A South Atlantic League. He started the season very well, hitting .325 after the first 25 games, but was transferred downward rather than up to Triple A. He was back with San Jose (the California League had been upgraded to Single A.) For whatever reason, he had a mediocre season, with stats very similar to the year before: After 102 games, he was hitting only .232. He had driven in 57 runs. And at one point, he even pitched in a game – striking out the one batter he faced.

Ardell was back in minor-league training camp in 1964, which proved to be his final season as a player. "Despite enjoying playing baseball," he recalled, "I was coming to realize that I did not enjoy the life of a minor league player." There were the difficult travels, the "sleeping in cramped beds in second rate hotels, and eating mediocre food at odd hours," and there was the "male tendency to descend to the lower common denominator."[10]

Ardell was getting a little older, and the prospect of making the majors again did not seem bright. He had, however, shone brightly in a March 31 exhibition game, playing first base for the Hawaii Islanders against the Los Angeles Angels. Ardell singled, doubled, and homered in four trips to the plate.

He played out the 1964 season based in Pasco, Washington, playing first base for the Tri-City Angels in the Single-A Northwest League. In 124 games, he showed significant improvement – .267 (.373 OBP), with 17 homers and 63 RBIs. But it wasn't enough of an improvement. Ardell finished his studies and graduated from college in June 1965.

"I hated the life," he said. "My brother could have played, but I said, 'I just don't think you're going to like it.' Once I realized what the life was going to be like, I actually quit before they fired me. I remember going to Roland Hemond. I said, 'I'm not doing very well. I'm not enjoying it. Can I quit?' And Roland being one of the most wonderful human beings in the world said, 'Yeah. You're the one who asked to spread the money over five years. That doesn't mean you're obligated to play.'"

Dave went to work for IBM out of college. "My dad, he and I started buying foreclosed apartments. Probably syndication before the term existed. We would buy one a year. Friends and relatives would put money in. After about seven or eight years, he and I formed our own company – DA Management, where we did more stuff like that and then we advised pension funds on real estate. (Dad) retired in his early 50s."

The interest in real estate had started while Dan was still in college.

"My dad had read a book somewhere along the way – *How I Turned a Thousand into a Million in Real Estate in My Spare Time*. Being a great student, I thought, 'Man, that sounds like a great book. I've got to check that out.' I talked to one of the professors and said I want to be in real estate. I had a minor in real estate. He said, 'Well, if you want to learn about real estate. There's only one place to go. Union Bank.' It ended up that I was able to get in there. I was there for five years.

"One of the guys I was working with moved to Wells Fargo in a real estate investment trust and asked me if I wanted to join him. I spent the next seven years with them. There were seven of us when we started and he and the fellow who started it both became chairman of Wells Fargo, back when it was a good company."

He was a banker, with a specialization in real estate. "I did construction lending. I did mortgages on industrial buildings. Offices. Apartments. It was all income property. Nothing to do with residential.

"I retired December 31, 1999. About six years ago, a guy who I played baseball with in high school called and he said, 'Are you a little bored?' Yeah. He said, 'I know you lost a lot of money in the Great Recession. Are you still broke?' We were very close. I called him some bad names. Then he said, 'The big question is, do you still have your faculties?' That was of issue. This was the right hand for the guy who started Public Storage."

ONE-HIT WONDERS

"It was the bottom of the housing market. He said, 'We're going to buy houses all over the country. We're going to fix them up and we're going to rent them.' When I joined the company, we had a thousand houses and 50 employees. Today, we have 50,000 and 1,350 employees."

"It has been something. We have 20 offices. I had to set the offices up, find people to get the offices started, and then mentor (for want of a better term) various people in the company."

Asked what his position at American Homes 4 Rent is, he chuckled and said, "I am officially a training manager. I do no training and I do no managing. They don't know what to do with me."

In 1981, some six years after his divorce, Dan married Jean Hastings. Jean had two children of her own. The marriage has endured. "She's still talking to me," Dan said some 37-plus years later.

Dan Ardell never begrudged his short run with the Angels, and remained a solid Angels fan more than 50 years later. He had won a couple of key games at different levels, and had that one base hit in the big leagues.

"My one base hit went to Al Kaline. He picks the guy off second and the game is over. I'm standing there on first base, batting 1.000, happier than hell, and thinking, 'Man, I should have gone long.' Twenty years old. You never know."

SOURCES

In addition to the sources cited in the Notes, the author consulted Retrosheet.org, Baseball-Reference.com, the *Encyclopedia of Minor League Baseball*, and the Dan Ardell player file and player questionnaire at the National Baseball Hall of Fame.

NOTES

1. Dan Ardell with author on January 27, 2019. Unless otherwise indicated, all quotations from Dan Ardell come from this interview.
2. Dan Ardell, "A Cup of Coffee in the Show: My Seven Games in the Majors," in William M. Simons, ed., *The Cooperstown Symposium on Baseball and American Culture, 2003-2004* (Jefferson, North Carolina: McFarland, 2005), 19. Dan Ardell's presentation at the Symposium is the source for a great deal of the material in this biography.
3. "A Cup of Coffee," 21.
4. Left-handed pitcher Bob Sprout appeared in only one major-league game, on September 27, 1961. He successfully executed a sacrifice bunt in his one and only major-league plate appearance. He pitched four full innings in the game, allowing three runs (two earned) on four hits and three walks.
5. "A Cup of Coffee," 21. The runner was Ken McBride.
6. Braven Dyer, "Dedeaux Says Ardell Cinch Future Great," *Los Angeles Times*, February 5, 1962: B8.
7. Dyer.
8. "A Cup of Coffee."
9. "A Cup of Coffee." The winning hit was a two-run single in the seventh inning, beating Reno, 5-3.
10. "A Cup of Coffee." He details a number of experiences on the road.

JEFF BANISTER

By Benjamin Sabin

"Probably my favorite part of the day is when I get up in the morning and put my feet on the floor. Because there were a couple of different times when I was told that would never happen. My legs were the two things that I was either not going to have or were not going to work anymore, and those two things carried me down the line to first base to etch a moment in time."

– Jeff Banister[1]

Jeffery Todd Banister was born on January 15, 1964, to Verda and Bob Banister in Weatherford, Oklahoma. The family lived in Weatherford until 1970 when, along with older sister Carey, they moved to La Marque, Texas. La Marque is a city in Galveston County, just south of Houston, and in 1970 was a residential community for employees of nearby refineries and chemical plants. Jeff's father, Bob, was a football coach at La Marque High School and his mother was an algebra teacher at the school. Jeff's father was busy with his coaching schedule and Verda played a pivotal role in Jeff's early athletic career. "She was the one that made sure I got to every Little League game, every practice," Jeff said. And "when coaches were late, she would step in."[2]

Jeff excelled at athletics and was a three-sport athlete at La Marque High School, where his father was

still the football coach. He played baseball, football, and basketball, being coached by his father in football and basketball. It was at this time, in his sophomore year, that Banister noticed that his ankle was swollen. It caused enough discomfort to warrant a doctor's visit. The doctor, family physician Dr. Lockhardt, discovered that Jeff had bone cancer and told him that if he did not get his leg amputated, he could possibly die. It was also found that day that he had cysts on the same leg, which had developed into osteomyelitis, which is an infection caused by bacteria eating away at bone marrow. Jeff and his family decided that taking the leg was the right course of action.[3]

Luckily for Jeff, the decision to amputate never came to pass. He persuaded the doctor to try to save the leg. Five months and seven operations later, Jeff came out of the hospital having beaten cancer and osteomyelitis.[4] The year was 1981, he was 16, and his dreams of playing major-league baseball were still intact. But that was not the end of his physical complications in high school. After a comparatively uneventful junior year, Banister injured his knee during his senior year and was almost cut from the team because the injury impeded his mobility. His father suggested that he try a different position, catching. Jeff took the advice.[5]

After finishing high school, Banister attended Lee Community College in Baytown, Texas. He caught for the Lee baseball team and during his freshman year was once again faced with adversity. On a play at the plate in a game in which Banister was catching, the baserunner tried to hurdle him to avoid his tag. The baserunner's knee hit Banister in the head, breaking three of his vertebrae and leaving him paralyzed for three days.[6] The accident led to another lengthy stay in the hospital, nearly six months. After three operations, a year of rehabilitation, and being told that he would never play ball again, Banister was back on the field with the baseball team. He finished out another year with Lee, and was named a Junior College

ONE-HIT WONDERS

All-American, before earning a scholarship to the University of Houston in 1986.

Banister stayed at the University of Houston for a brief period. It was there that he met his future wife, Karen Stanton. Shortly afterward, he was drafted by the Pittsburgh Pirates in the 25th round of the 1986 draft.[7] His first stop in the Pirates' minor-league system was with the Watertown Pirates in the Class-A short-season New York-Penn League in 1986. He put up dismal offensive numbers over 41 games, batting just .145.

In 1987 Banister moved to the Macon Pirates of the Class-A South Atlantic League. Playing in 101 games, he put up a more solid line of .254/.316/.378. His improved numbers and solid defense were enough to move him up to the Double-A Harrisburg Senators for the 1988 season. His hitting stayed consistent with the Senators: .259/.296/.376. His defense suffered, though, and he wound up with 17 errors in 71 games, tied for the league lead among catchers.

For the 1989 season, Banister returned to Harrisburg and even though his batting average dropped to .238, he was named the Eastern League All-Star catcher. The 1990 season began in Harrisburg again and improved offensive numbers, .269/.313/.386, were enough to get him called up to the Buffalo Bisons of the Triple-A American Association. His hot bat continued with Buffalo: a .320 average in 12 games.

Banister's cup of coffee came in 1991. While he was with Buffalo, Pittsburgh Pirates catcher Don Slaught was injured. The Pirates called up Banister on July 23 to fill Slaught's spot on the roster. Banister's moment in the sun came that same day when Pirates manager Jim Leyland had him pinch-hit for pitcher Doug Drabek with one out in the seventh inning in a game against the Atlanta Braves. On the hill for the Braves was Dan Petry. Banister laced a 1-and-1 pitch from Petry in the hole between short and third. Braves shortstop Jeff Blauser managed to field the grounder and make the throw to first. But Banister beat it out.[8] But neither of the next two batters could advance Banister.

After a series of roster moves, the Pirates sent Banister back to Buffalo after that one appearance. He finished the season with a .244 average in 79 games. While playing winter ball in the offseason, Banister blew out his elbow and needed surgery. He missed the entire 1992 season.[9] In '93 he joined the Carolina Mudcats of the Double-A Southern League as a player-coach. He played in only eight games and batted .333 (5-for-15). After the season, Banister retired as a player.

Although his playing days were finished, Banister remained with the Pirates organization. In 1994 he managed the Welland Pirates of the short-season New York-Penn League. The Pirates finished with a 30-44 record. In 1995 he managed the Augusta GreenJackets of the Class-A South Atlantic League to a 76-62 record. In 1996 and '98 he managed the Carolina Mudcats of the Double-A Southern League; between those two seasons he led the Lynchburg Hillcats of the Class-A Carolina League.

After the 1998 season, Banister worked from 1999 to 2001 as the Pirates' major-league field coordinator. In 2002 he was reassigned as Pittsburgh's minor-league field coordinator, a position he held until 2010. Banister briefly returned to managing with the Scottsdale Scorpions of the Arizona Fall League in 2009.

In the middle of the 2010 season, the Pirates fired their bench coach, Gary Varsho, and brought Banister in as the interim. After the season, Pirates manager John Russell was also fired. Banister and Clint Hurdle were interviewed for the position. Hurdle was hired; Banister retained the bench-coach position.[10] Along the way Banister learned about sabermetrics from Mike Fitzgerald, a quantitative analyst who was employed by the Pirates.[11]

After the 2014 season, Banister interviewed for manager positions with the Houston Astros and Texas Rangers. The Astros passed, but the Rangers on October 16 signed him to a three-year contract with an option for a fourth year.

In his first season with the Rangers, Banister took them from a last-place finish in 2014 to a division title in 2015. Although, they lost to the Toronto Blue Jays in the American League Division Series, Banister's about-face with Texas earned him American League Manager of the Year Award. The Rangers again won their division in 2016, but were swept by the Blue Jays in the ALDS. The 2017 and 2018 seasons were disappointing: fourth place and then last in the AL Central Division, and Banister was fired on September 21, 2018, just shy of the season's close.

In 2019 Banister briefly returned to the Pirates as a special assistant in baseball operations.[12] He held the position for only one season because the Pirates were in the midst of a restructuring that did not include Banister and 14 others. Banister interviewed with the Houston Astros after A.J. Hinch was fired, but lost out to Dusty Baker.[13] On September 2, 2020, the University of Southern Colorado announced that Banister would become its director of player development.

SOURCES

In addition to the sources cited in the Notes, the author consulted Baseball-Reference.com.

NOTES

1. Anthony Castovince, "They Had 1 Career AB, 1 Career Hit. Nothing Else," MLB.com, August 29, 2019. mlb.com/news/featured/mlb-ultimate-one-hit-wonders.
2. Stefan Stevenson, "Banister's Mom Played as Vital a Role in Athletics as Coaching Dad," *Fort Worth Star-Telegram*, May 13, 2017.
3. Brett Barnett, "The Story of Jeff Banister," *Bucs Dugout* May 8, 2020. bucsdugout.com/2020/5/8/21249547/the-story-of-jeff-banister.
4. Richard Justice, "Banister Cancer Scare Evokes Teenage Ordeal," MLB.com, February 24, 2016. mlb.com/news/jeff-banister-s-cancer-scare-evokes-ordeal-c165322978.
5. Barnett.
6. Barnett.
7. Barnett.
8. Castovince.
9. Castovince.
10. Associated Press, "Nick Leyva Hired as Third Base Coach," Espn.com, November 24, 2010. espn.com/mlb/news/story?id=5847952.
11. Ben Lindbergh, "The Pirates Sabermetrics Road Show," *Grantland,* September 23, 2014. grantland.com/the-triangle/pittsburgh-pirates-mike-fitzgerald-mit-sabermetric-road-show/.
12. Adam Berry, "Pirates Hire Jeff Banister as Special Assistant," MLB.com, January 6, 2019. mlb.com/pirates/press-release/pirates-hire-jeff-banister-as-special-assistant-302428658.
13. Jason Mackey, "Jeff Banister Among Pirates' 15 Layoffs in Baseball Operations," *Pittsburgh Post-Gazette*, June 26, 2020. post-gazette.com/sports/pirates/2020/06/26/Jeff-Banister-among-Pirates-15-layoffs-in-baseball-operations/stories/202006260146.

VINCE BELNOME

By Darren Gibson

Possibly the only "one-hit wonder" to belt a ground-rule double for his knock, one of the few to play only designated hitter, and one of the rare ones who (but only temporarily) had a second base hit, Vince Belnome is a unique twenty-first-century addition to the list of one-hit wonders.

Vincent Michael Belnome was born in Coatesville, Pennsylvania, on March 11, 1988, to Vincent Belnome (b. 1962), a carpenter, and Kimberly Ann Belnome (b. 1962), owner of a cleaning company. He has a younger sister, Kate.

Vince's father, also named Vince, "bought his son a batting cage and pitching machine when the younger Belnome was in ninth grade."[1] The younger Vince was a three-time team MVP for Coatesville High School, hitting .557 in his senior season, and setting a school career batting average record. He belted two home runs against Bishop Shanahan on March 30. His team won the Pennsylvania Interscholastic Athletic Association District 1 AAAA championship in 2006 with a perfect 23-0 record, but fell in its first state tournament game.

Belnome earned a half-scholarship to West Virginia University. In his freshman year he suffered a torn ACL in a game against St. John's. In 2009, Belnome's junior year, he slashed .418/.517/.648 with 84 RBIs, 9 home runs, 20 doubles, and 66 runs scored for the Mountaineers, one of three starters who hit above .400.[2] In the Mountaineers lineup, he regularly hit behind Jedd Gyorko, later also a minor-league teammate. Belnome hit a grand slam on March 21 against the University of Connecticut.[3] He went 6-for-6 with two home runs, four runs scored, and nine RBIs in an 18-3 blowout of the University of Cincinnati on May 10.[4] Belnome finished in the top 20 of NCAA regular-season batters for 2009.[5] He majored in sports management while in Morgantown.

After his junior season, Belnome was drafted by the San Diego Padres in the 28th round of the June 2009 amateur draft, one of two Mountaineers drafted, along with catcher Tobias Streich.[6] Belnome signed, and was assigned to Eugene (Oregon) of the low Class-A Northwest League, slugging .500 with 10 home runs and 16 doubles for the Emeralds. Later in the summer of 2009, he was promoted to Fort Wayne of the Midwest League and batted .500 in 10 games in helping the TinCaps win in the first round of the league playoffs. Belnome was selected to both the Northwest and Midwest League all-star teams. He worked extensively with Padres minor-league hitting coach Bob Skube.[7]

In 2010 Belnome moved up to Lake Elsinore of the high Class-A California League. He earned Organization All-Star status. His Bowman Padres prospect card listed these attributes of Belnome: a "selective hitter who rarely strikes out. ... Plays with great intensity. ... Can staff three positions. ... Keeps weight back and uses whole field. ... Shows burgeoning power." Belnome hit .273 (Brandon Belt led the California League with a .383 average) with an on-base percentage of .397, thanks to 102 walks, although he did also strike out 136 times.

ONE-HIT WONDERS

Belnome enjoyed a breakout 2011 campaign for San Antonio of the Double-A Texas League and manager Doug Descenzo. He slashed .333/.432/.603. He earned Texas League Player of the Week for the week ending on June 13 by going 11-for-23 with 5 home runs and 16 RBIs. However, he played in only 75 games due to a pulled groin and lower abdominal strain.

Belnome kept climbing the Padres organizational ladder, playing for the Padres' Triple-A affiliate in Tucson in 2012. He began the year as the starting second baseman in an infield that included catcher Yasmani Grandal,[8] but spent over six weeks on the disabled list in May and June with a separated shoulder. Belnome returned and became the starting third baseman. In 80 games with Tucson for manager Terry Kennedy, Belnome hit .275 with five home runs. Kennedy commented that Belnome was "a good teammate. You can't ask anything else of a player."[9] However, in December 2012, Belnome was traded by San Diego to Tampa Bay for Chris Rearick.

To begin 2013, Belnome was assigned by Tampa Bay to Durham of the International League. He batted cleanup, in a lineup including future major leaguers Brandon Guyer, Shelby Duncan, Tim Beckham, Mike Fontenot, and Chris Gimenez.[10] He was selected the Bulls' MVP by hitting .300 with an on-base percentage of .408, second in the league, and 77 runs (also second) in 127 games, including double-digit starts at third base, first base, and second base. Belnome earned IL Player of the Week honors in late April, and started in the IL all-star game.[11] He was batting .345 as of early July for the Bulls.[12] Even more than the production, however, was Belnome's influence in the clubhouse. "He's always upbeat," teammate Duncan commented, adding that to "have a positive, uplifting, encouraging personality like Vince makes everyone around him better."[13] The Bulls swept the Indianapolis Indians in the semifinals, then topped the Pawtucket Red Sox in four games to win the International League pennant. Belnome was also named a Tampa Bay organizational all-star.[14] In the winter, he played six games for Estrellas of the Dominican League.

Belnome began 2014 back in Durham for manager Charlie Montoyo as the primary first baseman, while also earning starts at third base and new professional positions of left field and right field. *Baseball America* pegged Belnome as having the best strike-zone discipline in the Rays system. However, Belnome actually began his year with the Rays, as he was recalled on April 4 while Sean Rodriguez was on paternity leave, arriving from Durham after the first pitch on Opening Night. Belnome did not see action in the game, and was returned to Durham the next day. For the Bulls in 2014, Belnome hit only .245 while striking out 128 times. Still, he was third on the team in doubles with 25 and tied for fourth in home runs with 10. It was certainly that potential power from the left side of the plate that intrigued the Rays.

Belnome was again recalled by Tampa in early July, earning his first start for manager Joe Maddon as the designated hitter in a game at Detroit on July 3. His parents made the seven-hour drive from Pennsylvania, and his fiancée drove up from Durham.[15] For his debut he drew Max Scherzer, the reigning American League Cy Young Award winner. Belnome struck out twice and flied out. Nonetheless, Belnome had a fond memory of the evening: "One of the greatest feelings in the world, playing in 'The Show' with 50,000 people there[16] including my family. The moment was incredible. I was facing a former Cy Young Award winner so I knew it wasn't going to be easy but I was up for the challenge."[17]

Belnome was returned to Durham two days later, but made it back with the Rays in August, earning starts at DH in home games on August 16 and 17 against the New York Yankees. He went 0-for-2 with a walk in each game, making his record 0-for-7 up to this point in his big-league career.

For his fourth career major-league starting assignment, on August 19 at Tropicana Field, Belnome drew, as luck would have it, Scherzer again. This time, though, the Rays jumped on Mad Max early, plating three runs in the first thanks to James Loney's home run. Belnome led off the bottom of the second, and hit a ground-rule double to right-center field,[18] after center fielder Rajai Davis lost the ball in the Tropicana Field ceiling. Belnome later scored on Ben Zobrist's single. Leading off the fourth inning, Belnome was momentarily banished from the list of "one-hit wonders," when he belted an opposite-field home run … or so everyone thought. As Belnome trotted around the bases and was about to accept his congratulations from third-base coach Tom Foley, Scherzer began arguing with home-plate umpire Greg Gibson. After Gibson convened the four umpires, crew chief Gerry Davis ruled the hit a foul ball instead of a home run. Belnome then struck out looking to complete the at-bat.

After a fly out in the sixth inning, Belnome later hit a crucial sacrifice fly in the eighth, which tied the game and ultimately sent it into extra innings. He was walked intentionally by the Tigers' Jim Johnson in the 10th inning, with the winning run in scoring position,

ONE-HIT WONDERS

but Detroit escaped the jam, and end up beating the Rays 8-6 in 11 innings.

Belnome soon was returned to Durham for its playoff push. The Bulls defeated the Columbus Clippers in the International League semifinals, earning a return trip to the finals, once again against the PawSox. This time, Pawtucket prevailed, in five games. Belnome was recalled a fourth time in the season by Tampa Bay, in late September, but did not play. In the offseason he was dropped off the Rays' 40-man roster, outrighted back to Durham.[19]

In 2015 Belnome began in Durham as the longest-tenured Bull on the roster, playing in 291 games over three years. He even saw spot pitching duty in a 17-6 blowout loss to Charlotte in early July.[20] His offensive production fell way off; he batted .169[21] before being released on July 22 to make roster space for outfielder Grady Sizemore.[22] Vince signed as a free agent on July 28 with New York Mets organization, and was assigned to Binghamton, which lost in the first round of the Eastern League playoffs.[23] After the 2015 season, he elected free agency, was not signed, and had not played professional baseball since 2015.

Belnome summed up his major-league experience:

> I love baseball, always have and always will. I had a dream when I was a young scrap and I told everyone that I would be a MLB PLAYER. Sure, it wasn't for 10+ years but I made it to the big leagues and ended up getting a hit off of a former Cy Young winner (and future Hall of Famer). No one can ever take that away. I will have plenty of stories to tell my children when they want to listen![24]

Vince Belnome and his wife, Abby, have a son Bowen (b. 1997) and another son who was due in November 2020. Belnome is a carpenter and co-owner/operator of Balance Hitting Academy in Parkesburg, Pennsylvania.

SOURCES

In addition to the sources cited in the Notes, the author relied on Baseball-Reference.com and MyHeritage.com Birth, Marriage, Death Records.

NOTES

1. Daniel Berk, "Belnome Traces Success to Batting Cage in Yard," *Arizona Daily Star* (Tucson), July 19, 2012: B003.
2. Phil Axelrod, "Duquesne Eyes First Baseball Title, Faces Xavier in A-10 Showdown," *Pittsburgh Post-Gazette*, April 29, 2008: 33.
3. "Baseball Notes," *Hartford Courant*, March 22, 2009: E02.
4. "Local Colleges: Baseball," *Cincinnati Enquirer*, May 11, 2009: 18.
5. "Final Regular Season Statistics: Batting Average" *Daily Advertiser* (Lafayette, Louisiana), May 26, 2009: 14.
6. Colin Dunlap, "Giants Select Dukes Recruit," *Pittsburgh Post-Gazette*, June 11, 2009: 25.
7. Daniel Berk, "Belnome Traces Success to Batting Cage in Yard."
8. Daniel Berk, "A Mix of New and Old," *Arizona Daily Star*, April 4, 2012: B003.
9. Daniel Berk, "Belnome Traces Success to Batting Cage in Yard."
10. "Boxscore," *Raleigh News and Observer*, July 20, 2013: C9.
11. Roger Mooney, "Longoria Content at DH – for Now," *Tampa Tribune*, July 4, 2013: 25.
12. Wade Rupard, "Perseverance Paying Off for Surprising Belnome," *Raleigh News and Observer*, July 5, 2013: C1.
13. Rupard.
14. Roger Mooney, "Minor-League Awards," *Tampa Tribune*, September 19, 2013: 25.
15. "Cobb Pleased with Progress" *Tampa Bay Times*, July 4, 2014: C4.
16. The attendance was 33,908.
17. Email correspondence with Vince Belnome, August 2, 2020.
18. Matt Baker, "Injured Trio Making Progress" *Tampa Bay Times*, August 20, 2014: C4.
19. Marc Topkin, "Rays to Be Flexible at Winter Meets," *Tampa Bay Times*, December 8, 2014: C8.
20. Marc Topkin, "Boxberger Sees Flaw to Fix," *Tampa Bay Times*, July 9, 2015: C3.
21. Nick Gray, "Snell's Latest Stop: Durham," *Raleigh News and Observer*, July 27, 2015: B2.
22. Roger Mooney, "Karns' Historic Homer Puts Him in Exclusive Company," *Raleigh News and Observer*, July 22, 2015: B2.
23. Lynn Worthy, "B-Mets Made Playoff Push Despite Moves," *Press and Sun-Bulletin* (Binghamton, New York), September 16, 2015: C1.
24. Email correspondence with Vince Belnome, August 2, 2020.

TIM BIRTSAS

By Steve Friedman

Timothy Dean Birtsas, a pitcher whose only major-league hit was a home run, spent five years pitching for Oakland and Cincinnati. He was born on September 5, 1960, in Pontiac, Michigan, a Detroit suburb. He grew up in nearby Clarkston, where, outside of his baseball career, he has spent most of his life. He attended elementary through high school in Clarkston, then came back home after his baseball career to work in business, founding a construction management company and remodeling a motel into a lakefront retreat. In his return to Clarkston, he lived within a mile of where he grew up.[1]

Besides his time in the major leagues, Birtsas also played professional baseball in Japan and Italy. He experienced the joy of being a World Series champion as well as on the winning team in the Italian Baseball League.

The Birtsas family arrived in the Clarkston area in in the fall of 1952, when his father, Gus, became a teacher in the Clarkston School District. Gus Birtsas spent 30 years teaching English and physical education and coaching baseball at Clarkston High School. He eventually became the principal at the local junior high school.[2]

Gus Birtsas coached baseball for many years, until Tim entered high school. At one point, when Tim's career hit a steak of bad luck, Gus flew to Las Vegas, received special permission to go onto the ballfield and, at 61 years old, squatted behind the plate to help coach his son.[3] "There was no limitation to the sacrifices he would make for us," said Tim. "I became a professional baseball player because of him. He put as much work into it as I did."[4] His mother, Carolyn, worked as a registered nurse until she and Gus retired in 1987.

Tim grew to 6-feet-7-inches, weighed 240 pounds, and was a dominating left-handed pitcher who also played basketball for Clarkston High School. After graduating in 1978 he entered Michigan State University on a baseball scholarship. He played baseball for three years at Michigan State, from 1980 through 1982. While the Spartans did not have a winning record during those years, Birtsas was a second team Big 10 selection in 1982 when he started 10 games and compiled a 6-4 record, striking out 68 batters in 64⅓ innings.[5] His eight complete games that season tied for the second most in a Spartan season.[6]

Birtsas's imposing height and live arm made him a good draft prospect. A scouting report submitted by a White Sox scout in May 1982 described him as having a good fastball (87 to 90 MHP) and good mechanics, but suggested that he needed to learn a curveball and a changeup. The scout commented, "great poise, good kid."[7]

ONE-HIT WONDERS

In June 1982 the New York Yankees selected Birtsas in the second round of the free-agent draft. Birtsas immediately began his minor-league career with Oneonta of the New York-Penn League. Through the next two seasons, 1983 and 1984, he continued his development in Fort Lauderdale of the Florida State League. During this period, he started 32 games and logged 225⅓ innings. He was out of action much of 1984 with a leg injury, but came back late in the season to make 10 starts as the team won the league championship.

After the 1984 season, Birtsas was packaged with outfielder Stan Javier and pitchers Jay Howell, Jose Rijo, and Eric Plunk in a trade with Oakland that brought Rickey Henderson, pitcher Bert Bradley, and cash to the Yankees.[8] It was the first of two trades in which Birtsas was bundled with Rijo.

Birtsas began the 1985 season in the minor leagues, playing in the Pacific Coast League for Tacoma, the A's Triple-A farm club. After making four starts, he was called up to Oakland and made his major-league debut on May 3, in a relief appearance late in the game when the A's were losing to the Boston Red Sox in Oakland. After two more relief appearances, he made his first major-league start on May 23 in Oakland, throwing six innings to earn a 4-2 win against the Baltimore Orioles and was soon added to the starting rotation.

On May 30 Birtsas made his second start, in Detroit against the Tigers. "From the time when I was seven years old, I used to dream of playing with the Tigers," Birtsas said after the game, in which he gave up three runs in five innings and took the loss. "It was a neat experience today. I always wanted to play in Tiger Stadium for many years. I just always thought it'd be in the other uniform."[9] In the third inning, Birtsas hit local star Kirk Gibson, a hometown friend and fellow Michigan State Spartan, in the mouth with a pitch that sent Gibson to the hospital for 17 stitches on his upper and lower lips. "I just missed with the pitch," Birtsas said. "I was trying to bust him inside and the ball took off. It was not meant to happen, but it did. The bases were loaded and the last thing I wanted to do was walk him. I can understand everyone being upset. He's their hero."[10]

Birtsas's initial performances cemented his role in the A's rotation. After the game, manager Jackie Moore announced that he would join the starting rotation permanently. "We felt from the first day he showed up at spring training that the kid had a lot of ability," said Moore. "We just didn't know when he was going to produce. He's a youngster that has a great feel for pitching."[11]

Birtsas went on to post a 10-6 record in 1985, making 25 starts. After an August 25 victory over the Orioles that improved his record to 10-4, there was talk about him being selected as Rookie of the Year, but he failed to win another game the rest of the season, making six more starts but throwing only 25 innings and accumulating an ERA of 6.12.

The 1986 season was a difficult one for Birtsas. Slated to be one of the left-handers in the A's bullpen, he started the major-league season by appearing in two games, pitching just two innings and yielding five earned runs. He was sent to Tacoma, where he spent the rest of the season, compiling a 3-7 record with an ERA of 5.07. Knee problems may have been a cause of his ineffectiveness.

Birtsas remained in the minors again in 1987, splitting his season between Tacoma and Huntsville of the Double-A Southern League. After the season he was packaged again with Jose Rijo and traded to the Cincinnati Reds for slugger Dave Parker.

Birtsas hoped to land a spot on the major-league roster as a long reliever. At the start of the 1988 season, he was optioned to Nashville of the Triple-A Pacific Coast League. After eight starts, he was recalled. For the Reds he appeared in 36 games (four starts), compiling a 1-3 record. At the end of August, he was again optioned to Nashville, but was recalled three days later to spend the rest of the season with the Reds after Rijo landed on the disabled list with a sore elbow.[12]

The 1989 campaign was Birtsas's only full season in the majors. Except for one start, he appeared in relief in 42 games. On July 2, he achieved his first major-league hit, a home run, off Sid Fernandez of the New York Mets in a game at Cincinnati's Riverfront Stadium. He hit it to right field on a 1-and-2 pitch in the bottom of the third inning. He had entered the game in the top of that inning in relief of starter Scott Scudder. On August 7 he earned the only save of his career, a four-inning effort against the San Francisco Giants in a 10-2 victory. It was his longest outing of the season.

On November 3, 1990, the Reds named Lou Piniella as their new manager. He replaced interim manager Tommy Helms, who ran the team during the latter days of the 1989 season after the suspension of Pete Rose.[13] Piniella took over leadership of a team that had lost 87 games in 1989 and guided them to become World Series champions.

ONE-HIT WONDERS

Birtsas began the 1990 season on the Reds' roster as the Reds raced out of the box, opening the season with a nine-game winning streak and never falling out of first place in the National League West. The drivers for the team were the Reds' outstanding relief core, known as the "Nasty Boys," Randy Myers, Rob Dibble, Norm Charlton, Tim Layana, and Birtsas. "We come after teams," said Myers. "And we do a lot of talking."[14] In their season-opening nine-game winning streak, the Nasties had four wins and five saves.[15]

Their bullpen depth took pressure off the starting pitchers, who needed to go only five, six, or seven innings before the game was turned over to the bullpen. The middle innings were the domain of right-handed pitcher Layana, known for his knuckle curve, and the left-handed Birtsas, who relied on his fastball. The late innings brought on Charlton, Myers, and Dibble.[16] Birtsas finished April without surrendering an earned run, appearing in four games and earning a victory.

On June 4 Birtsas struck out four batters in the seventh inning of a 10-1 loss to the Giants. In that inning, in which he also surrendered one run and two hits, he struck out Greg Litton, Will Clark, Matt Williams, and Gary Carter. The Williams strikeout was on a wild pitch on which he reached first base.

Birtsas's performance faded after April. By late June, with his ERA now over 4.00, it was apparent that Piniella had lost faith in him, and Piniella reduced his use to mopping up late innings during losses. On July 26 he was optioned to Nashville.[17] He was recalled in September and made the postseason roster, but did not pitch in either the National League Championship Series or the World Series.

On December 11, 1990, the Reds released Birtsas.[18] He continued his professional career in Japan, signing for the 1991 season with the Yakult Swallows of the Central League of Nippon Professional Baseball. He pitched in 18 games, starting 16, and ended the season with a 3-5 record. During a game in mid-April, Birtsas was ejected for fighting after a brushback pitch to Yoshihisa Komatsuzaki, who then rushed the mound. Birtsas received a warning, but Komatsuzaki was fined $1,500.[19]

After that one season in Japan, Birtsas signed to play for Rimini of the Italian Baseball League. In limited action during the regular season, he was 3-1 with a 2.31 ERA. In the league playoffs, however, he led the team to a three-game sweep in the championship finals. He won two of the three games, throwing a pair of complete games and surrendering only one earned run. Although Birtsas flirted with a return to the major leagues when he signed a minor-league contract with the Detroit Tigers in early 1993,[20] hip problems forced to him retire from baseball and he eventually had hip replacements in 2003.[21]

Birtsas has suggested that one reason he played internationally was to accumulate money to go into business.[22] After he retired, he founded RBI Inc., a construction and development company that specialized in real estate investments, management, and historical preservation.[23] Over time, he developed numerous local projects, often with his business partner Kirk Gibson. For example, in 2001, he purchased the land that contained Ellis Barn, an 1884 building that represented a significant period of Michigan's agricultural history. He began a five-year fight to rehabilitate the building, and in 2005 he and Gibson donated the barn to Springfield Township, adding a cash donation to support its rehabilitation.[24]

Birtsas told an interviewer in 2009 that he had grown to like the development business. "It was tough for me in the beginning (to leave baseball), but now that I've moved into business, I get the same rush as I did pitching a two-hit shutout," he said.[25]

SOURCES

In addition to the sources cited in the Notes, the author consulted Baseball-Reference.com, and Baseball-Almanac.com.

NOTES

1. Heather Clement, "Clarkston Loses Beloved Mentor," *Clarkston* (Michigan) *News,* July 27, 2005.
2. Clement.
3. Clement.
4. Clement.
5. Web1.ncaa.org/app data/statsPDFArchive/MBA1/Baseball Men's Division%20I 1982 416 michigan%20State%20University.pdf. Accessed October 5, 2020.
6. msuspartans.com/documents/2020/1/9/2019_Baseball_Record_Book_print.pdf. Accessed October 5, 2020.
7. collection.baseballhall.org/PASTIME/tim-birtsas-scouting-report-1982-may-09.
8. Murray Chass, "Yanks and A's Complete Deal for Henderson," *New York Times*, December 6, 1984.
9. Bob Tripi, "Tim Birtsas Grew Up with Dream of Playing," UPI Archives, May 30, 1985. upi.com/Archives/1985/05/30/Tim-Birtsas-grew-up-with-a-dream-of-playing/3426486273600/.
10. Tripi.
11. Tripi.
12. Associated Press, "Rijo Placed on 21-Day Disabled List," *New London* (Connecticut) *Day*, August 28, 1988.

ONE-HIT WONDERS

13 Associated Press, "Helms Managing Reds," *New York Times*, August 25, 1989.

14 Claire Smith, "Reds Find Relief with 'Nasty' Bunch on and off Mound," *New York Times*, April 23, 1990.

15 Smith.

16 Smith.

17 Charles F. Faber and Zacharia Webb, *The Hunt for Reds October: Cincinnati in 1990* (Jefferson, North Carolina: McFarland & Company, Inc., 2016), 145.

18 Faber and Webb, 156.

19 Associated Press, "Perfect Parks Have Best of Old, New," *Bowling Green* (Kentuckey) *Daily News*, April 19, 1991.

20 "Birtsas Signs with Tigers," *Clarkston News*, February 17, 1993.

21 "Birtsas Signs with Tigers."

22 "Birtsas Signs with Tigers."

23 Carol Hopkins, "Oakland County Cruisers hire former MLB player," *Oakland Press*, March 9, 2009.

24 oakgov.com/parks/parksandtrails/Springfield-Oaks/ellis-barn/Pages/default.aspx.

25 Hopkins.

JEFF BITTIGER

By Joel Rippel

Jeff Bittiger's professional baseball career spanned 23 seasons. But that long-playing career, which ended at the age of 40, included just 33 games – in parts of four seasons – in the major leagues.

The handful of highlights from his time in the major leagues includes four victories as a right-handed pitcher – including one for the Minnesota Twins in their pennant drive of 1987 – and one major-league hit.

Bittiger was born on April 13, 1962, in Jersey City, New Jersey. His father, Gary, was a chemical plant employee and his mother, Lois, was a secretary. He had a brother, Gary Jr., and a sister, Kerri.

Jeff attended Secaucus (New Jersey) High School. He joined the Secaucus varsity baseball team as a freshman as a catcher and infielder. He started pitching as a sophomore.

In a preview of his senior season, the 5-foot-10, 175-pounder threw a one-hitter with 14 strikeouts in the Patriots' 6-3 season-opening victory over Wallington on April 3. The team went on to win the New Jersey Group 1 state championship.

Bittiger, who played shortstop when he wasn't pitching, batted .490 with 9 home runs and 35 RBIs. On the mound he was 14-0 with a 0.29 ERA and 211 strikeouts in 102 innings. He finished his high-school career by tossing a four-hit shutout with 10 strikeouts – his lowest total of the season – in the Patriots' 6-0 victory over Monroe Township in the state championship game. Secaucus finished the season with a 26-2 record.

Bittiger, whose fastball was clocked at 93 MPH, "established himself as one of the best, if not *the* best in the state."[1]

Three days before pitching the Patriots to the title, Bittiger was selected in the seventh round of the June 1980 amateur draft by the New York Mets. Bittiger was the ninth pick for the Mets, who had three first-round picks and selected Darryl Strawberry with the first overall pick.

Bittiger, who had been offered a full athletic scholarship to play baseball for Clemson, signed with the Mets on July 1. The Mets announced they intended to use Bittiger as both an infielder and pitcher.

"He has a two-way shot, as a pitcher and a third baseman," said Mets director of scouting Pete Gebrian. "He can swing the bat with some power."[2]

Bittiger reported to Little Falls (New York) of the Class-A New York-Penn League. On the mound, he got off to a good start, striking out 10 and allowing no earned runs in his five innings. In seven pitching appearances, he was 0-1 with a 1.04 ERA and 33 strikeouts in 26 innings. In 37 at-bats, he batted .189 with 3 RBIs.

After the New York-Penn League season, Bittiger spent two months with the Mets Instructional League team in Florida.

ONE-HIT WONDERS

According to a newspaper, Bittiger made a good impression with the Mets as a pitcher – "one of the top one or two arms in the organization."[3]

Mets general manager Frank Cashen and manager Joe Torre agreed. Cashen said, "The No. 1 thing you have to be impressed with in Jeff is his poise. It's hard to believe he is only 18."[4] Torre said, "He's just a baby, and I saw him pitch only once down in the Instructional League. But he made an impression on me, and he showed me how he responds to pressure. … He's got a lot of velocity, and, if he stays healthy, there's no telling how well he could develop."[5]

Bittiger started the 1981 season with Lynchburg of the Class-A Carolina League. He went 11-7 with a 3.94 ERA in 24 starts and led the league in strikeouts (168 in 137 innings) to earn a promotion to Double-A Jackson. In four starts with Jackson, he was 2-1 with a 1.09 ERA.

He returned to Jackson for the 1982 season, going 12-5 with a 2.96 ERA in 25 starts and a league-record 190 strikeouts (in 164 innings). He allowed just 106 hits.

After the season Bittiger shared with Strawberry the Doubleday Award, as the outstanding Double-A player in the Mets organization.

Bittiger went to spring training with the Mets in 1983. He wouldn't turn 21 until April, and was the youngest pitcher in the big-league camp. He was sent to the Mets' minor-league camp on March 23. Two days earlier, he had pitched four shutout innings in the Mets' 3-1 exhibition victory over Toronto.

Bittiger spent the 1983 season with Triple-A Tidewater. With the Tides, he started slowly, winning just four of his first 12 decisions, but he finished with a 12-10 record in 28 starts.

Bittiger again went to the Mets' big-league camp in 1984 before spending the season in Tidewater. He was 8-8 with a 3.88 ERA in 23 starts.

In spring training with the Mets in 1985, Bittiger got caught in a numbers game. "Jeff reached a peak in '82, then dropped off some while others went past him," said Mets manager Davey Johnson. "Now another group has come up to that peak. His command (of pitches) hasn't improved as much as it should have by this time."[6]

Bittiger returned to Tidewater in 1985 for his third season with the Tides, going 11-7 with a 3.69 ERA in 24 starts. He started the season with a five-game winning streak and finished the season by winning five of his last seven decisions. But he missed seven starts after pulling a hamstring in early August.

In January of 1986, Bittiger was traded (along with catcher Ronn Reynolds) to the Philadelphia Phillies for a pair of minor leaguers, pitcher Rodger Cole and first baseman Ron Gideon. For the fourth consecutive season, he began in Triple A. With Portland of the Pacific Coast League, he went 13-8 (tying his career high for victories in a season that he set with two teams in 1981) in 26 starts. He was rewarded with a September call-up by the Phillies.

Bittiger made his major-league debut on September 2, 1986, against the San Diego Padres in Philadelphia. He allowed five runs in five innings and took the loss as the Padres defeated the Phillies, 6-2.

On September 22, in Pittsburgh, Bittiger made his second appearance. He allowed just two runs in 6⅔ innings to get the victory as the Phillies defeated the Pirates, 8-4.

Making the game more memorable for Bittiger, who had struck out in his only at-bat in his major-league debut, got his first major-league hit. In the top of the third, in his first at-bat of the day, Bittiger hit a solo home run to left field off Pirates starter Bob Kipper. After the game, he said, "More pitcher than third baseman, I think. I hit maybe eight or nine homers my senior year in high school, but pitching was what I did best."[7]

Bittiger made his final appearance of the season on October 4, the next-to-last game of the season, when he started and went three innings in the Phillies' 5-4, 14-inning victory over the visiting Montreal Expos.

Bittiger was released by the Phillies in December. He signed with the Atlanta Braves and was invited to spring training in 1987 but was released on April 4. He signed a minor-league contract with the Minnesota Twins in mid-April and was assigned to Portland (PCL). In a career-high 180 innings, he was 12-10 with a 3.40 ERA.

Bittiger was called up by the Twins, who were en route to their first World Series title. He made his American League debut on September 7 at the Metrodome against the Chicago White Sox. He went seven innings, allowing six hits and one run while striking out five, in the Twins' 8-1 victory. The victory left the Twins with a three-game lead in the AL West over second-place Oakland with 23 games remaining. Bittiger made two more appearances for the Twins, both in relief. After the season, he was released by the Twins, and he signed with the Chicago White Sox in January of 1988.

Bittiger opened the 1988 season with Vancouver (PCL). A 4-1 record, 1.04 ERA, and five complete

ONE-HIT WONDERS

games in seven starts earned him a call-up by the White Sox on May 13. In his White Sox debut on May 16, he allowed one earned run and struck out six in four innings in Chicago's 5-1 loss to Toronto. He spent the remainder of the 1988 season with the White Sox, going 2-4 with a 4.23 ERA in 25 appearances (seven starts).

Bittiger returned to Vancouver to start the 1989 season. He was recalled by the White Sox on May 22 and pitched 4⅔ innings of relief the next day. He allowed two earned runs in Chicago's 5-1 loss to the visiting Baltimore Orioles. On May 30 he started and took the loss in Chicago's 10-3 loss to the Tigers. He allowed five earned runs in five innings in what would be his final major-league appearance.

Bittiger left that start with a pulled muscle and was placed on the disabled list two days later. In late June he went to Sarasota for a rehab stint. He went 1-1 with a 0.75 ERA in two starts for the Gulf Coast League White Sox. He was activated from the disabled list on July 13 and sent back to Vancouver. With Vancouver, he was 9-5 with a 2.12 ERA.

In November of 1989, Bittiger was traded to the Los Angeles Dodgers for infielder Tracy Woodson. He was added to the Dodgers' 40-man roster and went to spring training with the team in 1990. But again, he got caught in a numbers game.

There was a 32-day work stoppage (a lockout by the owners) during spring training. After spring training resumed, there was talk that major-league rosters would be 27 players (three extra players) for the month of April. Ultimately, teams started the season with 24 players. Bittiger was sent outright to Albuquerque. He had agreed to the assignment, waiving his right to free agency.

"I was pretty disappointed," said Bittiger. "I knew the short three-week spring training was going to hurt my chance of making it. It's disappointing to go back (to the PCL). I felt I was the best pitcher in the league last year. I don't know what else I can prove."[8]

With Albuquerque in 1990, Bittiger won a career-high 15 games, going 15-6 with a 4.15 ERA in 28 appearances. After the season he signed with the Cleveland organization and spent the 1991 season with Colorado Springs (PCL). For the 1992 season, he signed with the Oakland organization. He started the season at Double-A Huntsville. He put together an eight-game winning streak to earn a promotion to Triple-A Tacoma. Between the two, he was 13-8 with a 2.97 ERA.

In 1993, for the first time, Bittiger didn't go to a spring camp. He pitched for an amateur team in New Jersey, then joined the Rochester (Minnesota) Aces of the newly formed independent Northern League. The franchise moved to Winnipeg after the 1994 season and Bittiger pitched for Winnipeg.

During the 1994-95 offseason, with the major-league players on strike, Bittiger signed a contract with the Oakland A's, whose general manager was Billy Beane, who had been taken by the Mets in the same draft as Bittiger. After the A's finished their Cactus League schedule with a 14-10-1 record, Bittiger was expected to be the A's Opening Day starter on April 3.

A settlement to end the work stoppage was reached on April 1 and the start of the regular season was postponed until April 26. Bittiger was assigned to Triple-A Edmonton (PCL).

"I just wanted an opportunity to pitch," said Bittiger. "I think I can still pitch, whether it's here (Edmonton) or in the big leagues."[9]

He appeared in six games with Edmonton – the sixth PCL team he had pitched for – going 2-0 with a 5.28 ERA. He was released by Oakland on April 30, and returned to Winnipeg of the Northern League for the remainder of the 1995 season, going 8-5 in 20 starts.

In 1996 Bittiger joined the expansion Fargo-Moorhead RedHawks of the Northern League. It would be the final team of his 23-year career. He spent the next seven seasons with the RedHawks.

In 1998 he was 12-1 with a 1.94 ERA in 16 starts as he tied the league record for victories and led the RedHawks to the league title. In 2000 Bittiger was named *Baseball America's* Independent Player of the Decade (for the 1990s). After the 2002 season, he retired as a player. In seven seasons with the RedHawks, he was 36-12 with a 3.46 ERA in 77 starts.

For his minor-league career, Bittiger won 193 games (135 in Organized Baseball and 58 in independent leagues) and struck out 1,994 (1,397 in Organized Baseball and 597 in independent leagues). At the time of his retirement, he was the Northern League career leader in victories and strikeouts.

After retiring, Bittiger spent the 2003 season as the RedHawks pitching coach. In 2004 he became a scout for the Oakland Athletics, a position he still held in 2020. In 2010 he was named the Oakland organization's Scout of the Year.

Bittiger and his wife Alicia live in Saylorsburg, Pennsylvania. Their son Brett was drafted by the

ONE-HIT WONDERS

Oakland Athletics twice. Oakland first drafted Brett, a shortstop, out of Pius X High School in the 41st round of the 2011 draft. He elected to play for Fairleigh Dickinson instead of signing. After one season, he transferred to Pace University, where he was a starter for three seasons. Oakland selected him in the 40th round of the 2016 draft. He played briefly for Oakland's Arizona Summer League team in 2016 before retiring.

SOURCES

In addition to the sources cited in the Notes, the author consulted Baseball-Reference.com, Newspapers.com, paceuathletics.com and Retrosheet.org.

NOTES

1. Greg Baumann, "Playoff Teams Offer Baseball's Best," *Passaic* (New Jersey) *Herald-News*, June 9, 1980: 13.
2. Patty LaDuca, "Bittiger Begins Met Career," *Passaic Herald-News*, July 2, 1980: 40.
3. "Ex-Secaucus Pitcher Already a Hit with Mets," *Hackensack Record*, December 12, 1980: 67.
4. "Ex-Secaucus Pitcher Already a Hit with Mets."
5. "Ex-Secaucus Pitcher Already a Hit with Mets."
6. Jack O'Connell, "Former Top Prospect Fights to Remain Met," *Hackensack Record*, March 12, 1985: 39.
7. Bill Conlin, "Bittiger Shows His Stuff," *Philadelphia Daily News*, September 23, 1986: 84.
8. Frank Maestas, "24-Man Roster Probably Cost Bittiger a Job," *Albuquerque Journal*, March 31, 1990: 29.
9. "Bittiger Travels Around PCL on Strength of Pitching Arm," *Edmonton Journal*, April 10, 1995: 32.

FRANK BOYD

By Chad Moody

1893 image of Boyd.

A bellicose player whose large stature cast an imposing shadow, Frank Boyd was tailor-made for rough-and-tumble late nineteenth-century baseball. Though he was a well-regarded and sturdy catcher, his big-league career spanned only two games – in which he improbably caught two future Hall of Fame pitchers. Without some unlucky contractual happenstances that befell him, however, it was suggested by noted baseball historian David Nemec that Boyd "might have proven to be a capable backup catcher in the majors for several seasons."[1]

Frank Jay Boyd was born on April 2, 1868, in West Middletown, Pennsylvania, a rural borough of Pittsburgh that was once a stop on the Underground Railroad.[2] There, his painter and merchant father, John, and homemaker mother, Eliza, raised three children. Boyd was the middle child; his brother, William, was the oldest and his sister, Mary (also known as Birdie), was the youngest. Boyd was of Scottish and Irish descent; his lineage interestingly runs through his great-great-grandfather, David Boyd, a Revolutionary War veteran who "resembled an Indian in appearance" after having previously been held captive and raised during his teenage years by Native Americans.[3]

After leaving home to pursue higher education, Boyd attended California State Normal School (California University of Pennsylvania) and Washington & Jefferson College. Although this soon enabled him to secure school teaching jobs "for a number of years" in the surrounding Pittsburgh area, Boyd's focus began to shift from academics to baseball.[4] By the age of 20, he was already "well known to all ball players of Washington County and the West Virginia 'panhandle'" for his fine play as a catcher for the independent West Middletown team.[5] After he played for that club for at least the 1887 and 1888 seasons – while moonlighting for the independent W.B. Cains club of nearby Burgettstown – the *Pittsburg Dispatch* had this to say about Boyd (and one of his batterymates): "They can hold their own in any minor league, being not only an excellent battery, but first-class batters, and Boyd a very fine baserunner."[6] The 6-foot-4, 195-pound "great hitter" reportedly hit .410 for West Middletown in 1888.[7]

The big backstop finally got his first nibble of professional ball in the 1889 campaign when he joined Wheeling of the Tri-State League.[8] But review of box scores indicates that he was released before Opening Day. Although records are sketchy, it is likely that the right-handed batter and thrower began the regular season with the independent club in Mingo Junction, a small village in Ohio less than 20 miles from his hometown.[9] What is certain, however, is that he joined the independent club in Scottdale, Pennsylvania, in

July.[10] He was called one of that team's "best" players, and it was reported by multiple sources in September that Boyd was slated to join the independent club in Jamestown, New York, to finish the season.[11] For unclear reasons, however, the catcher actually remained in his home state and wrapped up his busy year with the independent Erie Drummers.[12]

The hectic nature of Boyd's 1889 campaign continued into the offseason. In November he signed for the following season with Erie, which was in the midst of joining the newly formed New York-Pennsylvania League.[13] Although advancing from semipro to professional ball likely seemed at the time to be a progressive step for Boyd, it may have cost him an expedited path to the big leagues. In early December, (temporary) manager Harry Smith of the National League's Pittsburgh Alleghenys met with the big catcher. The *Pittsburgh Post* reported this of their meeting: "Smith wanted Boyd to sign a Pittsburgh contract, but he could not do it, as he had already signed an Erie contract. Smith wants him to ask for his release from Erie and join the Pittsburgh leaguers, but it is not likely the Erie team will so easily let him go, as he is a good man in his position."[14] Indeed, Erie did not release the "popular" player; this would not be the last time unfortunate circumstances caused a setback to Boyd's major-league career plans.[15]

Serving as the Drummers' backstop during the 1890 and 1891 seasons, Boyd received media praise for his play. Meaning it as a compliment, the *Pittsburg Dispatch* stated early in the 1890 campaign that "Boyd will bother many people" in the league.[16] And although the *Erie Daily Times* likewise lauded his play behind the plate, it additionally exposed a different, darker side of Boyd that arose during a June 30, 1891, game against Meadville. "Frank Boyd is a good catcher, but the public will not tolerate many displays of temper like that given yesterday," the newspaper opined.[17] Unsportsmanlike instances such as this continued to plague Boyd throughout his career, giving him a bad reputation among his opponents.

The offseason after the 1891 campaign proved to be filled with both intrigue and excitement for the 23-year-old. Leveraging his teaching background, Boyd was hired as a detective by the Edinboro State Normal School in Pennsylvania to surveil a principal thought to be stealing funds from the school's financial manager. "[Boyd] matriculated and began to 'brush up' in the day time, and watched [the principal] from a secret hiding place, covering [the financial manager's] safe and desk at night," reported the *Pittsburg Dispatch*. "After two months' watching Boyd gave up his job, failing to detect [the principal] or anybody else."[18] Although unsuccessful in ferreting out the alleged thief, the catcher was successful in generating interest from several minor-league clubs spanning the Illinois-Iowa League, Western League, and Wisconsin-Michigan League.[19] Boyd eventually opted to jump to the Eastern League, however, opening the 1892 season with the Elmira Gladiators before spending the second half with the Buffalo Bisons. All told, he hit a disappointing .227 in 97 games.[20]

While working as a hotel clerk during the offseason, Boyd was reportedly was being targeted by the NL's Boston Beaneaters, despite coming off an Eastern League campaign as a middling hitter at best.[21] Although a deal with Boston never came to fruition, another NL team, the Cleveland Spiders, signed Boyd to a contract for the 1893 season. "Though unlike most hotel clerks, he wears very few diamonds," observed Cleveland manager Patsy Tebeau upon meeting his new player. "The biggest he had on when I saw him was only an inch in circumference. That is quite modest, being that Boyd is a hotel clerk."[22] Initial scouting reports for the new Spiders catcher were generally favorable, with the *Cleveland Leader* noting that Boyd was reputedly "a fairly good man behind the bat," while the *Cleveland Plain Dealer* commented that he was "physically a big fellow and looks as though he could stand behind the bat for a week at a time."[23] *The Sporting News* offered this assessment of the backstop: "Boyd is a large, well-molded man, with the qualifications of a good catcher, in that he has a good arm and is an accurate thrower."[24] And Frank Knauss, an Eastern League competitor of Boyd's, deemed him to be "a clever catcher," and opined that "Cleveland has made no mistake in signing him."[25]

As Cleveland headed south for spring training, expectations indeed grew for the big catcher, with the *Cleveland Leader* now proclaiming that Boyd "from all accounts will develop into a really valuable player behind the bat."[26] Although a finger injury limited his preseason playing time, Boyd nonetheless was included on the club's roster to begin the 1893 regular season.[27] After spending the first nine games on the bench, Boyd was tabbed by manager Tebeau to get the start behind the plate in the May 18 game against the Cincinnati Reds. His batterymate that day was none other than future Hall of Famer Cy Young. In the 21-4 drubbing of the Reds, Boyd "rapped a beauty to left" for an RBI double in his first plate appearance "which a speedy man might have drawn into a triple."²⁸ All told, he went 1-for-5 with a walk, three runs scored, and three RBIs in his big-league debut. Despite some mild criticisms of his handling of foul flies, the 25-year-old acquitted himself quite nicely in the field.²⁹ "The young man is clean cut and vigorous looking and his work was like that of an old-timer," commented the *Cleveland Plain Dealer* on Boyd's performance. "He gave Young perfect support. His throwing was a sight for sore eyes."³⁰ And *The Sporting News* echoed the positive sentiment: "He caught well, giving 'Cy' Young excellent support and the opinion prevails that the youngster will do."³¹ The next day in another trouncing of Cincinnati, the rookie backstop caught John Clarkson, another future Hall of Famer. Unlike in his debut, however, this time Boyd only saw action as a ninth-inning defensive replacement. It was his final appearance in the big leagues – perhaps again due in large part to unfortunate circumstances.

Earlier in 1893, the Eastern League contended that the NL had been pilfering its talent without providing proper compensation as per an agreement between the two parties. Boyd, who had come to Cleveland via the Eastern League's Buffalo club, was one of the players stuck in the middle of the squabbling. Although the Spiders believed till the end that they held a legitimate claim on Boyd's services, NL President Nick Young intervened and opted to settle the dispute in June by returning the catcher to the Eastern League and Buffalo.³² "Boyd says with all possible emphasis that he will not play with the Bisons," reported the *Cleveland Plain Dealer* after Young's decision.³³ Indeed, Boyd did not immediately sign with Buffalo. He still kept himself sharp, however, by playing for independent Pennsylvania clubs in Marienville, Titusville, and Franklin, before finally relenting and rejoining the Bisons in August.³⁴

Although the catcher hit a respectable .313 in 39 games to cap his 1893 campaign back in Buffalo, his season was again tainted by instances of unsportsmanlike play. After an August game against Erie, the *Cleveland Plain Dealer* reported that "Boyd had a stick about 18 or 20 inches in length, sharpened on one end, which he used as his weapon, and during the earlier part of the game, while [Bill] Kuehne was about to field a ground hit he deliberately threw it in front of Bill, thereby causing him to slip up on the play."³⁵ Later in that game, he used the same tactic during a foul fly, and was this time fined by the umpire. And while coaching third base in a September contest again versus Erie, Boyd was "warned not to exercise his voice" while he "crazily danced" and "sonorously" taunted the opposition.³⁶ Nonetheless, the "lively chirruper" was back with Buffalo for the 1894 season, hitting a solid .318 in 82 games and impressing with his fine throwing arm.³⁷

After his three consecutive seasons in Buffalo, Boyd spent the rest of his baseball career hopping from town to town. In 1895 the "rowdy and scrappy" catcher became the player-manager for the Franklin (Pennsylvania) Braves of newly formed Iron and Oil League, where his uncivil behavior continued.³⁸ "Frank Boyd's team, down in Franklin, is getting itself badly disliked by their boorish and dirty ball playing of late," reported the *Buffalo Enquirer*. "One day last week the Oil City team was compelled to arm itself with bats and threaten to brain any of the spectators who laid hands on either the players or the umpire, whom they tried to mob at the instigation of Boyd, it is said."³⁹ Nonetheless, Franklin's mayor awarded a diamond pin to the "great favorite" in an August ceremony, after which the backstop departed to Detroit to join the Western League's Tigers upon receiving their more lucrative offer.⁴⁰ He hit .258 in 23 games with Detroit.⁴¹

Returning to the Eastern League for the 1896 campaign, Boyd joined the Rochester Blackbirds, for whom he posted respectable batting numbers while displaying "brilliant backstop work."⁴² There, the "ironman" became a fan favorite upon catching in nearly every game during the season.⁴³ After Boyd jumped to the league-rival Scranton Red Sox for the 1897 season, his batting average declined over 50 points to .204 – perhaps a result of the prior year's heavy workload.⁴⁴ His offensive struggles continued in 1898 when he hit .192 in 97 games back at Rochester (and Ottawa when the team relocated there during the season).

Despite now being deemed a "has been" and "bunco man" in the media, Boyd remained in the Eastern League to begin the 1899 campaign, this time with the Hartford Indians, but was released early on by manager Billy Barnie because he had been "so slow in throwing that bases were stolen with impunity."⁴⁵ He later briefly joined the Bristol Bell Makers of the Connecticut League but was commissioned to finish the season as an Eastern League umpire. While umpiring a game in Syracuse on Sunday, July 2, Boyd and some members of the home team were arrested and charged with Sabbath breaking.⁴⁶ Things did not improve after that incident. "It was the hardest work I ever put in in my life," Boyd said of his umpiring experience. "To begin with, knowing every player in the league, made the task still more severe, for where you would expect the men you formerly played with to help you out, they were the worst of the lot, and had no more respect for one's feelings than a dog would have. I would rather play than umpire any time."[47]

With his skills on the decline, the 32-year-old nonetheless was offered the opportunity to return to Bristol as a player-manager in 1900 – while simultaneously being pursued by the Wheeling Stogies of the Interstate League. Bristol, however, believed it held a legal claim to Boyd's services. "But Boyd will play here or in no league," proclaimed Bristol's secretary, James Cray. "We not only have his contract duly signed, sealed and delivered, but he has also accepted advance money from us. We intend to compel him to live up to his agreement if there is any baseball law that can be invoked to do so."[48] Once the dispute was settled, however, the catcher joined Wheeling's roster to begin the season. After he finished the campaign hitting a dreadful .208 in 84 games with the Stogies, Boyd's baseball career was over.

In his post-baseball years, Boyd settled down in Oil City, Pennsylvania, with his "well-to-do" wife, Mary.[49] Strange circumstances surrounded their marriage. According to the *Cleveland Leader*, Boyd's soon-to-be bride charged him with an unspecified crime while he was on the road during the 1893 baseball season. Arrested out of town, he posted bail, returned home, and got married the very next day. His new wife then dropped the charges.[50] Despite their rocky beginning, the couple raised five children: Frank, Jane, John, Loretta, and Mary. Census information indicates Boyd was an Oil City alderman in 1900. The next year he joined the South Penn Oil Company. There, Boyd spent 32 years primarily working in the land title and tax department before retiring. He was a member of St. Joseph (Catholic) Church and the Oil City Elks Lodge.[51] After a four-year battle, Boyd succumbed to hypertensive cardiovascular disease and decompensation on December 16, 1937. He was buried in St. Joseph's Cemetery in Oil City.

Despite his reputation for dirty play on the baseball field, Boyd exhibited a softer side in his later years. "He was a very modest, self-effacing man, very intelligent and well-informed on many subjects," wrote his daughter, Jane, in a 1973 letter to historian Clifford Kachline of the National Baseball Hall of Fame and Museum. "He had a very engaging smile and a good sense of humor. When the ball-playing boys on the block would see him coming home from work you could hear, 'Throw me one, Mr. Boyd, throw me one, please!' He never came in the home until he had thrown a ball to each boy."[52]

SOURCES

In addition to the sources listed in the Notes, the author accessed Boyd's file from the library of the National Baseball Hall of Fame and Museum in Cooperstown, New York; Ancestry.com; Baseball-Reference.com; Chronicling America; GenealogyBank.com; NewspaperArchive.com; Newspapers.com; Paper of Record; and Retrosheet.org.

NOTES

1 David Nemec, *The Rank and File of 19th Century Major League Baseball: Biographies of 1,084 Players, Owners, Managers and Umpires* (Jefferson, North Carolina: McFarland & Company, 2012), 92.

2 "West Middletown Walking Tour to Focus on Underground Railroad," *Observer-Reporter* (Washington, Pennsylvania), April 7, 2016, observer-reporter.com/news/localnews/west-middletown-walking-tour-to-focus-on-underground-railroad/article_3d24e0a8-c86a-5471-99f8-2f8793894d70.html, accessed June 24, 2019.

3 64th Congress 1st Session, *Senate Documents Vol. 14: Eighteenth Report of the National Society of the Daughters of the American Revolution October 11, 1914, to October 11, 1915* (Washington: Government Printing Office, 1916), 169.

4 "Frank J. Boyd Is Dead Here," *Oil City* (Pennsylvania) *Derrick*, December 17, 1937: 5.

5 "West Middletown Ball Players," *Canonsburg* (Pennsylvania) *Notes*, May 10, 1888: 1.

6 "West Middletown-Burgettstown," *Canonsburg* (Pennsylvania) *Notes*, September 15, 1887: 1; "Middletown in Line," *Pittsburg Dispatch*, February 12, 1889: 6.

7 "Base Ball," *Wheeling* (West Virginia) *Daily Register*, March 8, 1889: 4.

8 "Base Ball."

9 "Other Games," *Pittsburg Dispatch*, May 5, 1889: 6; "The Duquesnes Downed," *Pittsburg Dispatch*, July 12, 1889: 6.

10 "A Successful Trip," *Pittsburg Dispatch*, July 21, 1889: 6.

11 "Bad State of Affairs," *Erie* (Pennsylvania) *Daily Times*, September 17, 1889: 3; "Downed the Nocks Again," *Pittsburg Dispatch*, September 13, 1889: 6.

12 "Baseball Melange," *Erie* (Pennsylvania) *Daily Times*, September 26, 1889: 1; "The Situation in Pittsburgh," *Pittsburgh Post*, December 4, 1889: 6.

13 "City News in Brief," *Erie* (Pennsylvania) *Daily Times*, November 26, 1889: 4.

14 "The Situation in Pittsburgh."

15 "General Sporting Notes," *Erie* (Pennsylvania) *Daily Times*, November 29, 1892: 1.

16 "Mr. Schmitt Was Great," *Pittsburg Dispatch*, April 17, 1890: 6.

17 "On the Diamond," *Erie* (Pennsylvania) *Daily Times*, July 1, 1891: 1.

18 "Cooper Still Ahead," *Pittsburg Dispatch*, February 11, 1892: 7.

19 "Local Baseball Notes," *Erie* (Pennsylvania) *Daily Times*, February 9, 1892: 4.

20 "Eastern League," *Buffalo Courier*, March 4, 1893: 8.

21 "General Sporting Notes."

22 "Signed Two Men," *Cleveland Plain Dealer*, January 28, 1893: 5.

ONE-HIT WONDERS

23 "The Sporting World," *Cleveland Leader*, January 24, 1893: 3; "Signed Two Men."

24 "Cleveland Signs Two Players," *The Sporting News*, February 4, 1893: 1.

25 "Signed Two Men."

26 "On Their Way South," *Cleveland Leader*, March 28, 1893: 3.

27 "Cuppy Is Rounding To [sic]," *Cleveland Leader*, April 9, 1893: 3.

28 "Twenty-Three Hits," *Cleveland Leader*, May 19, 1893: 3; "A Farce," *Cleveland Plain Dealer*, May 19, 1893: 5.

29 "Twenty-Three Hits."

30 "A Farce."

31 "Those Awful Spiders," *The Sporting News*, May 27, 1893: 5.

32 Nemec.

33 "The Disabled Spiders," *Cleveland Plain Dealer*, June 17, 1893: 7.

34 "Boyd's Work Was Good," *Cleveland Leader*, June 25, 1893: 3; "Boyd Batted Well," *Cleveland Leader*, July 2, 1893: 3; "Base Ball Notes," *Cleveland Plain Dealer*, August 18, 1893: 5.

35 "Base Ball Notes," *Cleveland Plain Dealer*, August 20, 1893: 6.

36 "It Came in the Ninth," *Buffalo Courier*, September 6, 1893: 8.

37 "Sporting," *Buffalo Courier*, March 3, 1895: 20; "Down to Business," *Buffalo Courier*, April 19, 1894: 8.

38 "Four Straight," *Buffalo Enquirer*, August 24, 1895: 10.

39 "Luck Changed," *Buffalo Enquirer*, August 7, 1895: 8.

40 "Four Straight"; "Base Hits," *Evening Democrat* (Warren, Pennsylvania), August 23, 1895: 4.

41 "Work of a League," *Saint Paul Daily Globe*, December 1, 1895: 14.

42 "Eastern League Players' Averages," *Scranton* (Pennsylvania) *Tribune*, November 23, 1896: 3; "Base Ball Comment," *Wilkes-Barre* (Pennsylvania) *Record*, January 20, 1897: 7.

43 Nemec; "Morton Returned from His Trip," *Rochester Democrat and Chronicle*, February 18, 1898: 14.

44 "Averages of Eastern League," *Philadelphia Inquirer*, January 31, 1898: 4.

45 "World of Sports," *Waterbury* (Connecticut) *Democrat*, May 22, 1899: 8; "The National Game," *Hartford Daily Courant*, May 29, 1899: 2.

46 "Base Ballists Arrested," *Scranton* (Pennsylvania) *Times*, July 3, 1899: 1.

47 "It Sickened Boyd," *Ottawa Journal*, September 7, 1899: 3.

48 "Bristol Managers Anxious," *New Haven Register*, May 4, 1900: 9.

49 "A Catcher Caught," *Cleveland Leader*, July 1, 1893: 2.

50 "A Catcher Caught."

51 "Frank J. Boyd Is Dead Here."

52 Copy of letter written by Jane Boyd Thomas to Clifford Kachline dated September 22, 1973, from Boyd's file in the library of the National Baseball Hall of Fame and Museum in Cooperstown, New York.

MATT BROWN

By Joel Rippel

After two successful seasons at Triple A, Matt Brown was in his third spring-training camp with the Anaheim Angels in 2009. An exhibition game in late March showed what a challenge it was for Brown, 26 at the time, to make the Angels' Opening Day roster.

The Angels and Brown both got off to good starts in 2009. The Angels, who had won four of the previous five American League West Division titles, won 12 of their first 15 Cactus League games with Brown leading the team with 9 RBIs.

On March 22 Brown went 6-for-6 with two solo home runs and a run-scoring triple in the Angels' 18-12 victory over Kansas City. The effort raised his spring average to .543 (19-for-35) with a team-high 15 RBIs.

Despite those impressive numbers, Brown appeared destined to return to Triple-A Salt Lake for a third season.

"Leadoff batter Chone Figgins is entrenched at third base, the Angels are committed to Kendrys Morales at first base and veteran utility infielder Robb Quinlan is the likely backup at both positions," a sportswriter's analysis said. "And with Manager Mike Scioscia leaning toward opening the season with 12 pitchers, there could be one less bench player."[1]

Brown said he was just trying to get the attention of Angels management.

"I'm just showcasing what I can do, trying to make them look my way," Brown said. "I know they know I can hit in Triple A. They know I need an opportunity, a real opportunity in the major leagues. I've had tastes. I've never played (started) two days in a row."[2]

Scioscia said Brown had "jumped up on our depth chart. But we have some guys ahead of him at some spots. If there's no role, he'll be at Triple A."[3]

Despite hitting .468 for the spring with a team-high 19 RBIs, Brown was demoted to Salt Lake two days before the season opener. The demotion came after the Angels had presented Brown with the team's Fred Haney Award, as the team's outstanding player in spring training.

"This guy has opened a lot of our eyes," Scioscia said.[4]

Brown was born to Robert and Louanne Brown on August 8, 1982 in Bellevue, Washington.

The family moved to Coeur d'Alene, Idaho, soon after that and Matt grew up there. Robert Brown was a general contractor who ran his own firm, R.L. Brown Construction Company.[5] Matt started playing baseball when he was 5 years old and he developed into an All-State player.

Brown was a pitcher and shortstop during his three years on the Coeur d'Alene varsity baseball team. As a senior in 2001, he earned All-State honors after helping the Vikings win the Idaho state title. He batted .556 with 9 home runs and 41 RBIs. As a pitcher he was 6-1 with a 2.46 ERA.

"Matt is a great athlete," said Brian Holgate, Brown's high-school baseball coach. "Sports came easy for him. Once he started focusing on baseball, he really blossomed. He was recruited, but (I) wouldn't say heavily recruited."[6]

As Coeur d'Alene's season had progressed, Brown garnered a lot of attention.

"There was so much interest in the last month," Holgate said. "We had at least 10 scouts at every game and at practices. When we were taking (batting practice) before our first game at state, there were at least 10 scouts. From his sophomore to senior year, there's no kid I've ever seen improve as much as Matt Brown."[7]

Brown was selected by the Anaheim Angels in the 10th round of the 2001 amateur free-agent draft. Brown, who had scholarship offers from Oregon State and several smaller colleges, signed with the Angels on June 12, the day of his high school graduation.

"Before we met with (Anaheim officials), I sat down with my family and we talked about everything," Brown said. "This seems like the best opportunity right now."[8]

Brown began his professional career with the Angels' Arizona Summer League team in Mesa. He

ONE-HIT WONDERS

got off to a slow start, hitting .163 with one home run and 21 RBIs in 46 games. After the ASL season, he played in the Arizona Instructional League and was named a co-winner of the Angels' Dick Wantz Memorial Trophy as the organization's Instructional League player who showed the most dedication and improvement.

Returning to Mesa and the ASL to start the 2002 season, Brpwn batted .361 with 2 home runs and 22 RBIs in 28 games and made just one error at third base. He was sent to Provo of the rookie-level Pioneer League in July. With Provo, he batted .296 in 32 games.

Brown started the 2003 season with Cedar Rapids of the Class-A Midwest League. After hitting .207 in 49 games, he was sent back to Provo. With Provo, he regrouped to hit a team-high 11 home runs (third best in the Pioneer League) and drive in 52 runs (tied for second) in 65 games. The Angels won the Pioneer League South Division title with a 54-22 record and reached the championship series of the league playoffs, where they were swept by Billings, 2-0.

Brown spent the entire 2004 season with Cedar Rapids, hitting .233 with 23 home runs (third in the Midwest League) and 82 RBIs (fifth). He played in the Midwest League All-Star Game.

At Rancho Cucamonga of the Class-A California League in 2005, Brown hit .262 with 39 doubles, 12 home runs, and 65 RBIs. He was promoted to Arkansas of the Double-A Texas League for the 2006 season. He led the Travelers in hits, runs scored, at-bats, and games played as he hit .293 with 19 home runs and 79 RBIs. He was third in the Texas League in doubles (41) and fifth in extra-base hits (63). After the season he was added to the Angels' 40-man roster.

In 2007 Brown got his first invitation to spring training with the Angels, a promotion to Triple-A Salt Lake, and two brief stints with the Angels.

In 13 spring-training games with the Angels he went 6-for-17 with 3 home runs and 7 RBIs. Even though he was sent to the Angels' minor-league camp on March 18, his three home runs tied (with Gary Matthews Jr.) for the team lead in home runs.

Brown got off to a good start with the Salt Lake Bees, hitting .290 with 3 home runs and 21 RBIs in 29 games, to earn a recall by the Angels on May 8.

Brown made his major-league debut on May 10, 2007, in a day game at Angel Stadium of Anaheim. He entered the game against Cleveland as a defensive replacement at third base in the top of the eighth inning. In the bottom of the inning, facing Cleveland reliever Aaron Fultz, he flied out to left field in his first major-league at-bat.

In the top of the ninth, Brown made an outstanding defensive play for the final out of Kelvim Escobar's 8-0 shutout. With runners at first and third, Brown fielded a ball hit by Jason Michaels cleanly near the foul line and made a long throw to first baseman Robb Quinlan to retire Michaels.

That was the only appearance of his first stint with the Angels before he was returned to Salt Lake on May 15.

Brown was called up again on July 30. Over 17 days he played in three games (one start) before being returned to Salt Lake. He went 0-for-4 in the three games.

In 110 games with Salt Lake, Brown hit .276 with 30 doubles, 19 home runs, and 60 RBIs. He hit two home runs in a game three times. The Bees won the PCL's North Division with a 74-69 record before losing to Sacramento, three games to two, in the first round of the playoffs.

Brown was not recalled by the Angels in September. The team won the AL West title before being swept by Boston in the Division Series.

During the winter of 2007-08, Brown played briefly with Leones del Escogido of the Dominican Winter League. He batted .148 in eight games.

In his second spring training with the Angels, Brown appeared in 11 games, going 4-for-13. A highlight came in the Angels' 5-4, 10-inning victory over Arizona in Tempe on March 15. He tied the game with a solo home run in the eighth inning and then tripled to lead off the 10th inning and scored the winning run.

Brown began the season with Salt Lake, and he and the Bees got off to a torrid start. The Bees opened the season with eight consecutive victories. After a loss, they won their next 13 games and were 21-1 on April 27. The Bees had outscored their opponents 161-81 in their first 22 games as they fashioned the PCL's best season start.

Brown played a key role in the record-setting streak, hitting .429 with 6 home runs, 10 doubles, and 21 RBIs in the first 22 games.

"What's exciting about Salt Lake is they have a lot of guys who are going to help us," said Angels manager Mike Scioscia. "It's not a veteran team beating up on kids. All of those guys are on our depth chart."[9]

Brown was named the Angels' Organizational Player of the Month for April after hitting .425 for the month and leading all of the minor leagues in total bases (80), extra-base hits (tied with 20), and runs scored (26). He was third in the minor leagues in average and hits and fifth in slugging percentage (.755).

The Angels recalled Brown on April 29. He started on April 30, going 0-for-4 in the Angels' 6-1 victory over Oakland in Anaheim.

The next day, Brown got his first major-league hit. In the top of the eighth inning, with Oakland leading 15-6, Brown replaced Figgins at second base. With two outs in the bottom of the ninth, Brown hit a two-run double to right off Oakland reliever Dallas Braden. After the game, he was sent back to Salt Lake.

He was recalled on May 12 and made two starts, going 0-for-4 in each game, before being sent back to Salt Lake on May 22.

On July 16, Brown was the starting third baseman for the PCL in the Triple-A All-Star game in Louisville.

The PCL trailed the International League All-Stars 2-0 after eight innings before scoring six runs in the top of the ninth. Brown's RBI single – his second hit of the game – tied the game, 2-2. Brown eventually scored and the PCL added three more runs to take a 6-2 lead before holding on for a 6-5 victory. Brown was named the PCL's Top Star of the game.

At the end of July, Brown joined the US baseball team for the Beijing Olympics. Brown, who celebrated his 26th birthday on the day of the Opening Ceremonies, batted .281 with 2 home runs and a team-high 10 RBIs in nine games as Team USA, coached by Davey Johnson, earned the Bronze Medal. Brown drove in three runs in Team USA's victory over Japan in the Bronze Medal game.

Brown was recalled by the Angels on September 8. He played sparingly, going 0-for-6 in six appearances as the Angels repeated as the AL West champion.

For the season, Brown hit .320 with 21 home runs and 67 RBIs in 97 games with Salt Lake and was 1-for-19 in 11 games with the Angels.

After his torrid spring training in 2009, Brown got off to a slow start with Salt Lake. He was batting just .211 in the first week of May. He ended up hitting .245 with 13 home runs and 69 RBIs in 107 games. He was not recalled in September by the Angels, who earned their fifth AL West Division title.

In December of 2009, Brown was granted free agency and he signed a minor-league contract with the Texas Rangers in January 2010. The contract included an invitation to spring training as a nonroster player. He got an extended look by the Rangers during spring training, hitting .270 with 2 home runs and 6 RBIs in 27 exhibition games, but he was sent to Triple-A Oklahoma City.

In early May Brown was sidelined with a strained left oblique. He missed nearly two months of action, returning to the Oklahoma City lineup on July 1. He went 13-for-39 in his first nine games after returning to the lineup and hit .249 with 10 home runs and 32 RBIs in 79 games with Oklahoma City.

After the season, Brown signed a minor-league contract with the Minnesota Twins. With the Twins in spring training of 2011, he batted .304 with 3 RBIs in 17 games. He was sent to Rochester of the International League. He batted .225 with 3 home runs and 10 RBIs in 34 games before being released on June 3.

In 2012 Brown played briefly for Monclova of the Mexican League. He batted .169 in 17 games.

After 12 seasons and at the age of 30, Brown's playing career was over. His career minor-league totals show a .266 batting average with 137 home runs and 589 RBIs in 1,034 games. In his five seasons at Triple-A, he had a .270 average with 66 home runs and 238 RBIs in 427 games.

In 15 major-league games, he was 1-for-24 with 3 RBIs.

After retiring, Brown returned to Washington and went to work as a lineman.

SOURCES

In addition to the sources cited in the Notes, the author consulted Baseball-Reference.com, milb.com, Newspapers.com, Retrosheet.org, thebaseballcube.com, and the 2008 and 2009 Angels Information Guides.

NOTES

1   Mike DiGiovanna, "Brown's Efforts Appear Futile," *Los Angeles Times*, March 23, 2009: C4.

2   DiGiovanna.

3   DiGiovanna.

4   Kevin Baxter, "Brown Among Final Cuts," *Los Angeles Times*, April 5, 2009: C11.

5   Thank you to Melissa Searle of the Coeur d'Alene (Idaho) Public Library for providing information about the Brown family, which was found in the 1993 Coeur d'Alene city directory.

6   Brian Holgate, email correspondence, August 13, 2020.

7   Greg Lee and Jim Meehan, "Angels Draft CdA Star," *Spokane* (Washington) *Spokesman Review*, June 6, 2001: 12.

8   "Brown Hopes to Fly with the Angels," *Spokane Spokesman-Review*, June 13, 2001: 14.

9   Mike DiGiovanna, "Bootcheck Back, but Others Ill," *Los Angeles Times*, April 28, 2008: D7.

CRAIG CACEK

By Max Effgen

Craig Cacek (pronounced Cass-ek) played in seven games for the Houston Astros in 1977. From June 18 to July 10 he was in the major leagues for the only time.1 He had one hit, one RBI, and one walk in 21 plate appearances, a .050 batting average. The Astros' trade of Cliff Johnson to the New York Yankees created the opening for Cacek to be called up as a backup for two-time All-Star Bob Watson. Astros manager Bill Virdon told Cacek, "I don't know how much you're going to play, I don't know if you're going to play at all."[2] Consequently, Cacek spent most of his time in the majors acquiring splinters. Despite a solid .306 batting average in five minor-league seasons before the call-up and a .301 average through 11 professional seasons, he never saw the major leagues again, earning the legacy of a one-hit wonder.

Cacek was born to Vince and Betty (Nemec) Cacek in Hollywood, California on September 10, 1954. Vince Cacek was born in Bridgewater, South Dakota, and was raised in Cedar Rapids, Iowa, where he met Betty. He served in the Navy during World War II, and in management with Collins Radio Company, was transferred to California in 1952.[3] He later became an executive at Southland Marketing, which at the time was the largest liquor distributor in the world. Later in his career he was a consultant for Arthur Andersen and ITT.[4]

As a youngster Vince Cacek had played on a Cedar Rapids American Legion team that played against a St. Louis American Legion team that starred Larry Berra, later to be famous as Yogi. There is a story of Cacek hitting a smash 390 feet to the gap for a triple and Berra answering with a merely 300-foot home run down the line. In California, Vince played semipro baseball and caught the attention of the Hollywood Stars, the Los Angeles Angels, and even the Chicago Cubs. He opted not to join the low minors as a 24-year-old with a fine job, a wife, a young daughter, and a child on the way.[5] He was a relaxed and supportive role model for Craig, serving as president of the Panorama City American Little League and always as Craig's go-to hitting instructor. It was not unusual for him to say, "Stay aggressive, go up there and swing from your ass!"[6]

Betty Cacek was a strong influence as well. A homemaker who was involved in community affairs, she had rallied support for sewage improvements. Later she worked as the membership secretary at the Mid-Valley YMCA and as a receptionist at a travel agency. Craig's older sister, Christine, like her brother, made a career in special education.

Craig started playing organized baseball in Little League as an 8-year-old. As one of two younger boys in his first Little League season with Panorama City American, he was drilled by a 12-year-old pitcher. The

ONE-HIT WONDERS

beaning made young Cacek scared and afraid to "step in the bucket." Vince Cacek was there with supportive words that would go on to help Craig throughout his career: "If they hit you every time, it wouldn't be a game."[7]

Growing up in Los Angeles with the arrival of the Dodgers, it was often assumed that all baseball-loving boys would bleed Dodger blue. Not so for Cacek, who was a proud Yankees fan. With his parents' Iowa roots, they would visit family in Cedar Rapids. On television, the Yankees were broadcast. Quickly, Mickey Mantle became his favorite. The 1963 World Series between the Dodgers and Yankees brought 9-year-old Craig to devastation as the Dodgers won. He even wrote a poem to the Yankees that he sent to the team in consolation. Late in 1968, he got to see Mantle hit a home run in person, and it was a great thrill.[8]

Cacek starred for James Monroe High School under legendary high-school coach Denny Holt, who coached the Monroe Vikings from 1959 until 1981. "I didn't tolerate much foolishness," Holt recalled. "In fact, I didn't tolerate any."[9] The Monroe Viking teams made the Los Angeles City final five times, winning the championship with a 19-0 record in 1971. The California Interscholastic Federation – Los Angeles Section holds the city final annually at Dodger Stadium. Many try but few high school teams play on the hallowed grounds of their heroes. Cacek started in right field for the Vikings squad as a junior and earned All-League honors. On a talent-loaded roster, three players (John Flinn, Kim Andrew, and Cacek) eventually reached the major leagues. After winning the Los Angeles City championship, All-City right fielder Cacek said, "We all grew up watching [Sandy] Koufax and [Don] Drysdale and dreaming to play there and to be there, oh my God. I remember leaving the parking lot and being shocked."[10]

In 1972, as one of two returning starters from the 1971 squad, Cacek had the opportunity to sit with the Dodgers in the dugout for a 1972 game at Dodger Stadium.[11] Walt Alston, Bill Buckner, and Frank Robinson made an impression on the shaggy-haired high-school slugger. While the Dodgers were taking batting practice, Cacek saw a young Steve Garvey doing an interview with Vin Scully behind the cage. In awe, he approached Garvey afterward and learned sage ballplayer advice on interviews, "Take all you can get, kid."[12]

Cacek had an impressive senior season, batting .574 and earning Mid-Valley League Player of the Year, All City and Athlete of the Semester honors. The Vikings extended their winning streak to 34 games but fell short of repeating the City championship.[13] Cacek credited his father's people skills with advancing his case to be drafted. Vince Cacek had become friendly with Dutch Zwilling, the Federal League home-run king, and Harry Minor, both New York Mets scouts, Larry Barton Jr., a Reds scout, and even Casey Stengel. It was speculated that Cacek would attend the University of Southern California. Cacek, however, had no plans to go to college. "School and baseball together was not what I wanted to do. I was not the best student and I wanted to just play ball."[14] On June 6, 1972, he was drafted by the Mets in the ninth round of the amateur draft. He signed a contract with a $16,000 bonus.

The 1972 draft class was talented. Gary Carter and Dennis Eckersley would earn Hall of Fame honors. Several others became All-Stars and pennant-winning managers. Ellis Valentine, Mike Hargrove, Willie Randolph, and Chet Lemon, also from Los Angeles, started their professional careers in that draft.

After signing with the Mets, Cacek reported to the Marion (Virginia) Mets of the rookie-level Appalachian League. Cacek put up a solid .267/.376/.475 slash line (BA/OBP/SLG) with 54 hits in 61 games for the eighth-place squad. From Marion, he progressed through the Mets minor-league system with stops at Pompano Beach, Visalia, where he converted to first base, and then Jackson in the Texas League, where he set the team record for batting average.[15]

After the season the Mets traded Cacek to the Houston Astros for Manny Lantigua. Lantigua, a career minor-leaguer, would meet Cacek again as a teammate for the Pittsburgh Pirates Triple-A Portland Beavers club in 1979. Now firmly playing first base for the Memphis Blues in 1976 and the Charleston Charlies in 1977 when the Astros switched affiliates, both teams of the Triple-A International League. Cacek hit well, batting .324/.423/.429 in 1976 and putting up similar numbers with the Charlies before his 1977 call-up.

Cacek made his major-league debut on June 18 with a pinch-hit appearance in the seventh inning against the Mets at Shea Stadium. The game was tied, 3-3, when Julio Gonzalez tripled off Jerry Koosman. Cacek was sent to hit for relief pitcher, Gene Pentz. A groundball to short for a quick 6-3 out kept Gonzales at third. César Cedeño, the next batter, drove in the run on a sacrifice fly. The run held up for a 4-3 Astros victory. Welcome to the show, Craig Cacek.

ONE-HIT WONDERS

Cacek next played on June 20 against the Montreal Expos in Montreal. Bob Watson took a few days off due to a blood chemical imbalance.[16] Cacek played first base in the three-game series. Facing a wild Jackie Brown in the first inning, he walked on four pitches with the bases loaded, earning his only RBI. The next day Cacek again started at first. In the top of the fifth, he took a dominant Steve Rogers up the middle into center for his first and only major-league hit.[17] "It was a big hopper off the carpet over the head of Rogers. I think the shortstop scooped it up. There was no play at first," he said. Time was called and the ball collected.[18] Cacek reached second base on a fielding error but Roger Metzger struck out to retire the side.

Cacek started in two more games, pinch-hit and played first in two others, and was sent back to Charleston when Watson returned to the lineup. Terry Puhl took the roster spot and played 15 seasons with the Astros until 1990 and the Royals in 1991.[19]

Cacek recalled his time in the majors as traumatic for the 22-year-old. In a slump (0-for-30) at the time of his call-up, he never felt comfortable. It does not seem as if the Astros were really setting up Cacek for success. Virdon, like Holt, was a drill sergeant-style manager. Cacek never felt that Virdon liked him or that it was Virdon's decision to bring him up. "I had no connection with Virdon like I did with Holt," he said. "I felt pressure to perform in a way that I had not before. In retrospect, I was not ready. I did not know my teammates on the Astros, no connections. I know now I should have been kinder to myself." In 21 plate appearances, Cacek put the ball in play 17 times. "These were just hit on the nose and did not find a hole," he related, "There was a high fly drive in the fourth inning of a July 5 game versus the Padres that was foul down the line by half an inch. Had it been fair, it would likely have been a double and driven in two runs. Maybe that would have got me going."[20] Cacek lined out to short on the next pitch.[21] That foul ball and lineout is a metaphor for how close Cacek was to having the big-league career of his dreams.

In comparison, Cacek noted that Jim Fuller, a hitter with great power, was told he would have 100 at-bats. "When I was sent back, I was in shock. As a ballplayer that identified as a hitter, he could not believe that 'I went 0 for America.'" It was disappointment all around. Astros management in hindsight did not set up Cacek for success with comments such as "thought you were ready" remarked an unremembered scout in an uncomfortable elevator on the road that took a mental toll. Over time, Cacek has processed his cup of coffee in the show. In 21 at-bats, he had only three strikeouts. "I am proud about that. I always wanted to be a pure hitter and saw myself as a pure hitter."[22]

In 11 professional seasons, one is bound to earn a few nicknames. "Coma" is an odd nickname for a ballplayer. In 1977 Cacek had come down with the flu during spring training and was bedridden in the team hotel for three days. When the inevitable "where's Cacek?" questions in the locker room were bellowed, Dave Augustine answered, "He's in a coma." The name stuck and Cacek never minded it. "One-Speed" leaves less to the imagination. According to Cacek, "Honestly, I was never a real exciting ballplayer. I always hustled but it was always in one speed. Cannot recall when that one started but it fit."[23]

Cacek had a shot at making the Astros in 1978. Cacek had had a solid spring training and knew he was close. In a game at Cocoa, Florida, then the Astros' spring-training home, Cacek got to third base late in the game. According to Cacek, "The wind was blowing in and that always changed the way we had to play. There was a shallow fly ball to center and I went back to tag. The ball was caught, and I did not advance. They did not challenge with a throw. Just the ball back to the pitcher. The crowd began to boo. If third-base coach Bob Lillis had said anything, I did not hear it. Lillis and Virdon were livid. Jesus Alou would double in the next at-bat and I would score. I knew then and there that I was done with the Astros."[24]

Being sent back down, Cacek wanted to play in the Pacific Coast League and Dave Hersh, then the youngest owner in pro baseball, worked a deal that brought him to the Portland Beavers in the Pittsburgh system. "I had no thoughts of making the Pirates, I just wanted to play in the PCL. Playing on the West Coast and a few trips to Hawaii." Cacek loved Portland. It had a major-league town atmosphere and had a solid fan base, he said.[25] The Beavers were talented with Dale Berra, Vance Law, and others who later played in the majors. With the change of scenery, Cacek responded, leading the PCL with 180 hits, batting .319, and earning all-star first-base honors. Scoring 92 runs and driving in 102 runs was apparently not enough for a September call-up. "They were looking for pitching for the playoff run. I knew that there was no chance." Manager Johnny Lipon told him, "As far as I am concerned, you're a major league hitter." Cacek played winter ball in the Dominican Republic that year with Lipon. He struggled at the plate, but it was always something he wanted to do as a ballplayer.[26]

ONE-HIT WONDERS

Spring training in 1980 was a fun and loose clubhouse of the reigning World Series champions. Willie Stargell jumped on a table holding a driver and teed off on a baseball that rocketed through the locker room, destroying a clock on a distant wall. Again, it was clear that Cacek, playing behind Stargell, would not make the Pirates and would return to Portland.[27] In the 1980 season, Lipon moved to the Pirates Single-A ballclub and Doe Boyland saw more time at first base. After the 1981 season, the Pirates traded Cacek to the Angels as the Angels were preparing a trade to the Chunichi Dragons in Japan.[28] The Dragons settled on Charlie Spikes, who had more home runs and major-league experience. Gene Mauch was at the helm of the California Angels and his protégé Moose Stubing was manager of the Spokane Indians in 1982. "I knew that it was the end of the line," said Cacek. Stubing would bark, "You are in the lineup, it must be the second Tuesday of the month." After starting in 12 games at first base and hitting in a total of 64 games that season, Cacek, at 27, retired from professional baseball.[29] In 11 minor-league seasons, he had a slash line of .301/.401/.446.

Cacek quickly caught the attention of a Madison, Wisconsin, barnstorming team that went to the National Baseball Congress Tournament in Wichita, Kansas, in both 1982 and 1983. After that he did not hit a ball or put on a glove for nearly a decade. "When I hung it up, I had this thought to become a psychologist." Cacek returned to California and went back to school at San Diego State, Pepperdine Professional School, and Long Beach State. He earned credentials and became a school counselor in special education, a role that he has enjoyed for three decades.[30]

Thinking that his playing days were long gone, Cacek was walking his dogs in Los Angeles' Balboa Park in the summer of 1991. Reliving memories of a high-school playoff game at that ballfield 20 years earlier during the 1971 City championship, he saw a group of guys playing actual baseball, not men's league slow-pitch softball. Hardball, real baseball, this caught his attention. Cacek approached the team manager, Nick Newton, and learned more about the team that would become known for a time as the NALU Hawaiian Buffaloes.[31] In a legendary moment chronicled by teammate and *Los Angeles Times* writer Peter King, Cacek arrived late to a game, wheeling into the parking lot with his turn up to bat in the batting order. With his trademark "one-speed," he ambled to the plate and promptly deposited the baseball 20 feet beyond the left-field fence for a home run.[32] With the Buffalos, Cacek allowed himself to have fun with baseball again.

He played with the Buffalos and then three other teams – the Indians, Suns, and Padres – all of Santa Monica, in the Men's Senior Baseball Association for over 10 years, and even worked to become a pitcher. On the mound, Cacek would face some interesting competition. Jose Canseco would reportedly go 0-for-2 with a strikeout and a fly ball to left. Tom Hayden, the noted liberal activist and Chicago Seven member, had an at-bat.[33] Cacek tapped former Charlies teammate Randy Wiles for advice. Work fast, throw strikes, and change speeds, Wiles advised. Cacek threw mostly breaking stuff and even a knuckleball. He worked 100 innings per year for 10 years as a pitcher. At age 52, Cacek was the MVP in a 25-and-over league, having great hitting stats, and going 7-5 on the mound as a starting pitcher. Eventually, Cacek would play a game in Angel Stadium. Back in a major-league ballpark; fittingly, Craig Cacek got one walk and one hit.[34]

SOURCES

In addition to the sources cited in the Notes, the author consulted Baseball-Reference.com and baseballalmanac.com

NOTES

1. His last game was July 5. He was on the roster until July 10. "Astros Recall Puhl to Majors," *Terre Haute* (Indiana) *Tribune*, July 11, 1977: 11.
2. Author interview with Craig Cacek on November 6, 2019.
3. "Metro Deaths," *Cedar Rapids Gazette*, September 11, 1983: 14a.
4. Craig Cacek, email correspondence with author, November 15, 2019.
5. Craig Cacek, telephone interview with author, November 6, 2019. (Hereafter Cacek telephone interview.).
6. Craig Cacek, email correspondence with author, November 15, 2019.
7. Cacek telephone interview.
8. Cacek telephone interview.
9. Steve Henderson, "Going Against the Flow," *Los Angeles Times*, June 9, 1990: 302.
10. Eric Sondheimer, "Monroe's Perfect Season Withstands Test of Time," *Los Angeles Times*, June 5, 2001: 89.
11. John Stamm, "Consistent Cacek Trades Homers for Line Drives," *Clarion-Ledger* (Jackson, Mississippi), June 25, 1975: 39.
12. Cacek telephone interview.
13. Cacek telephone interview.
14. Cacek telephone interview.
15. Rick Cleveland, "Winningham Finds It's Getting Easier," *Jackson Clarion-Ledger*, June 22, 1983: 15.
16. "Giants Give Astros a Lift," *San Mateo* (California) *Times*, June 25, 1977: 8.
17. "Expos Crush Astros, 6-0," *Del Rio* (Texas) *News Herald*, June 22, 1977: 10.
18. Cacek telephone interview.

ONE-HIT WONDERS

19 "Astros Recall Puhl to Majors."
20 Cacek telephone interview.
21 Back to Baseball, backtobaseball.com/game/SDN197707050/san-diego-padres/versus/houston-astros/1977/july/5/all-plays-summary/.
22 Cacek telephone interview.
23 Cacek telephone interview.
24 Cacek telephone interview; "Alou Is Back as Astros Nip Blue Jays, 3-2," *Austin American-Statesman*, March 13, 1978: 29.
25 Cacek telephone interview.
26 Cacek telephone interview.
27 Cacek telephone interview.
28 "Names in the News," *Los Angeles Times*, December 18, 1981: 59.
29 Cacek telephone interview.
30 Cacek telephone interview.
31 Peter King, "The Boys of Fall," *Los Angeles Times*, October 22, 2000: 402.
32 King.
33 Robert D. McFadden, "Tom Hayden, Civil Rights and Antiwar Activist Turned Lawmaker, Dies at 76," *New York Times*, October 25, 2016: B, 14.
34 Cacek telephone interview.

CARLOS CASIMIRO

By Malcolm Allen

As of the end of the 2020 season, 789 players born in the Dominican Republic had played major-league baseball. Of the 363 who were primarily nonpitchers, 57 made All-Star teams and 35 appeared in a World Series for the eventual champions, but only 12 completed their careers with exactly one hit.[1] Before Orioles rookie Carlos Casimiro did it on July 31, 2000, none of those Dominican one-hit wonders had ever hit safely in the first at-bat of his big-league debut.[2]

Carlos Rafael Casimiro Shaw was born on November 8, 1976, in San Pedro de Macoris. His father, Felix Antonio Casimiro Santos, was a driver at Ingenio Porvenir, one of the city's signature sugar mills. Carlos's mother, Gladys Martinez Stapleton Shaw, worked in one of the nation's duty-free zones, designed to attract and stimulate foreign investment.

The couple had four children. Mercedes Luisa was the only girl, followed by Carlos and his younger brothers, Juan Pablo and the late Marcelo Augusto. In 2020 a middle-aged Carlos reflected on an alternate course his life could have taken. "If there was no professional baseball, the first thing that I would have focused on would've been my studies to become a lawyer, doctor, engineer, or an architect," he said. "And if, in any case, I had not been able to finish my studies due to the economic situation we had in my family, I would be working in the duty-free zone."[3]

Professional baseball was a possibility, of course. It had been played in the Dominican Republic since the late nineteenth century, but in the two decades before Casimiro's birth, the number of Dominicans to reach the majors was only 46. Before he turned 8, however, that figure more than doubled. From 1990 to 1993, 51 new Dominicans debuted in the big leagues in the first four years of his teens alone.

Casimiro grew up in the Inve-Cea barrio, within a mile of Tetelo Vargas Stadium, home to the professional Estrellas Orientales team of baseball's Dominican winter league. When he was 6, a sprawling sports complex opened just north of his home in preparation for the 1983 National Games, when more than 2,300 athletes competed in San Pedro de Macoris. Casimiro enjoyed playing basketball there, but baseball was king.

When outfielder Luis Mercedes became the 146th Dominican player on September 8, 1991, he made history as the first native of his country to be signed, developed, and deployed in a major-league game by the Baltimore Orioles.[4]

While the Orioles dove into the nation's pool of talent relatively late, scout Carlos Bernhardt hustled to make up for lost time. A 1991 *Baltimore Sun* article described him as "a thick-armed former minor-league pitcher whose task is to dive into the wretched Dominican mass of cane fields and muddy streets, separate the prospects from the thousands of players, and give them their first push as professionals."[5] From

Carlos Casimiro.

ONE-HIT WONDERS

1969 to 1971, Bernhardt hurled a total of 17 innings in the Seattle Pilots and New York Yankees' systems before his career was cut short by arm problems. His younger brother, Juan, played 154 games for the Yankees and Mariners.

When the Orioles fired two of their three Dominican scouts in 1987, Bernhardt became the club's scouting supervisor in the country.[6] They sent him some money to upgrade a ballpark in San Pedro de Macoris, and he rounded up supplies wherever he could. Months after Mercedes's first hit, for example, the Baltimore-based Oriole Advocates group shipped Bernhardt two tons of boxes containing 663 bats, more than 600 uniforms, 491 balls, 380 gloves, 286 helmets, and dozens of sets of catching gear.[7] Players like Armando Benitez and Manny Alexander – an All-Star closer and 11-year infielder, respectively – debuted with the Orioles over the next few years.

On April 15, 1994, a 17-year-old Casimiro joined the Orioles organization as well. "I managed to get signed by Bernhardt through my sister's husband, who recommended me to the Orioles so I could sign with them," he recalled. "The bonus was $2,500."

The Dominican Summer League started in 1989 specifically to help the country's prospects get started in pro baseball without the immediate additional pressure of adjusting to a new culture. The Orioles did not get their own DSL team until 1996, so Casimiro debuted with a combined team of Baltimore and San Francisco Giants prospects. Managed by former National League batting champion Matty Alou, it managed just an 18-52 won-lost record to rank 20th of the circuit's 21 teams.

Casimiro returned to the DSL in 1995, this time with a Bernhardt-managed squad of Orioles and White Sox youngsters. The team was a little better, but after batting .259 with four homers in 108 at-bats, Casimiro took his .454 slugging percentage to Sarasota, Florida, to finish the season with Baltimore's rookie-level Gulf Coast League affiliate. In 32 GCL contests, the 5-foot-11, 179-pound Casimiro hit .252 with a pair of home runs.

He played some shortstop in Sarasota but saw most of his action at second base. That offseason, Baltimore signed a perennial All-Star and Gold Glove Puerto Rican whom Casimiro admired to man that position in the majors. "My favorite player was Roberto Alomar," he recalled. "I like the way and the aggressiveness of how he played baseball, and how easy he made the plays."

The young Dominican was way below Alomar on the Orioles depth chart in 1996, but he helped the rookie-level Bluefield (West Virginia) Orioles win their division with an Alomar-like performance down the stretch. Mired with a .215 batting average on July 25, Casimiro batted .339 the rest the way to finish at .276.[8] His 10 home runs ranked third in the circuit behind 6-foot-5, 283-pound teammate Calvin Pickering, and he ranked in the league's top five in runs scored and steals, and the top 10 in doubles and total bases. His all-around performance earned him recognition as the Appalachian League's all-star second baseman.

That fall Casimiro joined the Estrellas Orientales for the first of four winter-ball seasons with his hometown team. Prior to the 1997 season, he got his first couple of mentions in the *Baltimore Sun*. "O's think 20-year-old could be strong offensively," reported Buster Olney.[9] Though beat writer Peter Schmuck noted that *Baseball America* rated the Orioles farm system the most barren in baseball, based on his conversations with major- and minor-league sources, he described Casimiro as the most promising second-base prospect in the Baltimore organization.[10]

The Orioles moved Casimiro up to the full-season, Single-A Delmarva Shorebirds in 1997. The team was based in Salisbury, Maryland, near the state's Eastern Shore. Early in the season, the local newspaper profiled him briefly. In addition to disclosing that he liked to eat pasta and preferred to hear merengue music when he came up to bat, the Dominican said that God was his hero, "faith in God" was his good luck charm, and all he knew about Salisbury was that it was by the beach. (Ocean City, Maryland, sits 30 miles to the east.) While Casimiro's prediction that the Baltimore Orioles would win the World Series looked good until the wire-to-wire AL East leaders stopped hitting in the ALCS, his goal "to have a good year and win the South Atlantic League championship" worked out nicely.[11]

On April 10 against the Greensboro (North Carolina) Bats, Casimiro became the first Shorebirds player to homer twice in one game.[12] He did it again against the Hagerstown Suns on June 28. Though he batted only .243 with nine homers overall, Casimiro led Delmarva with eight triples, swiped 20 bases, and tightened his defense after committing eight of his 21 errors in April.[13] When the Shorebirds beat the Bats, 8-1, in Greensboro to win the South Atlantic League title, he went deep and combined with Pickering for 7 RBIs.[14]

54

ONE-HIT WONDERS

The Orioles added Casimiro to their 40-man roster, and he spent part of his offseason playing for the Maui Stingrays of the Hawaii Winter League. When *Baseball America* released its updated prospect rankings in January, he was rated 13th in the Baltimore system overall, but the organization's top middle infielder.[15]

Casimiro's first big-league spring training was marred by a hand injury he'd suffered while lifting weights in the Dominican. Early in camp, he aggravated it on a check swing.[16] He spent the season with Baltimore's advanced Single-A Frederick (Maryland) Keys in the Carolina League, where he formed the keystone combination with shortstop Jerry Hairston Jr. early in the season. Prior to Hairston's promotion to Double-A that summer, Casimiro shifted to third base briefly to allow his double-play partner to gain experience at second.

By season's end, Casimiro topped the Keys with 47 extra-base hits, including 15 home runs, demonstrating the combination of soft hands and surprising power that made him a prospect. On the other hand, his .236 batting average and 98/25 strikeout-to-walk ratio illustrated how much progress he still needed to make in terms of patience and hitting breaking balls. "I'm feeling a little more comfortable at the plate," he remarked after blasting a grand slam and a solo homer against the Lynchburg Hillcats on July 29. "I'm just thinking of watching the ball and hitting it up the middle."[17]

Against Winston Salem on August 11, he hit another grand slam to win a game in the ninth inning,[18] but a broken left wrist he suffered in the final week of the month relegated him to spectator status. Casimiro's scheduled trip to the Maryland Fall League to gain more seasoning with the Bowie Nationals was canceled.[19]

When Alomar left the Orioles as a free agent in December, Baltimore signed Delino DeShields to replace him. DeShields fractured a thumb in spring training, however, and a healed Casimiro was one of the options to fill in for him. Instead, the Birds went with Jeff Reboulet as their Opening Day starter, while Jesse Garcia, a more experienced rookie, made the team as a backup. Casimiro wound up in Bowie, home of the Orioles' Double-A Eastern League Baysox.

Bowie skipper Joe Ferguson told reporters early in the year that he thought the Dominican could hit .300,[20] but Casimiro's average declined for the third straight season, to .221. "At that time, I didn't have much help from anyone," Casimiro said. "The only person who helped me a lot for me to become a major leaguer was David Stockstill. He was a hitting coach in the minors."

Stockstill, the 1979 Midwest League MVP when he clubbed 27 homers for the Wausau Timbers, was a Missouri native who'd played in the Mexican League for eight seasons. He later became the Orioles' director of international operations.

The good news for Casimiro in '99 was that he ripped 18 homers to lead the Baysox and missed only two games. His 73 runs scored tied for most on the team, and his 64 RBIs were his best single-season mark as a pro.

He returned to Bowie in 2000, albeit not until the final week of April after remaining in Florida to mend a spring-training shoulder injury.[21] With another young Dominican, Eddy Garabito, manning second base for the Baysox, Casimiro shifted to third and made a whopping 30 errors in 84 games. In early May, he was one of five players suspended after a 20-minute brawl with the Erie SeaWolves, ignited when Bowie's pitcher intentionally threw the ball at an opponent during a rundown.[22] After getting off to a strong start at the plate, Casimiro endured a two-month stretch in which he batted only .218 between May 10 and July 9.[23] When he blasted a game-winning three-run home run against the Akron Aeros on June 24, it was his first homer in 140 at-bats and snapped an 0-for-22 slump.[24] By the end of July, though, an opportunely timed .328 hot streak over 17 games raised the Dominican's average to .262.[25]

Meanwhile, in Baltimore the disappointing Orioles had the American League's next-to-worst record. In the four days before the July 31 trade deadline, they sent away seven veteran players in five separate deals. In return, the Orioles received only four players for their major-league roster, one of whom wouldn't arrive in time for that night's game. To supplement their shorthanded roster, the Orioles looked to Bowie, only a 30-minute drive south of Baltimore.

Casimiro woke up the morning of July 31 with a strong feeling that it would be his day. He called former Baysox teammate Luis Matos, an outfielder who'd been called up to the Orioles six weeks earlier, and told him, "Matos, when you go back to Baltimore, you will take me with you."

Matos picked him up and took him to Prince George's Stadium in Bowie, where manager Andy Etchebarren gave the Dominican the news. "When I heard him, I became frozen, I could not articulate a word from the emotion I felt," Casimiro recalled. "At

ONE-HIT WONDERS

that moment I told myself, 'You did it, your dream has come true.' Immediately, I phoned my family to give them the news that I had been called up to the big leagues."

That afternoon, in the locker room at Oriole Park at Camden Yards, Casimiro found a jersey with his name. He became the third Baltimore player to wear uniform number 36 in the 2000 season.

From the first-base dugout, he watched Albert Belle's two-run homer give Baltimore a first-inning lead against the visiting Twins. Designated hitter Jeff Conine followed by drawing a walk. By the time Conine's turn in the order came around again, the DH had left the ballpark to join his wife for the delivery of the couple's third child.

Therefore, with two on and two out in the bottom of the third against Minnesota southpaw J.C. Romero, Casimiro debuted as a pinch-hitter. The public-address announcer told the crowd of 32,661 that it was the 23-year-old's first major-league at-bat. After working the count to two balls and two strikes, he fouled off one pitch[26] before lining the next one into right-center field for a two-run, standup double. "Casimiro doffed his helmet at second base as the crowd rose to its feet with a thunderous ovation," reported Orioles beat writer Roch Kubatko in the *Baltimore Sun*.[27]

"Everyone rose from their seats to applaud and welcome my first hit and debut in the big leagues," Casimiro recalled. "That was a moment of great emotion for me."

By the time he got to bat again in the fifth, the Orioles led 5-2, and the Twins had gone to the bullpen. He struck out swinging to end the inning against fellow San Pedro de Macoris native Hector Carrasco. "I did know him well before we faced each other in the majors because he and I practiced together in a baseball program here in the Dominican Republic before I was signed by Baltimore," Casimiro explained.

He grounded out in his third at-bat, but the Orioles held on for a 6-5 victory. The next night Casimiro was in the starting lineup, batting fifth as Baltimore's DH against left-hander Mark Redman. He went 0-for-5 but his bases-loaded groundout in the first inning drew first blood in the Orioles' 10-0 rout behind Mike Mussina. There was a time in baseball history when Casimiro would have received credit for a game-winning RBI, but that statistic became defunct after the '88 season. "I've just got to do my job," the rookie told reporters afterward. "The manager at Bowie told me I was going to be here only four of five days, but I don't know."[28]

Casimiro watched from the bench as the Orioles' modest four-game win streak came to an end on Wednesday afternoon. Trent Hubbard, one of the players Baltimore had acquired, finally arrived from Atlanta and went straight into the starting lineup. On Friday in Tampa Bay, Conine returned to the team. When infielder Mark Lewis came off the disabled list before Saturday's contest, it was back to the minors for the young Dominican.

Casimiro joined the Rochester Red Wings for the last month of the International League play. In 24 games, he connected for four home runs, but batted just .222 in his first taste of Triple-A ball. He did not get called back up to the majors in September, and the Orioles outrighted him to Rochester after the season.

After attending Orioles spring training as a nonroster invitee in 2001, Casimiro returned to Rochester as a left fielder. He hit only .235 in 48 games, however, and was sent back to Bowie in June. Playing mostly third base in his 80 games there, his average sank to .222. By season's end, his overall .270 on-base percentage and .338 slugging mark between two levels were the worst marks he'd fashioned as a pro. His 122 strikeouts, versus 25 walks, showed him trending the wrong way, too.

That fall, Casimiro traveled to Taiwan as part of the Dominican Republic's roster for the Baseball World Cup tournament.[29] The Dominicans finished eighth out of 16 teams.

From 2002 to 2006, Casimiro played in the Italian Baseball League. "After being a free agent from Baltimore, I waited for several months to see if I could get a contract with another team in the USA," he said. "But seeing that I did not get with anyone, I decided to go to Italy to play. Because of the way in which the bosses treated me, I decided to come back for four more years."

His .409 batting average led the Serie A1 circuit in 2002[30] for an otherwise overmatched Paterno Citta dei Normanni club that was relegated to Serie A2 for 2003 after finishing last with a dismal 7-46 record. When the team returned to Serie A1 in 2004, it moved up to sixth place in the 10-team circuit, led by Casimiro's .945 OPS, the league's fifth best. Only Willie Canate, with 9, outpaced his eight homers.[31] Casimiro's 6 home runs won the crown in 2005, but Paterno sank bank to the basement. In 2006 he finished his Italian career with the T&A San Marino squad. "My best experiences were knowing the cities of Rome and Venice," he recalled.

ONE-HIT WONDERS

By the time he finished playing in Italy, Casimiro had married the former Wendy Margarita Santana Madrigal and become a father. Their son, Carlos Rafael Casimiro Santana, was born first, followed by brother Luis Ismael and sisters Dafne Isabel and Karla Maciel in the decade of the 2010s. "It drives me to work 100 percent in everything I do to give my family a better life, and that motivation is my children, my wife and my mother," he said. "If it wasn't for them, maybe I'd be involved in drugs trying to earn a lot of money but thank God I have them."

In 2014 Casimiro returned to baseball as the manager of the Oakland Athletics Dominican Summer League team, a position he still held as of 2020. "One of my friends, a coach who worked with them, recommended me to the bosses for a job. That's how I started working with Oakland," he explained.

At Oakland's Juan Marichal Complex in Boca Chica, about 25 miles west of San Pedro de Macoris, Casimiro sought to impart lessons he learned in pro ball to a new generation of prospects. "First, they must be on time to be able to take advantage of the moment and work on what they need," he said. "Second, they must work for a reason, something that encourages them to give 100 percent in everything, so that their development is more effective. For example, a good reason would be their mother, or a major leaguer that they choose to visualize playing like in the big leagues. Finally, think big, that they are always the best."

Reflecting on his all too brief Orioles career, he said, "I am very proud of the way I managed to hit safely in the majors although I was a little nervous about playing in the big leagues for the first time. But at the same time, I feel disappointed that I could not have played longer in the big leagues so I could help my family."

ACKNOWLEDGMENTS

Special thanks to Carlos Casimiro (email interview with Malcolm Allen on September 19, 2020) and to SABR colleagues Miguel Casey and Alberto Rondon for their help with translating.

SOURCES

In addition to the sources cited in the Notes, the author consulted baseball-reference.com.

NOTES

1. Three Dominicans, Estevan Florial, Cristian Pache, and Jesus Sanchez, got one hit apiece in their 2020 debuts.
2. Alberto Lois of the Pittsburgh Pirates collected his only hit in his first at-bat on October 1, 1978, but he'd appeared in two previous games without a plate appearance. On May 29, 2005, Napoleon Calzado matched Casimiro's feat. Calzado, like Casimiro, did it for the Orioles at Camden Yards.
3. Unless otherwise noted, all Carlos Casimiro quotes are from an email interview with Malcolm Allen, September 19, 2020.
4. Dominicans Ozzie Virgil, Jose Mesa, Jose Bautista, Juan Bell, and Francisco de la Rosa all played for Baltimore before Mercedes, but all five started their careers in other organizations.
5. John Eisenberg, "A Field of Dreams in the Third World," *Baltimore Sun*, December 22, 1991: 1A.
6. Eisenberg.
7. "Oriole Advocates Ship 2 Tons of Equipment to Dominican," *Baltimore Sun*, May 19, 1992: 5B.
8. *1998 Baltimore Orioles Media Guide*: 62.
9. Buster Olney, "Minor Goes Backdoor to O's," *Baltimore Sun*, January 390, 1997: 1C.
10. "Peter Schmuck, "O's Working Farm, but Far from Harvest," *Baltimore Sun*, April 9, 1997: 1D.
11. "Player: Carlos Casimiro," *Daily Times* (Salisbury, Maryland), April 11, 1997: 22.
12. "Casimiro's 2 HRs Lift Shorebirds, 5-0," *Baltimore Sun*, April 11, 1997: 5D.
13. *1998 Baltimore Orioles Media Guide*: 62.
14. "Shorebirds Batter Bats, 8-1, Capture South Atlantic Title," *Baltimore Sun*, September 12, 1997: 6D.
15. Peter Schmuck, "Once O's 'Twin,' Brewers Dream of Their Own Rise," *Baltimore Sun*, January 25, 1998: 11D.
16. Roch Kubatko, "Alomar Makes Strong Left Turn," *Baltimore Sun*, February 24, 1998: 5D.
17. Rich Scherr, "Casimiro Supplies Power with Slam, Solo Shot," *Washington Post*, July 30, 1998: C6.
18. Casimiro's 2000 Fleer Tradition baseball card.
19. *1999 Baltimore Orioles Media Guide*: 67.
20. Brian Straus, "Baysox Spruce Up in Spring," *Washington Post*, April 7, 1999: M22.
21. Kent Baker, "Young Baysox Ready to Grow Up," *Baltimore Sun*, April 6, 2000: 7C.
22. Kent Baker, "6-7 Stahl Has O's Thinking Big After Shaky Start," *Baltimore Sun*, May 8, 2000: 7E.
23. *2001 Baltimore Orioles Media Guide*: 58.
24. Roch Kubatko, "Pulled the Wrong Way in Spring, Maloney is on Tear Back to Majors Healthy," *Baltimore Sun*, July 3, 2000: 7E.
25. Roch Kubatko, "Chance for Casimiro," *Baltimore Sun*, August 2, 2000: 7D.
26. Dan Rodricks, "A Judge, a Senator and 30,000 Shriners," *Baltimore Sun*, August 2, 2000: 1B.
27. Roch Kubatko, "Casimiro Debuts in Fine Style as Young Cast Wins Again," *Baltimore Sun*, August 1, 2000: 6E.
28. Kubatko, "Chance for Casimiro."
29. "Aguilas Ceden Jugadores," *La Prensa*, October 31, 2001. prensa.com/impresa/deportes/Aguilas-ceden-jugadores_0_501699827.html (last accessed October 4, 2020).
30. "Tripla Corona," file:///C:/Users/Malcolm%20Allen/Downloads/2014%20MIKE%20ROMANO%20curriculum%20(2).pdf (last accessed October 4, 2020), 28.
31. "Le Statische del Campionato 2004," baseball.it/2004/09/22/le-statistiche-del-campionato-2004/ (last accessed October 4, 2020).

GUSTAVO CHACIN

By Tony S. Oliver

Baseball fans have always sought to quantify every aspect of their beloved game, no matter how picayune. Runs and outs came first, followed by individual marks like strikeouts, hits, and wins before technological advances allowed the proper measurement of pitch speed, much to the delight of aficionados eager to compare the exploits of Nolan Ryan to those of Randy Johnson beyond vivid memories and anecdotal evidence. While modern sabermetricians have waxed poetic over launch angle and exit velocity, only the connoisseurs of esoteric figures have measured the home-run trot, perhaps the least graceful of all gaits found on the baseball diamond. Unofficially, the Orioles' Luke Scott holds the record, rounding the bags in 35.76 seconds, thanks to a pulled hamstring shortly after he passed first base in a June 10, 2010, contest.[1] Less than 10 days earlier, on Memorial Day, one of the baseball calendar's holiest days, the Astros' Gustavo Chacín had accomplished the task in 27.28 seconds – a seeming eternity to those watching the video but likely a mere blur to those in attendance, cognizant of the sheer incongruity of the scene.

Gustavo Adolfo Chacín González was born on December 4, 1980, in the coastal city of Maracaibo, Venezuela, which sits between its namesake lake and the small gulf connected to the Caribbean Sea. A stocky 5-foot-11, 185-pound left-handed pitcher, he was scouted by Luis Feunmayo, who arranged a deal with the Toronto Blue Jays in 1998. He was quickly assigned to the Pioneer League (Rookie) for the 1999 season and appeared in 15 games (nine as starter). His 3.09 ERA over 64 innings placed second in the league among qualifiers.[2] He featured in eight decisions (four wins, three losses, one save) with the Medicine Hat (Alberta) Blue Jays, garnering an all-star selection.[3]

In 2000 the Toronto brass shipped Chacín to the Dunedin affiliate of the Class-A (Advanced) Florida State League as a member of the starting rotation. Chacín, the youngest member of the team, responded with a 9-5 record and 127⅔ innings but allowed a team-high 14 home runs. Nevertheless, he was added to the Double-A Tennessee Smokies later in the season. The Southern League gave the newcomer a rough welcome, victimizing him for 10 hits, seven runs (all earned), six walks, and two losses in 10 innings pitched. Countless others would have been traumatized by the rough landing, but Chacín took it in stride and returned for a strong 2001 campaign. He started 23 games and appeared as a reliever in two others, earning 11 victories with a 3.98 ERA, slightly above the league average of 3.89, along with one shutout. The card issuers seized on his strong minor-league performance to include him in the 2002 extended sets; Donruss, Topps, Leaf, and Upper Deck anointed Chacín a top prospect, fueling the fire of Blue Jays fans everywhere longing for a second banana to Roy Halladay's top-of-the-rotation presence.

The franchise opted to try Chacín as a bullpen arm for Tennessee in 2002, starting him in 13 contests while bringing him as a reliever in 22 others. As with many pitchers unsure of their role, Chacín struggled, with his ERA increasing to 4.66, a pattern that would continue the next year with the Eastern League's New Haven club. In a career-high 46 contests, Chacín's WHIP was an uncomfortable 1.543 but a key statistic caught the eye of the Blue Jays. He allowed only one home run during the entire campaign, an important concept the pitching-starved club sought to instill in their young arms' mindset. The Ravens advanced to the league finals, bringing a taste of collective success to the young left-hander. The team changed both its home (to New Hampshire) and its name (to the Fisher Cats) and won the circuit in 2004, with Chacín leading the league with 16 victories along with his team-high 25 starts and 141⅔ innings pitched. A brief call-up to the International League for the Syracuse club added two more wins (with 14 strikeouts in 11⅔ innings) for a minor-league high of 18. He loaded up on the hardware front, earning Double-A and Eastern League All-Star selections and the Eastern League Pitcher of the Year award.[4] *Baseball America* named Chacín to the Minor

ONE-HIT WONDERS

League 2nd All-Star Team and the Blue Jays selected him as their Minor League Player of the Year.[5]

Had the clock struck midnight at that juncture, and Chacín's regal carriage turned into a pumpkin, he likely would have been satisfied with a sensational year. Toronto, however, had other ideas, calling the young lefty to the majors. Many observers bemoan baseball's long season as tedious, with offerings like September 20's Blue Jays-Yankees game as all but meaningless, but the model allows the also-rans to give their prospects some valuable experience once the rosters expand. The Yankees strode in with a 94-55 record, tops in the AL East, while Toronto was 31 games behind, occupying the cellar. In fact, only 10,732 of the Bronx faithful attended, seemingly unworried about the 23-year-old making his major-league debut. Chacín never trailed, bolstered by Russ Adams's leadoff home run against Javier Vázquez, and through 98 pitches, 63 of which were strikes, limited the Yankees to four hits, three runs, and three walks. Newspaper chronicles the next morning revealed that this was the first win by a left-handed debutante in the Joe Torre era, a remarkable achievement. At the whim of the baseball deities, his even better follow-up against Baltimore (seven innings, one run, four hits, four strikeouts) was met by a dreaded loss as his comrades were unable to cross home plate.

The offseason brought hope north of the border with Chacín penciled in as the second starter behind Halladay for the 2005 Blue Jays. His impressive April numbers (4-1 record with a 2.48 ERA) earned him the Rookie of the Month Award, a feat he could repeat in July (five victories in six appearances). Chacín paced the American League first-year players with 13 wins; his 34 starts topped Blue Jays hurlers. He was selected for both the Topps and *Baseball America* versions of the All-Rookie Teams.[6] Perhaps his most impressive feat was allowing only 0.89 home runs per nine innings, good for ninth place in the American League despite facing the heavy boppers of the American League East. He had a strong claim to the Rookie of the Year Award and earned two first-place votes but paced behind five other greenhorns.

Frustration was the theme of the young hurler's 2006 season. Thanks to robust run support from his hitters, he finished April with a 4-1 record that belied ugly fundamentals: seven home runs allowed and 12 walks in 30⅔ frames. Early May brought seven runs in 8⅓ innings and a trip to the disabled list with a strained forearm and sprained elbow ligament. Returning to the team on May 30, he was lifted after 88 pitches against Boston while nurturing a five-run lead that would yield his sixth victory. He was not as lucky on June 9, leaving after three innings after re-straining his elbow; he did not come back until August.[7] During the stretch run, Chacín lowered his ERA by more than a full run but continued to struggle with control (1.27 strikeout-to-walk ratio), ending his 17-game season with a 5.05 ERA and nine wins against four losses.

However, Chacín's inactive stint was not without highlights. Since its beginning, baseball players have been used to sell tobacco, cars, sodas, and even coffee makers, so it was not a surprise when the Blue Jays marketing team concocted "Chacín: the fragrance." With tongue firmly in cheek, the always jovial pitcher filmed two 30-second promotional videos, eagerly shared over the local Toronto airwaves and on the Rogers Centre scoreboard. For months the team's broadcasters had a running joke that the pitcher, whose last name sounded like cologne, should have his scent immortalized.[8] The antics, which may have been forgotten in a prior era, were chronicled in various videos available on YouTube, as the left-hander told the audience his product "smell(ed) like victory."[9]

What began as a running joke in sports radio eventually took a life on its own, with the franchise giving the lucky first 10,000 fans to pass the turnstiles of its June 27, 2006, game a "free sample." Local newspapers did not chronicle the aroma in the ballpark, and Facebook was barely two years old when the giveaway took place; its success would have likely been quickly parroted in today's social-media-driven society.[10] A local company concocted the fragrance with Chacín himself lending a helping hand and nose to determine its ingredients.[11]

Chacín's darkest personal hour came during 2007 spring training, as Tampa police arrested him for driving under the influence. The organization was frank in its assessment, with manager John Gibbons stating that "it's a serious mistake and we all make mistakes," while general manager J.P. Ricciardi acknowledged that Chacín "made a mistake and we want to work with him, not against him."[12] With the incident fresh on his mind, he struggled mightily, allowing 17 earned runs in 27⅓ innings, good for a 5.60 ERA. Toronto placed him on the 15-day disabled list on April 29 due to a strained elbow; little did anyone know it was the last major-league pitch Chacín would throw for the franchise. The pain continued through bullpen sessions and a minor-league assignment before he had surgery in early September for a partially torn labrum.[13] He re-signed with the team on January 17, 2008, but was

ONE-HIT WONDERS

assigned to extended spring training after a slate of brutal performances. After a rough 11 games (7.88 ERA in 45⅔ innings) with Dunedin, having come full circle from 2000, Chacín was released by Toronto on May 9.

It is often stated that reaching the major leagues is awfully hard but staying is even harder. The Washington Nationals came knocking on December 16 with a contract. However, he did not play a game in the majors or minors for the franchise, which released him on April 1, 2009. The Philadelphia Phillies gave him an opportunity four days later, assigning him to the Lehigh Valley and Reading clubs before releasing him on November 9. Philadelphia was oddly not impressed with Chacín's performance, which included 115⅓ innings with a 3.20 ERA. He went back home to plot his move, confident another team would request his services. The Houston Astros beckoned on December 22, as an early Christmas present.

The road back to "The Show" began in Round Rock, the Astros' Triple-A affiliate. Chacín pitched six games early in the season, compiling a 3.60 ERA in 25 innings before being recalled by the Astros. Houston was caught in an identity crisis, with future Hall of Famers Craig Biggio and Jeff Bagwell recently retired and All-Stars Roy Oswalt, Carlos Lee, and Lance Berkman struggling to sustain an otherwise mediocre roster. The franchise hit rock bottom in 2011-2013, losing a combined 324 games, but the 2010 edition was merely uncompetitive, finishing fourth in the Central Division, 10 games under .500.

On May 7, more than a thousand days after last taking a big-league mound, Chacín threw two scoreless innings in a losing effort against the San Diego Padres. He was effective, throwing only 33 pitches (22 strikes) to the 10 batters he faced. A week later, he tossed 1⅓ frames in San Francisco, and on May 20 he obtained three outs against Colorado. The Astros' confidence in their reclamation project grew, and through his Memorial Day (May 31) outing, he boasted a 1.86 ERA in 9⅔ innings, all as a middle reliever in Houston defeats.

Before the May 31 game, and over more 339 career major-league innings, Chacín had given up 45 round-trippers but had never hit one himself. In fact, during his entire professional career (major leagues, minor leagues, and the Venezuelan winter league), he had never swatted a four-bagger. On the third pitch of his at-bat leading off the third inning, he connected to deep right field. While the theme of *Chariots of Fire* did not blare through Minute Maid Park's loudspeakers, no one would have blamed Chacín had he channeled the Academy Award-winning score in his mind.

He savored the moment, basking in the fans' adulation as the cheers got louder once the baseball disappeared, a few feet from the Chick-Fil-A's pole on right field. Chacín's run eased into a jog once he passed first base, breathing easier just prior to touching the keystone. His ill-fitting helmet wobbled at the pace, prompting Chacín to readjust it shortly after passing the opposing shortstop before resetting his goggles between third base and home plate. After crossing the dish for Houston's second run, he was engulfed in a sea of high fives in the Astros dugout from his teammates, perhaps as oblivious as many fans that this was Chacín's first major-league hit. In fact, it took one full replay cycle before the announcers confirmed his feat to the television audience; by then, Chacín's victim, the Nationals' Luis Atilano, was focused on the next batter, Michael Bourn.

Hitting-wise, the fairy-tale round-tripper was not just the highlight of Chacín's year, but also of his professional career. Chacín had not hit a home run in the minors, though he had a respectable .242 average (8-for-33) across all his stops. In the purest example of baseball symmetry, Atilano and Chacín are connected beyond that fateful swing. Exactly three weeks earlier, the Washington pitcher had singled off the Mets' John Maine. While Atilano registered the win by tossing 5⅓ strong innings, his safety was the only time he reached base in his short big-league career: He only played one year in the majors.

But the May 31, 2010, high was ephemeral. Chacín was lifted on the bottom of the fifth, with Cory Sullivan pinch-hitting as the Astros were down by three runs. The Nationals crossed the plate nine times in the seventh inning, putting the contest out of reach. Chacín picked up his last two wins and two losses as the season progressed, along with his only lifetime save. His final appearance came on September 30, when he tossed an inconsequential third of an inning by giving up a walk and a hit, and striking out his last batter.

Entering the 2011 season, Chacín was still relatively young, having just turned 30. The Astros re-signed him with an invitation to spring training, but he did not make the club. He threw 66⅔ innings for the Oklahoma City Redhawks but was released on July 14. The Mets inked him for the International League's Buffalo Bisons but his tenure was brief; 20 earned runs in 15 innings later, New York chose not to re-sign him.

ONE-HIT WONDERS

Eager to stay in the game, Chacín played independent ball in 2012 with the Rockland Boulders of the Canadian-American Association (3-5, 5.43 ERA) and the Atlantic League's Long Island Ducks (2-2, 3.93) before venturing south of the border in 2013 for one last run in Triple A with the Mexican League's Diablos Rojos of Mexico City (eight games, all in relief) and the Laguna Vaqueros (one game with no batters retired). For his entire major-league career, Chacín forged a 27-17 record across 102 games, 58 of which he started. His 4.23 ERA was consistent with his minor-league mark of 4.30.

But beyond franchise uniforms, Chacín also wore his country colors with great pride. In the original 2006 World Baseball Classic he registered a save against Australia in the preliminary round.[14] He did not feature in the decision against Puerto Rico in the first round, but Venezuela advanced to the semifinals, where he did not see action.[15]

Chacín's commitment to his motherland, however, had begun much earlier. A few months after his 18th birthday, he debuted for the Cardenales of Lara of the winter league. He would wear the team's colors for six consecutive campaigns, appearing in 72 games (56 as a starter) with a solid 3.44 ERA. His first four seasons included forays into the postseason. After several years away, Chacín returned to the winter circuit. Now wearing the Caracas uniform, he pitched in 13 games across the 2009-2010 and 2010-2011 campaigns. His 65 regular-season innings were supplemented by an additional 58 in the postseason, in which he picked up three wins for the Leones' 2009-2010 title. He saved the team from elimination with a stellar performance (seven innings, five hits, six strikeouts, no walks).[16]

Chacín next played for Magallanes in 2012-2013 and 2013-2014, starting 21 games and picking up another title, this time with the Navegantes against his former Lara franchise. He repeated the trick by thriving under pressure, scattering two runs over five innings to tie the series before Magallanes clinched the 2012-2013 crown the next day.[17] He was traded to La Guaira and tossed only three innings with a 15.00 ERA, with an additional 2⅔ scoreless frames in the playoffs. For his winter-league career, Chacín appeared in 113 contests, pitching 444 innings with a 3.77 ERA (111 ERA+) and a 23-29 mark. He added an additional 132 innings in the playoffs with a 4.09 ERA and a 10-8 record.

As of 2020 Chacin lives in Tampa, Florida, and was active with the Venezuelan exile community.

SOURCES

In addition to the sources cited in the Notes, the author relied extensively on Baseball-Reference.com.

NOTES

1   tatertrottracker.com/news/tater-trot-tracker-leaders-all-time.html.
2   Statscrew.com/minorbaseball/leaders/l-PION/y-1999.
3   thebaseballcube.com/minors/awards/history.asp?Award=PIO-AS.
4   thebaseballcube.com/players/profile.asp?ID=4858&View=Awards.
5   thebaseballcube.com/players/profile.asp?ID=4858&View=Awards.
6   thebaseballcube.com/mlb/awards/history.asp?Award=AllRookie.
7   Associated Press, "Blue Jays Score Eight Runs in the Eighth, Stun Tigers," ESPN.com, June 9, 2006, espn.com/mlb/recap?gameId=260609114.
8   Matt Maldre, "Blue Jays Pitcher Gustavo Chacín to Get His Own Cologne," Spudart.org, April 15, 2006. Spudart.org/blog/blue-jays-pitcher-gustavo-chacin-get-own-cologne/.
9   Youtube.com/watch?v=2mIAY8vRa3U https://www.youtube.com/watch?v=CnWbykpbbiA.
10 Ian Hunter, "Flashback Friday: Chacin Cologne," Blue Jay Hunter, October 15, 2010, bluejayhunter.com/2010/10/acid-flashback-friday-Chacin-cologne.html.
11 Lisa Altobelli, "Scene of a Pitcher: Batting Odor," *Sports Illustrated*, June 26, 2006, vault.si.com/vault/2006/06/26/scent-of-a-pitcher.
12 Associated Press, "Jays Pitcher Chacin Arrested, Charged with DUI," ESPN.com, March 17, 2007. espn.com/mlb/spring2007/news/story?id=2802353.
13 rotoworld.com/baseball/mlb/player/17947/gustavo-Chacín/news.
14 mlb.com/wbc/2009/stats/boxscore.jsp?gid=2006_03_09_venint_ausint_1.
15 mlb.com/wbc/2009/stats/boxscore.jsp?gid=2006_03_13_venint_purint_1.
16 pelotabinaria.com.ve/beisbol/box.php?game_id=MAG201001280&tem=2009-10.
17 Pelotabinaria.com.ve/beisbol/box.php?game_id=MAG201301290&tem=2012-13.

DOUG CLAREY

By Joe Schuster

Doug Clarey.

In many ways, Doug Clarey was an accidental major leaguer, someone who got there largely because of the convergence of a number of circumstances that allowed him to make the leap all the way from single-A ball to the big leagues for a few weeks in 1976. In those weeks, however, he managed to experience a moment that was the stuff of quintessential American dreams – hitting a game-winning home run in extra innings, in a ballpark near his boyhood home – before he slipped back into the minor leagues and then out of baseball not long after.

Douglas William Clarey was born on April 20, 1954, in Los Angeles.[1] His father, Elmer W. Clarey, was a dispatcher for United Airlines for 35 years.[2] His mother, Maxine Clarey, was a homemaker. Clarey had one sister, Sandra (Clarey) Larson. (Clarey's father died in 1995; his mother died in 2006.)

Even as a toddler, Clarey loved baseball. His father built him a backstop in the yard when he was only 2½ and Clarey said he spent every day throwing against it. The work helped him develop a strong arm and by the time he was in Little League ball, he was playing the positions that could exploit that attribute: pitcher, shortstop, and center field.

When Clarey was 12, the family moved north, to Los Altos, California, where he attended Homestead High School. (One of his classmates was Apple founder Steven Jobs.) There, Clarey, who became a Giants fan after the move, played baseball all four years, his first year on the freshman team and the other three as a member of the varsity.

His coach there, Jim Hemphill, later a scout for the Atlanta Braves organization, remembered Clarey as one of the best athletes he encountered in his years as a coach at Homestead.[3] There, Clarey helped the school win league championships in his sophomore and senior years, and set school records for the highest season batting average, .448, in his senior year, as well as the most home runs (7). He was selected first-team all-league his junior year and, in his senior year, was the league's most valuable player. That year, he was also chosen to the Northern California team for the annual California high school all-star game.

Days after his graduation in 1972, Clarey was chosen by the Minnesota Twins in the sixth round of the amateur draft in June, ahead of future All-Stars Jim Sundberg, Willie Randolph, and Rick Honeycutt, among others.[4] The Twins rated him "a good looking hitter with good running speed and decent power [with] the potential to be an above average major league hitter."[5]

It was potential that Clarey, for whatever reason, would struggle to realize.

The Twins assigned him to their rookie league team in Melbourne, Florida, in the four-team Florida East Coast League. There, appearing at shortstop in

ONE-HIT WONDERS

49 of the team's 57 games, he struggled as a hitter – a condition that would follow him through nearly his entire professional career, finishing with an average of .222, one home run, and an OPS of .578. In the field, he showed decent range but made 24 errors and his .900 fielding average was lowest among the league's regular shortstops.

For the next year, the Twins organization converted Clarey to a second baseman, assigning him to Geneva in the Class-A New York Penn League. There, he still did not hit as they expected (.237 with 5 home runs), but he continued to improve as a fielder, leading the league in assists at second base. In 1974 his fielding was good enough that, playing for Wisconsin Rapids in the Class-A Midwest League, he made the all-star team, despite batting .232 with 9 home runs. That year, he led the league's second basemen in assists, double plays, and fielding average.

That ability was enough to convince the St. Louis Cardinals organization to select him in the Rule 5 draft, and for the 1975 season they assigned him to Arkansas of the Double-A Texas League.[6] He continued to play solid defense – leading the league in assists and double plays at second base – but he suffered the worst year of his professional career at the plate, finishing at .206 – the third-lowest average in the league among all hitters with at least 200 plate appearances.

The season earned Clarey a demotion for 1976, back to Single A, at St. Petersburg in the Florida State League. Not surprisingly, Clarey was disappointed.

"I had a rough spring training," Clarey told the author. "I thought I had clinched a spot on the Triple-A roster but then the Cards sent down two infielders (Luis Alvarado and Mario Guerrero) so I went to Double A, but they had a couple of prospects like Ken Oberkfell, so I ended up at Single A."

Even worse, Clarey was not the starting second baseman at St. Petersburg. He told a sportswriter that year, "The reasons they gave me just didn't seem too clear. They told me I would be very important to the organization as a swing man, but that was hard for me to accept after having played every day."[7]

His fortunes turned fairly quickly that season, however.

In the second game of the year, Cardinals starting second baseman Mike Tyson injured his leg turning the pivot on a double play when Cubs third baseman Bill Madlock hit him hard trying to break up the play.[8]

The Cardinals initially listed Tyson as "day-to-day," but a week later, on April 17, put him on the 15-day disabled list. The ballclub would have preferred to call up either Alvarado or Guerrero from Triple-A Tulsa but both were out of options and would have to clear waivers before they could join the team. Because the Cardinals put Tyson on the disabled list on a Friday, they would have had to wait almost a week before either could join the team. As *St. Louis Post-Dispatch* sportswriter Dick Kaegel put it, "The club needed a body fast."[9]

That body was Clarey and the team recalled him.

"I was surprised," Clarey recalled. "I didn't expect it. No one sat down with me and told me what my responsibilities would be, but realistically I knew I was there to fill a spot on the roster. I would be a defensive replacement more than anything."

Clarey's first appearance in a major-league game was as a pinch-hitter for pitcher Mike Wallace in the sixth inning of a blowout loss to the New York Mets on April 20.[10] He struck out against Jon Matlack.

"He made me look bad," Clarey said. "I hardly even saw the ball when he was throwing it."

Four days later, Clarey entered the game as a pinch-runner in the top of the ninth inning of a 4-3 loss to San Diego and then stayed in the game at second base for the bottom of the inning, recording one putout, on a sacrifice bunt that pushed the eventual winning run into scoring position.

Four days after that, on April 28, against the Giants in Candlestick Park, with his parents and several of his high-school friends in attendance, Clarey had yet another chance, in the 16th inning of a 2-2 game. With two outs, Don Kessinger on first, and pitcher Mike Proly due up, Clarey was the only position player remaining on the bench who hadn't already gotten into the game.[11]

Clarey, who batted and threw right-handed, went to a one-ball, one-strike count, and then Giants hurler Mike Caldwell threw a pitch that his manager, Bill Rigney, later said came too far inside.[12] Clarey drove it down the left-field line, barely over the eight-foot-high fence, for his first, and as it would turn out, only major-league hit: a two-run home run that gave the Cardinals a 4-2 lead they held onto.[13]

After the game, Clarey told a sportswriter, "It's something you always dream about, ever since I was a little boy watching Giants games and just wishing I could be one of them. This is the greatest experience of my life."[14]

One sportswriter called Clarey a "Cinderella man."[15] Another said that Clarey's home run was "what's great about baseball" and reported that when

ONE-HIT WONDERS

Clarey came into the clubhouse after the game, "the place broke out in pandemonium."[16]

Clarey got into another game in extra innings six days after his game-winning home run, this time as a defensive replacement at second base in the 10th inning against the Braves in Atlanta on May 4. He collected an assist and had chance to hit in the 12th, but grounded out to the pitcher. Three days later, with the Cardinals back at home for the first time since Clarey's home run, the team presented him with a watch in a pregame ceremony commemorating the hit.[17] On May 7 St. Louis sent him back to St. Petersburg. There, he had three hits in eight at-bats before the organization promoted him to Triple-A Tulsa, where he remained for the balance of the season, save for one more brief stint with the Cardinals in late July and early August, when Tyson went on the DL again. During that stay, Clarey played in five games and had one at-bat, again in extra innings, this time in the 10th against the Cubs in Chicago, when he fouled out to the first baseman.

At Tulsa, Clarey continued the struggles at the plate that had marked his career as a hitter in the minor leagues, finishing the season batting .228, with 7 home runs, as he split his time among second base, shortstop, and third base.

The next spring, the Cardinals traded Clarey to the New York Mets for outfielder Benny Ayala. The Mets assigned him to Tidewater in the Triple-A International League, where Clarey hit only .125 with 3 home runs in 28 games before the Mets traded him to the Milwaukee Brewers organization, which assigned him to its Double-A Eastern League team at Holyoke, Massachusetts. There, he had, statistically, his most success in the minor leagues, hitting .268.

The Brewers traded Clarey to the Baltimore Orioles at the end of that season, and for 1978, Clarey ended up with Southern League Charlotte. There, while his average was not high (.226) he flashed power early on and was leading the league in home runs at the end of May with 12 before falling into a dry period in which he did not hit a single home run in June and July.[18] He finished the year with 19 home runs, fourth-best in the league.

After the season, the Orioles offered Clarey another contract to play at Double A, telling him they thought he had a future in coaching, but Clarey decided it was time to walk away from the game.

"It was time for me to go," he said. "All of the polish and luster that baseball used to have for me wasn't there anymore; it didn't mean the same thing to me and so I decided it was time to retire."

Clarey, who had married the former Marie Klarmann in 1977, settled in Los Angeles, and earned a California real estate license. He sold commercial real estate until 1993, when he left that and opened a gourmet pizza restaurant, Cheech's Pizza, located less than three miles from Dodger Stadium, and which he operated until passing the business on to his daughter, although he remained involved as he moved into what he termed "semi-retirement." He had two children, a son and a daughter.

NOTES

1. Doug Clarey player questionnaire on file in the archives of the National Baseball Hall of Fame.

2. Unless otherwise noted, all of the personal information about Clarey's life came from two interviews between the writer and Clarey: one in July 1986, for an article about Clarey that appeared in the July 6, 1988, issue of the *Riverfront Times* (St. Louis) and the second on January 6, 2012, for this biographical essay.

3. Details about Clarey's high-school career come from an October 24, 2012, interview with Jim Hemphill.

4. Unless otherwise noted, details about Clarey's professional career come from Baseball-Reference.com <baseball-reference.com/players/c/clared001.shtml>.

5. July 1986 interview with Bill Smith, then Minnesota Twins assistant minor-league director.

6. Art Voellinger, "15 Players Picked in Triple-A, Double-A Draft Sessions," *The Sporting News*, December 21, 1974: 45.

7. Rick Hummel, "Card Clarey Takes to Cloud Nine," *St. Louis Post-Dispatch*, April 21, 1976: 3F.

8. Dick Kaegel, "Cruz Learns a Lesson as Cubs Thwart Cards," *St. Louis Post-Dispatch*, April 11, 1976: 1F.

9. Dick Kaegel, "'Last Man' Clarey Gives Cards Victory in 16th," *St. Louis Post-Dispatch*, April 29, 1976: 1D.

10. Unless otherwise noted, accounts of Clarey's major-league appearances are from Retrosheet <retrosheet.org>.

11. Kaegel, "Last Man."

12. Ed Schoenfeld, "Unknown a Star After One Swing," *Oakland Tribune*, April 29, 1976: 39.

13. Kaegel, "Last Man."

14. Kaegel, "Last Man."

15. Neal Russo, "Maligned Redbird Firemen Doing a Super Rescue Job," *The Sporting News*, May 22, 1976: 27.

16. Schoenfeld.

17. Neal Russo, "Cards Bow to Astros High and Mighty Richard," *St. Louis Post-Dispatch*, May 8, 1976: 5A.

18. "Southern League," *The Sporting News*, August 26, 1978: 37.

VIBERT CLARKE

By Mitch Lutzke

A five-year veteran of the Negro Leagues, Ernesto Vibert Clarke was a one-hit wonder who followed the adage If at first you don't succeed, try, try again. The phrase may be a cliché, but in Clarke's case it's an accurate one.

The native of Panama recorded his first and only hit in the major leagues while part of a Washington Senators September call-up. The day – September 10, 1955 – marked a series of firsts for the left-handed hurler. The game was Clarke's first start in the major leagues and his first appearance in front of his home fans at Washington's Griffith Stadium. The club also claimed him as being the first to break the franchise's color line.[1]

Clarke, at 6 feet tall and around 165 pounds, was known for having a "good fastball, a pretty good curve," and not so good command.[2] Walking batters was an issue: He gave up nearly as many walks (14) as hits (17) in 21⅓ innings pitched in seven major-league games.

Most modern records say that Clarke was born on June 8, 1928, in Colon, Panama.[3] However, both the 1930 and 1940 federal censuses recorded in mid-April have Clarke born in 1922 or 1923 depending upon whether the census age indicated his actual birth year or the one he was going to celebrate in June. His father, Charles, was born in Barbados, while his mother, Annie, was born in Jamaica, and moved to the Panama Canal Zone around the time of Vibert's birth. In 1940 Vibert was recorded as being 17 years of age and employed as a dock worker; it said he had attended school through the seventh grade, which would support a birthdate of 1922 or 1923 and not 1928.[4] A 1948 article on the Cleveland Buckeyes Negro League team published the week of his birthday noted Clarke was 24 years old the previous season, making a birth year of 1923 or 1924.[5] As the Cleveland Buckeyes team story appears accurate, Clarke was either 32 or 33 years old and not 27 when he made his major-league debut in the summer of 1955.

In 1946 Clarke was 7-7 with the Negro American League Buckeyes and then became the ace of the staff in 1947, posting a record of either 11-2 or 13-2 and helping to capture the Negro American League pennant.[6] In 1948 the club failed to win the pennant and Clarke wasn't as effective that season, posting a mark of 8-9. In that season Clarke had the honor of giving up what is now – with the December 2020 determination by Major League Baseball that the NAL would be considered a major league – Willie Mays's first major-league homer, as the teen was an outfielder for the Birmingham Barons. He followed up in 1949 with a 4-10 record and a 4.50 ERA with the Buckeyes, now relocated to Louisville. Clarke pitched for the Memphis Red Sox from 1950 through 1953 and

Vibert Clarke.

ONE-HIT WONDERS

posted a much improved 13-10 and 2.98 ERA in his first season with the Tennessee club.[7]

When not stateside for the summer, Clarke played in his native Panama 10 consecutive winter seasons starting in 1945, the year before he signed with the Buckeyes. Clarke posted a 4-3 record and was apparently impressive enough to make the trek north to Cleveland in 1946. He posted only winning records in four of the 10 seasons in Panama winter ball.[8] He pitched a no-hitter in the 1947-48 winter and his best season was in 1950 (14-4, 2.87 ERA) with the Super Cola squad. By 1952 he held the Panamanian Winter League career wins record at 48.[9] In 1952, Clarke got himself into trouble as he attacked Carta Vieja player-manager Al Kubski after a game on February 7. Kubski was hospitalized with head injuries; Clarke was arrested and immediately suspended from the league by President Raul Arango.[10]

The next season, 1952-1953, possibly still under suspension, Clarke apparently spent some time in the Mexican League. In 1954 he signed with the Pampa (Texas) Oilers of the Class-C West Texas-New Mexico League. Clarke had a fine summer, being named to both the midseason and end-of-the-year all-star teams. Clarke posted an 18-7 record and struck out 234 batters in 232 innings (he walked nearly 100). He completed 19 of 23 games started, and batted .355.[11] The Oilers won the pennant and the league playoffs.[12]

In early December it was reported that Pampa had sold Clarke to the Senators.[13] During spring training in 1955, Clarke was assigned to Charlotte in the Class-A Sally League. He was 16-12, winning nearly one-third of 54-86 Charlotte's victories. Clarke was voted the team's most valuable player and was given a wristwatch.[14] Clarke and catcher Steve Korcheck were promoted to the Senators.

They were joining a woefully inept Senators team, led by manager Charlie Dressen. The best player on the last-place team (53-101) might have been 37-year-old first baseman Mickey Vernon, while none of the pitchers finished with a winning record. About a week before the call-ups, Dressen told sportswriters, "I don't have to point out that we don't have enough solid all-around players on the squad," and called it a "sad sack situation."[15] So, Clarke's lively arm offered the possibility of a welcome addition to this lackluster squad.

Clark made his major-league pitching debut on September 4, 1955 in relief against the New York Yankees at Yankee Stadium. He was greeted by Andy Carey's triple, got Whitey Ford out on a comebacker to the mound, and then saw Hank Bauer hit an RBI single to right field. Clarke then gave up a single to Gil McDougald before striking out Billy Martin and getting Yogi Berra to fly out to right field. The Senators failed to score in the top half of the ninth, losing 8-3. Clarke didn't bat in the game.

Clarke appeared both on the mound and at the plate in the first game of a doubleheader against Boston at Fenway Park the next day. Entering in the fourth inning in relief of Camilo Pascual, Clarke finished the contest and gave up two runs on Jimmy Piersall's home run, allowed three more hits, and walked six Red Sox as Washington dropped a 10-2 contest. He got his first major-league at-bat, hitting a fly ball off Tom Brewer in the seventh inning that was caught by Piersall in center field.

On September 10, before a slim crowd of 2,551 at Griffith Stadium, Clarke made his first major-league start, against the Kansas City Athletics. The Senators reached base 12 times against Johnny Gray in less than five innings, while the rookie Clarke cruised along, allowing no runs through five innings. In the Senators' fourth, after Gray loaded the bases with a walk to Roy Sievers, a single by newcomer Korcheck, and a walk to Jose Valdivielso, Clarke came to the plate. With an opportunity to help his cause, he struck out. Gray then walked Eddie Yost and forced in a run before he retired the final two batters of the inning.

In the bottom of the fifth, Washington loaded the bases again. Vernon reached base on an infield error, Sievers singled, and Valdivielso wrangled another walk from Gray. This time, with two outs, the Panamanian connected on a pitch and drove the ball to left field, clearing the bases. Ray Herbert relieved Gray and got the final out. Clarke ended the inning with his only major-league hit, three RBIs, and a 4-0 lead.

Gus Zernial connected for a solo homer to end Clarke's shutout bid in the sixth inning, but the lefty set down the Athletics in order in the seventh. The Senators got another run in their seventh and led 5-1 in the eighth, when it all unraveled for the rookie. He walked the first three batters. Chuck Stobbs came on to relieve, and five batters later the score was tied, 5-5. To make matters worse, after the Senators retook the lead in the bottom of the eighth, Pedro Ramos gave up Zernial's second home run of the day, a three-run shot, to hand Kansas City an 8-6 lead. With two outs in the bottom of the ninth, the Senators again loaded the bases, but couldn't score. Clarke's pitching and hitting heroics were all for naught.

ONE-HIT WONDERS

Clark started one more time, on the 16th against Baltimore, and didn't make it out of the fourth inning. His short stint allowed him to relieve the next day, when he gave up Brooks Robinson's second major-league hit and first RBI during his big-league debut.[16] Clarke opened the inning by getting two fly-ball outs, before a double and a walk gave Robinson his chance to shine. Clarke was saved from further damage when his Charlotte teammate and catcher, Korcheck, combined with third basemen Eddie Yost to pick off Hal Smith at third.

Clarke's final game in the majors was on September 24, against Baltimore at Griffith Stadium. It was his best appearance in the majors: He pitched a perfect last three innings.

Near the end of spring training in 1956, the Senators sent Clarke to Charlotte.[17] On March 31 he was suspended for three days by manager Rollie Hemsley, whose drill-sergeant attitude was apparently not to Clarke's liking. Hemsley had set an 11 P.M. curfew and took the ballplayers' car keys so they could log extra miles when walking to the ballpark. Clarke failed to show for a practice and lacked "the kind of hustle Hemsley demands." Hemsley announced, "There will be no prima donnas in camp, even if they can win a pennant singlehandedly."[18] Clarke's 1956 season with Charlotte was not good. He dropped to 3-10 by mid-June and was then sent to Louisville where he was 4-10. The following year he was 7-12 with three minor-league teams. He returned to Panama, where he had much improved numbers, but not enough to generate a return trip to the majors.[19]

Nearly a decade after his major-league debut, *The Sporting News* ran an article about Clarke pitching a three-hit shutout for his Cerveza Balboa club on December 17, 1964. The article mentioned Clarke's age as 35, giving him another birth year, 1930.[20]

Ernesto Vibert Clarke ended his career with no decisions on the mound and 1-for-6 at the plate. His ERA was 4.64 in 21⅓ innings, with 14 walks and 9 strikeouts. He had two bases-loaded chances in the same game and after failing in the first try, was successful in his second and proved that following a time-worn cliché was a good idea.

Clarke died in Cristobal, Panama, on June 14, 1970. Information on his later years has eluded researchers.

SOURCES

In addition to the sources cited in the Notes, the author consulted Baseball-Reference.com and Retrosheet.org.

NOTES

1. *Dayton* (Ohio) *Daily News*, April 15, 1997; *Detroit Free Press*, March 28, 1997.

2. James A. Riley, *The Biographical Encyclopedia of the Negro League Baseball Leagues* (New York: Carroll and Graf, 2002), 175.

3. As self-reported by Clarke. US Baseball Questionnaire, William J. Weiss, SABR. Though the nickname "Webbo" has been associated with Clarke, it has not been possible to locate even one newspaper article that mentioned the nickname. Colon was in the Panama Canal Zone, a US-administered 10-mile-wide strip of territory straddling the Panama Canal. It was turned over to Panama in 1979.

4. United States Federal Census Report, 1930. Silver City, Cristobal District, Panama Canal Zone, page 10B, Enumeration District 0041; United States Federal Census Report, 1940. Silver City, Cristobal, Panama Canal, page 24 B, Enumeration District 2-16.

5. "Outfielder Jethroe Is Star of Cleveland Buckeye Team," *Newark* (Ohio) *Advocate*, June 10, 1948.

6. Riley; *Newark Advocate*.

7. Riley. The figures for 1946-8 differ dramatically from those reported on Seamheads and Baseball-Reference.com.; T.J. Gorsegner, "The Senator who gave up Willie Mays' first Major League home run," SBNation Twinkie Town, December 19, 2020. https://www.twinkietown.com/2020/12/19/22190552/mlb-minnesota-twins-history-franchise-senator-webbo-clarke-willie-mays-first-major-league-home-run

8. Riley.

9. "Clarke Helps Brewers Sip Nifty Potion," January 2, 1965. Unidentified newspaper clipping dated January 2, 1965, in Clarke's file at the Baseball Hall of Fame Library.

10. Leo J. Eberenz, "Panama League Pennant Won by Carta Vieja Club," *The Sporting News*, February 20, 1952: 26; *Birmingham News*, February 19, 1952; *Sioux Falls* (South Dakota) *Argus-Leader*, February 19, 1952.

11. *Abilene* (Texas) *Reporter-News*, September 1, 1954.

12. *Pampa* (Texas) *Daily News*, September 9, 1954, and September 24, 1954.

13. *Knoxville News Sentinel*, December 2, 1954.

14. *The Sporting News*, September 5, 1955: 33.

15. Shirley Povich, "Chuck Plans Platooning to Prop Up Nats," *The Sporting News*, August 31, 1955: 8.

16. Lou Hatter, "There Were Good and Bad Days, All Memorable," *Baltimore Sun*, July 29, 1983: 67.

17. *Anderson* (Indiana) *Herald*, March 28, 1956; "Deals of the Week," *The Sporting News*, April 4, 1956: 26.

18. *Greenville* (South Carolina) *News*, April 1, 1956; Bob Quincey, "Hemsley Suspends Hill Ace; Hits Out at 'Prima Donnas,'" *The Sporting News*, April 4, 1956: 26.

19. Riley.

20. Eberenz, "Clarke Helps Brewers Sip Nifty Potion."

KEN CROSBY

By Tom Hawthorn

Ken Crosby's workday on a fine Southern California spring afternoon lasted only three innings. The Chicago Cubs right-hander, making the first major-league start of his career after eight seasons of professional baseball, gave up two singles, a double, and two triples; "three other drives were barely contained within the 410-foot confines" of Jack Murphy Stadium in San Diego.[1]

The Padres had scored four runs by the time Chicago manager Jim Marshall pulled Crosby for a pinch-hitter in the fourth inning. It was a sound managerial decision, as Joe Wallis tripled and later scored in a two-run inning that took Crosby off the hook. Alas for the Cubs, the Padres went on to score four runs in the bottom of the eighth to win, 9-5.

It was April 29, 1976. Gerald Ford was president of the United States. In two days, Republican challenger Ronald Reagan, a former California governor, would win the Texas primary. Jerry Brown, the sitting California governor, was battling Jimmy Carter and others for the Democratic nomination in the first post-Watergate presidential election. In a Las Vegas courtroom, three yellowed, handwritten pages were filed as the purported last will and testament of billionaire recluse Howard Hughes. In Europe, the Greeks witnessed their final solar eclipse of the twentieth century, while in San Diego 11,590 spectators witnessed an event even rarer — the only base hit of Ken Crosby's major-league career.

With one out in the top of the second inning, Crosby, batting ninth, knocked an offering from left-hander Brent Strom into right field, where it was gloved by future Hall of Famer Dave Winfield. ("I was very sick that day," Crosby recalled years later. He got behind in the count and gave me a fat one. I hit it to right!") Later in the inning, Crosby advanced to second on an error by first baseman Willie McCovey, another future Hall of Famer. Crosby would be stranded. For unfair comparison purposes, Winfield would end his career with 3,110 hits and McCovey with 2,211, compared with Crosby's standalone single.

On the mound, Crosby appeared in 16 games over two seasons with the Cubs, all as a reliever except for this lone start. His record was 1-0. He pitched 20⅓ innings, giving up 30 hits (including three homers) and 19 runs (all earned). He walked 15 and struck out 11. He finished seven of the 16 games in which he appeared, though he had no saves. His career earned-run average was 8.41.

In the field, he was flawless, handling a single putout and five assists without error.

At the plate, the 6-foot-2, 179-pound right-handed batter had three appearances with one walk and the single. The out occurred in unremarkable fashion at Dodger Stadium in a game remembered for a save,

ONE-HIT WONDERS

though not by a pitcher and it did not happen on the mound.

On April 25, four days before he got his hit against the Padres, Crosby and the Cubs were in Los Angeles. Chicago starter Steve Stone left in the second inning with a sore shoulder and Crosby was tapped to replace him. Crosby led off the third inning, grounding a Rick Rhoden pitch to shortstop Bill Russell, who threw to Steve Garvey to get him.

Crosby was on the mound in the bottom of the fourth. His first pitch of the inning, to Ted Sizemore, was outside. Suddenly, there was a commotion behind him in left field. A man ran onto the field with an American flag, which he spread out on the grass like a picnic blanket. He was soon joined by an accomplice, who would turn out to be his 11-year-son. The man poured lighter fluid on the flag. Racing toward them from behind, Cubs outfielder Rick Monday saw one of them strike a match. He had a revelation: "I thought, they can't light it if they don't have it."[2] He bent down to snatch the banner without breaking stride. Monday, who spent six years in the Marine Reserve, got a standing ovation from the crowd when he came to the plate to bat in the fifth and was treated as a hero for the rest of the Bicentennial Year season. After the man and his son were escorted off the field, Crosby got Sizemore to pop up to second, an anticlimactic ending to the at-bat.

The rest of the inning was a disaster for Crosby, who gave up a home run to Henry Cruz after a single by Garvey and a walk to Ron Cey. Steve Yeager's single followed by a stolen base (one of only three he would have that season) and Russell's single accounted for a fourth run. Scheduled to bat leadoff in the fifth, Crosby was pulled for a pinch-hitter. The Dodgers went on to win 5-4 in 10 innings in a game seen by 25,167 spectators.

Crosby, whose baseball nickname was Bing (of course), was a rare player from his era to have been born in Canada.

Kenneth Stewart Crosby was born on December 15, 1947, at New Denver, British Columbia. He was one of three sons for the former Alice Catherine Speed, the daughter of an English-born streetcar motorman and hotelier, and Frederick Homer Crosby, the son of parents who immigrated from Austria-Hungary. Both parents were born in British Columbia. (When Ken Crosby entered the United States as an infant, his ethnicity was described as Bohemian. His player contract card with *The Sporting News* lists his heritage as English-Austrian.) The couple met one summer when Alice was working at her family's resort and general store at Likely, an old Gold Rush town. Fred, a gold miner, was looking for a nearby mining camp. They married in Vancouver in 1940, a wartime marriage as Canada had declared war after Germany invaded Poland the previous year. Five of her brothers served with the Canadian forces.

On Ken's birth, Fred Crosby was superintendent of the Mountain Chief Mine in New Denver, a village of 1,671 people in the province's Kootenays region in southeastern British Columbia. The mine produced lead and silver. During World War II, the village was the site of an internment camp for 22,000 Canadians of Japanese ancestry who were forced from their homes. The camp is now known as the Nikkei Memorial Internment Centre, a national historic site.

Fred Crosby's work as a geological mining engineer for McFarland & Hollinger took him to mines on both sides of the border, forcing long separations from his family. In 1952 the Crosbys moved to Wells, Nevada, where they spent part of the summer living in a large tent with a wooden floor. Three years later, the family moved to Provo, Utah. In 1957, Fred was critically injured in an accident at the Oprih Hill Mine in Tooele County. He was hospitalized for a year and left paralyzed from the waist down.

Ken Crosby pitched for the Provo High Bulldogs, as well as a state champion American Legion team in 1965-66. In 1968 he started Brigham Young University's first-ever game in the College World Series. Though he had an undistinguished 4.01 earned-run average over the season, coach Glen Tuckett called on the right-hander to face a tough University of Southern California team under coach Rod Dedeaux. Crosby gave up just one hit through seven innings before losing 5-3 after a hit, two walks, a hit batsman, and an error led to four runs in the eighth. The winning pitcher was a left-hander named Bill Lee, a 22nd-round draft pick of the Boston Red Sox who had yet to be nicknamed "Spaceman" for his iconoclastic behavior.

Crosby, who majored in social psychology, was named outstanding BYU senior in 1969.

The pitcher spent the summer of 1968 with the Eureka Humboldt Crabs, who won the California state semipro championship. He was scouted by Ken Voller while with the Mesa (Arizona) Collegians the following summer. The New York Yankees picked him in the 10th round of the 1969 free-agent draft. The team signed him 12 days later, on June 17, 1969.

ONE-HIT WONDERS

Crosby pitched in the Yankees system for the Kinston (North Carolina) Eagles, the Johnson City (Tennessee) Yankees, the Manchester (New Hampshire) Yankees, and the Syracuse (New York) Chiefs before being traded to the St. Louis Cardinals on September 12, 1973, as the player-to-be-named later in a cash and player deal for reliever Wayne Granger, who had joined the Yankees the previous month.

In 1975 Crosby was in his second season with the Tulsa Oilers when the Cardinals swapped him to the Cubs for right-handed starter Eddie Solomon.

He made his major-league debut at Veterans Stadium in Philadelphia on August 5, 1975. Bill Bonham was pulled without recording an out in the first inning after surrendering three singles, two doubles, and two homers. Johnny Oates then singled off Crosby to make eight consecutive hits to start the game. The Cubs finally got an out when pitcher Dick Ruthven successfully dropped a sacrifice bunt to the first baseman. Two singles, three walks, a passed ball, and a balk later, and the Phillies were up 10-0. Crosby finally ended the inning by striking out Mike Schmidt, whose homer had chased starter Bonham.

Ruthven walked Crosby in the third and he scored on Monday's triple. The run scored in his debut was the only one he would make in the majors.

Crosby pitched in the Chicago system in 1975 and '76 for the Wichita (Kansas) Aeros and the Midland (Texas) Cubs. He also played winter ball in Puerto Rico.

In 1970 he married Marian Denler.

After baseball, Crosby worked in the sporting-goods industry before starting a career as a real-estate agent in Park City, Utah.

While he managed nine hits (seven singles, two doubles) over eight minor-league seasons for an .063 average, the lanky pitcher retired with a major-league career batting average of .500 and an on-base percentage of .667.

SOURCES

In addition to the sources cited in the Notes, the author consulted the following:

"Five sons on service, sixth, 16, 'rarin' to go,'" *Vancouver* (British Columbia) *Sun*, July 8, 1944.

Davis, David. "When Rick Monday Saved the American Flag from Being Burned at Dodger Stadium," *Vice*, April 25, 2016.

Dozer, Richard. "Monday Earns Fans' Salute for a Flag-Rescue Mission," *The Sporting News*, May 15, 1976.

Walker, Pat. "Ken Crosby, Young Man on His Way," *Orem-Geneva Times* (Orem City, Utah), October 16, 1969: 8.

The Sporting News Baseball Players Contract Cards Collection

Retrosheet.org

NOTES

1. Richard Dozer, "San Diego Spares Spoil Cubs' Pitching 9-5," *Chicago Tribune*, April 30, 1976: 61.
2. Tim Dahlberg, "Monday's Save a Fourth of July Memory," *Casper* (Wyoming) *Star-Tribune*, July 4, 2006.

JASON DAVIS

By Max Effgen

Jason Davis, a 6-foot-6-inch right-handed fireballer, pitched in seven seasons from 2002 through 2008 for Cleveland Indians, Seattle Mariners, and Pittsburgh Pirates. Known for a high-velocity sinking fastball in the upper 90s, Davis in 2003 led all American League rookie pitchers in innings pitched (165⅓), his first full season. Indians pitching coach Mike Brown compared Davis's velocity to that of a teammate, future Cy Young Award winner and 3,000-strikeout club member C.C. Sabathia.[1] Davis would see time as a starter and a reliever, compiling a record of 22-26 with one save in 144 games. All but his final 2008 season (with the Pirates) was in the American League, so Davis pitched with the designated hitter and had few interleague matchups. Over the seven seasons, he had only 19 plate appearances, and a .059 batting average. His one major-league hit was a home run against the Atlanta Braves on a career day, June 20, 2004, earning him the legacy of a one-hit wonder.

Jason Thomas Davis was born to Gary and Deborah Davis in Chattanooga, Tennessee, on May 8, 1980. His family has strong roots in Bradley County, Tennessee, and he was raised in the county seat, Cleveland. His father, Gary, coached Little League for Jason and his older brother, Nathan. Sister Michelle rounded out the Davis family. Jason was a tall (6-foot-6, 230-pound) multisport athlete, excelling in basketball and baseball. In a newspaper article, Davis recalled a humorous anecdote: He was playing outfield for his seventh-grade team, but his mind was on a Dixie Youth Baseball game he was scheduled to pitch later that day. "I ended up losing track of the game. I was bored out of my mind, so for a whole half inning I was out there working on my windup, having a good ol' time. What I didn't realize was everybody in the dugout was watching what I was doing. My coach even hollered out there (and) asked who I was playing for. My friends still bring that up from time to time."[2]

Davis excelled in baseball and basketball with his brother, Nathan, at Charleston High School playing baseball for Tennessee high-school coaching legend

Mike Turner. Talent on the court earned Davis a basketball scholarship to Cleveland State Community College in 1998. "I … wasn't going to play baseball," he recalled. There are two versions of what happened next. Nathan said in 2003 that he insisted on Jason joining the baseball team. "I knew Jason could pitch," he said. "I mean, he could really pitch. As soon as our coach saw him throw for the first time, he offered him a baseball scholarship on the spot."[3] Jason related the second version in 2016: "They had an issue in the fall and were struggling for pitching, and (coach) Mike Policastro approached me about coming to throw a little and see how I liked it." Davis loved pitching and decided to devote his time and talents to baseball, which he said "presented more opportunities."[4]

ONE-HIT WONDERS

Cleveland, Tennessee, has had a long history of producing major-league talent. Frank Bates pitched for two seasons in 1898 and 1899 for the syndicate-owned National League Cleveland Spiders and St. Louis Perfectos. The brothers Doc Johnston and Jimmy Johnston could be regarded as the town's most successful baseball products. Doc played for 11 major-league seasons with the Cincinnati Reds, Cleveland Indians, Pittsburgh Pirates, and Philadelphia Athletics from 1909 to 1922. He was the first baseman for the 1920 World Series champion Indians. Jimmy broke into the majors in 1911 with the Chicago White Sox, but did not stick in the majors until 1914, playing for the Chicago Cubs, Brooklyn Robins, Boston Braves, and New York Giants until 1926. He compiled a .294 batting average and stole 169 bases in 13 seasons. Jimmy set the Pacific Coast League record for stolen bases in a single season with 124 for San Francisco in 1913.[5] The brothers played against each other in the 1920 World Series. It was the first time brothers played against each other in the fall classic. Jimmy was called the "Greatest Utility Player" in 1926 by *Baseball Magazine*.[6] More recent ballplayers with ties to Cleveland, Tennessee, include Guy Lacy, Duff Brumley, Ray Stephens, Bubba Trammell, and Stephen Pryor.

Coach Mike Policastro had built the Cleveland State Community College Cougars baseball team into a regional junior-college powerhouse. Word of a 6-foot-6 right-handed fireballer throwing 90 miles per hour attracted area major-league scouts. Mark Germann, the Cleveland Indians area scout, first saw Davis in a playoff game. Quickly, Germann ran through his checklist. Did he have a major-league body? The physical tools to succeed at the game's highest level. Yes, Davis did and he worked well for a big guy. Everything about his motion was long. He threw hard but lacked a breaking pitch. Davis was interesting to the scout. Then Germann started researching what got Davis to this point. Attitude and a growth mindset are important. Is the player the type of person who is driven enough to put the team on his back? Does the team trust him enough?

Why did Policastro trust him in this playoff situation? How did that happen? Germann researched and found that Davis was a multisport athlete. He had even earned a basketball scholarship and played the sport during his first year. Davis was a good shooter, which Germann translated into "feel" and the ability to throw strikes. Davis's velocity was in the 88-89 range and would touch 93. Collegiate summer baseball, like the Cape Cod League, was a typical path. Davis had the physical tools. He passed the first test. Germann recommended a draft and follow to the Indians.[7]

The draft-and-follow system was eliminated with changes to the amateur draft in 2007. The drafting team had up to one year to sign a drafted player. Teams could draft high-school or junior-college players, follow them through the next season, and then sign them, or not, until one week before the next draft. Typically, later-round picks would be draft-and-follow. If the player blossomed during the "follow" season, the drafting team could end up with rights to a player who would warrant a high draft pick and compensation. Teams were expected to reflect this improved value in the contract offer. If not, the player could refuse to sign and return to the following amateur draft.[8]

Germann continued to scout Davis. Now the research went to the next steps. He investigated his character. He met Davis and his family. They were grounded. He looked at how they treated him as a scout as well as the interaction with each other. The Davises were a religious family and extraordinarily respectful with each other. It was clear that Jason had the support he needed to give him a firm grounding. By 2000 Jason's velocity was up to 94-95; however, the reliable breaking pitch still eluded him. Could he develop a splitter? Could he develop a swing-and-miss pitch? Germann told the author that the question for Davis, as well as all players, was and is, "Where is the ceiling?" As a scout it is always a question of risk. "There are so many variables that success is not predictable," he said. At this point, Germann brought in John Mirabelli, a longtime scout and executive with Indians, and he was positive. He liked what he saw in Davis. As the following draft in 2000 was shaping up, it was clear that Davis could go in the top five rounds. Still the question, the risk, was big arm, does it play at the major-league level without a secondary pitch?[9] The Indians made the decision and signed Jason Davis on May 18, 2000.

Davis was assigned to the Burlington Indians in the Rookie Appalachian League. Coming straight from the junior-college season, he posted a 4-4 record in 10 starts with 35 strikeouts and a healthy 2.19 K/BB ratio for a team that finished with 21-46 record. The next season, 2001, was Davis's breakout year. Assigned to the Columbus RedStixx of the Class-A South Atlantic League, he led the team in games started, wins, and innings pitched. Posting 115 strikeouts and keeping a 2.25 K/BB ratio, Davis earned a reputation for

ONE-HIT WONDERS

throwing hard and throwing strikes for the RedStixx and manager Ted Kubiak.

Davis began the 2002 season at high Class-A Kinston (Carolina League). Promoted to Double-A Akron (Eastern League) in midseason, Davis excelled (6-2, 3.51 ERA) and was called up to the Indians when rosters expanded in September. "If you could call any of our guys a nontraditional promotion, this is the guy but for right reasons," general manager Mark Shapiro said. The direction of Davis's season was onward and upward. "He was better in big games," Shapiro said. Davis had hit 97 MPH with a sinker paired with an effective split-finger fastball.[10] This was not expected to be a long-term promotion as Davis had not played at the Triple-A level; however by the Indians' estimation, he had not run out of gas and might benefit from a taste of major-league competition. "I don't think he is there yet," said Indians manager Joel Skinner, "But he does things you like to see a young guy do, in addition to having good stuff. He can control the running game and field his position."[11]

Davis was called up the same day as switch-hitting catcher, frequent batterymate and future five-time All-Star Victor Martinez.[12] He made his major-league debut on September 9, 2002, in a home loss to the Toronto Blue Jays. The game was described as an evening of contrasts by sportswriter Sheldon Ocker.[13] Jaret Wright, recovering from a second shoulder surgery, struggled. Davis made his debut in duress. Brought in at the top of the third inning with the Indians losing 6-0, he pitched four innings of relief. Davis got through the third, giving up one hit. In the fourth inning Eric Hinske hit a leadoff home run and Carlos Delgado doubled with one out, after which Davis retired the next eight batters he faced before being lifted. "I started to lose my butterflies and focus in on throwing strikes," he said after the game. "I cannot describe how nervous I was when I got in there."[14] Davis's performance earned him his first major-league start, against the Minnesota Twins in Cleveland on the 14th. Davis went 5⅔ innings, allowing six hits and one run. He left the game with the lead, but the Indians fell, 3-2. Six days later, Davis started and got his first major-league win, 1-0, against the Kansas City Royals on September 20 in Kansas City.

Before 2003 spring training, *Baseball America* ranked Davis as a Top Ten preseason prospect for the Indians. It was expected that he would begin the season in Triple A. But in 19 innings pitched in spring training, Davis posted a 1.42 ERA, and there was no stop in Triple A. Davis made the major-league roster.

Sports Illustrated commented, "Davis is a four-pitch package, but everything keys off the fastball."[15] Local sportswriter Terry Pluto wrote, "This kid throws 95 mph, and his ball moves all over the place. He needs a change up and experience, but what an arm!"[16]

Davis made his first start on April 4 in Kansas City. The dominant spring gave way to a disastrous first start. Davis gave up five runs in three innings. His second start was a struggle as well: five runs surrendered to the White Sox in four innings. Finally, at home on April 15, Davis earned his first win of the season. Manager Eric Wedge commented, "This was just a small piece of Jason Davis. He has a tremendous future."[17] Davis added another win and a loss in April to start the season 2-3. May and June were very good for Davis, but not the Indians, who were rooted in fourth place in the American League Central Division. Being down did not mean rolling over. Bad blood with the Minnesota Twins had been brewing most of the season and on July 4 it boiled over. With Davis on the mound, Torii Hunter took exception to an inside pitch at the waist. Hunter jumped back and pointed to Davis, who motioned for the hitter to come on out. Benches cleared. Three Indians, including Davis, and two Twins were ejected.[18] By the All-Star break, July 13-15, he was routinely mentioned as part of an emerging formidable rotation, along with C.C. Sabathia, Brian Anderson, and Billy Taber.

On August 8 Davis was one pitch from a 1-0 shutout of the Anaheim Angels. Garret Anderson, who had hit a grand slam off Davis on May 8, smacked a three-run homer to take the lead and snatch a victory in Cleveland. "I think I've learned a lot this year. I learned the hard way today. Sometimes that's the best way," Davis said.[19] Scratched for the final home game of the season on September 21, his season was done. Shoulder fatigue was the cause. He compiled an 8-11 record in 165⅓ innings, the second most on the staff and the most among all American League rookies.

Coming out of spring training in 2004, Davis earned the second position in the rotation behind Sabathia. The Indians remained confident; "Jason is talented enough that being in the minors last year would not have taught him as much or as fast as the things he learned with us," said manager Wedge.[20] Davis's outings were inconsistent. He would pitch well and then make mistakes that changed the game. The Indians bullpen was not a help, and the team hovered just below the .500 mark. Getting Davis to pitch to a win was beginning to gnaw on the Cleveland faithful. He had only two wins in his last 25 starts. The

ONE-HIT WONDERS

Indians simply were not winning when he pitched. Family always gave Davis a boost. Interleague play, Sunday baseball, and a 120-mile drive from Cleveland, Tennessee, to Atlanta aligned for a career day on June 20, 2004.

Davis's grandfather would take Jason and Nathan to games in Atlanta. Now Jason would pitch at Turner Field. Nearly 100 family and friends made the two-hour trip. He was masterful, holding the Braves scoreless for six innings. Back-to-back home runs by J.D. Drew and Chipper Jones were the only scoring by Atlanta. With interleague play at a National League park, Davis would get to bat, "I had almost 100 people here, so I did not want to strike out. I didn't want them to have anything on me when I go back home," he said. He delivered. In the top of the second inning, Atlanta pitcher Russ Ortiz missed his spot and Davis connected for a home run. This was his first, and last, major-league hit. Davis cruised through a career day: seven innings for the 5-2 win and his first major-league hit. He gave the ball to his grandmother, Maxie Davis.[21]

Davis's next three starts resulted in one loss and two no-decisions with 16 earned runs. Through July 8, the Indians were 5-13 in his starts. He was optioned to Triple-A Buffalo to take a deep breath and give himself a chance to become the pitcher the team believed he could be. For Buffalo Davis pitched in nine games, all starts, with a record of 3-2 and a 3.00 ERA. He was recalled in September, but questions about his ability to start and remain in the rotation at the major-league level arose.[22] After a decent start, Davis was moved to the bullpen. There were concerns about the move to this role. Erratic command paired with an overly emotional tendency doom the relief pitcher and both were becoming common in Davis's outings. He relished the opportunity, but the results were mixed. At season's end, Indians general manager Shapiro said, "We don't think Jason Davis is ready to close. Look at the best closers, most of them are veteran guys. They worked into their roles."[23]

The 2005 season brought uncertainly to Davis's role. A strained-oblique injury to C.C. Sabathia left a hole in the rotation. Davis pitched well enough to earn a start on April 10. He earned the win but returned to the bullpen. Now he was in middle relief. The ability to throw strikes and remain composed blew up on April 24. After entering the game in the bottom of the seventh inning and retiring the Seattle Mariners in order, Davis lost command in the eighth. He walked five batters in a row, throwing only three strikes to them. The game was a contrast of pitching styles. The crafty Jamie Moyer efficiently cruised while the Indians floundered.[24] Davis was sent to Buffalo and made the occasional spot start for the Indians.

During the 2006 season Davis was a reliever and pitched just 55⅓ innings. Again he shuttled between Buffalo and Cleveland. Finally, in 2007, out of options and his performance at an all-time low, Davis was designated for assignment on May 8. Quickly, the Indians and the Seattle Mariners made a trade. That he landed with the Mariners was not a surprise. Mariners manager Mike Hargrove was an assistant to the general manager with the Indians in 2004. He saw Davis at his best. A big guy with a big arm.

Davis saw spot relief duties for the Mariners and earned two wins in June. On the 22nd, the game against the Cincinnati Reds was out of hand at 9-0 when Davis took over with two outs in the top of the third. He allowed a run in the fifth, and in the sixth he was tagged for two home runs and six runs, leaving the game with the score 16-1. Davis saw action in two more games with Seattle before being sent to Triple-A Tacoma. He made five appearances for Tacoma and was granted free agency after the season.

In 2008 Davis went to spring training with the Texas Rangers, but was released. He was picked up by the Pittsburgh Pirates. He started the season in Triple-A Indianapolis and finished back in the majors. Davis made 14 appearances and four starts (2-4, 5.29). Now arbitration-eligible, he was given outright assignment. Davis re-signed with Pittsburgh as a free agent for 2009 but did not pitch at the major-league level again.

After comeback attempts in 2009 and 2011, Davis retired from professional baseball. With his wife, Sarah, he had four children, Lily, Jaxon, Landon, and Sadie. He worked as an individual pitching coach while taking a year off, and then he entered the workforce with M&M Mars at the candy maker's production plant in Cleveland, Tennessee.[25]

Jason Davis has an interesting hobby that gained him notoriety during his playing days, taxidermy.[26] The hobby started with a deer head in his Cleveland, Ohio, apartment, a basic instruction manual and taxidermy supplies. Working over the offseason, he focused on trophies from what he hunted. His trophy room included deer, ducks, bass, walleye, steelhead, pheasant, bobcat, and fox.[27]

Baseball continued to present Davis with opportunities, namely, coaching. His first foray in coaching came at Ocoee Middle School, in his hometown,

ONE-HIT WONDERS

where he became an assistant coach in 2016 and "had an absolute blast."[28] At the behest of his high-school coach turned athletic director, Mike Turner, Davis then joined Walker Valley High School at the varsity pitching coach. "… [W]orking with those kids and seeing them progress – I really developed a passion for that," Davis said.[29]

Davis was inducted into the Cleveland State Community College Hall of Fame in 2019.[30]

SOURCES

In addition to the sources cited in the Notes, the author consulted Baseball-Reference.com, baseballalmanac.com, retrosheet.org, and thebaseballcube.com.

NOTES

1. "Tribe Rookie Jason Davis Bidding for Starting Spot," *Tribune* (Coshocton, Ohio), March 2, 2003: 14.
2. "Pros Fondly Recall Playing as Youths," *Indianapolis Star*, July 31, 2008: D3.
3. "Davis Gets Jump-Start from Family," *Akron Beacon Journal*, May 13, 2003: C1.
4. "Former Indians Hurler Jason Davis Back at Home; Will Coach Walker Valley Pitchers," *Chattanooga Times Free Press*, September 22, 2016.
5. "Jimmy Johnston, Top Base Stealer Dies," *Los Angeles Times*, February 15, 1967: 35.
6. "'Greatest Utility Player' Leaves Glorious Record," *Jackson* (Tennessee) *Sun*, February 15, 1967: 12.
7. Mark Germann, telephone interview with author, July 6, 2020.
8. John Manuel, "The History and Future of the Amateur Draft," *Baseball Research Journal* (SABR), Summer 2010. https://sabr.org/journal/article/the-history-and-future-of-the-amateur-draft/.
9. Mark Germann, telephone interview with author, July 6, 2020.
10. "Davis a Surprise Addition," *Akron Beacon Journal*, September 10, 2002: C5.
11. "Tribe Notebook," *Akron Beacon Journal*, September 11, 2002: C5.
12. "Indians Recall Vic Martinez," *Telegram-Forum* (Bucyrus, Ohio), September 10, 2002: 11.
13. "Wright Blasted in Loss," *Akron Beacon Journal*, September 10, 2002: C1.
14. "Ex-Aeros Pitcher Davis Has Nice Debut in Relief," *Akron Beacon Journal*, September 10, 2002: C5.
15. Albert Chen, "Cleveland Indians: Patience Will Be Key as This Former Power Takes the Next Step in Rebuilding," *Sports Illustrated*, March 31, 2003. https://vault.si.com/vault/2003/03/31/3-cleveland-indians-patience-will-be-key-as-this-former-power-takes-the-next-step-in-rebuilding.
16. "Talking Tribe," *Akron Beacon Journal*, March 30, 2003: C4.
17. "No Woe Versus O's" *Akron Beacon Journal*, April 16, 2003: C1.
18. "Rivalry Hot, but Indians Offense Not," *Akron Beacon Journal*, July 5, 2003: C1.
19. "Davis' Consolation Prize," *Akron Beacon Journal*, August 9, 2003: C1.
20. "On the Mound, Learning Is a Slow Process," *Akron Beacon Journal*, March 28, 2004: C1.
21. "Davis Does It All for the Indians," *Akron Beacon Journal*, June 21, 2004: C1.
22. "Indians Summon Bard, Bartosh from Buffalo," *Akron Beacon Journal*, September 2, 2004: C5.
23. "Pitching Main Concern," *Akron Beacon Journal*, October 3, 2004: C4.
24. Larry Stone, "Moyer's Milestone: Lefty Ties Johnson for Most M's Wins," *Seattle Times*, April 25, 2005. https://www.seattletimes.com/sports/moyers-milestone-lefty-ties-johnson-for-most-ms-wins/.
25. Saralyn Norkus, "Former Major Leaguer Joins Mustang staff," *Cleveland* (Tennessee) *Daily Banner*, July 30, 2016. http://clevelandbanner.com/stories/former-major-leaguer-joins-mustang-staff,39406.
26. Ben Reiter, "The Right Stuffing," *Sports Illustrated*, August 15, 2005. https://vault.si.com/vault/2005/08/15/the-right-stuffing.
27. "Pitcher Hunts for Spot in Rotation," *Pittsburgh Post-Gazette*, February 24, 2009: 35.
28. Saralyn Norkus, "Former Major Leaguer Joins Mustang staff."
29. Ward Gossett, "Former Indians Hurler Jason Davis Back at Home; Will Coach Walker Valley Pitchers," *Chattanooga Times Free Press*, September 22, 2106. https://www.timesfreepress.com/news/sports/preps/story/2016/sep/22/former-indians-hurler-davback-home-will-coach/387907/.
30. Cleveland State Cougars, "Six to Enter Hall of Fame at Saturday Ceremony," February 5, 2019. https://www.cscougars.com/general/2018-19/releases/20190205hs3bdc.

RAOUL "ROD" DEDEAUX

By Richard Cuicchi

When Rod Dedeaux hit an RBI single in his first major-league start for the Brooklyn Dodgers in September 1935, it seemed a good omen for the beginning of a successful major-league career. Having graduated from the University of Southern California a few months earlier, he had been tapped by a struggling Dodgers organization as a prospect to watch. However, his hit was the only one of an abbreviated two-game major-league career.

Dedeaux didn't make a name for himself in the majors or even in minor-league baseball, but that wasn't the end of his story in the sport. He became one of the most renowned college coaches of all time at his alma mater, where he set the standard for modern-day collegiate baseball programs across the country.

Raoul "Rod" Martial Dedeaux (pronounced DAY-doe) was born in New Orleans on February 17, 1914. His father, Henry Dedeaux, of French descent,

Coach Rod Dedeaux.

migrated from the Mississippi Gulf Coast to New Orleans, where he married Valentine Boada. Rod was the youngest of their four children. Public records listed his father's occupation as an inspector in the farming industry. The records show Dedeaux's family moved to California between 1920 and 1930.[1]

Dedeaux attended middle school in Oakland before the family relocated to Southern California. He was an all-city selection in 1930 and 1931 at Hollywood High School and led the city league in hitting twice. He earned a bat signed by Babe Ruth for winning the Babe Ruth Slugging Award.[2] While in high school, he developed a relationship with Casey Stengel, who made his offseason home in nearby Glendale while he was then managing at Toledo in the American Association. He frequently worked out at Hollywood's Griffith Park under Stengel's supervision and then went to Stengel's home to discuss baseball.[3] That initial relationship fostered additional connections between the two later in Dedeaux's career.

Dedeaux attended the University of Southern California, where he was a three-year starter from 1933 to 1935 and was elected the team captain for his senior season.[4] He graduated with a bachelor's degree in education in 1935.[5] On the recommendation of Stengel, the Brooklyn Dodgers signed Dedeaux to a contract.[6]

Dedeaux joined the Dodgers in early May before he had a chance to attend his graduation ceremony and participated in several workouts with the team. Stengel was impressed with his fielding in practice drills and said of his protégé, "I like to see 'em make that play (after Dedeaux snagged a groundball far to his right in a fielding drill). When a shortstop can do that, he can do anything."[7] Dedeaux's initial minor-league assignment took him to Dayton of the Middle Atlantic League, where he hit well enough (.290) to earn a late-season call-up with the Dodgers. In Stengel's second season as manager, the Dodgers finished in the second division (fifth place) for the second time. He decided to assemble a group of veteran and minor-league players in September in order to preview

ONE-HIT WONDERS

his candidates for the team the next season. Dedeaux was among the prospects Stengel wanted to assess.[8]

Dedeaux made his major-league debut on September 28 as a late-inning defensive replacement in a game at Ebbets Field that drew only 194 fans. He subbed for shortstop Lonny Frey, who had homered and doubled. Dedeaux didn't get an at-bat in the Dodgers' 12-2 blowout of the Philadelphia Phillies. He played the next day in the second game of a doubleheader against the Phillies, starting in place of Frey. He went 1-for-4 with an RBI single off Hal Kelleher in the seventh inning of a game that ended in a 4-4 tie after eight innings because of darkness. Those two games were Dedeaux's only ones in the majors.

In 1936 Brooklyn initially optioned Dedeaux to its Allentown affiliate (New York-Penn League).[9] However, he and the Dodgers could not agree on contract terms, and his option was transferred to Hazleton, a Phillies affiliate in the league.[10] He played in 42 games before a back injury ended his season. He was out of baseball in 1937, but then returned for parts of the 1938 and 1939 seasons for several teams in the Western International League and Pacific Coast League. Dedeaux said of his abbreviated major-league career, "I had a cup of coffee but with no sugar. I think about it every day."[11]

With his baseball career in jeopardy, Dedeaux founded the DART (Dedeaux Automotive Repair and Transit) trucking firm in 1938 with an investment of $500 from his signing bonus with Brooklyn.[12] The company eventually became DART Entities and grew into a million-dollar trucking firm specializing in worldwide distribution. Even until his death, Dedeaux served as the company's president and was involved in its daily activities.[13]

But Dedeaux didn't leave the sport entirely. He played for and coached semipro teams in the Los Angeles area, often competing in practice games against local colleges and military service-based teams.

USC lost several of its athletic department coaches to military service in 1942, and Dedeaux was named the interim head coach of baseball when head coach Sam Barry (who was also the head football and basketball coach) was assigned full-time duties in football during the spring.[14] Then Barry was inducted into the Navy, and Dedeaux became the permanent coach. His first Trojans team won the California Intercollegiate championship in 1942.[15] They finished second for the next three seasons. Dedeaux's 65-year-old father died on the USC bench before the start of a Trojans game in 1943.[16]

When Barry returned from military service in 1946, they shared head coaching duties for the baseball program through the 1950 season. However, Dedeaux was the de facto head coach, as he was responsible for the major decisions for the team.[17] In the College World Series in 1948, the Dedeaux-Barry coaching combination led USC over Yale in a best-of-three series for the first of 11 national titles under Dedeaux.

Another of Dedeaux's connections with Stengel involved a 1951 preseason exhibition game on the USC campus between the Trojans and Stengel's New York Yankees. Except for games played at West Point, the Yankees had never visited a college campus to play the home team. The Yankees had won the 1950 World Series, and the squad included Joe DiMaggio, Phil Rizzuto, Yogi Berra, Johnny Mize, and Hank Bauer.[18] The Yankees' 15-1 victory included a mammoth home run by rookie Mickey Mantle that was measured years later by researchers to have been in the 650-foot range.[19]

Ten years after its first College World Series appearance, USC fought its way back from the losers bracket to defeat Missouri twice for the title. USC's dominance continued with three CWS titles during the 1960s. Dedeaux's Trojans captured a still unbroken record five consecutive championships from 1970 to 1974, including wins over other prominent national programs like Arizona State, Miami, and Florida State. In one of the most dramatic wins in College World Series history, the 1973 USC squad came from behind in the ninth inning to score eight runs and defeat Minnesota, 8-7. Gophers pitcher Dave Winfield had held the Trojans to one hit through eight innings. The 1978 team defeated Arizona State for the third time in the decade. As of 2020 Dedeaux still held the record with 11 College World Series championships as a coach.[20]

Dedeaux ended his 45-year tenure in 1986. His teams were 1,332-571-11 (.699), making him the then-winningest coach in collegiate baseball history.[21]

Dedeaux's previous exposure to Stengel was evident in dealing with his Trojan players. He was known to clown around with them but found opportunities to mix in life's lessons with his baseball teachings. Dedeaux said in a 1968 interview, "I have very definitely patterned my style after Casey's. Thirty-odd years ago I figured he had the best brain in baseball. That was long before his success with the Yankees. I never had any trouble understanding Case." Around USC,

ONE-HIT WONDERS

Rod Dedeaux during playing days.

Dedeaux was sometimes called the Young Perfessor, a play on Stengel's nickname the Old Perfessor.[22]

Dedeaux remained actively involved in his business during his coaching tenure at USC. During baseball season, he worked in the company's office in the mornings and carried out his coaching duties in the afternoons. It was often joked that Dedeaux coached a baseball team in his spare time. After he retired, family members continued to operate the business.

He was responsible for building the USC program into a national power and helping to elevate college baseball across the country. Before Dedeaux developed his program at USC, major-league organizations didn't look to collegiate baseball as a major source of amateur players. That changed with Dedeaux, who sent nearly 60 Trojans to the major leagues. Among the more successful players were Ron Fairly, Don Buford, Tom Seaver, Dave Kingman, Fred Lynn, Roy Smalley, Steve Kemp, Mark McGwire, Steve Busby, and Randy Johnson.[23] Altogether, he sent nearly 200 players to professional baseball careers.

Los Angeles Times sports columnist Jim Murray called Dedeaux's USC program, "the greatest farm club in the history of the major leagues," adding, "[T]he most consistent supplier of major league talent the past 10 years is a franchise maintained at no cost to baseball. It finds and signs its own prospects, suits them up, develops them, refines them, weeds them out – and then turns them over to the big leagues fully polished and ready for the World Series."[24]

The 1979 All-Star Game was indicative of Dedeaux's influence in the majors. Four of his former players (Kemp, Kingman, Lynn, and Smalley) appeared in the game. An article in *Collegiate Baseball Magazine* quoted him, "I don't believe any other school ever had that many all-stars in one game. I know it was one of the proudest moments of my life." When asked what he attributed his program's success to, he said, "First, you have to play smart baseball. … If you learn to do things right all the time, it doesn't matter who you're playing. Secondly, stay loose. When we work, we work hard; but we have fun, too. A little clowning always helps."[25]

Dedeaux had opportunities to enter the major leagues as a coach or manager, but always chose to remain with his alma mater. Stengel was reported to have asked Dedeaux to take a coaching job with the Yankees so that he could be groomed to become his successor.[26] Dedeaux did briefly hold a couple of jobs involving the majors, although not in the dugout. His *Sporting News* player contract card showed him as a scout for the Yankees in 1951, likely another result of his connection with Stengel. When the Brooklyn Dodgers relocated to California, they took advantage of Dedeaux's popularity in the Los Angeles area by adding him to the Dodgers public-relations staff in 1958.[27]

Dedeaux's sphere of influence also extended to international baseball. He founded the USA-Japan Collegiate World Series in 1972 and was its chairman from 1972 to 1984. President Richard Nixon selected Dedeaux in 1974 to supervise a baseball clinic in Panama. He coached the US amateur team that played in Tokyo in conjunction with the 1964 Olympics. He was involved in bringing baseball to the 1984 Olympics in Los Angeles as a demonstration sport and coached the U.S. team to a silver medal.[28]

Among the many honors Dedeaux garnered during his career were Coach of the Century in 1999 by *Baseball America* and *Collegiate Baseball*. As part of the 50th anniversary of the College World Series in 1996, Dedeaux was named the head coach of the All-Time CWS team by a panel of former World Series coaches, media, and college baseball officials. He was named Coach of the Year six times by the American Baseball Coaches Association and was inducted into the organization's Hall of Fame in 1970.[29]

After retiring as head coach in 1986, Dedeaux took an administrative job as director of baseball at USC, where he advised athletic director Mike Garrett and head coach Mike Gillespie in the development of Trojan baseball. He also helped with fundraising activities for the program and worked as a spokesman for the sport at the collegiate and international levels.[30]

As chronicled in Robert Leach's book about Dedeaux, *Never Make the Same Mistake Once*, Dedeaux's accomplishments went far beyond a magnificent record as coach of a successful program. He was noted for his role in the development of his players into men, frequently using a set of maxims that had application on and off the field for his players.[31]

One of his more famous quips was "Some day there will be a pop fly that doesn't come down." It was his way of telling his players to always hustle down to first on a fly ball. It was also his way of instilling in his players a philosophy of never taking anything for granted in life.[32]

Marcel Lachemann attributed his major-league accomplishments as a player, coach, and manager to having played for Dedeaux. He said, "Rod was always an underlying influence. The number of things learned under Rod are very hard to single out, but if I had to pick one, it would be the 'Never say die' mentality that he instilled in all of us. We were never out of a game and thus produced some of the all-time come-from-behind victories ever seen."[33]

Dedeaux's son Justin had been a player for his father and was his assistant coach for several years. Rod wanted his son to replace him as head coach when he retired but ran into disagreement from the USC athletic director.[34] His son Terry also played for USC.

Dedeaux was a fixture on the USC campus for 45 years and his legacy continued after he retired as the coach. The Trojan baseball field bears his name and a bronze statue of him ushers fans into the stadium. At the dedication of the statue in 2014, USC President C.L. Max Nikias said, "In the 134-year history of our university, very few people have had such a long and lasting impact on the University of Southern California community. Rod Dedeaux inspired our baseball players and enriched our campus spirit for more than half of the university's history."[35]

Dedeaux was married to Helen Louise Jones in 1940. In addition to Justin and Terry, their children included Denise and Michele. He died on January 5, 2006, at the age of 91.

SOURCES

In addition to the sources cited in the Notes, the author consulted Baseball-Reference.com, Ancestry.com, and the following:

Glick, Shav. "Rod Dedeaux, 91; Led USC Teams to 11 National Baseball Championships," *Los Angeles Times*, January 6, 2006.

Holmes, Tommy. "194 Pay Cash to See Dodgers Beat Phils, 12-2," *Brooklyn Daily Eagle*, September 29, 1935: D1.

Holmes, Tommy. "Casey Philosophizes: Dodgers Might Have Equaled Cubs' Winning Streak in Longer Season," *Brooklyn Daily Eagle*, September 30, 1935: 18.

Hughes, Ed. "Raoul Dedeaux, New Dodger, Clever Fielder," *Brooklyn Daily Eagle*, May 3, 1935: 24.

Leach, Bob. "Never Make the Same Mistake Once: Remembering USC Baseball Coach Rod Dedeaux," *The National Pastime*, 2011. sabr.org/research/never-make-same-mistake-once-remembering-usc-baseball-coach-rod-dedeaux. (accessed February 2, 2020).

Pietrusza, David, Matthew Silverman, and Michael Gershman. *Baseball: The Biographical Encyclopedia* (New York: Total Sports Illustrated, 2000), 277.

NOTES

1. Numerous sources about Dedeaux's life omitted the exact year and reason for the family's move to California.

2. David Rankin. *Rod Dedeaux: Master of the Diamond* (Monterey, California: Coaches Choice, 2013), 11.

ONE-HIT WONDERS

3. Bill Becker, "Dedeaux Uses Stengel's Style to Get Most Out of the USC Nine," *New York Times*, June 23, 1968.
4. "Dedeaux Leads Trojan Nine," *Los Angeles Times*, June 1, 1934: 2, 14.
5. "Trojans Lose Fifty-three Athletic Stars by Graduation Saturday," *Los Angeles Times*, June 6, 1935: 2, 11.
6. Becker.
7. Tommy Holmes. "Cards' Pilot on Sidelines, Feels Years," *Brooklyn Daily Eagle*, May 7, 1935: 14.
8. "Stengel Wavering on Youth Program," *The Sporting News*, September 19, 1935: 2.
9. Howard W. Davis. "Pitching Is Big 'If' as NYP Loop Opens," *The Sporting News*, April 30, 1936: 5.
10. Rankin, 14.
11. Rankin, 14.
12. DART Entities website. dartentities.com/about-us/our-history/ (accessed February 2, 2020).
13. 2019 USC Baseball Record Book, s3.amazonaws.com/sidearm.sites/usctrojans.com/documents/2019/1/17/2019_record_book.pdf. (accessed February 2, 2020).
14. "Trojans Sign Shelby Calhoun," *Los Angeles Times*, March 6, 1942: L, 19.
15. Paul Zimmerman, "Sport Postscripts, *Los Angeles Times*, May 1, 1942: L, 21.
16. "Dedeaux's Dad Dies on Bench," *Los Angeles Times*, April 24, 1943: 2, 8.
17. Rankin, 15.
18. Rankin, 18.
19. Robert McG. Thomas Jr. "Measuring a Blast," *New York Times*, June 23, 1986: C2.
20. USC Baseball History & Archive. usctrojans.com/sports/2017/6/15/usc-baseball-archive.aspx. (accessed February 2, 2020).
21. Florida State University's head coach Mike Martin retired in 2019 as the all-time winningest coach in NCAA baseball history with 2,029 victories. (https://seminoles.com/staff/mike-martin/).
22. Becker.
23. USC Baseball History & Archive.
24. 2019 USC Baseball Record Book.
25. "Rod Dedeaux: A Coach for a Century," *USC News*, February 1, 1999. news.usc.edu/9337/Rod-Dedeaux-A-Coach-For-the-Century/. (accessed February 2, 2020).
26. Mark Heisler. "Rod Dedeaux: Do You Measure This Man by Victories or Respect?" *Los Angeles Times*, June 16, 1986.
27. "Giles Loop Glint," *The Sporting News*, May 28, 1958: 26.
28. 2019 USC Baseball Record Book.
29. 2019 USC Baseball Record Book.
30. "Rod Dedeaux: A Coach for a Century."
31. Robert Leach, *Never Make the Same Mistake Twice* (Los Angeles: Figueroa Press, 2003), 12.
32. Leach, 69.
33. Leach, 104.
34. Heisler.
35. William Hanley, "Trojans Honor Former Coach Dedeaux," *Daily Trojan*, February 18, 2014.

JIM DERRINGTON

By Don Zminda

Jim Derrington's major-league career was brief, but historic. When Derrington took the mound for the Chicago White Sox at the age of 16 years, 306 days on the final day of the 1956 season, he became the youngest pitcher since Willie McGill in 1890 to start a major-league game. Derrington, who singled off Kansas City Athletics pitcher Bill Harrington in the fourth inning of that game, remains the youngest player in American League history to record a hit. Unfortunately for Derrington, his major-league career was over before he turned 18, and his career as a player in Organized Baseball ended due to injuries in 1961, when he was still only 21.

Born on November 29, 1939, in Compton, a Southern California city about 10 miles south of downtown Los Angeles, Charles James Derrington had baseball in his bloodlines. Derrington's father, Charles, played minor-league ball in the years just prior to America's involvement in World War II, and his maternal uncle, Herman Reich, had a 111-game career as a first baseman-outfielder with the Senators, Indians, and Cubs, all in 1949. The 1940 census lists Charles Sr. as a "ball-player" in the Middle Atlantic League. Charles, 20, and his wife, Evelyn, lived in the Reich family home. Herman's father, Carl, worked as a machinist in a paper mill. Herman Reich, 22, was listed as a ballplayer in the Pacific Coast League. Jim Derrington's birth may have prevented his dad from reaching the majors. "Dad was going with the Indians," he told *Chicago Tribune* writer David Condon, "and since I was just a baby, he wanted mom and me with him. But when Cleveland wouldn't pay the family transportation, dad stayed in California with us."[1]

Charles Derrington's career in Organized Baseball ended when the United States entered World War II, but both he and Jim's uncle Herman taught Derrington the nuances of baseball from an early age. "With my uncle and dad," he told Condon, "that's about all there has ever been for me: baseball. I've been playing since I could walk, and I would toddle with dad when he went to play in the semi-pro and minors."[2]

In grade school Derrington skipped the third and fifth grades, but with his size (he grew to be 6-feet-3 and 190 pounds) and athletic skills, he had no difficulty competing against often-older players at South Gate High School in South Gate, California, a city a few miles north of Compton. A pitcher-first baseman, he batted .452 at South Gate while posting a 10-2 record with an 0.23 ERA and 159 strikeouts in 88 innings. As a 16-year-old senior in 1956, Derrington batted .414 and went 8-2 on the mound, with two no-hitters. He was named the Los Angeles City Player of the Year by the Helms All-Southern California Board of Baseball. Paul Deitz, a boyhood friend of Derrington's who would go on to become a college baseball coach, told the *Los Angeles Times* in 1991: "I've coached in college and Alaska and sent 15 players to the major

ONE-HIT WONDERS

leagues and I could safely say that no one that I ever saw in my lifetime was as good as Jim was at that point in time. ... He was a man among boys."[3]

When Derrington graduated from high school, four major-league teams, including the New York Yankees, offered him large bonuses to sign, despite the fact that the rules of the time required that any player signing for a bonus greater than $4,000 was required to remain on his team's 25-man roster for the next two years. White Sox scout Hollis Thurston had been watching Jim for several years, and the White Sox eventually signed Derrington for a bonus of $78,000 (press accounts of the time significantly underestimated the size of the bonus, with reports ranging from $40,000 to 65,000). The actual signing did not take place until September 10, as Commissioner Ford Frick ruled that an agreement between the major leagues and the American Legion required Derrington to play a season of American Legion ball before signing.

When Derrington joined the White Sox in September of 1956, the club was far behind the eventual pennant winners, the New York Yankees, but was battling the Cleveland Indians and Boston Red Sox to finish second in the American League race (Chicago ultimately finished third with an 85-69 record). White Sox manager Marty Marion kept the 16-year-old on the bench until he gave the youngster a start against the last-place Athletics in Kansas City on September 30, the final day of the season.

Derrington retired A's leadoff man Vic Power, then surrendered three straight hits. He also walked two batters and committed a balk in the frame, with Kansas City scoring twice. After giving up three more hits and another run in the second inning, Derrington seemed to find his rhythm, working three scoreless innings while allowing only one hit. "After the first inning or so, I kinda settled down," he recalled. "It was really hell the first inning or two – I was all over the place with it."[4] But in the sixth inning Derrington weakened, permitting three runs on a walk to Joe DeMaestri and home runs by Power and Lou Skizas. He was removed for a pinch-hitter in the top of the seventh, having allowed nine hits and six runs (five earned), along with six walks and three strikeouts. He was charged with the loss in Chicago's 7-6 defeat. Although pitch counts aren't available for Derrington's performance, the online website Boyd's World Estimated Pitch Calculator estimates the 16-year-old's pitch count at 116, based on those stats.[5] As a batter Derrington also recorded his historic single in the top of the fourth. "The 6 foot 3 inch 190 pound southpaw was impressive in spots and obviously nervous in others," wrote Robert Cromie in the *Chicago Tribune*. "Five of Derrington's walks came on a 3-2 pitch, and he showed a slow curve that fooled several of the Kansas City hitters completely. All in all, it was a performance that should not have discouraged Manager Marion."[6]

Derrington had two at-bats in the game. George Brunet struck him out in the top of the second and then he singled to right field off Bill Harrington in the top of the fourth. He was left stranded at first base. Over the course of his brief career, he had nine plate appearances, with a total of six at-bats. This was his lone base hit.

The bonus rule required the White Sox to keep Derrington on their 25-man-roster for the entire 1957 season, and new manager Al Lopez, who had replaced Marion, used the youngster sparingly, with 20 appearances, including five starts. Overall he posted an 0-1 record with a 4.86 ERA. Lopez assigned veteran pitcher Dick Donovan to be Derrington's roommate, and Derrington later praised Donovan for assisting his development. As for his relationship with Lopez, Derrington commented that "I never said two words with him all the time I was there. But he did give me every opportunity I could ask for."[7] Derrington had some impressive moments in 1957, particularly in relief, posting a 1.54 ERA in his 15 appearances out of the bullpen. His biggest problem was control; overall he issued 29 walks in 37 innings pitched, with only 14 strikeouts. His season highlight came in a start against the Detroit Tigers on August 10 at Comiskey Park. In that game Derrington did not allow a hit until the sixth inning, permitted just three hits overall, and shut out the Tigers until the eighth inning, when he was lifted after surrendering a two-run homer to Reno Bertoia. The White Sox eventually lost the game, 6-4.

Under the bonus rules of the time, Derrington would have had to remain on the White Sox roster for most of the 1958 season, and offseason reports projected an expanded role as a lefty reliever in 1958. But in January of that year, the major leagues changed the rules to allow bonus players to be sent to the minor leagues without restriction. Although Derrington did not know it at the time, he had thrown his last major-league pitch at the tender age of 17.

Derrington spent most of the 1958 season with Colorado Springs of the Class-A Western League; he had a winning record (10-8) but an ugly ERA (7.06). He was also 0-1 in four games at Indianapolis of the Triple-A American Association. He seemed to break through in 1959, posting a 10-8 record with a 3.68 ERA

ONE-HIT WONDERS

for Charleston of the Class-A Sally League. He ranked among the league leaders in several categories and pitched in the league's All-Star game.

"After my second year in the minors, I was really pitching well," Derrington commented in 1991. "I knew I was going to be back up [to the majors] and be there for a long time."[8] The White Sox moved him up to their top farm club, San Diego of the Pacific Coast League, to start the 1960 season. But he tore ligaments and tendons in his left elbow in a spring-training game, and the team doctor "told me I'd be able to throw again but not like I did."[9] Demoted back to Class A, the former high-school pitcher-first baseman tried becoming a position player, but after batting only .223 in 84 games for Charleston, "found out there were a lot of things I couldn't do as a first baseman … or a hitter."[10]

Derrington attempted a return to pitching, but his old fastball was gone. "Against Tommy Harper one night," he recalled, "I threw eight breaking balls in a row, and I said to myself, 'He's going to be ready for what was left of my fastball.' He hit it over the center-field scoreboard. I said to myself, 'This isn't making it.'"[11] Pitching for two minor-league teams in 1961, Derrington went 7-5 with a 4.08 ERA; when he failed to land a job either as a pitcher or a coach in the spring of 1962, he decided to retire.

Married with three daughters, Derrington returned to South Gate and went to work in his father's TV and appliance store; he also helped his old friend Paul Deitz as an assistant coach at Chapman College in 1964-65. Derrington's father died in a car accident in 1968, and Jim took over the business, which had grown to five stores. In 1979 he sold the TV/appliance stores and got a job managing a produce company. Still interested in working in baseball, he switched to part-time work brokering produce in 1988; with his afternoons free, he became an assistant to baseball coach Dolf Hess of Fullerton (California) High School, also coaching the team in a summer league.

Derrington's last work in baseball came as a pitching coach and manager in the independent Western and Big South Leagues in the late 1990s. In 1995 he became pitching coach for the Sonoma County (California) Crushers in the Western League; in 1996, he held the same role for the Western League Tri-City (Washington) Posse. Then in 1997, Derrington became manager of the Greenville (Mississippi) Bluesmen in the short-season Big South League; he led the club to a second-place finish with a 39-20 record.

In 1998, Derrington returned to the Western League as manager of the Pacific Suns. The Suns had moved to Oxnard, California, from Palm Springs prior to the '98 season. Derrington was one of several ex-major leaguers in the league that year, joining Wally Backman, Dick Dietz, Charley Kerfeld, Bill Plummer, Buck Rodgers, and Derrel Thomas. This time, Derrington's managerial stint was unsuccessful; he was fired in midseason after the club got off to a 13-32 started.

Derrington remained in Southern California after his minor-league managerial career ended, settling in La Habra in Orange County. He expressed no regrets about being force-fed into the majors as a 16-year-old. "A lot of people said it came too soon, that I wasn't ready for that kind of pressure," he reflected. "But I don't know. I was throwing as hard as I could. I knew I could play at that level. I do know that for all the kids who play baseball, the biggest dream you ever have is to play in the big leagues, and that dream came true for me. All things considered, I wouldn't change a thing."[12]

Derrington died in Rancho Cucamonga, California on March 12, 2020, at the age of 80.

SOURCES

In addition to the sources cited in the Notes, the author consulted both Baseball-Reference.com and Retrosheet.org.

Author interview with Jim Derrington, October 16, 2019.

Booth, Steven. "Field of Nightmares." tht.fangraphs.com/field-of-nightmares-the-mis-adventures-of-the-pacific-suns/ (September 22, 2019).

"Derrington, Bernstein, Goss Gain All-City 9," *Wilmington* (California) *Daily Press Journal*, June 8, 1956: 8.

"Derrington Registers His Second No-Hitter," *Los Angeles Times*, May 30, 1956: 35.

Foster, Chris. "One-Time Pitching Prodigy Passes on Tips to Next Generation," *Los Angeles Times*, April 8, 1994: 170.

Hildebrandt, Chuck. "Sweet! 16-Year-Old Players in Major League History," *Baseball Research Journal*, Volume 48, Number 1, Spring 2019: 5-17.

Johnson, Lloyd, and Miles Wolff, eds. *Encyclopedia of Minor League Baseball*, third edition (Durham, North Carolina: Baseball America, 2007).

Mooney, Ron. "Diary: On the Road," *Petaluma* (California) *Argus-Courier*. July 4, 1995: 25.

Munzel, Edgar. "10 Will Make Pitch for Two Open Jobs on White Sox Staff," *The Sporting News*, February 19, 1958: 9.

Munzel, Edgar. "White Sox' Bullpen Not Nearly as Black as Painted," *The Sporting News*, November 20, 1957: 19.

Plunkett, Bill. "Suns Still Not Shining in Eyes of Western League," *Desert Sun* (Palm Springs, California), August 1, 1998: 23.

United Press, "Chisox Sign 16-Year-Old Pitcher from South Gate," *San Bernardino County Sun*, September 11, 1956: 24.

ONE-HIT WONDERS

NOTES

1. David Condon, "In the Wake of the News," *Chicago Tribune*, March 20, 1957: 57.
2. Condon.
3. Tom Birschbach, "He Started for the White Sox at 16, but Was Through at 22," *Los Angeles Times*, June 29, 1991: 266-67.
4. Brent Kelley, *Baseball's Biggest Blunder: The Bonus Rule of 1953-1957* (Lanham, Maryland: Scarecrow Press, Inc., 1997), 129.
5. Estimated Pitch Count Calculator, boydsworld.com/cgi/epccalc.pl (September 17, 2017).
6. Robert Cromie, "Bonus Hurler and Sox Lose to A's, 7 to 6," *Chicago Tribune*, October 1, 1956: 76.
7. Birschbach.
8. Birschbach.
9. Birschbach.
10. Dick Becker, "Derrington's Been Around – and He's Not Done," *Lincoln* (Nebraska) *Journal Star*, June 13, 1961: 13.
11. Birschbach.
12. Birschbach.

ALEX GEORGE

By Joel Rippel

Since World War I, six players have made their major-league debut before their 17th birthday. Alex George, the sixth-youngest when he debuted on September 16, 1955, at the age of 16 years, 11 months, 19 days, has the distinction of being the only one to make his first and last major-league appearance before his 17th birthday.

George's major-league career took up just nine days of his nine-year professional baseball career.

Alex George was born to Alex George Sr. and Elizabeth George in Kansas City, Missouri, on September 27, 1938. The elder George worked for the Kansas City Parks and Recreation Department and was the athletic director for the Kansas City Catholic Youth Organization. He was also the head of officials for the Big Eight Conference. His mother was a homemaker to the family, which included daughter Janice.

Alex Jr. was a three-sport standout for Rockhurst High School in Kansas City. He lettered four years in baseball and three each in football and basketball. He also competed in track and field. As a senior he led Rockhurst to league championships in football, basketball, and baseball.

After George was named the Most Valuable Football Player in the Kansas City area for 1954, his football coach described him as "one of the best quarterbacks in high school football."[1]

His final high-school baseball season saw Rockhurst go 17-1 and earn a spot in the state tournament. George accepted a scholarship offer to play basketball and baseball for the University of Kansas. In early September 1955, he enrolled and was on campus when he got a phone call from his father. His father told him the Athletics, who were in their first season in Kansas City after moving from Philadelphia, had offered the younger George a contract. George drove home from Lawrence that night.

The next day, he signed the contract and immediately reported to Municipal Stadium. He was in uniform that night as the A's opened a three-game series with the visiting Chicago White Sox.

In the bottom of the eighth inning, with the A's leading 13-7, Kansas City manager Lou Boudreau sent George to pinch-hit for rookie shortstop Jerry Schypinski. With two outs and a runner at first base, George faced White Sox reliever Al Papai, who was pitching in the big leagues for the first time since 1950.

George struck out.

"This is a story I love to tell," George recalled. "Sherm Lollar was a catcher for the White Sox at the time. Firmly entrenched major leaguer. So I approach the batter's box and get in the batter's box, and I got to tell you, my knees were shaking so hard, maybe he just felt sorry for me."

"He scuffles around a little bit, and he says, 'You ever hit a knuckleball?'"

"And I said, 'No.' He said, 'Have you ever seen one?'"

"And I said, 'No.' He said, 'That's all this guy throws. So you know what's coming.'"

"I said, 'All right.' He threw two or three knuckleballs and nothing. And then I fouled a couple off, whatever."

"And he reminded me, 'That's all this guy throws.' I said, 'OK.'"

"And I fouled a few more. I eventually struck out and it was a blessing just to get me out of the batter's box."

"So I take the field [George was a shortstop] and of course, and I'm sulking a little bit because I didn't at least get the ball in play and we have two outs. Jim Rivera, who played center field for the White Sox, he hit a line drive headed for left-center, and, out of reflex I just jumped and happened to catch it in the web of my glove for the third out of the inning."

"As I'm running off the field, Vic Power comes over, he's playing first base. He comes over and he's smiling, and pats me on the back. I flipped the ball to him and he said, 'No, no. You keep this.' Don't know whatever became of it. It was nice of him to do that."[2]

In recounting his major-league debut, George forgot to mention that he fielded another chance

ONE-HIT WONDERS

cleanly in the ninth inning. For the second out of the inning, he fielded a grounder off the bat of White Sox shortstop Chico Carrasquel and threw him out.

Two days later, in the series finale against the White Sox, George again pinch-hit for Schypinski. Facing right-hander Sandy Consuegra in the bottom of the eighth, he struck out. At shortstop in the top of the ninth, he handled one chance cleanly.

The next night, (September 19) in Detroit, George made his first start. Batting leadoff, he went 0-for-3. He struck out against Tigers starter Bud Black to lead off the game, and in his second at-bat, he grounded out to short. In the fifth inning he struck out. In the seventh inning, he was pinch-hit for by Vic Power. The Tigers defeated the A's 4-0 behind Black's six-hitter.

The teams played a day game the next day and George was again in the starting lineup. He led off the game against Tigers rookie right-hander Duke Maas. George beat out a bunt to the left side of the infield for his first hit (in six at-bats). He went 1-for-4 with a walk and two strikeouts in the Tigers' 7-3 victory.

George did not play in the next three games, before appearing in the A's regular-season finale on Sunday, September 25, in Chicago. George, who was days away from turning 17, replaced Schypinski at shortstop in the bottom of the seventh. In his only at-bat, he struck out against veteran left-hander Billy Pierce in the bottom of the eighth.

Chicago's 5-0 victory left the Athletics with a 63-91 record for their first season in Kansas City. The A's, who had gone 53-101 the previous season in their final season in Philadelphia, finished in sixth place (ahead of the Baltimore Orioles and Washington Senators).

In his nine days with the A's, George appeared in five games, going 1-for-10 with a walk and seven strikeouts. Defensively, he held his own. In his 18 innings in the field, he handled 12 chances, committing just one error. He was part of one double play.

After the season, George returned to Lawrence to begin classes.

"I plan to put on as much weight as possible," he told a sportswriter. "Then do a little running to get in shape."[3]

George joined the Athletics in West Palm Beach, Florida, for spring training in 1956. After playing in several "B" games he was sent to Kansas City's minor-league camp in Columbia, South Carolina, for reassignment.

He spent the 1956 season with Fitzgerald, Georgia, of the Class-D Georgia-Florida League. His season "started well, then (he) suffered a leg injury. Playing with the injury, his batting average slumped to .210."[4]

George, who rebounded to hit .268 with 15 doubles and 2 home runs in 138 games for lowly Fitzgerald, which was 47-92, "did well enough for the Fitzgerald (Ga.) club to warrant promotion."[5]

George spent the 1957 season with Seminole (Oklahoma) of the Class-D Sooner State League. He went 1-for-3 with a double in a season-opening 7-6 loss to Shawnee, but suffered a mild sophomore slump. He batted just .239 in 124 games, but he had a .393 slugging percentage with 19 doubles, 11 triples, and 9 home runs.

George blossomed in his third professional season. Playing for Pocatello of the Class-C Pioneer League, he had career highs in home runs (23), RBIs (90), and batting average (.282). He teamed with 18-year-old second baseman Lou Klimchock to form the Pioneer League's best double-play combination. Klimchock, who was batting .389 with 25 home runs and 112 RBIs, was recalled by the A's in September and made his major-debut 18 days before his 19th birthday. Klimchock was named the league's MVP and George was named to the league all-star team.

George slumped in 1959. He started the season with Albany (New York) of the Class-A Eastern League. After hitting .187 in 27 games, he was sent to Sioux City (Iowa) of the Three-I League. In 101 games with Sioux City, he hit .247 with 11 home runs and 53 RBIs. His combined totals for the season were a .234 batting average with 13 home runs and 58 RBIs in 128 games.

After the season George spent six months of active duty in the US Army at Fort Leonard Wood, Missouri. After his duty, George rebounded to put together back-to-back solid seasons in 1960 and 1961.

In 1960, with Lewiston of the Class-B Northwest League, he batted .275 with 12 home runs and 56 RBIs in 130 games. The next season, playing for Shreveport of the Double-A Southern Association, he batted .276 with 16 home runs and 68 RBIs in 137 games.

George's 1962 season was cut short. He opened the season as a utility infielder with the Albuquerque Dukes in the Double-A Texas League. He batted just .195 in 17 games before being released by the Dukes in late May.

George signed with the Washington Senators' organization for the 1963 season. He was assigned to York (Pennsylvania) of the Eastern League. An article in a local newspaper said, "The infield seems to be York's strongest point with (Danny) O'Connell at third, (future major leaguer) John Kennedy at short,

ONE-HIT WONDERS

Alex George at second, and Larry Stankey or (Bill) Edwards at first."[6]

The season got off to a good start for George. He was 4-for-4 with three singles and a double in the White Roses' 6-3 victory over Binghamton on May 5.

On August 7 George was traded to Reading for infielder Gene Giannini. But Giannini refused to report to York "and left for his home in Tennessee. As a consequence, the deal was canceled."[7]

The White Roses finished the season on September 5 with a doubleheader loss to first-place Charleston (West Virginia). The White Roses (63-77) finished 20 games behind Charleston (83-57). George finished the season with a .207 batting average with 6 home runs and 43 RBIs in 136 games.

After the season, George, who had been hampered by tendinitis in his throwing arm for two years, retired as a player. He was 24.

Over his eight seasons in the minor leagues, he batted .254 with a .393 slugging percentage in 942 games. He hit 81 home runs and drove in 320 runs.

After his playing career, he embarked on a long, successful career in TV advertising sales in Kansas City.

SOURCES

In addition to the sources cited in the Notes, the author also consulted Ancestry.com, Baseball-Reference.com, Findagrave.com, Newspapers.com, and Retrosheet.org.

NOTES

1. "Award to Alex George," *Kansas City Times*, December 16, 1954: 29.
2. Blair Kerkhoff and Rich Sugg, "Alex George Tells You What It's Like to Play in the Majors at Just 16 Years of Age," kansascity.com, June 8, 2018. kansascity.com/sports/mlb/article212804199.html.
3. "Vacation? No, Sir, Say A's Players," *Kansas City Times*, September 26, 1955: 21.
4. Ernest Mehl, "A's Bringing Up Homebred the Hard Way," *The Sporting News*, August 15, 1956: 12.
5. Ernest Mehl, "Many Names, Few Fixtures on A's Roster," *The Sporting News*, November 7, 1956: 16.
6. "White Rose Infield Set for 1963 Campaign," *York (Pennsylvania) Dispatch*, April 12, 1963: 15.
7. "Eastern League," *The Sporting News*, August 24, 1963: 39.

EDDIE GERNER

By Jack V. Morris

Here's how the story goes: a young lefty pitcher in the 1910s breaks into the big leagues but as time goes on, his hitting is too good to leave him out of the lineup in between starts. He eventually blossoms into an exceptional hitting outfielder on baseball's biggest stage, New York City.

If you thought Babe Ruth, you'd be correct. But the story also fits another player, lesser known because he created his own baseball path rather than allowing others to chart it for him.

Eddie Gerner was all of 17 when he broke into Organized Baseball with the Albany Senators of the New York State League in 1915. By 21, he was the youngest member of the World Series champion Cincinnati Reds. But instead of remaining within Organized Baseball, Gerner jumped his contract in 1920 and played semipro ball for the rest of his career. By the late 1920s, he had transitioned into a power-hitting outfielder on one of the best semipro teams, not just in New York City, but nationally, the Brooklyn Bushwicks.

Working a day job as a clerk, Gerner commuted from Philadelphia to New York on the weekends to play for the Bushwicks. For four seasons with the Bushwicks, he played against the best semipro teams, white or black, on the East Coast. He hit over .350 in all four seasons. His combination of day job and weekend ballplaying was so lucrative that in 1928 he reportedly turned down a $5,000 signing bonus offered by Otto Miller, catcher and acting scout for the Brooklyn Robins.[1]

Unlike Ruth, Gerner, who stood a quarter-inch under 6-feet-1 and weighed 182 pounds,[2] kept himself in great shape, playing high-level semipro baseball until he was 45. He ran a mile along railroad tracks every day during the baseball season. "You are only as young as your legs," said Gerner.[3]

Edwin Frederick Gerner was born on July 22, 1897, in Philadelphia to John and Maggie Gerner. John was listed as a huckster, someone who sold small articles or even vegetables, either door to door from a cart or a small stall, in the 1900 United States census. Eddie was the youngest of eight children born to John and Maggie.

A "Gerner" shows up as a pitcher in *Philadelphia Inquirer* box scores as early as 1910, playing for various semipro teams in Philadelphia. By 1914 he had made a name for himself as a pitcher in the semipro ranks. He was pitching for Stetson, one of the top Philadelphia semipro teams. No doubt it was there that Gerner caught the eye of Philadelphian Patsy O'Rourke who was the manager of the Albany Senators of the Class-B New York State League for 1915.

O'Rourke thought so much of the 17-year-old Gerner that he signed him as one of his pitchers. But

Ed Gerner.

ONE-HIT WONDERS

O'Rourke didn't put together much of a team. Albany was by far the worst team in the league with a 33-89 record, finishing 45½ games behind regular-season champion Binghamton. Gerner went 4-22 for the last-place Senators. In addition to little support from his teammates, he tended to be wild. In one game, he walked seven in a 1-0 loss to Elmira. But Gerner often played in the outfield for Albany. In fact, in mid-August, Gerner was the Senators' regular right fielder, taking a break from the outfield only when it was his turn to pitch. He batted a respectable .217 and set the groundwork for his transition to everyday player later in his career.

Playing for bad teams would be the norm for Gerner's career in the minor leagues. In 1916 he played for Albany again. The team was a little better, but in midseason it moved to Reading, Pennsylvania. Gerner's record was much better, 15-23 for the sixth-place (58-70) Albany Senators/Reading Pretzels. He also hit well, batting .285. Gerner pitched so well that the Cincinnati Reds drafted him in September.

Gerner attended 1917 spring training with the Reds and manager Christy Mathewson in Shreveport, Louisiana. Despite hitting and fielding well, he was "very wild" in a couple of games and the Reds sold him to the Montreal Royals of the International League.[4]

Gerner found himself on another terrible squad. The Royals finished seventh out of eight teams. However, Gerner had a brilliant season. He went 20-20, winning more than a third of the Royals' 56 wins. His teammate, future Hall of Famer Waite Hoyt, years later remembered Gerner's pitching prowess. "Eddie was the star of the club," said Hoyt 25 years later, "and the only guy who could win [games]."[5] After the season, Gerner was pitching again for Stetson, making some extra cash from his former employer.[6] This would be a theme throughout his career.

Gerner refused to report to spring training in 1918. It was reported that Mathewson placed Gerner on the voluntary retired list, then two weeks later Mathewson was quoted as saying that he had joined the US Navy. Neither was true – Gerner was playing with Stetson again. With the United States' entry into World War I, players were pressured to either enlist or work in a defense-industry job. In June Gerner took a job at the Hog Island Shipyard, which also meant he was pitching for Hog Island in the Delaware River Shipyard League.[7]

The Reds attempted to coax Gerner back but Gerner rebuffed them. Chances were he was making more money working at the shipyard than the Reds were willing to pay him. As nationally syndicated sportswriter Effie Welsh wrote about his refusal of the Reds' offer, "Gerner has a congenial position in Philadelphia and pitches on Saturdays for semi-professional clubs."[8]

Gerner continued to pitch for Hog Island throughout the summer. While many of the players around him were going to war, Gerner was still too young to be inducted. At the end of July, when he turned 21, he registered for the draft. The war ended a few months later without Gerner entering the military.[9]

The Reds wasted no time in getting Gerner under contract. He was among the first to be signed in 1919.[10] This time the Reds, under manager Pat Moran, kept Gerner on the squad when they moved north for the season opener. But Gerner found himself to be more of a batting-practice pitcher than a contributing member of the team. Despite being on the squad for the entire season, Gerber saw action in just six games, five as a pitcher and only one as a starter. The game he started, on July 28 against the Pittsburgh Pirates, was also the only major-league game in which he registered a hit. The Reds won the game 8-7 with Gerner pitching eight innings, giving up 12 hits and seven runs (four earned) to get the win. He also helped his cause, knocking in two runs, one of them on his only hit, a double in the fifth off the Pirates' Hal Carlson.

Gerner saw action in only two more games the rest of the season, both in mop-up roles in blowout losses. The Reds went on to win the National League pennant, then beat the Chicago White Sox in the tainted 1919 World Series. After the season, Gerner returned to his job as a clerk at Hog Island. Using his winners' share of the World Series money, he married fellow Philadelphian Marguerite Elizabeth "Daisy" White.[11]

Gerner signed for the 1920 season and again made the team. But as the Reds barnstormed their way back to Cincinnati, he left the team because his father was ill. He never returned.[12]

For more than a month, nothing was heard from Gerner. Then reports out of western Pennsylvania indicated he was playing for the town team of Franklin, a town about 85 miles north of Pittsburgh. He and Walt Kinney, a pitcher with the Philadelphia Athletics, had been signed in late May to bolster the Franklin team.

Starting in 1919, Franklin and its rival, Oil City, raided the major leagues for players. The two towns had been playing baseball against each other since 1866. Fueled by an influx of oil money after World War I, the two teams purchased players for a rivalry that drew thousands of people every time they played each other. James Borland, president of Franklin and the managing editor of the *Franklin News-Herald*, wrote, "We took players from the big-league teams and paid them exorbitant prices, all made possible by the easy money people were making after the close of the war."[13]

Gerner joined the Philadelphia Athletics' Scott Perry and Tom Rogers; the Cleveland Indians' Joe Harris; and future Philadelphia Phillies catcher Harry O'Donnell among others. The Reds didn't pursue legal action, instead sending scout Gene McCann to Franklin to induce Gerner to come back. All it did was pad Gerner's wallet. Franklin raised Gerner's salary by $1,000 to keep him.[14]

After a slow start, Gerner pitched and hit well. In an 11-game season-ending series with Oil City, Gerner won two of Franklin's four wins and batted .414. After the season he went back to his job as a clerk at the Stetson Hat Factory in Philadelphia.[15]

In 1921 Franklin offered the popular Joe Harris a salary of $6,000 for four months. Paying that much to one player, Franklin needed to cut some of its former players. Gerner was one of three players released. The Franklin team would finally dissolve halfway through the 1921 season under the burden of the huge salaries.[16]

Meanwhile Gerner went back to playing for semipro teams in Philadelphia. In 1921 he won 13 straight games for Fleisher Yarn before hurting his arm and losing in mid-June. After resting his arm for a couple of months, he ended the season playing for semipro teams Harrowgate and Nativity. From 1922 through 1924, Gerner played with various top Philadelphia semipro teams including South Philadelphia, Fleishers, and Germantown.

In 1925 he took his talents to New York, playing for George Lippe's Bay Ridge club of Brooklyn, commuting on the weekends from his home in Philadelphia. For two seasons, he played for Bay Ridge and it was with Bay Ridge that Gerner transitioned to full time as an outfielder and batting fourth in their lineup.

Bay Ridge's Brooklyn rival, the Bushwicks, took notice of the power-hitting Gerner and signed him for the 1927 season. He joined former major leaguers Stan Baumgartner and Eppie Barnes as well as the famous Hawaii-born semipro Buck Lai.

Batting cleanup, Gerner had an excellent season. Going into October's "Little World's Series" with the Farmers semipro club, Gerner led the team with a .374 batting average. Playing in all 49 games, Gerner pounded out 11 doubles, three triples, and four home runs. He was the only player to hit a home run for the Bushwicks that season.[17]

After the season, the Brooklyn Robins approached Gerner to play for them for 1928. In 1926 Gerner had been reinstated by Organized Baseball six years after jumping his contract to play with Franklin. Now, at a March meeting in Philadelphia, Gerner told Brooklyn's Otto Miller, who had a certified check in hand for $5,000, that he'd have to think about the offer and would answer him on April 1. Bushwick teammate Howard Lohr claimed he witnessed the meeting. "It made me feel sick to see Eddie refuse that five grand," said Lohr, adding, "If Eddie can see his way clear to leaving his business in [Philadelphia] he will join the Robins when they come North." He never did accept the check.

Working his day job and playing for various Philadelphia semipro teams during the week and the Bushwicks on the weekend was more appealing and probably more lucrative than signing with the Robins.

Gerner played three more seasons for the Bushwicks. In 1928 he again led the team in hitting, batting .353 in 54 games.[18] In 1929 Gerner had his best season yet, batting .423, best of all the regulars. He pounded out five home runs, six triples, and 13 doubles.[19]

With the addition of lights to the Bushwicks' Dexter Park in 1930, their schedule increased and included weekday games. Gerner played in 63 of the Bushwicks' 73 games and again led the team in batting with a .376 average. But the commuting had become too much. The combination of his day job as a shipping clerk at a drug manufacturing company and the travel to night games during the week for the Bushwicks was too much. The *Brooklyn Citizen* wrote at the end of the 1930 season, "Gerner suffered a breakdown in the last month of the season and had to give up baseball." The *Brooklyn Standard Union* said he "quit due to sickness."[20]

For the remainder of his playing days, Gerner stayed in the Philadelphia area. In 1931 he was a hired gun, playing for whoever paid him best. From 1932 through 1935, he played almost exclusively with the powerhouse Wentz Olney semipro team. In 1936 he hooked up with wealthy silk mill owner Oliver "Ollie" Schelly to play in the semipro Eastern Pennsylvania League. Schelly was the manager of the East Greenville team when he signed Gerner. From 1936 through 1942, wherever Schelly managed, Gerner played. Gerner played four seasons in East Greenville, then moved with Schelly in 1940 to Easton, Pennsylvania. The two

ONE-HIT WONDERS

then jumped to Nazareth, Pennsylvania, for the 1941 and 1942 seasons.

Gerner, who had turned 45 during the 1942 season, ended his career after the season. In the 1940 US census he was listed as a shipper working for a wholesale drug company.

After he retired from baseball, Gerner's name rarely made the newspapers. When it did, it was to reminisce about some of the great teams he had played on.

Gerner died on May 15, 1970, in Philadelphia. Surviving him was his wife, Daisy. The couple had no children. Gerner is buried in the Oakland Cemetery in Philadelphia.

SOURCES

In addition to the sources cited in the Notes, the author relied on the following:

Barthel, Thomas. *Baseball's Peerless Semipros* (Haworth, New Jersey: St. Johann Press, 2009).

Baseball-Reference.com

Retrosheet.org

Simkus, Scott. *Outsider Baseball* (Chicago: Chicago Review Press, 2014), 162-167.

NOTES

1. "Eddie Gerner May Yet Be a Robin," *Brooklyn Daily Eagle*, March 26, 1928: 4A.

2. According to his *Sporting News* contract card digital.la84.org/digital/collection/p17103coll3/id/64833/rec/1; Baseball Reference lists him as 5-feet-8, 175 pounds. Gerner's World War I draft registration card lists him as "Tall," making the contract card height more likely.

3. Stan Baumgartner, "Sandlot Star Ready For 26th Season," *Philadelphia Inquirer*, January 27, 1941: 20.

4. Jack Ryder, "Two Men," *Cincinnati Enquirer*, March 17, 1917: 6; "Eddie Gerner Released," *Wilkes-Barre Times Leader*, April 19, 1917: 15.

5. Waite Hoyt, "According to Hoyt," *Piqua* (Ohio) *Daily Call*, April 3, 1942: 6.

6. "Stetson to Play Stars of Mack in Final Game," *Philadelphia Evening Ledger*, October 5, 1917: 15.

7. "Mathewson to Take Reds Out," *Lima* (Ohio) *News*, March 11, 1918: 5; "Foster Wants $6,000 to Pitch for the Reds," *Scranton Times-Tribune*, April 12, 1918: 28; "New York Ship Has Close Call," *Philadelphia Inquirer*, June 9, 1918: 16.

8. "Little Bits of Baseball," *Pittsburgh Press*, June 16, 1918: 27; Effie Welsh, "Welsh Rarebits," *Wilkes-Barre Times Leader*, June 29, 1918: 9.

9. "Shipyard Ball Players Called by Draft Boards," *Scranton Tribune*, August 20, 1918: 12.

10. "Gerner, Rath Sign," *Lima News*, February 18, 1919: 10.

11. "Cincinnati Players Domestic in Plans for Coming Winter," *Sandusky* (Ohio) *Register*, October 16, 1919: 9; "World's Champions Scatter for Winter," *Sante Fe New Mexican*, October 24, 1919: 2.

12. "Jack Ryder, "No Game at Raleigh," *Cincinnati Enquirer*, April 3, 1920: 6.

13. James B. Borland, *Fifty Years in the Newspaper Game* (Boston: Chapple Publishing, 1928), 191, 193-194.

14. "Reds Will Not Disturb Pitcher Eddie Gerner," *Franklin News-Herald*, May 24, 1920: 3; Borland, 199.

15. "Oil City Was Leader in All Departments," *Franklin* (Pennsylvania) *News-Herald*, October 1, 1930: 10. "Season Is Over and Players Are Leaving Franklin," *Franklin News-Herald*, October 1, 1930: 3.

16. "Winter Baseball Gossip," *Franklin News-Herald*, October 1, 1930: 3; Borland, 197.

17. "Farmers and Bushwicks to Clash Today," *Brooklyn Citizen*, October 30, 1927: 13.

18. "Bushwicks and Farmers Resume Series Today," *Brooklyn Citizen*, November 4, 1928: 13.

19. "Bushwicks of 1929 Are Rated Best White Semi Pro Team in History," *Brooklyn Citizen*, November 3, 1929: 13.

20. "Bushwicks Had a Banner Season and Played Before Record Crowds, Night Baseball a Big Success," *Brooklyn Citizen*, November 2, 1930: 12; "Bushwick Nine in Dexter Bow" *Brooklyn Standard Union*, March 21, 1931: 9.

FRED GLADDING

By Paul Hofmann

One of the most dependable relief pitchers for the Detroit Tigers and Houston Astros during a 13-year major-league career that spanned 1961-1973, Fred Gladding was a 6-foot 1-inch, 220-pound, glasses-wearing right-hander. Given a variety of nicknames by teammates that characterized his demeanor on the field and physical appearance, Gladding was a strong-willed competitor with a gruff façade. Off the field, however, "He was as down to earth a person you could find, who took whatever life brought to him in stride."[1]

Fred Earl Gladding was born on June 28, 1936, in Flat Rock, Michigan. He was the youngest of three children born to Friedrich August and Elizabeth (Konaraska) Gladding. He had an older brother, Arthur, and an older sister, Lillian. Both were considerably older than Fred. Arthur was born in 1920 and Lillian was born in 1923. At that time, Flat Rock was a small rural community on the southern border of Wayne County, about 30 minutes south of Detroit. Fred's father was a second-generation Michigan farmer and diehard Detroit Tigers fan.

Born with a lazy eye – he was legally blind in his left eye – Fred realized early on that he could never make it as a hitter, so he turned to pitching. As a child, Fred was often found throwing a baseball against the side of the barn or a tennis ball against a boulder for hours on end. Ultimately, it was the same persistence that helped him overcome his disability that proved to be an asset as he navigated a circuitous route through the Tigers' minor-league system.

Following in his father's footsteps, Gladding grew up as a Tigers fan and like many boys growing up in southeastern Michigan, he dreamed of playing baseball at the corner of Michigan and Trumbull, at what was then called Briggs Stadium.[2] Later in life, when asked if he dreamed of one day playing for the Tigers, he smiled and with a gentle chuckle replied, "That's all I thought about."[3]

Growing up, Gladding's favorite player was another bespectacled pitcher, Dizzy Trout. The right-handed Trout carried a signature red bandanna that he used to wipe his glasses on the mound. Gladding later emulated his hero by carrying a red bandanna to the mound while he was in the minors.[4]

Gladding graduated from Flat Rock High School in 1955. In 1956 he achieved the first step of his dream when the Tigers signed him to his first pro contract.[5] He received a $4,000 signing bonus and was assigned to the Valdosta Tigers of the Class-D Georgia-Florida League.[6] In 35 games, 21 as a starter, Gladding went 11-9 with a 2.76 ERA as Valdosta ran away with the league title with a record of 94-45, 14½ games ahead of the second-place Waycross Braves.

The 20-year-old Gladding returned to Valdosta in 1957. He started 24 games and appeared in 37 in all, on his way to a 16-8 record with a 2.12 earned-run

ONE-HIT WONDERS

average. That year the Tigers finished in second place with a record of 77-62, seven games behind the Albany Cardinals.

Leaving spring training in 1958, Gladding made what appeared to be an improbable jump from Class-D Valdosta to Triple-A Charleston. After going 0-2 in three outings, he was demoted to the Birmingham Barons of the Double-A Southern Association. After three outings in Birmingham, he was sent down to the Augusta (Georgia) Tigers of the Class-A South Atlantic League. On May 25 he made his Sally League debut and pitched a seven-inning no-hitter in the nightcap of a doubleheader against the Macon Dodgers.[7] Gladding faced 23 Macon hitters as two drew walks and two reached on Tigers errors.[8] He was 12-7 with a 3.04 ERA for Augusta.

Gladding returned to the Sally League to start 1959. This time he was with the Johnny Pesky-led Knoxville Smokies, the Tigers' new Class-A affiliate. In 20 appearances with the Smokies (11 as a starter and nine in relief), Gladding went 6-2 with a 3.56 ERA. He finished the season by making seven starts for the Southern Association champion Birmingham Barons and went 2-3 with a 5.54 ERA.

It was during this second stint with the Barons that the Gladding was given one of his nicknames, The Bear. A journeyman minor-league catcher and batterymate, Ron "Gabby" Witucki, hung the moniker on Gladding, not because of his physical characteristics but more for his behavior on the mound. Gladding explained the origin of the name to *The Sporting News*. "I used to get mad on the mound and I'd stomp around like a bear in a berry patch," he confessed.[9] "He started calling me Bear."[10]

The 1959 season had another profound impact on the Gladding's future. While on the disabled list with the Smokies, Gladding was driving on Kingston Pike, a highway in Knoxville, and spotted a young University of Tennessee student who caught his eye. Her name was Margie Clotfelter. After following her, Gladding pulled up beside her, introduced himself, and asked her out.[11] The two hit if off immediately and on September 19, 1960, they were married. The marriage lasted nearly 55 years and was ended only by Gladding's death.[12]

Following a similar pattern established during the prior two seasons, Gladding started the 1960 back in Knoxville. In 23 games with the Smokies, 13 as a starter, he went 9-5 with a 2.43 ERA and three shutouts. He made a single appearance with Birmingham, the third consecutive year he played for the Barons, before being promoted to the Tigers' Triple-A affiliate Denver Bears. He appeared in 14 games with the Bears, nine as a starter, and had a record of 3-2 with a 2.35 ERA.

Gladding started the 1961 season with Denver, just one step away from his goal of playing for the Tigers. He was 7-3 with a 2.20 ERA when, after toiling in the minors for six seasons, he was finally called up by Detroit.

On July 1, 1961, Gladding made his major-league debut at Baltimore's Memorial Stadium when he came on in relief of right-hander Bob Bruce to start the bottom of the fifth. Orioles first basemen Jim Gentile, who had already hit a home run in the first inning, welcomed Gladding to the majors with a home run to deep center field to increase the Orioles' lead to 5-3. Gladding then settled down to pitch 2⅓ innings without yielding another run. He left the game with the Tigers leading 6-5 and was within one out of earning his first major-league victory when the Orioles scored two runs off Hank Aguirre to send the game into extra innings. The Tigers eventually won the game in 11 innings.

Gladding earned his first major-league victory a week later against the California Angels at Tiger Stadium. With the score tied 2-2, he came on and pitched a scoreless eighth inning. In the bottom of the inning, Tigers third baseman Steve Boros singled home Billy Bruton to put the rookie in line for his first career win. After Gladding allowed the first two Angels to reach in the top of the ninth, Terry Fox and Aguirre came in to nail down his first career victory.

Gladding appeared in eight games for the Tigers that summer and finished with a record of 1-0 and a 3.31 ERA. Despite his success, albeit limited, he spent the next two summers shuttling back and forth between the Tigers and their Triple-A affiliates.

Gladding started the 1962 season with the Tigers and was used sparingly in April and May. He was 0-0 with a 0.00 ERA over five innings in six appearances before being optioned back to Denver, where he endured a nine-game losing streak. The losing streak prompted thoughts of quitting baseball altogether.[13] He finished the year with a record of 6-12 and 3.82 ERA.

The Bear was optioned to the International League's Syracuse Chiefs to start 1963. Used almost exclusively as a reliever, he was 4-2 with a 3.93 ERA when he was brought up to fill the roster spot that was vacated when the team sold veteran right-hander Tom Sturdivant to the Kansas City Athletics.[14] Gladding pitched well for the Tigers. He appeared in 22 games and finished with a record of 1-1 and a 1.98 ERA.

ONE-HIT WONDERS

There was something else for the Gladdings to celebrate in 1963. Fred and Margie became new parents when they welcomed a daughter, Brenda, into the world. Brenda was the only child the Gladdings had.

Despite giving up some costly home runs during spring training in 1964, Gladding joined right-hander Alan Koch and left-handers Fritz Fisher and Dick Egan to form a balanced, if inexperienced, bullpen. Collectively the four had appeared in 63 games for a combined 79⅔ innings. Gladding, who had apprenticed in the Tigers system for eight years, was the most experienced of the quartet, having pitched 48⅔ innings in 36 games. However, he was hit hard in his first four appearances and when he was optioned back to Syracuse on May 10 he had an inflated ERA of 9.00.

Gladding quickly found his form at Syracuse. In seven games he was 2-1 with a 1.59 ERA and by the end of May he was back with the Tigers. He was effective for the remainder the season and solidified his spot in the Tigers bullpen. He was so successful that catcher Bill Freehan began to refer to him as "Little Monster," drawing a comparison to Red Sox relief ace Dick Radatz, who was known as The Monster.[15] From May 31 on, he made 38 appearances and went 7-4 with a 2.39 ERA and seven saves.

In an interview during his retirement, Gladding described his pitching repertoire as follows: "I was a sinkerball pitcher, threw hard and I sunk the ball all the time and ran the ball in on right-handed hitters and threw in a slider. Once in a great while I'd throw a slider."[16] Tiger backup catcher Jim Price described his work this way: "He threw hard, and had a very heavy sink. He'd break your bat in a hurry."[17]

By the mid-'60s Gladding had established himself as an integral and dependable member of the Tigers bullpen. In 1965 he appeared in 46 games and had a record of 6-2 with a 2.83 ERA and five saves. On June 15 he combined with two other Tiger hurlers to set a franchise record for strikeouts in a nine-inning game. Dave Wickersham was the Tigers starter that afternoon against the Boston Red Sox. The right-handed Wickersham failed to get out of the first inning, surrendering three runs on four hits, before being replaced by Denny McLain, who struck out the first two batters he faced to end the inning. McLain struck out 12 more Red Sox batters to finish with 14 over 6⅔ innings. With the Tigers trailing 5-2, Gladding came in to relieve McLain in the top of the eighth. He retired the side in order, striking out two, and then watched as his teammates rally for four runs in the bottom of the inning to take a 6-5 lead. Gladding then retired the Red Sox in order in the ninth, again striking out two, to earn the victory. The game total of 18 strikeouts is the Tigers record for a nine-inning game as of 2020, and has subsequently been tied three times.[18]

Gladding had another good season in 1966 when he went 5-0 with a 3.28 ERA and two saves. In 1967 he moved into the closer role for the Tigers and was one of the most dependable relievers in the American League. He appeared in 42 games and had a record of 6-4 with a team-leading 12 saves and a 1.99 ERA.

That season the Tigers were locked in a five-team pennant race when manager Mayo Smith, in an effort to give Denny McLain an additional day of rest, started Gladding in the second game of August 2 doubleheader in Baltimore. It was the only start of Gladding's major-league career and his first since 1963 with Syracuse. Gladding scattered five hits over five innings and was in line for the win when he was relieved in the sixth inning by Pat Dobson, who tossed three scoreless innings before giving up a two-run walk-off home run to Brooks Robinson.

A couple of weeks later, an injury to third baseman Don Wert necessitated that the Tigers make a trade. On August 17 the Tigers acquired veteran Eddie Mathews from Houston. In return the Tigers agreed to send the Astros a pair of players to be named later. The Tigers remained in contention until the very end and finished in a second-place tie with the Minnesota Twins, a single game behind the American League champion Boston Red Sox. This was the closest Gladding came to experiencing postseason baseball, as it turned out that Gladding would be one of the two players traded to Houston.

Despite going 26-11 with a 2.70 ERA and 33 saves in 217 games over seven seasons with the Tigers, Gladding was one of the five players they allowed the Astros to pick from. The Astros selected Gladding and his career with his hometown team was over.[19] At the time the Tigers had four young relievers, John Hiller, Mike Marshall, Fred Lasher, and Dobson. The Tigers thought Gladding, who was 31 years old at the time, was the most expendable. Only Hiller would go on to enjoy long-term success with the Tigers and Gladding's .703 winning percentage (26-11) remains second highest among Tigers pitchers with at least 200 games pitched.[20]

In 1978, when Mathews was inducted into the Hall of Fame, Gladding quipped, "This is probably as close as I'll ever come to getting into the Hall of Fame – having a guy I was traded for make it. It's the highlight of the twilight of my career."[21] However, this was not

ONE-HIT WONDERS

the twilight of his career. Gladding had lots of good baseball left in him.

His first season in Houston was not what he, or the Astros, expected. Unable to throw his fastball, Gladding was limited to seven games before floating bone chips in his right elbow forced the Astros to shut him down for the year.[22] While he recorded two saves, his ERA was a gaudy 14.54. Meanwhile the Tigers were on their way to winning the team's first World Series title since 1945.

Years later, Margie Gladding shared how surprised and devastated her husband was by the news of the trade. "It hurt him when he was traded to Houston," she said.[23]

With his arm trouble behind him, Gladding bounced back nicely in 1969. He appeared in 57 games and finished with a 4-8 record and a 4.21 ERA to go along with a National League-leading and career-high 29 saves.[24] This was also the season when Gladding recorded the only base hit of his major-league career.

Two years earlier Gladding told a sportswriter, "If I ever get a hit up here, I'm going to ask the umpire to stop the game and get me the ball."[25]

On July 30, in the first game of a doubleheader against the New York Mets at Shea Stadium, Gladding enjoyed success both on the mound and (for the first time) at the plate. In addition to throwing 2⅔ innings of perfect baseball to earn his 20th save, the left-handed-hitting pitcher, who was literally 0-for-the-decade, blooped a bases-loaded single off Mets right-handed reliever Ron Taylor in the ninth inning of a 16-3 Astros victory. Gladding's RBI single was part of an 11-run ninth inning highlighted by grand slams by Denis Menke and Jimmy Wynn.[26] The hit was his first in 48 major-league at-bats. Gladding failed to hit safely in his subsequent 15 at-bats and finished with a career batting average of .016, the lowest of any player in the major leagues with a career batting average above zero (.000).

Though never confused with a pitcher who handled the bat well, Gladding's record-low batting average may not have necessarily been predicted. In 10 minor-league seasons, he compiled a .127 batting average (49-for-386).[27]

Gladding was again the Astros' primary closer in 1970. Appearing in a career-high 63 games, he was 7-4 with a 4.06 ERA and a team-leading 18 saves, the seventh highest total in the National League.

By 1971 Gladding had lost some of the zip on his fastball and reinvented himself as a finesse pitcher. While his strikeouts per inning were nearly cut in half (in 51⅓ innings he struck out 17 batters), he was no less effective. He finished with a record of 4-5 with a 2.10 ERA and a team-leading 12 saves.

Gladding enjoyed another solid year for the Astros in 1972. He appeared in 42 games and finished 5-6 with a 2.77 ERA and 14 saves. On June 9 he recorded his 100th major-league save when he pitched scoreless eighth and ninth innings in the Astros' 4-2 victory over the New York Mets at Shea Stadium.

During his time in Houston, Gladding's playing weight increased to 240 pounds and some of his teammates took to calling the chunky hurler "Fred Flintstone," in reference to the character from the popular TV cartoon of the 1960s, or "Fat Freddy." Fellow Astros right-hander Jack Billingham, in reference to Gladding's rotund physique, once told a reporter, "Fred seems to hold his beer more than the rest of us."[28] The good-natured and ever-humble Gladding took the ribbing in stride and never seemed to mind the kidding.

Gladding was the Opening Day winner in 1973 when he came on in relief to get the last out in the bottom of the 12th inning before the Astros scored the winning run in the top of the 13th to beat the Atlanta Braves, 2-1. However, it was soon apparent that the 36-year-old Gladding's arm had begun to show the signs of 18 years of professional baseball. Although he was 2-0 with a 4.50 ERA, he was inconsistent in his 16 early-season appearances. In June he reluctantly accepted an assignment to the Triple-A Denver Bears. Gladding was hit hard at Denver, giving up 28 hits in 19 innings pitched. He finished with a record of 0-2 and a 4.74 ERA. Following the season, he was released by the Astros.

In six seasons with the Astros, four of them as the team's closer, Gladding was 22-23 with a 3.68 ERA and 76 saves. His final major-league record was 48-34 with a 3.13 ERA and 109 saves.

Following his career, Gladding returned to the Tigers organization. He began his coaching career as a minor-league instructor for the Tigers in 1974 and 1975. From 1976 to 1978 he was the Tigers pitching coach under manager Ralph Houk. The first year of his stint was highlighted by the emergence of Mark Fidrych and "Bird Mania" that swept the nation.[29] He also tutored right-handers Jack Morris, Milt Wilcox, and Dave Rozema, all of whom were part of the 1984 World Series champion pitching staff.

After he was hired as the Tigers pitching coach, Gladding summarized his approach to his new role. "I know myself, when I pitched, I like a little pat on the back," he said. "But I also know, once in a while, every pitcher can use a good, swift boot in the hind end to wake him up. That was the approach, I took when I started out coaching in Triple A. And it worked there. Those kids really appreciate it. When you have people come up to you later and thank you for getting them straightened out, you can't help but feel you've done something right."[30]

Gladding, who was born into a Lutheran tradition, was baptized at Faith Presbyterian church in 1981. He and his daughter, Brenda, were baptized together.[31] According to Margie, Fred was extremely close to his daughter and three granddaughters.[32]

After Fred retired from coaching, the Gladdings settled in Knoxville. They were comfortable there and the area offered Fred plenty of hunting and fishing opportunities. In later years his health began to fail. He had open-heart surgery and he also suffered from kidney disease. Eventually he and Margie moved to Columbia, South Carolina, to be closer to their daughter. On May 21, 2015, he died at the age of 75. His life was celebrated at Faith Presbyterian Church in Knoxville and he was buried at Woodhaven Memorial Gardens in Powell, Tennessee.

Because he missed out on the 1968 Tigers World Series championship, Gladding has been forgotten by many. However, for those who follow the game closely, he is remembered as one of the most consistent relievers during his 13-year major-league career. In fact, he went well beyond having a solid baseball career. He was able to "live his boyhood dream" of playing for the Detroit Tigers.[33]

SOURCES

In addition to the sources cited in the Notes, the author relied on Baseball-reference.com and Retrosheet.org.

NOTES

1. Thomas Sweet, personal correspondence, May 22, 2020. Pastor Thomas Sweet is Senior Pastor at Beaver Creek Cumberland Presbyterian Church. Pastor Sweet baptized Fred Gladding and presided at his funeral.
2. The ballpark was renamed Tiger Stadium in 1961.
3. Billy Staples, "Before the Glory" – Fred Gladding – Detroit Tigers, Houston Astros, youtube.com/watch?v=IuvMYIAxJb4.
4. Staples.
5. The Tigers also signed his high-school baseball coach, Marvin Mittlestat, as a scout. In 32 years at Flat Rock High School, Coach Mittlestat led the Rams to 20 league championships.
6. John Wilson, "Gladding, of Old School, Makes Astros Foes Sit Up," *The Sporting News*, August 7, 1971: 24.
7. Gladding's no-hitter was one of three pitched by Tigers farmhands that weekend. On May 24 John Aehl, a 22-year-old left-hander, tossed a no-hitter in the Durham Bulls' 2-0 victory over the Greensboro Yankees. On May 25 Joe Laughlin, pitching in his first professional game, pitched a no-hitter in the Montgomery Rebels 5-0 victory over the Pensacola Dons. Neither Aehl nor Laughlin made it to the majors.
8. "Gladding Hurls No-Hitter in Sally League," *Tampa Times*, May 26, 1958: 10.
9. Watson Spoelstra, "Bengals Beam, Rivals Frown Over Gladding's UFO Pitches," *The Sporting News*, May 27, 1967: 9.
10. "The Bear Stomps on Tigers' Foes With Nifty Relief Jobs," *The Sporting News*, April 29, 1967: 22.
11. Thomas Sweet, personal correspondence, May 10, 2019.
12. Margie Gladding, personal correspondence, May 9, 2019.
13. Bruce Markusen, "Flat Rock Native Fred Gladding Spent Seven Seasons with the Tigers in the 1960s." Retrieved from vintagedetroit.com/blog/2015/01/09/flat-rock-native-fred-gladding-spent-seven-seasons-tigers-1960s/.
14. Tigers Drop Sturdivant, *Detroit Free Press*, July 24, 1963: 25.
15. Bruce Markusen.
16. Billy Staples.
17. Tony Paul, "Ex-Tigers Pitcher Fred Gladding, Flat Rock Native, Dies at 78," *Detroit News*, May 26, 2015. Retrieved from detroitnews.com.
18. Steve Kuehl, "June 15, 1965: Denny McLain Sets Tigers Record with 14 Strikeouts in Relief," SABR Games Project, sabr.org/gamesproj/game/june-15-1965-denny-mclain-sets-tigers-record-with-14-strikeouts-in-relief/.
19. The Tigers sent Leo Marentette to the Astros on December 10, 1968, to complete the trade.
20. Tony Paul.
21. Jim Hawkins, "Even as Sub, Mathews Led Tigers in '68," *The Sporting News*, August 26, 1978: 12.
22. Bruce Markusen.
23. Margie Gladding.
24. Minnesota Twins Ron Perranoski led the majors with 31 saves.
25. Watson Spoelstra.
26. "Pitcher-Batter Briefs," *Great Hitting Pitchers* (Phoenix: Society for American Baseball Research, 2012), 80.
27. Gladding hit .158 (23-for-146) in Class D, .157 (19-for-121) in Class A, .000 (0-for-15) in Double A, and .067 (7-for-104) in Triple A.
28. Bruce Markusen.
29. Tony Paul.
30. Jim Hawkins, "Gladding to Use Firm Hand in Tutoring Tigers' Pitchers," *The Sporting News*, May 8, 1976: 10.
31. Thomas Sweet, personal correspondence, May 22, 2020.
32. Margie Gladding.
33. Margie Gladding.

ROY GLEASON

By Charlie Bevis

While he made one hit in his only major-league at-bat in 1963, Roy Gleason is better known for the unfortunate one hit of shrapnel he incurred in 1968 from an enemy bomb explosion while serving in the US Army during the Vietnam War. Gleason, who had played five years in the minor leagues before he was drafted into the military in 1967, earned a Purple Heart and recovered from his wounds to play one more year of minor-league baseball.

Roy William Gleason was born on April 9, 1943, in Melrose Park, Illinois, the middle child of Richard, a truck driver, and Molly (Gorr) Gleason.[1] Roy and his two sisters initially grew up in La Grange, Illinois, a town 15 miles west of downtown Chicago, before the family moved to Southern California in 1954 and resided in a ranch-style house in Garden Grove, a suburb 35 miles southeast of Los Angeles.[2]

In 1956 Roy was stunned when his father left the house "to make a phone call" and never returned. "Now what do we do?" Roy thought at the time, in his newfound role as 13-year-old man of the house. "I knew that I couldn't undertake the responsibility of supporting my mother and sisters. I remember telling myself that baseball was the answer. If I worked really hard at what I excelled in, perhaps I'd be able to do it."[3] When Roy entered Garden Grove High School in the fall of 1957, the Brooklyn Dodgers formally announced that the ballclub was relocating to Los Angeles for the 1958 season. The Los Angeles Dodgers provided the big break that Roy sought to support his now-fatherless family.

Roy had a spectacular varsity baseball career at Garden Grove High School as a tall, lanky outfielder and right-handed pitcher. But it was summer ball where Roy captured the attention of scouts from several major-league clubs. Playing for the local American Legion team in the summer of 1958, he attracted the attention of Dodgers scout Kenny Myers, who was so smitten with his potential as a ballplayer that he worked with Roy during the winter to hone his batting skills and turn him into a switch-hitter.[4] During the summer of 1960, Roy advanced to play for the Dodger Rookies, an elite amateur team managed by Myers.[5] Since the summer team was sponsored by the major-league Dodgers, Roy had increased visibility within the Dodgers organization during his high-school years.

All the attention by the Los Angeles Dodgers hooked Roy, who signed with the club on June 16, 1961, the night of his high-school graduation.[6] "I wanted to play for the Dodgers, and I wanted to repay Kenny for his investment," Gleason explained his decision many years later.[7] He was so eager to sign with the Dodgers that he turned down a $100,000 offer from the Los Angeles Angels, the American League expansion club. Instead, Roy accepted a $55,000 deal from the Dodgers, which consisted of a $50,000 signing bonus, payable in five annual installments, plus $5,000 payable directly to his mother as "agent."[8]

Roy Gleason.

Courtesy of the Los Angeles Dodgers.

ONE-HIT WONDERS

Because many publications reported his signing bonus to be $100,000, Gleason was included in the informal listing of the dozen or so "bonus baby" high-school players who had signed six-figure contracts in 1961, topped by Bob Bailey and Lew Krausse.[9] In this era before the institution of the amateur draft in 1965, a big contract given to an inexperienced 18-year-old created enormous expectations by the ballclub that signed him. The Dodgers touted the 6-foot-5, 220-pound, switch-hitting Roy as a top outfield prospect, expecting this "Dodger-of-tomorrow" to mature into a five-tool player at the major-league level.[10] Dodgers coach Pete Reiser told sportswriters that "Roy Gleason has such tremendous power he could become a better long-ball hitter than Duke Snider."[11]

The Dodgers placed Roy on the club's 40-man roster to avoid losing him in the minor-league draft.[12] This meant that he was paid the major-league minimum salary, which in 1962 was $7,000, in addition to his annual $10,000 signing-bonus installment.[13] Roy was now the breadwinner in the Gleason family. During this Cold War era when young men were actively being drafted into military service, Roy's local Selective Service board issued him a 3-A draft classification, which exempted him from the draft because he was the sole support for his mother and younger sister.[14]

Rather than send Roy to the minor leagues in 1961, the Dodgers directed him to play another summer with the Dodger Rookies, a team now comprising recently signed high-school players, and then sent him to the Arizona Instructional League that fall.[15] For the 1962 season, the Dodgers assigned Roy to their Reno (Nevada) farm club in the Class-C California League, where he had a decent year with 22 home runs, 76 RBIs, and a .234 batting average, but also a league-high 214 strikeouts.

For the 1963 season, Gleason played for Salem (Oregon) in the Single-A Northwest League, where he hit 15 home runs, had 60 RBIs, and batted .254. He finished strong, though, hitting 12 homers during the last two weeks of the season after he modified his batting stance to lower his hands, a change the exhausted ballplayer adopted after a late night out on the town.[16]

Despite his modest hitting numbers, Gleason was called up to the Dodgers in September when major-league rosters were expanded, primarily for his speed on the basepaths. The Dodgers, in a heated battle with the St. Louis Cardinals for the National League pennant, needed an ace pinch-runner during the stretch drive to run for hard-hitting but slow-footed Bill Skowron. Gleason appeared in seven games for the Dodgers as a pinch-runner. On September 3 he made an impact in his first appearance, scoring the tying run on a sacrifice fly in a game the Dodgers went on to win. He scored another run on September 5, an insurance run in the eighth inning of another Dodgers victory.

After the Dodgers had clinched the pennant, manager Walt Alston gave Gleason an opportunity to bat in the eighth inning of the September 28 game, when the Dodgers were losing 12-2 to the Phillies. "Gleason, get a bat. You're batting for Ortega," Gleason recalled how Alston barked at him while he sat at the far end of the bench. "I guess it was good in that I didn't have time to think about it. It was an adrenaline rush, 'Holy cow, I'm going to hit.' I had been frustrated, pinch-running but not getting any at-bats."[17] However, "He didn't tell me until Philadelphia was already on the field and the pitcher was already warmed up. So I barely had time to grab a bat and run up to the plate as the umpire is looking over at the dugout to see who is hitting."[18]

On the second pitch from Dennis Bennett, Gleason doubled to left field. When he eventually scored a meaningless third run, the few remaining spectators at Dodger Stadium politely applauded. "When the game ended, I realized that my at-bat was an amazing moment in my young life. It signaled the accomplishment of a goal, the manifestation of a dream," he recalled. "I hoped that Walt would give me more opportunities during the next season."[19] However, Gleason was destined to finish his big-league career with a 1.000 lifetime batting average.

After the Dodgers swept the Yankees to win the 1963 World Series, Gleason received $250 as his share of the players' proceeds (much less than the full share of $12,794).[20] The Dodgers also awarded him a ring for his September pinch-running contribution to winning the pennant.[21]

In 1964 when Gleason didn't make the Dodgers roster in spring training, he was sent to the Albuquerque (New Mexico) farm club in the Double-A Texas League. However, after just 15 games, he was optioned back to Single-A Salem, where he finished the season with a .254 average (and 148 strikeouts). After this mediocre performance, the Dodgers dropped him from their 40-man roster and assigned him to their Spokane (Washington) farm club in the Triple-A Pacific Coast League.[22] With this demotion in status, the Dodgers seemed to give up on the once-promising prospect.

ONE-HIT WONDERS

Gleason never played in a game with Spokane in 1965, though, due to a spring-training injury.[23] When he was ready to play again, Spokane optioned him back to Single-A Salem, where he hit a miserable .144 in 51 games.[24] By July he had tried unsuccessfully to convert into a pitcher to try to remain a prospect for the Dodgers.[25] He then spent the rest of the 1965 season with Santa Barbara of the Single-A California League, where his performance remained poor, with a .129 batting average in 47 games. Gleason, 22 years old and in receipt of the final installment of his signing bonus, had a minimal chance to once again wear a Dodgers uniform. He was no longer a vaunted Dodger-of-tomorrow.

Although he was exposed to the minor-league draft after the 1965 season, no other club sought to obtain his services, probably leery of a future change in the bachelor's military-draft status in light of the escalation of the Vietnam War. Ballclubs usually encouraged their young unmarried players to join the National Guard or Army Reserve to avoid the military draft. Gleason claimed the Dodgers never advised him to enlist in either organization, though, under the belief that his 3-A draft exemption would last the duration of the war.[26] During 1965, however, draft inductions of men aged 18 to 26 doubled and the draft exemption for married men was curtailed to apply just to those who supported a family, not just a wife without children, which ballclubs might have believed would imperil his "hardship to dependents" deferment.[27]

During the 1966 season, there was little uptick in Gleason's baseball performance, as he hit .173 in 45 games at Double-A Albuquerque before finishing the season with the Tri-City team of the Single-A Northwest League. Although he had his best minor-league stint at the team in Washington state (.281 average, league-leading 16 home runs), it was too little, too late. The Dodgers, who had won consecutive National League titles in 1965 and 1966, were focused on the development of other young outfielders.

When Gleason went to 1967 spring training with the Dodgers in Vero Beach, Florida, local draft boards were reconsidering the draft-exempt status of professional athletes amid congressional concern about "the apparent immunity of professional athletes from the military draft."[28] Although he had a draft deferment during his five years in the Dodgers minor-league system, he was supporting his mother and soon-to-be-18-year-old sister, not a wife or children. In 1967 during a firestorm of public concern about the apparent favoritism of athletes to avoid military duty, his case for supporting dependents was much weaker than when he had signed with the Dodgers back in 1961. An omen surfaced when the Army drafted New York Yankees rookie Bobby Murcer in February of 1967.[29]

Gleason's local draft board reclassified him 1-A and "fit for service" in March of 1967.[30] According to Gleason, the Dodgers advised him to hire a lawyer to appeal the decision. "Listening to this advice turned out to be very foolish on my part," he later said. "I put my entire stock in their wisdom, and I made a mistake."[31] When he received his draft notice in April of 1967, he went to basic training and advanced infantry training before shipping out to Vietnam in December of 1967 during the height of the Vietnam War.

In March of 1968, Gleason received the Bronze Star for his bravery during a search-and-destroy mission, when he transported two wounded soldiers to safety. "I couldn't help feeling that I really needed to be at spring training instead of sitting in the God-forsaken land of Vietnam," he recalled about his early months in the war. "Here I was dodging bullets each day, fighting a war that half our nation opposed."[32] Buzzie Bavasi, general manager of the Dodgers and a World War II veteran, regularly wrote to him while he was in Vietnam, to update him on the Dodgers. "Everything Buzzie sent me reminded me I had a future," Gleason recalled. "I thought, this will be a springboard for me, because I was in good [physical] shape over in Vietnam. As soon as I get home, I'll be ready to play."[33]

Gleason's hopes to return to the Dodgers were derailed on July 24, 1968, when he was leading a patrol through the jungle and a Viet Cong mine exploded in his path. "Seeing the blood from my wounded wrist, I quickly made a tourniquet to stop the blood flow," Gleason said of his reaction to the bomb blast. "At first, I didn't feel the shrapnel in my lower leg. The adrenaline pumping through my body and instinct to survive helped overcome the pain."[34] Gleason, along with several wounded soldiers in his platoon and three men killed in action, was evacuated by helicopter to their base camp. He was soon transported to a military hospital in Saigon and then transferred to a hospital in Osaka, Japan.[35] Left behind in his foot locker at base camp was Gleason's cherished 1963 World Series ring, which was missing (stolen) when his locker was returned to him stateside.[36]

Roy Gleason received the Army Commendation Medal for his heroism in the evacuation of his wounded soldiers and also the Purple Heart for being wounded himself in combat. "Although the ceremony wasn't very extravagant, I knew that my sacrifice had been recognized," he later said. "I was only worried that the sacrifice would include my baseball career."[37]

An Associated Press article published in August of 1968 told Gleason's story to millions of Americans across the country. "Charley's a darn good fighter," he told writer John Roderick from his hospital bed in Japan, referring to the Viet Cong. "But not as strong as he was. He's a pretty bad shot, too. Look how he missed me."[38] By September Gleason was convalescing at Letterman Army Hospital in San Francisco. "Shrapnel from the blast ripped open his left calf, put a hole in his left wrist, and damaged his right arm," Michael Leahy wrote of Gleason's wounds in his book *The Last Innocents*. "He discovered that his calf wound had robbed him of virtually all his speed. The wrist wound had the effect of leaving his left index finger numb, so he no longer could grip a bat quite right."[39]

Despite the obstacles, Gleason actively pursued physical therapy, telling the medical staff that he "was on a mission to return to baseball."[40] However, because he had lost 40 pounds from his previous 235-pound frame, there were serious questions about his return to baseball after being away from the sport for two years. Discharged from the Army in January of 1969, he went to spring training with the Dodgers. Unfortunately for Gleason, Bavasi, his top supporter while in Vietnam, had left the Dodgers to become president of the expansion San Diego Padres.

Gleason was a big story at 1969 spring training, as Los Angeles sportswriters wrote lengthy pieces about the Vietnam War hero. John Wiebusch of the *Los Angeles Times* wrote an eloquent story about Gleason's time in Vietnam and the resulting "purple-red gash on his left wrist" and "lumps on his calf where eight pieces of shrapnel are imbedded in the flesh."[41] Bob Hunter of the *Los Angeles Herald-Examiner* penned a full-page article in *The Sporting News*, noting how Gleason joked, "I guess I got the lead out" when doctors removed some of the metal shell fragments from his leg.[42] Everyone, though, knew that he was a long shot to play again for the Dodgers.

In reality Gleason, nearing 26 years old and eight years removed from his bonus-baby signing, was auditioning for a spot with the Triple-A Spokane farm club, which held his contract when he was drafted. Spokane optioned him to the lower minors at the end of spring training.[43] Following subpar stints with Double-A Albuquerque (.121 average in 27 games) and Single-A Bakersfield (.209 average in 74 games), his career with the Dodgers ended in December of 1969 when the California Angels selected him in the minor-league draft.[44]

The Angels played in a new ballpark in Anaheim, just a few miles from Roy's hometown of Garden Grove. While the Angels didn't have a spot for him in their minor-league system for the 1970 season, the ballclub did arrange for him to play with the Jalisco club in the Mexican League, which lacked affiliation with major-league farm systems. Gleason's baseball career ended in January of 1971 when he was severely injured in a truck accident while working an offseason job in the mountains of Northern California.[45]

Gleason finished with a lifetime batting of .223 in six minor-league seasons, in addition to the 1.000 batting average he compiled during his abbreviated tenure in the major leagues. "I just wish I'd had a real chance at baseball. Being drafted killed my career," he later mused. "Nothing was going to be the same after that. But the draft and Vietnam did things like that to all kinds of people. That year [1968] I got hurt was a bad time for a lot of guys."[46] In his post-baseball life, Roy was married and divorced twice, had two sons (Troy and Kaile) in his second marriage, and settled into working as a car salesman at Hardin Honda in Anaheim after trying out a number of different occupations, including furniture mover and bartender.[47]

In 2001, more than 30 years after leaving professional baseball, Gleason's baseball career finally turned positive when he met Wally Wasinack, a customer at Hardin Honda.[48] While they easily conversed about Roy's baseball life, Wasinack was more intrigued by Roy's military service and embarked on a mission to get Roy more recognized. He connected with Mark Langill, the publications director for the Dodgers, who arranged for Gleason to visit Dodger Stadium on July 17, 2003. As part of a tour of the ballpark, Gleason visited the wall that is inscribed with the names of all former Dodgers players. After locating his name there, he remarked, "I'd rather be on this wall than the other one," referring to the Vietnam Memorial in Washington, D.C., that honors those killed in action during that war.[49]

On September 20, 2003, the Dodgers honored Gleason in a pregame ceremony at Dodger Stadium to celebrate the 40th anniversary of his lone major-league base hit. After the ballclub showed a two-minute video of him on the scoreboard, narrated by legendary announcer Vin Scully, he threw out the ceremonial first pitch. Manager Jim Tracy and the Dodgers players then trotted out to the mound to surprise him with a

ONE-HIT WONDERS

box containing a replica of his 1963 World Series ring that he had lost in Vietnam.

"I was in shock when he handed me the World Series ring, and it remains one of the most incredible instances of my life," he wrote in his 2005 book *Lost in the Sun: Roy Gleason's Odyssey from the Outfield to the Battlefield*, co-written with Wasinack. "I felt like I was 20 years old again, and the only regret I have now is that it couldn't continue." During the playing of the National Anthem, he recalled that "emotion overwhelmed me, as I realized that the Dodgers and the fans were recognizing all those who have gone to war. I was merely a figurehead for veterans from all wars, especially the thousands who perished in the jungles of Vietnam."[50]

The media soon labeled Gleason as the only professional baseball player to serve in Vietnam after having played at the major-league level.[51] However, that aspect of his military service was not the recognition Gleason sought. The ring ceremony at Dodger Stadium inspired him to become a public proponent for all veterans, not just ballplayers and not just those of the Vietnam era.

Following his participation in a Memorial Day ceremony held by the San Diego Padres in 2006, Gleason began pitching major-league clubs to adopt his Operation ERA concept (Earned Recognition and Appreciation), to honor veterans by conducting ballpark programs.[52] His mission helped to spark Major League Baseball to create the Welcome Back Veterans initiative announced in June of 2008. At the games on Memorial Day in 2009, all major-league clubs first wore special caps to honor veterans. Gleason was later recognized for his efforts on behalf of veterans during a pregame ceremony at Game Two of the 2017 World Series.[53]

In a 2015 interview, the 72-year-old Gleason was sanguine about his baseball experience as a one-hit wonder. "The only way I can look at it is that I was blessed to be able to have the tools to get there in the first place," he told Sam Gardner of Fox Sports. "Every kid dreams about playing in the major leagues, and I got that chance. It was only one at-bat, but I was there. How many guys in America today wish they could have had just one at-bat in the majors? So I was fortunate. It wasn't meant to be, and I'm happy where I'm at now, and that's all that counts."[54]

NOTES

1. *The Sporting News Baseball Players Contract Cards Collection*, Roy Gleason.
2. Roy Gleason, *Lost in the Sun: Roy Gleason's Odyssey from the Outfield to the Battlefield* (Champaign, Illinois: Sports Publishing, 2005), 1, 31.
3. Gleason, *Lost in the Sun*, 49.
4. Gleason, *Lost in the Sun*, 57, 69.
5. "Dodger Rookies Appear," *San Bernardino* (California) *Sun*, July 1, 1960: 28.
6. "Dodgers Give Prep $75,000," *Los Angeles Times*, June 17, 1961: 17.
7. Gleason, *Lost in the Sun*, 77.
8. Gleason, *Lost in the Sun*, 78-79.
9. Allen Lewis, "Baseball Bonus Spree Is 'Suicide,' Phils' Quinn Says," *Philadelphia Inquirer*, June 20, 1961: 35.
10. Bob Hunter, "Moeller Rated Tops in Dodger Kiddies' Class," *The Sporting News*, November 29, 1961: 15; "Taking Shortcut in Climb Up Dodger Ladder," *The Sporting News*, December 20, 1961: 4.
11. Frank Finch, "Reiser Pins No. 1 Tag on '62 Dodgers' Kids," *The Sporting News*, April 4, 1962: 4.
12. "Dodgers Juggle Farm Hands to Set Up 40-Man Roster," *Palm Springs* (California) *Desert Sun*, October 20, 1961: 8; Dodgers 40-man roster, *The Sporting News*, January 10, 1962: 11.
13. Bob Hunter, "'Wide Open,' Smokey Says in Sizeup of '62 NL Race," *The Sporting News*, February 7, 1962: 17.
14. Gleason, *Lost in the Sun*, 141.
15. "Braves Tackle Dodger Rookies," *San Bernardino Sun*, July 4, 1961: 9.
16. Keith Sharon, "A Rookie at Peace: The Only Major-League Ballplayer Sent to Vietnam Got Back One Thing He Lost," *Orange County Register* (Anaheim, California), March 1, 2006: 1.
17. Michael Arkush, "Five-Star Ball Player Roy Gleason: The Only Major Leaguer Who Served in Vietnam," *The VA Veteran*, May/June 2004: 27.
18. Sam Gardner, "One & Done: Roy Gleason Only MLB Player Wounded in Vietnam," *Fox Sports* website, August 11, 2015. foxsports.com/mlb/story/one-done-roy-gleason-was-only-mlb-player-wounded-in-vietnam-war-081115.
19. Gleason, *Lost in the Sun*, 120.
20. "Splitting Swag," *The Sporting News*, October 26, 1963: 6.
21. Sharon, "A Rookie at Peace: The Only Major-League Ballplayer Sent to Vietnam Got Back One Thing He Lost."
22. "Deals of the Week," *The Sporting News*, October 24, 1964: 21; Dodgers 40-man roster, *The Sporting News*, January 23, 1965: 21.
23. "Coast Loop Crews," *The Sporting News*, May 1, 1965: 38.
24. "Deals of the Week," *The Sporting News*, May 22, 1965: 34.
25. "Salem Conversion Project," *The Sporting News*, July 3, 1965: 39.
26. Gleason, *Lost in the Sun*, 150.
27. "Induction Statistics," *Selective Service System* website, sss.gov/About/History-And-Records/Induction-Statistics; John Finney, "New Husbands Face Draft as Exemption Is Removed," *New York Times*, August 27, 1965: 1.
28. John Herbers, "Congress Panel Is Studying Draft," *New York Times*, December 8, 1966: 1; B. Drummond Ayres, "Reserves Told to Enlist Men as Names Come Up," *New York Times*, December 23, 1966: 11. The congressional report was issued in April of 1967 ("360 Pros Reported Exempt from Draft," *New York Times*, April 8, 1967: S23).
29. Robert Lipsyte, "Murcer, Yanks, Called by Army; Shortstop Is Lost for 2 Years," *New York Times*, February 25, 1967: 32.

ONE-HIT WONDERS

30 Gleason, *Lost in the Sun*, 150.

31 Gleason, *Lost in the Sun*, 151.

32 Gleason, *Lost in the Sun*, 174-176.

33 Michael Leahy, *The Last Innocents: The Collision of the Turbulent Sixties and the Los Angeles Dodgers* (New York: Harper Collins, 2016), 415.

34 Gleason, *Lost in the Sun*, 8.

35 "Bonus Baby Hurt in Vietnam," *Los Angeles Times*, July 31, 1968: 38.

36 Gleason, *Lost in the Sun*, 222.

37 Gleason, *Lost in the Sun*, 184-185.

38 John Roderick, "Roy Gleason: Charley Is a Darn Good Fighter," *Asheville* (North Carolina) *Citizen-Times*, August 4, 1968: 23.

39 Leahy, *The Last Innocents*, 416.

40 Gleason, *Lost in the Sun*, 185.

41 John Wiebusch, "Gleason: War-Wounded Dodger Starts Comeback at Vero Beach," *Los Angeles Times*, February 28, 1969: 2.

42 Bob Hunter, "A Vietnam Hero Prizes Ted's Letter," *The Sporting News*, March 22, 1969: 12.

43 "Deals of the Week," *The Sporting News*, April 26, 1969: 28.

44 "Minors Cut Back in Draft Selections," *The Sporting News*, December 13, 1969: 34.

45 Bill Plaschke, "At Ease, At Last," *Los Angeles Times*, September 19, 2003: 33.

46 Leahy, *The Last Innocents*, 416.

47 Gleason, *Lost in the Sun*, ix, 213-216.

48 John Hunneman, "Roy Gleason, the Only Ball Player Wounded in Vietnam, Urges Baseball to Honor His Fellow Vets," *San Diego Union-Tribune*, August 12, 2007.

49 Plaschke, "At Ease, At Last."

50 Gleason, *Lost in the Sun*, 238.

51 Sharon, "A Rookie at Peace: The Only Major-League Ballplayer Sent to Vietnam Got Back One Thing He Lost"; Hunneman, "Roy Gleason, the Only Ball Player Wounded in Vietnam"; Arkush, "Roy Gleason: The Only Major Leaguer Who Served in Vietnam."

52 Hunneman, "Roy Gleason, the Only Ball Player Wounded in Vietnam."

53 Alyson Footer, "Vietnam Veterans Honored Before Game 2," MLB.com, October 25, 2017.

54 Gardner, "One & Done: Roy Gleason Only MLB Player Wounded in Vietnam."

ED GLENN

By Mike Cooney

"These are the saddest of possible words: 'Tinker to Evers to Chance.'" Thus begins the iconic eight-line poem written in 1910 by Franklin Pierce Adams. Joe Tinker was a rookie in 1902. That was the year that Ed Glenn, whose only major-league hit had come four years earlier, was called up by the Chicago Orphans/Cubs to replace Tinker. Glenn's career with the Orphans/Cubs was representative of his entire career.

Eddie Glenn had the ability to be a star in the major leagues. Instead, he had a vagabond career, playing often brief stints with a bewildering number of teams. In 12 years of professional baseball, he played for at least 24 teams. The fact that Glenn continued to be signed by team after team shows he was considered an accomplished baseball player despite the fact that his personal life decisions continued to sabotage his career due to his chronic addiction to alcohol. Without alcohol, Franklin Pierce Adams might have written: These are the saddest of possible words: *Glenn* to Evers to Chance.

For Eddie Glenn, the saddest of possible words were controlled by alcohol.

Edward D. Glenn was born on October 28, 1874, in Cincinnati.[1] He was the fourth of eight children born to Nicholas Glenn, a laborer, and Bridget Glenn.

When Edward was young, the family moved to Ludlow, Kentucky, just across the Ohio River from Cincinnati. At the age of 19, Glenn was still learning his baseball skills when he was arrested for participating in a strike against the Louisville and Nashville and Kentucky Central Roads. Glenn was arraigned and released on bail on July 12, 1894.[2]

The following year, Glenn began his baseball career as a pitcher when he and "Ed Gallagher left … for Omaha, Ohio where they will be the battery of the Omaha Baseball Club."[3] There is no information for his Omaha team experience. By August, Glenn was playing shortstop for the Covingtons of Covington, Kentucky.[4]

Then, by September, Glenn was pitching for the Cincinnati Shamrocks.[5] Coming off a successful pitching performance for the 1895 Shamrocks, Glenn signed with Portsmouth of the Virginia League for the 1896 season.[6]

Instead of pitching or playing shortstop for Portsmouth, Glenn spent most of his time in right field. Early in the 1896 season, the *Norfolk Virginian* wrote that Glenn was said to be a "crack-a-jack."[7] Of Norfolk's second game of the season, on April 17, the *Virginian* wrote: "The only thing worthy of mention up to the seventh was Glenn, sensational catch. …"[8] Three days later Glenn started in right field, but in the fourth inning was called on to pitch the remainder of the game. While giving up five hits, he showed "a very deceptive curve," the *Virginian* wrote.[9]

After playing 13 games, Glenn left the team and on May 12 signed a contract with league rival Lynchburg "to play right field"[10] where he appeared in 13 games. Glenn finished the season playing shortstop for a Paris, Kentucky team.[11]

In January of 1897, Glenn signed to play for Parkersburg of the Ohio-Western Virginia League.[12] By July he was playing shortstop for the New Bedford Whalers of the New England League.

The 1898 season became somewhat confusing. On June 30 the *Cincinnati Enquirer* reported: "Ed Glenn, one of the best ball players [of] this vicinity and a graduate of Ludlow baseball players, left last night for Rochester, N.Y., where he will join the Grafton (Mass.) team of the New England League."[13] Glenn was actually reporting to Worcester. (The New Bedford team had been transferred to Worcester; Grafton was a suburb of Worcester.) On July 1, Glenn hit a home run in the team's first game at Worcester.[14] After playing four games for Worcester, Glenn left the team. He did report to Grafton, perhaps a semipro team, in August.[15] At some point Glenn was obtained by the Washington Senators. He made his major-league debut on September 7, 1898. Playing shortstop and batting seventh, Glenn went 0-for-4 as Washington lost to Boston, 5-1.[16]

ONE-HIT WONDERS

With no transaction information available, it is unclear how Glenn, after making his debut with Washington found himself playing for the New York Giants three days later. With New York playing Boston, he got his first base hit. "Glenn, the young New England league shortstop, put up a fine game at short, taking Jack Doyle's place after the latter opened an old cut on his right hand," reported the *Boston Globe*. "Glenn opened the ninth with a single."[17] It was his only major-league hit. The *New York Times* wrote, "Glenn, a new man, had a trial. He did well."[18] The next day Glenn went hitless while making two errors.[19]

Glenn finished his two-team, three-game, major-league debut season with one hit, three walks, and two errors.[20]

In 1899 Glenn returned to the minor leagues, playing for a new Cambridge (Massachusetts) team in the New England League.[21] On the eve of the season the *Boston Globe* wrote: "There are few better minor league shortstops than Eddie Glenn."[22]

Glenn opened the season against Portland on May 10 as the starting shortstop.[23] On the 13th he had a game to forget when he made five errors in a 19-8 loss to Fitchburg.[24] On May 24 Glenn almost had a game to be remembered when he started "a clean triple play in the fifth inning ... but the umpire allowed only a double on it."[25]

After a game on May 26,[26] Cambridge folded[27] and transferred its players to the new Lowell Orphans. By Lowell's opening game on May 31, Glenn was playing shortstop for the Orphans.[28]

On June 6, after playing 20 games for Cambridge/Lowell, Glenn was the starting shortstop for the Taunton Herrings.[29] He left the team after playing in 13 games. After leaving Taunton, it appears, Glenn played shortstop for Bristol for a few games.[30] By the end of June, Glenn left Bristol and "signed to play third base with the New Haven Club."[31] He played 62 games to finish out the 1899 season for New Haven.

The 1900 season found Ed Glenn with yet another team. The *Cincinnati Enquirer* reported: "Edward Glenn, one of the most promising young ballplayers in this vicinity, has gone to Youngstown, Ohio, where he will play shortstop for that team."[32] By mid-June he was released and reportedly wound up with Columbus of the Interstate League.[33]

Selma, Alabama, of the Southern Association became the next team to sign "Eddie Glenn, our fast shortstop," in March of 1901.[34] Glenn reported early and besides "putting in a few hours of good practice every day,"[35] he was instrumental in the preparation of the baseball diamond at Selma's Riverside Park.[36]

On the eve of the season the *Selma Times* predicted: "... the infield will be a particularly strong one. Each one is a hard worker and go into a game with their whole soul and with a determination to win."[37]

That opinion would soon change.

Though Glenn's primary position for Selma was at shortstop, on May 13, after "the wild pitching of Sechrist," he replaced Doc Sechrist and pitched the last four innings.[38] Four days later Glenn again took the mound, this time as the starting pitcher.

The *Selma Times* reported: "For nine innings yesterday afternoon, Eddy Glenn, the fastest shortstop in the Southern League, who was pitching the first game with Chattanooga, had the Missionaries guessing, and they could never guess right. All during the game, Glenn sent a lot of speedy shoots and curves over the slab that puzzled the visitors' batsmen, and they could score but seven scattered hits and one run off his deceptive delivery."[39] The following day, the *Times* commented: "Eddy is a great favorite and he wears his honors becoming his generous nature.[40]

Two weeks later everything changed when on May 29, "Glenn, Selma's fast short stop[,] jumped the Selma club at Memphis ... and signed with Manager Jack Gorman's fast Jackson, Tenn. Independent team. Glenn has been dissatisfied for some time with his job with the Senators and as he is at outs with the manager and players it is perhaps the best thing for the club that he left, as he would have always caused strife if he had staid [sic]. ... Glenn will not be missed."[41]

Glenn's reputation continued to spiral downward when he agreed to sign with Nashville of the Southern League. "The latest caper reported to have been cut by Eddy Glenn, Selma's erstwhile crack short-stop, is that after accepting advance money from Manager

Ed Glenn, #10 in front row.

ONE-HIT WONDERS

Fisher, Eddy has decided to stay with the Jackson, Tenn. Independent club and give Nashville the go by. Glenn is a good player, but his recent action in jumping Selma at Memphis and accepting Manager Fisher's advance money in bad faith will always cause him to be regarded with suspicion by reputable players and lovers of the national game."[42]

Two days later, June 16, "Eddy Glenn, the clever short stop for the independent team here (Jackson, Tennessee), and who was formerly considered the fastest infielder and best all-around player in the Southern League when he played with Selma the early part of the season, fell from a window in the Southern Hotel ... to the pavement nearly a hundred feet below. The accident was caused by Glenn going to sleep while sitting in the window and becoming overbalanced. The ... fall was broken by telegraph wires running along the street in front of the hotel and this circumstance undoubtedly prevented his instant death. His attending physicians say that he has a slight chance of recovery."[43]

The *Selma Times* commented: "... [W]hile Glenn's action in jumping the local team at Memphis without notice or reason is universally condemned, he still has many personal friends among the local fans."[44]

One week after his fall, Jackson club President Gorman said that Glenn "had a very poor chance to pull through."[45] That dire prognosis was apparently overstated: A little over a month later the *Times*, reported: "It is said that Eddy Glenn will soon join the team again. It is to be hoped that he will, as Selma is badly in need of a shortstop."[46]

It is unclear whether Glenn actually returned to finish out the season with Selma, but his recovery was sufficient to have him choosing to wait on a call from a major-league team in 1902, rather than signing any of "no end of offers to join minor league teams."[47]

Glenn's confidence in himself was rewarded when "he received a dispatch from Frank Selee, of the Chicagos requesting his terms. Glenn replied with figures which he thought were prohibitive, but, to his surprise, he received a contract yesterday, together with a dispatch accepting his terms and ordering him to report at once."[48]

The *Cincinnati Enquirer* reported a concern about Glenn's recovery from his three-story fall, stating: "he has never fully recovered. If the ailment caused by the injury does not break out afresh, it's a 100-to-1 shot that Glenn will more than hold his own with the Chicago team."[49]

Before leaving for Chicago, Glenn told the *Enquirer*: "It has always been my ambition to become a member of the Cincinnati team, and I would have played my legs off for the Reds."[50] Instead of the Reds, on June 25, Glenn left Cincinnati to join the Chicago Colts (Orphans/Cubs)."[51]

Chicago wanted Glenn to replace shortstop Joe Tinker, suspended after a scrap involving Pittsburgh's Wid Conroy.

Glenn played his first game with Chicago on June 26. The next day Tinker was reinstated. But Tinker had gone home to Kansas City,[52] so, Glenn played a second game with Chicago on the 27th while the team waited for Tinker's return.

Tinker was back for Chicago's next game. The *Cincinnati Enquirer* wrote: "Joe Tinker will get into the game at once and Eddie Glenn, who was signed by the Chicago Club last week, will be released. [Manager Frank] Selee says that Glenn fielded well, but showed up weak at the bat."[53]

The *Enquirer* commented: "Glenn only played in two games and many a slugger has failed to get a hit in two consecutive days."[54] In Glenn's two games with Chicago, he walked once, and went hitless in seven at-bats while making six assists at shortstop with no errors.

After being cut by Chicago, Glenn joined the Utica Pent-Ups of the New York State League, where he finished the 1902 season playing 70 games.

Glenn started the 1903 season with the Memphis Egyptians of the Southern League. With the Egyptians paying him $175 per month,[55] Glenn played in 80 games before Natchez Indians manager Al Haupt "approached the Egyptians about purchasing Glenn from them. Initially, Haupt was concerned because Glenn wanted "$300 (per month) for his distinguished services."[56]

On August 14 the *Natchez Democrat* reported that Glenn would join the Indians. "Charlie Frank (Egyptians president) was given a nice sum of coin for the release of Glenn. ... Much persuasion was required to get Glenn in a notion to go with the Cotton State team, but he finally (agreed) to do his best with Haupt."[57]

After playing three games with Natchez, Glenn jumped the team. He told the *Nashville Tennessean*: "I'm through. As John L. said, 'Booze done it.'"[58]

The *Tennessean* continued: "Thus mused Eddy Glenn, the erratic shortstop, who has consumed enough pousse cafes, anisettes, old-fashioned toddies, mugs full of amber fluid, Manhattans, Martinis,

ONE-HIT WONDERS

absinthes, vermouth, and Chartreuse to float a battleship during his two weeks' absence from diamond struggles. [Glenn says,] 'The water wagon route for me in the future. There's nothing like clear, sparkling aqua pura. I'm on the front seat in the Appollinaris chariot, and don't forget to mention it.' Glenn seems to be in earnest. He rues the day that he fell from sober grace just as he disremembers the celebration in Jackson which caused him to fall from the second story window of a hotel."[59]

The *Tennessean* reported that Natchez manager Al Haupt had pleaded with Glenn to return to the Indians. Haupt even sent Glenn money for transportation, but at that time, Glenn had not responded.[60]

Glenn's "retirement" lasted less than two weeks. By August 29, he was back at shortstop for Natchez.[61] Glenn finished out the 1903 season with the Indians.

In April 1904 Glenn signed a contract to play with the Bloomington Bloomers of the Illinois-Indiana-Iowa League.[62] Before the season opened and after an exhibition game between Bloomington and St. Paul, the *Davenport Morning Star* commented: "Glenn on short ... will be (a) fixture."[63]

But Glenn struggled, and was benched in early May.[64] His popularity quickly faded as indicated by a fan who yelled, "You couldn't steal a bucket of water out of the river" after he was thrown out trying to steal second base.[65]

On May 27, after playing in 15 games and batting .195 with an .832 fielding average,[66] Glenn was suspended for the rest of the season "and unless he improves in conduct and in playing he will probably not get on next year. ... Glenn says he don't care what the Bloomington team does to him, and expresses contempt for the suspension."[67]

The summer-long suspension did not last long. Glenn was back at shortstop for Bloomington in less than two weeks.[68] But his return did not go well. He was quickly released. He signed with the Dubuque Dubs of the Three-I League. The *Quad-City Times* commented: "Funny the way cast-offs are passed around the Three-I League. ... Glenn, who wasn't good enough for the Bloomers, is on third for Dubuque."[69]

It is not certain whether Glenn finished out the 1904 season with Dubuque, nor is there evidence that he played in Organized Baseball in 1905. As the 1906 season approached, Glenn signed to play for the Augusta (Georgia) Tourists of the South Atlantic League. The *Cincinnati Enquirer* commented: "Ed Glenn, at shortstop, is a sensational infielder, of considerable experience who intimates that his work this season will prove that he is fit for faster company."[70]

Glenn started the season with the Tourists, but eventually moved on to the Charleston Sea Gulls of the same league. Glenn played a total of 98 games between the two teams.

There is no indication that Glenn played in Organized Baseball in 1907. In 1908 he began the season with the semipro Hamilton (Ohio) Krebs of the Kentucky, Indiana, Ohio (K.I.O.) League. But on July 14 the *Dayton Herald* reported: "Ed Glenn ... expected to reach (Grand Rapids, Michigan) this afternoon in time to play in today's game. Glenn is a shortstop ... (who) has played all over the South and knows the game thoroughly."[71]

With the Grand Rapids Soldiers in the Central League, Glenn once again was playing in Organized Baseball. Meanwhile, the league's Dayton team had four injured players who needed to be replaced.[72] And on July16, instead of playing for Grand Rapids, Glenn was playing for Dayton. The *Herald* reported that the Dayton club had secured Glenn from the Hamilton Krebs.[73] There is no indication whether Glenn decided against joining Grand Rapids in favor of Dayton, or if the management of the Hamilton Krebs decided they had a better deal from Dayton.

It appears Glenn played little, if any, for Dayton. A review of 1908 Central League statistics does not show evidence of any official appearances at bat.[74]

In any event, Glenn's return to Organized Baseball was short-lived. By early August he was back playing in the K.I.O. League, this time playing for Middletown.[75]

Glenn started the 1909 season back in Organized Baseball, playing for the Richmond (Kentucky) Pioneers of the Blue Grass League. While Richmond was considered "the class of the Blue Grass League,"[76] Glenn on June 4 "for some unknown cause left the team and went to his home."[77]

The Pioneers immediately felt the effect of Glenn's desertion. The *Richmond Climax* newspaper reported: "The Richmond team was somewhat crippled by the absence of Glenn, who took a leave of absence without the knowledge of the management, a short time before time to play. So sudden was his leaving it seemed to disorganize the entire team."[78] In a "good-riddance" suggestion, the paper commented, "Glenn will not be missed ... when the boys have had time to get over the shock."[79]

ONE-HIT WONDERS

By mid-July, Glenn was back playing, and apparently managing,[80] in the Blue Grass League – this time for the Shelbyville Grays.[81] In early August, Glenn, after a Shelbyville player had been ejected for abusing the umpire, "became angry and began to abuse (umpire) Dunbar and he too was ordered out of the game."[82]

One week later, Shelbyville traded Glenn to the Frankfort Statesmen of the Blue Grass League. Perhaps tellingly, the *Richmond Climax* commented: "Frankfort will likely be shy a short stop in a few days for Eddie is a quitter."[83]

The *Climax*'s comment became prophetic when two weeks after the trade to Frankfort, "Glenn, the Frankfort shortstop, was taking a nap in the city and didn't awaken until the game was almost over."[84] Still, he was soon back in the starting lineup.[85] Glenn ended the 1909 season having played a total of 84 Blue Grass League games.

Glenn once again changed teams in 1910. In February 1910, the *Bourbon News* of Paris, Kentucky, reported: "Eddie Glenn will not be signed by the Frankfort club to play short this season. Manager Warren says Glenn is a brilliant player, but is very unreliable on account of certain habits, and will not keep himself in the proper condition."[86]

With Frankfort declining to sign Glenn, manager Kuhn of the Shelbyville Grays decided to re-sign him, regardless of Shelbyville's experience with him during the 1909 season.[87] Playing for Shelbyville, Glenn was often lauded for his exceptional fielding ability[88] while holding his own at the bat.[89] Still, by July, Glenn found himself playing for yet another Blue Grass team, the Lexington Colts.[90] Glenn played a total of 77 games during the 1910 season.

The Colts were Glenn's last team in Organized Baseball. The 1911 season found him playing for several local semipro teams.

With his baseball career spiraling downward, Glenn's private life hit rock-bottom on August 3, 1911, when "Ed Glinn [sic], well-known baseball player, was bound over to the Kenton County grand jury from the Ludlow Police Court yesterday in the sum of $1,000 for assault and battery. Glenn was arrested yesterday ... on a warrant sworn out by his mother, who charged him with beating and severely wounding his brother Andrew with a flatiron. ... The mother and two brothers were in Court and testified against Glenn, who claimed he was intoxicated at the time the trouble occurred and remembered nothing of it."[91]

Four months later, Eddie Glenn was dead.

As reported by the *Bourbon News*: "Eddie Glenn, aged 35 ... was found dead in a locomotive pit in the Ludlow shops of the Southern railway Thursday by fellow employees. Glenn ... had been working as a machinist, and when ... it was found that he had not 'punched out' ... Wednesday night a search was begun, Death was due to concussion of the brain."[92]

According to his death certificate, Edward Glenn was born in 1874 and died on December 6, 1911, at the age of 37.[93] As with conflicting birth years, the actual date of his death is also in question.

While most documents, including his death certificate, show his death on December 6, 1911, a lawsuit brought by his brother[94] seeking $25,000 from the railroad asserts that Glenn died ... on or about December 7, 1911.[95] (The difference in the date of death results from the fact that Glenn did not return home on the evening of December 6 while his body was found the morning of December 7.)

The lawsuit accused the railroad of responsibility for Glenn's death due to negligently failing to cover, light, or block off the locomotive pit.[96] It was rejected by the county Circuit Court and the United States District Court.[97]

Ed Glenn was buried at Saint Joseph New Cemetery in Cincinnati.

NOTE

A special thank-you to Alisha Lee of the Kenton County (Kentucky) Circuit Court for researching and providing court documents for Andrew Glenn's lawsuit.

SOURCES

In addition to the sources cited in the Notes, the author consulted Baseball-Reference.com.

NOTES

1. Early census reports support an 1874 birthdate while later documents support an 1875 date. The Ed Glenn family tree developed by a Glenn relative, the 1880 Federal Census, and Glenn's death certificate all indicate an 1874 birthdate.
2. "Strike Incidents," *Cincinnati Enquirer*, July 13, 1894: 5.
3. *Cincinnati Enquirer*, May 7, 1895: 6. The quotation is as presented in the *Enquirer* article, though efforts to locate a community by that name have not proved successful.
4. "Terrible Tumble," *Public Ledger* (Maysville, Kentucky), August 2, 1895.
5. "Shamrocks Won Easily," *Cincinnati Enquirer*, September 3, 1895: 2.
6. "Little Problem," *Cincinnati Enquirer*, March 2, 1896: 2.
7. "The Agony Has Begun," *Norfolk Virginian*, April 16, 1896.
8. "Second Day's Game," *Norfolk Virginian*, April 18, 1896: 6.
9. "Grangers Go Down," *Norfolk Virginian*, April 21, 1896: 6.
10. "Around the Bases," *Norfolk Virginian*, May 13, 1896: 6.

ONE-HIT WONDERS

11. "The Tail-Enders," *Marietta* (Ohio) *Daily Leader,* January 27, 1897.
12. "The Tail-Enders."
13. *Cincinnati Enquirer,* June 30, 1898.
14. "First Game at Worcester," *Boston Globe,* July 2, 1898: 2.
15. "Milfords 7, Graftons 5," *Boston Globe,* August 14, 1898: 2.
16. "Won in the First," *Cincinnati Enquirer,* September 8, 1898: 8.
17. "Great Game of the Season," *Boston Globe,* September 10, 1898: 7.
18. "The Game at Boston Yesterday," *New York Times,* September 10, 1898: 4.
19. "New Yorks Lose Again," *New York Times,* September 11, 1898: 5.
20. "New Yorks Lose Again." Baseball-Reference.com shows Glenn committed only one error in his three games. The *New York Times* shows Glenn with two errors in the September 10 game.
21. "Bates Defeats Cambridge," *Boston Globe,* May 5, 1899: 2.
22. *Boston Globe,* May 8, 1899: 4.
23. "Portland 9, Cambridge 6," *Boston Globe,* May 11, 1899: 3.
24. "Fitchburg 19, Cambridge 8," *Boston Globe,* May 14, 1899: 16.
25. "Pawtucket 20, Cambridge 8," *Boston Globe,* May 25, 1899: 4.
26. "Manchester 8, Cambridge 5," *Boston Globe,* May 27, 1899: 5.
27. *Boston Globe,* May 27, 1899: 4.
28. "Newport 10, Lowell 5," *Boston Globe,* June 1, 1899: 5.
29. "Made Good Previous Day's Defeat," *Boston Globe,* June 7, 1899: 5.
30. "Made Good Previous Day's Defeat." Bristol was in the Connecticut State League. As a side note, Glenn also played a few games for a Greensboro team (probably a semipro team) in the first week of July.
31. *Hartford Courant,* June 28, 1899: 13.
32. "Ludlow," *Cincinnati Enquirer,* April 25, 1900: 8.
33. "Outfielder Bay Signed," *Cincinnati Enquirer,* June 16, 1900: 3.
34. "In Real Earnest," *Selma* (Alabama) *Times,* March 31, 1901: 3.
35. "In Real Earnest."
36. "Diamond Notes," *Selma Times,* March 17, 1901: 3.
37. "Baseball Projects," *Selma Times,* April 21, 1901: 3.
38. "Lost the First Game," *Selma Times,* May 14, 1901: 3.
39. "Pitcher Eddy Glenn," *Selma Times,* May 17, 1901: 3.
40. *Selma Times,* May 18. 1901: 4.
41. "Eddy Glenn Jumps the Selma Club," *Selma Times,* May 30. 1901: 3.
42. "Eddy Glenn's Latest," *Selma Times,* June 15, 1901: 3.
43. "Fell Three Stories," *Selma Times,* June 18, 1901: 3.
44. "Fell Three Stories."
45. *Selma Times,* June 25, 1901: 3.
46. "The Wanderer's Return," *Selma Times,* August 9, 1901: 3.
47. "Lost to Reds," *Cincinnati Enquirer,* June 26, 1902: 4.
48. "Lost to Reds."
49. "Lost to Reds."
50. "Lost to Reds."
51. "Another Shortstop for Colts," *Chicago Tribune,* June 26, 1902: 13. In 1902 the team was variously referred to as the Colts, the Orphans, and the Cubs.
52. "Tinker Reinstated," *Chicago Tribune,* June 28, 1902: 6.
53. "Baseball Gossip," *Cincinnati Enquirer,* June 30, 1902: 3.
54. "Baseball Gossip."
55. "Big Salary Lists," *Tennessean* (Nashville), July 25, 1903: 5.
56. "Baseball," *Natchez* (Mississippi) *Democrat,* August 13, 1903: 8.
57. "Baseball," *Natchez Democrat,* August 16, 1903: 8.
58. "No Double Headers," *Tennessean,* August 17, 1903: 3.
59. "No Double Headers." Reports of Glenn falling from a window differed, with the fall described as one of 100 feet, to one from the third floor, and one from the second story.
60. "No Double Headers."
61. "Baseball," *Natchez Democrat,* August 30, 1903: 8.
62. "Pa Hill Getting Ball Park Ready," *Cedar Rapids* (Iowa) *Gazette,* April 7, 1904: 8.
63. "New Players in Three-I League," *Davenport* (Iowa) *Morning Star,* April 24, 1904: 4.
64. "Three-I Notes," *Daily Times* (Davenport, Iowa), May 7, 1904: 2.
65. "Home for Fans," *Quad-City Times* (Davenport, Iowa), May 18, 1904: 4.
66. "Something Must Be Wrong," *Quad-City Times,* June 7, 1904: 7.
67. "Glenn Suspended," *Davenport Morning Star,* May 28, 1904: 6.
68. "Strengthened Team Wins from Bloomers," *Moline* (Illinois) *Dispatch,* June 10, 1904, 2.
69. "Fodder for Fans," *Quad-City Times,* June 24, 1904: 9.
70. Jack Ryder, "LIO," *Cincinnati Enquirer,* February 18, 1906: 10.
71. "K.I.O. Boys to Join Soldiers," *Dayton* (Ohio) *Herald,* July 15, 1908: 8.
72. "Some Artistic Bunching," *Cincinnati Enquirer,* July 15, 1908: 4.
73. "Vets to Tumble if Rowan Loses," *Dayton Herald.* July 17, 1908: 10.
74. John B. Foster, ed., *Spalding's Official Baseball Record 1909,* Central League, 109.
75. "K.I.O. Jottings," *Dayton Herald,* August 8, 1908: 6.
76. "Blue Grass League," *Cincinnati Enquirer,* May 16, 1909: 10.
77. "Glenn Returned Home," *Cincinnati Enquirer,* June 5, 1909: 9.
78. "Lost to Lexington," *Richmond* (Kentucky) *Climax,* June 9, 1909: 2.
79. "Notes," *Richmond Climax,* June 9, 1909: 2.
80. "Forfeit Second Game," *Richmond Climax,* August 4, 1909: 2.
81. "Blue Grass League," *Courier-Journal* (Louisville, Kentucky), July 19, 1909: 6.
82. "Forfeit Second Game," *Richmond Climax,* August 4, 1909: 2.
83. "Notes," *Richmond Climax,* August 11, 1909: 2.
84. "Bluegrass League," *Louisville Courier-Journal,* August 26, 1909: 8.
85. "Blue Grass League," *Cincinnati Enquirer,* September 5, 1909: 6.
86. "Notes," *Bourbon News* (Paris, Kentucky), February 25, 1910: 4.
87. "Notes," *Bourbon News,* March 4, 1910: 1.
88. "Millers Defeat Bourbonites," *Bourbon News,* June 21, 1910: 4.
89. "Blue Grass League," *Courier-Journal,* (May 31, 1910: 7.
90. "Baseball," *Bourbon News,* July 29, 1910: 4.
91. "Ludlow," *Cincinnati Enquirer,* August 4, 1911.
92. "Eddie Glenn, Ball Player, Dead," *Bourbon News,* December 12, 1911: 1.
93. Kentucky, Death Records, 1852-1965 for Edward Glenn.
94. Glenn's brother was the administrator of his estate.
95. Kenton County Circuit Court, Petition #13558.
96. Kenton County Circuit Court, Petition #13558.
97. Kenton County Circuit Court, Petition #13558.

KEITH GORDON

By Tim Deale

People from all walks of life play the great game of baseball. They play in Little League, Babe Ruth League, high school, American Legion baseball, and college, just to name a few. During those years they dream of one day playing in the major leagues and they are told that if they work hard and practice enough, they can do it.

A study showed that between 2006 and 2017, an average of 14.21 million people six years old and up played baseball in the United States each year.[1]

Based on the amount of high school seniors and college players eligible for the major-league amateur draft, there were 140,435 players available to be drafted in one year.[2] From 2012-2019 just over 1,200 players were drafted by major-league teams each year. That amounts to 0.8% being drafted as an eligible high-school or college player.

One of those fortunate few was able to make his dream come true: Keith Gordon, who was born on January 22, 1969, in Bethesda, Maryland. He did all of the above. Appropriately, he played at Walter Johnson High School, as a shortstop and pitcher.

His father, William Gordon, introduced Keith to football, basketball, and baseball at an early age. William knew about the world of sports from playing college basketball at Maryland-Eastern Shore and being drafted by the NBA's Seattle SuperSonics.[3]

All of the hard work of practicing and playing throughout his younger years started to pay off in high school. Gordon played all four years on the varsity team as a hard-hitting, good-fielding shortstop and pitcher and led his team in hitting starting in his freshman year. He was named to the "All-Met" team in his junior and senior years. He was the Maryland Athlete of the Year in his senior year. While in high school, Gordon also played American Legion ball and was a Selective All-Star three times.[4]

Asking what made him so good, Gordon responded, "I received a lot of help starting with my mother, Carolyn, and father, and my grandparents. They were always running me somewhere to a practice, or a game. My sister Erica, and brother Ali, and friends and coaches all helped me to be better. And then hard work, determination, and wanting to be the best."

Gordon went to college on a scholarship, majoring in communications and business at Wright State University in Dayton, Ohio, for one year and then to Arizona State for two years. While in college he continued to be a shortstop and pitcher and was drafted by the Cincinnati Reds in the second round of the June 4, 1990, amateur draft. He was 6-feet-1, weighed 200 pounds, and batted right and threw right-handed.

How did he find out he had been drafted? "I received a phone call from the Cincinnati Reds telling me I had just been drafted in the second round." What happened next? "My father was handling

Keith Gordon.

ONE-HIT WONDERS

everything up to that point but we realized I needed an agent. Then we met with the Reds and signed the contract."

Gordon started his minor-league career with the Billings (Montana) Mustangs of the Pioneer League, a Rookie classification. He played in 49 games, hitting .234 with a .346 on-base percentage playing shortstop.

The next year, 1991, he was promoted to the Charleston (West Virginia) Wheelers, who won the Class-A South Atlantic League championship. Switched to the outfield, he hit .268 with a .358 OBP and 25 stolen bases.

In 1992 Gordon was sent to the Cedar Rapids Reds of the Class-A Midwest League, where he batted .251 with a .329 OBP and had 21 stolen bases.

Gordon was promoted to the Chattanooga Lookouts of the Double-A Southern League for the 1993 season. A big surprise soon followed. In July he was called up by the Reds and on July 9 he made his major-league debut, in a game against the Pittsburgh Pirates in Pittsburgh. He was the starting left fielder and batted eighth. In his first at-bat, against the Pirates' Bob Walk, he lined out to shortstop. His second at-bat produced a fly ball to center field. In the top of the seventh inning, Joel Johnston was pitching for the Pirates and with one out and the pitch count at 1-and-2 Gordon hit a line drive single to right field. He finished the night with one hit in four at-bats.

The next night, Reds manager Davey Johnson put Gordon in as a pinch-hitter for pitcher Scott Service in the top of the ninth inning. Facing Pirates pitcher Cliff Otto with teammate Chris Sabo on third and two outs, Gordon hit a groundball to first base for the third out.

For the third game in a row, Gordon found himself in the action. With the score tied 2-2 in the top of the seventh inning and one out, Reds first baseman Brian Dorsett hit a double. Needing a run, manager Johnson decided to bring in some speed and used Gordon as a pinch-runner. The next batter, Jacob Brumfield struck out. Jose Rijo tried for a bunt but popped it up. Gordon stayed in the game and played left field. He batted in the top of the ninth inning and struck out against Blas Minor.

The three games he played in July of 1993 were the only games Gordon played in the major leagues. He had one hit in six at-bats.

Asked about being called up to the majors, Gordon replied, "It was everything I had worked for, it was great. Walking out onto the field was awesome. It was a bit overwhelming for a minute but then I remembered what the manager, Davey Johnson, and shortstop Barry Larkin told me, 'Don't get wrapped up in the moment, it's still baseball. Get back to what made you comfortable when you played at the other levels and enjoy it. Go have fun. "That is exactly what I did."

Gordon did not give up on his dream of playing in the majors. He went back to the minors and finished the season with Chattanooga, batting .291 with a .327 on-base percentage and a .468 slugging percentage. "I then went to something new, the Arizona Fall League, I think it was the second year for it."

In 1994 Gordon played in 82 games with Chattanooga and then was promoted to the Indianapolis Indians of the Triple-A American Association, where he batted .207 in 18 games. He played for Indianapolis in 1995, batting .264 and helping them to a division title.

A change in scenery happened during the offseason: Gordon was a free agent and remembering his youth and how much time his family and friends devoted to helping him, he wanted to play near enough so they could watch him play. Knowing the Baltimore Orioles had minor league teams close enough to drive to their stadiums he signed with the Orioles organization and was sent to the Bowie Baysox of the Double-A Eastern League, Gordon batted .261 and a .679 OPS (On-base plus slugging) in 82 games. Gordon showed he still had the base stealing ability by stealing 13 bases which were second most on the team, just two shy of the team leader who played in 129 games. Gordon was promoted to the Rochester Red Wings of the Triple-A International League, where he batted .250 with a .762 OPS in 33 games. The increase in OPS was due to having 10 extra-base hits in his 26 hits, five of which were home runs.[5]

In 1997, a huge change of scenery took place. Gordon received an offer from the Mercuries Tigers of the Chinese Professional Baseball League (Taiwan). Since he was a free agent he wanted to give it a try. There are no statistics readily available but according to Gordon the competition was similar to Double A/Triple A, and there were a few Americans on each team. During the season he learned the Cincinnati Reds had interest in him again and he packed his bags to head for the United States where the Reds sent him to Chattanooga.[6]

Always willing to try something new, Gordon was a free agent again and began 1998 with the Cancun Langosteros of the Mexican League, then signed with the New Jersey Jackals of the independent Northeast League. Batting .312/.354/.527, Gordon was an all-star outfielder for the Jackals and led the team to a division title. He was second in the league in RBIs (70) and third in home runs (16). No statistics are available for the Cancun team.

Winning a batting title is a big deal and Gordon did just that in 2000, batting .339 for the Atlantic City Surf of the independent Atlantic League. In 2001 he was with the same team, had the same batting average and ranked fifth in the league. He also played 24 games for the Saltillo Saraperos of the Mexican League.

In 2002 Gordon enjoyed another all-star season with Atlantic City: 20 home runs, 83 RBIs, and 28 stolen bases with a slash line of .293/.349/.511. The Surf won a division title.

Gordon played in the minor and independent leagues from 1990 through 2002. He was in the Reds organization for seven seasons, the Orioles one season, and the Seattle Mariners one season (New Haven of the Double-A Eastern League for 23 games in 2000). He definitely improved with age: His batting average for his final three seasons with the Atlantic City Surf (2000-2002) was .321, his slugging average was .544, and his OPS was .909.

Looking back on his time in baseball, Gordon said, "Spring trainings with the major-league teams were so much fun. I was practicing and playing with the major-league players and learned so much from them and the coaches, it was great. Also, each day we would receive gear from different equipment manufacturers so I always had the best stuff."

Toward the end of Gordon's professional playing days, he met his future wife, Julie, from Pittsburgh. When their daughter, Jenna, was born, family and fatherhood became the priority. Knowing the salary of a minor-league player and independent-league player cannot support a family. Playing professional baseball was a dream come true and now Gordon had to decide between his dream and his priorities with his loved ones. He retired from playing baseball. Leaving the baseball world was not easy but he decided to start a career in finance as a loan officer. He knew one day he would return to baseball in some capacity. A few years later he began teaching and coaching at Bullis School, a prestigious private school in Potomac, Maryland. He became the head coach of the varsity baseball team, a post he still held in 2020.

Realizing how much he enjoyed coaching and teaching baseball, Gordon began to coach a local travel team during the summer. A couple of years later, he became the coach of the 17U Mid Atlantic Red Sox, a showcase travel team.[7]

In 2019 the team finished second in its bracket in the Perfect Game in the Georgia tournament, which attracted 400 teams.[8] Some of the players Gordon coached have gone to major universities or have been drafted by major league teams. One of the players was drafted by the Philadelphia Phillies in 2019, and during the previous couple of seasons, two were drafted by the Cleveland Indians, one each by the Houston Astros, New York Mets, Seattle Mariners, and Toronto Blue Jays.[9]

Over the past few seasons members of the team have committed to colleges including Duke, Eastern Kentucky, Florida State, Georgetown, Johns Hopkins, LaSalle, Maryland, Miami, MIT, Navy, North Carolina, Notre Dame, Penn, Penn State, South Carolina, St. Joseph's, Stanford, Virginia, Virginia Tech, and West Virginia.[10]

Although some might look at Gordon's professional playing career as a short time in the major leagues without any evident impact on baseball, he sees his experience as a positive. "I was able to achieve a childhood dream. Now I can use all of my experiences and everything I've learned and pass it on to the young people of today and help them achieve their dream," he said.

ONE-HIT WONDERS

SOURCES

All minor-league and major-league information and stats came from Baseball-Reference.com.

The author had personal interviews with Keith Gordon on July 10, December 10, December 14, 2019 and September 16, 2020. Unless otherwise attributed, all quotations come from these interviews.

NOTES

1. https://www.statista.com/statistics/191626/participants-in-baseball-in-the-us-since-2006/
2. http://hsbaseballweb.com/inside_the_numbers.htm
3. https://www.sonicsrising.com/pages/1974-seattle-supersonics-nba-draft
4. Keith Gordon interview. July 10, 2019.
5. Keith Gordon interview, September 16, 2020.
6. Keith Gordon interview, September 16, 2020.
7. Keith Gordon interview. December 10, 2019.
8. Keith Gordon interview. December 14, 2019.
9. www.midatlanticredsox.net/copy-of-teams-2
10. www.midatlanticredsox.net/copy-of-teams-2.

BOBBY GUINDON

By Bill Nowlin

Bobby Guindon in 1964.

Bobby Guindon's major-league career spanned nine days in 1964, but he worked hard for six more years hoping for another shot, even converting from a first baseman/outfielder to a pitcher after a horrific encounter with a snow blower permanently hampered his ability to grip a baseball bat.

Robert Joseph Guindon was born just down the street from Boston's Fenway Park, in the bordering town of Brookline, Massachusetts, on September 4, 1943. His parents were Henry and Mary Guindon, and they had three other children – Henry Jr., Paul, and Marie. The family lived in Roslindale at the time, later moving to West Roxbury. Henry Guindon worked in the retail shoe business as a salesman for Coward Shoe. May Guindon was a homemaker, "a very, very good homemaker," Bob Guindon said in a February 2018 interview. "She sewed at home and she also worked along with her sister, who owned a dress shop. And she also made curtains. She loved to sew. The shop was in the White City, a little area at the end of the MTA tracks around Forest Hills. It was kind of like a village within a village. It was a small area, with everyone involved with other families. All the parents and mothers knew exactly where their kids were and where the other kids were. It was just a nice place to live."[1]

The Guindon parents discouraged him from playing sports. "Bobby had a blood disease when he was very young," Mary Guindon said the day he signed with the Boston Red Sox, "and the doctor said he would never be able to engage in sports. Since then we were always worried. He was big for his age and had to play with the older boys and the field is far away from our house. We were afraid he'd get hurt and we wanted him to try for college instead."[2] He was indeed an all-scholastic honoree his last three years in high school.[3]

He had been discouraged from playing Little League when the family had first moved to the West Roxbury neighborhood of Boston because he was already large and strong for his age and local League officials felt he would overpower the other children.[4]

Bobby attended the Robert Gould Shaw School in West Roxbury and then Boston English High School. He played basketball and ran track, but by age 16, it was his baseball playing that was already attracting the attention of local scouts. He played first base for Boston English, and semipro ball in the summertime for the Malden City Club in the Suburban Twilight League. He led that league in home runs and RBIs in the summer of 1960.[5]

In 1960 he became the only player in the country to make the Hearst All-Stars two years in a row, one of the top 18 players selected in the six weeks of tryouts and games in the national competition. He was 15 years old at the time he played in the 1959 game at Yankee Stadium, which he believes made him the youngest player to appear in the national Hearst

ONE-HIT WONDERS

game.[6] Wilbur Wood, also from the Boston area, was selected in 1959. Wood won the game and Guindon was 2-for-5 with a single and a double.

Manager Ossie Vitt predicted they'd be back at Yankee Stadium playing in big-league uniforms after they were old enough to sign. "They're the two kids who came through when the pressure was on. We could have blown the game big, but with Wood pitching and Guindon coming up with that hit we broke through and it was all downhill from there."[7]

One of his favorite days at the plate came in a game between English High and Watertown High School in 1960. "We were behind 8-2 entering the last of the ninth. I batted twice in the inning and hit consecutive homers to drive in five runs and we rallied to win."[8]

A *Boston Globe* report said that Guindon came to Fenway Park for the 1960 Hearst trials limping due to a hurt ankle and figured he had no chance to make the team, but the left-handed youngster pulled three of the five pitches he was thrown into the bullpens in right field.[9] He had struck out in the championship Hearst game at Yankee Stadium in the summer of 1960, but not before hitting three "foul ball homers" into the upper deck. At age 16, he was already 6-feet-1 and weighed 185 pounds; he later added another inch and is listed with a playing weight of 195 pounds. He attracted the attention of a number of former big-league players who took time out to help tutor him. "Mr. [Eddie] Waitkus has been wonderful to me," Guindon said in July 1960. "He's been out to every one of our games for three weeks and he gets out on the field during our practice and gives me advice [on fielding at first base.]"[10]

He was scouted heavily during his senior year at Boston English. He hit .538 in his final high school season. In the end, it was reported that 14 clubs made offers, each team representative given a half-hour to make his pitch to Bobby and his parents. The winning team was the Boston Red Sox, who offered a reported $135,000 signing bonus, which at the time was said to be $10,000 more than the largest bonus previously paid (to Lew Krausse of the Athletics two days earlier).[11]

Mary Guindon said, "We've always been Red Sox fans." Bobby himself said they selected the Red Sox because, "they made the top offer and I've always wanted to play for them." Mary Guindon added, "Naturally, we wanted him to be close to home and we're glad that he's going to be."[12]

These were the years between the bonus rule and the major-league draft. There were no player agents yet. How did he know what to ask for? It turns out he didn't know. Bob Guindon told the story at length in the February 2018 interview:

"My parents were hard-working people. They had no concept about working as a professional baseball player. My dad always felt as though it was a game. If it got in the way of school, you wouldn't be able to play. They never watched any of my games, before the Hearst games at Yankee Stadium. They just had no idea. It was all a big surprise to them. They didn't have any reason to come watch my games, or they just couldn't.

"Four or five scouts started to call. They talked to my parents. They could talk to me back then, but that was useless because I didn't know anything – what to say. They would talk to my parents and say they were very interested, and they would like to be considered, to make an offer to me for my contract when I graduated from high school. They [my parents] didn't know what that meant.

"We had a friend of ours who was in the newspaper business, by the name of Ralph Wheeler. He was with the *Globe*, I think, and he was the high school reporter. He come over to the house once and talked to my mom and dad and said this was going to happen. The scouts are very interested in talking with you and making an offer. They asked, 'What do we do?' So he helped guide them a little of what to expect. He had some knowledge and it was his recommendation – by this time, there were 10 or 12 teams that wanted to bid on my contract. They were shocked. They said, 'Well, we don't know much about this. We don't know how to handle it.' Back then there was no attorneys involved, no agents. Nothing like that. He said, 'Well, there's a lot of interest. To make it easy for you people, and for them as well, set aside a day after graduation. Just pick a day, a day after or two days after, and give them each a half-hour or whatever they need - but keep it less than an hour – give them a time they can come out.'

"So they did. My dad was working all the time, but my mother would take those calls and set them up with their appointments. I don't know what the hell is going on; I had no idea. As far as money was concerned, we were pretty excited because they were throwing around numbers of $10,000 or $15,000. My parents thought that was just crazy."

Given the times, that was more than his father would ever make in a year as a shoe salesman.

"Oh, absolutely. It was crazy to even consider this. My dad was going to take the day off to make sure I got the right kind of support. There was about 13 or 14

ONE-HIT WONDERS

clubs interested. They were all going to make an offer. They filled up the schedule.

"And then the night before they were all to come in, we had them calling us and canceling. Wishing us well. They were talking to my parents, obviously, saying how happy they were to have scouted me, what a nice boy I was, congratulations for bringing up a wonderful boy, 'You people must be nice' and 'We wish you luck. Be very careful with the kind of money that you're going to get.' It was just too much for my parents. They started to believe that maybe – just maybe - it *could* be $10,000.

"The next day, they started to come in, and the first guy that come in, he was apologizing. He wanted to show up, to show his respects to my parents, but said, 'My team is just not going to make an offer. We think he's wonderful and yada, yada, but we're just not going to be able to afford the kind of numbers that we hear are being passed around.' He's ready to walk out the door and my father asks, 'You're not going to say anything? Are you sure? You don't want to leave us with some kind of number? Well, give us an idea.' So he says, 'I'll tell you what, Sir. I'll just give you a verbal offer. If you don't get an offer over $35,000 today, you call this telephone number and I'll be here in a half an hour.' And he left. And my mother started bawling her eyes out.

"The whole day, my parents were very emotional. The Red Sox came in as the last team. I'm not going to mention the other teams. It doesn't matter. But the Red Sox came in – this was Neil Mahoney -- and said, 'OK, we would love to have you. Mr. Yawkey has given me permission to offer you whatever you need for us to have you on our team. But we're not interested in making this a bidding war. Just tell us, would you like to play for the Red Sox? If you really want to do that, then we're very interested in having you.' He asked me, 'Do you want to play with the Red Sox?' I said, 'Yes, I do.' He said, 'OK, then tell us what it is that we have to match.' My dad said, 'It's $125,000.' Neil Mahoney almost fell off the couch. [laugh]

"He said, 'Hold on. I have to call back Mr. Yawkey. We expected it to be high but we had no idea it would be that high.' It was the highest ever [highest bonus ever offered to that point in history]. It was just crazy.

"I had three other teams that had offered over $100,000. There was one other team that had offered me $125,000.

"I think there were some players [the Red Sox] had missed [just earlier] and I think the local press was giving them a little bit of a hard time about not showing as much interest in the local talent. I think they felt it would be smart not to pass on me at that point. I was that young. I was on all these all-star teams – national teams as well as state all-star teams for three years. So there I was, and it began."

Guindon was assigned to play in Alpine, Texas, for the Sophomore League (Class D) Alpine Cowboys. In 1961, he got into 64 games playing first base, and hit .284 with 43 runs batted in. That winter he worked on a crew surveying for an engineering firm in Boston.

In the spring of 1962, Guindon went to spring training with the Boston Red Sox. He did indeed play closer to home in '62, in the New York-Penn League (also Class D) for the Olean Red Sox in Olean, New York. He played in 111 games and hit .320 with 37 homers and 121 RBIs. Guindon led the league in the latter two categories and was named Rookie of the Year. He had been the only unanimous selection to the league All-Star team.

That fall, he worked out in the outfield during the Florida Instructional League. Rico Petrocelli roomed with him and later said what Guindon had already acknowledged – that he felt a lot of pressure due to signing the large contract. He needed to forget that, Petrocelli said, "and play every day as though he didn't have a dime for a cup of coffee. If he does that, he'll make it big."[13]

He had, as one might expect, taken a good deal of flak from other players, some good-naturedly and some likely with an edge, regarding the big bonus he'd been given. In spring training in 1962, he said a few years later, "When I got into the batting cage, they needled me pretty good. I couldn't take it. I talked back to them fresh and acted like a pop=off." He told one of them he'd wrap the bat around his neck. Another time, when he couldn't even hit the ball out of the batting cage, "I stepped out and threw the bat all the way into the first base stands." He confessed, "I think I pulled all that stuff because I thought I was another Ted Williams. I found out the hard way I wasn't… There are times I wish that I never got the money. I mean that. Sometimes I wish I was just another kid that signed for nothing and that no one paid any attention to."[14] He let it be known that he'd lost 30 pounds during his time with Alpine, worried about shaping up to expectations.

Before 1963 spring training began, Guindon had asked not to train in Scottsdale with the Boston ball club, but to go to spring training with Boston's Triple-A club, the Seattle Rainiers.[15] He was assigned to play Double-A ball in 1963, for the Reading

ONE-HIT WONDERS

(Pennsylvania) Red Sox in the Eastern League. It was a down year; he played in 118 games but only hit .238 and drove in 56 runs. That fall he returned for more work in the Instructional League, and later said that he had learned a lot at Reading.

It was in 1963 that Bob married Patricia Dorsey. She lived in West Roxbury, too. "We knew each other for…forever, it seemed like. She was my sweetheart. I was hers."

In 1964 he was assigned to Seattle and improved to .264 in the higher classification, with again 56 RBIs but with 20 homers. The Red Sox finished in eighth place in 1964, 27 games out of first, and had a decision to make as to whether or not to protect Guindon in the draft. The team wasn't going anywhere so they figured they'd give him a look.

Guindon had a very busy couple of weeks. He was called up to the Red Sox on September 10. He joined the team, and became a father on September 14. Five days later, he had his major-league debut. "A very busy time, yes. A little bit of stress on my part. Of course, my wife had the biggest challenge. But, yeah, to have all that going on at once…and I was a kid…I had just turned 21 on the 4th."[16]

Pattie and Bob's son Christopher Guindon was joined about 2 ½ years later by Craig. "Christopher has two wonderful children, both girls. He lives in Houston. Craig lives in Dallas and he has two boys and a girl."

His major-league debut came in the September 19 game against the visiting Minnesota Twins, pinch-running for Dick Stuart in the bottom of the seventh inning. The next batter up hit into the third out of the inning, and Guindon was replaced. The next day, he pinch-hit and drew a base on balls, but again languished on the base paths. He got a start on September 23 in Detroit, playing first base, and was 0-for-4 in the game with one strikeout. On the 26th, he pinch-ran again. On the 27th, still at Tiger Stadium, he got another start, this time playing left field. He struck out his first time up, and his second, but then stroked a double to left field in the top of the seventh off Joe Sparma. In top of the ninth, he got a fourth at-bat. There were two outs and the Red Sox were losing, 3-0. He struck out for the third time on the day. It proved to be his last appearance in a big-league game.

There was no way to know that at the time, and Guindon put in a lot of hard work over ensuing years hoping to make it to the majors again.

Playing the two positions, first base and left field, in the two games he had started, Guindon handled eight fielding chances without an error. He might have played more for the Red Sox, at first base, but Dick Stuart – the reigning American League RBI king – was in the hunt for the title again. Stuart finished with four RBIs fewer than Baltimore's Brooks Robinson.

So Guindon finished the season with one base hit. That earned him a chapter in the book *One Hit Wonders*.[17] "I only had one hit," he said in 2018, "but I had two line drives that were caught. Those don't count. You never see those in the stats, but if [those had dropped in] instead of being 1-for-8, you were 3-for-8 and all of a sudden the stats count."

Guindon trained with the Red Sox at Scottsdale in 1965 and had a legitimate shot at the first-base job but came up short and was cut from the squad on April 5 and sent to Florida to join the Toronto Maple Leafs, Boston's Triple-A club of the day. He had a very rough year. In early May he was obtained by the Seattle Angels, the Triple-A club of the California Angels, on option from the Red Sox. In 31 games, he batted just .207 with 14 RBIs.

On June 13 the Red Sox recalled him from Seattle, and placed him with Toronto after they brought Tony Horton up from Toronto to play in Boston. He had liked playing in Seattle, but now found himself with the Maple Leafs. He hit .206 with 24 RBIs in 83 games, more or less the same as he had hit in Seattle. On October 22, Boston sold his contract outright to Toronto, which made him subject to the minor-league draft. He was dejected. "I wish now I'd gone to college," he said. With a wife and child, he was working in a clothing store and taking a real estate course.at night.[18]

He was, indeed, still quite young. Dick Williams, his manager in Toronto, said, "He was confused and wanted to quit after the season. But I told him he could

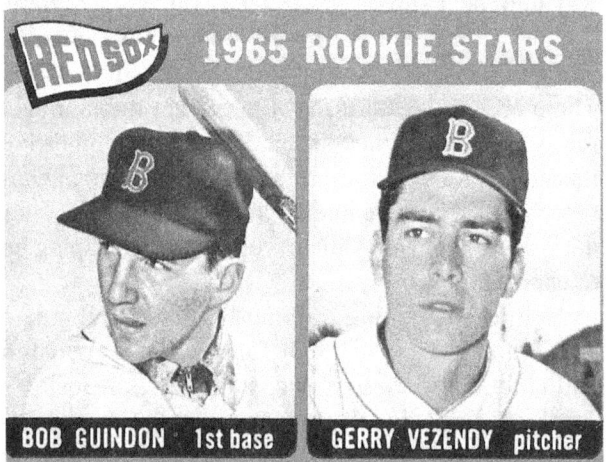

ONE-HIT WONDERS

be my first baseman next year. He's only 21 and has all the equipment to be a good ball player."[19]

Guindon started the season with Toronto, but didn't fare that well at the plate, batting .225 after 78 games. At the start of August, he simply left the club and appeared to be missing, but he had spent a couple of days driving back to Boston. He let Neil Mahoney know that he wasn't happy, that he wasn't playing enough.[20] It was worked out that he would play in Double A for the Pittsfield Red Sox. He got into 31 games and hit .330. But he was far from satisfied. He said he couldn't play for an organization that didn't really want him. "I still want to play baseball," he said, "but I won't play for the Red Sox. If they won't release me, I'll quit." Sox GM Haywood Sullivan wasn't pleased with the attitude. "As long as he feels that way, then we don't want him. Yes, we're trying to deal him off."[21]

They didn't trade him, tempers cooled, Mahoney offered some advice, and Guindon played for Pittsfield again in 1967, batting .242 in 80 games. But he also started trying his hand at pitching (even though he had never pitched before, even in high school), and was 2-0 with a 0.69 earned run average in four starts and four other pitching appearances. "I think Bobby can make it as a pitcher. I really do," said Pittsfield manager Billy Gardner. "He's got the arm and looks really good. Bob throws as good as any left-handed pitcher in this league. He has a heck of a slider, a good fork ball and a fast ball that really moves."[22]

As it happens, over the winter of 1966-67, Guindon had caught his right hand in a snow blower and it had taken somewhere around 100 stitches to close the cuts on the two fingers which were damaged. He was late to spring training, and apparently couldn't grip the bat quite the way he previously could. "I don't have tendons there anymore," he revealed a few years later.[23] But his left hand was still good, and he proved he could pitch. He filled in during a stretch of makeup doubleheaders. He even threw a 5-0 seven-inning no-hitter in the first game of a doubleheader against York on August 25. Two runners reached base by way of walks.[24]

The Boston Red Sox won the American League pennant in 1967, under skipper Dick Williams. And Williams, who had managed Toronto when Guindon skipped out in '66, said that Guindon would never play for the Red Sox if he had anything to say about it: "If Guindon comes, I leave."[25]

Guindon stayed in the organization, though, for another year. He went back to Florida Instruction League that fall to work on his pitching (and worked in a combined no-hitter there), and then started 20 games for Pittsfield in 1968. He was 10-6 with a 2.46 ERA. Pittsfield won the Eastern League pennant that year.

In the December 2 minor-league draft, Tulsa selected Guindon from Pittsfield and Guindon joined the St. Louis Cardinals system. He was assigned to the Arkansas Travelers (Double-A) in the Texas League. He didn't get much mound work – only 21 innings – and was 1-1 with a 4.67 ERA, but the Travs had him play in 92 games at first base. He hit .281 in 113 games.

His final season in pro ball was with the Triple-A Tulsa Oilers in 1970. Again, he was used more as a position player, only working a total of six innings as a pitcher. He played in 53 games in the outfield and 23 at first base. He hit .276 with 44 RBIs. Guindon resigned after the season.

He had begun training to become a bank officer with a bank in Boston, in case baseball didn't work out.

In his post-baseball career, Guindon earned exceptional success in business at a variety of different positions. During the offseasons he had worked doing outdoor surveying work for an engineering firm for 70 cents an hour. He went to school at night and got his real estate broker's license, and spent two offseasons working for a real estate firm. Then he got the invitation to join State Street Bank and Trust in their advanced executive training program. When he saw that baseball wasn't going to pan out for him, he already had this other opportunity available to him and he worked for State Street for three years after retiring as a ballplayer.

Another friend invited him to apply for a position with Wang Laboratories, and he started in sales for the rapidly-growing Massachusetts-based computer company. He worked for Wang for the next 14 years. From sales, he become involved in sales training, even working overseas. He then moved to Chicago as a district sales manager, then came back to Massachusetts to head up the company's services department as the company moved more in the direction of providing services such as programming. He later became a regional vice president.

After 14 years, the Guindons bought a country inn in Jackson, New Hampshire – the Inn at Thorn Hill. They ran that for three years, then sold it. Another opportunity came up. "A friend of mine had been doing a wonderful job helping a small company grow. They reached a point where they needed to expand their executive group and reached out to me. I don't know if you've ever heard of Stephen R. Covey. He wrote *The 7 Habits of Highly Effective People*. It sold over

ONE-HIT WONDERS

20 million copies. He had a top executive training program. I went out and helped them grow and grow and grow, until we merged with another company about 15 years ago. And I retired. It worked out tremendously. We all were happy." He had served as Chief Operating Officer and as Senior Vice President.

Now he and Pattie live in Florida and have been enjoying retirement.

Looking back on his baseball career, Guindon says, "Ten years is a good run, isn't it? My baseball career was full of challenges. But I enjoyed some wonderful years in the minor leagues. It was a great experience. I tried hard. We played hard. A lot of great things happened to me in baseball. I had my chances. I had a lot of chances. The Red Sox gave me chances. The Cardinals gave me chances. I played Triple A for a long time, and I guess I wasn't good enough. I'm happy going to bed every night – and I have been since I left the game – feeling I did the best I could."

SOURCES

In addition to the sources noted in this biography, the author also accessed Guindon's player file and player questionnaire from the National Baseball Hall of Fame, the *Encyclopedia of Minor League Baseball*, Retrosheet.org, and Baseball-Reference.com. Thanks to Rod Nelson of SABR's Scouts Committee.

NOTES

1. Author interview with Bob Guindon on February 23, 2018. Unless otherwise indicated, all quotations attributed to Guindon come from this interview.
2. Will McDonough, Sox Pay Top Bonus," *Boston Globe*, June 10, 1961: 15.
3. Warren Walworth, "Sox Get Guindon With $135G Bonus," *Boston American*, June 10, 1961: 3.
4. Red Hoffman, "Guindon Expects to Reach Majors by 1963," *Boston Traveler*, June 10, 1961: 4.
5. Will McDonough, "Bird Dogs Flying to Hub Again," *Boston Globe*, April 6,1961: 39.
6. Author interview.
7. Bill McSweeny, "Sandlot Aces Hits on B'way," *Boston American*, August 19, 1959: 17.
8. Red Hoffman.
9. Art Ballou, "Bird Dogs Like Hub's Guindon Like They Liked Elbie, Murphy," *Boston Globe*, September 4, 1960: 54.
10. Pat Horne, "Waitkus Aids Hearst Star," *Boston American*, July 27, 1960: 35.
11. Will McDonough, "Sox Pay Top Bonus." His signing was credited to Red Sox farm director Neil Mahoney. See "Guindon Thrice Honored, HR Mark Within Reach," *Boston Globe*, August 19, 1962: 75.
12. McDonough, "Sox Pay Top Bonus."
13. Ed Costello, "Murphy Case Tops Guindon," *Boston Herald*, March 31, 1963: 200.
14. Will McDonough, "Guindon Poorer, Wiser Than in '62," *Boston Globe*, March 3, 1965: 21.
15. Hy Hurwitz, "Guindon Spurns Scottsdale Camp," *Boston Globe*, February 13, 1963: 16.
16. Author interview. "She came back three weeks early. She wanted to stay and have the baby in Seattle. Her mother wanted her to come back. I had had some indication that I might be called up at the end of the year. Having a baby in Seattle alone and all that responsibility when I might go with the Red Sox, she didn't want to do it but she agreed to come back early. We had an apartment in Foxborough. We had that lined up, to be able to move into that whenever we got back home."
17. George Rose, *One Hit Wonders* (iUniverse, 2004). Second edition 2009 available at www.baseballwonders.com.
18. Tim Horgan, "Guindon, 22, At Crossroads," *Boston Traveler*, October 22, 1965: 37.
19. Herb Ralby, "Toronto Players Seen Great Help to Sox," *Boston Globe*, September 30, 1865: 50. Guindon was 22 at the time, but indeed quite young.
20. "Guindon in Boston, Future Still in Air," *Boston Globe*, August 4, 1966: 41.
21. Tim Horgan, "Bonus Gone, Guindon Now Seeks Trade," *Boston Traveler*, December 15, 1966: 41.
22. George Sullivan, "Guindon Fighting Back As Pitcher," *Boston Traveler*, June 14, 1967: 53.
23. John Ferguson, "Home-Run Punch Not An Uppercut, Guindon Discovers," *The Sporting News*, May 16, 1970: 33.
24. A good account of the no-hitter is provided by Roger O'Gara, "Guindon Glitters With A No-Hit Job," *The Sporting News*, September 9, 1967: 35.
25. Larry Claflin, "O'Connell Feels Sox Draft Cupboard Bare," *Boston Record American*, November 28, 1967: 42.

JOHN LOUIS HAIRSTON SR.

By Richard Cuicchi

A case could be made for the Hairston family to be labeled the "First Family of Baseball." Former major leaguer Sam Hairston Sr. and his ballplaying descendants' careers spanned nearly 70 years, including the Negro Leagues of the 1940s, the early days of the integration of major-league baseball, and the modern-day game. The family includes three generations of players, one of only four families in history who can make the claim as major leaguers.[1] Their baseball family tree has many branches, with 10 members who played for or were drafted by professional baseball organizations. One of the second-generation players was John Louis Hairston Sr.,[2] whose major-league batting record included only one hit.

Hairston's first call-up to the majors occurred in 1969 during one of the most exciting, as well as most depressing, times in Chicago Cubs history. During what is normally one of the highlights of a major-league player's career, Hairston's big-league promotion turned out to be bittersweet. An injury in the minors in 1970 affected his ability to get another opportunity, and thus his major-league career consisted of only three games.

Hairston was the son of Sam Hairston Sr., a former Negro League player and one of the early African-American trailblazers in the Chicago White Sox organization. When the younger Hairston made his major-league debut with the Cubs on September 6, 1969, they became the first African-American father-son duo in the majors. They were the first Black catchers for their respective teams. The catcher position was the last in Cubs history to be integrated.

Sam Hairston Sr. originally played in the Negro Leagues with the Birmingham Black Barons and Indianapolis Clowns. He was the Negro Leagues' Triple Crown winner in 1950.[3] He became the second African-American player in Chicago White Sox history on July 21, 1951 (after Minnie Miñoso debuted on May 1), four years after Jackie Robinson broke the major-league color barrier. Sam Hairston Sr.'s major-league career consisted of only four games. After he retired as a player in 1960, he became a well-respected longtime coach and scout for the White Sox until the late 1990s. His White Sox connection would have influence over several of his offspring's baseball pursuits.

Sam Hairston Sr. had another son, Jerry Hairston Sr., who played 14 seasons with the White Sox and had two of his own sons, Jerry Jr. and Scott, with extensive careers in the majors.

The three generations of Hairstons add up to the most representatives from one family to play at the major-league level, tying the Delahanty brothers (Ed, Frank, Jim, Joe, and Tom). All five Hairston major leaguers had a Chicago connection: Sam Sr. and Jerry

ONE-HIT WONDERS

Sr. played for the White Sox, while John, Jerry Jr., and Scott played for the Cubs.

John Louis Hairston Sr. was born on August 27, 1944, in Birmingham, Alabama, to Sam Hairston Sr., and Jessie (Merritt) Hairston.[4] He played baseball, football, and basketball at Hooper High School. He led his baseball team to three conference championships.[5] After graduating in 1962, he attended Southern University in Baton Rouge. He led his team to the 1965 NAIA national baseball tournament. Southern had a quick exit though, losing shutouts to Sam Houston State (Texas) and Glassboro State (New Jersey).[6]

Hairston was selected by the Cubs in the 16th round of the first major-league baseball amateur draft, in 1965. He was the third catcher picked in the draft by the Cubs, after Ken Rudolph (second round) and Ronald Drake (sixth round but did not sign).

In 1966 he was one of four Hairstons in pro baseball. Sam Sr. was a coach in the White Sox organization while his brother Sam Jr. and his uncle Jack Hairston were playing in a rookie league on the same team in the White Sox organization.[7]

Despite two uneventful seasons in the low minors in his first two years, Hairston was one of 15 Cubs farmhands invited to spring training in Scottsdale, Arizona, in 1967. He was one of four catchers returned to the minors.[8] He was assigned to Class-A Lodi, where he began to flourish. He was named Topps Player of the Month for July in the California League.[9] For the season Hairston had a slash line of .280/.380/.456, with 14 home runs and 76 RBIs in 121 games. He was named to the league's postseason all-star team.

Hairston earned a promotion to Double-A San Antonio (Texas League) for the 1968 season, but his overall numbers regressed with a .239/.308/.343 slash line, 7 home runs and 30 RBIs.

Hairston's 1969 season started at San Antonio in a similar fashion, but on May 12 he received a promotion to Tacoma (Pacific Coast League) when Bill Heath was called up by Chicago. He responded exceptionally to Triple-A pitching with the best stint of his career, batting .451 with 2 home runs and 9 RBIs in 25 games. His four singles in a game on August 18 against Phoenix were one of his highlights.[10]

A week later, on his 25th birthday, Hairston was called up by the Chicago Cubs to shore up an injury-plagued catching corps when outfielder Jim Qualls went on the disabled list with an injured right shoulder. Hairston's short stint with the Cubs occurred during one of the most momentous times in their history.

The Cubs had held first place since Opening Day. By August 16, they enjoyed their largest lead (nine games) of the season. By the time Hairston arrived on August 27 their lead over the New York Mets had dwindled to 3½ games. The Mets had reached that point by winning 11 of 12 games since August 16. The Cubs were in panic mode to maintain their lead.

Cubs manager Leo Durocher stuck with veteran Randy Hundley as his everyday catcher, and Hairston wound up playing sparingly. On the 50th anniversary of the Cubs' ill-fated season, he said, "Randy was having a rough time. I wondered on the bench, 'Why not put in someone else?'"[11] Hairston's assessment was correct: Hundley played in 36 consecutive games from August 24 until the end of the season, sitting out only 24 total innings. During that stretch he had a slash line of .153/.237/.220.

Hairston made his major-league debut on September 6, replacing left fielder Billy Williams in the sixth inning against the Pittsburgh Pirates. He flied out in his first major-league at-bat, against lefty Bob Veale in the seventh inning. Veale caught him looking in a strikeout in the ninth inning as the Pirates won, 13-4.

The Mets defeated the Cubs on September 8 and 9, effectively putting a nail in the coffin for the Cubs' season. Baseball lore has it that an errant black cat brought bad luck to the Cubs when it ran onto the field in front of their dugout during the game on September 9. When the Mets took two games from Montreal in a doubleheader the next day, they took possession of first place and never relinquished it for the remainder of the season.

Hairston got into the game against Philadelphia on September 18 as a pinch-hitter for Ted Abernathy in the seventh inning. With Hundley and Don Young on base, Hairston swung hard and hit a roller up the third-base line. Pitcher Grant Jackson fielded the ball and made a hurried throw over the head of first baseman Dick Allen. Two runs scored to give the Cubs a 3-2 lead. Hairston was credited with his first (and only) major-league hit. The Phillies scored three times in the next inning and won the game, 5-3.

On the last day of the season, against the Mets (who had clinched the division title on September 24), Hairston finally got a start as catcher and struck out against Gary Gentry in his only plate appearance in the third inning. Although it was little consolation for their disastrous season, the Cubs won the game, 5-3.

The Mets finished eight games ahead of the Cubs and went on win their dramatic first-ever World Series championship. The Cubs didn't recover from their collapse until they won their first World Series in over 100 years in 2016.

Looking ahead to the 1970 season, the Cubs didn't have an established backup behind Hundley. Hairston had been one of six catchers used in 1969. Going into spring training, Hairston, Ken Rudolph, and Randy Bobb were tabbed as potential candidates. However, when Hundley suffered a chip fracture of his left thumb in late March, the Cubs weren't comfortable with their relatively inexperienced backup receiver corps. Eleven-year veteran catcher J.C. Martin was acquired in a trade with the Mets for Bobb.[12]

Hairston returned to Tacoma to start the regular season. He played in 44 games before suffering a serious knee injury on June 3 that stemmed from a fight triggered by a collision play at home plate. Hairston was the catcher when Portland baserunner Bobb, his former teammate, ran home from third base on a groundball to third with the bases loaded. To break up a double play, Bobb slid hard into Hairston, who took the force-out throw at the plate and wheeled to throw out the batter at first base. A fight broke out between Bobb and Hairston, and the benches of both teams emptied onto the field before order was restored by the umpire. It was later determined that Hairston suffered torn ligaments in his knee and required immediate surgery, ending his season.[13]

The 1971 season found Hairston fighting for a backup catcher spot with Triple-A Des Moines in the Oakland A's organization.[14] However, he started the regular season with their Double-A affiliate Birmingham, where he had a good showing with a .278 average, 5 home runs, and 32 RBIs in 69 games as an outfielder and first baseman. Cleveland Indians Triple-A affiliate Wichita purchased Hairston shortly after midseason; he played behind the plate again and posted a .286 average, 5 home runs, and 15 RBIs in 33 games.[15]

Still suffering from the effects of the knee injury, Hairston retired in 1971 at age 26. He said after his career had ended, "If that (injury) hadn't happened I think I would have become Randy Hundley's backup. Leo Durocher liked me."[16]

Hairston married Evelyn Rose Lagarde in 1966.[17] The family's baseball bloodlines continued when they encouraged their sons (John Jr., Jeff, and Jason) to play the sport. Each reached a level of success, ultimately being drafted and playing in the minors.

John Hairston Jr. was drafted by the Chicago White Sox in 1985 out of high school. He played three seasons in the White Sox organization and one in the Yankees system between 1991 and 1996. He had four daughters (Alex, Juli, Mady, and Lizzie), all of whom continued the Hairston athletic legacy by playing college soccer.[18]

Jeff Hairston was drafted out of high school by the Pittsburgh Pirates in the 11th round in 1992. He played two seasons in the rookie Gulf Coast League.

Jason Hairston was drafted out of high school in the 10th round by the Baltimore Orioles in 1994, but he chose to attend Washington State University. He was selected by the Atlanta Braves in the 16th round in 1997 and played two minor-league seasons.

John Hairston's brother Jerry Sr. stayed in baseball after his 16-year major-league career. He became a minor-league manager (seven years in rookie leagues with the White Sox) and coach. In addition to Jerry Sr.'s major-league sons, Jerry Jr. and Scott, son Justin was drafted in the 50th round by the White Sox in 1998.

Hairston's brother, Sam Hairston Jr., missed an opportunity to advance in pro baseball because of his military service in Vietnam. He had played briefly in the rookie leagues for the White Sox organization in 1966 and 1967.

John Hairston said in the book *The Cubs of '69*, "I didn't even have a cup of coffee. I was just the cream in somebody's coffee."[19] However, he never questioned his decision to quit baseball at an early age. He said, "I had a chance to raise my children, which was more important to me than if I had won four World Series. That may sound crazy to some other people who'd say, 'What's the matter with you.' But my children were more valuable to me than making a couple of bucks."[20]

Jerry Hairston Sr. gives credit to his older brother for being a role model. He said, "He really helped me out not only in baseball, but also in life. What to look for in the community, how to stay out of trouble. He was an inspiration for me.[21]

Third-generation Scott Hairston remarked about his baseball heritage, "It's nice to be part of a unique family, and I hope I can pass it on to my children."[22] It would be unprecedented if the Hairston baseball family tree was eventually extended with a fourth-generation ballplayer.[23]

After retiring, Hairston obtained master's degrees in physical education and counseling and taught at the high school and community college levels in Portland, Oregon.[24] He also coached baseball for several years in the Portland Interscholastic League.[25]

ONE-HIT WONDERS

SOURCES

In addition to the sources cited in the Notes, the author consulted Baseball-Reference.com and the following:

Baseball Reference Bullpen. baseball-reference.com/bullpen/John_Hairston_Jr. (accessed October 25, 2019).

Dozer, Richard. "No Relief for Cubs; Lose to Phils, 5-3," *Chicago Tribune*, September 19, 1969: 3, 1.

Rini, Joe. "Scott Hairston Is Heir to a Baseball Legacy," *Rockland County Times* (Nanuet, New York), May 31, 2012. rocklandtimes.com/2012/05/31/scott-hairston-is-heir-to-a-baseball-legacy/. (accessed October 25, 2019).

NOTES

1 The other three-generation families to play in the majors are the Bells (Gus, Buddy, David, Mike), the Boones (Ray, Bob, Aaron, Bret), and the Colemans (Joe P., Joe H., and Casey). The players Jayson Werth, his grandfather John Richard "Dick" Schofield, and his uncle Richard Craig "Dick" Schofield are sometimes referred to as a three-generation major-league family.

2 Hereafter in this biography, "Hairston" without a first name, refers to John Louis Hairston Sr.

3 Rory Costello, "Sam Hairston Sr.," SABR Bioproject. sabr.org/bioproj/person/211ac89e. (accessed October 25, 2019).

4 Costello.

5 *1970 Chicago Cubs Official Roster Book, Press-Radio-TV*: 12.

6 NAIA Championship History. Naia.Org/Sports/Bsb/Records/BSB_Championship.Pdf. (accessed October 25, 2019).

7 Costello.

8 "Gigon Signed to Cubs Pact; 21 Players Sent to Minors," *The Sporting News*, April 8, 1967: 22.

9 "Millan Named Topps Player of the Month," *The Sporting News*, August 19, 1967: 21.

10 "Pacific Coast League Roundup: August 18," *The Sporting News*, September 6, 1969: 37.

11 George Castle, "'He Was Inspiration to Me.' John Hairston Broke Barriers with Cubs, Motivating Next Generation," *Chicago Tribune*, August 20, 2019. chicagotribune.com/suburbs/naperville-sun/sports/ct-nvs-spt-baseball-chicago-cubs-john-hairston-st-082119-20190820-lpikj7htf5f4zfry3ldlxmyjry-story.html. (accessed October 25, 2019).

12 Edgar Munzel, "Martin Fills Cub Void – Sub for Injured Hundley," *The Sporting News*, April 11, 1970: 52.

13 "Bobb's Slide Boils into Fight at Plate," *Oregonian* (Portland), June 4, 1970: 3, 1.

14 Ed Honeywell, "Parents Send Help to Bolster Young T-Cubs," *Tacoma News Tribune*, April 5, 1971.

15 "Deals of the Week," *The Sporting News*, July 24, 1971: 36.

16 Rick Talley, *The Cubs of '69* (New York: Contemporary Books, 1990), 253-254.

17 *The Sporting News* Player Contract Cards. digital.la84.org/digital/collection/p17103coll3/id/63259/rec/1. (accessed December 17, 2019).

18 Lael Tate and Jessica Griepenburg, "Family First," *Grant Magazine*, grant-magazine.com/hairston/. November 11, 2015. (accessed October 25, 2019).

19 Talley.

20 Castle.

21 Castle.

22 John Shea, "Hairston's Lengthy Baseball Heritage," sfgate.com/sports/article/Hairston-s-lengthy-baseball-heritage-3224261.php, July 10, 2009. (accessed October 25, 2019).

23 A fourth-generation Boone was selected by the Washington Nationals in the 2017 draft. Jake Boone, son of Bret Boone, did not sign with the Nationals and entered Princeton University.

24 Castle.

25 *Oregonian*.

BILL HARMAN

By Niall Adler

Bill Harman was a shy country boy who became a leader. He was a star basketball and baseball player at the University of Virginia. As the basketball team's captain, he led the Cavaliers into the 1941 National Invitational Tournament. And then he played one summer for the Philadelphia Phillies, collecting exactly one base hit. He was a broad-shouldered, 6-foot-4 catcher, who could also pitch. He did the dirty work, cleaning up missed shots underneath the basket and playing one of baseball's most grueling positions, catcher. He was a leader, captain of both collegiate teams, and student body president. Regularly referred to as "cool under pressure," he was tested in 1945 as a Marine crewman at the Battle of Okinawa.

William Bell Harman achieved a lot as the second of four children born to Fred and Margaret (Bell) Harman on January 2, 1919, in Bridgewater, in rural Virginia's Shenandoah Valley. His brother, Fred Jr., was born a year earlier and his sister Virginia followed two years later. Sister Anne was born just before the 1930 census. Fred and Margaret, in their mid-20s when Bill was born, were farmers, living on the farm of Margaret's parents, Samuel and Sallie Bell, in North River, Virginia.

Image of Harman from the 1941 yearbook.

By 1930 Fred and Margaret and their four children were living with their mother-in-law. Fred owned a farm and they were one of the few families in the area with a radio.[1] By 1940, it was college-aged Bill, his parents, and Anne on the farm. Bridgewater is located on a bend of the North River and is susceptible to floods. Fewer than 1,000 people lived in the town during Bill's youth.

"Virginia farmers tended to fare better than farmers elsewhere, largely because of the prevalence of truck and dairy farming and the continued popularity of tobacco. Nonetheless, drought and the Great Depression in the late 1920s and early 1930s hit Virginia farmers especially hard. It would take another world war to help them recover."[2] The Harman farm was likely one of the fortunate ones, being able to send a son to boarding school and having some of life's luxuries.

In the 1930s, the State of Virginia was sending more children to school from the country to the city. And Bill, it seems, had a thirst for knowledge. Before Bill's arrival at Episcopal High in Alexandria, the school had 220 students.[3] On his departure the the school was one of the five private schools in the state to have "outstanding records in college deans' offices."[4]

For most farmers, "money for necessities was scarce—for luxuries nonexistent,"[5] so the fact that Bill's family was able to send a son to a boarding school says the family likely produced products that for "poverty-stricken people (they) could not do without, such as food, clothing, and cigarettes."[6]

Bill attended Episcopal High from 1935 to 1937 and was a member of the basketball and baseball teams. Annual tuition for the boarding school was $850 and there was a limited amount of scholarships. Bill did not receive one. Students attended from all over – New York, New Jersey, Louisiana, Alabama, and Mississippi, and as far away as Texas, Ohio, and even Ireland. The Harman farm was about 150 miles away.

Offdays consisted of Sundays and Mondays with many of the boys venturing into the District of Columbia by train. The boys would hold "hops"

ONE-HIT WONDERS

with local girls schools. The curriculum was rigorous as students also took Latin, Greek, and of course, religion.

Harman attained a leadership position at the school, serving as "monitor," an extremely high honor for students. For two years running, he was voted the school's best basketball player, but also the "most bashful." The yearbooks regularly said he was "cool under pressure."

His first year in 1935 the basketball team had its "most successful season in a decade," going 10-3. In the rivalry game against Woodbury High the newcomer, Harman, along with A.J. Wilson, led the come-from-behind victory for the first win in the series. The team's "dark horse" averaged 10-12 points per game. The *Whispers Yearbook* noted it was "unusual for a new boy to make a letter" but that didn't faze him. He was a "large boy with a few odd characteristics that made him noticeable."[7] In baseball, he was a "country boy," who made good as a dependable catcher on a young team that won two games.

The 1936 basketball team was built around Harman and another boy. Harman was the team's captain and was noted in the yearbook as "tall, rangy and smooth" with a "coolness under fire." He achieved honorable mention all-state honors. Late in the year of a .500 season, Harman hit the game-winning jumper with 15 seconds left after pouring in 16 points two games prior. Harman was one of only four returning players on the 1936 baseball team. He split time with another player at catcher, but when he hit cleanup the *Whispers Yearbook* wrote he "broke many a pitcher's heart ... (and was) a terror to opposing runners." He regularly had at least one hit in a game.

The 1937 team featured seven boys over 6 feet; Harman was the "sparkplug" who led them one win shy of the state championship. (A team outbreak of the mumps interrupted their season.) Harman was again one of "outstanding hitters" on the team, which finished just over .500.[8]

After high school, Harman went on to the University of Virginia, where he played for the freshman basketball and baseball teams, along with another talented freshman, Billy McCann. During their three years at Virginia, the Cavaliers went 49-16 on the hardwood, 28-1 at home. Rules at the time put McCann and Harman on the freshmen teams. The freshman basketball team went 9-3 and outscored opponents 440-290; Harman and McCann were regularly the leading scorers. The freshman baseball team of 1938 went undefeated and in April the "flashy Virginia catcher" homered and caught Harold Brosnan's 14-strikeout performance of Washington and Lee.[9] Harman, McCann, and Brosnan all played professional baseball.

With the two sophomores, the Cavalier basketball team went 15-5 in 1938-39, after going 6-10 the year before. They won the Big Six Virginia state championship amongst the other Virginia universities and went 10-2 against state opponents. They won their last five games of the season.

Harman, listed at 6-feet-6 (he was really a few inches shorter), began his varsity career with 13 points over the Young Italian American Progressive Club. The "big, rangy" center just missed all-state honors scoring 186 points, second to Armand Feldman.[10]

In his first varsity baseball game in 1939, Harman drove in four runs with a double and triple against Haverford.[11] The team finished 14-6 with three of the six losses coming over the last four games. The year before, the Cavaliers were 8-8. The turnaround was in large part because of McCann and Harman.

In June 1939, coach Gus Tebell led 17 players to Cooperstown, New York, to take part in a college tournament at the new Hall of Fame's Doubleday Field. They played two tune-up games against Rutgers and New Brunswick on the way up before taking on Ivy League champion Cornell and Illinois Wesleyan on June 15 and 17. The event ended in a three-way tie. Virginia defeated Cornell 8-1 on Thursday. Cornell won 3-2 in 10 innings over Illinois Wesleyan on Friday. Virginia lost to Illinois Wesleyan 10-9 in the Saturday finale. The Cavaliers lost in the bottom of the ninth after leading 7-2 early. With a chance to go ahead, Harman was walked to load the bases in the top of the ninth with the score tied, 9-9. Virginia did not score. Harman ended with one hit in each game.[12]

Back on the hardwood, the 1939-40 basketball team was even better, going 16-5. Harman was one of four starters returning and was the team's sharpshooter. The January 13 *Richmond Times-Dispatch* called him "big, rangy, active and husky" as he scored half the points against Medical College (20 points), Hampden-Sydney (20), William and Mary (19), and Roanoke College (17).

After Harman scored 12 of the team's 34 points in a win over Virginia Tech on January 29, the paper said he "rates with the State's finest." In early February, Harman's 165 points and George Washington guard Red Auerbach's 102 points were the tops in the state.[13] George Washington, averaging more than 50 points

ONE-HIT WONDERS

a game, was slowed by a Cavalier defense in early February but still won 35-32 in overtime.

Harman bruised his leg soon after and entered the hospital, missing games to state champion Washington and Lee (loss), VMI (win), and Richmond (loss). With the state championship out of reach, the season ended with a win over Virginia and 12 points from Harman. The Associated Press named McCann and Harman all-state. Harman led the state with 217 points, just under 13 points a game.[14]

Back on the diamond a few weeks later, McCann and Harman were two of seven returning starters. Harman hit sixth as a junior in 1940. The team won the state title behind an 18-4 record.

Harman also began to pitch, striking out three in a perfect ninth against Pittsburgh and allowing one run on seven hits in seven relief innings in a 12-11 win over Michigan. He also had two doubles and three runs in that game. Tebell insisted that Harman only pitched "in case of need." In mid-April he was hitting .360 with four doubles, a triple, and two homers.[15] The "need" continued with five innings of two-hit ball against Virginia Tech and a tally of two runs on six hits given up over 13 relief innings.[16]

In the big game of the season, Virginia moved to 10-2 after Harman outpitched undefeated Richmond and top pitching prospect Porter Vaughan, 2-1. Harman allowed one run on two hits in the first and then no-hit the Spiders the rest of the way. He struck out 10 and retired the last 12 batters in a row.[17]

Early newspaper accounts had Harman facing off against Vaughan again before 4,000 fans in Charlottesville in the season finale. But instead, Harman caught reserve pitcher John Willey and he spotted Richmond three runs in the first. Virginia lost 5-4. Harman was 0-for-3. Porter Vaughan signed an $8,000 bonus contract with the Philadelphia Athletics after the season.[18]

Harman had one more year to go, a memorable 1941 that consisted of an NIT berth, his university degree, his debut with the Phillies, and his enlistment in the US Marine Corps.

For men coming of age in 1941, the time before Pearl Harbor was different. One wrote, "For me and my generation 1941 was not a year of Pearl Harbor and war, but of peace, the last year of peace, a shaky, fraying, disintegrating peace, but nonetheless peace."[19] By the end of World War II, more than 300 Virginia alumni had died in the war.[20]

Harman's last year of basketball at Virginia ended at the National Invitational Tournament, then bigger than the NCCA Tournament, in March at Madison Square Garden with an 18-6 record. Harman and McCann combined for 42 points in the season opener and kept rolling. The pair and sophomore Dick Wiltshire finished in the top 10 in state scoring.[21] Two years after graduation, in 1943, the *Richmond Times-Dispatch* conducted a fan poll of the top players in University of Virginia history, McCann was one of the top six players selected. Harman finished seventh with 59 votes.[22]

Harman also continued to be a school leader as team captain, a part of the Inter-Fraternal Council as a member of Phi Kappa Sigma fraternity, and as the 1940-41 student body president.

For the 1941 basketball season, the Cavaliers were known for their offense and defense, a rarity for the era. The team's January victory over an undefeated Tennessee team, 41-30, when Harman had 18 points, propelled the Cavaliers to the NIT in mid-March.

Harman battled for the state scoring lead all season, as the Cavaliers brought in large crowds, as they cheered Harman's 41-40 game-winner on what a newspaper described as the flight of a "snowbird" type pass from McCann at William and Mary in February.[23]

To finish the regular season he scored 15 points in his prep hometown of Alexandria in a win over George Washington and then before 3,000 home fans, in what was believed to be his last collegiate game, he had 27 points in a win over Washington and Lee. He finished with 351 points, a 16-point-a-game average, to win the state scoring championship.

Everyone believed the basketball season was over. Players took exams and McCann and Harman prepared for their final baseball season. Three weeks later, the NIT committee decided that the Cavaliers' January win over Tennessee was worthy of an invite to the eight-team tournament. Virginia, without the benefit of playing for nearly a month, was invited to play CCNY in New York City.

Against 1940 NIT runner-up CCNY, the Cavaliers closed to within 23-19 at the half but soon were without their two stars. Harman fouled out five minutes into the start of the second half. McCann followed five minutes later. Virginia lost 64-35.

"There was no way we could beat a good New York team," said McCann. "New York was so much better than we played down there. ... (With the layoff) we were a long way from being organized for the NIT."[24]

Virginia basketball did not make another postseason until 1972. That included six seasons under coach McCann, who went 40-106 (1957-63).[25]

ONE-HIT WONDERS

Another image of Harman from the 1941 yearbook.

Back on the diamond in spring 1941, Harman was listed at 205 pounds and hit cleanup behind second baseman McCann. His seven home runs remained a school single-season record until 1976.[26] The team faltered, though, finishing 11-8, losing five of seven late in the season after a 5-0 start.

In late May both McCann and Harman signed professional deals. McCann to the Petersburg Rebels of the Virginia League and Harman to the last-place Philadelphia Phillies on May 28, after commencement.[27]

After signing, Harman remained a civilian, waiting for his draft number to be called. The Phillies, also seeing the writing on the wall, took just about anyone to get better and field a team. In a 1991 recollection, *Sports Illustrated* noted, "The inevitable dilution of talent eventually required team owners to make do with the oddest, and perhaps the most inept, contingent of players ever seen on major league playing fields."[28]

Like a tall, rangy basketball player who could catch and pitch.

Harman was one of four catchers for the Phillies and was one of the tallest players in the majors. He also pitched. In the 1930s, 83 players pitched at least 50 innings and had at least 300 at-bats in the minors.

None made the majors. A few Negro League players had done so, but again, it was rare.[29]

Harman made his major-league debut on June 17, 1941, making the last out as a pinch-hitter in an 11-3 loss to the Cardinals against Mort Cooper on an 84-degree day in St. Louis.[30]

On June 25, 1941, the day Joe DiMaggio hit in his 37th straight game, Harman was a two-way reserve. He pinch-hit in the eighth in game one of a doubleheader against the Cincinnati Reds at Crosley Field, fouling out, before catching the ninth. In game two, he pitched the ninth inning and gave up one run on a single, a sacrifice, and another single in a 5-1 loss.[31]

For the season Harman had a 4.85 ERA in five appearances and 13 innings. He did pitch a perfect eighth in a loss to the Pirates on July 23 that included retiring Vince DiMaggio. He pitched three innings on the mound against the Giants on September 23 in his last pitching appearance.

After going hitless the month of June (0-for-5) and July (without an at-bat) Harman ran for Phillies catcher Bennie Warren in the seventh inning on a 96-degree day in St. Louis on August 2. He caught the seventh and the eighth before coming to bat against Cardinals starter Howie Krist in the ninth. Harman singled to left field to lead off the ninth and scored on Jim Carlin's home run, finishing off an 11-7 defeat. Harman played seven more games as a reserve going 1-for-14 (.071). On September 28 at Ebbets Field, he flied out to left against Bob Chipman in the ninth. It was the first of 51 career wins for Chipman over a 12-year major-league career and the last game for Harman.

Harman went to Marine boot camp in July 1941 in Parris Island, South Carolina.[32] In anticipation of the United States entering the war, boot camp was reduced from eight weeks to four.[33] It consisted of marching, parades, drilling, firing a rifle, and learning how to clean, disassemble and reassemble the rifle.[34] The "lucky ones" lived in Quonset huts by the sandpits. Others lived in tents, in the "oppressive heat" of a South Carolina humid summer.[35] After Parris Island, Harman was assigned to the officer training cadre training officer cadets in 1941-42.[36] He was discharged after that but joined again prior to the 1945 Battle of Okinawa.

In late December 1941, Harman assisted McCann with the Virginia freshman basketball team while coach Tebell was away at the Rose Bowl as an official. The game had been moved from Pasadena, California, to Durham, North Carolina, because of

ONE-HIT WONDERS

fears of a Japanese attack on the West Coast following the attack on Pearl Harbor on December 7, 1941.[37]

Harman and McCann both fought in the Pacific in 1945. McCann, a paratrooper, was hit in the neck by shrapnel at Iwo Jima and received two Purple Hearts.[38] Harman was a part of the invasion of Okinawa in April 1945. In 1942 the Phillies had not heard from Harman. Reports had him enlisting in the Marines, but also undergoing treatment for an old ankle injury. He was released by the Phillies in May 1942.[39]

Harman was added to the faculty of the Augusta Military Academy in April 1942.[40] He did, however, play at least one more pro season. As an outfielder and catcher, he played in 26 games for the Petersburg (Virginia) Rebels of the Class-C Virginia League in 1942. He hit .197 with four doubles and one home run. The Rebels were 74-52 and finished third in the Virginia League for manager Steve Mizerak.

In the fall of 1942, Harman began working as a teacher and coach in the Waynesboro (Virginia) public schools. He resigned in March 1943.[41] Before resigning he married Janet Lorraine Cline in early 1943.[42] In November 1943 he was a part of a group of former basketball players playing for the DuPont company. DuPont is where he spent his career after the war.[43] He was listed on the roster of the Wellsville Yankees in 1944, but no statistics could be located and it is not known if he ever played.

In 1945 and 1946 he served as an assault amphibious vehicle crewman. In 1945 Harman took part in the invasion of Okinawa, serving with the 1833 3rd Amphibious Corps. "Crewmen likely rotated between ship to shore transporting casualties, casualty replacements, and supplies, working on tractors that needed repairs, and manning a machine gun in a nearby defensive position so all of the above and other things like getting sleep and eating could be accomplished," a Marine Corps historian told the author.[44] The 80-plus-day battle was the largest amphibious landing in the Pacific Theater.

The Allies faced 155,000 Japanese soldiers and another 500,000 civilians on the island of Okinawa, 350 miles from Japan. The enemy set up positions above the terrain and overlooked the terrain.[45] The Allies not only had to advance over deserted terrain, of which Harman's Amphibious Corps helped bring them forward, but also through knee need mud with little sleep, food or dry clothes.[46]

Some well-known fellow Marines on Okinawa who played in the majors were future Yankees All-Star outfielder Hank Bauer, Dodgers All-Star first baseman Gil Hodges, and longtime Braves announcer and pitcher Ernie Johnson Sr.[47]

Harman returned to the States and settled into a 41-year marketing career with DuPont's textile fibers department, retiring in 1984 at the age of 65 but remaining as a consultant for the company. His marketing career took him to watching models strut down runways in Paris and New York as the company promoted its new Lycra product and had some of its best years.[48] He died at the age of 88 on September 22, 2007, in Greenville, Delaware. He had two sons, William Bell Harman Jr. and Thomas Asher Harman. At the time of his death he had three grandsons and a great-granddaughter.[49]

SOURCES

In addition to the sources cited in the Notes, the author consulted Retrosheet.org and Baseball-Reference.com. Point totals and other statistics from game reports at the University of Virginia are from the *Richmond Times-Dispatch* from 1938 to 1941.

NOTES

1. Early family information via the 1920, 1930, and 1940 Censuses. According to the Census, in 1930 about 40 percent of the population owned a radio.
2. "Rural Life in Virginia," Virginia Museum of History and Culture, viewed September 26, 2020. virginiahistory.org/collections-and-resources/virginia-history-explorer/rural-life-virginia.
3. "Large Student Enrollment in State Expected," *Richmond Times-Dispatch*, August 22, 1933: 7.
4. "Scholarship, Books Given to Alexandria High School," *Richmond Times-Dispatch*, March 11, 1938: 4.
5. Ron Heinemann, "The Great Depression in Virginia," Encyclopedia Virginia, viewed September 26, 2020, encyclopediavirginia.org/great_depression_in_virginia#start_entry.
6. Heinemann.
7. Information about Episcopal High is from the 1935, 1936, and 1937 Whisper yearbooks and research done by school archivist Laura Vetter.
8. Whisper yearbooks.
9. "Brosnan Whiffs 14 as Va. Frosh Defeat W&l," *Richmond Times-Dispatch*, April 13, 1938: 15.
10. "Four Maroons on All-State Cage Team," *Richmond Times-Dispatch*, March 1, 1939: 15; "Virginia Star," *Norfolk Virginian-Pilot*, December 27, 1939: 8.
11. "Haverford Nine Is Turned Back," *Richmond Times-Dispatch*, March 31, 1939: 18.
12. "College Series Ends in Three-Way Tie," *Freeman's Journal* (Cooperstown, New York), June 21, 1939: 1-2.
13. "Virginia Risks Court Records Against G.W.," *Richmond Times-Dispatch*, February 3, 1940: 13. Auerbach, the future Hall of Fame coach, finished with 162 points.
14. "3 Schools Contribute to All-State Quintet," *Richmond Times-Dispatch*, February 24, 1940: 14.
15. "Spiders Risk Perfect Record Against Cavalier Nine Today," *Richmond Times-Dispatch*, April 19, 1940: 20.
16. "Virginia Engages Tar Heel Nine This Afternoon," *Richmond Times-Dispatch*, April 25, 1940: 17.

ONE-HIT WONDERS

17 Tom Wiley, "Harman Hurls 2-Hit Game as Cavaliers Defeat Spiders," *Richmond Times-Dispatch*, May 1, 1940: 10.

18 Tom Wiley, "Cavaliers Defeat Spiders 5-4," *Richmond Times-Dispatch*, May 18, 1940: 12. Vaughan went 2-11 with a 5.83 ERA in 24 games in the majors (1940-41, '46), and was also an Army captain.

19 Ron Briley, "Baseball and Other Matters in 1941," *NINE: A Journal of Baseball History and Culture*, January 2002, abstract, researchgate.net/publication/236794782_Baseball_and_Other_Matters_in_1941_review.

20 Jennings L. Wagoner and Robert L. Baxter, Jr. "Higher Education Goes to War: The University of Virginia's Response to World War II," *Virginia Magazine of History and Biography* 100, no. 3 (1992): 399-428. Accessed September 6, 2020. jstor.org/stable/4249294.

21 "Cavalier Five to Meet Legion in Return Go," *Richmond Times-Dispatch*, March 6, 1941: 14.

22 Dick Williamson, "Pinck, Knox, Spessard, McCann, Iler Make All-Time 'Big Six,'" *Richmond Times-Dispatch*, February 17, 1943: 12.

23 Morris Siegel, "Cavaliers Nose Out William and Mary 41-40," February 12, 1941: 16.

24 Chauncey Durden, "The Sportsview," *Richmond Times-Dispatch*, March 23, 1980: 36.

25 In 1976, McCann and Wiltshire watched sixth-seeded Virginia upset North Carolina in the "Miracle in Landover" at the ACC Tournament. Virginia then lost to DePaul in their first-ever NCCA Tournament appearance and third-ever postseason.

26 In 1976 Tony Zentgraff broke the single-season record of seven homers that had been set by Harman and tied by Don Aichol (1951), Chuck Arnold (1956), and Pete Anderson (1974). "Cavalier Breaks HR Mark with 8," *Richmond Times-Dispatch*, April 15, 1976: 58.

27 "Bill Harman Signs Contract with Phillies," *Richmond Times-Dispatch*, May 30, 1941: 12.

28 Eventually 428 major leaguers served in the armed forces. William Jeanes, "Baseball in World War II," *Sports Illustrated*, August 26, 1991, viewed September 22, 2020. vault.si.com/vault/1991/08/26/baseball-in-world-war-ii-fdr-let-baseball-continue-so-we-had-a-pastime-played-by-graybeards-no-beards-and-other-marvels.

29 Negro League and major-league Hall of Famers Martin Dihigo, Bullet Rogan, and Leon Day all were two-way stars in the 1920s and '30s. After Ruth, another player didn't have 50 innings and 300 at-bats until Shohei Ohtani did so in 2019.

30 "MLB Flashback: Bill Harman, Alan Knicely, Jon Rauch." News Break. Accessed September 6, 2020. newsbreak.com/virginia/bridgewater/news/1585330238033/mlb-flashback-bill-harman-alan-knicely-jon-rauch. The Retrosheet and Baseball-Reference play-by-plays of the game both describe the type of out as "unknown."

31 Boxscore, June 26, 1941, National Baseball Hall of Fame Archives.

32 "William Bell Harman page," Togetherweserved.com. Accessed September 6, 2020. marines.togetherweserved.com/usmc/servlet/tws.webapp.WebApp?cmd=ShadowBoxProfile&type=Person&ID=362425.

33 "Training for War," US Marines website, mcrdpi.marines.mil/Portals/76/Docs/CentennialCelebrationBook/MCRDPI-history-book-4.pdf.

34 James Salerno, "Joining the Raiders," interview by National World War II Museum, 2015, Digital Collections of the National WWII Museum, National WWII Museum, New Orleans, Louisiana. ww2online.org/view/james-salerno.

35 Don McLoud, "Parris Island in the '40s: A Rude Awakening for One New Yorker," *Island Packet* (Bluffton, South Carolina), October 15, 2015, Accessed September 20, 2020. islandpacket.com/latest-news/article39413739.html.

36 Edward Nevgloski (chief of Marine Corps History and director of Marine Corps History Division) in email with author, September 2020.

37 Bill Diehl, "Billy McCann Named Coach of Cavalier Frosh Cagers," *Richmond Times-Dispatch*, December 31, 1941: 15.

38 Morris Siegel, "Fork Union Position Agrees with McCann," *Richmond Times-Dispatch*, December 16, 1945: 31.

39 "Missing Phil Discovered," April 30, 1942, National Baseball Hall of Fame Archives.

40 "Harman Joins Augusta Staff to Replace Craft," *Richmond Times-Dispatch*, April 16, 1942: 14.

41 "Harman to Coach Waynesboro," *Richmond Times-Dispatch*, August 27, 1942: 14.

42 Barton Pattie, "Virginia Sports Reel," *Free Lance Star* (Fredericksburg, Virginia), February 9, 1943: 9.

43 "Al Hawkins Coaches Du Pont Cage Team," *Richmond Times-Dispatch*, November 12, 1943: 16.

44 Nevgloski.

45 "Battle of Okinawa: Operation Iceberg," *World War II* magazine / Historynet.com, June 2005, accessed September 20, 2020. The Allies faced 155,000 Japanese soldiers and another 500,000 civilians on Okinawa, an island 350 miles from Japan. Marines sailed from the West Coast of America to Hawai'i to Guam before continuing to Okinawa. The Allies landed on the Western side of the island as the "Japanese chose to dig deep and fight on their terms," away from the beach and overlooking terrain.

46 Seth Paridon, "The Invasion of Okinawa: One Damned Ridge After Another," April 15, 2020, National World War II Museum, accessed September 20, 2020, nationalww2museum.org/war/articles/okinawa-invasion-1945. The Japanese were holed up in caves that dotted the Awacha Mountain range. The topography of ridge lines and lack of vegetation favored the enemy, making the caves difficult to reach. The amphibious tractors got stuck in the mud and tanks were "knee-deep in mud." The Allies continued to advance while getting shot at by the Japanese from an elevated position. The rains allowed for no sleep, little food, or dry clothes. "Generally a Marine could take three or four steps before his boondockers, already caked in inches of mud, were literally sucked off his feet," said Seth Paridon, who took part in the invasion. "(The Marines') forte is amphibious landing and they took us under their wing," said Len Lazarsrick, who was part of the invasion. The Japanese had embedded coconut logs on the beach, facing out to the sea at 45 degrees to deter amphibious vehicles from landing. Soldiers had to jump out and go on foot, he continued. In May, soldiers had to deal with monsoon season as well. "The foxholes would fill up with water and you had to bail them out when there was an air raid." – air raids, sometimes a half dozen times a night, left little time for sleep. ... If you got four hours of good sleep, you did good," said Melvin Munch. "Your view of the warfare is not the big picture, it's your narrow view. And part of that view is trying to stay alive," continued Lasarick, whose 96th Division was trained by the Marines. As the battled continued the "smell of war stayed with you constantly. You hated to breathe the odor of death," said Munch. In the end the Allies suffered 50,000 casualties and the Japanese suffered 100,000. The atomic bombings of Hiroshima and Nagasaki essentially ended the war in the Pacific in August and avoided a much larger invasion of Japan. Len Lazasrick, "Segment 3," interview by National World War II Museum, 2015, Digital Collections of the National WWII Museum, National WWII Museum, ww2online.org/view/len-lazarick#segment-3 and Melvin Munch, "Battle of Okinawa," interview by National World War II Museum, 2015, Digital Collections of the National WWII Museum, National WWII Museum, ww2online.org/view/melvin-munch#boot-camp-to-okinawa.

47 Gary Bedingfield, "Baseball in Wartime," accessed September 20, 2020, baseballinwartime.com/marine_corps.htm.

48 "Opening New Doors, Retiree Locks into Construction Firm," *Wilmington* (Delaware) *News Journal*, February 4, 1995: 29.

49 Obituary, *Charlottesville* (Virginia) *Daily Progress*, September 25-27, 2007, viewed September 20, 2020 legacy.com/us/obituaries/dailyprogress/name/william-bell-harman-obituary?n=william-bell-harman&pid=95048587.

AARON HEILMAN

By Peter Seidel

For every baseball player's great triumph, someone must suffer the agony of defeat. While Bobby Thompson's "Shot Heard 'Round the World" was undoubtedly his greatest triumph, it was also a crushing moment for Ralph Branca. As Branca and Thompson are forever linked by that one moment, so are St. Louis Cardinals catcher Yadier Molina and New York Mets pitcher Aaron Heilman.

Aaron Michael Heilman was born on November 12, 1978, in Logansport, Indiana, also the hometown of baseball's first commissioner, Kenesaw Mountain Landis. Heilman's father, Joseph, ran track at Indiana University. Joseph met Deborah Simmons at the university and the two married in 1971. Beau Wicker, the sports editor of the *Pharos-Tribune* of Logansport, said Heilman's parents owned a bulk cleaning supplies company that was located inside a hardware store.[1]

Aaron Heilman was an outstanding pitcher at Logansport High School and pitched a perfect game his freshman year. During his junior year, Heilman led Logansport to the state finals, sporting a 10-3 won-lost record, a 0.98 ERA, 87 strikeouts in 81 innings pitched, and only 17 walks. Heilman fanned 17 batters in an American Legion regional contest.

Success followed Heilman his senior year, when he went 11-1 with a 1.06 ERA with 105 strikeouts in 79 innings. Heilman was his team's most valuable player and earned All-State honors.

The New York Yankees selected Heilman in the 55th round of the 1997 amateur draft but he opted to attend the University of Notre Dame. "Coming out of high school, I really wanted to get a degree," Heilman said. "I wanted to go to school and get that experience. I made it pretty clear that I was very serious about that, and said, 'Don't even bother, thanks for the interest, but come talk to me in three or four years when I'm done.'"[2] While pitching for the Fighting Irish, Heilman compiled a 43-7 record and an ERA of 2.49. His freshman year he pitched primarily out of the bullpen and finished with a 7-3 record, striking out 78 and walking 19 in 67 innings. Heilman led the nation with a 1.61 ERA and earned third-team All-American honors.

Heilman started 14 of his 20 games his sophomore year and finished 11-2 with a 3.14 ERA and 118 strikeouts in 109 innings. He earned third-team All-American and first-team Big East honors. In his junior year he posted a 10-2 record with a 3.21 ERA and 118 strikeouts in 103⅔ innings. The highlight was when he struck out 18 batters in one game. The Minnesota Twins selected Heilman with the 31st pick in the 2000 draft, but he opted to stay at Notre Dame for his senior year. Heilman's senior year, 2001, was his breakout season: a perfect 15-0 record and a 1.74 ERA, 111 strikeouts in 114 innings, 12 complete games, three shutouts,

ONE-HIT WONDERS

and a 0.89 WHIP. He was the Big East pitcher of the year and a first-team All-American. It is considered one of the most dominating pitching seasons in Notre Dame history, and it led to a 49-13-1 record and first place in the Big East. Heilman graduated from Notre Dame with a dual major in management information systems and philosophy.

The New York Mets selected Heilman as the 18th overall pick in the first round of the 2001 draft. He pitched that summer for the St. Lucie Mets in the Florida State League. In seven starts, Heilman finished with a 0-1 record, a 2.35 ERA, and 39 strikeouts in 38⅓ innings. In 2002 he was moved up to Double-A Binghamton (Eastern League), and in 17 starts he pitched to a 4-4 record with a 3.82 ERA, and 97 strikeouts in 96⅔ innings. Late in the season he was promoted to Triple-A Norfolk, where he was 2-3 with a 3.28 ERA.

Heilman started the 2003 season at Norfolk but was called up on June 26 to make his first major-league start against the Florida Marlins, at Shea Stadium. "It was incredibly exciting and nerve-wracking, you kind of feel like it's the culmination of all your hard work, but really it's just the beginning," he said.[3] Heilman tossed six innings and gave up just one earned run, but the Mets made four errors while their offense scored only one run against Dontrelle Willis, eventually the National Rookie of the Year. "I thought he did his job. We just didn't do it behind him," Mets manager Art Howe said of Heilman. "He pounded the strike zone. If we catch the ball behind him, he's right in the game."[4] "Hats off to the other guy," Willis said of Heilman. "One play, if they make that play, it's a different type of ballgame."[5] Heilman reserved 25 or 30 tickets for his wife, parents, relatives, and Notre Dame baseball coaches. "It was special for me because I had guys who I hadn't seen since graduation flying into New York to come watch me pitch," he said. "Coach [Paul] Manieri and Coach [Brian] O'Connor flew in, so it was very special because all of these people went out of their way to show their support for me."[6]

Five days later Heilman started against the Montreal Expos and came close to earning his first major-league victory. After giving up three runs through seven innings, the Mets broke a 3-3 tie with three runs in the bottom of the seventh. In the top of the eighth inning, reliever Armando Benitez coughed up the lead, and the Expos tied the game. Tony Clark's RBI single in the bottom of the ninth inning gave the Mets a 7-6 victory. "Certainly, I would have liked to get the win," Heilman said, "but as long as we win, that comes first."[7]

After two quality starts to begin his major-league pitching career, Heilman was roughed up in his third start, allowing five earned runs on six hits and four walks in four innings. "I pretty much fell behind hitters," he said. "It's tough to be successful that way."[8] His fourth start was even rougher: He surrendered eight earned runs to the Philadelphia Phillies in 4⅓ innings. The Phillies scored four runs with two outs in the first inning, which particularly upset manager Howe. "I don't know if his concentration went, but he's just got to get us off that field with a zero."[9] "I thought I made some pretty good pitches," Heilman said, "but it didn't work out."[10]

The fifth time proved to be the charm for Heilman. Although he struggled in the first and fifth innings, overall he pitched well enough to beat the Phillies this time and earn his first major-league win, 8-6 in Philadelphia on July 21. "I wanted it to come," said Heilman, who was given a clothes-soaking beer shower and also an "anonymous bottle" of Korbel champagne. "It's nice to get it out of the way."[11]

On August 12 Heilman notched his only major-league hit, a single off San Francisco Giants starter Sidney Ponson, a grounder just to the right of the second baseman in the third inning that drove in a run and helped Heilman earn his second major-league win, 5-4. Heilman surrendered a home run and an RBI single to Barry Bonds. "Certainly, he doesn't miss many pitches," Heilman said of Bonds. "I made some good pitches, but unfortunately, he took all of those."[12]

While there were a few quality starts, much of Heilman's rookie season was a struggle as he finished with a 2-7 record and a 6.75 ERA. He started the 2004 season at Norfolk, where he went 7-10 with a 4.33 ERA. While not stellar, Heilman was their first-round draft pick in 2001 and once a top pitching prospect, and on August 23 he got the call to return to the majors and start against San Diego. Heilman allowed four earned runs on eight hits and three walks over 3⅔ innings as the Mets lost 9-4 to the Padres. Heilman made four more starts and finished the 2004 season with a 1-3 won-lost record and a 5.46 ERA.

There was cause for optimism entering the 2005 system. New Mets manager Willie Randolph liked the way Heilman pitched in spring training. "I liked the way he was throwing at the end of spring training," Randolph said. "He made a little adjustment in his delivery and I liked the way the ball was moving. I think it gives us a nice shot."[13] That plus an injury

ONE-HIT WONDERS

to starting pitcher Kris Benson guaranteed Heilman not only a start in April, but for the first time in his brief major-league career a start before August. His first start did not go very well: The Atlanta Braves scored five earned runs against him on eight hits in five innings. However, Heilman's next start gave fans a tantalizing look at his potential as a major-league pitcher, a one-hit 4-0 shutout of the Florida Marlins at Shea Stadium on April 15.

The optimism lasted only five days as the Marlins beat up Heilman in his next start, in Miami, scoring seven earned runs on 11 hits in four innings. After a few quality starts, Heilman was asked to pitch in relief. He responded on May 5 with 3⅓ shutout innings propelling the Mets to a 7-5 victory over the Phillies. "His changeup is a thousand times better than it was last year," said Mets closer Braden Looper. "He is throwing [the change] ahead and behind in the count."[14] Benson's return from the disabled list and Heilman's relief success saw him transfer from a starting pitcher to the bullpen. When Heilman moved to the bullpen, his ERA was 4.37. By the end of the 2005 season it was 3.17.

In spite of his success in the bullpen, Heilman entered 2006 spring training competing for the fifth starting pitcher role. He had started in the Dominican Republic winter league to prepare himself for the 2006 season. By the end of March, Randolph had decided to give the starting assignment to rookie Brian Bannister and keep Heilman in the bullpen. "I'm certainly disappointed," Heilman said.[15] Despite his disappointment, Heilman became a workhorse in middle relief. In 74 appearances he compiled a 4-5 won-lost record and a 3.62 ERA with 26 holds. He was used primarily as the eighth-inning set-up man for the closer, Billy Wagner, and was a key contributor to the Mets finishing the season in first place in the National League East.

The Mets swept the Dodgers in the National League Division Series and Heilman pitched the eighth inning of all three games. In Game Two of the Championship Series against the St. Louis Cardinals, he helped preserve a 6-6 tie with late relief, but the Cardinals scored three runs off closer Wagner to win. Heilman pitched a scoreless eighth inning to help the Mets win Game Six. With Game Seven game tied, Heilman entered in the eighth inning and struck out two Cardinals. He remained in the game to pitch the ninth inning. With one out, Scott Rolen hit a single to left field to bring up Yadier Molina, who hit Heilman's first pitch to him over the left-field wall at Shea Stadium to give the Cardinals a 3-1 lead, which they held in the bottom of the inning to go to the World Series.

Heilman returned to the Mets bullpen in 2007 and appeared in exactly half of the Mets games (81 appearances), going 7-7 with a 3.03 ERA. However, things took a turn in 2008 as he finished the season with a 3-8 record and a 5.21 ERA. He allowed 75 hits and 46 walks in 76 innings pitched, giving him a high 1.59 WHIP. By the end of the season Heilman wanted to return to the starting rotation, and requested a trade if the Mets insisted on keeping him in the bullpen. According to Heilman's agent, "the object the entire time has never been to get out of New York. The object is to get out of the bullpen."[16] On December 11, a three-team trade sent Heilman to the Seattle Mariners. In January 2009 the Mariners traded Heilman to the Chicago Cubs, who kept him in the bullpen. (70 games pitched, 4-4). After the season, Heilman was traded to the Arizona Diamondbacks. He pitched out of the bullpen in 2010 and for 3½ months in 2011 until the Diamondbacks released him on July 19. Heilman signed minor-league deals with the Phillies, Pirates, and Rangers after being cut by Arizona.

Heilman required Tommy John surgery in both 2012 and 2013, effectively ending his professional baseball career. "I had two elbow surgeries two years in a row. I tried to come back and rehab just blew out again after the first one," he said. "I had the revision done and just didn't quite come back. I decided to just hang out and had a pretty good career, so I decided to spend some time with the family. I'm just enjoying retirement and fixing stuff around the house and trying to keep busy, We do a lot of stuff for the school and PTO and different charities. We try to keep busy, but nothing major on the horizon."[17]

SOURCES

In addition to the sources cited in the Notes, the author consulted Baseball-Reference.com, The Baseball Cube, and YouTube.

NOTES

1. Beau Wicker email to author on January 13, 2021.
2. Sean Tenaglia, "Heilman Happy to Be Home," UND.com, March 4, 2014. https://und.com/heilman-happy-to-come-home/.
3. Tenaglia.
4. Michael Morrissey, "Aaron 'D' Victim in Debut – Four Met Miscues Sabotage Heilman," *New York Post*, June 27, 2003. https://nypost.com/2003/06/27/aaron-d-victim-in-debut-four-met-miscues-sabotage-heilman/.
5. Morrissey, "Aaron 'D' Victim in Debut."
6. Tenaglia.

ONE-HIT WONDERS

7 Paul Schwartz, "Same Old Benitez – Blows Save, Aaron's 1st Win, but Mets Roll," *New York Post*, July 3, 2003. https://nypost.com/2003/07/02/same-old-benitez-blows-save-aarons-1st-win-but-mets-roll/.

8 Michael Morrissey, "Lowering the Broom – Unlikely Mets Heroes Sweep Up in Cincy," *New York Post*, July 7, 2003. https://nypost.com/2003/07/07/lowering-the-broom-unlikely-mets-heroes-sweep-up-in-cincy/.

9 Mark Hale, "Art's Mad and Howe; Blows His Stack After Phils Rip Sloppy Mets," *New York Post*, July 12, 2003. https://nypost.com/2003/07/12/arts-mad-and-howe-blows-his-stack-after-phils-rip-sloppy-mets/.

10 Hale, "Art's Mad and Howe."

11 Michael Morrissey, "Scrappy Heilman Clinches 1st Win; Three HRs Lead Mets Past Phils," *New York Post*, July 22, 2003. https://nypost.com/2003/07/22/scrappy-heilman-cinches-1st-win-three-hrs-lead-mets-past-phils/.

12 Michael Morrissey, "Mets Upstage Bonds: Hold Off SF Despite Two HRs by Barry," *New York Post*, August 13, 2003. https://nypost.com/2003/08/13/mets-upstage-bonds-hold-off-sf-despite-two-hrs-by-barry/.

13 Mark Hale, "On-the-Spot Starter; Heilman Gets Call in Place of Benson," *New York Post*, April 9, 2005. https://nypost.com/2005/04/09/on-the-spot-starter-heilman-gets-call-in-place-of-benson/.

14 Andrew Marchand, "Heilman Changing for the Better," *New York Post*, May 6, 2005. https://nypost.com/2005/05/06/heilman-changing-for-better/.

15 Ben Shpigel, "Mets Make Bannister's Day; Heilman to Bullpen," *New York Times*. March 29, 2006 https://www.nytimes.com/2006/03/29/sports/baseball/mets-make-bannisters-day-heilman-to-bullpen.html.

16 Adam Ruben, "Aaron Heilman Wants Starting Role with Mets or a Trade," *New York Daily News*, November 20, 2008. https://www.nydailynews.com/sports/baseball/mets/aaron-heilman-starting-role-mets-trade-article-1.337292.

17 Beau Wicker, "Heilman Throws Out First Pitch for Ohio Valley Regional," *Pharos Tribune* (Logansport, Indiana), July 19, 2018. https://www.pharostribune.com/sports/local_sports/article_3c45d0a5-b770-54c4-b424-c55f82983e35.html.

CHRIS JELIC

By Tara Krieger

When Chris Jelic was traded from Kansas City to New York in 1987, the Mets picked up a future All-Star. It just wasn't him.

Jelic's place in baseball history endures as the answer to two trivia questions: He was the other guy the Mets got when they traded for David Cone, and he remains the only player whose lone hit was a home run in his final major-league at-bat.

Jelic's big-league career spanned four games in the last week of the 1990 season; the home run was his only hit in 11 appearances at the plate.

He would like to set the record straight, though – he could've easily had two more (and then not be included in this book). Two days before, he had hit a "bullet down the first base line"[1] in the fifth inning that was ruled an error when Sid Bream couldn't handle it.

"Everybody else in the game said it should've been a hit," Jelic said.[2] The next day, "I had another ball that I hit in the hole between third and short that Jay Bell couldn't make the play on, but they never would've had me anyway, and they made [it] an error. So I had a few guys on the team saying, 'You got at least two other at-bats you should've had a hit.'"

He doesn't dwell on what could have been, though – his life has been pretty good. Ever the optimist, he just adapts to whatever comes next. If you can't be the star quarterback, become a punter. If you can't be a pro football player, focus on baseball. If you can't be a catcher, be a supersub. And if you can't play anymore, be ready to move on.

A former two-sport athlete at the University of Pittsburgh, Jelic grew up in the Steel City suburb of Mt. Lebanon in a family and a community that was sports-mad.

"Western Pennsylvania at the time (it has really changed) was full of people that valued toughness and looked down on whiners," wrote Jeff Jelic, Chris's older brother. "Most of us were first or second generation immigrants and working hard for anything you got was admired and expected.

"As a result, and we did not know it or fully appreciate it at the time, Western Pennsylvania in the 70's and 80's was an unbelievably competitive area. Just the number of HOF athletes coming out of W.PA at that time was quite remarkable.

"We grew up with it so it seemed normal, but once we started competing nationally, we realized how special the area was. If you could compete in W.PA athletically, you could play at a high level anywhere."[3]

According to Jeff Jelic, Chris's graduating high-school class at Mt. Lebanon featured 11 Division I scholarship athletes on the football team alone. Two years ahead of Chris in school was John Frank, who won two Super Bowls with the San Francisco 49ers. A few years behind Chris were tennis player Don

Chris Jelic.

ONE-HIT WONDERS

Johnson, who won a Wimbledon doubles title, and professional wrestlers Eric and Kurt Angle, the latter also an Olympic gold medalist.[4]

"Our neighborhood pickup games were better than a lot of varsity high school teams in other states," mused Jeff Jelic.[5]

Chris's father, Ralph Jelic, was a good enough running back at the University of Pittsburgh to be selected by the Pittsburgh Steelers in the 10th round of the 1957 NFL draft. He signed a contract for $6,500, but never played a game, and went on to coach several colleges and scout for the Raiders, Chiefs, and Buccaneers, before a decades-long career in marketing and sales in construction and geotextiles. Chris's mother, Cynthia (Agnew) Jelic, an elementary-school teacher, was the top female athlete at Pitt 1959, as a basketball player in the pre-Title IX era.

"I don't think I could beat her in a race until I was a freshman in college," said Jeff Jelic, a former all-American college wrestler, in his father's 2018 obituary. "I still don't know if I could beat her in tennis that well."[6]

The Agnews were of Scots-Irish and German ancestry and were natives of Western Pennsylvania. But Ralph's father (Chris's grandfather), Frank Jelic, immigrated from Zagreb, Yugoslavia (now Croatia), at age 7. He dropped out of school in third grade and worked at a slaughterhouse on the North Side. The work ethic was passed down to Ralph Jelic.

"Most people idolize athletes," Jeff Jelic said. "For him, it was his dad, who got up every day, went to work, didn't fuss, would eat whatever you put in front of him. If you want to be proud of somebody, that's who you be proud of. That's how my brother and I were raised."[7]

Ralph and Cynthia Jelic married in 1959. Ralph was coaching at Lehigh and had moved the family to Bethlehem, Pennsylvania, when Jeff came along three years later. A second son, Christopher John, was born on December 16, 1963.

When Chris was still a baby, the Jelics relocated to Natick, Massachusetts, where Ralph took assistant coaching jobs at Boston University – earning a master's degree in education there – then, in 1968, at Harvard. In 1971 the family returned home to Pittsburgh, where Ralph served as the university football team's defensive coordinator for the next two seasons. The South Hills seemed as good a place as any to raise kids.

"He wanted us to have 'roots' instead of wandering around the country every few years," said Jeff Jelic, who has a medical and a dental degree and specializes in maxillofacial surgery.[8]

Chris also has a sister, Jane, four years younger. She lettered twice in volleyball at Indiana University of Pennsylvania and now teaches special-education students.

Their talents notwithstanding, Ralph and Cynthia Jelic never forced their kids to follow in their footsteps, nor did they coach them. They just played the role of supportive parents, stressing commitment.

"Whatever you went into," Chris said, "whether it was a sport, classwork, if you were going to go into the band, whatever you were going to do, you need to give 100 percent. You need to give your best effort."

Jeff was the more studious of the two boys; an article in the *Pittsburgh Press* said he averaged B's to Chris's C's. Chris was the gregarious one.

"Everyone in Mt. Lebanon knows Chris," Ralph Jelic said in 1983. "He's in the middle of everything. He's always been a leader. He just seems to have that extra drive."[9]

Chris excelled at football and baseball. Despite being 5-feet-11 and 180 pounds, he played quarterback and punter on what longtime Mt. Lebanon high-school assistant athletic director Russ Jones dubbed the best teams the school ever had.[10] In 1980 and 1981, Mt. Lebanon lost a total of one regular-season game (undefeated in the latter year) en route to back-to-back championships in the Western Pennsylvania Interscholastic Athletic League (Class AAAA). In baseball, he was in the top three in the league in home runs and RBIs his junior and senior years.

"My dad never pushed us into anything," Chris Jelic said. "In fact, one of the benefits of growing up with him having played and coached in college – he also scouted in NFL for a number of years as well – he would always say, 'Look, you have some ability in both sports, as long as you're enjoying them, play them as long as you can, or as long as you want and the decision will make itself,' which it did. It just didn't happen until after my junior year in college."

Major Division I schools came calling with full scholarship offers – Indiana, Boston College, Michigan, North Carolina State.[11] But when the University of Pittsburgh made him an offer, "it was kinda like a no-brainer." His parents had both been Panthers, and Jeff was already there on a wrestling scholarship. And the football program was only five years removed from an NCAA national championship. "I had been to a lot of Pitt's football camps in the summer," Jelic said. "So I knew some of the coaches

ONE-HIT WONDERS

and got to know the vibe. It was close to home." Foge Fazio's eleven it was.

Still, Jelic made clear when he was recruited for football that he be allowed to play baseball in the spring. (But for the commitment to play football – "because I kind of always figured baseball was gonna be my sport just based on my size" – Jelic speculated that he might have been taken in the amateur baseball draft out of high school.[12]) He made an exception his freshman year for spring football, because the quarterback position would be a free-for-all, due to the departure of graduating senior and future Pro Football Hall of Famer Dan Marino.

Jelic said he had positive memories of Marino, who "was a pretty good baseball player in high school at Central Catholic" in Pittsburgh. Marino's future sister-in-law was a high-school classmate of Chris's at Mt. Lebanon; his wife, Claire Veazey, was in Jeff's grade.

"Danny always had the reputation of being a cocky guy, but if you look at a lot of the good athletes, a lot of the good football players, they always have a little cockiness to them, that kind of confidence thing," Jelic said. "I had a pretty good relationship with Dan. Although I respected him, one of the things that happened with me, growing up with my dad being a college coach, I really wasn't impressed with it. There really wasn't any of that idol worship, no matter what sport I was in."

With Marino starting and the backup quarterback also about to graduate, Chris knew his playing time as a freshman would be limited. So he would catch punts "to keep myself busy during practice." Then the free safety, Tom Flynn (who had a short career in the NFL), injured himself, and Tony "Dino" Fellino, the defensive backfield coach, suddenly found himself without a reliable receiver who would not drop punts. Jelic got the call, returned five punts, and played two games at free safety. Pitt made the Cotton Bowl, losing, 7-3, to Southern Methodist.

Jelic positioned himself in the top two for the starting quarterback job that spring. Then he went off to play summer-league baseball to make up for lost time. Meanwhile, Pitt hired a new quarterbacks coach, Ron Turner, who took umbrage at Jelic's splitting time between two sports. No one serious about football would have other priorities.

"Going into my sophomore year, there was a little bit of a contentious relationship, so to speak, because they wanted me to quit baseball, and I didn't do it," Jelic said.

Jelic lost the starting quarterback job twice that year – first to John Cummings; then, when Cummings fractured his clavicle in the season opener, to John Congemi. Jelic would generally be a late-game replacement – notably, he engineered what proved to be the winning touchdown in the fourth quarter of a 21-16 victory over Notre Dame. The Panthers made the Fiesta Bowl that year, losing to Ohio State, 28-23. Jelic subbed in for the final two plays (seven seconds), but Pitt's hopes died on Ohio State's 24-yard line.

Having played baseball that spring, Jelic was third on the depth chart at quarterback going into his junior year, and he volunteered to play the defensive backfield, at safety and as a punter. He also backed up at quarterback, even starting two games. The reduced role didn't bother him; he was just looking for playing time. And that summer, he had caught a glimpse of his future in Cape Cod.

Pitt was not known as a baseball school – in fact, in Jelic's sophomore year, 1984, it was not even in an athletic conference. And scouts were not devoting much attention to a school where weather prevented year-round practice.

"My dad would say to me, 'You know, you're one of the best players around here, probably one of the best players in the state, but that really doesn't tell us where you fit,'" Jelic said. His cousin knew Mickey White, the scouting supervisor for the Cincinnati Reds in New England at the time. "So Mickey made some phone calls and pulled some strings to get me into the Cape."

For an aspiring professional ballplayer, playing in the Cape Cod Baseball League was the equivalent of sending a self-proclaimed wine connoisseur to the South of France. Think you have real talent? Now is the time to test it against other college players who think the same.

Jelic, assigned to the Hyannis Mets, competed against dozens of would-be big leaguers, including future All-Stars Joey Cora [Chatham], Joe Girardi [Cotuit], Greg Vaughn [Cotuit], and Walt Weiss [Harwich].[13] Not to mention the entire 1984 Olympic team, which practiced on the Cape that summer.

The difference was not so much running or hitting, Jelic said, but in the pitching. "In the Northeast, you might play a team that would have one real good pitcher," he said. "And what would one real good pitcher mean? Would it mean one of the best pitchers in the country? Maybe not, but it may be a guy that was noticeably a good pitcher on that particular team. Whereas you go up there, every guy on the staff was

ONE-HIT WONDERS

probably the ace at whatever their college was – the ace at Stanford, the ace at USC, at Oklahoma State – and you saw them every night."

Jelic hit .320 for Hyannis, and scouts noticed. "That's where the reality set in I'm probably going to end up getting drafted at some point for baseball," he said.

Jelic had pitched in high school, and his sophomore year Pitt coach Bobby Lewis used him occasionally as "kind of our closer," Jelic said, coming in from right field to pitch out of a jam, then going back to right when a new pitcher was summoned the next inning, "so that my bat stayed in" the lineup.

However, his speed was not quite the same level as a typical outfielder. Scouts suggested that with his "quick release" and "extremely strong arm" (honed at quarterback), he would increase his draft value if he learned to be a catcher.

"He adapted like a duck to water," Lewis said.[14]

"But the other good thing was, I could play infield, I could play outfield, I could do a bunch of different things," Jelic said. "I'm sure a lot of that had to do with athletic ability, but later in pro ball that ended up helping me."

The strategy worked – in the spring of 1985, Jelic hit .371 with 6 home runs and 27 RBIs; made all-Big East, in Pitt's first year in the conference; and was ranked among *Baseball America's* top 50 amateur prospects – a likely second-rounder.

Laurels notwithstanding, Jelic remained clueless about how the draft would actually go. "I can remember from that day, my dad said, 'Are you gonna wait around?' I'm like, 'Wait around for what? Whatever!'" Jelic said. He drove to Pitt's campus – about 11 miles from his house – to play basketball.

He returned home later to find his teenage sister, Jane, standing in the front door.

"Kansas City Royals, second round!" she said. A telegram revealed Jelic was the 45th overall pick, as a catcher.

Ralph Jelic spoke to family friends who were lawyers and agents to gauge the amount of money they should ask for. But Chris was eager to sign – he knew that if he returned to Pitt for his senior year, he probably would not go much higher the next year that would make returning worth it.

"It's like, you know what, you're going to haggle over a couple of bucks, you're good enough to make it, let's get on with it," he said. Though sometimes for fun these days, he will ask a friend who is a baseball executive, "'Hey, out of curiosity, what did the 45th pick get this year?' And he'd tell me, and I'd go, 'Oh my gosh, you gotta be kidding me! I could've retired.' It's insane."

One thing they did agree to: In addition to his $65,000 signing bonus, the Royals would pay for Jelic to finish the three semesters of college he had left, whenever he chose to go back.

"He's born to be a catcher, in our opinion," Royals director of scouting Art Stewart said, observing that Jelic "catches like he's a five-year veteran," and that he was "the type that can see the big leagues quick."[15]

Two weeks later, Jelic was catching for the Eugene Emeralds in short-season A-ball. He hit .313 as the Emeralds were crowned Oregon division champions in the Northwest League. On August 22 he inadvertently instigated one of the most brutal brawls in league history against the Salem Angels, who then were within striking distance of first. Jelic was behind the plate when a retaliatory pitch sailed over Angels batter Bill Geivett's head. Geivett and Jelic exchanged words.[16]

"The next pitch was right down the middle, but Bill threw his bat at our pitcher," Jelic said. "So when he threw the bat at the pitcher, I actually picked him up and slammed him on the ground and landed on top of him. And I remember, we were throwing punches, and I can remember I landed facing their dugout, and

their whole dugout just charged us. And it just opened up the floodgates."

The bench-clearing melee stopped play for 15 minutes, as inebriated Emerald fans threw debris on the field – appropriately, it was quarter-beer night. Four were ejected, though Jelic – who at the time said he tackled Geivett "to keep him from going anywhere and doing anything"[17] – was not among them. A few days later, Geivett and Jelic apologized to each other "and we ended up kinda being buddies."[18]

Jelic spent the offseason in the instructional league honing his catching skills, then reported to Class-A Fort Myers in 1986, then back to the instructional league that fall. He had an "above average year" (his words) in the Florida State League – batting .256 with 50 RBIs in 108 games, including a .403 on-base percentage – but admitted not having a break "wore me out a little bit."

In 1987, the Royals invited Jelic to big-league camp for the first time, though predictably, he was sent to their minor-league facility in Sarasota before the month was out. On March 27, with about a week left in spring training, he was kicking back with his teammates in the complex's common room when his name came over the intercom to report to the minor-league director's office. The Royals needed a catcher to replace an aging Jim Sundberg,[19] so they had traded promising pitching prospect David Cone to the Mets for Ed Hearn, fresh off an auspicious rookie season behind the plate. To balance out the transaction, the Mets also sent over Mauro Gozzo and Rick Anderson, two hurlers with middling expectations – and the Royals threw in Jelic.[20]

After Jelic broke the news to his disbelieving teammates, he loaded up his car and drove to the Mets' minor-league camp in St. Petersburg.

He wasn't too concerned about integrating himself into the wild bunch of World Series champions. He had also played alongside George Brett and Bret Saberhagen and some formidable Royals teams in big-league camp, after all, and was not easily star-struck.

Growing up, "I was never one of those guys that was like this diehard follow all these baseball teams," he said. "So I got traded, it was like, 'OK, pack it up, here we go, here's my next team.'"

At Class-A Lynchburg in the Carolina League, Jelic was among the league leaders in hitting (.330, 8 home runs, 48 RBIs) at the all-star break when he was promoted to Double-A Jackson. He didn't fare as well the second half, but the Mets put him on their 40-man roster in the offseason and he spent most of spring training in big-league camp before returning to the Texas League.

But in Jackson in 1988, his shoulder started to fall apart. Perhaps it was from all those years throwing harder than ever, year-round every day, first as a quarterback, then as a catcher. Pitchers have pitch counts, but no one keeps track of what catchers and quarterbacks throw.[21]

"My mindset was always, football, you're always playing hurt, so if you're not feeling good or something's bothering you or whatever, if I could put up with the pain, I'm just gonna keep playing," Jelic said.

That included catching every pitch of a 26-inning game against San Antonio that began the evening of July 14, was suspended in the 25th inning at 2:28 A.M., and ended in a 1-0 loss two days later. It was the longest game in Texas League history, both by innings and time (7 hours 23 minutes), and the longest game to remain scoreless in Organized Baseball history.[22]

But the janky shoulder, along with a torn rib-cage muscle, limited him to 88 games, and a .209 batting average.

It also prompted a visit with Dr. James Andrews in Birmingham, Alabama.

Aggressive rehab from surgery on a loosened shoulder socket occupied Jelic that winter. The doctors advised him he might need a full year to recover from the procedure completely. He reported to Mets camp in Port St. Lucie the spring of 1989 as a nonroster invitee and was optioned back to Jackson.

Initially, he was used as pinch-hitter and DH, but the dearth of playing opportunities[23] suppressed his batting average to .206 by late July.[24] As the shoulder healed, he started working out at first base, third base, and the outfield. The additional work helped raise his average to .257 by season's end.

Coming back from an injury, especially in the minors, can be "tedious," Jelic said, but "my thing was, I could always hit, so I figured having some versatility and doing some other things, even when I couldn't really catch, I always felt pretty comfortable in what I could do."

Jelic attributed this "versatility" as a reason for why he ultimately was called to the big leagues.

But that was a year away. There was still Triple-A ball to conquer, and in 1990 Jelic headed to Tidewater. Although Jelic enjoyed the "camaraderie" of the minor leagues, he admitted "the bus rides can be brutal."[25] He welcomed the use of airplanes at the farm system's highest level.[26]

ONE-HIT WONDERS

"But even here we only get $14 in meal money on the road," he mused at the time. "And $10 of that has to go to clubhouse dues. That leaves you with four bucks a day. That's not even enough for McDonald's unless you bring your own money."[27]

Jelic's arm still was preventing him from catching much, so he played first and third instead.[28] He hit .306 – with a .406 on-base percentage – with 49 RBIs in 92 games. His roommates in Tidewater, Darren Reed and Rocky Childress, both had some major-league experience; it seemed only a matter of time.

The call came in early September,[29] with the Mets and the Pirates separated by a half-game atop the National League East. Jelic said he had been "limping around" for a couple of days with a bruised hip, having run into a concrete barrier down the third-base line at Tidewater's Met Park.

He thought manager Steve Swisher was checking on his injury when he delivered the news. He couldn't believe it.

"And we were joking," Jelic said, "he said, 'You know, you idiot, I saw you run into that wall, I knew you were getting called up a couple days ago. I saw you run into that wall, all I could think about was, 'Oh no!' That's how I found out."

Jelic met the team in St. Louis, but his role was limited to that of a spectator over the next four weeks, watching the Mets' postseason hopes slowly wither.

"By the time I got into a game, I hadn't seen live pitching for probably close to a month," Jelic said.

But he would take early batting practice and shag fly balls before each game, which caught the eye of manager Bud Harrelson and bench coach Doc Edwards.

"They're like, 'Hey, you look pretty good in the outfield,'" Jelic said, "and I told them, 'I played outfield most of my life, so this is nothing new.'"

At Shea Stadium on September 30, the day the Mets were mathematically eliminated, right fielder Daryl Boston had to be removed after running into the wall in the fifth inning.

As Harrelson pondered who should take his place, Edwards had the bright idea: "Put Jelic in!"[30] Boston was on deck in the bottom of the inning, so Jelic was barely able to grab his helmet and bat before Cubs pitcher Steve Wilson finished his warmups.

"I didn't even have time to think about it," he said.

Jelic had faced Wilson in the minors, so he knew exactly what he threw, but struck out on a 3-and-2 count.

"I almost fell over, I was swinging so hard," he said.

Jelic went to left field in the top of the sixth and was replaced by a pinch-hitter in the bottom of the inning.

The Mets then headed to Pittsburgh for the season's final series. Jelic started all three games in left field, a section of which was packed with his hometown faithful. Although the Pirates had already clinched the division, the fans still booed the Mets lineup mercilessly.

"Except that when they announced my name, they would cheer," Jelic said. Pittsburgh may be a big city, but everybody knew the Jelics.

In the opener at Three Rivers Stadium, Jelic went 0-for-4, but reached base on the aforementioned Sid Bream error. He scored his first big-league run on a single by – of all people – David Cone. In the second game, he *would* have had his first RBI had the grounder to Jay Bell been ruled a hit instead of an error, as it scored Pat Tabler.

Going into the season finale, October 3, Jelic was a career 0-for-7. After two groundouts and a fly ball, he was 0-for-10. In the top of the eighth, the Pirates brought in 41-year-old Doug Bair, a 15-year veteran making his final major-league appearance.[31] The Mets were ahead by one, and Jelic led off the inning.

The count was 3-and-1, and Jelic, thinking fastball, pounced on one down the middle that sailed out into the left-center-field seats.

"It was kind of like a line drive, so I took off running," Jelic said. "I'm thinking, this is going off the wall, and I'm running full speed as I hit first base, when I looked up and saw the ball go out of the park."

Jelic slowed to a trot amid scattered cheers.[32] The Pirates saved him the ball, which Bair signed.

"Tell him I said thanks," Jelic said that day.[33]

The Mets ultimately won, 6-3.[34]

"The last game, my last at-bat and in my hometown," Jelic told the Associated Press. "You couldn't write a better script."[35]

He was referring to the season, of course, but shortly after it ended, he was in Birmingham again for a second shoulder operation. He also had another procedure that offseason to repair a perforated eardrum (and two follow-up surgeries the next two years when that one didn't take).

The Mets front office figured that Jelic would be of little value to the organization if he could not catch – and coming off a second surgery, with so much uncertainty, Jelic knew, "I'd be wasting my time." The Mets released him on November 13.

ONE-HIT WONDERS

Luckily, he had somewhere to go, as Joe McIlvaine, who had been the Mets' assistant general manager in 1990, had just become the Padres GM.

"He said, 'Look, if you can catch, great; if not, we know you can hit, and we know you can play other positions. So catching will be a bonus,'" Jelic said. "That sold me there."

Jelic signed with the Padres organization and was sent to Triple-A Las Vegas. Doctors recommended he take his time with recovery, as the aggressive approach he took after the first surgery might have necessitated the second one. But the road back still proved challenging, as he found out when he and a buddy tried to play catch a month after the operation.

"I couldn't even throw it like 10 feet," Jelic said. "I'm like, 'Oh, this isn't good! This is not good. I may need to go back to school earlier than I think.'"

It got better, but he didn't catch at all in 1991, limited to 49 games at first base, third base, the outfield, and designated hitter. But still had a .436 on-base percentage and 23 RBIs.

The Padres knew Jelic needed more playing time, so they sent him to Double-A Wichita to start 1992, then brought him back up to Las Vegas in midseason. He continued to play first, third, and the outfield.

"But I tried to come back a little too quickly, and I ended up hurting my elbow," he said. "So I had my elbow scoped twice in '92, once in the middle of the season, and about six weeks later, like an idiot, I was playing, even though I was hurt. So in the offseason, '92, I had it scoped a second time."

But for timing that season, he might have had another brush with "The Show." Jim Riggleman, his manager in Las Vegas, had been promoted to manage San Diego. Riggleman favored having "that kind of utility guy that could hit and play multiple positions" on the roster, Jelic said. And there was an opening right around the time Jelic had his first shoulder surgery.

Four or five weeks later, Tony Torchia, the Las Vegas hitting coach, pulled Jelic aside. "He goes, 'I don't wanna tell you this to make you feel bad. I'm telling you this because you're being recognized: you were gonna fill that spot. And now you're hurt,'" Jelic said. "So it's one of those, I appreciate that he told me that, but it was kinda like, aw, you gotta be kidding me."

Jelic still showed up at camp in 1993 and earned the starting first baseman's job and the cleanup spot in Las Vegas. Then, on April 7, Las Vegas picked up Mike Simms, who had a few stints with the Houston Astros and was three years younger than Jelic.

"He was playing first base every day, and I was pretty much DH'ing and playing a couple days a week," Jelic said, "and I'm like, 'OK, I can see where this is going.'" He was 29, and he didn't want to be "bouncing around the minor leagues until I'm in my 30s. It's time to move on."

So in June, he asked for his release, and he and Organized Baseball parted ways at the All-Star break.

As planned eight years earlier, he returned to Pitt to finish his degree, attending nights and weekends to graduate with a BA in communications in 1994. He began working in sales in 1995.

No stranger to travel from his playing days, he spent the next decade traversing the Midwest and Mid-Atlantic regions, pitching to steel mills and automotive plants in Baltimore, Chicago, and along the Rust Belt.

Then in 2015 he moved into management, at Quaker Houghton, an industrial chemical company based in Conshohocken, Pennsylvania. Jelic is the regional sales manager for the Great Lakes, dispatching representatives and supervising budgets on accounts between Western New York and Michigan, as well as a small portion of Canada.

A lifelong bachelor, his home life has been somewhat nomadic, as well – he spent time living in Pittsburgh, Cleveland (twice), and parts of Michigan. As of 2020, he lived in Wyandotte, Michigan, about a half-hour south of Detroit along the Canadian border. He is an avid fisherman and golfer.

Although he does not coach any Little League teams, he has a niece and several nephews to throw the ball around with, including Jeff's teenage son, Jason, in whom he sees prospect potential.

"When I go home and visit my mother, my nephews will come in and sometimes they'll want to go to the batting cage, or they'll call me, and tell me what's going on, ask me questions," Jelic said. "I like to play catch, and then for three days I can't lift my arm above my head."

He added, "I always make a joke, I say, 'I have one good throw in me.' So if you need, like, one good throw, I got one good throw, and then I'm on the DL for about three weeks. But it's not like I'm going out throwing every day, either."

He has several friends still working in sports – in front offices, as coaches, or in media – and sometimes he will drop by when they are in town facing the Tigers, or when he is in Pittsburgh.

"The evaluation of players are a lot different nowadays," he said. Though, he added, "That sabermetrics stuff drives me nuts." He doesn't necessarily mean it

ONE-HIT WONDERS

negatively – just that maybe he is of an older-school mentality. As he tells his nephew when he starts questioning him about what he thinks about his exit velocity, "You know what? See the ball, hit the ball! You're worrying about all these numbers. You don't have to."

He remains a bit of a local celebrity in the Pittsburgh area, where many of the residents enjoy hearing about his brushes with greatness in football and baseball.

"I don't look back and regret anything," Jelic said. "Had I never made it to the big leagues, maybe I could say, 'Well, was I ever good enough to get there?' Well, you know what, I got there. It's not a 'what if?'"

SOURCES

Professional baseball statistics, unless otherwise indicated, are from baseball-reference.com; college football statistics are courtesy of Pitt media guides from 1982-1984; college baseball statistics are gathered from articles within the Associated Press, *Pittsburgh Post-Gazette*, *Pitt News*, and *Pittsburgh Press*. All quotes from Chris Jelic, unless otherwise noted, are from an interview with the author on October 11, 2020. Special thanks to John Fredland for helping make the connection, and to Jeff Jelic for his additional information and insight.

NOTES

1. Interview with author, October 11, 2020. All quotations from Chris Jelic, unless otherwise noted, are taken from this conversation.
2. Jelic postulated in his interview with the author that the scorers made the call because Zane Smith had a no-hitter at that point; actually, he'd already allowed two hits. Jelic came around to score that inning what was ultimately the go-ahead run in the Mets' 4-1 victory.
3. Jeff Jelic email to author, October 5, 2020.
4. Dallas Mavericks owner Mark Cuban also attended Mt. Lebanon High School in the 1970s – and was cut from the basketball team.
5. Jeff Jelic email to author, October 5, 2020.
6. Jerry DiPaola, "Ex-Pitt Standout Ralph Jelic Remembered for Impact as Father, Community Contributor," *Pittsburgh Tribune-Review*, July 25, 2018, archive.triblive.com/sports/college/pitt/ex-pitt-standout-ralph-jelic-remembered-for-impact-as-father-community-contributor/.
7. DiPaola.
8. Jeff Jelic email to author, October 5, 2020.
9. Bob Smizik, "The Jelic Boys are Chips Off the Old Block," *Pittsburgh Press*, January 17, 1983. Ralph Jelic influenced Jeff's decision to become a wrestler in high school, because he was too small for football.
10. "Mt. Lebanon's Jones Retires after 36 years," *The Almanac* (South Hills Community News), June 23, 2015, thealmanac.net/news/mt-lebanon-s-jones-retires-after-years/article_83554966-272f-5dfa-b29a-300d2ccf1e28.html.
11. Jelic notes that NC State offered him a baseball scholarship.
12. Jelic said that he went to some baseball tryouts his senior year and had some discussions with area scouts, but they shied away from "if we draft you" hypotheticals, because "back then, there wasn't anyone who was going to waste a draft pick on me for baseball knowing I was going to play football at Pitt. But the experience was the first time it "started creeping in" to Jelic's mind that he might be more than just a top local talent.
13. Hyannis had three future major leaguers: Jelic, Scott Hemond, and Scott Jordan.
14. Associated Press, "Jelic May Switch to Baseball," *Gettysburg* (Pennsylvania) *Times*, May 30, 1985.
15. "Pitt's Jelic Drafted by Kansas City in the Second Round," *Pittsburgh Post-Gazette*, June 4, 1985. Ironically, Jelic told the author that because his last year of college was his first year catching, at that point, "I probably only caught 20 games in my entire life."
16. Jelic said the Angels had hit Eugene's Rafael DeLeon, one of the smallest guys on the team, twice. He recalled that the "words" he exchanged consisted of Geivett turning around and saying, "Hey, you guys better –" and Jelic responding, "Well, your guy is the one who is gonna get you hurt! Your pitcher did it."
17. Stan Pusieski, "Ems Win the Fight for First, 12-4," *Eugene Register-Guard*, August 23, 1985.
18. Interview with author, October 11, 2020. Injuries prevented Geivett from making the majors, but he bounced around baseball front offices in the decades following. He self-published a book about his experiences in 2017. mlb.com/news/former-rockies-exec-bill-geivett-writes-book-c212930158.
19. Sundberg, nearing 36, had batted .212 in 1986, and was himself traded to the Cubs a week later.
20. The rest of Cone's career would include two 20-win seasons, a Cy Young Award (with the Royals, after he returned as a free agent), a perfect game, and five All-Star team selections, not to mention five World Series championships. The rest of Hearn's career would include 13 games.
21. Email between Jeff Jelic and John Fredland, October 4, 2020. Chris Jelic confirmed that the year-round throwing might have messed up his shoulder, in an email with the author on November 15, 2020.
22. For a detailed retrospective on all 26 innings that cites to these records, see John Whistler, "The Game That Wouldn't End," *San Antonio Express-News*, July 13, 2013.
23. Jackson, as a National League franchise, did not use the designated hitter at home, and only three of its Texas League opponents were American League farm clubs – meaning DH opportunities were not plentiful.
24. David Assad, "Mets Farmhand Chris Jelic on a Hitting Tear," *Pittsburgh Post-Gazette*, August 24, 1989.
25. Interview with author, October 11, 2020.
26. Scott Campbell, "Former Pitt Baseball Player Now Major League Prospect," *The Pitt News*, June 6, 1990.
27. Campbell.
28. The Mets exhausted seven catchers in 1990, including Dave Liddell, whose major-league career also consisted of one hit; it's possible that had Jelic been at full strength, he would have been called up earlier as one of them.
29. Several newspapers ran the item on September 5, 1990. Jelic could not confirm the exact date, but he said the Mets were in St. Louis, and they played two games there September 3 and 4.
30. Chris Jelic interview with author, October 11, 2020.
31. The game was also the last for Pirates starter Jerry Reuss, whom Jelic faced his first two at-bats.
32. One person remembered Jelic getting a "standing ovation" from Pirates fans after the home run, see "Gravybill" (October 23, 2002), *The Ultimate Mets Database*, Ultimatemets.Com/Profile.Php?Playercode=0439&Tabno=7. Archive video footage of the crowd at that moment was too blurry for the author to verify this.
33. Paul Meyer, "It's NL Playoff Time for Bucs," *Pittsburgh Post-Gazette*, October 4, 1990.
34. The winning pitcher that day was Frank Viola, who became the 18th pitcher in history to win 20 games in both leagues.
35. Associated Press, "Viola Gets No. 20 as Mets Beat Pirates," *Spokane* (Washington) *Spokesman Review*, October 4, 1990.

STAN JOHNSON

By Alan Cohen

It is the stuff of dreams. Coming to bat with the bases loaded, representing the lead run. Stan Johnson, in just his ninth major-league at-bat, was in that position. Little did he know that it would be his last major-league at-bat. Perhaps had he not hit into a rally-killing double play, he would have had more opportunities. We will never know.

In his very first season as a professional, he had a similar opportunity while playing for the Davenport White Sox of the Three-I league. On July 15, 1957, against Keokuk, Johnson came up in the sixth inning with the bases loaded and his team clinging to a 3-1 lead. He "picked out a fast pitch delivered by (Harold) Dodeward, and when the ball finished traveling, it was somewhere in the Mississippi River."[1] Davenport won the game, 7-3.

Stanley Lucius Johnson was born on February 12, 1937, in Dallas, Texas. He was the second child of Lucius and Versey Johnson. His sister, Barbara, had been born a year earlier. At the time of the 1940 census, Lucius Johnson worked as a waiter in an athletic club. The family lived in the Dallas home of William M. Lyton, Versey Johnson's father and a church pastor. Ten family members and two lodgers lived in the home.

The family moved to San Francisco when Stan was young, and he first attended the High School of Commerce, where he was named to the second-team All-City squad in his sophomore year. Commerce was closed after his sophomore year and he transferred to Galileo High School. He played American Legion ball in 1952 for the A.H. Wahl Post.

Before the 1953 high-school baseball season, Johnson, while a junior at Galileo High School, worked out with the San Francisco Seals. This was in violation of California Interscholastic Federation rules and Johnson and four other players received suspensions. No sooner had the suspensions been announced than the city's superintendent of schools, Herbert C. Clish, pursued an investigation as to whether the boys involved had received appropriate notification that they were in violation of a rule.[2] After a week's investigation, the clash was resolved, and Johnson was reinstated. In his first appearance of the season, on April 17, he pitched his team to a 7-5 win and had three hits.

In the summer of 1953, Johnson played American Legion ball for Galileo Post 236. He was selected to play for the San Francisco team in the annual *Examiner* game. The game was a 12-inning, 12-12 tie. Of those who played that day, five players, including Johnson, made it to the major leagues. The others were Gene "Lefty" Hayden, Jim Small, Joe Gaines, and Earl Robinson.

In 1954 Johnson, a pitcher-outfielder, batted .407 and was named to the All-City team. He was selected to play in the annual Lions Club East-West game at Seals Stadium. He was also selected, for the second year, to play in the *Examiner* game. Playing left field, he went 1-for-5 with an RBI as his City team lost to the Northern California team, 5-4.

In the fall of 1954, Johnson entered City College of San Francisco. After the 1955 season he was the only unanimous choice for the All-Conference team in the Big Eight Junior College Baseball Conference.[3] He transferred to the University of San Francisco in the fall of 1955 and was at the school at the same time as basketball players Bill Russell and K.C. Jones were completing their college careers. Although Johnson played with the USF baseball team in a couple of exhibitions in 1956, he did not play in any regular-season games.

During the summer of 1956, Johnson batted .392 playing for the semipro Klamath Falls (Oregon) Lakers of the Northwest League, a league made up of collegiate players. Klamath Falls, managed by former big-leaguer Dino Restelli, went 30-5 and on August 25 Johnson went 6-for-6 with a triple and a homer. In the seven-run first inning of a 16-8 win, he singled and tripled. The next day, in the season finale, he went a more pedestrian 3-for-5 with a triple.[4] The first-inning triple led to his team's first run in a 7-0 win.[5] The performances did not go unnoticed.

ONE-HIT WONDERS

Johnson was signed by Chicago White Sox scout Dario Lodigiani on February 2, 1957. He signed for a bonus of $4,000, the maximum amount to avoid being subject to the Bonus-Baby Rule, which would have had him sit on the White Sox bench for two years. He was thus allowed time to develop in the minor leagues.[6] Johnson's numbers in the minors were formidable. He broke in with Davenport, Iowa, in the Three-I League in 1957. His hope for a hit in his first game was thwarted by a great play by Cedar Rapids right fielder Bob Norris. The first hit came in the fifth inning the next day, but when Johnson was thrown out trying to steal, a skirmish developed at second base and he was ejected.

After a slow start, Johnson's bat caught fire on May 6 and 7. In two games he went 7-for-9 with seven RBIs and his first two extra-base hits of the season, a triple in a 4-3 win over Cedar Rapids on May 6 and a two-run homer in an 18-9 drubbing of Keokuk on May 7. He put together a nine-game hitting streak in June and batted safely in 13 of 14 games at one point.

For the season, Johnson batted .282 with 8 homers and 69 RBIs. He finished fifth in the league with 138 hits and tied for sixth with 22 stolen bases.

In 1958 Johnson batted .364 with 58 extra-base hits and 110 RBIs at Colorado Springs in the Class-A Western League. His average was the third best in the league, and he led his team with 35 doubles, 11 triples, and 15 stolen bases. George Redden in the August 9 *Chicago Defender* said, "Stan Johnson, the Skysox's fleet outfielder, is currently atop of the heap in the batting department as he has an average well above the .300 mark."[7] Colorado Springs was the class of the Western League that season, winning the pennant by three games and placing its entire outfield, including Johnson, on the league's All-Star team.

In 1959 Johnson was promoted to the Indianapolis Indians of the Triple-A American Association and began the season with 11 hits in his first 23 at-bats.[8] On May 8 and 9, his bat keyed wins over St. Paul that brought his team's first-place record to 19-7. His seventh-inning grand slam off St. Paul's Bob Darnell highlighted a 6-1 win on May 8, and his seventh-inning homer the next night provided insurance in a 7-4 win. The Indians, after 35 games, were 26-9 and held a four-game lead over Minneapolis. However, Indianapolis, after its great start, lost momentum, slumped seriously, losing six of seven games after the American Association All-Star Game in mid-July, and slipped to third place.

Johnson's average was standing at .286 after a superlative performance on June 19. In his team's 5-3 win over Charleston, he had driven in a run with a double, homered, and made a game-saving catch in the seventh inning, leaping to corral a high liner with two runners on base. However, he pulled a leg muscle while making the catch and his availability was limited for much of the next month. He missed 13 games and pinch-hit in 11 others.

Nine consecutive losses at the beginning of August, the last seven by one run, dropped Indianapolis to fourth place. The Indians finished the season in third place in the league's Eastern Division and missed the playoffs. For the season, Johnson batted .281 and drove in 61 runs. He led his team with 16 stolen bases, only five of which came after his injury in June.

"A ballplayer who feels the juices running strongly in his veins once the bell rings."[9]

In 1960, Johnson was with the San Diego Padres of the Triple-A Pacific Coast League. On Opening Day, his team played a day-night doubleheader and he started off his season with a very productive day. He singled in a run in the opener and his three-run homer keyed a come-from-behind rally as the Padres won the nightcap, 7-6. He also excelled in the field, leaping to rob Seattle's Bud Podbielan of a homer in the first game.[10] Johnson began the month of May with a 13-game hitting streak, and hit safely in 16 of his first 17 games to raise his average from .246 to .325. He stayed hot for the balance of the PCL season. After batting .333 (third best in the league) with 50 extra-base hits, he was called up to the White Sox at the end of the PCL season. He was chosen the Padres' most valuable player and was named to the postseason all-star team. His manager at San Diego, Jimmie Reese, said, "They'd be wise to give him an opportunity to play, the way he has been going with the Padres."[11]

Johnson got into five games with Chicago and had his only major-league hit. He made his first appearance on September 18 in the second game of a doubleheader. He pinch-hit for pitcher Russ Kemmerer and struck out against Bob Bruce of the Tigers. His second chance came on September 23, at Cleveland. The White Sox were ahead 6-0 in the ninth inning. After Ted Kluszewski homered off Frank Funk, the Cleveland pitcher knocked down Chicago's Minnie Miñoso. In anger, Miñoso threw his bat toward the mound and was ejected from the game by umpire Bob Stewart. Chicago manager Al Lopez replaced Miñoso with Johnson, and Stan homered on Funk's first pitch to him.[12] In the bottom of the inning, Johnson played

ONE-HIT WONDERS

left field. He went hitless in his remaining four at-bats with the White Sox. He was put in the pool of eligible players for the expansion draft after the season but was not selected by either the Washington Senators or Los Angeles Angels.

Johnson went to spring training with the White Sox in 1961 and hit a two-run triple in the first spring-training game. On April 5 he was sent outright to San Diego. After batting .321 in his first 26 games, Johnson went into a slump. Through June 9, he had played in 43 of 54 games with the San Diego. His average was only .276 with no homers and only 12 RBIs.

On June 10 Johnson was part of an eight-player trade and went to the Kansas City Athletics along with Wes Covington, Bob Shaw, and Gerry Staley. In return, Chicago got Don Larsen, Ray Herbert, Andy Carey, and Al Pilarcik. Johnson was hitless in three games with Kansas City. He made his last major-league appearance on June 13. In the top of the eighth inning, the bases were loaded with one out and the A's trailed 7-4. Pedro Ramos had been summoned from the bullpen by Twins manager Cookie Lavagetto to face Hank Bauer. The lefty-swinging Johnson was sent up to pinch-hit for the right-handed Bauer. Johnson pulled a groundball to second base that was converted into a 4-6-3 double play. Johnson stayed in the game and played in right field.

At the trading deadline, the A's acquired Deron Johnson and Art Ditmar from the Yankees and Stan Johnson was sent to Honolulu. Johnson's major-league career was over after eight games and 11 plate appearances. His homer in 1960 was his only hit in nine at-bats.

Johnson finished the 1961 season at Hawaii in the PCL, playing in 86 games and batting .275 with 6 home runs and 53 RBIs. Although he never returned to the majors, he continued to play professionally through 1969.

In the offseason between the 1961 and 1962 seasons, Johnson was traded to the Dodgers organization and spent 1962 at Spokane in the PCL. He got off to a great start with Spokane and was leading the PCL in batting with a .352 average on June 17. The team did not fare well in the standings, finishing in last place with a 58-96 record. Johnson finished the year with a .286 batting average.

After the season Johnson was dealt to Seattle of the PCL for pitcher Bill Thom. He was with Seattle, then a Triple-A affiliate of the Boston Red Sox, for two years. In 1963 he led his team in batting (.297), homers (13), and RBIs (55) and tied for the lead in runs scored (78).

The Red Sox did not bring him back to the majors. The next season, 1964, he batted .289 and led the team in hits (134) and doubles (33). Once again the call did not come. Johnson remained in the Red Sox organization in 1965 when they switched their Triple-A affiliation to Toronto.

With Toronto, playing for manager Dick Williams, Johnson batted .268 with only 4 homers and 42 RBIs in 1965. He was no longer a prospect. The team finished in third place and, in the postseason playoffs, swept Atlanta and defeated Columbus four games to one to win the International League championship. In the final series, Johnson, batting leadoff in the first two games, went 3-for-8 with an RBI as the Maple Leafs took a 2-0 lead in the series. Game Three was a pitchers' duel between Billy Rohr of Toronto and Steve Blass of Columbus. The game was scoreless going into the bottom of the ninth inning at Toronto. Johnson reached first on an error by Gene Michael and, with two out, scored the winning run on a single by Russ Gibson, only the second hit allowed by Blass. Columbus averted the sweep in Game Four, but Toronto closed up the series in Game Five.

In 1966 Johnson was back with Toronto and batted .274 with 24 extra-base hits. He had 6 homers and 25 RBIs. The team contended all year and finished in a tie for second place, one game behind Rochester. Once again Toronto excelled in the playoffs, defeating Columbus 3-2 in a best-of-five series. In the decisive fifth game, Johnson singled in his team's first run in the second inning as the Maple Leafs won, 6-1. They defeated Richmond in five games in the best-of-seven Governor's Cup Series. In Toronto's Game Three 7-6 win, Johnson had two hits, including a double that brought home two runs when his team took a 3-0 lead in the second inning.

The next season with Toronto, 1967, Johnson played in 105 games, as he had in 1966, and batted .293. His suffered three on-field injuries during the season. He fouled a ball off his foot in early June, missing 10 games, and twice he was hit by pitches. He was platooned on occasion by manager Eddie Kasko. Speaking toward the end of July, Johnson said, "Sure, I'm older than most of these kids [he was 30], but I'm not exactly an old man. I don't mind resting once in a while, but I can still play every day – in fact, I'd like to."[13] A torrid stretch during June and July raised Johnson's batting average to .336, and he was named to the North team in the International League All-Star Game. For the season, he had 19 extra-base hits, including two homers. He had 29 RBIs, four more than

ONE-HIT WONDERS

in 1966. There was no return visit to the playoffs for the team, which finished sixth.

The summer of 1967 was notable for a number of reasons – in and out of baseball. It was a time of high racial tension and in the predawn hours on Sunday, July 23, rioting began in Detroit and lasted five days. Those tensions spread 57 miles south to Toledo, Ohio, where two nights of rioting resulted in the postponement of scheduled doubleheaders between Toronto and Toledo on July 25 and 26.[14]

In the majors, the Red Sox were en route to their first World Series appearance in more than two decades and one of their leaders was Reggie Smith, who finished second in that season's Rookie of the Year balloting. In 1966 at Toronto, Smith had roomed with Johnson, and he credited Johnson's tutelage with having been a key to his .320 batting average with the Maple Leafs.

With major-league expansion pending and attendance at the Toronto minor-league games woefully low, the Red Sox switched their Triple-A affiliation to Louisville in 1968 and Johnson batted only .206 in 84 games with the fifth-place Colonels. The 31-year-old Johnson was cut loose during the offseason and traveled to Japan for the 1969 season. Playing for the Taiyo Whales of the Japanese Central League, he batted .242 with 5 homers and 29 RBIs. He retired from professional baseball at the end of the season.

In 1970 and 1971 Johnson was a scout for the Red Sox.

Johnson married Jacqueline C. Miles on February 12, 1961. They had two children, Stacey Clair Johnson-Randolph, born in 1962, and Stan Jr., born in 1964. Stan's father, Lucius, died on May 13, 1972, from injuries suffered in a traffic accident.

Stan contracted Parkinson's disease in 2007. In his final days, he was also being treated for Alzheimer's disease. He died on April 17, 2012, and is buried in Holy Cross Catholic Cemetery at Colma, California.

SOURCES

In addition to the sources cited in the Notes, the author used Ancestry.com, Baseball-Reference.com, and *The Sporting News*, the *Daily Times* (Davenport, Iowa), the *Indianapolis Star*, and the following:

Hayward, Harry M. "5 S.F. Preps Ineligible for Attending Camps," *San Francisco Examiner*, April 7, 1953: 27.

MacCarl, Neil. "Rest Cure Helps Johnson Become Leafs' Bat Terror," *The Sporting News*, August 12, 1967: 31.

Prell, Edward. "Sox Farm Clubs Start to Produce," *Chicago Tribune*, November 13, 1958: D4.

Reich, Carl. "S.F. Legion Nines Bow in Openers," *San Francisco Examiner*, July 20, 1952: 28.

NOTES

1. John O'Donnell, "Dav-Sox Take Keokuk Series, 7-3," *Davenport* (Iowa) *Morning Democrat*, July 16, 1957: 11.
2. Harry M. Hayward, "Clish Orders Probe of Ban on 5 Preps," *San Francisco Examiner*, April 8, 1953: 30.
3. "CCSF's Johnson Tops Big Eight All-Star Nine," *San Francisco Chronicle*, June 12, 1955: 2-H.
4. "Lakers Sweep Series Against Cheney Studs," *Medford* (Oregon) *Mail Tribune*, August 27, 1956: 6.
5. "Leopold Shuts Out Studs with Three-Hitter," *Herald and News* (Klamath Falls, Oregon), August 27, 1956: 11.
6. "White Sox Sign Former Galileo Star Stan Johnson," *San Francisco Chronicle*, February 3, 1957: 4-H; "Chisox Sign Star USF Outfielder," *San Francisco Examiner*, February 3, 1957: II-15.
7. George Redden, "Colorado Springs," *Chicago Defender*, August 9, 1958: 20.
8. *The Sporting News*, April 29, 1959: 30.
9. Jack Murphy, "Mayor's First Pitch Goes Astray, but Padres Sparkle," *San Diego Union*, April 16, 1960: A-17
10. Murphy, "Mayor's First Pitch Goes Astray, but Padres Sparkle," *San Diego Union*, April 16, 1960: A-17
11. Keller, Earl, "Jolter Johnson Rated Dazzler by Padre Pilot," *The Sporting News*, August 17, 1960: 31.
12. Richard Dozer, "2 Home Runs Help Wynn Beat Indians," *Chicago Tribune*, September 24, 1960: 2-1.
13. Neil MacCarl, "Rest Cure Helps Johnson Become Leafs' Bat Terror," *The Sporting News*, August 12, 1967: 31.
14. John Hannen, "Mud Hens Postpone Tonight's Doubleheader," *Toledo Blade*, July 26, 1967: 49.

ED KENNA

By Phil Williams

One might think Ed Kenna a genteel soul who overachieved in his baseball life by appearing in two games with the Philadelphia Athletics in 1902. After all, the "poet pitcher" was a well-educated son of a US senator who authored two volumes of verse.[1] Yet for years after his Philadelphia stint, Kenna starred in the high minors and impressed onlookers as being a major-league talent. But he was too often his own worst enemy or fell victim to misfortune. Kenna found maturity in his post-baseball life as he served his native city of Charleston, West Virginia, as a newspaper editor. But for an early death at age 34, he was perhaps destined to follow in his father's footsteps.

Edward Benninghaus Kenna was born on October 17, 1877, in Charleston, the county seat of Kanawha County. He was the first of six children born to John and Annie (Benninghaus) Kenna.[2] His father was born in Kanawha County in 1848, when it was part of Virginia.[3] After John's father died in 1856, his mother moved her young family to Missouri. John worked the family farm, then, at 16, joined the Confederate Army, serving in General Joseph O. Shelby's forces.[4] Among the friends he made in this youth: the outlaw Jesse James.[5]

After the Civil War, John Kenna returned to Kanawha County and studied law. In 1870 the state repealed oaths enacted immediately after the Civil War to disenfranchise former Confederates. These voters allowed West Virginia's Democrats to "redeem" the state from Reconstruction.[6] John Kenna rose quickly in the party ranks, elected as Kanawha County attorney in 1872, to the US House of Representatives in 1876, and to the US Senate in 1882. In Washington, he championed West Virginia internal improvements and battled Republican tariffs. Yet Kenna's health deteriorated, and he died from heart disease in January 1893.

Senator Kenna left his young family with little more than a $10,000 life insurance policy.[7] Democratic President Grover Cleveland appointed his widow as Charleston's postmistress.[8] These means undoubtedly helped the family's eldest son, Edward, to continue

EDWARD BENNINGHAUS KENNA.

Ed Kenna.

his education. In these endeavors, athletics played a prominent role. At Mount St. Mary's College in Emmitsburg, Maryland, Ed captained the football team and was the baseball nine's star pitcher before graduating in 1898. Then he moved onto graduate work at Georgetown University. He shot put for their track and field team, played fullback, punted, and kicked for their football squad, and twirled and patrolled right field for Hoya baseball. Led by Kenna and Doc White, Georgetown's 1899 baseball team was considered the strongest collegiate nine in the nation.[9]

ONE-HIT WONDERS

Eligibility requirements varied considerably among colleges in this era. By pitching for Washington area semipro teams after the Hoyas' season concluded, Kenna was seemingly barred from further participation in Georgetown's athletics.[10] That fall he joined the faculty of Horner Military School in Oxford, North Carolina.[11] He captained their football team then, the next spring, starred on the diamond for them, with a Raleigh sportswriter labeling him "easily the best college twirler in the state."[12] Once the 1900 Horner baseball season concluded, he made his professional debut with the North Carolina Association's Statesville outfit. A Charlotte observer opined that "Kenna outclasses any pitcher in the league."[13] After the Association's season concluded, Kenna moved up to Toledo of the Class-B Interstate League in September. Often rattled in faster company, he went 0-4 with the Mud Hens. That fall, he coached football at Richmond College (now the University of Richmond).[14]

Kenna returned to his native state in 1901. First, he pitched for and studied law at West Virginia University.[15] After their spring campaign concluded, he signed with the Western Association's Wheeling Stogies. Kenna won his first five games with the Stogies.[16] Fred Knowles, the New York Giants' team secretary, scouted Kenna in Wheeling on July 20, but after seeing the pitcher lose his first game in an error-filled affair, left without making an offer.[17] Connie Mack, scurrying to find talent for the Philadelphia Athletics in their inaugural season, inquired as to Kenna's availability.[18] But Wheeling's management wasn't interested in selling him, and the pitcher wanted to stay in West Virginia. Down the stretch, Kenna and Frank Killen were the team's only twirlers, and worked hard.[19] Wheeling finished in fourth place, with a 70-64 record. Per a contemporary source, Kenna went 17-7 with the Stogies.[20]

Returning to West Virginia University that fall, Kenna was elected president of the senior law class and played quarterback for the Mountaineer football team.[21] In November the American League's Cleveland Blues signed him.[22] Days later, he broke his shoulder on the gridiron, ending his football season.[23]

For some time, at least back to his Georgetown days, Kenna had been writing poetry. West Virginia served as a muse, and he spent much of his free time as a Stogie writing.[24] That offseason, as his shoulder healed, he completed a volume.[25] *Lyrics of the Hills* appeared in 1902. One of its poems begins:

Huntin' time is comin'

For the pheasants are a drummin'

And the ches'nut burrs are turnin' on the south side of the tree;

And the "*whicker, whicker, whicker,*"

Of the raspin', screamin' flicker

Comes a driftin' from the mountain top across the crick to me.[26]

Kenna was a strapping 6-foot, 180-pound right-hander. It is uncertain what shoulder he broke playing football. But at Cleveland's 1902 spring training camp in New Orleans, he battled arm and shoulder soreness and a bout of dysentery.[27] He also found time to make "a world of friends since his arrival."[28] Cleveland manager Bill Armour later criticized his lack of concentration, reportedly stating, "Kenna was too busy writing verses, instead of paying attention to the national game."[29] The team released him on April 25.

Meanwhile, in Philadelphia, court injunctions upheld the National League's reserve clause and prevented Napoleon Lajoie, who had jumped from the Phillies to the Athletics before the 1901 season, from playing in-state with Mack's team. These injunctions affected three Athletics pitchers – Bill Bernhard, Bill Duggleby, and Chick Fraser – who had also jumped from the Phillies.[30] On May 1, Mack signed Kenna.[31]

On May 5, after starter Snake Wiltse allowed four hits and three runs in the first inning against the visiting Senators, Mack put Kenna in. "He held Washington down to five hits, and also showed that he is something of a 'sticker,' smashing the ball on the nose every time he came to bat," the *Philadelphia Record* observed.[32] One smash resulted in a double off Washington starter Watty Lee. Another, in the seventh, put Kenna on base with a fielder's choice. Three batters later, Harry Davis launched a three-run homer, propelling Philadelphia to a 7-5, come-from-behind, victory.

Four days later, Kenna started against visiting Baltimore. The Orioles eventually finished in the AL cellar in 1902, while the Athletics won their first pennant. But on this chilly, windy day, Baltimore pounced upon Kenna's offerings, hit-and-run perfectly, and ran the basepaths with abandon. Regarding Philadelphia's play: "While Kenna was easy [yielding 15 hits, eight walks, and six steals], his support was frightful and the manner in which the locals threw the ball around, got caught off bases and went to sleep was enough to make Connie Mack feel that the very air was full

ONE-HIT WONDERS

of injunctions," wrote the *Philadelphia Times*.[33] The Athletics lost, 13-6. Despite the poor play behind Kenna, Mack must have concluded that a veteran squad (Baltimore's lineup featured John McGraw and Wilbert Robinson that day) capably executing small ball was too much for his raw recruit. He released Kenna.

Soon afterward the American Association's Milwaukee Brewers sought to sign him. Yet, due to their inability to immediately locate Kenna and send advance money, another Milwaukee outfit – the Class-A Western League's Creams, beat them to the punch.[34] Kenna's new team stood at 18-22 when he debuted with them on June 15. His 19-8 record helped the Creams finish the campaign with an 80-54 record, only a game off first place. Among league regulars, Kenna's .739 winning percentage was topped only by Kansas City's Kid Nichols (.794). Contemporary statistics suggest that no pitcher in the league allowed fewer hits (5.63) per game than Kenna, while only Omaha's Frank Owen allowed fewer runs per game than Kenna's 2.56.[35]

In 1903, pitching a full season for the Creams, Kenna went 28-9 with 186 strikeouts. In early July, Washington offered Milwaukee manager Hugh Duffy $4,000 for five of his players, including Kenna. Duffy declined, in part because the Creams were in first place (and would eventually win the pennant).[36] Another factor may have been his decision to leave Milwaukee to manage the Philadelphia Phillies. By early September rumors toward this end were afoot, as was talk that Kenna would follow Duffy in signing with the Phillies.[37]

Simultaneously, Cincinnati Reds President Garry Herrmann, fresh from helping to broker peace between the National and American Leagues – for which he was appointed chair of baseball's new ruling National Commission – sought to bring the sport's minor leagues under this aegis.[38] Such an agreement was signed on September 11.[39] Ten days later, the Phillies drafted Kenna.[40] Soon afterward, news of Duffy's pre-draft negotiations with Philadelphia for the purchase of Kenna (and third baseman Jim Cockman) reached Herrmann. As these negotiations occurred during the Western League season, and because Duffy failed to pay the players their final checks, Herrmann awarded the two players to Milwaukee. For this action, "Mr. Herrmann was warmly congratulated by managers, players and newspaper men for his manly and sportsmanlike decision in so delicate a manner."[41]

The Western League, however, abandoned Milwaukee after the 1903 campaign. Kenna signed with the circuit's Denver Grizzlies.[42] In the aftermath, Duffy stated of Kenna, "I think [he] would be as good a pitcher as there was in the country, if he took care of himself."[43]

Kenna employed an underhanded "cannon-ball-like delivery."[44] From the beginning he possessed "a beautiful drop ball" that would be recalled well after his career ended.[45] In addition to this (likely) curve, Kenna possessed "speed to burn" and gradually evolved into a "careful and deliberate" pitcher "who uses his head" against the opposition.[46]

Yet, as Duffy implied, undisciplined behavior accompanied these talents. Kenna later admitted the need to curb his drinking.[47] He possessed a hot temper and, in 1901, perceived insults led him to assault an African-American at a Dayton hotel.[48] In poetry, he strove to tell a maiden "I love you" in "an honest manly way."[49] In life, he was a playboy, denying a story of him being wed to a young Milwaukee woman after he arrived in Colorado, and forever flirting with female fans in the stands.[50] A Denver paper noted in the midst of the 1904 season that no Western League player received more "mash notes" than Kenna. "He reads them and then passes them around among his team mates, all to have a good laugh at the expense of the foolish girl that writes them," the paper said.[51]

Denver led the pennant race until the very end of the season, when Omaha and Colorado Springs overtook the Grizzlies. Kenna posted a 21-12 record and 168 strikeouts.[52] Yet "Eddie constantly complained that the altitude interfered with his work" and sought to get out of Denver.[53] George Tebeau owned both the Grizzlies and the American Association's Louisville Colonels and in January 1905 traded Kenna to the Kentucky franchise. Afterward, a Denver paper struck a familiar tone: "If Kenna had taken care of himself during the season of 1904 he would have been drafted by the big leagues, and he would have made good up there."[54]

In early 1905, Kenna stated that he was on the wagon and planned to return to the majors after the coming Association season ended.[55] In April exhibition games against National League competition, he "pitched masterly ball" against the Giants, showed "midseason form" against the Reds, and two-hit the Pirates.[56] His efforts sagged in midseason due to illness, but by late August he was back in form and attracting the interest of two unspecified American League teams.[57]

ONE-HIT WONDERS

On August 31, after the visiting Colonels won three of four in Kansas City, the team sped back to a hotel in a horse-drawn wagon, hoping to catch a 6:15 train to Toledo. With a trolley car barreling down at them from behind, the wagon driver made a sharp turn, tipping over the vehicle and spilling its occupants. Several players were seriously injured, none more so than Kenna, who was dragged under the trolley's fender until it came to a stop. "Kenna's left elbow was dislocated, his left arm fractured, his nose broken, his body bruised, and his face scratched and lacerated."[58] His season was over, with a 16-13 record. Louisville finished in fourth place with a 76-75 mark.

Whether it was the lingering effects of his injuries or a failing pitching arm, Kenna never got on track in 1906, finishing the campaign with a 12-21 mark and allowing a league-high 139 walks (versus 95 strikeouts).[59] By midsummer, Kenna began to play right field, and finished with a .325 average in 55 games. "I certainly will try to persuade Tebeau to let me play the outfield instead of pitch next season," he said in December.[60]

Yet Kenna was back on Louisville's mound in 1907, battling injuries and increasingly ineffective. When released by the Colonels in July, he had a 3-7 record.[61] He pitched a little semipro ball in Kentucky that summer, then hung up his spikes.[62] Years earlier, Kenna had flirted with newspaper work but instead committed to professional baseball.[63] With this career over, he returned home and joined the *Charleston Gazette* as a reporter. By 1909, he became the newspaper's editor.[64]

Under Kenna's watch, the *Gazette*'s editorial page often engaged in boosterism befitting a small city. In 1910, the Class-D Virginia Valley League's Charleston Senators arrived. As the season began, the *Gazette* told its readers, "The support of the home team is one of the best ways to make its career one of success, and the successful ball team is one of the best advertisements that a town can have."[65] By August, however, the paper turned its ire upon loud-mouthed "pinheads" in the stands: "If this brand of self-sufficient, conceited and absolutely incompetent critics would but know they are fools, then the task of the base ball booster, the base ball players and the base ball owner would be easier."[66]

The *Gazette*'s editorial page also argued passionately for bettering Charleston's civic life. It raised concerns over increasingly polluted local rivers and the lack of public playgrounds.[67] On January 29, 1911, on behalf of the Associated Charities, a three-column editorial took readers on a detailed tour of the city's poorest neighborhoods and the suffering within. The piece concluded, "Let it not be said that Charleston cannot look after her own. Let us bring hope to the hopeless, food to the hungry, comfort to the afflicted. These are the deeds that make men blessed."[68]

Such a sense of localized responsibility was consistent with Kenna's political ideology. Like his father, he turned to Thomas Jefferson and Andrew Jackson for guidance. "The only check against autocracy and empire, is the power of the states – the vitality and integrity of local government," stated a February 1910 *Gazette* editorial.[69] "Laws cannot reform men, they cannot make men better, they cannot change their point of view," the paper argued later that year.[70]

The paper's editorials sometimes treated African-Americans in bluntly racist terms.[71] Yet the *Gazette* also forcefully denounced "the evil of lynching."[72] After Kenna's death, Charleston's principal black newspaper, the *Advocate*, graciously recognized his lack of demagoguery: "He was too kind-hearted to impose upon the weak and defenseless; too indifferent to popular acclaim to win it by ways that are dark or tricks that are vain."[73]

Like his father, Kenna identified with the largely Southern-based Democrats of this era. He was passionately partisan but could also be admiring of independent Republicans on a larger stage, such as Wisconsin Senator Robert La Follette.[74] Indeed, as Kenna's editorship progressed, so did his editorial page's focus upon national politics. Although a small city, Charleston was a state capital, not an isolated backwater. Kenna increasingly considered both its, and possibly his own, ambitions within a larger scope.

His temper remained intact. Local temperance advocates, whom he considered opportunistic Republican machine politicians, particularly angered him. In 1911 the Reverend Thomas Hare, superintendent of the West Virginia anti-saloon league, brought a speaker to Charleston to promote a "dry" vote. The speaker questioned the integrity of Kenna's late father. Kenna, who periodically went after "the 'Reverend' Tom" in the *Gazette*, decked Hare.[75] The "wets" triumphed in the ballot box.

This scrap aside, Kenna was becoming a respectable member of society. In February 1910 he wed Frances Beardsley, the 21-year-old daughter of a Charleston lawyer. Democrats urged him to run for a State Senate seat soon afterward, but he declined, reportedly stating he was afraid he might win.[76] West Virginia's Republican Governor William Glasscock issued a commission adding Kenna (at least symbolically) to his staff, with the honorary rank of colonel. A son, William, arrived in 1911. In January 1912 the Mountain States League (the Senators' new circuit) elected him its vice president.[77]

By that time, Kenna was in Grant, Florida, recuperating from a "nervous stomach disorder." He gradually improved, but in mid-March was suddenly afflicted by an attack of tonsillitis.[78] His health worsened quickly, and he died of heart failure on March 22. Survived by his wife and son, Ed Kenna was buried in Charleston's Spring Hill Cemetery. Soon afterward, a second volume of his verse, much of which initially appeared in the *Gazette*, was published posthumously. One of its shorter poems is *Trailing Arbutus*:

> Oh, modest flower, 'tis thine to bring
>
> The herald perfume of the spring;
>
> So silent death, 'tis thine to be
>
> The herald of Eternity.[79]

SOURCES

In addition to the sources noted in this biography, the author used Kenna's file from the National Baseball Hall of Fame, the *Encyclopedia of Minor League Baseball*, and the following sites: ancestry.com, genealogybank.com, and ohiocountywv.advantage-preservation.com.

The author is grateful to the staff of the West Virginia State Archives for their assistance in accessing their collection of the *Charleston Gazette*.

NOTES

1. In his day, Kenna was nicknamed the "poet pitcher." The "pitching poet" moniker arose posthumously. Baseball mythology may remember him as a poet who happened to pitch; his contemporaries thought him a pitcher who happened to write poetry.
2. A younger brother, John Edward (Jack), also played baseball, first playing for West Virginia University then pitching with minor-league teams in Chattanooga and Worcester, Massachusetts, from approximately 1909 to 1911.
3. Kanawha and the other counties that constitute West Virginia were part of the state of Virginia until the Civil War. Residents of the counties were generally anti-Secessionist and broke away from Virginia after it seceded from the Union. West Virginia was admitted to the Union as a state in 1863.
4. For a brief biography, see *Memorial Addresses on the Life and Character of John Edward Kenna* (Washington: Government Printing Office, 1893), 5-10.
5. "Kenna and Jesse James," *Clarksburg* (West Virginia) *Telegram*, January 27, 1893: 1.
6. For background on West Virginia Reconstruction, see Ralph Mann, "Reconstruction," *e-WV: The West Virginia Encyclopedia*, wvencyclopedia.org/articles/28, October 22, 2010. Accessed August 12, 2019. Also see Stephen D. Engle, "Mountaineer Reconstruction: Blacks in the Political Reconstruction of West Virginia," *The Journal of Negro History*, Vol. 78, No. 3 (Summer, 1993): 137-165. Available online at tinyurl.com/yymcvl6s.
7. *Weekly Register* (Point Pleasant, West Virginia), February 7, 1893: 3.
8. *Weekly Register*, May 16, 1893: 2.
9. Henry Chadwick, ed., *Spalding's Official Base Ball Guide, Season of 1900* (New York: American Sports Publishing Company, 1900), 125-128.
10. For examples of his semipro endeavors: "Victory for the Bureaus," *Washington Times*, June 18, 1899: 8; "Tarboro's Ball Pitcher," *Wilmington* (North Carolina) *Messenger*, July 29, 1899: 4. On Georgetown barring him, see "Gone to Pieces," *Sporting Life*, September 18, 1899: 1.
11. For more on his stay at Horner, see Edward B. Kenna, ed., *The Oxonian*, Vol. 3, No. 4 (December 1899). Available online at tinyurl.com/y4yffrm5.
12. "It Was Horner's Game," *Raleigh Morning Post*, May 1, 1900: 2.
13. "Kenna Did It," *Charlotte News*, July 5, 1900: 1.
14. "Football Team at the College," *Richmond Times*, September 30, 1900: 2.
15. For references to his pitching with WVU, see "W.&J. Team Shut Out," *Pittsburgh Post*, June 9, 1901: 13; "West Virginia's New Captain," *Pittsburgh Post*, June 18, 1901: 6.
16. "Young Collegian," *Cincinnati Enquirer*, June 30, 1901: 10; *Wheeling Daily Intelligencer*, July 17, 1901: 3.
17. "Two Games," *Cincinnati Enquirer*, July 21, 1901: 10; *Wheeling Daily Intelligencer*, July 22, 1901: 3.
18. "Pitcher Kenna," *Cincinnati Enquirer*, July 24, 1901: 4.
19. "Pitcher Kenna," *Cincinnati Enquirer*, August 14, 1901: 4.
20. "Notice Served on Kenna," *Cleveland Plain Dealer*, April 26, 1902: 4.
21. *Wheeling Daily Intelligencer*, October 19, 1901: 3.
22. "Kenna to Pitch for Cleveland," *Baltimore Sun*, November 14, 1901: 6.
23. "Kenna Is Out of the Game," *Pittsburgh Post*, November 16, 1901: 6.
24. "Baseball Gossip," *Cincinnati Enquirer*, February 4, 1902: 4. Notably, as a poet, Kenna never wrote of baseball.
25. *Wheeling Daily Intelligencer*, November 20, 1901: 3.
26. Edward B. Kenna, *Lyrics of the Hills* (Morgantown, West Virginia: Acme Publishing Co., 1902): 33.
27. "With the Leaguers at Athletic Park," *New Orleans Picayune*, April 4, 1902: 8; Ginger [pseud.], "Pelicans Beaten," *The Sporting News*, April 12, 1902: 6; "Bradley Again in the Game," *Cleveland Plain Dealer*, April 12, 1902: 6.
28. Ginger [pseud.], "Wright Was Wild," *The Sporting News*, April 5, 1902: 6.
29. "Around the Park," *New Orleans Picayune*, May 3, 1902: 8.
30. For a discussion of these court rulings, see Norman Macht, *Connie Mack and the Early Years of Baseball* (Lincoln: University of Nebraska Press, 2007), 264-269.
31. "Baseball Gossip," *Washington Times*, May 1, 1902: 4.
32. "Timely Home Run Drive," *Philadelphia Record*, May 6, 1902: 11.
33. "A Weird Exhibition," *Philadelphia Times*, May 10, 1902: 10. Also see "Win a Game at Last," *Baltimore Sun*, May 10, 1902: 6.
34. "A Little Mix-Up," *Sporting Life*, June 28, 1902: 15.
35. Francis C. Richter, ed., *Reach's Official American League Base Ball Guide, for 1903* (Philadelphia: A.J. Reach Co., 1903), 198.
36. "American League Notes," *Sporting Life*, July 11, 1903: 9.
37. "Phillies Get Kenna," *Minneapolis Journal*, September 5, 1903: 8.
38. J. Ed Grillo, "Is Not Worrying," *The Sporting News*, September 5, 1903: 1.
39. J. Ed Grillo, "Slight Changes," *The Sporting News*, September 19, 1903: 1.
40. "The Commission's First Work," *Sporting Life*, September 26, 1903: 4.
41. "Draft of Minor League Stars," *Cincinnati Enquirer*, October 27, 1903: 4.

ONE-HIT WONDERS

42 "Milwaukee Pitcher Signed with Denver," *Pittsburgh Press*, November 21, 1903: 10.

43 "Tips by the Managers," *The Sporting News*, December 12, 1903: 2.

44 "Lost to the Misfit Team," *Toledo Bee*, September 7, 1900: 6. On his delivery being underhanded: "Colonels Open the Season with a Splendid Victory Over St. Paul Club," *Louisville Courier-Journal*, April 20, 1905: 6.

45 "Baseball," *Norfolk Virginian-Pilot*, July 30, 1899: 15; "Only Three Years Off Toledo Sand Lots, 'Doc' Watson Is Major League Prospect," *Pittsburgh Press*, December 7, 1912: 8.

46 "Field of Sports," *Wheeling Daily Intelligencer*, August 9, 1901: 3; "Denver Wins Two Games," *Denver Post*, September 5, 1904: 11; Frank E. Force, "Opinions," *Minneapolis Tribune*, August 27, 1905: 39.

47 Brownie [pseud.], "Rough Treatment from the Fans," *Milwaukee Journal*, April 27, 1905: 9.

48 "Out of the Game," *Dayton Daily News*, September 21, 1901: 2.

49 Edward B. Kenna, *Lyrics of the Hills* (Morgantown, West Virginia: Acme Publishing Co., 1902), 68.

50 The report of him being wed to Miss Victoria Towell: *Racine (Wisconsin) Daily Journal*, March 24, 1904: 8. His denial: Brownie [pseud.], "Rough Treatment from the Fans," *Milwaukee Journal*, April 27, 1905: 9. An example of his flirting: "Colonels Now in Last Place," *Louisville Courier-Journal*, May 22, 1907: 6.

51 Otto Floto, "Eminently Fitting," *Denver Post*, August 1, 1904: 7.

52 Henry Chadwick, ed., *Spalding's Official Base Ball Guide, 1905* (New York: American Sports Publishing Company, 1905), 197.

53 Otto Floto, "Dan Patch Is Going into Winter Quarters After a Very Successful Advertising Season," *Denver Post*, November 15, 1904: 11.

54 "Fans Do Not Like the Trade," *Louisville Courier-Journal*, February 10, 1905: 6. [Note this article quotes a *Denver Times* sportswriter at length.]

55 Brownie [pseud.], "Rough Treatment from the Fans," *Milwaukee Journal*, April 27, 1905: 9; "New Pitchers in Good Shape," *Louisville Courier-Journal*, March 21, 1905: 6.

56 "Giants Twirlers in Rare Form," *Louisville Courier-Journal*, April 3, 1905: 6; "The Colonels Win with Ease," *Louisville Courier-Journal*, April 7, 1905: 6; "The Game at Louisville," *Pittsburgh Post*, April 13, 1905: 11.

57 "Even Break in Doubleheader," *Louisville Courier-Journal*, July 5, 1905: 6; "Boston After Clay," *Minneapolis Journal*, August 26, 1905: 24.

58 "Kenna's Condition Improved," *Kansas City Star*, September 1, 1905: 7. See also "Pitcher Kenna Seems Better," *Louisville Courier-Journal*, September 2, 1905: 10.

59 Francis C. Richter, ed., *Reach's Official American League Base Ball Guide, 1907* (Philadelphia: A.J. Reach Co., 1907), 156.

60 "Kenna Retires as a Pitcher," *Louisville Courier-Journal*, December 22, 1906: 9.

61 "The American Association," *Sporting Life*, December 14, 1907: 9; "Condensed Dispatches," *Sporting Life*, July 27, 1907: 2.

62 "Bardstown 10, Bowling Green 0," *Louisville Courier-Journal*, July 19, 1907: 6.

63 "Locals," *Observer* (Concord, North Carolina), August 16, 1900: 3.

64 For background of his association with the *Gazette*, see "Col. Edward B. Kenna Dies Suddenly of Heart Failure," *Charleston Gazette*, March 23, 1912: 1, 6. It is unclear when in 1909 he became editor. No editor was listed on the paper's editorial page that year. By early 1910, Kenna is.

65 "The Ball Season Opens," *Charleston Gazette*, May 4, 1910: 4.

66 "Foolish Knocking," *Charleston Gazette*, August 24, 1910: 4.

67 "The Need for Playgrounds," *Charleston Gazette*, April 8, 1910: 4; "Where Is the End," *Charleston Gazette*, April 8, 1910: 4.

68 "Succor to the Needy," *Charleston Gazette*, January 29, 1911: 4.

69 "Democratic Opportunity," *Charleston Gazette*, February 1, 1910: 4.

70 "Rum and Reform," *Charleston Gazette*, December 1, 1910: 4.

71 For example: "A Pathetic Fallacy," *Charleston Gazette*, December 24, 1910: 4.

72 "Congratulations," *Charleston Gazette*, August 18, 1910: 4.

73 "Edward B. Kenna," *Charleston Advocate*, March 28, 1912: 5.

74 "La Follette for President," *Charleston Gazette*, June 20, 1911: 4. Despite this editorial's title, one suspects that Kenna would have supported Woodrow Wilson in the 1912 race. The *Gazette*'s editorial page argued that Taft was too weak to rise above Republican Party brokers and that Roosevelt had dangerously consolidated the federal government's powers during his presidency. Toward a Wilson speech in December 1910, the *Gazette* suggested, "There is nothing of the New Nationalism nor centralization, nor paternalism, in it." See "Wilson's Sanity," *Charleston Gazette*, December 17, 1910: 4.

75 For Kenna's contempt for Hare, see *Charleston Gazette*, January 28, 1911: 4. For their scrap, see John C. Bond, "Wets Win," *Wheeling Daily Intelligencer*, June 3, 1911: 1.

76 John C. Bond, "Democrats Prepare to Make Fight in Kanawha," *Wheeling Daily Intelligencer*, June 2, 1910: 3.

77 "Latest News by Telegraph Briefly Told," *Sporting Life*, February 3, 1912: 2.

78 "Col. Edward B. Kenna Dies Suddenly of Heart Failure," *Charleston Gazette*, March 23, 1912: 1, 6.

79 Edward Benninghaus Kenna, *Songs of the Open Air and Other Poems* (Charleston, West Virginia: Tribune Printing Co., 1912), 43.

JOHN LEOVICH

By Eric Vickrey

Growing up in the Pacific Northwest, John Leovich excelled at baseball, football, and hockey with the talent to play each sport professionally. He made national headlines in 1941 when he decided to leave college to pursue a baseball career with the Philadelphia Athletics. That same summer Leovich joined the elite fraternity of players who have made it to baseball's highest level when he appeared in a game versus the Cleveland Indians. Leovich, a catcher, played four innings, batted twice, and hit a double off one of the greatest pitchers of all time in what was his only major-league game.

John Joseph Leovich was born on May 5, 1918, in Portland, Oregon. He was the youngest of five children born to parents Michael and Theresa (Mladanov), who had immigrated from Croatia. John grew in Slabtown, a neighborhood in northwest Portland that largely comprised Croatian and Yugoslavian immigrants. The name Slabtown came from term slabwood, the leftover wood from milling that residents used to heat their homes.[1] Like many in the neighborhood, Michael worked in a lumberyard, as a foreman. He died when John was just 5 years old.

John was a natural athlete and played baseball, football, and hockey throughout his youth. Among his childhood friends and classmates at St. Patrick School were Johnny Paveskovich and Mike Stepovich. Paveskovich later legally changed his last name to Pesky. Johnny Pesky went on to have a successful major-league career with the Boston Red Sox while Stepovich would eventually become governor of Alaska before the territory gained statehood. The trio played baseball together and formed a double-play combination of "Leovich to Paveskovich to Stepovich." Pesky later reminisced: "We all grew up around the old Vaughn Street Stadium (home of the Pacific Coast League's Portland Beavers). In the summertime you had to be a ballplayer to be someone and in the wintertime you played hockey at Marshall Street Ice Arena."[2] Leovich worked as a clubhouse boy for the Beavers during his grade-school years, and Pesky was a batboy.[3] The boys got to see many future big leaguers come through Portland, and Leovich recalled seeing Joe DiMaggio during his 61-game PCL hitting streak in 1933.[4]

Leovich played shortstop through his freshman year of high school. He switched to catcher when his team needed a backstop, and Pesky shifted from second base to shortstop. It did not take long for Leovich to become the top young catcher in Oregon. As a 16-year-old he was named to the Portland American Legion all-star team. A year later he caught for Astoria in the Oregon State Baseball League, and according to one Oregon newspaper "was offered contracts by several professional clubs."[5] The following season he played for Hop Gold, a Portland-based team

John Leovich.

ONE-HIT WONDERS

sponsored by Star Brewery. According to a 1936 article in Salem's *Capital Journal*, Leovich was considered "a likely prospect for major league service."[6] Vince Paveskovich, Johnny's brother, recalled Leovich's impressive physique: "He was built like a brick shithouse. Wide shoulders, big bottom, strong and very knowledgeable behind the plate."[7]

After attending Lincoln High School in Portland, Leovich transferred to Lakeside Preparatory School in Seattle for his senior year. He was a star player on Lakeside's football team as a fullback and, according to one report, "the greatest line smasher and passer off the west slope of the Cascades."[8] After the football season, Leovich put on ice skates and was "one of the finest amateur hockey players in the northwest," playing defenseman for a Seattle All-Star team.[9] In fact, both he and Pesky were both offered professional hockey contracts.[10] Ted Leovich, John's son, recalled that hockey was his favorite sport.[11]

In the fall of 1938, Leovich enrolled at Oregon State College in Corvallis as a physical education major. He was elected freshman class president and played football and baseball for the Beavers. Listed at 195 pounds, he played left end on the gridiron and catcher on the baseball diamond. In his sophomore year, Leovich led the team with a .423 batting average; the Beavers finished as conference champions.[12] After his junior-year football season he was given honorable mention when the Associated Press named its All-American team.

On February 7, 1941, Oregon State athletic director Percy Locey announced that Leovich was withdrawing from the college to sign a professional baseball contract with the Philadelphia Athletics. Locey issued a statement criticizing major-league baseball for luring athletes away from college before graduation: "It is regrettable, to say the least, that a boy who is earning his way through college should be tempted by all the money a big league baseball club can offer him."[13] Connie Mack, owner and manager of the Athletics, responded to this criticism by explaining that Leovich was signed at the encouragement of a Portland-area scout and claimed he was not aware he was still in school. "I don't know if he has signed the papers we sent him yet, but if he has, we'll tear 'em up if he wants. I hope the kid finishes school," said Mack.[14]

George Vranizan, who signed Leovich, had "ascertained beyond all doubt that Leovich was determined to quit college sport for a professional contract and decided as long as the die was cast the A's might as well grab the boy."[15] Leovich later confirmed that his decision to leave Oregon State was due to his financial situation: "I was going to take any job – day labor if necessary – but because I had some ability at baseball I turned to that," he said.[16] His contract with the A's was reported to have paid him $4,000.[17] Leovich also received a contract offer from the Detroit Tigers. He later explained why he chose the Athletics: "Tom Turner, the owner of Portland, had a working relationship with Philadelphia, and I was familiar with them."[18]

Leovich reported to training camp with the A's later that month in Anaheim, California. An Associated Press photo of Mack, wearing his trademark suit and bowler and instructing a group of players that included Leovich, was published in newspapers across the country. Leovich explained the financial challenges he faced in college to a reporter for the *Philadelphia Inquirer*. His words gave some context to why he decided to leave college for professional baseball: "There are no scholarships, and the most conference officials will allow an athlete to earn a month is $50. To do this he has to work at least 60 hours a month – two hours a day. This means that the young man has to get up at 5:30 A.M., do janitor service for an hour, eat breakfast, go to classes, study, participate in his sport, eat dinner, work, try to study – and go to bed."[19] At the end of spring training, it was announced that Leovich would remain with the A's heading into the 1941 season. "He ought to hit where I wind up puttin' him," said Mack.[20]

With Frankie Hayes and Hal Wagner ahead of him on the catching depth chart, Leovich did not see any action during the first 13 games of the 1941 season. He spent time working with coach Earle Brucker, warming up pitchers between innings, and serving as the bullpen catcher.[21] He would also sit next to Mack in the dugout and relay steal signs.[22]

On May 1 the Athletics played Cleveland in the final game of a three-game series. The A's were off to a rough start with a record of 4-9 and had lost the first two games of the series to the red-hot Indians. To make matters worse, they were tasked with facing one of the game's best young hurlers, Bob Feller, in the series finale. Feller, just 22 years old, was already a veteran with 85 career victories and three All-Star Game appearances under his belt. Jack Knott started the game for the Athletics.

A crowd of 4,000 showed up to League Park II for the Thursday afternoon tilt. The game went as one might have scripted with Feller shutting down the A's through five innings without allowing a hit. His strikeout of Knott in the fifth inning was the 1,000th of his career, an astonishing number for a 22-year-old. Feller helped himself with the bat and gave his team an 8-0 lead when he hit a three-run home run off Knott in the bottom of the fifth.

With the game seemingly out of reach against Cleveland's ace, Mack replaced starting catcher Hayes with Leovich in the bottom of the sixth. Leovich caught A's relievers Rankin Johnson and Herman Besse. In the eighth inning, with Feller still on the mound, the rookie catcher stepped up to the plate in a major-league game for the first time. With a runner on first, Leovich hit a groundball to shortstop Lou Boudreau, who stepped on second and threw to first for a double play. Later in life, he recalled facing the Hall of Fame pitcher: "I had faced kids in high school and college who were just as fast as Feller although they didn't have the good curve he had. I was not overawed and was able to relax."[23]

Staked to a 13-3 lead heading to the ninth inning, Feller took the mound looking for a complete-game victory despite having walked eight batters. Possibly tired or perhaps pitching to the score, Feller allowed the first four batters of the inning to reach before Bob Johnson hit a grand slam to cut the Cleveland lead to 13-8. After the next two batters were retired, Leovich got another opportunity against Feller. The rookie made the most of his second chance and doubled to right field. The game ended when the next batter, Pete Suder, lined out.

A week later, Leovich was optioned to the Toronto Maple Leafs, Philadelphia farm team in the International League. This was the first of many stops for Leovich that summer. On May 21 he was optioned to Wilmington of the Class-B Interstate League after the team asked Mack for a right-handed-hitting catcher.[24] The *Corvallis* (Oregon) *Gazette-Times* reported that Mack thought Leovich was "about two years away from big league form."[25] Through 25 games with Wilmington, Leovich was hitting .239 with no extra-base hits and nine runs batted in.[26] He was again on the move in July when he was sent from Wilmington to Class-C Newport News when the teams exchanged catchers. In eight games with Newport News, Leovich was 6-for-22.[27] After serving as the A's bullpen catcher in late July and early August, Leovich found himself back in the Interstate League when the A's sent him to Lancaster.[28] In 54 games played between Wilmington and Lancaster, Leovich finished with a batting average of .190.[29]

Leovich was released by the Athletics after the season. A newspaper report said Mack wanted to give

John Leovich.

the catcher "ample opportunity to make other connections."[30] Mack was later quoted as saying that Leovich "wasn't quite as advanced as I expected him to be, and I paid him a large salary last year – more than I felt was justified. When it came to deciding whether to sign him again I mentioned I couldn't possibly continue to pay that amount. Had he said he would take half, I would have signed him."[31] The *Los Angeles Times* reported that a shoulder injury suffered playing football for Oregon State hampered his throwing ability and "quite likely ruined his major league career."[32] Later in life, Leovich had nothing but good things to say about Mack and said he was a real gentleman.[33]

That fall Leovich went to work in the Portland shipyards. In early 1942 he signed a contract with the Portland Beavers. He played in 117 games, hitting .190 with one home run and 31 runs batted in. The Beavers finished last in the eight-team league with a record of 67-110. Though he and the team failed to have much success on the that season, Leovich had a highlight off the field: On June 20, 1942, he married Janet Goresky of Portland.

After the 1942 season, Leovich enlisted in the US Coast Guard. During the summers of 1943-1945 he played for Coast Guard baseball teams in Portland and Seattle. He also saw action for the Norvans in the

ONE-HIT WONDERS

Vancouver (British Columbia) Senior League when time allowed. The Seattle Coast Guard team he played for in 1944 finished with a record of 55-5 and at one point won 30 consecutive games.[34]

In early 1946 Leovich lived in Eugene, Oregon, and worked as a hockey referee. That spring, he moved back to Seattle to work for Solo-Tone, which marketed jukeboxes for restaurant tables.[35] He also worked with his sister and brother-in-law in their Seattle tavern business. In June of 1946, he appeared in a handful of games with the Vancouver Capilanos of the Class-B Western International League. Later that summer he made his last appearance in professional baseball playing for another WIL team, the Bremerton Bluejackets. Bremerton manager Sam Gibson, whom Leovich played against in the PCL, recruited him to play.

John and Janet later moved back to Portland. John played some semipro ball, and for a time, he worked for a beer distributor. They had a son, Ted, who attended Lincoln High School and the University of Southern California. Along with an Italian partner, the Leoviches operated two Portland restaurants: Il Trovatore and Tony's. In a 2020 interview, Ted recalled helping at the restaurant as a child, and on Sundays when the restaurant was closed, his job was to go around and remove gum from under the tables.

In 1970 John and Janet purchased a restaurant in Lincoln City on the Oregon coast that they reopened under the name Captain John's. They operated the business until they retired in 1979. John still went to the restaurant every morning to have coffee with friends. He also enjoyed trout and salmon fishing and watching sports on TV in his later years.

Though his major-league career lasted just four innings, Leovich looked back fondly on his time playing baseball and, according to Ted, was very proud of getting a hit off Feller. In an interview conducted more than 50 years after his baseball career ended, he said the lifelong relationships he made in the game were the most enjoyable part of his career.[36]

John Leovich died on February 3, 2000, at the age of 81.

ACKNOWLEDGMENTS
Special thanks to Ted Leovich for sharing his memories and helping with details about his father's life off the field.

SOURCES
In addition to the sources cited in the Notes, the author relied on Baseball-Reference.com.

NOTES

1. Donald R. Nelson, *The Sons of Slabtown and Takes of Westside Sports* (Self-published, 2016): 3.
2. Bill Mulflur, "Slabtowners' Reminisce with Johnny Pesky," *Oregon Journal* (Portland), January 15, 1974.
3. Richard Tellis, *Once Around the Bases: Bittersweet Memories of Only One Game in the Majors* (Chicago: Triumph Books 1998), 37.
4. Tellis, 39.
5. "Hop Golds Open Season in Bend," *Bend* (Oregon) *Bulletin*, May 19, 1936: 2.
6. "'Red' Miller Scheduled to Face Solons," *Capital Journal* (Salem, Oregon), June 13, 1936: 7.
7. Bill Nowlin, *Mr. Red Sox: The Johnny Pesky Story* (Cambridge, Massachusetts: Rounder Books, 2004), 22.
8. "Lakeside Looms as Real Threat," *Spokane* (Washington) *Spokesman-Review,* November 18, 1936: 31.
9. "Shining Stars of Amateur Ice Game Coming Saturday," *Spokane Chronicle*, February 11, 1938: 20.
10. Tellis, 39.
11. Author's telephone interview with Ted Leovich, October 6, 2020.
12. "Berry, Leovich Top Collegiate Batters," *Corvallis* (Oregon) *Gazette-Times*, June 4, 1940: 5.
13. "Locey Condemns Signing of Star," *Salem* (Oregon) *Statesman Journal,* February 9, 1941: 6.
14. Al Wolf, "Connie Mack Pauses Here, Explains Leovich 'Kidnap,'" *Los Angeles Times*, February 10, 1941: 27.
15. Fred Hampson, "Oregon Sports Notes," *Klamath News* (Klamath Falls, Oregon), February 14, 1941: 11.
16. Paul Zimmerman, "Sports Postscripts," *Los Angeles Times*, October 23, 1941: 22.
17. Hampson.
18. Tellis, 39.
19. "Jimmy Wilson Say He's Through, But –," *Philadelphia Inquirer*, March 7, 1941: 35.
20. "Baseball Briefs," *Harrisburg* (Pennsylvania) *Evening News,* April 4, 1941: 22.
21. Tellis, 39.
22. Tellis, 40.
23. Tellis, 41.
24. "Blue Rocks Get John Leovich," *News Journal* (Wilmington, Delaware), May 21, 1941: 23.
25. Fred Hampson. "Army Taking Toll of Oregon Prep Coaches; Medford Has Only Bowerman, May Lose Him," *Corvallis Gazette-Times*, July 1, 1941: 7.
26. Interstate League Statistics, *Harrisburg Telegraph*, July 7, 1941: 15.
27. "3 Builders Post Averages of .338; Madden Up 21 Points," *Newport News* (Virginia) *Daily Press*, July 27, 1941: 19.
28. "Roses Cop Twin Bill, Aim at 6th Place in Series with Trenton," *Lancaster* (Pennsylvania) *New Era*, August 6, 1941: 10.
29. "Cox Takes Inter-State Batting Title for 1941 With His Average of .363," *Allentown* (Pennsylvania) *Morning Call,* September 7, 1941: 14.
30. "Hadley Released by Athletics," *New York Daily News*, October 21, 1941: 153.
31. Fred Hampson, "Durdan Enters New Field of Athletics; Other Sports Notes," *Corvallis Gazette-Times*, May 7, 1942: 7.
32. Zimmerman.
33. Ted Leovich interview.
34. *The Sporting News*, November 2, 1944: 12.
35. Dick Strite, "Highclimber," *Eugene* (Oregon) *Guard*, May 5, 1946: 18.
36. Tellis, 43.

DAVE LIDDELL

By Alan Raylesberg

David Alexander Liddell is the only New York Mets position player to bat a perfect 1.000 for his career.[1] Born on June 15, 1966, in Los Angeles,[2] Liddell had the proverbial "cup of coffee" in the major leagues, getting a pinch-hit single in what turned out to be his only at-bat in the major leagues.

Liddell grew up in Riverside, California, part of the greater Los Angeles area. He was selected by the Chicago Cubs in the fourth round of the June 1984 major-league amateur draft, out of Rubidoux High School in Riverside. Liddell was the sixth player in the school's history to be signed or drafted by a major-league baseball team; one, Mike Corkins, played in the majors for six seasons.[3] After Liddell, 10 more Rubidoux alumni were drafted (as of October 2020) and two of those, Sean Mulligan and Dan Giese, made it to the majors.[4]

Liddell was drafted as a catcher, a position he played growing up. As a teen, he played with and against another catcher, Greg Myers, who would go on to play 18 seasons in the majors. While Liddell played at Rubidoux, Myers was playing at neighboring Riverside Polytechnic High School, whose alumni include former major-league great Bobby Bonds. Liddell and Myers continued to cross paths when Myers was selected 74th overall and Liddell 83rd in the 1984 draft.[5]

The draft then consisted of over 50 rounds with more than 800 players selected. The number-one pick, Shawn Abner (New York Mets), never lived up to his potential, while later picks included future stars such as Mark McGwire, Tom Glavine, and Al Leiter. Before selecting Liddell, the Cubs picked college pitcher Drew Hall in the first round.[6] Their second-round pick, a high-school pitcher from Las Vegas, Nevada, was future Hall of Famer Greg Maddux.[7]

After signing with the Cubs, Liddell was assigned to the Pikeville Cubs rookie-league team in the Appalachian League, where his roommate was none other than Maddux.[8] The 1984 season was the third and final one for minor-league baseball in Pikeville,

a Kentucky city with about 7,000 residents.[9] Liddell played 22 games, mostly at catcher, but struggled offensively, getting only three hits in 46 at-bats (.065 batting average). Maddux performed much better, starting 12 games and going 6-2 with a 2.63 ERA.[10] While Maddux earned a promotion to Class A in 1985, Liddell remained in the Appalachian League.

After finishing last in attendance for the second straight year, the Pikeville franchise folded and the Cubs moved their Appalachian League team to Wytheville, Virginia. It was there, in 1985, that the 19-year-old Liddell caught 36 games with a much-improved batting average of .231, with four home runs in 104 at-bats. That performance resulted in Liddell moving up to Class A in 1986.

ONE-HIT WONDERS

Liddell's new "home" in 1986 was Peoria, Illinois, and the Peoria Chiefs in the Midwest League. Maddux had played there in 1985. Maddux now was on the fast track, moving up to Double A and then Triple A during the 1986 season before making his major-league debut in September 1986. Liddell, meanwhile, was finding his groove with Peoria. In 37 games, Liddell batted .264 in 125 at-bats, while performing solidly behind the plate. That performance led the New York Mets to acquire Liddell from the Cubs in a June 30, 1986, trade for 30-year-old Ed Lynch, who had been a reliable pitcher for New York over six seasons.[11]

The trade was significant for the Cubs, as Lynch was acquired to replace Rick Sutcliffe (the 1984 NL Cy Young Award winner) in the rotation, after Sutcliffe went on the disabled list. In reporting the trade, the *New York Times* focused on the departure of the popular Lynch, who was "surprised and disappointed" at leaving New York.[12] The *Times* article about Lynch barely mentioned Liddell, noting only at the end that the Mets "got Dave Lenderman, 24, a right-handed relief pitcher in the Eastern League, and Dave Liddell, 20, a catcher in the Midwest League."[13]

Liddell was assigned to Columbia, the Mets team in the Class-A South Atlantic League, and also played at Lynchburg in the Class-A Carolina League. The Mets promoted him to Double A in 1987. After a short stint in Double A, Liddell was back in Single A, again splitting his time between Columbia and Lynchburg. In 1988 Liddell remained in Single A, splitting his time between St. Lucie in the Florida State League and the Reno Silver Sox in the California League. After he hit a career-best .329 in 26 games at Reno, the Mets promoted him to their Triple-A International League farm team in Tidewater (Norfolk, Virginia) for the 1989 season.

With Mets starting catcher and future Hall of Famer Gary Carter 35 years old and a lack of depth behind him, there was opportunity lurking for the 23-year-old Liddell. Veteran coach Vern Hoscheit, who worked with the Mets minor-league catchers, observed that Liddell was "receiving high marks,"[14] and Liddell was one of four nonroster players invited to spring training in 1989.[15] Things did not go well at Tidewater, however, as Liddell batted only .151 in 24 games,and was sent back to Double A, this time to Jackson in the Texas League. His struggles continued there; he batted only .178.

Despite his mediocre minor-league statistics, Liddell was back at Tidewater for the 1990 season. Carter was gone[16] and the Mets' primary catcher was Mackey Sasser.[17] At Tidewater, Liddell was the primary catcher, with Barry Lyons and Orlando Mercado splitting time between Tidewater and the parent Mets.

On June 1, 1990, Mercado was recalled from Tidewater. After playing in that day's game, he left the team due to the death of his father. Needing a backup catcher, the Mets called Liddell up on June 3. Liddell's offensive struggles were continuing at Tidewater and so when his manager, Steve Swisher,[18] approached him, Liddell's reaction was "I'm getting sent down to Double A, right?" only to be told that he was going to the Mets.[19] After toiling in the minors for six-plus seasons, Liddell was finally in "The Show."

And that afternoon, in Philadelphia, opportunity came his way. With the Mets trailing the Phillies 8-1 in the eighth inning and the lefty-hitting Sasser due to lead off, new manager Bud Harrelson[20] decided to give the righty-hitting Liddell his chance, sending him up as a pinch-hitter against left-hander Pat Combs. In an 8-1 game in which the Mets had only one hit, Mets television announcers Tim McCarver and Ralph Kiner recognized the excitement that the longtime minor leaguer felt as he came to bat for the first time in the major leagues. And that excitement increased when Liddell hit a groundball through the middle for a single and his first major-league hit. McCarver exclaimed, "How about that" while also remarking that Liddell "had been hitting .178 in Jackson."[21]

Watching that at-bat today on YouTube, one can see the pure joy on Liddell's face standing at first base, as the batted ball was retrieved and thrown to Dave Magadan in the Mets dugout so that Liddell would have a memento of his moment in the spotlight. Kiner declared that it was "something that he [Liddell] will never forget."[22] Of course, no one knew at the time that this would be not only Liddell's first major-league hit but also his last.[23]

After coming around to score, following his single, Liddell stayed in the game to catch in the bottom of the eighth. He was credited with a putout on a strikeout. Thus, in addition to a career batting average of 1.000, Liddell had a career fielding percentage of 1.000. Writing about the game in the *New York Times*, Claire Smith added a line at the end of her article, titled "Fine Debut," stating, "Dave Liddell, the rookie catcher purchased from Tidewater Saturday, pinch-hit in the eighth and singled, his first major-league-hit."[24] Liddell never again appeared in a major-league game.[25]

After the 1990 season, Liddell became a free agent and signed with the Cincinnati Reds. He never played

ONE-HIT WONDERS

a game in their organization and ended up in the Milwaukee organization for the 1991 season before ending his professional career with the Baltimore organization in 1992, at the age of 26. In nine minor-league seasons, Liddell hit .215 with 24 home runs in 1,749 plate appearances.

Needing a job, Liddell took up a career installing and maintaining highway lighting, city traffic signals, and fiber-optic systems, as a member of the International Brotherhood of Electrical Workers (IBEW).[26] Yet, the baseball bug did not leave him. In August 1994, the Major League Baseball Players Association went on strike, resulting in the remainder of the season, and the postseason, including the World Series, being canceled.[27] As spring training got underway in 1995, the Players Association remained on strike and the owners prepared to use replacement players for spring training and the regular season. Among those replacement players was none other than Liddell.

Still living in his native California, Liddell joined the California Angels, playing in spring-training games, including the home opener at their Tempe, Arizona, training camp.[28] Interviewed by *The Sporting News* at the time, Liddell described himself as "below average in hitting, power and running, average in receiving, and above average in throwing."[29] He compared himself to his longtime friend Greg Myers, who was in his eighth year in the majors and on strike. Liddell remarked that "[e]very year we played together [as teenagers] I was his backup" and that Myers advanced further in his career on superior hitting ability. "He's better," Liddell said, "[p]eople don't get to the big leagues on appearances."[30]

The use of replacement players was very controversial, with at least one major-league manager refusing to manage them and some owners also opposed.[31] The strike ended late in spring training, followed by a shortened regular season. The replacement players were never used, and Liddell did not get another chance at baseball glory

In retirement, Liddell continued his work as a member of the IBEW. He married and still lives in Southern California. Maddux and Myers, drafted at the same time as Liddell, had long, successful careers in major-league baseball, while Liddell appeared in only that one game. When interviewed by Anthony Castrovince for his article on "ultimate one hit wonders," Liddell expressed no regrets about his very brief major-league career and post-baseball life, summing things up this way:

"Realistically I was barely over .200 as a minor-league hitter. I got called up because of the death of another player's father. It's not like I earned it. The game owed me nothing. I never dwelled on it, because a man has got to make a living."[32]

As of October 2020, only 17 position players in the modern era had a hit in their only plate appearance in the major leagues.[33] Chances are few baseball fans would remember Dave Liddell but for this fact. However, because of what he accomplished on the evening of June 3, 1990, he is and always will be part of baseball lore.

SOURCES

In addition to the sources cited in the Notes, the author relied on Baseball-Reference.com Retrosheet.org and Baseball-Almanac.com.

NOTES

1. As of October 2020. Two Mets pitchers, Eric Cammack and Jason Roach, batted 1.000 in their major-league careers, with Roach going 2-for-2. Four other players were 1-for-1 with the Mets but did not have a career average of 1.000, having played for other teams (Gary Bennett, Buddy Carlyle, Rodney McCray, Ray Searage). Source: *Complete Baseball Encyclopedia*, baseball-encyclopedia.com/.

2. According to the 2006 *ESPN Baseball Encyclopedia*, Liddell was born Desmond Lane Liddell.

3. Corkins was signed by San Francisco in 1967 and played in the majors from 1969 to 1974. Five others – Ray Elder (1967), Gary Schafer (1968), Rex Jackson (1970), Dale Sanner (1970), and Pride Evans (1981) – were drafted but never played in the the majors. See The Baseball Cube thebaseballcube.com/hs/profile.asp?HS=2107.

4. Mulligan was drafted by San Diego in 1991 and played one season (1996) in the majors. Giese was drafted by Boston in 1999 and played in the majors from 2007 to 2009.

5. Myers was selected by Toronto in the third round.

6. Hall had a brief major-league career, pitching for the Cubs from 1986 to 1988, Texas in 1989, and Montreal in 1990.

7. The Cubs' third-round pick was shortstop Julius McDougal from Jackson State University. He played nine seasons in the minor leagues.

8. Anthony Castrovince, "MLB's ultimate one-hit wonders," MLB.com, August 29, 2019 mlb.com/news/featured/mlb-ultimate-one-hit-wonders.

9. In 1982 the franchise was affiliated with Milwaukee as the Pikeville Brewers, before becoming a Cubs affiliate in 1983.

10. Maddux was inducted into the Appalachian League Hall of Fame in 2019, as part of the inaugural class. mlb.com/appalachian-league/hall-of-fame.

11. In what became a World Series championship season for the Mets, Lynch injured his knee early on and there was no longer room for him in the rotation when he was ready to return. Lynch finished the 1986 season with the Cubs, then pitched one more season for Chicago (1987), his last season in the majors.

12. Joseph Durso, "Ojeda Leads Mets Past Cardinals 7-0; Lynch Sent to Cubs," *New York Times*, July 1, 1986. With the Mets "on the brink of success," Lynch said, "I'm speechless. It's like living with a family the whole year and getting thrown out on Christmas Eve." Mets manager Davey Johnson added,

ONE-HIT WONDERS

"He's been the mainstay here for five years [and] did everything I asked. But we've got young arms at Tidewater who could pitch here right now."

13 After the trade, Lenderman was assigned to the Mets' team at Jackson in the Double-A Texas League. He never advanced above Double A and was out of baseball after the 1987 season.

14 "Baseball – Around the Minors," *The Sporting News,* August 8, 1988: 35.

15 "Baseball," *The Sporting News,* February 3, 1989: 39.

16 After five seasons, Carter was released by the Mets in November 1989. He then signed as a free agent with the San Francisco Giants. After playing for the Giants in 1990, Carter played for the Dodgers and Expos before retiring after the 1992 season.

17 Twenty-one-year-old Todd Hundley was also in the mix. Hundley played most of the 1990 season at Double-A Jackson, while playing 36 games with the Mets.

18 Swisher, a major-league catcher, played nine seasons. His son, Nick, played 12 seasons in the big leagues.

19 Castrovince.

20 Harrelson took over as Mets manager on May 29, 1990, after the Mets parted ways with Davey Johnson.

21 Actually, Lindell hit .178 in Jackson the year before.

22 youtube.com/watch?v=07RB7S28VTU

23 Anthony Castrovince's article includes a photograph of Liddell, then age 52, holding the very ball that he had hit through the middle of the infield nearly 30 years earlier. mlb.com/news/featured/mlb-ultimate-one-hit-wonders. Topps also memorialized the moment, issuing a Dave Liddell card as part of its 1991 Topps Debut '90 set. The back of the card is from "The Register" and states, in part, "[On June 3] made his major league debut by delivering Single on the first pitch as a pinch-hitter leading off 8th inning at Philadelphia that evening. Time was called and Dave was given the baseball as a souvenir."tcdb.com/GalleryP.cfm/pid/37434/col/1/yea/0/Dave-Liddell?sTeam=New%20York%20Mets&sCardNum=&sNote=&sSetName=.

24 Claire Smith, "A Wheel of Misfortune in Mets' Loss," *New York Times,* June 4, 1990: C1.

25 Pitcher Wally Whitehurst was sent to the minors to make room on the roster for Liddell. Under the rules then existing, Whitehurst was required to remain in the minors for a minimum of 10 days. After that, Whitehurst was recalled and Liddell was sent back to Tidewater

26 Castrovince.

27 It was the first time the World Series was not played since 1904.

28 Mike Digiovanna, "Silent Spring for Angel Replacement Games: Baseball: California and San Diego play 12 innings before settling for a tie 3-3," *Los Angeles Times,* March 4, 1995, latimes.com/archives/la-xpm-1995-03-04-sp-38699-story.html.

29 "Baseball," *The Sporting News,* March 27, 1995: 36.

30 "Baseball," *The Sporting News,* March 27, 1995: 36. Drafted out of high school at the same time as Liddell, Myers had a very different career path. In his 1984 rookie league season, he hit over .300 and was promoted to A ball in 1985. He was in the majors for seven games with Toronto in 1987 before ending up in the majors for good in 1989. He played for Toronto and six other teams before finishing his career back in Toronto in 2003-05.

31 Detroit manager Sparky Anderson said he would not work with replacement players, stating "[t]here ain't no place in our game for replacement players." The Baltimore Orioles announced that they would not play games with "strikebreakers" and Toronto excused its manager, Cito Gaston, from managing games. "Cracks Form in Owners' Strategy," *Spokane Spokesman-Review,* February 18, 1995, spokesman.com/stories/1995/feb/18/cracks-form-in-owners-strategy/.

32 mlb.com/news/featured/mlb-ultimate-one-hit-wonders.

33 As of October 2020. Source: *Complete Baseball Encyclopedia,* baseball-encyclopedia.com/.

ERNIE LINDEMANN

By Phil Williams

Few one-game major leaguers led a baseball life as rich as pitcher Ernie Lindemann's. From 1903 through 1915, he was a dominant force in the New York City area's thriving semipro scene. He routinely faced, and often succeeded against, major-league teams and elite African-American independents. Indeed, Lindemann's sole major-league appearance, with the Boston Doves in 1907, stands as an almost comical footnote to his accomplished career.

Ernest Theodore Lindemann Jr. was born on June 10, 1883, in New York City.[1] He was the fourth of six children born to Ernest and Martha (Herman) Lindemann. His father was Prussian-born, his mother American-born with German parents. Ernest Sr. was a policeman. The family moved to Brooklyn's Bensonhurst neighborhood when Ernie was young.[2] He attended Public School 101 and the Manual Training (now John Jay) High School.[3]

By 1900, Lindemann was pitching for the Bensonhurst Field Club.[4] He began the 1901 season with Bensonhurst, then made his professional debut with the Connecticut State League's Waterbury Rough Riders.[5] Lindemann remained with Waterbury in 1902, and provided memorable efforts such as a two-hit shutout of Hartford.[6] But Waterbury sank into the cellar. The teenager began pitching semipro ball on Sundays, first with a Freeport, Long Island, team, then with Brooklyn's Brighton Athletic Club.[7] On November 16 his Brighton season culminated with a 12-strikeout, 3-3 draw against pitcher Harry Howell and an "All Americans" outfit featuring several other major leaguers.[8]

Sunday baseball was then among the greatest controversies in American sporting life.[9] Along the East Coast, defenders of an established cultural morality sought to hold off the recreational impulses of a booming urban population. Not until after World War I could New York's three major-league teams host Sunday games without fear of police action. The area's semipro teams, although not immune to crackdowns, attracted less attention. They mostly played in northern New Jersey cities and in Brooklyn's less densely populated eastern stretches, where state laws were less likely to be enforced. Drawing impressive crowds, semipro teams capitalized on the blue laws.

In March 1903 Lindemann married Marie Vanderbilt who, despite a notable Gilded Age last name, was a policeman's daughter. That October, their daughter Thelma arrived. Having police on both sides of the family enabled Ernie to better navigate the fluctuating permissibility of Sunday baseball. On at least one occasion Ernest Sr., who captained Brooklyn's Sheepshead Bay station, led an arrest of his son's Sabbath-breaking team that failed to net his offspring.[10] His father reportedly favored semipro baseball for Ernie, possibly because it kept him grounded with his young family.[11] As Lindemann's Waterbury stay wound down, Doc Reisling, Hartford's manager in 1902, signed the young pitcher for the American Association's Toledo Mud Hens squad he was poised to take over the following year. But as the 1903 season

Ernie Lindemann

ONE-HIT WONDERS

dawned, Lindemann ignored this Organized Baseball future.

Instead, Lindemann worked at Equitable Life Insurance's Manhattan office during the week as a clerk. On Saturdays he played with the Equitable company team, often as an outfielder. On Sundays, at St. George Cricket Grounds he pitched for the Hoboken semipro nine. Details regarding his salary are elusive. Six years later, negotiating with the New York Giants, pitcher Hooks Wiltse estimated he could earn the same $3,500 the team offered him playing semipro ball.[12] Lindemann probably wasn't earning major-league money in 1903, but his showing that season may have ensured that he soon would.

It began on April 5, when he no-hit a squad of New York State Leaguers.[13] Two weeks later, in front of 12,000 fans, he took an 8-5 lead into the ninth against the New York Giants. But an error helped the Giants plate six runs, and they triumphed, 11-9.[14] Lindemann faced major-league teams five more times that year: beating the Boston Beaneaters, 7-5, on May 10; losing a rematch to the Giants, 5-2, on May 17; falling to the New York Highlanders, 5-3, on July 19; four-hitting the Brooklyn Superbas for a 3-1 victory on July 26; and losing to the Giants, 6-0, in a November 1 benefit game.[15]

Major-league teams occasionally rested top talent and rarely offered front-line pitching in such exhibition games. In these six games, Lindemann faced Jack Cronin (twice), Wiley Piatt, Roscoe Miller, Harry Howell, and Bill Reidy. Yet, besides Lindemann, only one other Hoboken player appeared in the majors: 36-year-old Tuck Turner. Moreover, semipro defenses could be subpar: Hoboken committed 19 errors in the six matches, the major leaguers 12.

Independent African-American teams threw their best pitching at Lindemann and might be considered his truest tests. Several times he passed with honors: besting José Muñoz and the All-Cubans, 8-1, on May 24; three-hitting Rube Foster and the Cuban X-Giants in a 13-0 thrashing on June 28; and outlasting Kid Carter and the Philadelphia Giants, 6-4, in front of 6,000 on August 2.[16] Both Muñoz and Carter defeated Lindemann twice on other occasions that season.[17]

Although Lindemann had seemingly forsaken Organized Baseball, after his breakout 1903 campaign several major-league teams were reportedly interested in his services. Billy Murray, the gifted minor-league manager then leading the Eastern League's Jersey City club, was as well.[18] Lindemann rebuffed the advances. Hoping to apply harder measures, and angered by independents attracting interest away from his product, Eastern League President Pat Powers lobbied baseball's National Commission to forbid any team under its governance to play Hoboken.[19] The ban came on July 2, 1904.[20]

The New York Giants had already visited Hoboken once that season. On April 24 they beat Lindemann, 8-5.[21] Hoboken filled its Sunday schedule with other independents. Most notably, Lindemann split four games with Foster, now with the Philadelphia Giants.[22] That summer, he suffered "an illness that threatened to develop into typhoid fever."[23] That September, the Giants drafted him.[24]

It was a remarkable moment: After cruising to the pennant with a 106-47 record, John McGraw added a 21-year-old semipro phenom to a staff headed by Joe McGinnity and Christy Mathewson. Yet Lindemann expressed no interest in heading south for spring training and balked at McGraw's contract offer.[25] New York released its claim on him, and he again belonged to Toledo.

Instead, Lindemann began 1905 pitching for a Perth Amboy squad. On April 30 he no-hit a visiting Crescents team from Philadelphia.[26] Soon afterward the National Commission backed away from its earlier ruling against Hoboken (and other semipros), indicating Lindemann was no longer considered ineligible.[27] In late May he joined Ambrose Hussey's Ridgewood team. Twirling Sundays at Wallace's Ridgewood Grounds, located just past Brooklyn's border in Queens, Lindeman formed a lasting battery with catcher Alex Farmer.[28] Three times that season, he battled the Philadelphia Giants, then at the very height of their powers, each time losing to Emmet Bowman.[29] Lindemann enjoyed greater fortune against major leaguers: outlasting the Highlanders, 13-8, on October 8; a week later beating the Giants, 5-2, immediately after they won the World Series; before losing to Chief Bender and his "Philadelphia Professionals," 7-4, on October 22.[30]

"There is nothing altruistic about Linde in baseball," a sportswriter later observed and, after a falling-out with Hussey in May 1906, he led an exodus of Ridgewood players.[31] This cast played for several Brooklyn semipros (Brighton, Manhattan Beach, and Marquette) on Sundays, while Lindemann also twirled on Saturdays with a Summit, New Jersey, team. His season's highlight: holding the Brooklyn Superbas to two singles as he and Doc Scanlan dueled to a scoreless draw on October 14.[32]

ONE-HIT WONDERS

Lindemann was listed at 5-feet-10 and weighing 182 pounds. Contemporaries referred to the right-hander as "the big blond," suggesting such metrics might be understated.[33] He was a "crafty" pitcher noted more for breaking balls than fastballs early in his career, but sportswriters later referenced his spitballs.[34] His struck out more batters and pitched to less contact than his peers. For example, in a 5-4 victory over the Cuban X-Giants on April 26, 1903, Lindemann struck out nine while Ed Wilson fanned none. The X-Giants accumulated 17 assists in the field, the Hobokens only five.[35]

Lindemann began the 1907 season with the Elizabeth (New Jersey) Stars, pitching six Sundays against major-league teams over May and June. Twice he lost convincingly: to the Reds, 9-0, and to the Highlanders, 8-4.[36] Twice he pitched well and lost narrowly: to the Pirates, 4-3, and to the White Sox, 6-5.[37] Twice he pitched masterfully: four-hitting the Athletics and beating Rube Waddell, 3-2, on May 5, then two-hitting the Giants and besting Dummy Taylor, 2-1, on June 23.[38]

The hapless Boston Doves, already scheduled to play a four-game series in Brooklyn on surrounding days, booked a Sunday game in Elizabeth for June 30. Somehow, likely through manager Fred Tenney's overtures and with new owner George Dovey's blessing, Boston recruited Lindemann to face Brooklyn that Friday. Boston also recruited his batterymate, Alex Farmer, although – for unclear reasons – he stayed on the bench that day.[39]

Most of the several thousand Brooklyn fans present that Friday assumed that when the lineups were announced, it was the Doves' Vive Lindaman in the box. Yet word quickly spread through the stands that it was indeed their hometown semipro ace. Lindemann pitched well, allowing only two runs over the first six innings, in large part due to poor defensive play by the Doves.

Boston scored five runs in the top of the seventh, aided by Lindemann (who had singled earlier in the game) successfully laying down a sacrifice bunt. But, leading 5-2, he loaded the bases in the bottom of the frame. At that point Tenney pulled him, and the Doves eventually won in the 10th, 6-5.[40] Lindemann's game line: four walks, three strikeouts, and four earned runs over 6⅓ innings. Two days later, in Elizabeth, he shut out Boston, 2-0.[41]

Pointing toward "a National agreement rule which distinctly says that no major league player may play with independent clubs during the season," a Brooklyn scribe asked, "Is President Dovey of the Bostons bigger than the National League?"[42] Brooklyn President Charles Ebbets quickly stated that he believed Dovey was unaware of Lindemann's status and that to protest the game "would be poor sportsmanship."[43] Lindemann, content to profitably play the field, finished the campaign pitching for Elizabeth, Summit, and – in another foray into Organized Baseball – the Connecticut State League's Hartford Senators.[44]

Lindemann returned to Hussey's Ridgewoods in 1908 and for the next four seasons spent most of his Sundays pitching at Meyerrose Park. He was salaried for his efforts and reportedly belonged to the park's ownership group.[45] "He is as popular in Ridgewood as Mathewson is at the Polo Grounds," an onlooker noted.[46]

Lindemann's efforts against major-league teams were limited in this span, in part as Brooklyn aggressively asserted the territorial rights the National Commission granted it.[47] Twice he faced the Giants. On October 17, 1908, a quartet of New York starters (including Mathewson and McGinnity), overcame Lindemann in 10 innings, 3-1.[48] Exactly one year later he dueled Red Ames and Doc Crandall to a 4-4 tie.[49] He also beat a Hoboken squad with Chief Bender in the box on October 30, 1910.[50] His finest Ridgewood performance was against José Muñoz and the Cuban Stars on July 26, 1908. In the first inning, Lindemann allowed three runs (two likely unearned), and Muñoz two. But other than the Cuban allowing a tying tally in the sixth, neither ace allowed another run in a match finally called after 17 innings. The 5,000 fans present "were for the most part on their feet" throughout "the later stages of the game."[51] Lindemann's 16 consecutive scoreless innings, a sportswriter noted, "was about as fine an exhibition of pitching as has ever been seen in a semi-professional game."[52]

A detailed look at Lindemann's 1909 season provides a snapshot of his career.[53] Per present-day newspaper databases, 36 appearances (all starts) are evident, and he fashioned a 22-13-1 record. He pitched for Ridgewood 28 times, Richmond Hill (a Queens County team also controlled by Hussey) four times, twice with a Northport, Long Island, team, once with an Underwood Utes squad in Connecticut, and once with a club assembled for a political retreat. Mostly he pitched on weekends: 27 Sundays and 7 Saturdays.

His appearances were split evenly, 18 apiece, between black and white teams. He fared better against the white squads (13-4-1) than the black ones (9-9). Twice he faced Organized Baseball: in addition to

ONE-HIT WONDERS

the 4-4 draw vs. the Giants, he beat Hartford, 5-3, pitching for the Underwoods on April 17. His most frequent opponent was the Brooklyn Royal Giants, likely the finest Eastern black team at the time, and starring infielders Bill Monroe and Grant "Home Run" Johnson. Lindemann split eight games with the Royals, losing all three of his matches against their ace Harry Buckner.

Box scores are available for 31 of 36 of these appearances. Lindemann went 18-12-1 in this subset. He failed to complete a game only once, when the Royals drove him from the box on June 6. Lindemann pitched 267⅓ innings and allowed 105 runs (earned and unearned), or 3.43 every nine innings. He yielded 215 hits and 75 walks, for a WHIP of 1.093. He struck out 207 opponents, for a strikeouts per nine innings ratio of 7.0. A capable batter, he claimed 24 hits in these 31 games.

By 1911, the Ridgewoods were in decline. Their starting outfield signed with New Brunswick and Lindemann's longtime batterymate Farmer was sidelined by illness.[54] Lindemann signed "a contract to pitch and furnish a team for Bath Beach promoters" in March 1912.[55] He recruited several Ridgewood players. Their new team, the West Ends, played at the West End Oval at Cropsey Avenue between Bay 19th and Bay 20th Streets in Brooklyn.[56] Yet the venture met with little success, with an illustrative moment coming on June 30, when the rebuilt Ridgewoods behind Doc Scanlan beat Lindemann, 10-2.[57] The West Ends didn't survive beyond the summer. Lindemann spent September pitching for a Long Branch, New Jersey, club.[58] He spent 1913 with the Ridgewoods and several central New Jersey teams. An observer: "He's not the pitcher he was a few years ago."[59]

Lindemann staged a comeback in 1914 pitching for Brooklyn's Suburbans, whose oval was in the borough's Kensington neighborhood.[60] He commonly mowed down lesser competition. Against greater challenges, Lindemann's results were mixed. He lost, 3-0, to Cyclone Joe Williams and the New York Lincoln Giants on June 21.[61] Yet that fall, Lindemann won two of three games against future major leaguer Jimmy Ring.[62] One of these affairs came against "Cobb's Stars" on October 11. Lindemann yielded two walks, a double, and a homer to Ty Cobb, but hit two doubles himself and prevailed, 7-5.

Perhaps his most notable performances that season came against the Bushwicks. Then in their initial campaign, as a freshly renamed Ridgewoods squad, the team eventually became the most famous of all Brooklyn semipros.[63] On June 26, Lindemann whitewashed the Bushwicks, then "the same old star as of yore" beat them again on October 25, 10-3.[64]

His renaissance continued into 1915. Lindemann opened the season by two-hitting the New York State League's Wilkes-Barre Barons in a 3-1 win.[65] Andy Coakley, who built an accomplished semipro career after leaving the majors, joined Lindemann to face the Bushwicks in two key midsummer doubleheaders. In the first showdown, on August 1, Coakley lost the opener. Lindemann faced Charlie Girard in the second match and led, 4-3, before an error-filled ninth inning cost him the game.[66] A week later both pitchers avenged their defeats, with Lindemann winning the opener, 5-1.[67]

Later that August, pitching in Hackettstown, New Jersey, Lindemann injured his back.[68] He struggled to return to healthy form that season. His 1916 debut came in mid-June with another Brooklyn semipro franchise, the Cypress Hills.[69] He pitched several times that summer. Then, at age 33, his career ended. Perhaps it was the back injury. Perhaps it was the arrival of a second child, son Ernest, in the Lindemann household in early 1917. Whatever the case may have been, his name disappeared from the box scores.

Later accounts credited Lindemann with 600 or more victories.[70] Half this total seems more likely. His Equitable career limited his ballplaying almost exclusively to weekends. Although durable, he rarely pitched on both Saturday and Sunday. Also, there is no indication Lindemann ever played under an assumed identity – his own name was too marketable. Consequently, his 36 appearances in 1909 seem representative. He pitched 16 complete seasons, from 1900 to 1915, and may have averaged 20 wins per season, thus giving him 300 or more career wins.

After baseball, Lindemann remained in Bensonhurst, becoming a widower when Marie died in 1938. A decade later he retired from Equitable.[71] He died from cancer on December 27, 1951, and was survived by his daughter, Thelma, son, Ernest, and two grandchildren. Ernie Lindemann was buried in Lutheran All Faiths Cemetery in Queens.

SOURCES

In addition to the sources noted in this biography, the author accessed Lindemann's file from the National Baseball Hall of Fame and the following sites:
ancestry.com
chroniclingamerica.loc.gov/newspapers/
digifind-it.com/elizabeth/newspapers.php
fultonhistory.com
genealogybank.com
newspapers.com

ONE-HIT WONDERS

NOTES

1. There was another Ernest T. Lindemann whose life ran roughly parallel to, and is sometimes confused with, the subject of this biography. Born in 1878 (also on June 10) to Otto (a birdcage manufacturer) and Bertha Lindemann, he also was of German heritage. Like the pitcher, he married, early in the new century, a Marie. In his case, Marie Kohlmann in 1905. The couple had three children: Marion, Arthur, and Edward. A graduate of New York Law School, he became a noted Staten Island lawyer. For a biographical profile of this Ernest Lindemann, see Charles W, Leng, *Staten Island and Its People, A History, 1609-1929, Volume III* (New York: Lewis Historical Publishing Co., 1930), 397. He died on February 19, 1941. (For an obituary, see *New York Daily News*, February 20, 1941: 39.) Census records, his WWI Draft Registration, contemporary newspaper articles referencing his age (and his policeman father), and his death certificate all support that the pitcher Ernie Lindemann was born in 1883, with June 10 the most likely date.

2. The 1900 census finds the Lindemanns residing at 84th Street between 21st and 22nd Avenues.

3. "'Ernie' Lindemann, 68, Famed Semi-Pro Baseball Moundsman," *Brooklyn Eagle*, December 28, 1951: 9.

4. "On Baseball Diamonds," *Brooklyn Standard Union*, July 16, 1900, 9; "Baseball," *Brooklyn Standard Union*, August 11, 1900: 12.

5. "Amateur Games," *Brooklyn Standard Union*, July 24, 1901: 3; "State League," *Hartford Courant*, August 23, 1901: 2.

6. "Hartfords Shut Out," *Hartford Courant*, June 11, 1902: 14.

7. "Rockville Centres Win 'The Citizen' Pennant," *Brooklyn Citizen*, August 18, 1902: 4; "On Amateur Diamonds," *Brooklyn Standard Union*, September 27, 1902: 9.

8. "All American Team Was Played to a Standstill," *Brooklyn Standard Union*, November 19, 1902: 9.

9. For more on the subject, see Charles DeMotte, *Bat, Ball & Bible: Baseball and Sunday Observance in New York* (Washington: Potomac Books, 2013).

10. "Six Captains Retired," *New York Sun*, March 30, 1909: 2; "Lindemann's Son Escaped," *Brooklyn Eagle*, June 25, 1906: 5.

11. "'Duke' Farrell Has Lots to Tell the World About Bensonhurst, Its People and Places," *Brooklyn Eagle*, June 15, 1952: 29.

12. "Wiltse to Play in New Jersey," (New Brunswick) *Central New Jersey Home News*, March 11, 1909: 5.

13. "Hoboken Opened with Victory," *Jersey Journal* (Jersey City), April 6, 1903: 7.

14. "New York's Close Game," *New York Times*, April 20, 1903: 5.

15. "Hoboken Wins from Boston," *Jersey Journal*, May 11, 1903: 7; "New York, 5; Hoboken, 2," *New York Times*, May 18, 1903: 8; "New York, 5; Hoboken, 3," *New York Times*, July 20, 1903: 5; "Hoboken, 3, Brooklyn, 1," *New York Times*, July 27, 1903: 5; "Hoboken Wound Up with Shutout," *Jersey Journal*, November 2, 1903: 7.

16. "All Cubans Beaten in Hoboken," *Jersey Journal*, May 25, 1903: 7; "Hoboken Shut Out Cuban X Giants," *Jersey Journal*, June 29, 1903: 7; "Hoboken Club's Great Victory," *Jersey Journal*, August 3, 1903: 9.

17. "Hoboken Beaten by All-Cubans," *Jersey Journal*, June 8, 1903: 9; "Hoboken Lost to All Cubans," *Jersey Journal*, August 10, 1903: 7; "Hoboken Club Escaped a Shut-Out," *Jersey Journal*, May 4, 1903: 8; Hobokens Are Shut Out," *New York Press*, July 6, 1903: 6.

18. "Pitcher Lindeman, Who Has Made Good Record This Year," *New York Evening World*, October 31, 1903: 6. [Note, as this example illustrates, that Lindemann's name was commonly misspelled in contemporary accounts.]

19. "Gossip on the Diamond," *Perth Amboy* (New Jersey) *News*, April 7, 1904: 3.

20. "Lindeman Under the Ban," *Brooklyn Citizen*, July 3, 1904: 5.

21. "New Yorks Defeat the Hobokens," *Jersey Journal*, April 25, 1904: 9.

22. "Hobokens Beat the Phila. Giants," *Jersey Journal*, April 18, 1904: 7; "Hoboken Shut Out by Phila. Giants," *Jersey Journal*, June 20, 1904: 9; "Hobokens Won from Phila. Giants," *Jersey Journal*, July 18, 1904: 5; "Hoboken Lost in Record Game," *Jersey Journal*, August 15, 1904: 5.

23. "Baseball," *Trenton Times*, September 4, 1904: 13.

24. "Lindemann Drafted by New Yorks," *Jersey Journal*, September 21, 1904: 7.

25. "Baseball," *Trenton Times*, March 19, 1905, 8; "Linderman Will Pitch," *Perth Amboy News*, March 23, 1905: 4.

26. "Crescents Shut Out by the Local Team Yesterday," *Perth Amboy News*, May 1, 1905: 4.

27. "Lindeman Vs. Giants," *New York Evening World*, May 2, 1905: 10; "Warning to Players," *The Sporting News*, May 13, 1905: 1.

28. For more on the ballpark, see "The Parks of Ridgewood," BrooklynBallParks.com.

29. "Amateur Baseball," *Brooklyn Standard Union*, June 12, 1905: 3; "Ridgewoods Lost After Pitcher's Battle," *Brooklyn Standard Union*, August 21, 1905: 3; "Amateur Baseball," *Brooklyn Eagle*, September 18, 1905: 12.

30. "Defeated the Highlanders," *Brooklyn Citizen*, October 9, 1905: 5; "McGraw's Men Lost," *New York Times*, October 16, 1905: 10; "Lindemann Had Bad Inning," *Brooklyn Citizen*, October 23, 1905: 5.

31. "'Old Man' Lindeman," *Hackettstown* (New Jersey) *Gazette*, July 9, 1915: 1; "Hussey Tried to Butt," *Brooklyn Citizen*, May 18, 1906: 5.

32. "Not a Run Was Scored," *Brooklyn Citizen*, October 15, 1906: 5.

33. "Diamond Flashes," *Plainfield* (New Jersey) *Courier-News*, August 24, 1912: 9.

34. "Exciting Game in Hoboken," *Jersey Journal*, April 27, 1903: 7; "Hoboken Beaten by All-Cubans," *Jersey Journal*, June 8, 1903: 9; "See Old Baseball Heroes at Outing," *Brooklyn Times*, July 21, 1909: 3; "Bushwicks Make Reply," *Brooklyn Times*, August 4, 1915: 8.

35. "Exciting Game in Hoboken," *Jersey Journal*, April 27, 1903: 7.

36. "Reds Have Easy Time with Stars," *Elizabeth* (New Jersey) *Daily Journal*, May 20, 1907: 13; "Highlanders Dump Stars into Bog," *Elizabeth Daily Journal*, June 10, 1907: 13.

37. "Pittsburgs Win from Stars, 4-3," *Elizabeth Daily Journal*, May 13, 1907: 12; "Stars Lose to Chicago in Eleventh," *Elizabeth Daily Journal*, June 17, 1907: 10.

38. "Athletics Beaten by Stars, 3-2," *Elizabeth Daily Journal*, May 6, 1907: 15; "Giants Lose Game to the Stars," *Elizabeth Daily Journal*, June 24, 1907: 10.

39. "Notes of the Game," *Brooklyn Standard Union*, June 29, 1907: 8.

40. "Lindeman, Ex-Ridgewood Twirler, Tries to Fool Dodger Misfits," *Brooklyn Standard Union*, June 29, 1907: 8; "Tenney's Boys Win in 10 Innings," *Boston Globe*, June 29, 1907: 9; "Crippled Superbas Lose Game After Hard 10-Inning Battle," *Brooklyn Eagle*, June 29, 1907: 4.

41. "Stars Blank Boston by Score of 2-0," *Elizabeth Daily Journal*, July 1, 1907: 11.

42. "Many Pennant Races Close; Chicagos Sure of National Flag," *Brooklyn Eagle*, July 1, 1907: 20.

43. "Lindemann Is Ineligible," *Brooklyn Eagle*, July 2, 1907: 5.

44. For his Hartford stay, see "Hartford Downs Holyoke Leaders," *Hartford Courant*, August 8, 1907: 10; "Hartford Beats Norwich Champs," *Hartford Courant*, August 15, 1907: 10; "Forfeited Game Must Be Played," *Hartford Courant*, August 17, 1907: 14.

ONE-HIT WONDERS

45 A.R. Cratty, "Pirate Points," *Sporting Life,* October 31, 1908: 7; "Season Opens March 28 at Meyerrose Park," *Brooklyn Eagle,* March 15, 1909: 24; "News and Notes of the Amateur Players," *Brooklyn Times,* March 25, 1910: 10.

46 "Notes of the Game," *Brooklyn Standard Union,* May 24, 1908: 6.

47 As an example, see "Ridgewood Won Easily," *Brooklyn Times,* October 17, 1910: 5.

48 "Giants Defeat Ridgewoods in Ten Inning Game 3 to 1," *Brooklyn Standard Union,* October 18, 1908: 6.

49 "Ridgewoods Tie Giants," *Brooklyn Times,* October 18, 1909: 9.

50 "Ridgewoods Beat Bender," *Brooklyn Times,* October 31, 1910: 5.

51 "Results in a Tie After 17 Innings," *Brooklyn Eagle,* July 27, 1908: 18.

52 "A 17-Inning Tie Game," *Brooklyn Citizen,* July 27, 1908: 3.

53 A spreadsheet with specifics for his 1909 season may be found at tinyurl.com/y224dlzt.

54 "Manager R.B. Bliss Signs Entire Ridgewood Outfield for Brunswicks," (New Brunswick, New Jersey) *Home News,* March 22, 1911: 9; "Hobokens Beat Ridgewood," *Brooklyn Times,* April 24, 1911: 10.

55 "Hail – Snow – Spring and Baseball Chat," *Newtown* (New York) *Register,* March 21, 1912: 8.

56 For more on the ballpark, see "Brooklyn's Semipro Fields," covehurst.net/ddyte/brooklyn/semipro_parks.

57 "New Ridgewoods Beat Lindemann's West Ends," *Brooklyn Eagle,* July 1, 1912: 19.

58 On the West Ends' demise, see "'Duke' Farrell Has Lots to Tell the World About Bensonhurst, Its People and Places," *Brooklyn Eagle,* June 15, 1952: 29. For a Long Branch moment, see "Long Branch Loses Twice," *Long Branch* (New Jersey) *Record,* September 17, 1912: 2.

59 "Doc Scanlan Will Work for Brunswicks Friday," (New Brunswick) *Central New Jersey Home News,* May 27, 1913: 8.

60 For more on the ballpark, see "Brooklyn's Semipro Fields," covehurst.net/ddyte/brooklyn/semipro_parks.

61 "Double-Header Won by Lincoln Giants," *Brooklyn Eagle,* June 22, 1914: 18.

62 "Sensational Victory Won by Suburbans," *Brooklyn Eagle,* September 21, 1914: 18; "Ring's Team Turns Tables," *Brooklyn Citizen,* September 28, 1914: 4; "Ty Cobb Shows How to Use the Willow," *Brooklyn Standard Union,* October 12, 1914: 8.

63 Hussey had sold his share of the Ridgewoods in 1913, and the remnants of the team were renamed the Bushwicks. See "Ridgewoods to be Known as Bushwicks This Year," *Brooklyn Eagle,* January 2, 1914: 22.

64 "Suburbans Shut Out the Crack Bushwicks," *Brooklyn Standard Union,* July 27, 1914: 4; "Suburbans Cinch Game in the First Inning," *Brooklyn Standard Union,* October 26, 1914: 8.

65 "Lindemann Pitches Suburbans to Victory," *Brooklyn Eagle,* April 19, 1915: 19.

66 "Bushwicks Twice Defeat Suburbans," *Brooklyn Eagle,* August 2, 1915: 3.

67 "Suburbans Even Bushwick Series," *Brooklyn Eagle,* August 9, 1915: 19.

68 "Bushwicks Champions," *Brooklyn Standard Union,* August 23, 1915: 8.

69 "Lindemann to Twirl Against Fast Ironsides," *Brooklyn Standard Union,* June 16, 1916: 14.

70 Charles Heckelmann, "Major Leaguers 'Meat' for Semi-Pro Hurler," *Brooklyn Eagle,* March 1, 1935: 16; "Necrology," *The Sporting News,* January 9. 1952: 21.

71 "'Ernie' Lindemann, 68, Famed Semi-Pro Baseball Moundsman," *Brooklyn Eagle,* December 28, 1951: 9.

CHUCK LINDSTROM

By Richard Bogovich

More than 9,000 men played in the major leagues before Chuck Lindstrom, but he was the first to achieve an incredibly rare distinction. In fact, 15 more years passed before another player matched him. He is also among the few twentieth-century major leaguers whose fathers were Hall of Fame players, and though none of these sons were superstars, Lindstrom will long be known as the only player in major-league baseball's first century to retire with a slugging percentage of 3.000.[1]

Charles William Lindstrom was born in the Chicago suburb of Evergreen Park on September 7, 1936, the third son of Freddie Lindstrom and the former Irene Kiedaisch.[2] In the 1920 census she was living with her German-immigrant parents on Chicago's South Side, and her father was a baker. Chuck's father had recently played his final major-league game and voluntarily retired young, at the age of 30. By mid-1939 he was a radio broadcaster for WLS-AM,[3] and that was his occupation in the 1940 census, which showed the Lindstroms residing at 7808 S. Michigan Avenue. Later in 1940, however, he returned to pro baseball as manager of the Knoxville Smokies in the Southern Association. He continued there in 1941, then switched to managing the Fort Smith Giants of the Western Association in 1942. In early 1943 the elder Lindstrom became postmaster in north suburban Evanston, home of Northwestern University,[4] and that set the stage for a decision that would affect the course of Chuck's life: In 1947 Freddie Lindstrom became Northwestern's baseball coach, a position he held for 14 years.[5]

Meanwhile, the older of Chuck's two brothers, Fred Jr., started attending their father's high school, Loyola Academy, and by the autumn of 1945 was making a name for himself on its football team.[6] In the early 1950s Fred gave his brothers and parents a much more important reason to be proud of him, when he served as a lieutenant in the US Air Force during the Korean War.[7]

It should come as no surprise that the Lindstrom boys would excel at several sports. Andy, three years older than Chuck, was a starting guard on Loyola Academy's basketball team during the winter of 1950-1951.[8] Chuck also played basketball during high school, except at New Trier in suburban Winnetka.[9] Naturally, baseball was in the mix. "When I played ball, my father never stuck his nose in," Chuck recalled. "He never told a coach he was wrong, was never in conflict with anyone about my playing."[10] Chuck received some attention in mid-1952 when Winnetka's junior American Legion team played in a regional title game. It was noted that the team included sons of three celebrities. The other two famous fathers were former NFL Commissioner Elmer Layden (also one of Notre Dame's legendary Four Horsemen) and national radio personality Don McNeill (Senior).[11]

In mid-1953 Andy was signed by the Phillies and sent to their farm team at Mattoon, Illinois, in the Class-D Mississippi-Ohio Valley League.[12] He made his professional debut on July 11 and in 5⅓ innings he gave up seven hits but just one run.[13] Andy pitched in four more games over the following month.[14] There is no record of his having appeared in a pro game after that season.

Chuck Lindstrom, on left, with coach.

ONE-HIT WONDERS

Chuck Lindstrom had vastly more success in baseball that summer than his brother. For starters, in the opening game of a regional American Legion tournament in Columbus, Ohio, on August 19, he hurled a 5-0 one-hitter.[15] And when the double-elimination finals opened in Miami, Florida, on September 1, his three-hitter helped Winnetka's team win, 2-1.[16] Three days later, he went up to bat in the sixth inning against the favored team, from Yakima, Washington. His single with runners on base was the crucial hit in that frame, which decided a close game. His girlfriend heard the action live, during a special FM radio broadcast while she hosted a slumber party at her Winnetka home. "The room shook with screams of joy," reported one Chicago newspaper. "Popcorn flew."[17] Lindstrom started the final game against Yakima, and his father provided play-by-play for an Evanston radio station. A reporter for *The Sporting News* said Freddie was reasonably impartial until a Yakima baserunner on first, who thought Chuck was ignoring him, broke for second. During that quiet moment Freddie couldn't help but scream, "God almighty, he's going down, Chuckie!" Whether or not he needed his dad's help, Chuck pivoted in time and threw out the would-be thief.[18] Though Yakima ultimately won the game and thus the championship, Lindstrom was chosen the American Legion Junior Baseball Player of the Year, and one result was that his photograph was added to a plaque in the National Baseball Hall of Fame in Cooperstown, New York.[19]

As Chuck Lindstrom neared his graduation from New Trier in June of 1954, the Chicago White Sox reportedly offered him $50,000 to sign with them. By late June, however, he decided to enroll at Northwestern.[20] He kept busy around then by playing in the annual game between Chicago high-school all-stars and their suburban counterparts. It took place on June 26 before 5,000 fans in Comiskey Park. He caught the entire game and scored the winning run in the ninth inning on a wild pitch.[21] Two days later he began a two-week stint in the semipro Iowa State League with his brother Andy's team, the Estherville Red Sox. Andy had pitched in the season opener, before his younger brother joined, but an arm injury kept him from playing with Chuck.[22] Chuck left the team after July 9 because he had been invited to accompany the White Sox on their road trip to Washington, Philadelphia, New York, and Boston from the 15th through the 25th.[23]

August 9, 1954, was a big day in Lindstrom's life up to that point, because he was honored in Cooperstown for his American Legion achievement the prior summer. At home plate prior to an exhibition game between the New York Yankees and Cincinnati Redlegs, he was handed an "official designation scroll" by Lou Brissie, the new commissioner of the Legion's junior baseball program. Lindstrom didn't linger in Cooperstown, because two days later he joined the Kenosha Chiefs of the Illinois-Wisconsin League briefly, before starting classes at Northwestern.[24]

Not surprisingly, Lindstrom starred for the freshman baseball team during the spring of 1955.[25] As a sophomore he made the All-Big Ten Conference first team as its catcher, and was on the second team a year later.[26] After both of those collegiate seasons he played with the Watertown Lake Sox in South Dakota's Basin League.[27]

As Lindstrom finished his junior year in June of 1957, he was already facing life-altering events. He was preparing for tryouts with the Detroit Tigers and the Yankees, and he'd already worked out for the White Sox. And he was engaged to be married in December to Elsie McCloud Fellows, a native of Columbia, Missouri, who was a vocal music major at Northwestern.[28] The White Sox signed him in mid-month, with a $4,000 bonus, and sent him to the Colorado Springs Sky Sox of the Class-A Western League, a team short on catchers.[29]

Lindstrom made his professional debut on June 18 in a loss at home to Topeka. He singled as a pinch-hitter in the ninth inning and eventually scored. He made his first start behind the plate the next day, in a 6-5 win that kept Topeka from winning an 11th consecutive game.[30] One high point came in late July when he helped sweep a doubleheader against first-place Topeka with a grand slam in the nightcap.[31] He played in 66 games that summer and batted .222. *The Sporting News* reported that on September 6 Lindstrom "called it a season" due to a sprained wrist and returned to Chicagoland. However, he'd just been recalled by the White Sox and was put on a short list of prospects to receive trials at their 1958 spring-training camp in Tampa, Florida.[32]

In late February of 1958, a Chicago paper confirmed that Lindstrom was among "about 45 guys around camp" who also included Hal Trosky Jr., whose major-league career would consist of two relief appearances for the White Sox that year. Lindstrom was mentioned in the context of a six-inning split-squad game in early March, but on the 24th the White Sox optioned him to their Davenport team of the Class-B Illinois-Indiana-Iowa (Three-I) League.[33] On March 29 Lindstrom left the minor-league camp in

ONE-HIT WONDERS

Hollywood, near Miami, reportedly saying that he was quitting baseball, but about a week later he was back. "Chuck was a little discouraged with his hitting but he realized he didn't give himself enough of a chance," said his father. "He just came home to have a talk with me before he reported."[34]

Things worked out very nicely for Chuck Lindstrom in 1958. In 127 games for Davenport, he batted .276 with 14 homers and 71 runs batted in. He helped lead his team to the Three-I League's first-half championship and in late August he was named the first-team catcher among the circuit's honorary all-stars.[35] He was recalled by Chicago on September 4 but remained with Davenport until it concluded a championship series against Cedar Rapids with a loss on September 13.[36]

Lindstrom warmed the bench for the White Sox without seeing any action until the last game of the season, at Comiskey Park vs. the Kansas City Athletics on September 28, and he also didn't find himself in the starting lineup for that daytime contest. The White Sox led 3-1 after four innings, and suddenly the home team had a brand-new battery, consisting of Trosky and Lindstrom. It was reportedly the first time in major-league history that a battery featured the sons of major leaguers.[37] Lindstrom had turned 22 three weeks earlier.

The first batter the new duo faced was Joe DeMaestri, who was well into an 11-year major-league career. DeMaestri grounded out. After a walk and a fielder's choice, up stepped slugger Roger Maris. Lindstrom committed a passed ball but then Maris grounded out to end the inning. By the bottom of the sixth inning the White Sox led 6-4, and Lindstrom led off that frame against pitcher Bob Davis, who was eight games into a two-year major-league career. Lindstrom drew a walk and eventually scored.

Lindstrom then caught three scoreless innings for Bob Shaw, who would lead the American League with a .750 winning percentage (18 wins, 6 losses) a year later for the pennant-winning White Sox. In the meantime, he had a second plate appearance in the bottom of the seventh inning, again against Davis. Johnny Callison led off with a walk but after two flies to left field he remained at first base. Up stepped Lindstrom. Many years later he recalled working the count to three balls and one strike. Kansas City's veteran catcher Frank House decided to help his young counterpart and said, "I would be looking for a fastball if I were you." Lindstrom replied, "I appreciate that but I'm already looking for one!" That was indeed Davis's next pitch, and Lindstrom recalled pounding it into the power alley between right and center fields, where it struck the top of the wall. It traveled about 375 feet. Callison scored as Lindstrom pulled into third with a triple. Shaw batted next and ended the inning with a grounder to Davis.

The White Sox added more runs in their half of the eighth but that inning ended with Lindstrom on deck. The game ended four batters later with the White Sox winning, 11-4. Lindstrom was told that he'd get to play that day, so his parents were in the stands. "My mom had seen many a major-league baseball game, but this was probably as excited as I had ever seen her," he recalled many years later. "Her knuckles were standing out as white as could be from squeezing her hands so tight. She was just thrilled to death, much more thrilled than I was, because I honestly thought there would be many other times."[38]

Shortly before Thanksgiving the White Sox announced a 38-man winter roster, and Lindstrom was on it. In early 1959 the White Sox announced that only two players were under contract, and Lindstrom was one of them.[39] By the end of February, he was among the catchers in the major-league spring-training camp, but in late March he was among six players sent to the minor-league camp in Hollywood.[40]

Lindstrom ended up spending the 1959 season with Charleston of the Class-A South Atlantic League. Though he played in as many games as in his successful campaign with Davenport the year before, his batting average dropped to .219, and he didn't generate much power. One factor may have been that he started wearing glasses at bat. Previously he'd only worn a pair at Northwestern to see distant blackboards during class.[41] However, his father provided a different explanation: "They tried to make a pull hitter out of him," Freddie Lindstrom said. "Chuck compiled his big average[s] at Northwestern hitting straight away. But the majors want the home run."[42] In any case, helping to offset any disappointment he felt was the fact that by that point he and Elsie had welcomed their first child, Kathy.[43]

Over the final month of the season, Lindstrom pitched in three regular-season games for Charleston, and made one more appearance on the mound during the playoffs in early September.[44] That may have set the stage for additional disappointment on his part, because he was assigned to Chicago's San Diego farm team in the Triple-A Pacific Coast League in October, only to learn by early March of 1960 that his new club planned to convert him to a pitcher.[45] A week after he

ONE-HIT WONDERS

reported to San Diego that month, his second child, Laura Ann, was born.[46] By mid-April he was facing demotion, so he decided to quit baseball instead. By then he had completed his Northwestern degree, so he decided that he'd go into business in Elsie's hometown of Columbia, Missouri.[47]

Lindstrom didn't stick to that decision for long. Toward the end of June he was again playing for Chicago's affiliate in the Three-I League, now the Lincoln (Nebraska) Chiefs.[48] His batting average of .218 nearly matched his low mark of the previous year, but with Lincoln he played in only 59 games, not quite half of his 1958 and 1959 totals.

In early 1961 Lindstrom was pursuing a master's degree at the University of Missouri, in Elsie's hometown, but he was reportedly pursuing high-school coaching jobs not far from Winnetka and Evanston.[49] He began the 1961 baseball season by returning to Charleston, his team in 1959, but he played in only three games before being shipped back to Lincoln by mid-May.[50] He had even fewer appearances than in the previous season, just 54 games, but two things contributed to that. In June he went on the disabled list for 10 days with torn chest muscles.[51] More significantly, on July 13 it was announced that he had accepted a coaching position at Lincoln College in Lincoln, Illinois for the 1961-1962 school year. Because he had completed his Missouri master's, he was also expected to teach physical education and social science courses.[52]

As a result of his new job looming, Chuck Lindstrom finished the 1961 season early. Though he departed with a batting average of .194, his last time at bat was the most one could ask for. On August 20 it was known that he'd leave the team the next day for Lincoln in central Illinois. The Chiefs played a tripleheader of sorts at home, because the two teams began the day by resuming a suspended game. Lindstrom caught the entire day because Lincoln's regular receiver was injured. In the nightcap, Lindstrom helped pitcher Bob Locker scatter four hits and retire 15 batters in a row in one stretch, on the way to a 5-0 outcome. Late in the game was Lindstrom's "swan song," as a *Lincoln Evening Journal* sportswriter noted. "Loudest applause of the evening may have gone to Chuck Lindstrom," he wrote. "Chuck blasted a home run over the scoreboard in the 8th inning."[53] That proved to be his final plate appearance as a professional ballplayer, a few weeks before his 25th birthday. A month later he said he was done with professional baseball, and that time he meant it. "I don't know, it may be my temperament or my personality, but I'm very glad to get out of it," he told a sportswriter. "I can't enjoy baseball when it becomes a real business."[54]

During the summer of 1962, he was presumably the Chuck Lindstrom who caught and pitched for a club in Elsie's hometown, the Columbia Western Auto team. In late July that team was competing in the Missouri State Non-Pro Baseball Tournament, and on August 2 he hurled a complete game in a 3-0 loss in the losers' bracket. He gave up eight hits and a walk but struck out 15 opponents.[55] Otherwise, for the first two decades after his time as a White Sox prospect, his sporting focus was in Lincoln.

In 1963 Lindstrom managed Lincoln's team in the brand new summertime Central Illinois Collegiate League. The club's president was Lincoln native Emil Verban, the former Cardinals second baseman. Lincoln had a team in the CICL during its first six seasons (and again from 1988 through 1990). Lindstrom's first squad included future major leaguers Del Unser and Tom Heintzelman, and his rosters in 1967 and 1968 included two more, Skip Pitlock and Art Howe.[56] Lindstrom's team won the CICL pennant in 1967 despite a .224 team batting average.[57]

In the spring of 1964 Lindstrom was promoted to Lincoln College's athletic director.[58] At that point and for more than a decade after, his brother Andy was Lincoln's soccer coach. The brothers also worked together with the CICL team, because Andy became club President Verban's secretary at some point.[59]

By 1973 Chuck and Elsie had divorced, though after daughters Kathy and Laurie they also had two sons, Charles and John.[60] In 1972 or early 1973 he married the former Elaine McCombs of Humeston, Iowa, a science teacher who had graduated from Illinois State University during the winter of 1971-1972. They had one daughter, Lisa.[61]

In 1973 Lindstrom returned to the CICL as a manager, except for the team in Macomb, about 80 miles to the west. He coached yet another future major leaguer, pitcher Bob Shirley. It turned out to be the last of Macomb's five seasons in the league.[62] Lindstrom continued to oversee all sports for Lincoln College while still leading its baseball team, the Lynx. "Chuck Lindstrom has built what many observers believe is one of the finest junior college baseball programs in the state, if not the U.S.," commented a longtime central Illinois sportswriter in the mid-1970s.[63] In 1974 the Lynx had the second best season in the state, with a 23-11 record. That came on the heels of Lincoln basketball coach Al Pickering leading that crew to the

ONE-HIT WONDERS

fourth best mark in the state with a record of 26-11.[64] One of Lindstrom's baseball players who graduated in 1975, Brian Snitker, began a stint as manager of the Atlanta Braves in 2016.[65]

In 1976 Freddie Lindstrom was named to the National Baseball Hall of Fame by its Veterans Committee. Andy was instrumental in the campaign to add his father. Reportedly more than 60 of Freddie's relatives traveled to Cooperstown for his induction. Freddie was thus able to bask in that glory for five years, until his death in 1981 at the age of 75. Irene died in 1980.[66]

In mid-1980 Chuck Lindstrom stepped down as Lincoln College's athletic director, and was succeeded by Al Pickering. Lindstrom remained baseball coach but left Lincoln College entirely two years later. He left with some bitterness, and alluded to conflict with administrators going back at least four years. He was the baseball coach for 21 seasons and athletic director for 17.[67] By the late 1970s he'd begun to pursue sports-related business interests, including a product for drying waterlogged ballfields more rapidly, called Diamond Dry. Upon his departure from Lincoln College he also worked for Musco Sports Lighting, which eventually led to the creation of his own business, Universal Sports Lighting.[68]

Lindstrom didn't always pursue such ventures full-time; he also spent 13 years as the City of Lincoln's parks and recreation director. However, his lighting work received a boost from one of his star players from the 1960s, Art Howe, who coached and managed in the majors for more than a decade starting in the mid-1980s.[69]

In the 2000s Lindstrom has received several honors at Lincoln College. He was named an honorary athletic letterman in 2003 and received the college's Honorary Alumni Award in 2009. The Lynx hall of fame recognizes him online with a biography that credits him as a women's athletics pioneer for "starting Women's Basketball, Softball and Volleyball" and notes that in 2013 the College baseball coach's office was dedicated in his name. By the 2007 baseball season there was a Chuck Lindstrom Field in Lincoln.[70]

In 2016, Lindstrom was interviewed for the American Legion. Asked about his honor by the Legion 63 years earlier, he shifted the conversation to much more recent events, such as his pride in the award bestowed upon one his children, Charles Jr., for being the first allied weatherman during Operation Desert Storm in 1990 to enter Iraq, as a sergeant with the 101st Airborne Division. His most meaningful baseball memory was even more recent: He talked about a gathering about a year earlier when his Lincoln College baseball players came back, more than 30 years later, after the campus's baseball office had been named for him.[71]

SOURCES

In addition to the sources cited in the Notes, the author relied on Baseball-Reference.com as the primary source for baseball statistics.

NOTES

1. See baseball-reference.com/bullpen/Chuck_Lindstrom. His baseball-reference.com statistics page calls him "Charlie." However, in newspapers throughout his life, "Chuck" has been standard. For an overview of sons of Hall of Famers who played in the majors, see Joe Posnanski, "Fathers, Sons and Hall of Fame," July 9, 2015, at joeposnanski.substack.com/p/fathers-sons-and-hall-of-fame.

2. Birth records for Cook County, Illinois, identify his birthplace as the adjacent Village of Evergreen Park rather than Chicago itself. His mother's maiden name appeared in a photo caption in the *Chicago Daily News*, February 17, 1928: Photogravure section, page 5. (The date of this section is February 18 but it apparently came with the prior evening's paper.)

3. "Radio Programs for Tonight, Tomorrow," *Chicago Daily Times*, April 17, 1939: 24. Don Foster, "How TIMES Comic Strips Are Dramatized," *Sunday Times*, June 11, 1939: 19-M.

4. "Fred Lindstrom Takes Evanston Postal Job," *Chicago Daily Times*, February 10, 1943: 30.

5. Charles F. Faber, "Freddie Lindstrom," SABR BioProject, sabr.org/bioproj/person/b4f653b8.

6. For example, see Bob Tatar, "St. Philip Shades Loyola 18 to 14," *Chicago Sun*, October 29, 1945: 19. See also "All Catholic League All-Star Teams," *Chicago Daily News*, November 30, 1945: 33. Though Chuck's oldest brother was often called Fred Jr., his findagrave.com entry shows his name as Frederick Charles Lindstrom III.

7. See his obituary, at dignitymemorial.com/obituaries/des-plaines-il/frederick-lindstrom-5063016.

8. Bud Nangle, "Loyola Rambles Without Fanfare," *Chicago Daily News*, February 1, 1951: 37.

9. "Pontiac Tourney Top Bracket Looks Strong, Well Balanced," *Bloomington* (Illinois) *Pantagraph*, December 27, 1952: 9.

10. George Rose, *One Hit Wonders: Baseball Stories* (Lincoln, Nebraska: iUniverse, Inc., 2004), 68.

11. Tony Weitzel, "The Town Crier," *Chicago Daily News*, July 26, 1952: 21. Lindstrom and Mike Layden, who were sometimes batterymates, received national exposure the following summer when pictured together. See Franklyn J. Adams, "Sons and Brothers of Name Players Dot Legion Rosters," *The Sporting News*, August 19, 1953: 4.

12. "Lindstrom's Son Signed by Phillies," *Chicago Daily News*, July 7, 1953: 23.

13. "Weekend Woeful for Phils Twice," *Daily Journal-Gazette and Commercial-Star* (Mattoon, Illinois), July 13, 1953: 6.

14. Andy's entry at that baseball-reference.com/register/player.fcgi?id=lindsto01and simply indicates he pitched in five games for Mattoon, but it has no statistics (nor does it identify him as Freddie's son). He also appeared in box scores published by the *Mattoon Daily Journal-Gazette* on July 22, 23, and 27 and August 13. Those box

ONE-HIT WONDERS

scores excluded earned runs and runs allowed but his five-game totals were 18⅔ innings pitched, 24 hits, 10 walks, and 12 strikeouts.

15   "Lindstrom's One-Hit Job Beats Edison," *Columbus* (Ohio) *Dispatch*, August 19, 1953: 8B. Bud Nangle, "Winnetka Wins in Legion Playoff," *Chicago Daily News*, August 19, 1953: 50. The Columbus paper said Lindstrom walked four batters and struck out seven, but Nangle said he walked six and struck out nine.

16   "Winnetka Goes After 2d Straight in Finals," *Chicago Daily News*, September 2, 1953: 30.

17   "N. Shore Gripped by 'Series Fever,'" *Chicago Daily News*, September 5, 1953: 28. This account said Lindstrom's RBI single broke a 2-2 tie, but at least one other report said he drove in the tying run, and that what proved to be the winning run scored moments later on a wild pitch. See "Surprise Starter Thompson Keeps Winnetka in Running," *The Sporting News* (Junior Baseball Edition), September 16, 1953: 2.

18   Jimmy Burns, "Legion Ball Saving Game, Say Ex-Stars," *The Sporting News* (Junior Baseball Edition), September 16, 1953: 4.

19   Jimmy Burns, "Winnetka's Versatile Lindstrom Chosen as Legion Player of Year," *The Sporting News* (Junior Baseball Edition), September 16, 1953: 2.

20   Howard Brantz, "A Sporting Glance," *Carroll* (Iowa) *Times Herald*, May 28, 1954: 2. Fred Young, "Young's Yarns," *Bloomington Pantagraph*, July 1, 1954: 9.

21   "Suburban Wins All-Star Prep Baseball, 4-3," *Chicago Tribune*, June 27, 1954: 2, 5.

22   N.E. Demoney, "Red Sox Down Cardinals, 6 to 4," *Estherville* (Iowa) *Daily News*, June 30, 1954: 11. See also Hoyt Luithly, "Red Sox in Weekend Split with Braves," *Estherville Daily News* June 28, 1954: 4. Andy's full stats for his lone appearance happened to be on the latter page, in the table beneath the headline, "1954 Record of the Red Sox."

23   "Red Sox Drop Third Game in Row," *Estherville Daily News*, July 10, 1954: 4. "Will Represent Red Sox in All-Star Game," *Estherville Daily News*, July 12, 1954: 4. "Chuck Lindstrom was voted among the top five Red Sox players but he has left the team to return to Chicago where he has been invited to accompany the White Sox on their swing around the eastern half of the American League." His cumulative stats were printed in a table in that same paper the next day, on page 6.

24   "Great Lakes Plays Chiefs Here Tonight," *Kenosha* (Wisconsin) *News*, August 12, 1954: 19. Apparently this paper had the odd habit of excluding positions from its box scores.

25   Howie Geltzer, "'Cat Nine Eyes Next Year after Successful Season," *Daily Northwestern* (Evanston, Illinois), May 26, 1955: 3.

26   "All-Big Ten Team Named," *Rockford* (Illinois) *Morning Star*, June 2, 1956: 8. "3 Teams Supply 2 Big 10 Stars," *Chicago Daily News*, June 10, 1957: 16.

27   "Lake Sox Overcome Yankton 5-0 Lead," *Huronite and Daily Plainsman* (Huron, South Dakota), June 23, 1955: 13. "Lake Sox Score 8 in 3rd, Down Mitchell, 16-3," *Huronite and Daily Plainsman*, June 26, 1956: 9. A baseball historian named David Trombley compiled biographies of many Basin League players at usfamily.net/web/trombleyd/BasinBios.htm and included details in Lindstrom's not squeezed into this biography (though Lindstrom was said to have played briefly for Winona in the Minnesota State League in June of 1957 when in actuality he was with that circuit's team just over the border in Mason City, Iowa).

28   "Sox Delay Lindstrom Decision," *Chicago Daily News*, June 6, 1957: 48. Details about Elsie were provided at findagrave.com/memorial/166287440/elsie-madden.

29   Harvey Duck, "Sox Sign Lindstrom," *Chicago Daily News*, June 17, 1957: 23. "Only two base runners tried to steal on him this year," Duck noted. "One was retired, while the other was safe at second when the shortstop failed to cover the base." See also "Lindstrom Signs Pro Pact with White Sox," *Mason City* (Iowa) *Globe-Gazette*, June 18, 1957: 11. He had played four games with the Mason City Braves in the Southern Minnesota League before the White Sox signed him.

30   "Hawks Bat Skymen," *Amarillo* (Texas) *Daily News*, June 19, 1957: 11. "Hawks Fly Down," *Amarillo Daily News*, June 20, 1957: 18. The starting catcher for the Sky Sox during Lindstrom's debut was presumably Charles Schaffernoth, but his Baseball-Reference stats for 1957 show him only with Des Moines, another Western League club.

31   "Topeka Lead Is Slashed," *Ottawa* (Kansas) *Herald*, July 29, 1957: 6.

32   "Western League," *The Sporting News*, September 18, 1957: 47. "Sox Recall 7 for Trials; Add 7 More," *Dixon* (Illinois) *Evening Telegraph*, September 5, 1957: 10.

33   John P. Carmichael, "Sox Renew Drive to Get Sievers," *Chicago Daily News*, February 25, 1958: 22; John P. Carmichael, "Sox Best Behind Plate," *Chicago Daily News*, March 7, 1858: 33; "Sox Option Lindstrom and Ditusa," *Chicago Daily News*, March 25, 1858: 27.

34   "Lindstrom Rejoins Sox Farm Camp," *Chicago Daily News*, April 7, 1958: 26; "Chuck Lindstrom to Stay in Baseball," *Daily Northwestern*, April 9, 1958: 3. For a much longer version of Freddie's pep talk, see David Condon, "Condonsations," *The Sporting News*, April 16, 1958: 16.

35   "Dav-Sox Dominate All-Star Balloting," *Muscatine* (Iowa) *Journal*, August 30, 1958: 4.

36   "Cedar Rapids Is Three-I King, 9-8," *Cedar Rapids* (Iowa) *Gazette*, September 14, 1958: 4, 1.

37   "Sons of Ex-Stars Make Up Battery," *Omaha World-Herald*, September 29, 1958: 9.

38   Dave Reidy, "One Hit Wonder," *The Morning News*, September 26, 2003, themorningnews.org/article/one-hit-wonder (*The Morning News* is an independent web magazine.) According to Paul Munsey and Corey Suppes at ballparks.com/baseball/american/comisk.htm, Comiskey Park's power alleys were 375 feet from home plate from 1956 through 1958, after which they were each 10 feet shorter until 1968.

39   "Chisox List Winter Roster," *Logansport* (Indiana) *Pharos-Tribune*, November 20, 1958: 21. "Ask Sox Players to Take Pay Cut," *Chicago Daily News*, January 8, 1959: 45.

40   Lindstrom was one of three White Sox catchers in a photo in the *Racine* (Wisconsin) *Sunday Bulletin*, March 1, 1959: 3, 2. See also "Sox Ship Six to Minors," *Chicago Daily News*, March 30, 1959: 28.

41   "Chisox Catcher's Batting Improves With New Glasses," *Charleston* (South Carolina) *News and Courier*, May 13, 1959: 2-B.

42   "Lindstrom Eyes Top," *Daily Northwestern*, April 7, 1960: 7.

43   Marvin West, "Fans Measure Young Chuck Lindstrom on Basis of Dad's Accomplishments," *Knoxville (Tennessee) News-Sentinel*, May 28, 1959; 30. Elsie and Kathy weren't named in the article but were both named in "Lindstrom Eyes Top," *Daily Northwestern*, April 7, 1960: 7.

44   Lindstrom's baseball-reference.com stats lack details for the three regular-season games in which he pitched, but at least one newspaper provided them as follows: "Gastonia Bucs Rout Charleston Sox 8-4," *Charleston News and Courier*, August 1, 1959: 10 -- ⅔ IP, 2 H, 4 R, 0 ER, 1 BB, 0 K; "Macon Trounces Chasox 13 to 3," *Charleston News and Courier*, August 15, 1959: 12 -- ⅔ IP, 0 H 0 R, 1 BB, 1 K; "Asheville Wins over Chasox in Opener 13-8," *Charleston News and Courier*, August 31, 1959: 2-B -- 6⅔ IP, 7 H, 4 R, 4 ER, 5 BB, 7 K. He also pitched in the first game of the playoffs, according to "Smokies Blast Sox," *Charleston News and Courier*, September 3, 1959: 30. His pitching line for that contest was 3⅓ IP, 5 H, 4 R, 4 ER, 1 BB, 3 K.

45   "Doby's Career May Be Over," *Knoxville News-Sentinel*, October 20, 1959: 19. "Curve-Tossing Wojey Signs '60 Padre Contract," *San Diego Union*, March 4, 1960: 23.

46   "Lindstrom Eyes Top."

ONE-HIT WONDERS

47 "Chuck Lindstrom Quits Pro Baseball," *Daily Northwestern*, April 15, 1960: 8.

48 After 1956 there were no Illinois or Indiana teams in the Illinois-Indiana-Iowa League, but it did include Nebraska, Kansas, and Wisconsin teams.

49 Fred Young, "Young's Yarns," *Bloomington Pantagraph*, February 18, 1961: 7. Young said Lindstrom was tempted by the possibility of coaching at a new high school in Skokie, less than four miles inland from Evanston. On the same day, another sportswriter in central Illinois instead wrote that Lindstrom had applied a few miles farther west, in Niles. See Bob "Dry" Drysdale, "The Dope Bucket," *Illinois State Journal* (Springfield), February 18, 1961: 8.

50 "Chasox Send Two to Lincoln Team," *Charleston News and Courier*, May 10, 1961: 10.

51 Dick Becker, "Chiefs Run Into 4-Hitter," *Lincoln* (Nebraska) *Evening Journal*, June 9, 1961: 15.

52 "Lindstrom Gets Lincoln Post," *Illinois State Journal*, July 14, 1961: 26.

53 Dick Becker, "Sunday Rest Idea Shattered," *Lincoln Evening Journal*, August 21, 1961: 11. See also "Foxes Win 3 of 5, Play Here Tonight," *Appleton* (Wisconsin) *Post-Crescent*, August. 21, 1961: A11, A12.

54 John Hillyer, "Speaking of Sports," *Illinois State Journal*, September 19, 1961: 11.

55 "Iberia Merchants Shut Out Springfield in Tough Game," *Sedalia* (Missouri) *Democrat*, July 29, 1962: 12; "Stockton Walnuts Win Over Jefferson City Red Birds," *Sedalia Democrat*, August 3, 1962: 6. Lindstrom's first name was used in both accounts, though the latter misspelled his surname as Lindstrum. See also "Carling's Dealt 5-4 Loss by Columbia Western Auto," *Sunday News and Tribune* (Jefferson City, Missouri), July 1, 1962: 10.

56 "Verban Named President of Lincoln Group," *Illinois State Journal*, May 21, 1963: 11.

57 Robert J. Herguth, "People," *Chicago Daily News*, August 29, 1967: 15. See alsotciclbaseball.com/index.php?view=about&show=teams for a year-by-year account of CICL teams and champions. For full 1967 CICL statistics, see *State Journal-Register*, August 20, 1967: 66. Howe played in all 49 of Lincoln's games and batted .284, while Pitlock went 11-3 with an earned run average of 2.12.

58 "Lindstrom New Director," *Illinois State Journal*, April 25, 1964: 9.

59 "Griggas Joins Lincoln College Athletic Staff," *Illinois State Journal*, June 26, 1964: 21. "Lincoln's CIC Entry to Play," *State Journal-Register*, February 13, 1966: 56. Andy was also a history professor at Lincoln College, according to "Lindstrom, Hubbard Earn Berths in Hall of Fame," *Bloomington Pantagraph*, February 3, 1976: B-2.

60 The names of Elsie's first four children were confirmed in her second husband's obituary, which is posted at his findagrave.com entry.

61 Lisa worked at Universal Sports Lighting, her father's business before he retired, as still indicated at pitchbook.com/profiles/company/62960-14.

62 "Tab Lindstrom for CICL Post," *Illinois State Journal*, January 30, 1973: 11; Joe Morrissey, "Pioneers Lose 12-Inning Battle in Opener," *Galesburg* (Illinois) *Register-Mail*, June 13, 1973: 38; "Caps Hammer Macomb 5-3," *State Journal-Register*, July 7, 1973: 21. See also the CICL website, ciclbaseball.com/index.php?view=about&show=teams.

63 Fred Young, "Young's Yarns," *Bloomington Pantagraph*, March 19, 1975: D-4.

64 Bob McBride, "Looping the Loop," *Henry* (Illinois) *News Republican*, September 18, 1974: 8.

65 See lincolncollege.edu/lincoln-college-alumnus-brian-snitker-named-atlanta-braves-interim-manager/.

66 Charles F. Faber, "Freddie Lindstrom," SABR BioProject, sabr.org/bioproj/person/b4f653b8. Also see Irene's findagrave.com entry.

67 "Pickering Named Lincoln College A.D.," *State Journal-Register*, June 13, 1980: 26. Bryan Bloodworth, "Lincoln College's Lindstrom Resigns as Head Baseball Coach," *Bloomington Pantagraph*, April 17, 1982: 10.

68 Chuck Rigsby and Stan Hieronymus, "State Tournaments Will Be at One Site," *Peoria* (Illinois) *Journal Star*, June 8, 1979: C-2. "Legion Field Soon Will Be Well Lit," *Bloomington Pantagraph*, May 27, 1982: B7. Paul Swiech, "Firms Team Up to Light Sport Fields, *Bloomington Pantagraph*, September 13, 1992: E1. John Schmeltzer, "Ex-Sox Player Lighting 'em up," *Chicago Tribune*, April 12, 2004: 4, 1. For Musco Lighting, see musco.com/.

69 Jason Blasco, "Former Chicago White Sox Player Uses Lessons Way Beyond Legion Baseball," *Lincoln* (Illinois) *Courier*, June 20, 2013, accessible at lincolncourier.com/article/20130620/NEWS/306209914.

70 "Honorary Athletic Letterman Standing Awarded to Jones and Lindstrom," *The Log* (Lincoln College alumni publication), Spring 2003: 5, accessible at alumni.lincolncollege.edu/wp-content/uploads/sites/7/spring2003.pdf; "Reunion 2009," *Lincoln Log*, Spring 2009: 1, accessible at alumni.lincolncollege.edu/wp-content/uploads/sites/7/Spring09.pdf. See also http://www.lincolnlynxsports.com/halloffame/ID/24; Hal Pilger, "Little Things Lead to Big Losses for Southeast," *State Journal-Register*, April 19, 2007: 28.

71 Cameran Richardson, "Legion Baseball Alum Recalls Valuable Lessons Learned," February 18, 2016, accessible at legion.org/baseball/231261/legion-baseball-alum-recalls-valuable-lessons-learned.

RED LUTZ

By Bob Webster

During the 1922 season, Cincinnati Reds second baseman Lew Fonseca raced back to catch a pop fly in short right field. The right fielder also raced in and the two collided, knocking each other dizzy. Seeing the ball lying on the field with the runners circling the bases was too much for Red Lutz, the Reds' bullpen catcher, to take. He raced in from the bullpen, picked up the ball, and threw a perfect strike to nail a runner at third. After the dust settled, the baserunner was awarded home by the umpire and the red-faced Lutz returned to the bullpen.[1]

Louis W. "Red" Lutz was born on December 17, 1898, in Cincinnati to Wilhelm and Rosa (Geiger) Lutz. Rosa Geiger was born in 1862 in Schomberg, Kingdom of Wurttemberg, German Empire. She migrated from Bremen, Germany, to New York City in 1884 and lived in Cincinnati from 1888 until her death in 1935. The housemaid and laundress married Herman Wilhelm Sontag in 1888. They had three children; Freda, Herman Aloysius, and Rose Sontag Thieman. Herman died in 1894. Rosa then married Wilhelm Lutz in Cincinnati on December 30, 1897, and about a year later their son, Louis, was born. Wilhelm, a cabinetmaker, had also migrated from Bremen to New York City, in 1872. Rosa and Wilhelm were married for only a little over four years when Wilhelm died.[2]

Louis moved with his widowed mother and step-siblings to the Mount Adams neighborhood of Cincinnati in 1904 and he lived there until he entered the Navy. He was baptized in the Church of the Immaculate Conception on February 2, 1899. Beginning in 1903, Louis attended grade school and high school at the church's Immaculata School in Mount Adams. He played baseball, basketball, and football during his younger years for Immaculata, the Fraternal Order of Elks, and other local teams.[3]

Father John Philip Maerder was appointed pastor of the church in 1914 and revitalized the Immaculata Athletic Club, which enjoyed great prominence on baseball fields and basketball courts around Cincinnati.[4] The pastor and the Immaculata Athletic Club had quite an influence on Lutz's teenage years and developing his baseball skills.[5]

Lutz also developed his baseball skills at the Fenwick Club, a young men's residence and club similar to the YMCA, but with a Catholic approach. The Fenwick Club also had an impact on the youngster's teenage years, but to a lesser extent than the Immaculata. Lutz played baseball and basketball there as a teenager and returned to play handball at the Fenwick Club after he retired from baseball.[6]

Lutz enlisted in the US Navy in May 1918 during World War I. He was stationed at the Naval Air Station in Miami, Florida, and was discharged on January 28, 1919.[7]

Red Lutz.

Courtesy of Bill Eggemeier.

ONE-HIT WONDERS

Lutz broke into Organized Baseball in 1920, playing for three Class-D Florida State League teams; the Orlando Caps, the St. Petersburg Saints, and the Sanford Celeryfeds. He started the season in Orlando, spent a short time with the Celeryfeds in May because they were out of catchers,[8] and then returned to the Caps. In June he was sold to the St. Petersburg Saints, but apparently did not report right away; it was reported that he was sold to the team from Orlando but was fined $25 and suspended for not reporting to the St. Petersburg team.[9]

In 1921 Lutz played for a semipro Southern Indiana Baseball Association League team in Greensburg, Indiana, and was in the Cincinnati Reds training camp in 1922.[10] The Reds already had two catchers who were assured of making the roster, Ivey Wingo and Bubbles Hargrave. The 31-year-old Wingo began his career with the St. Louis Cardinals in 1911 and had been with the Reds since the 1915 season. He hit .260 in his 17-year career with the Cardinals and Reds while throwing out 46 percent of potential basestealers. Wingo was the subject of the bidding war between the Federal League and the American and National Leagues, and his salary with Cincinnati was $6,500 in 1915, a $2,000 raise over the 1914 season. When the Federal League folded after the 1915 season, the Reds attempted to trade Wingo and his large contract. But Reds fans signed a petition to keep Wingo in Cincinnati and the owners obliged. With that popularity, the Reds kept him around through the 1926 season.[11]

Wingo had not mastered left-handed pitching, so the Reds picked up the good-hitting Bubbles Hargrave to platoon with Wingo for the 1921 season. Hargrave played for Cincinnati for the next eight seasons, hitting over .300 in six consecutive seasons.[12]

With competition like that, Lutz did not have much of a chance to land a catching job with the Reds. He was, however, able to make the team and spent most of the 1922 season warming up relief pitchers. On May 31 the Pirates led the Reds 11-1 going into the eighth inning. Lutz came in to catch and made a plate appearance. He took advantage of the opportunity by hitting a double.[13] Then it was back to the bullpen until Wingo or Hargrave sustained a significant injury, but that didn't happen for the remainder of the season. He was being paid $450 a month.

Lutz was released by the Reds on May 2, 1923, and returned to minor-league baseball.[14] He joined the Oklahoma City Indians of the Class-A Western League and batted .235 in 72 games, splitting time as catcher with Jack Roche and Jimmie Long, who had both seen playing time in the major leagues. "I got more money in the minors," he said.[15]

In 1924 Lutz played for the Shenandoah Braves of the independent Anthracite League in Eastern Pennsylvania.

Lutz played for three teams in 1925, the Bridgeport Bears and Worcester Panthers of the Class-A Eastern League and the Shamokin Shammies of the Class-B New York-Penn League, where he hit .320 in 100 at-bats. He played the full year in Shamokin in 1926, batting .256 in 96 games.

Lutz kept his minor-league career going for a few more years. In 1927 he played 25 games for the Haverhill Hillies of the Class-B New England League and 126 games for the Burlington Bees of the Class-D Mississippi Valley League in 1929, where he hit .290 with 130 hits in 449 at-bats. He followed those two impressive seasons by hitting .256 in 73 games with the Fairmont Black Diamonds of the Class-C Middle Atlantic League in 1930. His baseball career appeared to be over after the 1931 season when he played for the Dubuque Tigers and the Moline Plowboys, both of the Class-D Mississippi Valley League.

Lutz stayed in touch with Hargrave and was liked well enough by the Reds organization to be asked to return in 1938 as the player-manager if the Union City Greyhounds of the Kentucky-Illinois-Tennessee (Kitty) League. As a player, the 39-year-old appeared in 15 games in addition to managing the team.

He finished his major-league career having gone 1-for-1 with a double, for a batting average of 1.000, an on-base percentage of 1.000, slugging percentage of 2.000, and an OPS of 3.000.

Except for his time in Union City, Lutz played for some local teams in Cincinnati including Heidelberg Brewing and Coca-Cola between 1936 and 1940.[16]

In 1923 Lutz had begun working for the New York Central Railroad as a baggage handler, and throughout the years he also worked as a brakeman and conductor on the James Whitcomb Riley passenger train, which operated between Chicago and Cincinnati via Indianapolis. During his baseball career he worked at the railroad during the offseason and during periods of being laid off from the railroad, he did odd jobs like selling coffee and candy door to door. In his early years with the New York Central, he played for the railroad's basketball team.[17]

Lutz stayed with the New York Central until August 10, 1968. When the train pulled into Union Terminal in Cincinnati at 11:15 that night, Lutz decided to call it a day after 44 years with the railroad.

ONE-HIT WONDERS

Courtesy of Bill Eggemeier.

Lutz, 1923.

On February 25, 1922, before reporting to the Reds training camp, Lutz had married Louise Gillming in Greensburg, Indiana. They had two children, Robert L. Lutz and Ruth Ellen (Lutz) Eggemeier, and eight grandchildren.[18]

After their marriage, Red and Louise moved to a home in Newport, Kentucky, across the Ohio River from Cincinnati. In 1950 they moved to Cincinnati. Louise died in 1964 and Red lived in their house until 1970, when he had a stroke and moved in with his daughter's family in Newport.[19]

After his baseball career, Lutz liked to go to the racetrack once in a while and fished occasionally. He enjoyed traveling with his wife and, after she died, with his daughter's family. He enjoyed trips to Florida and on a couple of occasions attended Reds spring-training games at Al Lopez Field in Tampa. He loved his dogs and cats and taking long walks. He also enjoyed going to Cincinnati Reds games and was very active until his stoke in 1970.[20]

Besides his stroke in 1970, Lutz had a heart attack in the early '50s. Because of circulation problems resulting from the stroke, Red had his left leg amputated in 1980.[21]

Red Lutz died at the Veterans Hospital in Cincinnati on February 22, 1984, of congestive heart failure. He is buried in St. Stephen Cemetery in Fort Thomas, Kentucky.[22]

SOURCES

The author used Retrosheet.org and Baseball-Reference.com for stats and game information, as well as a telephone interview and multiple emails with Bill Eggemeier, a grandson of Red Lutz.

NOTES

1. Joe Heffron and Jack Heffron, *The Local Boys: Hometown Players for the Cincinnati Reds* (Birmingham, Alabama: Clerisy Press, 2014), 123.
2. Bill Eggemeier (grandson), telephone and email correspondence in January/February 2020.
3. Eggemeier.
4. Jim Steiner, "The History of Immaculata School," Retrieved from: 2011.hci-parish.org/wp-content/uploads/2011/02/History-of-Immaculata-School.pdf.
5. Eggemeier.
6. Eggemeier.
7. Eggemeier.
8. Larry, "Sports Chatter by 'Larry,'" *Orlando Sentinel*, May 6, 1920: 10.
9. "Florida State League; Dope for the Fans," *Orlando Sentinel*, June 25, 1920: 4.
10. Henry Farrell, "Many Rookies in Training Camps," *Daily Republican* (Rushville, Indiana), March 16, 1922: 6.
11. Jim Sandoval, "Ivy Wingo," SABR BioProject, sabr.org/bioproj/person/bac1fa27.
12. Greg Erion, "Bubbles Hargrave," SABR BioProject, sabr.org/bioproj/person/bac1fa27.
13. "Brief Sports," *Dayton Daily News*, June 1, 1922: 8.
14. Eggemeier.
15. Stephen Karan, "Lutz Up … Powie, a Double," *Cincinnati Enquirer*, August 13, 1968: 6.
16. Eggemeier
17. Eggemeier.
18. Eggemeier
19. Eggemeier.
20. Eggemeier.
21. Eggemeier.
22. Eggemeier.

EMIL MAILHO

By Dan Schoenholz

In his long and accomplished baseball career, San Francisco Bay Area native Emil "Lefty" Mailho managed over 2,500 hits, yet all but one – a pinch single in a 1936 contest – came in the minor leagues. One writer described Mailho as "arguably the best .056 lifetime hitter the majors (have) ever seen."[1] Mailho, who crossed paths with such all-time greats as Joe DiMaggio, Connie Mack, Babe Ruth, and Lefty O'Doul, was never able to gain a toehold in "The Show," but was a star outfielder in the Pacific Coast League and the Southern Association in the 1930s and '40s. A go-to source of reminiscences for Coast League historians in his later years, he was one of the oldest living former major leaguers before his death in 2007 at the age of 98.

Mailho was born in Berkeley, California, on December 16, 1908, to Pierre Mailho, a grocer, and his wife, Marie, both from the Pau region of southwestern France. Emil was the second oldest of six children (five boys), and grew up playing baseball at Berkeley's San Pablo Park, where many other big leaguers (including Hall of Famer Chick Hafey, Augie Galan, and Billy Martin) also cut their teeth on their way to Berkeley High and then the majors.[2] Mailho attended the University of California, Berkeley, beginning in 1928 and pitched and played outfield for the Bears under coach Carl Zamloch for two seasons while studying architecture. One of Mailho's memorable moments from his time at Berkeley was watching Roy Riegels' infamous wrong-way run in the 1929 Rose Bowl.[3]

In 1930 Zamloch, who had left Berkeley to become manager and part-owner of the Oakland Oaks, recruited the 5-foot-8, 160-pound Mailho to play professionally. The Great Depression was taking hold, and he couldn't pass up the chance to earn some money.[4] "I might have been an architect now," Mailho said in a 1968 interview. "But, oh, well, I don't regret it."[5]

Mailho didn't stick with the Oaks, but was sent for more seasoning to Phoenix in the Class-D Arizona State League. His impressive numbers there – a .328 batting average in 1930 and .363 in 1931, highest on the team – earned him a return to the Bay Area, where he appeared in 10 games with the Oaks late in the 1931 campaign.

Thanks to his success in Phoenix, Mailho was expected to compete for a starting job in Oakland in 1932. Despite his diminutive size, noted the *Oakland Tribune*, "count on the half-pint outfielder to attract more attention in camp than will a lot of the big fellows."[6]

It wasn't easy: In the midst of the Depression, veteran players weren't necessarily eager to help up-and-coming youngsters like the left-handed-batting, left-handed-throwing Mailho show their stuff in training camp. "When I was a rookie, they wouldn't let me

Eric Mailho.

ONE-HIT WONDERS

hit," Mailho said. "They were protecting their jobs, afraid you'd take their job."[7] Nevertheless, he became the Oaks' center fielder, hitting .316 in 135 games in 1932. In 1933 Mailho played in 180 of his team's 192 games and batted .303, with 209 hits. Though stolen-base totals weren't kept as an official statistic, he and his teammates ran with abandon – so much so that Mailho earned another nickname, "Fast Mail."[8]

"Ray Brubaker was a good manager," Mailho said of the Oaks' skipper that year. "He liked to do a lot of running. We had Frenchy Uhalt, Leroy Anton, myself. We stole a lot bases – our club didn't have a lot of power, so we had to. We drove the catchers nuts."[9]

The Oaks expected big things from the 25-year-old Mailho in 1934, but a home-plate collision in an early April game left him with a knee injury that would sideline him for almost two months.[10] Unable to play, he made good use of the time off, as he eloped to Reno with the former Lola Silva of Berkeley.[11]

Mailho eventually returned to the diamond in 1934, but managed only a .198 average in 96 at-bats. The lost season was a bitter disappointment to Mailho, who had hoped a big year would vault him to the majors.[12] But, healthy again in 1935, he got off to a sizzling start, hitting .433 in April.[13] At midseason, his average was a still-robust .364, good enough for third in the Coast League, and the Oaks were battling for first place for the first time in several years.[14]

Around this time, a group of Oaks fans worked with the club to organize Emil Mailho Day in honor of the popular outfielder.[15] In what Mailho later characterized as his greatest thrill in baseball, on July 21, 1935, the second game of a Sunday doubleheader was dedicated to him.[16] After receiving a variety of gifts from the team, Mailho proceeded to pound out five hits – four for extra bases – in a storybook performance.[17] Although the Oaks faded from contention in August and September, Mailho saw continued success at the plate, finishing with a .353 average and 230 hits in 172 games. At season's end, he made at least one sportswriter's Coast League all-star team along with another Bay Area outfielder, Joe DiMaggio of the San Francisco Seals.[18] Then, in October, Mailho received the news he'd been hoping for: The Philadelphia Athletics drafted him from the Oaks.[19]

Mailho reported to the Athletics' training camp in Fort Myers, Florida, intent on not only securing a roster spot but also winning regular playing time. "The big league is faster than the Pacific Coast circuit in that the pitching is better and the defense snugger, but I feel I have the skill to stay in the fast set," he said.[20] His chances were improved by the scarcity of established major-league talent on the club: After a disappointing 1935 campaign, manager-owner Connie Mack had sold the last well-known members of Philadelphia's 1929-1931 World Series teams – Jimmie Foxx, Doc Cramer, and Eric McNair – to the Red Sox. Sportswriter John Lardner saw fit to satirize the situation in a profile entitled "Mack Has Difficulty Recognizing [His] Players."[21]

Things got off to a promising start for Mailho in the Athletics' very first spring-training game, against the Cincinnati Reds. The contest drew 793 paying customers, one of whom was a recently retired big-leaguer named George Herman "Babe" Ruth.[22] With the greatest slugger of all time looking on, Mailho launched a long home run off Si Johnson. "Nice hit, kid," said Ruth.[23]

Mailho continued to play well throughout camp, and secured his roster spot by rapping five hits in a 19-0 A's victory over the minor-league Newark Bears.[24] But as soon as the club headed north to begin the regular season, he found himself in an unfamiliar position: at the end of the bench. Mailho was used almost exclusively as a pinch-hitter, a role he struggled with. "That pinch-hitting is tough," he said. "I was used to being in there every day on the coast. And it's a lot different."[25] In his first major-league at-bat, Mailho pinch-hit on Opening Day and struck out against Wes Ferrell of the Red Sox. He made outs in his next two pinch-hitting appearances as well before drawing a walk from Johnny Broaca of the Yankees and scoring on Wally Moses' triple in a game on April 21. For the next four weeks, Mack continued to use Mailho intermittently as a pinch-hitter, and Mailho continued to struggle, drawing an occasional walk, but failing to hit safely.

On May 15, Mailho pinch-hit in the seventh inning with runners at first and second and the A's trailing Detroit by a run. The situation called for a sacrifice, but he twice bunted foul. Things worked out for the best, however, as he lined a two-strike single to right off Tommy Bridges of the Tigers, that year's league leader in wins and strikeouts.[26] It was Mailho's first (and as it turned out, his last) major-league hit. He ended up scoring the winning run on a single by Rabbit Warstler, helping the A's post a rare road win.

As Philadelphia quickly settled into last place in the American League, Mack refused to start Mailho, or even to give him playing time in their many lopsided losses. Why? One theory had to do with Mailho's size. "My uncle could hit, and he was fast, but he was short.

ONE-HIT WONDERS

Connie Mack was tall, and he didn't like short guys," said Mailho's nephew, Tim Mailho.

Regardless of the reason, Mailho grew increasingly frustrated. "My uncle finally said, if you aren't going to play me, trade me, or I'll quit," nephew Tim said. Mack optioned Mailho to Atlanta, but said he would be recalled later in the season.[27] At the time of his demotion, Mailho was hitting .056, with one hit in 18 at-bats, although he had worked five walks and scored five runs.

Emil and Lola (along with newborn son Bobby) headed south to Atlanta, where Emil found himself immediately penciled into the starting lineup. He made a good first impression. "The new French center fielder of the Crackers gave the fans an idea of his ability last night by getting two hits, driving in a run and scoring himself, and making several fine catches," reported the *Atlanta Constitution* after one of Mailho's early efforts.[28] A week later, after he went 7-for-10 in an Atlanta doubleheader sweep, the headline read: "Mailho Is Star."[29] In his half-season, he hit .315 and helped lead the Crackers to the Southern Association pennant.

At season's end, the Athletics announced that they would recall Mailho in 1937.[30] For the next couple of months, references to Mailho in the Atlanta sports pages were mostly in the context of the gap his departure would leave in the outfield. It turned out, though, that the Crackers still had designs on him. Team President Earl Mann, on his way back from the minor-league owners' meeting in Montreal in December, made a stop in Philadelphia and purchased Mailho's rights from Connie Mack.[31] It was as close as Mailho would ever get to returning to the big leagues.

Mailho signed his contract with the Crackers in February 1937 and declared: "I hope to have my best year in baseball."[32] He got off to a fine start, hitting in 14 straight games in the early going.[33] By June he had a .398 average. "[T]he fiery French rightfielder ... is setting a burning pace among Southern League hitters," noted the *Atlanta Constitution*. "He hopes to be back in the majors next season."[34] Mailho faded in the second half, but still finished with a .344 average, good for third in the batting race.

In 1938 Crackers catcher Paul Richards was named player-manager, his first opportunity as a skipper in what would turn out to be a long managerial career. As noted in his SABR biography, Richards was ahead of his time in appreciating the importance of nontraditional statistics like on-base percentage. Thus he was well aware of the value that Mailho – who walked often in addition to regularly topping .300 in batting average – brought to the Crackers' lineup.

With Mailho hitting at a .304 clip with power (10 homers) and speed (21 steals) despite being hampered for much of the season with a leg injury, Atlanta reclaimed the Southern Association crown in 1938. The Mailhos also celebrated the birth of their second son, Gary, that summer. At season's end, future Hall of Famer Burleigh Grimes, manager of the Montreal Royals of the International League, tried to pry Mailho loose from the Crackers, but Richards refused to deal him.[35]

In 1939 Mailho got off to another torrid start and was hitting over .400 well into June. Still, he drew no interest from a big-league team. Jack Troy, a sports columnist for the *Atlanta Constitution*, didn't understand it. "Mailho can do everything well. He has a strong, accurate arm; he is a steady, dependable hitter, and … a fine base runner," wrote Troy. "… [I]t's a break for the Crackers that he didn't fill the big league bill in the astute eyes of Connie Mack. But everyone is entitled to a mistake and it may not be too late yet to rectify the one made on Mailho."[36]

After battling some midseason injuries, Mailho finished fifth in the league in 1939 with a .343 batting average, and led the league in walks and hit-by-pitches (for an on-base percentage of .472) as well as runs scored with 122.[37] He continued to be immensely popular with Atlanta fans. They appreciated "the dazzling Frenchman," and the feeling was reciprocal.[38] "He loved Atlanta – my aunt loved it, too," said Tim. "He was a sharp dresser, and the local store owners were always giving him fancy clothes. He loved that. And the food, too: When my aunt and uncle were old and I'd shop for them, my aunt always made me get chicory. That was something that they'd gotten a taste for in Atlanta."[39] Before the final regular-season game at Ponce de Leon Park, Mailho was voted the most popular Cracker and received a trophy.[40]

In March of 1940, Richards named Mailho as the Crackers' field captain.[41] Joining him in the outfield that year was young slugger and future three-time major-league All-Star Willard Marshall. Perhaps because of the presence of a bona-fide power hitter behind him, Mailho put together his best season. He hit .364, good for second in the Southern Association, while leading the circuit with 304 total bases and 144 runs scored.[42] He also walked 121 times.[43] In recognition of his outstanding campaign, Mailho was named the co-recipient of the league's Most Valuable Player award (with catcher Greek George).[44]

ONE-HIT WONDERS

Sports columnist Troy continued to struggle with the notion that Mailho wasn't worthy of another shot in the majors. "Mailho is the mystery ballplayer of the Southern league," he wrote. "For years he has been considered by writers and managers as the league's finest all-around outfielder. ... Why Mailho hasn't gone up is still a puzzle."[45]

Mailho got off to his typical hot start in 1941, hitting .375 through late May, but then was laid low by a bout of arthritis that kept him out of the lineup for a couple of weeks. When he returned, he slumped, and he finished with a .298 average, the first time in his career that he hit under .300 for a full season, though the Crackers again won the Southern Association crown.

In the fall there was some speculation that Mailho would be tapped to succeed Fred Lindstrom as manager of the Knoxville Smokies, but instead the Crackers announced that Mailho had been sold to the Oakland Oaks. "In making the deal, President Earl Mann respected the wishes of Mailho, who is nearing the end of a fine playing career and prefers to be near his California home," said the *Atlanta Constitution*.[46]

It was with Oakland in 1942 that Mailho was in the middle of an unusual incident in Portland that resulted in the game being postponed, as recounted in a 1994 book. "Oaks outfielder Emil Mailho had just caught a flyball to end the inning. He was jogging in from the outfield when he disappeared! Mailho's weight caused the ground to collapse under him into a sinkhole. The only thing visible was the top of Mailho's cap."[47]

Unfortunately for Mailho, his power also did a vanishing act in 1942, as he managed only one homer in 599 at-bats to go with his still-solid .297 batting average. Mailho blamed at least part of his power outage on the low-quality baseballs used during wartime. "The ball we hit was like a rock because they couldn't use good rubber in them. It was all synthetic rubber, so the ball didn't have any life in it."[48]

Throughout the war years, Mailho was working a defense job during the day and playing baseball at night. "We worked at the Hubbell Galvanizing Plant while we were at home. ... Of course, when we went on a road trip, we didn't have to work. Les Scarsella, Cotton Pippen, and about five or six of us were there."[49]

Mailho got his average back up to .314 in 1943, but in 1944, at age 36, he managed only a .277 mark. He also got into a spat with the team owner that caused the Oaks to cut him loose. "In 1944, Brick Laws (the Oaks' owner) sold me to the Seals," he said. "I had a little squabble with his son, Bill. He was clowning around in the dugout, and I had a bad inning and said, 'get the hell out of here.' Oh, geez, it hit the fan! Laws said, 'He can't call my kid names like that and get away with it.' So that was the end of it. Dolph Camilli was the manager, and he said to Laws, 'Are you going to let a little thing like that get in the way of the best hitter you have?' When I went to the Seals, I killed the Oaks. All the Oakland guys were for me."[50]

Wearing the uniform of his longtime rivals and playing for instead of against veteran Seals manager Lefty O'Doul, Mailho led the league in hitting for much of the 1945 season before slumping, though he still finished with a .306 average in 149 games. In December, the Seals sold him to Oklahoma City in the Texas League. Far from home, he played in only 55 games in 1946 before calling it quits and returning to the Bay Area. His career line in the minor leagues: a .318 average with 2,511 hits.

Mailho had been interested in construction ever since his childhood, when he helped his father remodel some apartments owned by the family.[51] He obtained his contractor's license in 1947, and, as with baseball, he was good at it. "He was a master carpenter and a bricklayer, too," said Tim. "Whatever he did, he did to the full extent. He didn't do anything halfway."[52]

For the next 20 years, Mailho built custom homes in the Bay Area. In the late 1960s he closed his contracting business and briefly opened a boat-building operation near San Jose. A 1968 feature in the *San Jose Mercury News* profiled his painstaking construction of the 34-foot sloop *Ne Libre* (Born Free). The article reinforces the notion that Mailho was a perfectionist in everything he did.[53]

Mailho subsequently worked for several cities as a building inspector, including Fremont, where he also ended up building his own home. In retirement, he regularly participated in Coast League reunions and gave interviews to Coast League historians, but as his old friends and teammates died and his own health began to decline, his baseball past was at risk of being forgotten. When he was well into his 90s, however, Mailho was interviewed by Oakland A's broadcaster Marty Lurie for a segment on Lurie's "Right Off the Bat" pregame show. The interview revived the connection between Mailho and the franchise he'd played for – however briefly – and culminated with him being asked at age 97 to throw out the ceremonial first pitch before an A's game in 2006. Mailho, his mind still razor-sharp, saw the irony in being honored on the mound at the Oakland Coliseum. "Emil told me, 'I don't want to throw out the first pitch (today), I want to hit it,'" said Tim.[54]

Mailho died a few months later at age 98 in Castro Valley, California. He had been the fourth oldest living former major-leaguer at the time of his death.

SOURCES

In addition to the sources cited in the Notes, the author utilized Baseball-Reference.com. The author would also like to thank Tim Mailho for his assistance and generosity.

NOTES

1. George Rose, *One-Hit Wonders: Baseball Stories* (iUniverse, 2004), 10.
2. "Berkeley Park Produced Galaxy of Sports Stars," *Oakland Tribune*, October 16, 1994; "Oaks Launched Careers of Baseball Legends," *Oakland Tribune*, July 24, 1994. The latter article notes that Emil Mailho's younger brother, Pete, also played for the Oakland Oaks, and that his little brother Johnny played semipro ball.
3. Author interview with Tim Mailho, September 24, 2018.
4. Tim Mailho interview.
5. "When He Makes Hit Now – It's a Boat," *San Jose Mercury News*, June 24, 1968.
6. "Emil Mailho Signs Contract With the Oaks; May Become Regular," *Oakland Tribune*, February 13, 1932: 10.
7. Dick Dobbins, *The Grand Minor League* (Emeryville, California: Woodford Press, 1999), 194.
8. Tim Mailho interview.
9. Dick Dobbins, 194.
10. "Mailho Injury Sends Jakucki to Centerfield," *Oakland Tribune*, April 11, 1934: 22.
11. "Oak Fielder Takes Bride," *Oakland Tribune*, July 2, 1934: 17.
12. "Pool Again Denied Raise, Spurns Offer," *Oakland Tribune*, February 5, 1935: 18.
13. "Mailho Clouts at .433 Clip," *Oakland Tribune*, April 30, 1935: 25.
14. "Oaks 2 Games from Top, Battle for Lead," *Oakland Tribune*, July 9, 1935: 18.
15. "Vitt Banished by Umpire; Oaks Win 10-Inning Battle," *Oakland Tribune*, July 13, 1935: 8.
16. "Oaks Launched Careers of Baseball Legends," *Oakland Tribune*, July 24, 1994.
17. "Oaks Take Series from Angels, Head for Portland," *Oakland Tribune*, July 22, 1935: 12.
18. "The Sports X-Ray," *Los Angeles Times*, September 17, 1935: 30.
19. "Mailho, Oaks Fielder, Drafted by Athletics," *Oakland Tribune*, October 16, 1935: 12.
20. "Tips from the Sports Ticker," *Philadelphia Inquirer*, March 22, 1936: 46.
21. "Mack Has Difficulty Recognizing Players," *Nebraska State Journal* (Lincoln), March 19, 1936: 13.
22. "A's Hopefuls Lose Camp Opener to Reds, 10-7," *Camden (New Jersey) Courier-Post*, March 7, 1936: 24.
23. "At 97, Feisty Mailho is 2nd Oldest Living Athletic," *East Bay Times* (Contra Costa, California), August 13, 2006.
24. "Five Out of Five," *Columbus Telegram*, March 27, 1936: 6.
25. "Mailho Looms as a Tough Batter," *Atlanta Constitution*, June 11, 1936: 19.
26. "3-Run Flare-Up in 7th Brings A's 2nd in Row," *Philadelphia Inquirer*, May 16, 1936: 15.
27. "Athletics Farm Out Mailho to Atlanta," *Philadelphia Inquirer*, June 8, 1936: 17.
28. "Crackers Take Baron Opener, 4-2; Lindsey Hurls Today," *Atlanta Constitution*, June 13, 1936: 10.
29. "Crackers Take Double-Header from Little Rock, 7-3, 12-1," *Atlanta Constitution*, June 20, 1936: 11.
30. "Macks, Dodgers Recall Mailho, Pitcher Leonard," *Atlanta Constitution*, September 18, 1936: 18.
31. "Purchase of Leonard Sets Hurling Corps," *Atlanta Constitution*, December 18, 1936: 22.
32. "Emil Mailho Signs Contract; 13 Crackers Are Now in Fold," *Atlanta Constitution*, February 12, 1937: 22.
33. "Mailho Stopped at 14 Straight," *Atlanta Constitution*, May 7, 1937: 25.
34. "Fiery French Outfielder Sets Burning Pace in Southern League Hitting," *Atlanta Constitution*, June 6, 1937: 17.
35. "All in the Game," *Atlanta Constitution*, December 9, 1938: 23.
36. "All in the Game," *Atlanta Constitution*, June 12, 1939: 13.
37. "Haas Officially Wins Southern Batting Crown," *Atlanta Constitution*, October 31, 1939: 19.
38. "They're the First Five Hitters in Cracker Lineup," *Atlanta Constitution*, March 10, 1938: 16.
39. Tim Mailho interview.
40. "Crackers End Regular Season with 7-6 Victory," *Atlanta Constitution*, September 11, 1939: 13.
41. "Emil Mailho Named Captain of Crackers," *Atlanta Constitution*, March 10, 1940: 20.
42. "Mailho's Greatest Season Gives Him 2d Place in Batting Race," *Atlanta Constitution*, September 15, 1940: 18. Baseball-Reference.com shows him with 304 total bases.
43. "Dejan Official Batting Champ at .371," *Atlanta Constitution*, November 20, 1940: 18.
44. southernassociationbaseball.com/timeline.pdf.
45. "All in the Game," *Atlanta Constitution*, September 11, 1940: 22.
46. "All in the Game," *Atlanta Constitution*, December 6, 1941: 16.
47. Dick Dobbins and Jon Twitchell, *Nuggets on the Diamond* (Emeryville, California: Woodford Press, 1994), 203.
48. Dick Dobbins, *The Grand Minor League*, 194.
49. Dick Dobbins, 194.
50. Dick Dobbins, 262-63.
51. "When He Makes Hit Now – It's a Boat," *San Jose Mercury News*, June 24, 1968.
52. Interview with Tim Mailho, October 12, 2018.
53. "When He Makes Hit Now – It's a Boat."
54. "At 97, Feisty Mailho Is 2nd Oldest Living Athletic."

DAVID MATRANGA

By Joel Rippel

Even though David Matranga's major-league career featured just one hit – a home run in his first at-bat – it gave him credibility for his post-playing job.

"It changed the course of a lot of things for me," said Matranga. "I played (professional baseball) for 12 years. Some people can say I was one of the fortunate ones."[1]

Matranga was born on January 8, 1977 in Orange, California, to Dan and Linda Matranga. Dan was an insurance agent and Linda was a homemaker. Matranga has a brother, Robert.

Matranga was a standout at Orange High School, less than three miles from Anaheim Stadium. As a senior he batted .494 with 3 home runs and 24 RBIs and was named second-team All-Orange County by the *Los Angeles Times*.

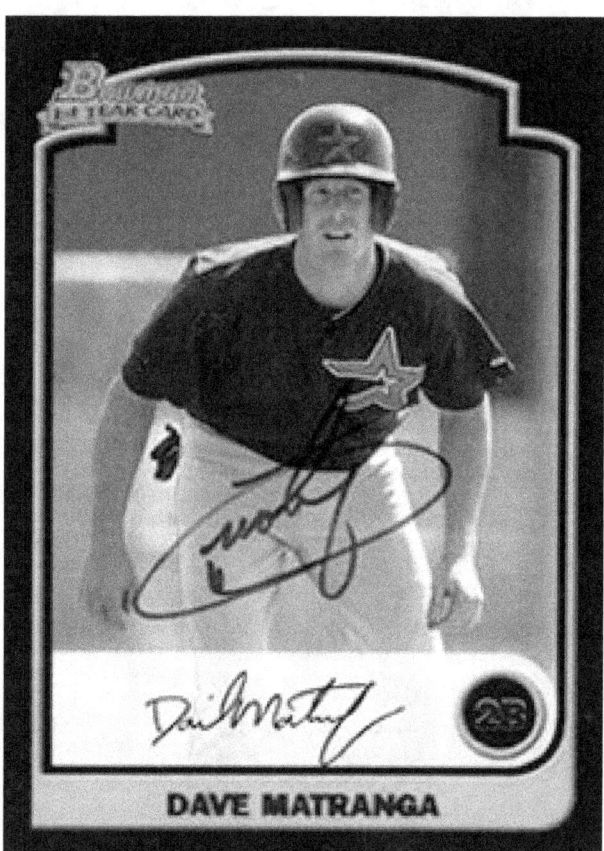

After his senior season, Matranga was named to the USA Baseball Junior (Under-18) team. The 18-member team played 16 games in 24 days with the schedule capped by its 10-0 victory over Taiwan at Fenway Park in Boston.

As a freshman in 1996 at Pepperdine University in Malibu, California, Matranga earned honorable mention All-West Coast Conference honors after batting .292 while playing second base for the Waves. After his freshman season, he played in the Alaska Summer League.

Going into his sophomore season, Matranga was moved from second base to shortstop.

"He's a player we are building around," said Pepperdine coach Frank Sanchez. "He is an outstanding college shortstop."[2]

As a sophomore, Matranga batted .305 with 11 home runs and 50 RBIs in 59 games and was named first-team All-West Coast Conference. After the season, he played on Team USA.

As a junior Matranga batted .299 in 50 games for the Waves. He was selected by the Houston Astros in the sixth round of the June amateur draft. He signed and was assigned to Auburn (New York) of the Class-A New York-Penn League. His professional career got off to a good start as he hit .306 with 4 home runs, 24 RBIs, and 16 stolen bases in 40 games.

Matranga spent his second professional season with Kissimmee (Florida) of the Class-A Florida State League, where he batted .231 with 6 home runs, 48 RBIs, and 17 stolen bases in 124 games.

In 2000 Matranga was promoted to Round Rock (Texas) of the Double-A Texas League. He batted .233 with 6 home runs and 44 RBIs in 120 games. The team, in its inaugural season, won the Texas League championship, broke the Double-A single-season attendance record and was named the top team in minor-league baseball by *Baseball America*.

Matranga returned to Round Rock in 2001. In July he was hitting .315 when he was promoted to Triple-A New Orleans. He went 5-for-16 with a home run and

ONE-HIT WONDERS

three RBIs in four games with the Zephyrs before being sent back to Round Rock. He finished the season with a .302 batting average, 10 home runs, 60 RBIs, and 17 stolen bases in 103 games with the Express. Matranga was named a Double-A All-Star.

Matranga spent the 2002 season with New Orleans, batting .273 in 101 games. He returned to New Orleans for the 2003 season. The season included two brief stays in the major leagues. In May Matranga was recalled and, without seeing any action, was returned to New Orleans a day later. A month later he was summoned by the Astros again after they placed second baseman Jeff Kent on the disabled list with a wrist injury. Matranga arrived in Houston and made his major-league debut the same day.

On June 27 the slumping Texas Rangers, who had lost 12 consecutive road games and were 29-48, and the Astros, who were just 5-9 in their previous 14 games, opened a three-game interleague series with a day game.

The Astros, who had swept a three-game series from the Rangers the previous week in Arlington, scored two runs in the first inning and one in the second to open a 3-0 lead. After the Rangers scored twice in the top of the fourth to make the score 3-2, Matranga was sent to pinch-hit for pitcher Kirk Saarloos. But Matranga's first major-league at-bat had to wait an inning after the third out of the inning was made with Matranga on deck.

The Rangers took a 4-3 lead with two runs in the top of the fifth inning. Rookie reliever Nate Bland relieved Saarloos during the inning. With Bland scheduled to lead off the Astros' fifth inning, Matranga was again sent up to pinch-hit.

The 6-foot, 170-pound Matranga, using a bat he borrowed from New Orleans teammate Alan Zinter and brought with him, lined a 1-and-1 fastball from Rangers starter Joaquin Benoit to left for a solo home run. The home run tied the score, 4-4. The Rangers scored a run in the sixth inning and then extended their lead to 8-4 (in an eventual 10-7 victory) on a three-run home run by Rafael Palmeiro in the seventh. It was the 508th career home run for Palmeiro.

Matranga became the 84th major leaguer – the second in Astros history – to hit a home run in his first major-league at-bat. (The first was Jose Sosa in July of 1975.)

After playing in five more games (going hitless in four at-bats). Matranga was returned to New Orleans. His season totals for the Zephyrs were a .241 batting average and 3 home runs and 25 RBIs in 102 games.

Matranga spent the 2004 season with Round Rock, hitting .242 with 7 home runs and 48 RBIs in 112 games. After the season, he became a free agent and signed with the Anaheim Angels. He was placed on the Angels' 40-man roster and went to spring-training camp. When the Angels played host to the Los Angeles Dodgers in an exhibition game at Anaheim Stadium on April 1, Matranga pinch-hit in the eighth inning to fulfill a promise he had made to his father.

"To just walk in the clubhouse and be a part of this team and see my name on the back of a uniform means a whole lot," said Matranga. "I've been waiting a long time for this."[3]

When he was 5 years old, Matranga and his father attended an Angels game and David vowed he would play for the Angels. He played the game with a picture of his father, who died in 1998, taped inside his cap.

Matranga started the 2005 season with Triple-A Salt Lake. On April 28 the Angels recalled him after placing Maicer Izturis on the disabled list. Matranga joined the team for the final game of a three-game series at Yankee Stadium. The Angels played six games in Minnesota and Seattle before returning home for a three-game series with Detroit.

In the series finale, a 10-1 victory for the Tigers, Matranga made his American League debut. He entered the game as a defensive replacement in the top of the eighth. In the bottom of the ninth, he grounded out to shortstop for the final out of the game.

Three days later Matranga was sent back to Salt Lake. In early July he was taken off the Angels' 40-man roster and designated for assignment. He accepted the assignment and rejoined Salt Lake. For the season, he batted .243 in 55 games with Salt Lake.

Matranga spent the next four seasons as a utility infielder at the Triple-A level with four different organizations.

In 2006 with San Diego's Portland farm team, he batted .219 in 91 games. In 2007, with Oklahoma (Texas Rangers), he batted .266 in 77 games. He spent 2008 with Omaha (Kansas City), hitting .269 in 61 games. In 2009 he returned to New Orleans (now a Florida Marlins farm team), hitting .272 in 95 games.

After the 2009 season, Matranga considered continuing his career in Japan. He had negotiations with the Yomiuri Giants before deciding to retire.

Over 12 minor-league seasons, he batted .254 with 82 home runs, 433 RBIs, and 105 stolen bases in 1,097 games.

His major-league totals saw him play in both leagues, and 1-for-6 as a batter. He played second base for a total of five innings in three games, handling five chances without an error.

Matranga's agent, Page Odle, who had played at Oral Roberts University and for three seasons in the minor leagues, offered Matranga a job with Odle's firm, PSI Sports Management.

Matranga has had a successful career as an agent and as of 2020 was the vice president of the firm, which is based in Southern California. Among the players the firm has represented are Kole Calhoun, Aaron Judge, Scott Kingery, and Kolten Wong.

"Going back to that home run, and what I did in the big leagues, in such a small moment in time – it's affected my entire life," Matranga said. "It's affected how I've been able to relate and communicate with people on this side of the game. The respect that you get from doing something like that, from just getting there. Being a minor leaguer versus a guy who got to the big leagues, even if it was for only (six) at-bats, you have a different sort of credibility."[4]

Including Matranga, only 22 players made their one major-league hit a home run. And only four of those players homered in their first major-league at-bat: Luke Stuart in 1921, Mark Worrell in 2008, Eddy Rodriguez in 2012, and Matranga.

SOURCES

In addition to the sources cited in the Notes, the author consulted Baseball-Reference.com, Newspapers.com, and Retrosheet.org.

NOTES

1. Andy McCullough, "Before He Was Aaron Judge's Agent, David Matranga Was a Literal One-Hit Wonder," theathletic.com, April 9, 2020.
2. Steve Henson, "Diamond in the Rough," *Los Angeles Times*, January 30, 1997: 46.
3. Bill Shaikin and Ben Bolch, "Team, City Discuss a Settlement," *Los Angeles Times*, April 2, 2005.
4. McCullough.

SPARROW MCCAFFREY

By Bob LeMoine

"Of the other new catcher, McCaffrey," wrote F.W. Arnold in *Sporting Life*, "not much can be said. He is claimed by his friends to have all the requirements for a successful catcher, a good arm, a good eye and a stout pair of legs that are speedy. We don't know about this, but will have an excellent opportunity to judge before the season is ten days older."[1] Actually, there is still little to say about Sparrow McCaffrey over 100 years later, and the 10 days Arnold referred to would nearly cover the 120-pound, 21-year-old catcher's entire major-league career.[2] He batted 1.000, having a hit in his only at-bat while playing two games in his career, stretching from August 13 to August 15 of 1889.

Charles P. McCaffrey was born 1868 in Philadelphia in the annexed borough of Frankford, to Irish immigrant parents Charles P. and Sarah (McDevitt) McCaffrey. Charles Sr. worked as a laborer, and the oldest children also had jobs: John (dyer), Hannah (weaver), Mary ("stands in store"), and young Charles (varnisher). Three younger siblings: James, Susan, and Henry, were at school, while Joseph was still too young to do any of these tasks. Also occupying the house on Melrose Street was Sarah's widowed mother, Hannah McDevitt.[3] Frankford was one of the working-class "river wards" areas a few miles northeast of Philadelphia, where Irish Catholics generally settled at the time.[4]

McCaffrey played for the semipro Frankford team of the Inter-State League, also called the Philadelphia Region League, during the 1887-1888 seasons.[5] The team won the championship while one by one other teams dropped out of the league as they struggled to break even.[6] "One of the features was the season's work of McCaffrey," wrote the *Philadelphia Times*, "who caught 73 of the 82 games and had but 25 errors." The paper also listed him batting .204.[7]

McCaffrey moved on to the Norristown team of the Middle States League in 1889. "McCaffrey and [Lewis] Graulich are stone walls before any pitcher, and both are good hitters," wrote the *Philadelphia Times*.[8] He was a batterymate of Sadie McMahon, who would play nine seasons in the major leagues. The *Philadelphia Inquirer* referred to McCaffrey as "the crack young catcher of the Norristown club," adding, He is McMahon's old catcher, and the latter says he is a good one, being a fine thrower to bases."[9] McMahon had already been signed by the Philadelphia Athletics, as major-league teams started plucking talent from the minor leagues. By early August of 1889 McCaffrey too had been spotted, and Columbus (Ohio) of the American Association acquired him for catching help.[10] The Solons were a woeful bunch, 32-52 at the end of July, 24½ games out of first place.

McCaffrey made his first of two major-league appearances on August 13 at St. Louis. Columbus starter Hank Gastright was getting clobbered by St. Louis, 11-2, through seven innings. Veteran catcher Jack O'Connor called it a day by that point "and then the little Norristown catcher, McCaffrey, went in. He did good work," remarked *Sporting Life*.[11] McCaffrey didn't get an at-bat as the game finished as a 12-3 St. Louis win. He bowed out two days later, also in St. Louis, in a game called a "comedy of errors" by the *St. Louis Republic* as the home team prevailed 19-11.[12] McCaffrey again replaced O'Connor late in the game and singled off Silver King to close out his career. McCaffrey did play at least one more exhibition game with Columbus, taking the field against Terre Haute on August 16, a foe one newspaper called "Somebody Columbus can Beat."[13]

St. Louis writer Joe Pritchard quipped, "Columbus is carrying a pitcher [*sic*] named McCaffrey who isn't any larger than a grasshopper, and when he was called off the bench recently to face Gastright's fast delivery, the people in the grand stand thought he would be knocked to pieces in a jiffy. But the 'sparrow' pulled in Gastright's delivery just as easy as falling off a log."[14]

After his stint in Columbus, McCaffrey had no team to return to. "Norristown's baseball club at last has succumbed to the inevitable – financial disaster," wrote a correspondent of the *Philadelphia Times*. The team was $1,000 in the hole "by reason of wet weather

ONE-HIT WONDERS

and hard luck," and disbanded on August 19. "The club is still sighing for a good round of bonus money from the Athletics for pitcher McMahon. Several hundred would also be acceptable from Columbus for catcher McCaffrey."[15]

In 1890 McCaffrey joined Lebanon, which played in the Eastern Interstate League and later jumped to the Atlantic Association, where the team won the pennant.[16] McCaffrey batted .294 and .221 in these two distinct seasons. He returned to Lebanon, now in the Eastern Association, in 1891, and batted .209 in 56 games, missing time with a broken thumb.[17]

McCaffrey was arrested in April of 1892 "on the charge of drunkenness and wantonly pointing a revolver," the *Daily News* of Lebanon reported. "He threatened to shoot Minnie Lee, residing on Elizabeth Street, and behaved in a disorderly manner. Mack is well known at the place, but his behavior caused the woman to refuse him admission." McCaffrey had a hearing before a judge and paid a $10 fine.[18] He was later appointed a substitute postal clerk and his address was given as Lee Street in Philadelphia.[19]

McCaffrey spent 1892 with both Troy and Philadelphia of the Eastern League but played only a few games.

Sparrow McCaffrey died of consumption (tuberculosis) on April 29, 1894, at the age of 26. He was living in his parents' house and was an ironworker at the time of his death.[20]

SOURCES

In addition to the sources cited in the Notes, the author consulted Baseball-reference.com and Familysearch.org.

NOTES

1. F.W. Arnold, "Columbus Chatter," *Sporting Life*, August 7, 1889: 6.
2. McCaffrey's height is unknown.
3. 1880 census.
4. See William E. Watson, "Irish (The) and Ireland" in The Encyclopedia of Greater Philadelphia. philadelphiaencyclopedia.org/archive/irish-the-and-ireland/ Retrieved April 23, 2019.
5. "Among the Base Ballists," *Daily News* (Lebanon, Pennsylvania), March 24, 1890: 1.
6. Charlie Weatherby, "Brandywine Baseball Club (West Chester, Pennsylvania)," sabr.org/bioproj/topics/brandywine-baseball-club Retrieved April 23, 2019.
7. "The Frankford's Record," *Philadelphia Times*, October 14, 1888: 15.
8. "At Norristown," *Philadelphia Times*, May 12, 1889: 16.
9. "Notes of the Diamond Field," *Philadelphia Inquirer*, August 2, 1889: 6.
10. "Base Ball Notes," *Sunday Leader* (Wilkes-Barre, Pennsylvania), August 4, 1889: 8.
11. "Games Played Tuesday, August 13," *Sporting Life*, August 21, 1889: 3.
12. *St. Louis Republic*, August 16, 1889: 6.
13. *Indianapolis Journal*, August 17, 1889: 5.
14. Quoted in the *Kansas City Times*, August 25, 1889: 10.
15. "Base Ball at Norristown," *Philadelphia Times*, August 25, 1889: 10.
16. "Wind-up of the Atlantic," *Lebanon Daily News*, October 1, 1890: 1.
17. "Passed Balls," *Lebanon Daily News*, June 13, 1891: 4.
18. "Base Ball Catcher Arrested," *Daily News*, April 7, 1892: 1; "Fined $10," *Daily News*, April 8, 1892: 1.
19. "Will Work in the Post Office," *Philadelphia Times*, July 27, 1893: 6.
20. "Died," *Philadelphia Inquirer*, May 4, 1894: 7.

ROGER HORNSBY MCKEE

By Jack Zerby

With his one major-league hit, Roger Hornsby McKee never came close to his namesake's Hall of Fame total. He did, though, channel Rogers Hornsby with an Organized Baseball batting title.[1] And while the namesake Hornsby was a player-manager for 12 seasons during an era when such skippers had a penchant for giving themselves a turn on the mound from time to time,[2] he resisted the temptation to pitch. Named for the second baseman, Rogers McKee was a major-league pitcher and became the youngest player in the modern era to notch a nine-inning complete-game win – just after he turned 17. Although this accomplishment is not recognized as an official record, given twenty-first-century trends in the usage of pitchers and the minuscule number of complete games by starters, however, it may well be a distinction that will remain Roger McKee's as long as professional baseball is played.

Signed by the Philadelphia Phillies as a left-handed North Carolina high-school and American Legion pitching phenom in the midsummer of 1943, McKee stayed with the big club through the end of that season and hurled his complete-game win on October 3. He got his first minor-league experience in 1944, with a brief late-season recall to Philadelphia before a year-plus of military service in 1945-46. Then, his pitching velocity diminished by what he attributed to throwing too hard, too soon, in a shortened, cold and wet 1944 spring training, he began an odyssey through the minor leagues as a first baseman and occasional outfielder before returning home with his family to work for the Postal Service, coach baseball, commit himself to civic affairs, and live a rich, full life with his spouse of 70 years.

Roger Hornsby McKee was born on September 16, 1926, in Shelby, Cleveland County, North Carolina, the eldest child of Broadus Lee McKee and Gertie Spencer McKee. Broadus McKee's ancestry was Scots-Irish; Gertie Spencer's was English, and they and their parents were all native North Carolinians. Located 40 miles west of Charlotte in the North

Photo courtesy of Roger McKee's family, Shelby, North Carolina.

Roger McKee.

Carolina Piedmont region, by 1926 Shelby was a textile-mill town with a burgeoning population due to New South industrialization.[3] Broadus McKee worked in the LeGrand family's Shelby Mill cotton factory and later as a fireman for the City of Shelby. Gertie tended the McKee home and also worked at Shelby Mill. The family – by 1940 it included Broadus, Gertie, Roger, a younger son, Bill, and two younger sisters, Elissa and Margie – lived in the mill village, on-site housing provided by Shelby Mill.[4]

Broadus McKee was an avid fan of baseball, and especially followed the St. Louis Cardinals and their player-manager, Rogers Hornsby.[5] On September 16,

ONE-HIT WONDERS

1926, when Broadus and Gertie welcomed their first-born, the Cardinals closed the day's play tied with the Cincinnati Reds for the National League lead. By October 2, when the Cardinals had eked out the pennant with a two-game edge on the Reds and opened the World Series against the Yankees in New York, the son had his name: Rogers Hornsby McKee. Reported as "being bashful about his name,"[6] McKee dropped the "s" from his first name, becoming simply "Roger," when he started school.[7]

Roger McKee's athletic skill set matched his father's baseball ambitions for him. By the age of 8 he was pitching for a Shelby youth team,[8] and as a 15-year-old junior in in 1942 was unbeaten on the mound for Shelby High School.[9] That same season he pitched the Shelby Post 82 American Legion team to the North Carolina state championship with a 3-2 win in the state final.[10] In the spring and early summer of 1943, the whip-thin (6-feet-1, 160 pounds) 16-year-old lefty was 9-1 for the Shelby Legion team, with a no-hitter. He averaged 14 strikeouts per outing and hit .500, but the team reached only the state semifinals.[11] McKee and another future major leaguer, Smoky Burgess, from nearby Forest City, were Shelby's go-to battery. McKee pitched 29 innings in three games over five days in the 1943 Legion tournament, but lost the elimination game to Albemarle, 7-4.[12]

Philadelphia Phillies scout Cy Morgan[13] first spotted McKee as a high-school and Legion sensation in 1942. "I've looked all over the world for this kid and I'm staying here till I get him," Morgan enthused just before McKee signed for a reported $5,000 bonus[14] on August 12, 1943, at the end of the Legion season.[15]

Morgan immediately hustled McKee to Philadelphia, where Freddie Fitzsimmons had taken over managerial duties from Bucky Harris on July 28.[16] With Organized Baseball then in its second of four seasons of the personnel scrambles necessitated by World War II, Fitzsimmons, as most managers did, needed pitching; at age 16 and a week removed from Legion baseball, McKee was a major leaguer.

When play closed on August 17, 1943, the Phils were only 10 games under .500 at 51-61 but had dropped to seventh place in the National League, 22½ games behind the Cardinals. In the midst of a lengthy homestand, they trailed those Cardinals 5-0 after six innings in the first game of a doubleheader on August 18 when Fitzsimmons gave McKee his major-league baptism at the age of 16, sending him out to face Harry Walker, Stan Musial, and Walker Cooper in the top of the seventh inning with the Phillies trailing 5-0.[17]

Showing some understandable nerves, McKee allowed Walker a bunt single and then walked Musial. But he recovered to get Cooper on a 5-4-3 double play before retiring Whitey Kurowski on a fly ball to right field. He yielded a run in the St. Louis eighth on a walk, sacrifice, and double, but shut down the Cardinals in the ninth, this time besting Musial, who bounced a fielder's choice groundball to second base after Walker's leadoff single.

McKee pitched a third of an inning of ineffective relief against Cincinnati on August 22 as the Reds thrashed the Phillies 20-6. The next night Fitzsimmons started McKee in an exhibition game at Wilmington, Delaware, against the Phillies' Class-B Blue Rocks farm club in the Interstate League. The lefty responded with a five-hit, complete-game win. Wilmington bunched two of its hits against McKee to cost him a shutout in the ninth inning as Philadelphia won, 5-1.[18]

After the successful exhibition outing however, the rookie rode the bench for more than a month[19] before Fitzsimmons gave him another inning of work, on September 26 in St. Louis.

But then, as the Phillies closed out the season in Pittsburgh on October 3, McKee got what would be his only major-league start in the 1943 finale – the second game of a doubleheader at Forbes Field. The Phillies had won the opener, 3-1, behind Dick Barrett.[20] McKee's second-game mound opponent, Cookie Cuccurullo, another lefty, was himself making his major-league debut but was, at age 25, an elder statesman compared with the just-turned-17 North Carolinian.

This day, greater youth prevailed, as Cuccurullo gave up seven runs through seven innings and Bill Brandt, his replacement, yielded another four. Meanwhile, McKee was solid, scattering five hits and holding Pittsburgh to three runs. At the plate, with the game tied 3-3 in the top of the seventh inning, Cuccurullo's last turn on the mound that day, McKee worked a leadoff walk and scored the go-ahead run on Benny Culp's single; the Phillies tallied three more to take a 7-3 lead. Then, with two outs in the Philadelphia ninth and his team comfortably ahead, McKee drilled a single off Brandt to drive in the final Phillies run before closing out the Pirates without a baserunner in their half. It ended as an 11-3 Philadelphia romp.

McKee thus became and remains (as of 2020) the youngest major leaguer (at the age of 17 years, 17 days) in the modern era to pitch a complete-game win.[21]

Wartime travel restrictions continued to impact baseball as the Phillies, now sporting the additional nickname Blue Jays,[22] traveled 33 miles from

ONE-HIT WONDERS

their home at Shibe Park to 1944 spring training in Wilmington, Delaware. Camp didn't open until April 1, and extended only through April 15, with 10 exhibition games scheduled.[23] It was cold, wet, and windy, and with limited time to prepare, the 17-year-old began to throw full-throttle early – probably too early. "It was cold. There was snow on the ground. We worked out in a big field house, then we finally got to go outside. I don't know what it was, but the speed of my pitches wasn't wasn't there. My arm didn't hurt and I could throw without pain, but the ball didn't get to home plate as fast. That made a big difference," McKee recalled many years later.[24] The portside velocity that had so excited scout Cy Morgan just the summer before and had carried McKee to a complete-game win in his first major-league start just wasn't there anymore. McKee was on the Phillies roster when the 1944 season opened,[25] but his out-of-nowhere lack of velocity concerned the Philadelphia brass. The game was then decades away from today's sophisticated handling of young pitchers to preserve their arms; after nine games over which the Phillies were 5-4 and McKee never threw a pitch in competition, all the club did was option him to Wilmington.[26]

McKee gave his all in 106 innings over 20 games for Wilmington in 1944 with his diminished arm, posting a 6-8 record and a 4.25 ERA. A trio of successive Wilmington managers, including Cy Morgan, used him in an additional 34 games at first base and center field; he batted .225 in 151 at-bats and hit three home runs, tied for third on the club. The Phillies recalled the lefty at the end of the season – he got two innings of mop-up relief in a 15-0 loss to the Chicago Cubs on September 26.

This was the final appearance of McKee's five-game major-league career, which featured a quintet of "ones" – a historic game-winning pitching accomplishment in his one start for a 1-0 pitching record; one hit, one run scored, and one RBI as a hitter.

That year, 1944, had acquainted McKee well with the disappointments professional baseball career could bring, but there was happiness as well. He married the former Denice (pronounced "Dennis") Spangler in Gaffney, South Carolina, on July 19.[27] Denice and Roger had gone to separate high schools – she at smaller Piedmont High in Lawndale in northern Cleveland County; Roger at Shelby[28] -- but they both played high-school basketball and met at one of her games in 1942. After traveling with Roger throughout his minor-league career, Denice earned a bachelor's degree in business education and a master's degree in business economics at Appalachian State Teachers College (now University) in Boone, North Carolina, and taught business classes and did counseling in the Shelby city school system.[29] She also worked in the office of her family's Spangler Roofing and Siding business and still, in her 90s, kept books for various Spangler family businesses.

The couple had one child, Rogers Hornsby McKee Jr., born November 9, 1947. He is now retired after a career as an industrial engineer with PPG in Shelby.[30]

Two days after his 18th birthday in September 1944, Roger McKee registered for the Selective Service draft. He entered the US Navy as a draftee early in 1945, went through basic training with a group that included Stan Musial at Bainbridge (Maryland) Naval Training Center, and was part of a detachment from Bainbridge called to Washington to participate in funeral services for President Franklin D. Roosevelt in April 1945. McKee later played in an eight-team service league at Pearl Harbor,[31] and was posted in Japan with US occupation forces after the war ended There, he saw the aftermath of both the Hiroshima and Nagasaki atomic bombs. McKee was discharged on April 30, 1946.

This was early enough in the baseball season for him to join the Terre Haute Phillies of the Class-B Three-I League. With Terre Haute, McKee pitched eight innings in four games and picked up a win. But he was now essentially a first baseman and occasional outfielder,[32] hitting a useful .318 in 280 at-bats. The Phillies, however, had signed McKee as a pitcher and when they elected to expose McKee to the Rule 5 draft in November 1946, the Cardinals selected him.[33]

McKee had told a Shelby-area writer, "Well, I'd rather play ball than anything else I know of. It just gets in your blood,"[34] when he signed as a 16-year-old. Now, 3½ years later and no longer a Phillie, he embraced that philosophy and embarked on a 10-year minor-league journey with St. Louis and three other organizations that included 12 teams across classification levels from Triple A to D.[35] Except for a single appearance in 1955 in Class B, he had stopped pitching, but he had some serviceable years as a hitter. He seemed to do it best for the Baton Rouge Red Sticks of the Class-C Evangeline League, where he won the league batting title at .357 in 1953. He had 13 home runs that season, but showed more power the next year – still with the Red Sticks, he clouted 33 homers, good for third-best in the power-happy 1954 Evangeline League, and hit .321 in another solid year at the plate.[36]

ONE-HIT WONDERS

McKee played at higher levels in 1955 and 1956 before returning to Baton Rouge for 75 games at the end of the 1956 season and hitting .307. He finished his career at age 30 in 1957, getting into 54 games with Baton Rouge and sipping a cup of coffee with Topeka of the Class-A Western League in the Milwaukee Braves organization.

Roger McKee returned home to Shelby after baseball. He worked for a while for a polyester fiber manufacturer, then went to work as a city route mail carrier for the US Postal Service, retiring after 30 years of service. He assisted the baseball coaching staff at Shelby High School and in the early 1960s was head coach of the American Legion Post 82 team for which he had pitched so well himself. Jim Horn, a North Carolina Legion baseball co-chair, remembered, "I know he was one of the greatest to come through our area. I followed him [when I was] a little guy and always looked up to him." When I was playing Legion ball, if we were going to be facing a left-hander, he'd come out and pitch batting practice to us. His whole life was that way – he was there to help you if he could."[37]

McKee had taken courses as Southern Business College in Shelby during some of his offseasons. In 1966, at the age of 40 and a decade after he had played his final minor-league game, McKee took courses at Gardner-Webb University in nearby Boiling Springs, and although he didn't graduate with a degree, ultimately received a distinguished alumni designation for his service to the school. He served on the board of directors of Gardner-Webb's athletic booster group, the Bulldog Club, and established the Roger McKee Baseball Scholarship at Gardner-Webb. McKee was inducted into the Cleveland County (North Carolina) Sports Hall of Fame in 1977. He served on the Shelby Parks and Recreation Board.

Roger, a 10-handicapper, taught Denice to play golf – well enough that she has two holes in one; Roger never had one. Roger also "loved to travel,"[38] and the couple did so widely, visiting all 50 states and parts of Canada and Mexico. Denice also told the author of Roger's avid interest in reading, where his tastes tended to history, biographies, and other nonfiction. He paid little attention to baseball after his time in the game, and on the rare occasions when he would watch a televised game, tended to dismiss it with "the game these days is entirely too long."[39] Instead, he closely followed Duke University basketball and football.

By August 2009, when the Phillies invited Roger to their Alumni Weekend event, he had limited mobility and was reluctant to attend. Roger Jr. contacted the Phillies for his dad, and the club arranged an all-expenses-paid trip for the entire family. Despite being in a wheelchair, Roger had a "wonderful time" being recognized in the on-field ceremonies at Citizens Bank Park along with Phillies' standouts such as Robin Roberts, Steve Carlton, and Mike Schmidt. "The Phillies couldn't have been kinder or more considerate."[40]

Roger and Denice McKee celebrated their 70th wedding anniversary on July 19, 2014.

Shortly thereafter, on September 1, 2014, Roger McKee died at Cleveland Regional Medical Center in Shelby after a brief series of strokes.[41] He was 87 and was survived by Denice, son Roger Jr. and wife Barbara, sister Elissa McKee Bright, two grandsons, and a great-grandson. He and Denice had been longtime members of the Shelby First Baptist Church and his memorial service was held there on September 5, 2014.

Roger McKee is buried at the Double Shoals Baptist Church Cemetery in Shelby.[42]

ACKNOWLEDGMENTS

I sincerely appreciate the time Denice McKee and Roger McKee Jr. spent with me at Roger's home near Shelby on August 8, 2018, and the hospitality accorded my wife and me by Roger Jr.'s wife, Barbara. Their collective recollections of Roger McKee, both during his baseball career and over the 56 years back in Shelby after he hung up his spikes, certainly make this biography better than anything I could have produced without their kind assistance and interest.

SOURCES

In addition to the sources cited in the Notes, I used the Newspapers.com website for minor-league game stories, box scores, and general reference material, and the Baseball-Reference.com and Retrosheet.org websites for major-league box scores, player and team pages, and pitching and batting logs. I accessed US Census data and other information on the McKee and Spangler families through Ancestry.com at my hometown Transylvania (North Carolina) County Library. My SABR colleague Kevin Larkin reviewed Roger McKee's file in the Giamatti Research Center at the National Baseball Hall of Fame Library and provided copies of pertinent material.

NOTES

1 Rogers Hornsby collected 2,930 hits in his 23-year career. He won seven National League batting titles between 1920 and 1928. He was inducted into the Hall of Fame in 1942. Roger McKee hit .357 with the Baton Rouge Red Sticks to win the 1953 Evangeline League batting title.

2 For an account of a game in which two player-managers, Ty Cobb of the Tigers and George Sisler of the Browns, got into the act, see the author's "October 4, 1925: Heilmann Grabs AL Batting Title; Cobb 'Saves' the Day," SABR Baseball Games Project, sabr.org, accessed July 9, 2018.

3 US Decennial Census figures report Shelby's 1920 population as 3,609. By 1930, it was 10,789, an increase of 198.9 percent.

ONE-HIT WONDERS

4. Author's conversation with Denise McKee, Roger McKee Jr., and Barbara McKee, Shelby, North Carolina, August 8, 2018. (*Hereafter:* "August 8 conversation.")

5. "Rather Play Than Eat – That's Phils' McKee," *Harrisburg Telegraph*, October 21, 1943: 21.

6. John H. Whoric, "Sportorials" column, *Daily Courier* (Connellsville, Pennsylvania), November 1, 1943: 7.

7. "Rather Play Than Eat." The hand-printed name and signature on McKee's Selective Service registration card, dated September 18, 1944, are both "Roger Hornsby McKee."

8. Whoric.

9. "Rather Play Than Eat."

10. "Gardner-Webb Alum, Pro Baseball Player, Passes Away," gardner-webb.edu/newscenter/gardner-webb-alum-pro-baseball-player-passes-away/. September 4, 2014, accessed June 29, 2018.

11. Whoric.

12. *Shelby* (North Carolina) *Star* clipping, August 1943 date missing, unattributed, from McKee family baseball scrapbook; August 8 conversation.

13. William Prestwood "Cy" Morgan never played in the major leagues. He was a steady .300-plus-hitting outfielder over 11 minor-league seasons from 1926 through 1939 for teams ranging in level from Class D to Class A. He scouted for three major-league organizations from 1941 through 1965. Cy Morgan (scout) entry, Baseball-Reference Bullpen, accessed September 6, 2018.

14. The $5,000 figure is from the newspaper item cited in Note 15. In a profile of McKee done in connection with the Phillies' 2009 Alumni Weekend observance however, McKee himself recalled the figure to have been $3,000. Larry Shenk, Roger McKee profile in *The Phillies – An Extraordinary Tradition*, Scott Gummer, ed. (San Rafael, California: Insight Editions, 2009), 53. Whatever the amount, Denice McKee told the author that Roger McKee used a significant portion of it for a down payment on a house for his parents and siblings.

15. Catherine Bailey, "Shelby Youth in the Majors," *Rocky Mount* (North Carolina) *Telegram*, August 20, 1943: 6. The signing date is from the status card in Roger McKee's file at the Giamatti Research Center, National Baseball Hall of Fame, Cooperstown, New York.

16. The 41-year-old Fitzsimmons had begun the 1943 season as a pitcher with the Brooklyn Dodgers. He was released on July 27, the day before he took over the Phillies.

17. With his debut, McKee became the youngest player in the 1943 National League. Rogers Hornsby was long gone from St. Louis by 1943. After his 1926 Cardinals won the World Series against the Yankees, he moved on to manage the New York Giants in 1927. By 1943 he was signed to continue managing the Fort Worth Cats of the Texas League, but the circuit suspended operations from 1943 to 1945 due to World War II. C. Paul Rogers, "Rogers Hornsby," SABR Baseball Biography Project, sabr.org, accessed July 5, 2018.

18. "Phils Trounce Wilmington, 5-1," *Philadelphia Inquirer*, August 24, 1943: 23.

19. McKee turned 17 on September 16, 1943.

20. Roger McKee Jr. recalls his father's telling him that had the Phillies not won the opener, Fitzsimmons may well have used a different starter for the second game. August 8 conversation.

21. "Rogers [*sic*] McKee, 'Teenage Tar Heel Twirler,'" DiamondsInTheDusk.com, accessed July 6, 2018. The baseball term "modern era" refers to all National League and American League seasons from and after 1901. The American League joined the older (1876) National League as a major league for the 1901 season.

22. The additional name came from a 1943-44 offseason contest aimed at boosting fan interest. Stan Baumgartner, "Bobo"s First Press Confab Balks Philly," *The Sporting News*, March 9, 1944: 18. According to the 1944 Phillies' team page at Baseball-Reference.com, "Blue Jays" was used by the team for the 1944 and 1945 seasons only, then dropped "due to fan outrage/apathy."

23. *The Sporting News*, January 13, 1944: 14, and March 9, 1944: 6.

24. Shenk, McKee profile.

25. *The Sporting News*, April 6, 1944: 15.

26. "Five Players Dropped by Phils," *The Sporting News*, May 4, 1944: 18.

27. "We loved each other, and we eloped," Denise McKee told the author. Gaffney is just across the state line from Shelby and at the time was "the place" for eloping young couples to be married. Denice McKee recalled that Roger had pitched the night before he left for Shelby but the newlyweds were back in Wilmington in time for his next start. August 8 conversation.

28. Denice McKee explained that at the time, high school in North Carolina consisted of only three years. August 8 conversation.

29. "70th Anniversary: Mr. and Mrs. Roger McKee," ShelbyStar.com, accessed June 28, 2018; August 8 conversation.

30. August 8 conversation.

31. Gary Bedingfield, "Those Who Served,' BaseballInWartime.com, accessed July 6, 2018; August 8 conversation. Roger McKee Jr. notes that his father told him one of the few times he recalled being booed was when he got Ted Williams out in a service game. "They wanted to see Ted hit the ball out."

32. Box scores from various Midwestern newspapers covering the 1946 Three-I League show McKee playing first base and batting either fourth or fifth for Terre Haute. At the end of the season, a story reporting his selection in the draft by the Cardinals described McKee as a "star ... first baseman" for Terre Haute. *Davenport* (Iowa) *Daily Times*, November 6, 1946: 23.

33. *Davenport* (Iowa) *Daily Times*, November 6, 1946: 23.

34. Bailey.

35. McKee did not play anywhere during the 1951 season.

36. Denice and Roger Jr. accompanied McKee most of these summers. Denice remembers "enjoying meeting new people wherever we went." Having been only nine years old when his father retired from baseball, Roger Jr. has few memories from those years other than "playing under the bleachers and looking for nickels, probably in Baton Rouge." August 8 conversation.

37. Alan Ford, "Local Baseball Legend McKee Passes Away," *Shelby Star*, September 4, 2014: online edition, ShelbyStar.com, accessed June 28, 2018.

38. August 8 conversation.

39. August 8 conversation.

40. August 8 conversation.

41. Author's telephone conversation with Roger McKee Jr., July 9, 2018.

42. Roger McKee obituary, *Shelby Star*, undated, accessed through Legacy.com June 28, 2018.

BILL MILLS

By John Heeg

The 1994 major-league baseball season came to an abrupt end on August 11 because of a player strike. The strike lasted for 232 days, which meant that the 1994 postseason was not played. This was the first time a major professional sports league did not play a post-season because of labor struggles. Before the strike ended on April 2, 1995, teams began spring training using replacement players.

While the members of the Players Association were waiting for their union and the owners to come to agreement, players who had dreamed of playing in the major leagues now had a window of opportunity to achieve their dreams. Many of them players had seen time in the minor leagues while others played independent ball. When the strike ended, many of those players were cast aside with only a few earning minor-league contracts.

Los Angeles Times writer Mike DiGiovanna characterized the opening of the 1995 season as a six-week fantasy camp, as an embarrassment when reflecting on his experience as a writer in a 2019 article, "MLB 1994 strike: Replacement Players Provided Comic Relief, Farcical Baseball."[1] The last time the major leagues used "replacement players" was during World War II, when many established major leaguers were in the armed forces.

During World War II, more than 5,000 major- and minor-league players served in the military or worked in defense plants. The void created by their absence sent club owners and executives scrambling in search of serviceable talent. More than 400 ballplayers made their big-league debuts between 1943 and 1945, the period that saw the largest concentration of departing players. In baseball, it sometimes doesn't hurt to be in the right place at the right time.[2] Massachusetts native Bill Mills was in the right place and the right time and able to record his only major-league hit in the 1944 season.

William Henry Mills Jr. was born on November 2, 1919, in Boston, the second of four children of Massachusetts natives William and Mary Mills. Mills Sr. was a veteran of World War I and worked as a wholesale meat salesman.

Young Bill played football and baseball at Arlington (Massachusetts) High School and was the captain of both teams in his senior year. After high school, he attended Coburn Classical Prep in Waterville, Maine, where he played football and baseball, and he continued to play both sports at the College of Holy Cross in Worcester, Massachusetts.

Bill began his college studies and baseball career at Holy Cross in 1939. At about the same time, World War II began. In September of 1940, with the United States not yet in the war, Congress established a

Bill Mills.

Courtesy of Roger Erricson.

ONE-HIT WONDERS

military draft, at first calling up men for one year of service. Mills registered for the draft, but was rejected for military service because of a perforated eardrum. By the time Mills was a senior, the existence of military programs on campus led to extensive curriculum changes, with more focus on mathematics, physical sciences, and physical training, and less on philosophy and the classics.

In the spring of 1943, opposition groups were uniting to overthrow Mussolini in Italy. In Massachusetts, Mills, by now a senior at Holy Cross, became the captain of the baseball team. That season he batted .586, leading the league in batting average. When word got out that the Crusaders had on their roster a catcher with a great hitting eye, above-average speed, and a fantastic arm, scouts made their way to Worcester.

Connie Mack's Philadelphia Athletics were struggling. After the breakup of their pennant-winning teams from 1929-31, the A's declined rapidly. Since 1935 they had consistently finished the season in last place. During the war, Athletics fans hoped that the losses to military service by other teams would maybe level the playing field for the A's, but that was not the case, especially after Sam Chapman and Benny McCoy went off to war in 1942; the A's record that season fell to 55-99, and in 1943 it dropped to 49-105. The A's struggled in many categories particularly in hitting. In 1943 the team batting average was .232. The team's catchers, Hal Wagner and Bob Swift, together batted .218. Since Mills had put up impressive numbers in college and Mack was in need of some offense, the A's manager signed Mills in the fall of 1943 as an amateur free agent. In *The Sporting News*, Stan Baumgartner reported that Mills was "described by some to have all the actions and physical characteristics (minus the ears) of Mickey Cochrane."[3] It was anticipated that he would team with Hal Wagner.

In November 1943, Mills married Grace Marie Herlihy of Winchester, Massachusetts. He worked that winter as a physical-education instructor at the Sidney Hill Health Institute in Boston.[4]

Mills was right-handed, stood 5-feet-10, and was listed at 175 pounds. He joined the A's for spring training at Frederick, Maryland.

Before spring training began, the Athletics reacquired Frankie Hayes, who became the team's primary catcher in 1944, playing in every game that year.

Mills began the 1944 season in the minor leagues. When spring training ended, his hitting ability was not a concern, but it was feared that his throwing arm was not strong enough for him to make the Opening Day roster, and he was sent to the Toronto Maple Leafs of the Double-A International League. He played in eight games and was 3-for-17, two of his hits being a double and a triple. On May 7, the Athletics traded catcher Wagner to the Boston Red Sox for Ford Garrison, and this created an opening for Mills. Despite his .176 batting average, the evident need of the A's was enough to get him called up to the major leagues.

On Friday, May 19, 1944, the 24-year-old Mills made his major-league debut, against the Cleveland Indians in Philadelphia. He entered the game as a pinch-hitter in the eighth inning, facing Indians starter Al Smith with one out. He singled and later moved up to second base but was stranded there. The next day against Cleveland, he pinch-hit again, in the eighth inning with runners on first and second and one out, but hit into an inning-ending double play. His third plate appearance came on the road – again facing the Indians during a May 28 doubleheader in Cleveland, he walked in the top of the ninth inning of the second game. The A's were down, 5-1, and his walk loaded the bases with one out. He was retired on a force play, but a throwing error allowed two runs to score. Cleveland won, 5-3.

Mills's next chance at the plate came five days later, on June 2, when he pinch-hit against the St. Louis Browns on June 2 at Sportsman's Park. Facing Bob Muncrief with two on and one out, he hit into a double play that ended the fifth inning in a game the Browns won, 3-0.

Mills played his final major-league game the next day. In an 18-8 blowout loss, Mills was able to get some playing time behind the plate. With the Browns leading 8-1 in the bottom of the fourth inning, Mack sent Mills behind the plate to give starting catcher Frankie Hayes a rest. In his final at-bat as a major-leaguer, Mills struck out. In the sixth inning, as the Browns were scoring five more runs, he split his finger on a foul ball off the bat of Mark Christman and had to leave the game, replaced by Tony Parisse.[5]

After five major-league plate appearances, Mills was sent down to the minor leagues – reportedly at his own request, so he could get more work, given that Hayes was catching every game. He played 17 games for the Lancaster Red Roses of the Class-B Interstate League.[6] In 47 at-bats, Mills batted .277.

After the season, Mills was traded by the Athletics to the Milwaukee Brewers of the American Association for Jim Pruett, cash, and a player to be named later. For reasons unknown to us today, he went on the voluntarily retired list from April 1945 until March 1946.

ONE-HIT WONDERS

At the age of 26, Mills returned to baseball in 1946 to play for the Providence Chiefs of the Class-B New England League. Splitting time between playing for the Chiefs (who actually played in adjoining Cranston) and working as a junior-high teacher and coach in Pawtucket, Mills spent four seasons on the Chiefs roster, mostly part-time after the first season.

In 1949, at the age of 29, Mills played his last season in Organized Baseball. He continued his newfound profession as a math teacher and baseball and football coach at Goff Junior High School in Pawtucket. Sources differ on where he lived and worked after his baseball career. He retired from teaching and coaching in 1976.[7] In retirement, Mills and his wife, Rita, spent the summer on Cape Cod and the winters in Port Charlotte, Florida. The couple were married for 37 years and had one son and three daughters. Mills died in hospice at Gainesville, Florida, on August 9, 2019.[8] At the age of 99, he was the second oldest living major leaguer.

SOURCES

In addition to the sources cited in the Notes, the author consulted Baseball-Reference.com, Retrosheet.org, thebaseballcube, statmuse.com, and the following:

"A's Spring Training 1944," Philadelphia Athletics Historical Society. January 9, 2019. https://www.philadelphiaathletics.org/history/as-spring-training-1944/.

"Holy Cross: 1900-1949." https://www.holycross.edu/175th-anniversary/historical-timeline-holy-cross/1900-1949.

Rose, George. *One Hit Wonders: Baseball Stories*. IUniverse, 2004.

Nowlin, Bill, ed. *Who's on First: Replacement Players in World War II* (Phoenix: Society for American Baseball Research, 2015).

Ancestry.com. *U.S. WWII Draft Cards Young Men, 1940-1947* [database on-line]. Lehi, Utah, USA: Ancestry.com Operations, Inc., 2011.

NOTES

1. Mike DiGiovanna, "MLB 1994 Strike: Replacement Players Provided Comic Relief, Farcical Baseball," *Los Angeles Times*, August 12, 2019. https://www.latimes.com/sports/dodgers/story/2019-08-11/mlb-1994-strike-anniversary-replacement-players-provided-comic-relief.

2. Craig Allen Cleve, *Hardball on the Home Front* (Jefferson, North Carolina: McFarland, 2004), 2.

3. Stan Baumgartner, "Phillies Lose to Uncle Sam, Judge Landis," *The Sporting News*, November 11, 1943: 6.

4. "A's Buster Mills Weds," *The Sporting News*, December 23, 1943: 16.

5. See the Retrosheet game account at https://www.retrosheet.org/boxesetc/1944/B06030SLA1944.htm.

6. "Interstate League," *The Sporting News*, June 22, 1944: 18.

7. Legacy.com, and Legacy. "William Mills Obituary (1919 - 2019) – The Providence Journal." Legacy.com. August 19, 2019. https://www.legacy.com/obituaries/providence/obituary.aspx?n=william-h-mills&pid=193658540.

8. Sam Gazdziak, "Obituary: Bill Mills (1919-2019)," RIP Baseball, August 19, 2019. https://ripbaseball.com/2019/08/19/obituary-bill-mills-1919-2019/. One former student, Jane Cairns, offered a touching posthumous memory of him as a teacher, writing in part, "I attended Goff from 1966 to 1969. Mr. Mills was my math teacher for 8th grade. Just seeing this passing of him reminds me of how kind he was to me. It is because of him that I loved math. He treated his class with a sweet and loving manner. I was a shy student so it meant a lot to me to have him be so open." https://www.legacy.com/obituaries/providence/obituary.aspx?n=william-h-mills&pid=193658540.

FRANK MILLS

By Mike Cooney

On September 22, 1914, Shoeless Joe Jackson sat on the Cleveland Naps dugout bench watching his newest teammate, 19-year-old Frank LeMoyne Mills, make his major-league debut. Seconds later, Shoeless Joe applauded Mills as he stood on first base after hitting a single. At 19 years old, with a batting average of 1.000, the baseball future of Frank Mills looked bright. Thus began a baseball odyssey that would years later, once again, intersect with Shoeless Joe Jackson.

Frances Lewis Mills was born on May 13, 1895, in Knoxville, Ohio. While he was still identified as Frances L in the 1900 Federal Census, the 1910 Census identified him as Lemoyne Mills.[1] With his 1914 debut with the Cleveland Naps, as well as in the 1920 and later Federal Census reports, he was identified as Frank L. Mills.

Frank Mills's father, Fred G. Mills (from the 1910 census on, he was referred to as Ford) was a grocer who later became a laborer making his living doing odd jobs. His father was also at one time the mayor of Sebring, Ohio, as well as the postmaster for Sebring. Frank's mother was identified as Jennie Edwards. Jennie, whose full name was Mary Virginia Edwards, married Fred Mills later in 1895. Frank had three brothers and one sister.

By 1914, at the age of 19, Mills was beginning to show his baseball potential while catching for the Business Men in the Alliance (Ohio) City League.[2] At least two professional baseball teams expressed interest in him.

The Dallas Base Ball Club, a Class-B Texas League team, recognizing Mills's potential, offered him a minor-league contract on July 15, 1914. In the contract, Mills, who was to be paid $150 per month, was identified as Lemoyne Mills.[3]

Instead of signing the contract with Dallas, Mills chose to sign with Cleveland when, after a two-day tryout, manager Joe Birmingham "offered young Mills a very flattering contract and offered to take him on at once for work with the Naps."[4] Cleveland offered to pay Mills $350 per month.[5]

Mills made his major-league debut on September 22, 1914, in a game against the Philadelphia Athletics at Cleveland's League Park. Pinch-hitting against the Athletics' Bullet Joe Bush, Mills "delivered with a single," after which "Birmingham presented him with a new baseball on which were inscribed the name of all the Philadelphia players."[6] It was Mills's only major-league hit.

Mills pinch-hit again two days later (he walked) and started two games at catcher, including catching 12 innings in a 12-inning 6-5 victory over the Chicago White Sox on September 30. In all, Mills was 1-for-8. While behind the plate, he threw out three of the five baserunners who attempted to steal.

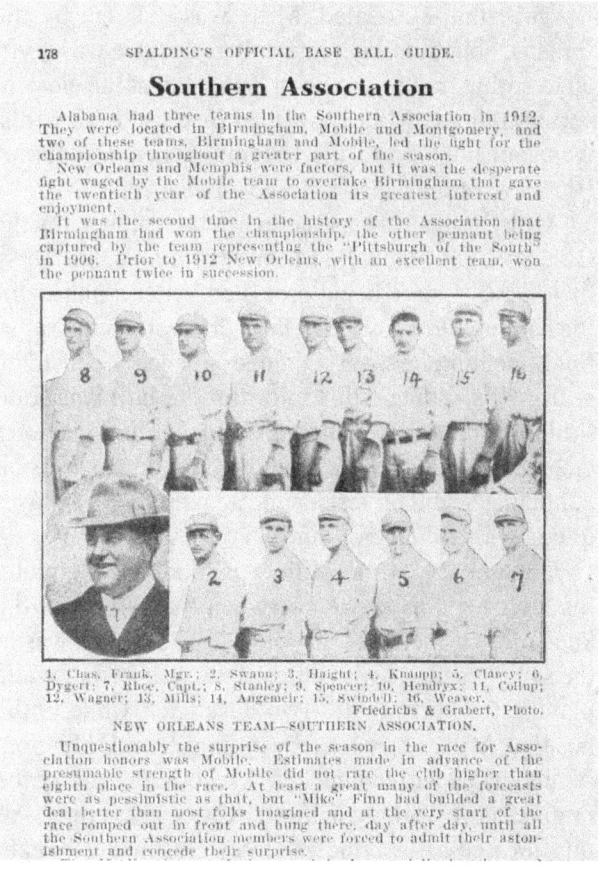

Frank Mills, #13, from the 1913 Spalding Guide.

ONE-HIT WONDERS

Mills was invited to spring training with the 1915 Indians[7] (Cleveland changed its team name from Naps to Indians after the 1914 season), but never played in another major-league game.

Failing to make the major-league roster in 1915, Mills was sent to the Portsmouth Cobblers of the Class-D Ohio State League. He made his presence known in the first game of the season when "none of the opponents tried to steal off of him after seeing an exhibition of his throwing."[8]

Mills played in 23 games for the Cobblers, hitting .271 and fielding .964.[9] His Portsmouth career ended on June 3 when he "suffered a broken shin bone" while trying to block the plate in an effort to keep a runner from scoring. "The crunch of the bone as it snapped could be heard through the stands, and Mills fell to the ground groaning with pain," the local paper reported.[10]

Later, in spite of his broken leg, Mills told Portsmouth president Gahleman that he "was doing as well as could be expected," and that he "expects to catch a good many games for Portsmouth before the season is closed."[11] Two weeks later, a league umpire visited Mills at the hospital and reported that he had been operated on to remove "poisonous matter from his broken leg." Mills was still confined to bed.[12]

Once the leg healed, Mills was recalled by the Indians,[13] but didn't get into any games. He was invited to spring training again in 1916,[14] but at the close of spring training, Mills, now identified as "Lee" Mills, was sent outright to the Indians-owned Davenport Blue Sox of the Class-B Three-I League.[15]

Mills began 1916 as the everyday catcher for the Blue Sox. On June 1, he became part of a controversy that led to a game being protested. After a player for the Moline Plowboys hit a high drive down the right-field line, umpire Jerry Eddinger allegedly consulted with Mills. When Mills told him the ball was foul, Eddinger then called the ball foul. Moline manager George Hughes said "he had no protest on the decision ... but that he did protest having an umpire ask a player to make his rulings for him."[16]

On June 24, while Mills was blocking the plate, his "left leg was broken between the ankle and the knee midway between the joints."[17] This break was in the same place as Mills suffered the year before while playing for Portsmouth. Two days later, while in the hospital, Mills was visited by umpire Jerry Eddington. As a local paper recounted it, "According to Jerry the umpires now working in the Tri-Cities ... felt throbs of pity for Lee Mills lying at Mercy Hospital ... bought a cargo of fruit for the injured player. (Mills) greeted them suspiciously and eyed the packages with wonder. When they were opened and spread about the room, Lee failed to make any remarks but reached for the bell and summoning a nurse ordered her to have the fruit analyzed in the laboratory. If it was all right, the player (Mills) further instructed her, he would eat some of it."[18]

With the severity of the broken leg, Mills was expected to spend six weeks in the hospital and to miss the entire season.[19] However, he was out of the hospital and returned to the Blue Sox five weeks later. Two days after his return, he was "let go... it being necessary to cut down on expenses on account of the small attendance at the games."[20]

Upon his release, the local newspaper commented: "Mills indicated he would leave ... for his home in Ohio, where he has been offered a position as traffic manager for a wholesale china house. If Lee is as prolific in breaking china as he is with his legs, he'll soon draw a release there too."[21]

In the spring of 1917 Mills was again invited to spring training with the Indians, but was not offered a contract. That spring he married Mildred H. Lembright. The couple had a son, Jack, and a daughter, Marion.[22] On June 5 Mills registered for the military draft. On his registration he indicated he was a "Railroad Employee" working for the "Pennsylvania Lines, Eastern Division."

There is no discernible documentation that Mills served in the military. In fact, in a contemporary *Youngstown Telegram* political cartoon, Mills, in a baseball uniform, is shown shaking hands with a soldier. The caption reads: "Make A Good Start Frank, Give The Fans The Best (Nothing Too Good For 'Jambar') Make 'EM STAND THE TEST"[23]

As the 1917 baseball season opened, Mills thought Cleveland still "had a string" on him, but that he had "not been forbidden to play semi pro ball."[24] With this in mind, Mills joined McElroy, a Youngstown semipro team.[25] Perhaps socially significant at the time, one of Mills's McElroy teammates was an African-American named Claude Johnson.[26]

While Mills was with McElroy, umpire and former major-league player Bill Powell "voiced the opinion that right now Mills is a better catcher than some of the National League's backstops who are drawing down big pay."[27]

Mills continued playing semipro ball for McElroy in 1918 and 1919.[28] At some point during this time Mills went to work as a clerk for Carnegie Steel (later part of US Steel).[29]

ONE-HIT WONDERS

At age 25, after beginning the 1920 season playing for the semipro Castle Cords,[30] Mills joined the Atlanta Crackers of the Class-A Southern League. The move from the Cords to the Crackers was not without controversy. Shortly after the Crackers persuaded Mills to sign with them, the Castle Cords sued the Crackers, claiming a "contract with [an] Independent Club is as binding as one with [a] league team." The Crackers, who viewed the Cords as an "outlaw" team, did not respond, even though Mills had signed a contract to play with the Cords for the entire 1920 season.[31] Still, even though Mills had broken his agreement with the Cords, he said he would have left Atlanta and gone back to New Castle if Fred Carta, a Cords pitcher who had been sent to Atlanta to persuade Mills to return, had "come at him in the right manner," which he did not, so Mills chose to stay with Atlanta.[32]

Mills batted .205 in 54 games for the Crackers. A highlight came on July 17 when, according to the *Atlanta Constitution,* his "work behind the platter for the Crackers was worthy of commendation. Frank scored the only tally of the Crackers' side of the game by tripling to the scoreboard. ... In addition to the greatly improved brand of stick work Frank cut down three Bears trying to slip over the second by stealing method."[33]

The Crackers offered Mills a contract for the 1921 season. The new contract called for a salary of $250 per month. It contained the standard reserve clause binding Mills to the Crackers after the season.[34]

Mills decided not to sign the contract due to having a "good position with the Carnegie Steel Company ... (and) that the Southern League climate did not agree with (him) or his family."[35] Mills asked the Crackers for permission to catch for a semipro team.[36]

The Crackers denied permission and, exercising the reserve clause from his 1920 contract, sold him to the Brooklyn Dodgers.[37]

The move from Atlanta to Brooklyn was viewed differently by journalists from the two cities.

One article reported, "The Brooklyn club has acquired a promising catcher in Mills. He ... is very active, especially in blocking low pitches; he hits well and he can run."[38] The *Brooklyn Daily Eagle* opined that "Mills ... was worth a gamble," but commented that "he would not have been considered if he had not refused to report to Atlanta."[39]

The *Atlanta Constitution* wrote that Mills "is regarded as a major-league possibility by Richard Guy, sporting editor of the *Pittsburg Leader*."[40] The next day, the *Constitution* commented, "We are still wondering what in blue blazes Brooklyn will do with Frank Mills, whose only claim to recognition was ... a fairly good throwing arm," and noted, "If the Dodgers retain Mills until April 1, the Crackers are certain to come in for a few extra dollars."[41]

In any event, Mills refused to report for Brooklyn spring training "because he wanted to be guaranteed his salary for a season," and on March 28 it was reported that the club had returned him to Atlanta.[42]

Once again Mills refused to report to Atlanta and signed a semipro contract with McElroy.[43] Having made the choice to report neither to Brooklyn nor Atlanta, Mills was violating the reserve clause from his 1920 contract and, in effect, violating a rule passed by the National Association in May of 1920 that "players who had ignored reservation rights of their clubs or jumped contracts would be ... barred."[44]

Then came the November 1920 National Association[45] meeting where, as a result of the 1919 Black Sox scandal that resulted in the lifetime ban of Joe Jackson and seven other White Sox, the "barred" clause was changed to add that "any player taking part in games with discredited players who have been barred ... will automatically be barred themselves."[46]

Disregarding this rule, Mills played the 1921 season for the McElroy Furniture Men. Their first game was against "the fast colored aggregation ... American Giants."[47] The Furniture Men went on to play a series of games against other semipro teams and occasionally against visiting major-league teams. As a result, Mills was barred from Organized Baseball for violating his obligations to the reserve clause and for playing with "discredited players."[48]

Mills quickly challenged the decision and asked that he be reinstated and declared a free agent. National Association Secretary J.H. Farrell denied Mills's requests. Mills appealed to major-league Secretary-Treasurer Leslie O'Connor, who responded that since Mills was a minor leaguer, the major leagues had no authority over his disbarment.[49]

O'Connor added, "There is no major league club which would give you a contract with the special provisions you demanded from Brooklyn. Your return by Brooklyn to Atlanta was not significant ... as they purchased your services on condition that you should make good to their satisfaction.

"If you thought there was something suspicious about the transactions, why did you wait a year before presenting the matter, meanwhile playing (presumably) with ineligible players?"[50]

ONE-HIT WONDERS

Having been rejected by both the National Association and the major leagues, Mills continued to play semipro ball while continuing to work for U.S. Steel. By 1926 Mills was playing for the General Tires team in the Ohio and Pennsylvania League.[51]

Technically, Mills, as a banned player, was not eligible to play in the Ohio and Pennsylvania League. As a result, while he continued to play for the General Tires, he continued to petition for his reinstatement to good standing in professional baseball.

In preparation for a personal appeal to Commissioner Kenesaw Landis, during the 1926 Joint Meeting of the major leagues in Cincinnati, Mills reported that he and General Tires business manager Jake Reisinger would draw straws to see who would meet with Judge Landis first. The local newspaper commented: "This is a delicate task and it will behoove Frank and Jack to leave the door open for a hasty retreat, as the Judge is a man of very uncertain temper."[52]

Part of Mills's argument for reinstatement concerned the reason he chose not to report to the Brooklyn Dodgers or Atlanta. According to Mills, he "had one more fling at professional baseball when he got a leave of absence from U.S. Steel in order to play with Atlanta. When he was sold to Brooklyn in 1921, U.S. Steel canceled his leave and he had to return to the steel company."[53]

Meanwhile, perhaps in an effort to distance himself from his participation in the Ohio and Pennsylvania League, Mills agreed to join the semipro Coshocton Regulars.[54] Mills played out the 1926 baseball season with Coshocton, a member of the Eastern Ohio League,[55] while continuing to prepare for his face-to-face appeal with Judge Landis.

After meeting with Landis in Cincinnati, Mills said, "Everything looks favorable that I will be reinstated within a few days." He added that "Landis listened to his plea with much more patience than he has been said to show 'jumpers' in the past."[56] (A player barred for violating his reserve clause was considered a "jumper.")

While waiting on the response from Judge Landis, Mills agreed to a contract to become manager of the 1927 Coshocton Regulars.[57] An important part of his agreement to manage the Regulars was the fact that they played only on Sundays,[58] and he could stay on at U.S. Steel. In addition, Mills was able to recruit other players who had full-time jobs.[59]

In an interesting twist, Emmett Cain, a three-year starter for the Regulars, decided not to sign a 1927 contract. Cain said he wanted to be reinstated in Organized Baseball "and to do so must necessarily lay out of the Eastern Ohio League this year, because of the ineligible players connected with the loop."[60]

While waiting for his own reinstatement, Mills continued to manage in a league that welcomed ineligible players. And he responded to Cain's decision not to sign his contract by placing him "on the suspended list of the Regulars so as to be available for service with the local club if he does not succeed in being reinstated."[61]

The 1927 season opened on April 24 with a 5-4 win against "Hans Wagner's Twin Cities club."[62] A month into the season, Mills received a hand-written letter from Landis in which the commissioner wrote, "It is never a joy to me to have to say 'no' to a player." He then denied Mills's appeal for reinstatement and directed him to again consult with National Association Secretary Farrell.[63]

Having been rejected for reinstatement, Mills continued as the Regulars' player-manager. By early September, they were in a battle for first place and Mills "set the hitting pace ... having swung his bludgeon at a .356 clip."[64] By the end of the season the Regulars were the Eastern Ohio League champions.[65]

Mills was lauded by the *Coshocton Tribune* for arousing "the admiration of the fans in rival league cities by his clean playing and sportsmanship in not "squawking" at every adverse decision in a game."[66] The paper went on to say: "It is hoped that the business management of the Coshocton Club will exert every effort to bring Mills (back in 1928)."[67]

Though he had stated a desire to return as manager of the Regulars, Mills couldn't get a commitment from the club, and in January 1928 he agreed to play for the Beaver Falls, Pennsylvania, team.[68] Then, in spite of having signed to play for Beaver Falls, Mills in late March ended up signing a contract to again manage the Regulars.[69]

Before Coshocton's April 29 opening game, Mills was named manager of the Eastern Ohio League All-Stars for a game with the Homestead Grays, but the game was rained out.[70]

Then, a week after the opening game, Mills resigned. The *Coshocton Tribune* wrote that he and the backers of the Regulars were at odds and "it was decided to let him out."[71] Having resigned from the Regulars, Mills rejoined the General Tires team.[72]

In 1929 Mills was hired to manage the Youngstown Oaklands in the Ohio State Baseball Association.[73] He was instrumental in the formation of the new league,

ONE-HIT WONDERS

which took teams from the Eastern Ohio League and the Ohio and Pennsylvania League."[74] Once again, the new Association teams would play only Sunday games.[75]

By the end of the 1929 season, Mills "was no longer on the active list as a playing manager," choosing to concentrate on his duties as manager,[76] as well as on his new position as a salesman in the slag division of U.S. Steel.[77]

In late June of 1930, Mills put together a team to play against the Pittsburgh Pirates.[78] The Pirates won 16-3. The *Coshocton Tribune* reported: "The Mills aggregation ... looked like the Mudville team of the bush leagues, and the Pirates made them look even worse."[79]

While still hoping for reinstatement, during the following years Mills "managed Youngstown semipro teams and played in exhibition games against major leaguers under many aliases.[80]

In 1931 Mills gave up his attempts for reinstatement to Organized Baseball.[81] In 1932 his wife, Mildred, died at the age of 34.[82] (Mills married Velma Viola Weining sometime prior to 1940.)[83]

While continuing to be involved with semipro baseball in the Youngstown area, Mills learned that Judge Landis was "cleaning up" the banned lists. Mills again applied for reinstatement.[84] This time he was successful. In 1934, Mills was informed that he was "restored to the good graces of Organized Baseball after having been outlawed 13 years."[85]

Mills was 39 years old when he was reinstated. Too old to resume a career in Organized Baseball, he concentrated on his career at U.S. Steel. At the same time, he remained involved with the baseball world. Shortly after Pittsburgh's Three Rivers Stadium opened in 1970, Mills had the honor of throwing out a game's first pitch.[86]

Over the years, perhaps as a result of playing with or against each other on barnstorming teams,[87] Mills and Casey Stengel had become close friends, often traveling between Pittsburgh and New York together.[88] In 1978 Mills sent several photographs taken at Stengel's home to the Baseball Hall of Fame. In a letter dated September 22, 1978, Hall of Fame Director Howard C. Talbot wrote: "The president and the board of directors of the National Baseball Hall of Fame and Museum, Inc., gratefully accept your generous gift of photos taken at Casey Stengel's home."[89]

In addition, a picture of Mills, Charlie Deal, and Dutch Zwilling at a Stengel memorial service once hung in the Hall of Fame's Stengel exhibit.[90] Mills, sometimes with Stengel in attendance, would often get paid for his recitation of "Casey at the Bat."[91]

Meanwhile, while concentrating on his U.S. Steel career, Mills became the company's top slag salesman. (Slag was originally considered a waste product by the steel industry.) By 1957, he was selling over a million tons of slag each year."[92]

Family lore says that early in his U.S. Steel career, Mills learned about a meeting scheduled to discuss plans for construction of the Ohio Turnpike. He worked his way into the meeting as part of the catering crew. Listening carefully to the conversations, he went back to his office and prepared a quote using slag as the base. The quote was accepted and, as a result, springboarded his career.[93]

Mills took courses in salesmanship and law and received a Bachelor of Law degree from LaSalle Extension University.[94]

Mills was promoted to manager of the slag sales division in 1953. He held that position until he retired in 1960.[95] That year Mills was named to the Curbstone Coaches Hall of Fame.[96]

After his retirement, Mills continued his community-service activities while pursuing a favorite hobby, building purple martin houses and observing their habits.

Mills's second wife, Velma, died on July 25, 1979. Frank Mills died on August 31, 1983.[97] Frank and Velma are buried in Forest Lawn Memorial Park Cemetery in Youngstown, Ohio.

Frank Mills had a baseball career that spanned three decades. He had the high of a major-league hit when he was 19 and the low of being "outlawed" by Organized Baseball when he was 26. Neither defined Frank Mills.

One hit! But not just a "one-hit-wonder."

SOURCES

Thank you to Frank Mills's granddaughters Janice Conroy and Marilyn Lahiff for sharing their memories and the Frank Mills family scrapbook.

NOTES

1. 1910 United States Federal Census via Ancestry.com.
2. "Cleveland – Try Out Was Very Satisfactory to Nap's Management," Undated, unidentified clipping from Mills's family scrapbook.
3. Contract Approved by the National Association of Professional Baseball Leagues, Class B.
4. "Cleveland – Try Out Was Very Satisfactory."
5. "Frank Mills Has Made Successful Career Selling Slag, Formerly Waste Product," *Youngstown Vindicator*, August 11, 1957: A32.

ONE-HIT WONDERS

6   "Old" Poke, "Went Direct to Cleveland from Semi-Pro Club," *Davenport* (Iowa) *Daily Times*, April 3, 1916: 13.

7   Western Union Telegram, March 16, 1915 (Mills family scrapbook).

8   J.W. Collins, "Large Crowd Out for Opening Day; Big Parade Ushers in the 1915 Season," Mills family scrapbook.

9   "Old" Poke.

10   "Local Catcher Was Cut Down at Plate, Score Was 3 to 0," *Portsmouth* (Ohio) *Daily Times*, June 4, 1915: 10.

11   "Mills Not Discouraged," *Portsmouth Daily Times*, June 5, 1915: 10.

12   "Mills Improving," *Portsmouth Daily Times*, June 19, 1915: 2.

13   "Old" Poke.

14   "Here's First Group of Indian Squad at Training Camp," *Cleveland Press*, March 3, 1916: 16.

15   "Old" Poke; Jerry Mack, "O'Leary to Work Gould in Getaway Tilt Against Peoria Next Wednesday," *Quad City Times* (Davenport, Iowa), April 23, 1916: 22.

16   "Duggan Doubles in Eighth for Blue Sox Win," *Davenport Daily Times*, June 2, 1916: 16.

17   "Blue Sox Catcher Breaks Left Leg in Collision at Plate; Out for the Season," *Quad City Times*, June 25, 1916: 10.

18   "Just an Earful," *Davenport Daily Times*, June 27, 1916: 10.

19   "Just an Earful."

20   "Sure Bite Bug Bait," *Quad City Times*, August 1, 1916: 8.

21   "Just an Earful," *Davenport Daily Times*, August 5, 1916: 11.

22   1930 United States Federal Census via Ancestry.com.

23   "Keeping the Home Fires Burning," *Youngstown Telegram*, undated article from Mills family scrapbook.

24   "Breaks Same Leg Twice but Won't Permit Double Mishap to Interfere With Aspirations," undated, unidentified article from Mills family scrapbook.

25   "Breaks Same Leg Twice."

26   Photograph with team member identification provided by Janice Conroy (Frank Mills's granddaughter).

27   Photograph with team member identification provided by Janice Conroy.

28   "Composite Box Score of M'Elroys Shows Mills Away Out in Front" Undated, unidentified article from Mills family scrapbook.

29   1920 United States Federal Census via Ancestry.com.

30   "Brooklyn Infielders Aboard Band Wagon," *Brooklyn Standard Union*, February 12, 1921: 8.

31   "Atlanta Club to Be Sued for Signing Markle and Mills," Undated, unidentified article from Mills family scrapbook.

32   "Frank Mills Tells Why He Failed to Come Back," Undated, unidentified article from Mills family scrapbook.

33   *Atlanta Constitution*, July 18, 1920: 3

34   Contract Approved by the National Association of Professional Baseball Leagues Uniform Players Contract, Class A.

35   Untitled, undated, unidentified article from Mills family scrapbook.

36   Untitled, undated, unidentified article from Mills family scrapbook.

37   "Brooklyn Infielders Aboard Band Wagon."

38   "Catcher Mills Is Capable Player," Undated, unidentified article from Mills family scrapbook.

39   "Mills Has Low Batting Mark," *Brooklyn Daily Eagle,*" February 14, 1921: 18.

40   "Frank Mills Subject of Pitt Comment," *Atlanta Constitution*, February 19, 1921: 10.

41   "Sammy Mayer Made Two Great Deals," *Atlanta Constitution*, February 20, 1921: 3.

42   "Rain Stops Dodgers; Mamaux on Sick List," *Brooklyn Standard Union*, March 29, 1921: 12.

43   "Stambaugh Leases Park?" Undated, unidentified article from Mills family scrapbook.

44   Undated, unidentified article from Mills family scrapbook.

45   The National Association was the governing body for the minor leagues.

46   "To Keep Game Clean," *Reach Official American League Baseball Guide 1921*, A.J. Reach Company, 204.

47   "M'Elroy Team Ready to Start," *Youngstown Vindicator*, April 30, 1921: 13.

48   Letter to Frank Mills from major-league Secretary-Treasurer Leslie O'Connor, March 13, 1922.

49   O'Connor letter to Mills.

50   O'Connor letter to Mills.

51   "Frank Mills," *Coshocton* (Ohio) *Tribune*, January 18, 1927: 6.

52   "Mills and Reisinger Draw Straws to See Which Must Face Landis First," undated, unidentified article from Mills family scrapbook.

53   "Frank Mills Has Made Successful Career Selling Slag, Formerly Waste Product," *Youngstown Vindicator*, August 11, 1957.

54   "Hildebrand Released; Mills or Durant Will Take Place with Regs," *Coshocton Tribune*, July 20, 1926: 7.

55   "Sixth Club in E.O. Loop to be Named Today," *Coshocton Tribune*, February 27, 1927: 5.

56   Frank Mills Is Confident of Early Reinstatement," undated, unidentified article from Mills family scrapbook.

57   "Mills, New Manager of Regulars, Has Enviable Record; 31 Years of Age," *Coshocton Tribune*, January 18, 1927: 6.

58   "Contracts Sent Out to Full Team; Only Cain and Storch to Be Kept," *Coshocton Tribune*, January 23, 1927: 16.

59   "Contracts Sent Out."

60   "Emmett Cain Will Not Be with Regulars This Year; Placed on Suspended List," *Coshocton Tribune*, February 28, 1927: 6.

61   "Emmett Cain."

62   "Regulators Defeat Twins, 5 to 4, in Opening Contest," *Coshocton Tribune*, April 25, 1927: 4.

63   Letter to Frank Mills from Commissioner Kenesaw Landis, May 24, 1927.

64   "Regular-Tuscora Battle for Pennant Expected to Be Fiercely Fought," *Coshocton Tribune*, September 9, 1927: 7.

65   "Manager Mills Makes Enviable Record and Brings Pennant Here," *Coshocton Tribune*, September 27, 1927.

66   "Manager Mills."

67   "Manager Mills."

68   "Coshocton May Withdraw from Eastern Ohio Baseball Loop," *Coshocton Tribune*, January 10, 1928: 1.

69   "Mills to Manage Coshocton Team," *Coshocton Tribune*, March 25, 1928: 1.

70   "Coshocton Regs Look as Strong as Last Year; New Men in Box, Field and at Second," *Coshocton Tribune*, April 15, 1928: 12.

71   "Frank Mills Resigns as Coshocton Regs' Manager; Ed. Kelly to Hold Reins," *Coshocton Tribune*, May 7, 1928: 1.

ONE-HIT WONDERS

72 "Pearson Hurls Game for Tires," *Coshocton Tribune,* May 21, 1928: 3.

73 "Mills to Manage Youngstown Team in Coming Season," *Youngstown Vindicator,* March 4, 1929: 2.

74 "Baseball Fans Keenly Interested in Confab at New Philadelphia," *Coshocton Tribune,* March 3, 1929: 10.

75 Youngstown to Be in League," *Youngstown Vindicator,* March 4, 1929: 10.

76 "The Sport Market," *Coshocton Tribune,* August 25, 1929: 10.

77 "Frank L. Mills; USS Executive," *Youngstown Vindicator,* September 1, 1983: 1.

78 "Pittsburgh Pirates to Play Here July 10," *Coshocton Tribune,* June 30, 1930: 7.

79 "Pirates Win From Opponents, 16 to 3," *Coshocton Tribune,* July 11, 1930: 9.

80 "Frank Mills Given Reinstatement by Czar of Baseball," undated, unidentified article from Mills family scrapbook.

81 "Frank Mills Given Reinstatement."

82 findagrave.com/memorial/141285125/mildred-h_-mills.

83 1940 United States Federal Census, Ancestry.com

84 "Frank Mills Given Reinstatement."

85 "Frank Mills Given Reinstatement."

86 Photograph with inscription provided by Janice Conroy (Frank Mills granddaughter).

87 Toni Harsh (Casey Stengel grandniece) interview, August 3, 2019.

88 Janice Conroy interview, May 24, 2019.

89 Letter to Mills from Howard C. Talbot, director, National Hall of Fame and Museum, September 22, 1978.

90 Photograph with inscription provided by Janice Conroy.

91 Janice Conroy interview, May 24, 2019.

92 "Frank Mills Has Made Successful Career Selling Slag, Formerly Waste Product," *Youngstown Vindicator*, August 11, 1957.

93 Janice Conroy interview, May 24, 2019.

94 Frank Mills Testimonial, May 21, 1960.

95 "Frank L. Mills; USS Executive," *Youngstown Vindicator*, September 1, 1983: 1.

96 "Frank L. Mills; USS Executive."

97 "Frank L. Mills; USS Executive."

GUY MORRISON

By Bob LeMoine

Guy Morrison was a four-sport athlete with plenty of energy and drive. He excelled in college and on the pitching mound in the 1920s for minor-league teams, mostly in the Midwest in the Three-I League. After years of minor-league mound dominance, which he accomplished while coaching high-school and college sports on the side, Morrison finally made it to the major leagues with the 1927-28 Boston Braves at the age of 31. His major-league career was brief: On the mound he accomplished one win; at bat he accomplished one hit. He then went back to the minors and coaching. When he received a devastating medical diagnosis, he took his own life at the age of 38.

Guy Morrison, from the 1917 yearbook, West Virginia Wesleyan College.

Walter Guy Morrison was born August 29, 1895, in Hinton, West Virginia, to Moffett and Jeanetta (Neff) Morrison. Moffett worked as a lumber inspector and the couple had three children at the 1910 census: Charley, Grace, and Guy. In 1910 they were living in the town of Beckley in southern West Virginia. Morrison attended grammar school there and did college prep work at the Beckley Institute. He enrolled at West Virginia Wesleyan College in Buckhannon and graduated in 1917 with a bachelor of arts degree. Morrison was a four-sport athlete while in college: baseball, football, basketball, and track. He was an all-state defensive end in football and an all-state guard in basketball, and won the West Virginia Intercollegiate 100- and 400-yard dashes. He was a top pitcher in baseball and was a teammate of Earl "Greasy" Neale, who had an eight-year major-league career as well as a professional football career that led him to one day coach the Philadelphia Eagles in the NFL and be inducted into the Pro Football Hall of Fame.

Morrison served as an artillery lieutenant during World War I, and when he returned he briefly played independent baseball, then signed a contract in 1919 with the Evansville club of the Three-I League. He was traded in July to Moline in the same league and finished with a 3.67 ERA in 25 games, while a later article credited him with a 14-14 record.[1] He returned to Evansville in 1920 and racked up a 17-7 record with a 2.36 ERA in 26 games. He also became a coach in the athletic program at Bloomington (Illinois) High School that fall.[2] He continued pitching at Evansville in 1921 and compiled a strong 16-8 record with a 3.23 ERA in 32 games, even more impressive considering he didn't pitch on Saturdays in the fall when he was coaching football. Since commuting didn't make sense, Morrison announced his wishes to be traded to Bloomington to make his tasks of pitching and coaching easier.[3] That's where he would spend 1922, but not before he helped Bloomington High win the county basketball tournament.[4]

ONE-HIT WONDERS

Morrison's pitching was outstanding for his new team in 1922: 19-15 with a 2.28 ERA in 41 games. He pitched shutouts on July 1, 4, 13, and 19, and lost 1-0 on July 9, to earn the reputation as an "iron man." Rumors circulated of major-league scouts taking interest.[5] Despite his hectic pace, Morrison found time to get married on August 9 to Blanche Lindsey, a secretary at Bloomington High School. The couple were "numbered among Bloomington's most popular young folks," *The Pantagraph* celebrated.[6] Imagine the shock Bloomington fans had when they picked up the newspaper on November 2 and read, "Guy Morrison Sold to New York Giants." Morrison resigned his athletic position to join the world champions for spring training in Texas.

But impressing legendary manager John McGraw and earning a spot on the pitching staff was a tough task, and Morrison was assigned to San Antonio of the Texas League with an option to recall if needed. "Lack of a good curveball of major league proportions was all that kept the handsome West Virginia Wesleyan alumnus from sticking with the McGraw forces," wrote H. Lee Watson in the *Decatur* (Illinois) *Herald*.[7] He finished 13-17 (3.75) in 41 games and never received an invitation to New York. Instead, he secured a position as athletic director and coach at a San Antonio high school.[8] That position was only temporary, however, as Morrison was sent back to Bloomington for 1924.

In 24 games that season, Morrison was still dominant with a 2.72 ERA despite a 10-9 record. He also became assistant athletic director and baseball coach at DePauw University in Greencastle, Indiana.[9] He was also sold to Decatur of the Three-I League. He was traded in the offseason to Quincy (Illinois) but refused to report. Instead, he purchased his release from the club in June to become a free agent.[10] He signed with Idaho Falls of the Utah-Idaho League, where he had a stellar 1926 season (17-4) that helped the team win the pennant. He returned to DePauw in the fall but was soon on the move again.

Columbia of the South Atlantic League drafted Morrison away from Idaho Falls and then allowed the Pittsburgh Pirates to acquire him, giving Morrison another shot at the major leagues.[11] But the Pirates sold him during spring training to Shreveport of the Texas League.[12] However, Morrison was soon acquired by Waterbury (Connecticut) of the Eastern League. Morrison went 16-7 with a 2.43 ERA in 33 games. That was enough for the nearby Boston Braves to take notice and purchase him from Waterbury at the end of August. Guy had finally made it onto a major-league roster at the age of 31.[13]

Morrison made his major-league debut on August 31 at Braves Field in the ninth inning with the Braves trailing Cincinnati, 1-0. "Guy Morrison, the husky right-hander brought from Waterbury, worked the last inning," wrote James C. O'Leary in the *Boston Globe*. "He looked pretty good. Although two hits were registered against him, one of them was a scratch."[14] The Reds secured the shutout.

Morrison pitched in eight games out of the bullpen for the Braves, mostly in middle relief. He fared well, throwing 18 innings and compiling a 2.50 ERA, but was wild with seven walks to only one strikeout. He pitched poorly, however, in the three games he started for manager Dave Bancroft. He couldn't get out of the third inning in the second game of a doubleheader on September 5 against the New York Giants, walking three and allowing two earned runs. His next start, at Wrigley Field against the Cubs, was much better. The Braves jumped on the board with four runs in the first, knocking out starter Lefty Weinert, who lasted two-thirds of an inning and was replaced by Percy Jones. The Cubs got two back in the first after an error and a home run to deep right by Cliff Heathcoate. But in the top of the second, Morrison led off with the only hit of his career, another deep shot into the right-field seats to give the Braves a 5-2 lead. As of 2020 Morrison was one of 23 major-leaguers whose lone hit was a home run.[15]

The Cubs tied the score, 5-5, in the bottom of the second with three runs, two of them unearned on two Braves errors and three hits. Jones and Morrison barred further scoring until the Cubs got a run in the seventh and two in the eighth (one unearned). Morrison pitched the complete game, allowing only four earned runs but 13 hits. He fared poorly in his last start, surrendering six earned runs in six innings at St. Louis. He finished the season pitching two innings of relief in the second game of a doubleheader against Philadelphia on October 1, and picked up his only career win when the Braves scored five runs in the bottom of the eighth for an 8-6 victory. Morrison finished the year 1-2 with a 4.46 ERA in 34⅓ innings.

Morrison spent the winter at Columbia University in South Carolina, working on a master's degree in physical education.[16] He joined the Braves for spring training in 1928 in St. Petersburg, Florida, where O'Leary commented that Guy had "plenty of speed, splendid control, and other 'stuff' required by a successful pitcher, including mental equipment and confidence in himself," adding, "All he asks, he says, is a thorough tryout and a chance to show what he can do."[17] Morrison had only one more appearance, however, when he entered in the seventh inning on April 27 with the Braves trailing Brooklyn, 5-0. Morrison pitched a scoreless seventh and eighth but allowed four runs in the ninth on two walks, a single, and a three-run homer by Del Bissonette. The 9-0 loss closed the book on Morrison's major-league career, with his ERA soaring to 5.06.

Morrison was sent to Providence of the Eastern League the next day and resumed his minor-league career.[18] He also became the football, baseball, and basketball coach at Montclair State Teachers College (now University) in New Jersey.[19] Morrison finished two seasons pitching in Providence, going 16-14 (4.36) and 9-12 (4.55). When his pitching was done that season, he moved to Grand Rapids, Michigan, to become athletic director for the city school system. That brought him back to his old Three-I League stamping grounds and in 1930 he pitched one last time each for Bloomington, Peoria, and Decatur.[20]

Morrison remained in Grand Rapids as athletic director until 1934. He developed a blister after a golf game that developed into an infection and blood poisoning. He was hospitalized for a week and told by a physician that to save his life his right leg needed to be amputated. Morrison committed suicide by shooting himself in the head at the age of 38. "Always a well-conditioned athlete who took exceptionally fine care of himself and not being able to reconcile himself to the fact he had to have his leg amputated is said to be the real reason [for the suicide]," said the *Decatur Daily Review*.[21] Morrison left behind his wife, Blanche. They had no children.

Morrison is buried at Sunset Memorial Park in South Charleston, West Virginia.

SOURCES

In addition to the sources cited in the Notes, the author consulted the following:

Baseball-reference.com

Familysearch.org

Find a Grave, database and images (findagrave.com, accessed April 24, 2019), memorial page for Walter Guy Morrison (29 Aug 1895-14 Aug 1934), Find A Grave Memorial no. 48086234, citing Sunset Memorial Park, South Charleston, Kanawha County, West Virginia, USA ; Maintained by Harrison G. Moore IV (contributor 47091968).

Cassidy Lent of the A. Bartlett Giamatti Research Center at the Baseball Hall of Fame provided a copy of Morrison's Hall of Fame file, which included the following:

"Pitcher Guy Morrison Wages Worthy Fight for Fame on Diamond," 1927 article of unknown origin.

NOTES

1. "Morrison May Be C.H.S. Coach," *Evansville Press*, July 31, 1919: 1; "Guy Morrison Sold to New York Giants," *The Pantagraph* (Bloomington, Illinois), November 2, 1922: 9.

2. "Eva Fans in Riot," *The Dispatch* (Moline, Illinois), September 6, 1920; "B.H.S. First Game on September 25," *The Pantagraph*, September 13, 1920: 10.

3. "Home from Evansville," *The Pantagraph*, December 8, 1921: 6.

4. "Bloomington High School Wins the County Tournament," *The Pantagraph*, February 13, 1922: 10.

5. Fred H. Young, "Just Between You and Me," *The Pantagraph*, July 15, 1922: 10; "Guy Morrison Is Master of Rox," *The Pantagraph*, July 20, 1922: 9.

6. "Miss Lindsey to Wed Guy Morrison Today," *The Pantagraph*, August 9, 1922: 8.

7. H. Lee Watson, "Guy Morrison, Bloomer Star, Bought by Commodores," *Decatur Herald*, March 15, 1925: 26.

8. "Morrison to Coach San Antonio High," *The Pantagraph*, August 24, 1923: 10.

9. Fred H. Young, "On the Sport Trail," *The Pantagraph*, September 8, 1924: 10.

10. Fred H. Young, "Just Between You and Me," *The Pantagraph*, June 17, 1926: 10.

11. "Another Morrison Added to Pirates; Guy, Star Hurler of Utah Loop, Bought," *Pittsburgh Daily Post*, December 10, 1926: 13.

12. "Bucs Release Guy Morrison," *Pittsburgh Post-Gazette*, April 3, 1927: 25.

13. "Waterbury Pitcher Bought by Braves," *Boston Globe*, August 30, 1927: 22.

14. James C. O'Leary, "Fielding Lapses Allow Reds to Bag Game, 1-0," *Boston Globe*, September 1, 1927: 13.

15. Available through Baseball-reference.com Play Index. baseball-reference.com/tiny/6ZbNs.

16. Ernest J. Lanigan, "Brown and Morrison Seek Degrees in Winter Courses," *Hartford Courant*, January 4, 1928: 14.

17. James C. O'Leary, "Guy Morrison Showing Well," *Boston Globe*, February 27, 1928: 20.

18. Burt Whitman, "Braves to Put High Wire Net on New Bleachers; Unwise to Move Stands This Year," *Boston Herald*, April 29, 1928: 23.

19. "Sport Comment," *Montclair* (New Jersey) *Times*, January 28, 1928: 13; "Former Montclairite Takes Life in Grand Rapids," *Montclair Times*, August 24, 1934: 5.

20. "Young's Yarns," *The Pantagraph*, June 22, 1930: 16.

21. Howard Millar, "Bait for Bugs," *Decatur Daily Review*, August 17, 1934: 36; "Morrison Shot Self, Fearing Amputation, Inquest Verdict Says," *The Pantagraph*, August 17, 1934: 10.

AL NAPLES

By Bill Nowlin

Shortstop Al Naples' major-league career was limited to two back-to-back games at the end of June 1949. He doubled to right field his first time at bat. It turned out to be the only base hit of his brief time in the big leagues.

Naples was born on August 29, 1926, in Staten Island, New York. Aloysius Francis Naples Jr. was the son of Aloysius and Mae Naples. The elder Aloysius worked as the office manager in a stock brokerage house. Mae raised three children – Al, Donald, and Richard. The family was of Irish, Spanish, and German heritage.

Al attended St. Peter's High School, an all-boys Catholic high school on Staten Island. The school was founded in 1917. He was active in both baseball and basketball at the school and graduated in 1944. St. Peter's won the New York City championship in both sports, in 1944. Al's brother Don was also on the championship team.

When he was still in his middle teens, Al also played Catholic League baseball on Staten Island and on some of the playgrounds around New York City.

The Second World War was still in progress. After he graduated from high school, there followed 23 months of service in the United States Navy.

He entered the Navy right after graduation. The choice of the Navy was probably dictated by his envisioning a career on the water. "I was going to be a Sandy Hook pilot," Naples explained in a November 2019 interview. It's in our family. My oldest cousin was a pilot. Another cousin became a pilot. Bringing the ships into New York City into the Harbor. I spent a year and a half in the North Atlantic with the [USS] *Franklin Delano Roosevelt*[1] and the ship I was on, [USS] *Charles R. Ware* [DD-865, a destroyer]. I think I had enough of the Navy. So I reneged on going into the Sandy Hook pilots and went to Georgetown when I got the call."[2]

The *Roosevelt* was an aircraft carrier. The *Charles R. Ware* was one of two escort destroyers, on the lookout for German submarines. They never encountered any. "But we knew that they were in the area. They were off Cape Cod, off the Virginia coast. We patrolled all the shores in Europe, to the fjords and so on. We went from Guantanamo all the way up to the Arctic. Greenland and so on."

"I was a seaman third class. I did a lot of navigational stuff with the captain."

Al's wife, Rose, prodded him to tell about his time boxing in the Navy. "It was the second or third day I was at Great Lakes for training, working out in the gym, and this one man who was a coach in the Golden Gloves. He asked me if I wanted to go into boxing. I thought about it. My father was a boxer, a lefty. He'd probably be proud of me if I went into boxing so I said, 'Sure.' It got me out of KP, running the grinder in the morning and all. He was a good teacher. After the war, he used to write me and ask me to continue with it, but it was a dangerous sport even though we had helmets and gloves. They used to do it at smokers, at boot camp. On Saturday night, you'd get up and do three rounds. I enjoyed it."

"One time at Guantanamo Bay, they had a thing with six fights. I won it and they gave me a five-gallon thing of ice cream I took back to the ship."

After separation from the Navy, he returned home to Staten Island. He was talented enough that he earned a position on the semipro Gulf Oil baseball team in New York City, gaining valuable experience alongside teammates including Heeney Majeski, Herb White, Chuck Connors, and Danny Gardella.

"We used to play against all the black teams like the Kansas City Monarchs, the [New York] Black Yankees and so on, so I was playing against high-level players when I was just a junior in high school. That's basically where I learned my game, playing against the Negro League teams, the House of David, semiprofessional teams and so on. That got me the opportunity to play in all-star games in the New York City area, some of which were played at Yankee Stadium."[3]

An opportunity presented itself. He received a basketball scholarship to play for Georgetown University.

ONE-HIT WONDERS

Elmer Ripley had been coaching Notre Dame basketball and then left to coach Georgetown. "He called me up when I got out of the Navy, a couple of weeks later. I knew nothing about Georgetown. I went down there and I got a good education. I think I had enough of the Navy. So I reneged on going into the Sandy Hook pilots and went to Georgetown when I got the call." Naples majored in mathematics and spent three years at Georgetown – receiving attention for his play in both basketball and baseball.

In the spring of 1947, his work at shortstop for the Georgetown Hoyas was earning some attention in the press. On April 15 the Hoyas were trailing the University of Maryland Terrapins 5-0, but scored two runs in each of the seventh, eighth, and ninth innings to win. The Washington Post credited Naples with "two timely hits" – an eighth-inning triple driving in one run and a two-out ninth-inning single that drove in the tying and winning runs.[4]

A sophomore majoring in mathematics, he had caught the eye of Georgetown baseball coach Joe Judge, the former major leaguer who in April 1948 predicted that he had a chance of making the majors despite his small stature (Naples was 5-feet-9 and listed at 168 pounds).[5] Naples was right-handed.

He enjoyed a big day kicking off the 1949 season on March 30, playing Dartmouth and going 3-for-5 with two singles and a triple.[6] His clutch two-run double in the 11th drove in both runs as Georgetown beat Maryland, 2-1, on May 18.[7]

On June 23 Naples signed a contract with the American League's St. Louis Browns. Apparently the Browns had made a move. Both Bob Dillinger and Jerry Priddy had been injured and the Browns had an urgent need for a shortstop.

The June 24 *Boston Globe* reported that Naples had joined the Browns, in Boston to play the Red Sox. The paper wrote, "Naples was to have worked out with the New York Yankees Newark farm, but Vice Pres. Charley DeWitt's long distance call weaned him to St. Louis."[8]

Dillinger had suffered an ankle injury, and Priddy was expected to be out for a number of days with a pulled muscle in his right leg.

As Naples told the story, "I was from the metropolitan area and I used to work out with the Yankees. I was All-City in baseball and so on."

"I had a few scouts from the New York City area that were talking to me all the time. When I was in high school, and I was picked on an all-star team, I was hitting .500. The East All-Stars played the West in the New York Giants' stadium [Polo Grounds]. I couldn't tell you who was following me. What happened was, I was working out with the Yankees and the St. Louis Browns were in there. I was taking infield with them. Then the Browns went to Boston. When they went to Boston, Eddie Pellagrini was hurting. He was a shortstop at the time. I got a call from Charley DeWitt, the [Browns'] owner, from Boston. He asked me if I would be interested in the Browns."

"The coach that I had at Georgetown was Joe Judge. He played first base for the Washington Senators for a number of years and then I think he went with the Dodgers. He had connections. I used to work out with the Washington Senators, too."

"I went up to Boston and signed a contract. Back then, they didn't have agents. I signed on Friday and I played Saturday and Sunday. It was real bang, bang, bang."

Naples reported being given a bonus of $5,000 – rather large for a team like the Browns, but perhaps reflecting both their urgent need and the hope to persuade him not to sign with any of the competition. His salary was $800 per month. The bonus money and $2,000 more from his father allowed Al and Rose to purchase a home in Silver Lake, Staten Island, upon their marriage the following year.

Naples was in Boston but manager Zack Taylor "decided to let him ride the bench for the present as he tested the combination of [Roy] Sievers on third, [John] Sullivan at short and [Andy] Anderson at second."[9]

The Browns had come to Boston in last place with a record of 18-42. The Red Sox were in fourth place, at 31-28. Naples apparently did ride the bench for the first two games of the scheduled four-game set, and saw the Browns lose, 7-0 and then 21-2. Taylor may have felt it incumbent to give Naples a start.

Starting for St. Louis was Bill Kennedy (0-4) and for the Red Sox it was Mel Parnell (9-3). Naples was eighth in the Browns batting order. Leading off the top of the third inning, he doubled to right field. He was left stranded there by two strikeouts and a groundout. The Red Sox scored seven times in the bottom of the third.

On his second time up, Naples grounded back to Parnell and was thrown out at first. He grounded out third to first in the seventh, and again hit the ball back to Parnell in the top of the ninth, the play going 1-3. The final score, a complete-game 10th win of the season for Parnell, was 13-2, Boston.

ONE-HIT WONDERS

Harry Mitauer of the *St. Louis Globe-Democrat* wrote of Naples' debut: "Naples slammed out a double on his first trip to the plate, but failed to get the ball out of the infield on the next three tries. He looked good in the field, handling five assists and one putout at shortstop."[10]

Jack Barry of the *Boston Globe* offered pretty much the same assessment: "Young Al Naples, a junior at Georgetown, playing his first major league game, looked good. He slapped a double to right on is first appearance at the plate in the majors, and handled himself well at shortstop."[11]

Naples played again on Sunday, going 0-for-3 at the plate. He fumbled Vern Stephens's infield roller in the bottom of the sixth inning. Stephens scored a bit later with the first of three runs scored in the inning. The final score was a more respectable 5-3. Chuck Stobbs held the Browns to seven hits. He struck out Naples his first time up, induced a groundball to second base, and then a ball hit back to the mound. Naples was in the on-deck circle when the game ended.

Priddy was back in the Browns infield for their next game.

Naples never got another chance to play in the majors. He was injured, suffering a "broken finger on his right hand during fielding practice."[12]

He tells the story: "We went out to Cleveland and Chicago and then Detroit and I was supposed to play a game out in Detroit. My name was on the list to start. I was taking infield and they had a catcher playing first. He threw the ball and I tried to catch it with my right hand. It broke my finger and I had to go in and tell Taylor, the manager, that I didn't know what happened to my finger but I couldn't throw. I didn't play that game. We went to St. Louis the next day and I had it X-rayed."

"I had to go down to one of their farm teams and get rehab."

That was Springfield. On July 17 the Browns optioned Naples to their Class-B farm club, the Springfield (Illinois) Browns. The team ultimately finished in last place in the Three-I League.

He appeared in 56 games for Springfield, batting .232 in 181 at-bats. His extra-base hits were three doubles and four triples.

"Yeah, Springfield. I finished the season out with them and I was supposed to go back up, but I never did. Of course, I wanted to finish my college education. I guess a year and a half later, the St. Louis Browns put me on the restricted list. That's where I was for a number of years.

"I never went to San Antonio. That's where the Browns had sent me to [in the spring of 1950]. I never went there and that was the end of my career." He was, he explained in an email, actually kept on the restricted list until sometime in 1961.[13]

On January 7, 1950, Naples married Virginia Penny on Staten Island. The couple remain married as of the end of 2019. Virginia goes by the name "Rose."

Indeed, Naples did want to complete his college education. He did so, and then some. Rose urged him to go into teaching after he completed college, and he continued to pursue advanced degrees. "I spent a lot of time going to college. I went six years going to NYU nights. At that time Rose and I had five children, and it was a chore because we lived in Jersey and I had to travel over the George Washington Bridge and all the way down to NYU. I got my master's up at Fordham."

He took a position as a math supervisor at Regis High School in New York City, for one year. "It was just too much traveling since I lived in Staten Island. I finally got a job at the school I graduated from – St. Peter's High School."

At Regis, Naples also coached both baseball and basketball. The same was true at St. Peter's, where he coached for five years.

Al Naples.

Courtesy of the National Baseball Hall of Fame.

ONE-HIT WONDERS

Another opportunity presented itself. "I got a national foundation scholarship to Columbia University with Watson Labs, a full scholarship. Watson was the founder of IBM. The intent was to get teachers – I was teaching at the time – to try to get them computers into the high schools. It was just a promotional type thing. I was picked out of 30 teachers from the metropolitan area; 12 completed the course. I was able to get with the president of the Board of Education of Oradell and River Edge, New Jersey. His name was George Howitt. He was one of the vice presidents for Hewlett-Packard and he got the computer in our school."

The school was the River Dell School, named after two New Jersey towns – River Edge and Oradell.

"I was able to contact other teachers that I knew in Jersey that were tied up with our computer. They were able to get time. It meant that we didn't have to pay anything. We just housed it."

"We were using punch cards for computers back then. It was quite an experience because nobody really knew much about them at the time. I had to get a teacher. He had to give up his job. He was a bartender down on the Jersey shore. He ended up teaching it. It was very successful. The students loved it. We used an Apple computer, the desk computer that they had at the time."

He taught from 1956 to 1958 at Dwight Morrow, and then began to teach at River Dell. "I lasted 30 years with that school, from 1958 to 1987." He also kept his hand in coaching, helping coach both baseball and basketball. He helped coach baseball for two years and basketball for five.

Al Naples calls his wife, Rose, "my right-hand person. She's 93, too. We had seven children. We have 15 grandchildren." They had met in August 1944. She worked as a playground supervisor. At the time of their marriage in 1950, she was a physical education teacher at the College of New Rochelle. Their seven children are Alyce, Virginia, Aloysius Jr., Bill, Thomas, Adrienne, and Kevin.

After he retired, more than 30 years ago, Al and Rose moved to Massachusetts.

Why Massachusetts? "Because all our kids basically moved this way. Tom was in the Coast Guard up in this area. We had kids in Wayland and Gloucester. We just have one who's out of the area, living in Florida."

At the time of the November 2019 interview, Naples was undergoing chemotherapy. He had beaten leukemia once before after going through some experimental and extended treatment that lasted from 1985 to 1992. "It came back again eight months ago. I'm taking this chemo and they're whacking the hell out of me."

He had just the two brothers. "My brother Don, he was a year behind me. When we went to St Peter's we won the New York City championship in both baseball and basketball."

Don got a scholarship to St. Michael's. He was a Yankee. He played in Wellsville [52 games in 1945 for the Class-D PONY League Wellsville Yankees, where he hit for a .313 batting average] and in the Mexican League. "He was going in, breaking up a double play or something, and got hit in the eye. He got some publicity in the New York papers and they took his scholarship away. He got into the Fire Department. He ended up dying of cancer. Smoke. He was a hero, cited twice by the New York mayor for heroism."

"My other young brother, Richard, he was killed in the Korean War in 1950. He was young. He was 21. He was in the Army."

Naples is very appreciative of the attention given him and his fellow St. Louis Browns alumni. "A lot of people don't even know the St. Louis Browns existed," he notes. The franchise moved to Baltimore after the 1953 season and became the Baltimore Orioles.

When St. Peter's High School celebrated its 100th anniversary (the school was founded in 1917), it started a school hall of fame and inducted Naples into it.

Reflecting on his baseball career from his home in Orleans, Massachusetts, Al Naples says, "You know, when you went onto a team like that, nobody really took you under their wing. You're on your own."

"I managed to survive and sort of went my own way."

"I enjoyed the little trip that I had, but I always say what happened to me out in Detroit was the best break I ever had. I broke my finger, and that changed the whole complexion towards playing baseball. I stayed in Springfield until the end of August and that's when I took off. They didn't particularly care for that."

"It was a short-lived thing. It was a different life then."

Naples died on February 26th in Orleans, Massachusetts, just 18 days following the passing of his wife, Rose. They were both 94.

SOURCES

In addition to the sources cited in the Notes, the author relied on Baseball-Reference.com and Retrosheet.org.

ONE-HIT WONDERS

NOTES

1. The USS *Franklin D. Roosevelt* was the second Midway-class aircraft carrier and the first ship in the Navy named after President Franklin D. Roosevelt. Initially, the carrier was launched as the Coral Sea but was renamed on May 8, 1945, following the death of the president.

2. All direct quotations from Al Naples come from an interview with the author on November 3, 2019, and from email exchanges over the following few days, unless otherwise indicated.

3. Ronnie Joyner, "Al Naples," Pop Flies (*St. Louis Browns Historical Society and Fan Club Spring Newsletter* Vol. XXII, No. 1), 2006.

4. "Hoyas Edge Terps, 7-6," *Washington Post*, April 16, 1947: 13.

5. Lewis F. Atchison, "Basket Ball Castoffs Shine for GU Nine," *Washington Evening Star*, April 23, 1948: 42.

6. "Hoyas Beat Dartmouth, 4-3, In 9th Inning of Opener," *Washington Post*, March 31, 1949: 20.

7. "Hoyas Beat Terps in 11," *Washington Post*, May 19, 1949: 21.

8. "Red Sockings," *Boston Globe*, June 24, 1949: 22.

9. "Brownie Notes," *St. Louis Globe-Democrat*, June 24, 1949: 21.

10. Harry Mitauer, "Browns Roll Over Before Bosox Again," *St. Louis Globe-Democrat*, June 26, 1949: 43.

11. Jack Barry, "Sox Slaughter Browns Again, 13-2, Gain on Leaders," *Boston Globe*, June 26, 1949: 36.

12. "Browns' Notes," *St. Louis Globe-Democrat*, July 6, 1949: 11.

13. Al Naples email to author, November 12, 2019.

TITO NAVARRO

By Rory Costello

Puerto Rican shortstop Tito Navarro played in 12 games for the New York Mets late in the 1993 season. He came to the plate 18 times, reaching base once – with a game-winning RBI single in extra innings. He appeared twice in the field. That was his only major-league experience. Navarro's injury-plagued career ended in the spring of 1995, when he was still just 24 years old.

Norberto Navarro Rodríguez was born on September 12, 1970, in Rio Piedras, which is part of the San Juan municipal area. Information on his family and early life has not yet come to light

Navarro attended Colegio Nuestra Señora del Carmen in Trujillo Alto, which is also in the San Juan urban area. He signed with the Mets on September 2, 1987, when he was only 16. At that time, Puerto Rican players were not subject to the amateur draft.[1] The scout was Junior Román, a former minor-league infielder (1976-79) who then covered Latin America for the Mets.[2]

For his first pro season, 1988, Navarro was assigned to Kingsport in the Appalachian Rookie League. He batted .244-0-23 in 54 games and moved up to Pittsfield in the New York-Penn League in 1989. That was short-season Class-A ball, and the schedule's late start was significant because that spring Navarro had his first operation on his right (throwing) shoulder – ongoing problems with this shoulder eventually required two more surgeries and severely hindered his career. Navarro did not make his debut until the end of June, a couple of weeks after the season opened.[3] In 46 games, his average improved to .280; he had no homers and 14 RBIs. Navarro ran well, but at a slender 5-feet-10 and 155-160 pounds, power was not part of his game.

Navarro spent a full season in Class A in 1990 with Columbia in the South Atlantic League. After recovering from a very slow start, he lifted his average to .314 in 136 games. He also showed his good batting eye, drawing 69 walks, which lifted his on-base percentage to .395. In addition, he stole 50 bases, after totaling just 16 in his first two seasons. Furthermore, as one would hope for a shortstop, he was dazzling on defense. All in all, Navarro was rated the league's best prospect.[4]

The Mets recognized Navarro's play by promoting him to Jackson in the Double-A Texas League, where he played three games. After the season ended, they invited him up to Shea Stadium and presented him with a Doubleday Award, the prize given to the organization's top player at each level of the minors. Navarro felt happy and proud but underscored that he'd worked for the honor. He found the competition tough, and the very hot temperatures (up to 107-108 degrees at times) were another challenge.[5]

Navarro then played winter ball in his homeland during the 1990-91 season. He competed for time at

ONE-HIT WONDERS

shortstop for the Arecibo Lobos with fellow Mets prospect Kevin Baez and Yankees farmhand Héctor Vargas. He said, "I want to play ball. At best, they won't put me in to play every day, but I'll play hard. It's a question of doing the work. If they give me the opportunity, I'll take advantage of it."[6]

He did just that, getting into 48 of the Lobos' 59 games, hitting .267-0-12 in 161 at-bats, and stealing 10 bases. It was a good showing, but another promising young *boricua* shortstop was the league's Rookie of the Year that winter: Wil Cordero.[7]

In February 1991, the *Hackensack* (New Jersey) *Record* presented snapshots of various Mets farmhands, one of whom was Navarro. The line on him was "he makes contact and puts the ball in play. Also possesses a strong arm."[8] At least then, the latter observation still held true.

Spending a full summer in Double A, Navarro continued to perform well. With Williamsport in the Eastern League, he hit his only two professional home runs and drove in 42 runs in 128 games. He hit .288 and his OBP was .380; he also stole another 42 bases. At the end of the season, *The Sporting News* said "keep an eye out for shortstop Tito Navarro, who showed good bat control."[9] At that point, he had earned consideration as the Mets' shortstop of the future.[10]

Navarro returned to Arecibo in the winter of 1991-92. He got into just 23 games that season (.286-0-7 in 77 at-bats). One may conjecture both that his shoulder may have been bothering him and that the Lobos had other shortstops.

Navarro was in big-league spring training in 1992 but was sent to minor-league camp for reassignment in mid-March. In early April he underwent reconstructive surgery on his right shoulder to repair a rotator cuff tendon and ligament damage.[11] It caused him to miss the subsequent summer season. Had his arm been sound, he probably would have played for the Mets' top affiliate, Tidewater in the International League. There he would have competed with his old Arecibo teammate, Kevin Baez, and Tim Bogar for time at shortstop.

Navarro might even have made it to the majors at some point that year because the Mets' incumbent shortstop, Kevin Elster, was struggling with his own recurring shoulder problems. Elster was able to play just a handful of games in April and then was disabled for the rest of '92 as well. When the outlook for Elster became increasingly bleak, the team traded for good-field, no-hit Dick Schofield. That August, Joe Sexton of the *New York Times* asked pointedly, "Can the Mets absorb the costs of Schofield's unproductive .205 bat in their lineup?" He called Navarro, despite being sidelined, the organization's "only bona-fide prospect for the [shortstop] position."[12]

Veteran utility infielder Bill Pecota was Schofield's primary backup. When Pecota went on the 15-day DL in late April, Baez was called up. Baez also returned in September, but Navarro wasn't ready. That October, the Mets traded with San Diego for Tony Fernandez, who'd won four Gold Gloves with Toronto. Fernandez was also viewed as an upgrade on offense over Schofield, a free agent whom New York did not seek to re-sign. Elster was no longer in the picture either.

As for Navarro, the Mets left him unprotected in that November's expansion draft. He was not selected by either Colorado or Florida, though at least one report thought that one of the new clubs might take a shot at him.[13]

Navarro still couldn't play in the Puerto Rican league that winter either, but he returned to action in spring 1993 after New York re-signed him to a one-year contract that February. In camp, he had the benefit of tutelage from infield instructor Bud Harrelson. The Mets' former two-time All-Star shortstop noticed something with the prospect's throwing form and showed him a cleaner, more efficient way to set up.[14]

Tony Fernandez was dealt away from New York after less than half a season in 1993. (In a curious twist, he went back to Toronto, replacing the injured Schofield, who'd signed with the Blue Jays.) The Mets then went with Bogar and Baez at short. Meanwhile, Navarro finally reached Triple A, spending most of the year with the Tides. In 96 games, he posted a line of .282-0-16, nearly all as a designated hitter. He was frequently held out of the lineup and played in just eight games at shortstop so that his shoulder would not be taxed.[15]

Nonetheless, when rosters expanded that September, Navarro was called up to join the big club. In his debut, at Houston's Astrodome on September 6, he went 0-for-5 and his arm was called into question.[16] Two days later, he struck out as a pinch-hitter, making the second-to-last out in Darryl Kile's no-hitter. The shortstop's only other start and only other appearance in the field came on September 11 at Shea Stadium. He received a total of 15 chances at short in those two outings and did not commit an error.

Navarro's lone hit in 17 big-league at-bats came at Atlanta-Fulton County Stadium on September 18. With two outs in the top of the 10th, Darrin Jackson and Jeff McKnight singled off Mike Stanton. Navarro

ONE-HIT WONDERS

batted for Jeff Innis, and Braves manager Bobby Cox brought in righty Steve Bedrosian for the lefty Stanton. However, Navarro – a switch-hitter – just changed from the right side of the plate to the left.[17]

On the first pitch, the rookie dropped a flare into short right field, bringing Jackson home.[18] "You can't think about what a tough situation that is," he said. "You just have to go up there and do it."[19]

Mauro Gozzo pitched a one-two-three inning to get the save, and the Mets' win trimmed Atlanta's lead over the San Francisco Giants to three games. "That first hit was slow in coming," Navarro said, "but I guess it came at a good time. Maybe the Giants will buy me a steak dinner."[20] Indeed, the NL West race was decided on the season's last day.

Meanwhile, it was a dismal year for the Mets, who finished at 59-103. Yet as they closed in on 100 losses, Navarro saw no shame in being with the club and didn't think the folks at home would either. "No," he said. "That's the big show. Not too many can play in that league, not from Puerto Rico. They will not make fun of me. They like the New York Mets. Really."[21]

Navarro came to the plate six more times that season, all as a pinch-hitter. He was 0-for-5 with a sacrifice. In the last game of the season, at Florida on October 3, he pinch-ran for Dwight Gooden and scored an insurance run in a 9-2 Mets win.

Not long after the season ended, on October 19, Navarro underwent surgery on the front of his right shoulder. His throws to first base were weak, and another operation on the joint was deemed necessary if they were to firm up at all. Initial estimates called for him to miss another whole season.[22] As one might expect, Navarro was again not able to play winter ball. He began throwing lightly in February 1994, however, and the club expected him to be able to play by May.[23] As it turned out, he was in action in early April.[24]

To start the 1994 season, Navarro went to St. Lucie in the Florida State League (Class A) on a rehab assignment. He began the year as a DH, and the organization then moved him from shortstop to the outfield. The experiment went well enough that Navarro returned to Norfolk in June. Gerry Hunsicker, then an assistant vice president with the Mets, said that Navarro's arm motion was "more conducive" to center field. Hunsicker noted, "If you didn't know his background, you wouldn't know he hadn't played the outfield. His strength is back, his arm seems fine." The organization still wanted Navarro to play some infield, to enhance his chances of sticking in the majors. However, his arm wouldn't let him.[25]

In 51 games for the Tides, Navarro hit .275-0-18. In late July, the press noted that he had a long-shot chance of being recalled to New York because of Kevin McReynolds' bad knee.[26] Injury struck again, however; this time Navarro tore muscles in the wall of his abdomen. Once more he was out of action during the winter season. The following February, *The Sporting News* wrote that his inability to recover from the abdominal tear was a concern. "In the best of all possible worlds, he would be fully healthy, playing left field, and filling the team's need for a leadoff hitter." But the organization doubted that his skills would be sharp, even if he were healthy.[27]

There was a sad irony in Navarro's situation. He was on the Mets' 40-man roster, making him a member of the major-league players union, which was then on strike. A fellow Puerto Rican, outfielder Ricky Otero, was in the same boat. Unless they became strikebreakers, they couldn't work for the big club in spring training, and the minor-league facilities were not available to them either.[28]

The crippling strike ended in early April 1995, and the Mets signed Navarro to a one-year contract. A little later that month, though, they released the "one-time 'shortstop of the future,'" who was out of options.[29] His playing days thus concluded (he never performed again in Puerto Rico either).

As of 2020, Navarro was living in Puerto Rico. Among other things, he was working in the construction business and helping take care of his grandchildren.[30] Efforts to reach him during 2020 for further insights into his life and career proved unsuccessful.

It's impossible to project how this prospect's career would have turned out had he not gotten hurt. As it developed, the Mets went with veteran José Vizcaino at short in 1994 and 1995. For several seasons after that, the position was manned by Rey Ordóñez – a spectacular fielder whose production at the plate was limited. With a healthy Navarro, the organization might not have felt the need to take part in the October 1993 lottery for the rights to sign Ordóñez, or to trade for Vizcaino ahead of the '94 season. At the very least, one can imagine Navarro in a utility role, or he might have brought value in a trade.

ACKNOWLEDGMENTS

Continued thanks to SABR member Jorge Colón Delgado for Navarro's statistics in the Puerto Rican Winter League. Thanks also to Alexis Figueroa for his contact with Navarro.

ONE-HIT WONDERS

SOURCES

In addition to the sources cited in the Notes, the author consulted Baseball-Reference.com, Retrosheet.org, and the trading card database comc.com

NOTES

1 That changed in 1989, following a bidding war over Melvin Nieves.

2 Tito Navarro, phone call with Alexis Figueroa, September 14, 2020.

3 "Mets Fall to Pirates," *Berkshire Eagle* (Pittsfield, Massachusetts), July 1, 1989: D-5.

4 Tito Navarro baseball card, Continental Cards Play II series, 1991. *Baseball America's 1991 Almanac* (Durham, North Carolina: American Sports Publishing, 1991). 182.

5 Rubén A. Rodriguez, "'He Trabajado Para Esto' – Tito Navarro," *El Nuevo Día* (San Juan, Puerto Rico), September 15, 1990. The Mets also honored Columbia teammate Tim Howard, making that team the only one in the system with two Doubleday Award recipients that year. See also *2006 New York Mets Media Guide*.

6 Rodriguez, "'He Trabajado Para Esto' – Tito Navarro."

7 José A. Crescioni Benítez, *El Béisbol Profesional Boricua* (San Juan, Puerto Rico: Aurora Comunicación Integral, Inc., 1997).

8 Untitled sidebar, *The Record* (Hackensack, New Jersey), February 10, 1991.

9 Mike Eisenbath, "Organizations of First Rank," *The Sporting News*, September 23, 1991: 13.

10 Tom Friend, "[John] Franco Hurls His Stool; No Runs Score," *New York Times*, September 23, 1993: B-17.

11 "Mets: It's a New Beginning," *The Record*, April 6, 1992: 34.

12 Joe Sexton, "Mets Aren't in Position to Contend," *New York Times*, August 23, 1992.

13 "OK, Take Your Picks," *Boston Globe*, November 15, 1992.

14 Mike Lupica, "Buddy System Is Mets' Again – for One Day," *New York Daily News*, March 16, 1993: 55.

15 Tom Friend, "Sour Old St. Nicholas Fed Up with [Pete] Schourek," *New York Times*, September 7, 1993: B-11.

16 "Sour Old St. Nicholas Fed Up with Schourek."

17 Furman Bisher, "Braves Hit by No-Name Once Again," *Atlanta Constitution*, September 19, 1993: E-1.

18 Joe Sexton, "What Began as the Mets' Embarrassment Becomes the Braves'," *New York Times*, September 19, 1993.

19 Bill Madden, "Unheralded Mets Spoil Braves' Luck," *New York Daily News*, September 19, 1993.

20 "Navarro Stars in Clutch as Mets Cool Off Braves," *Asbury Park* (New Jersey) *Press*, September 19, 1993.

21 Tom Friend, "Lowly Mets' Temperature Reaches 100," *New York Times*, September 21, 1993: B-11.

22 "Franco Hurls His Stool; No Runs Score."

23 Marty Noble, "New York Mets," *The Sporting News*, February 14, 1994: 27.

24 Chuck Otterson, "Expos Lose Opener 4-0 to St. Lucie," *Palm Beach* (Florida) *Post*, April 8, 1994.

25 Steve Adamek, "[Jason] Jacome Offers Glimpse of Future," *The Record*, July 19, 1994: 56.

26 Frank Isola, "Mets Mull DL for K-Mac," *New York Daily News*, July 22, 1994.

27 Marty Noble, "New York Mets," *The Sporting News*, February 6, 1995: 32.

28 Jennifer Frey, "To One Mets Hopeful, Promotion Is a Hardship," *New York Times*, February 16, 1995.

29 Steve Adamek, "[Rico] Brogna Bruised but Not Broken," *The Record*, April 23, 1995: 10.

30 Emails from Navarro's acquaintance Alexis Figueroa to Rory Costello, September 12 and October 14, 2020.

CURLY ONIS

by Mike Huber

Curly Onis's major-league career batting line read: "1 game. 1 at-bat. 1 hit." A perfect batting average. A total of 22 major-league players have stroked a hit in their sole plate appearance, and Onis, a catcher, is one of that elite group. Further, according to Baseball-Reference.com, 127 catchers had a single hit in their careers in the majors.[1] Seven of them (including Onis) had just a single plate appearance in the big leagues, giving each of them a 1.000 career batting average.

Onis's story, though, has a few unique twists to go with his perfect batting line. He was born Manuel Dominguez Onis in Tampa, Florida, on October 24, 1908. His parents, Manuel and Manuela, were both born in Asturias, Spain, and came to the United States in 1900 and 1905, respectively. Manuel Sr. worked as a tobacco wetter in a cigar factory in Tampa. The younger Manuel once explained that process, saying, "The tobacco came in dry, and he wetted it and fixed it so you could handle it."[2]

Tragedy struck the family while both children were of school age; their father died. By 1920 Manuela was a widow, raising her son, Manuel, and daughter, Josephine.[3] After the death of her husband, Manuela went to work in the same cigar factory to earn money to support her family.

Onis always wanted to be a baseball player. At 5-feet-9 and weighing 180 pounds, he became a catcher. He attended George Washington High School in Tampa, but the school didn't have a baseball team, so the young catcher played sandlot ball in pickup games. That's when he earned the nickname Curly.[4] According to Onis, "I had a thick, black, curly head of hair, and you know how it is. We all had nicknames. One kid started calling me that and then another one and soon everybody was calling me Curly."[5]

When not playing baseball, Onis had various jobs to help the family. He dropped out of high school to work for the Tampa Electric Company. The catcher was told that if he played for one of the four teams in the company's league, he could get a job driving a streetcar. "Since jobs were scarce, I took it and played ball for them. We won 24 out of 25 games."[6]

Onis was born the same year as future Hall of Famer Al Lopez, another Tampa native whose father worked in the cigar factory. Curly and Al became fast friends and played in many of those pickup games (both were catchers). Onis credited Lopez with getting him into professional baseball. By 1928 Lopez was playing for the Brooklyn Dodgers. In 1931 Lopez told Wilbur Good, an 11-year veteran of the major leagues and the manager of the Johnstown Johnnies of the Middle Atlantic League, about Onis, and persuaded Good to sign his friend to a contract. As a 22-year-old, Onis played in 42 games for the Johnnies. He caught in 30 of those games and was used as a pinch-hitter in the others. In his first season in professional baseball, Onis batted .212 with three home runs.

Onis was released at the end of the season. He played for the Cuban Stars in 1933, and then in 1934 with Jacksonville in the Florida-Georgia League. (No stats are recorded for the league.) While with Jacksonville, Lopez called his boyhood friend again, asking him to come to Brooklyn. Onis didn't have any money, so Lopez sent him a train ticket. Onis spent two months in Brooklyn, warming up pitchers. At the end of the season, he rode back to Tampa with Lopez.

Once back in Florida, Onis received a letter from the Dodgers, offering him a contract for the next season. According to Onis, "I think it was for $400 a month."[7] The 1935 Tampa City Directory listed his occupation as "ballplayer,"[8] living with his mother. The 26-year-old catcher was both excited and nervous as he reported to Brooklyn's spring-training camp. The Dodgers gave him a true opportunity, and he played in many of their spring-training games.

Onis's major-league debut took place on April 27, 1935. The Boston Braves visited Ebbets Field to play the Dodgers in a Saturday afternoon contest. Brooklyn had a five-game winning streak heading into the game. A crowd of 28,000 went through the turnstiles, with many of them hoping to get a glance at the Braves'

ONE-HIT WONDERS

left fielder, Babe Ruth.[9] In his final season, Ruth had started the 1935 campaign hot, going 6-for-15 (.400) in his first five games. This included a home run in four games against the Brooklyn Dodgers, played at Braves Field. Six days later (April 27), Ruth and the Braves were in Brooklyn, once again playing the Dodgers.

The game was a pitchers' duel for five innings, matching Boston's Ed Brandt against Brooklyn's Ray Benge. Brandt was making his third start of the season, while Benge was making start number two. The crowd saw just three singles through the first five innings.

In the sixth inning, the Braves' Billy Urbanski and Buck Jordan hit back-to-back singles to start the inning. Ruth walked to load the bases. Wally Berger blasted a double to left, driving in two runs and sending Ruth to third, and "the dust he raised hook-sliding to the bag did not settle for half an inning."[10] Randy Moore bounced a ball to second baseman Tony Cuccinello, who fired home to catch Ruth at the plate. (Different accounts had Ruth out by as much as 10 feet when Dodgers catcher Babe Phelps received Cuccinello's throw.) Les Mallon then doubled, plating two more runners, and the Braves had a 4-0 lead. Brooklyn answered with two runs in its half of the sixth, on a walk to Len Koenecke, a double by Sam Leslie, and a two-run single by Cuccinello, who was thrown out at second trying to advance. That was all the scoring in the game.

Bobby Reis pinch-hit for Phelps to start the Dodgers' seventh inning. Phelps had caught a pop fly off the bat of Berger to end Boston's half of the seventh. There was no mention of an injury in the newspapers, and Phelps had gone 1-for-2 off Brandt. Perhaps Dodgers manager Casey Stengel was looking for an offensive spark. Reis grounded out, short to first. This forced Stengel to insert Onis as his new catcher with Boston coming to bat. Years later, Onis recalled, "I was sitting on the bench with two guys between me and Stengel. I remember Casey leaned forward and turned to me and said, 'Hey, kid. Wanna play?' I said, 'That's what I'm here for.' So he says, 'Okay, get yourself ready and go on in there.'"[11]

A strange event took place with Onis behind the plate in the top of the eighth. He "lost" a ball down his shirt front with Shanty Hogan batting. Hogan swung and foul-tipped an offering from Bob Logan. Onis appeared to have caught the ball, but then it disappeared. The *New York Daily News* told its readers that home-plate umpire Bill Stewart "produced a new baseball and the game was about to continue when Hogan made strange motions in the direction of Onis's bosom. Onis blushed, fumbled and produced the missing baseball from beneath his chest protector."[12]

In the ninth, Jordan bunted a ball into the frozen ground in front of home plate. Onis ran out to pick it up and slipped while throwing to first base. The ball sailed into right field and Jordan scampered to second on the error. Logan then struck out Hal Lee, giving Onis the sole putout of his career. In the home half, with one out, Joe Stripp hit a grounder to short and, according to the *Daily News*, "Stripp beat out Urbanski's throw to Jordan but Umpire Ziggy Sears saw it differently. At least 25,000 boos and a cannon cracker tossed at his heels from the upper tier couldn't change his mind."[13] Stripp argued vehemently, causing the first-base umpire to eject him from the game.

With the Dodgers down to their last out, Onis took his turn in the batter's box, making his big-league batting debut. "I couldn't stand up, I was so nervous," he recalled. "The first pitch was a strike and I took it. I stepped out of the box and walked away from the plate about five feet and stooped down and picked up some dirt and rubbed it on my hands. The umpire sort of walked by me and said, 'Get up there, kid, and hit that ball.' Well, that sort of pepped me up and I went back. The next pitch was a curveball and I hit it right over third for a single. Oh, man! I can't tell you how great I felt."[14] He reached first and stayed there, afraid

Curly Onis.

213

to be picked off, but he was stranded when Jimmy Jordan, pinch-hitting for Logan, flied out to left to end the game. In his sole plate appearance, Onis had delivered a hit.

Of interest is the fact that Onis owned a career fielding percentage lower than his career batting average. His fielding record line was two innings, one putout, one error, for a fielding percentage of .500.

A few weeks after the game in Brooklyn, Onis was optioned to the minors. Phelps returned to the Brooklyn lineup in the next game; he ended the 1935 season batting .364 in 47 games. Lopez did the majority of the catching duties for the Dodgers, appearing in 128 games. Meanwhile, Onis played 16 games as a catcher (27 overall) with the Class-A Reading/Allentown Brooks of the New York-Pennsylvania League. On July 13 he was sent to the Dayton Ducks of the Class-C Middle Atlantic League. According to the *Tampa Tribune*, Onis got into a fight with an umpire in one of the Dayton games. Onis was behind the plate and the umpire called a ball that Onis thought was clearly strike three. "We got into an argument and finally he says to me, 'You get back down there and catch or I'll throw you outta here,' and I said, 'If you throw me outta here, I'll hit you in the head with my mask.' So he threw me out and I hit him with my mask."[15] The umpire was Bill Grieve.[16] Onis found himself subsequently suspended without pay for 30 days. When the suspension was served and Onis "was ready to play again, teams stayed away from [him] fearing retribution from the umpires."[17] He was recalled to Brooklyn again, where he was immediately released, giving him the one career at-bat in the majors. For his two teams in the minors in 1935, Onis batted a combined .254, but he also made 11 errors in 51 games behind the plate.

Onis started the next season (1936) with the Double-A Toledo Mudhens (still in the Dodgers farm system), but he played only one game (going 0-for-3) before being shipped back to the Class-A Allentown Brooks. He put up better offensive numbers (.293 with 11 doubles and 11 triples), but he also had 15 defensive miscues.

For five seasons, from 1935 through 1939, Onis played for two different teams in the minors. He started the 1937 season catching for the Sioux City Cowboys (Class-A Western League). The Cowboys were affiliated with the Detroit Tigers. After 76 games, he was sent to the Fort Worth Cats of the Texas League.

Onis started the 1938 season in Fort Worth, but he did not make any appearances. Instead, he was sent down (the Cats were a Class-A1 team) to the Class-D Leesburg Gondoliers, part of the Florida League. This brought Onis closer to his home in Tampa, and in 116 games he batted .255 with four home runs. He also made 28 errors.

In 1939 Onis began the season with the Hartford Bees (Class-A Eastern League, an affiliate of the Boston Braves). He did not make much of an impact, collecting seven hits in 14 games. But then an opportunity came up. Onis was offered a chance to manage in the minors, and at the age of 30, he became the skipper in Leesburg (with the team now called the Anglers). Leesburg was not affiliated with any major-league franchise but was part of the eight-team Florida State League. Onis played in 80 games while managing, batting .274. Nelson Leach also managed for part of the season.

A year later, Onis was player-manager for the Orlando Senators (still in the Florida State League, but now part of the Washington Senators farm system). He hit .284 in 139 games and was named the league's all-star team catcher.[18] There was a pretty good right-handed pitcher on that all-star team. His name was Stan Musial, and he was becoming a star in St. Louis's minor-league franchises. The 1940 season was the last for Onis in professional baseball. Another player in the St. Louis farm system, Lou Klein, slid into Onis and broke his knee. After two surgeries, he still couldn't squat and, at the age of 31, announced his retirement. He kept a slight limp for the rest of his life. In eight minor-league seasons, Onis had appeared in 671 games. His official batting record is incomplete, but the only defensive position he played was catcher.

Onis returned to Tampa and got his old job as a streetcar motorman with Tampa Electric. Two years later, he became a fireman for the City of Tampa. Curly Onis married Zoraida Diaz on November 27, 1942, in Tampa. The couple had met as youngsters, when Zoraida had played softball. A week later on December 4, he enlisted in the US Coast Guard. He did not deploy overseas and was released from service on August 8, 1944.

In 1950 Onis worked as a station fireman at the Gulf Beaches in St. Petersburg, Florida, across the Tampa Bay from Tampa. He worked for the City of Tampa Fire Department until his retirement. Onis stayed active in his community, as a member of Masonic Lodge 240, the Tampa Consistory Scottish Rite, the Retired Firefighters Organization, the Kentucky Colonels and the Seminole American Legion Post 111.[19]

ONE-HIT WONDERS

In his later years, Onis battled diabetes and suffered from a heart condition. He was diagnosed with cancer in August 1994 and entered the hospital shortly before Christmas with an infection. He died on January 4, 1995, at the age of 86 and was buried in Centro Asturiano Memorial Park Cemetery in Tampa. Curly and Zoraida had been married for 52 years. They had one daughter, Sandra Onis Mims.

In 1963 Onis completed a series of surveys for the National Baseball Hall of Fame and the Dodger Alumni Association. Under the position played for the Dodgers, he wrote "third string catcher."[20] He couldn't remember which number he wore on his jersey, and he listed that his hobbies were "golf, fishing, and watching the Dodgers on TV."[21] Despite appearing in only one game for the Brooklyn Dodgers and getting only one at-bat in that one game, Curly Onis, the third-string catcher, retired with a perfect batting average in the majors.

SOURCES

In addition to the sources mentioned in the Notes, the author consulted Curly Onis's file from the Giamatti Research Center at the National Baseball Hall of Fame and Museum; baseball-reference.com; and retrosheet.org.

NOTES

1. This figure is current as of the beginning of the 2020 regular season.
2. Richard Tellis, *Once Around the Bases* (Chicago: Triumph Books, 1998), 21-28.
3. 1920 United States Federal Census, Tampa Ward 7, Hillsborough County, Florida (Enumeration District 55), T625_223: page 13A, found on ancestry.com. Accessed April 2019.
4. Both retrosheet.org and baseball-reference.com list his playing name as Ralph. Later references, to include several obituaries, list his nickname as Curly.
5. Tellis.
6. Tellis.
7. Tellis.
8. "1935 Tampa City Directory," found on ancestry.com. Accessed April 2019.
9. Several sources incorrectly state that Babe Ruth made his National League debut on April 27, in this game against the Dodgers. The truth is that Ruth debuted on April 16 in a game against the New York Giants at Braves Field. He singled in his first plate appearance. See retrosheet.org/boxesetc/1935/B04160BSN1935.htm. The game played on April 27, 1935, was Ruth's eighth of the season.
10. Stuart Rogers, "Brandt Hurls as Braves Top Dodgers, 4-3," *Daily News* (New York), April 28, 1935: 414. Interestingly, the final score was 4-2, not 4-3.
11. Tellis.
12. "The Ball Disappears," *Daily News*, April 28, 1935: 34C.
13. Rogers.
14. Tellis.
15. Tellis.
16. Tellis.
17. "Ex-Brooklyn Dodgers Pitcher Onis Dies," *Tampa Tribune*, January 6, 1995: 110. Unfortunately, the *Tampa Tribune* informed its readers that Onis had been a pitcher, not a catcher.
18. Tellis.
19. Onis obituary, *Tampa Tribune*, January 6, 1995: 25.
20. *Dodger Alumni Association Update*, part of Onis's file at the National Baseball Hall of Fame and Museum. Accessed May 2019.
21. *Dodger Alumni Association Update*.

STEVE ONTIVEROS

By Clayton Trutor

Steve Ontiveros played in 10 major-league seasons (1985-1990, 1993-1995, 2000). A long and lithe right-handed pitcher, Ontiveros played for the Oakland Athletics (1985-1988, 1994-1995), Philadelphia Phillies (1989-1990), Seattle Mariners (1993), and Boston Red Sox (2000). A model of perseverance, the right-handed-hitting Ontiveros twice overcame injuries and struggles in the minors to return to the major leagues after extended absences. Despite making just 207 big-league appearances, Ontiveros had considerable success both as a long reliever and a starting pitcher. In his two stints with the Athletics, Ontiveros proved to be a successful starting pitcher, solidifying the middle of Oakland's staff in both the late 1980s and mid-1990s. In 1994 Ontiveros excelled as a part-time reliever/part-time starter for the A's and boasted an AL-best 2.65 ERA. His success in the strike-shortened season helped him earn a spot on the 1995 American League All-Star team.

Steven Ontiveros was born on March 5, 1961, in the village of Tularosa, New Mexico, not far from the larger city of Alamogordo and Holloman Air Force Base, where his father, Ramon "Ray" Ontiveros, served in the US Army. Ray and his mother, Jeannine Michelle (LaCroix) Ontiveros, whom he met while serving in France, raised four children. Steve was the second oldest. The family later relocated to Portage, Indiana, in the Michiana region of northwestern Indiana/southwestern Michigan. Ray was an avid sports fan who encouraged his son's interest in baseball.[1] The family is not related to Steve Ontiveros, the Chicago Cubs and San Francisco Giants infielder of the 1970s.[2]

Ontiveros was a standout pitcher as a freshman and sophomore at Brandywine High School in Niles, Michigan, and as a junior and senior at St. Joseph's High School in South Bend, Indiana. As a junior he posted a 22-1 mark and led St. Joseph to a number-four ranking in the state.[3] Ontiveros earned a baseball scholarship to the University of Michigan, where he played alongside future big leaguers Chris Sabo, Jim Paciorek, and Gary Wayne for coach Bud Middaugh, who oversaw the Wolverines' 1980s heyday. Ontiveros was Middaugh's relief ace in the early 1980s. The Wolverines earned bids to the College World Series in Ontiveros's freshman (1980) and sophomore (1981) years.[4]

After Ontiveros's junior year at Michigan, the Oakland Athletics selected the 21-year-old in the second round of the 1982 amateur draft. His ascension through the A's system was rapid. In 1982 he spent most of the summer with West Haven of the Double-A Eastern League and appeared to be out of his depth. He posted a 6.33 ERA in 16 appearances. The young righty remained in Double-A in 1983, pitching for the relocated Albany A's of the Eastern League. This time, Ontiveros showed he was ready for Double-A baseball, tying for the team lead in wins with 8 and putting up a 3.75 ERA. He made 32 appearances, including 13 as a starter.

After missing most of the 1984 season with ligament damage in his right arm, Ontiveros impressed with Tacoma of the Triple-A Pacific Coast League early in the 1985 season. In 15 relief appearances, he posted a 3-0 mark with a 2.94 ERA. Ontiveros was called up to the Athletics on June 13. He impressed working out of the bullpen in the waning days of manager Jackie Moore's regime. Ontiveros posted a 1.93 ERA in 39 appearances, earning eight saves and boasting a WHIP of 0.857. The rookie told the *South Bend Tribune* that his efforts to diversify his pitch selection had helped him become a successful major-league pitcher. No longer did he simply rely on his heavy fastball to get hitters out. "My fastball," he said, "I can throw one that runs away from left-handed hitters and one that cuts in." At the time, he was also working on a curveball that would serve him well as he adjusted from being a fireballer to being a crafty veteran later in his career.[5]

In 1986 Ontiveros suffered through a sophomore slump. He made a career-high 46 appearances, all in relief, for the Athletics, as both a long reliever and a closer. His ERA ballooned to 4.71, but he had a career-best 10 saves.

Ontiveros's 1987 season was much more robust. In his first full season as Oakland's manager, Tony La Russa moved Ontiveros into the starting role the pitcher had aspired to since early in his big-league career. The right-hander made 22 starts and a total of 35 appearances. He proved to be one of Oakland's most dependable starters in 1987, winning a career-high 10 games against 8 defeats. He lowered his ERA to 4.00 while working a career-high 150⅔ innings.

Ontiveros made 10 starts for the 1988 AL champion Athletics, nine of which were in the first three months of the season. He went 3-4 with a hefty 4.61 ERA, the lion's share of which came from a couple of rough starts early in the season. Ligament damage in his right arm forced Ontiveros to undergo arthroscopic surgery, which cost him most of the season.

On February 16, 1989, Ontiveros signed as a free agent with the Philadelphia Phillies. He made just six appearances for the club, missing most of the season to undergo a second major reconstructive elbow surgery.[6] Ontiveros had five starts and one relief appearance for Philadelphia, posting a 2-1 record with a 3.82 ERA. He opened 1989 with a pair of strong starts, earning a victory on April 6 against the Cubs at Wrigley Field and a win over the Montreal Expos at Veterans Stadium on April 11. In the win over Montreal, Ontiveros threw seven scoreless innings while surrendering just five hits.

During that Expos game, Ontiveros recorded the only base hit he ever made as a batter – a double in the bottom of the fourth inning. The score was tied, 1-1, as he came to bat against Pascual Perez with the bases loaded. His double to right field cleared the bases and gave the Phillies a 4-1 lead. Three batters later, he scored the fifth Phillies run on a sacrifice fly by Von Hayes. The final score was 6-2, Phillies.

Primarily an American League pitcher, Ontiveros had only 13 plate appearances – all in 1989 – and the one hit.

Ontiveros struggled to make it back into the Philadelphia bullpen. He made a total of five appearances, all in relief, for the 1990 Phillies, posting a strong 2.70 ERA in 10 innings pitched. In 1991 Ontiveros made just seven appearances, all for Triple-A Scranton/Wilkes-Barre. After the season the Phillies released the 30-year-old right-hander, who began the first of his two mid-career minor league odysseys.

Ontiveros signed with the Detroit Tigers in early 1992 but he never made an appearance for the club, still trying to heal his injured right arm. He spent most of 1993 with the Minnesota Twins organization, rebuilding his career with the Portland Beavers of the Triple-A Pacific Coast League. Ontiveros boasted a 2.87 ERA with Portland as well as a 7-6 record, mostly as a starter.

On August 10, 1993, the Seattle Mariners got a steal when they flipped minor-league outfielder Greg Stockey for Ontiveros, who made a significant late-season contribution for the Mariners. In arguably the most effective stretch of his career, the 32-year-old Ontiveros made 14 appearances in August and September for Seattle. He allowed just two earned runs in 18 innings pitched for an ERA of 1.00. Oakland, his original big-league home, scooped him up as a free agent after the season.

Once again Ontiveros became Tony La Russa's jack of all trades. He made 14 relief appearances and 13 starts for the Athletics in 1994. He won six games against four defeats with an AL-leading 2.65 ERA, besting second-place Roger Clemens and third-place David Cone for the title. After the season Ontiveros signed the biggest deal of his career – a one-year pact worth nearly $1 million.

Ontiveros had another solid season for Oakland in 1995. Holding down the number-two spot in the rotation, he made 22 starts and went 9-6 with a 4.37 ERA. He was picked to play in the All-Star Game and played a prominent, if dubious, role in the midsummer classic. He entered the game, which was tied 2-2, in the top of the eighth inning and surrendered a game-winning home run to the Florida Marlins' Jeff Conine. Conine was named the game's MVP and Ontiveros took the loss.[7]

The 1995 season proved to be Ontiveros's final full big-league campaign. A free agent after the season, he signed with the California Angels, but his 1996 campaign was over before it began, shut down due to right shoulder surgery.

The latter half of the 1990s was a second minor-league odyssey for Ontiveros. He bounced from the Angels organization to the Baltimore, St. Louis, Milwaukee, and Colorado systems between 1996 and 2000, never staying in any minor-league city too long. Released by the Rockies on July 7, 2000, he signed with the pitching-starved Boston Red Sox as they pursued a third consecutive trip to the postseason. The Red Sox failed to make the playoffs but Ontiveros did make three late-season appearances (two starts), posting a 1-1 record with a 10.13 ERA. The Red Sox released the 39-year-old after the season. He was signed by the New York Mets in January 2001 and spent part of the season with their Triple-A affiliate in Norfolk. Ontiveros made one final shot in professional baseball, finishing out the 2001 season with Oakland's Triple-A affiliate in Sacramento before calling it a career.

After retirement, Steve and his wife Cindy settled in Scottsdale, Arizona. He has remained in baseball, serving as the head coach for Scottsdale Preparatory Academy and several baseball instructional academies in Arizona. He has worked there as recently as 2017. In 2008 he was the pitching coach for the Chinese national baseball team at the 2008 Beijing Olympics.[8]

NOTES

1. "Ramon 'Ray' Ontiveros," *South Bend Tribune*, June 21, 2015: C5.
2. Curt Rallo, "This Ontiveros Is Out to Make a Name for Himself," *South Bend Tribune*, June 20, 1985: 41.
3. Curt Rallo, "This Ontiveros Is Out to Make a Name for Himself."
4. Ryan Zuke, "Michigan's History in the College World Series," MLive.com, September 19, 2019. Accessed on July 20, 2020: mlive.com/sports/g66l-2019/06/214ec6eeff5716/michigan-baseballs-history-in-college-world-series.html.
5. Curt Rallo, "A Happy Reliever, Ontiveros Hopes to Start," *South Bend Tribune*, September 25, 1985: C1.
6. Sam Carchidi, "Ontiveros Out for Season," *Philadelphia Inquirer*, July 2, 1989: 5C.
7. "Nationals Put on a Power Display," *Quad City Times* (Davenport, Iowa), July 12, 1995: 3S.
8. "Steve Ontiveros Is the Spin Doctor," *SpinDoctor.us*, 2019. Accessed on July 20, 2020: spindoctor.us/about.html.

BILL PETERMAN

By Chris Rainey

On May 1, 1983, the Philadelphia Phillies celebrated their 100th anniversary in baseball. The festivities that day included 93-year-old John Enzmann, the oldest living member of the team. He was invited to toss out the ceremonial "first pitch." Former Phil Bill Peterman was also on hand to take part in the festivities.[1] Peterman was one of more than 50 Philadelphia natives to play for the Phillies and before he was called to duty in World War II, he posted a 1.000 batting average with his hometown team.

Peterman was a catcher who began his professional career in 1940. He earned a roster spot with the Phillies during the spring of 1942. He was used as the bullpen catcher until April 26, when manager Hans Lobert beckoned "to me to come in from the bullpen."[2] The Dodgers were pounding the Phillies, 10-2; Peterman caught the ninth inning and then led off the bottom half against pitcher Ed Head.

Peterman recalled, "My legs were shaking. He threw the first two pitches by me. I decided to start swinging as he wound up. ... I hit the ball through the middle for a single."[3] The next batter, Bert Hodges, forced Peterman at second base. The Phillies left the next day for a two-week Western swing. Peterman was sent a different direction, joining Williamsport in the Eastern League. He never played in another regular-season major-league game.

William David Peterman was born on March 20, 1921, in Philadelphia. He was the youngest of seven children born to Issachar and Amanda Louise (Walters) Peterman. The Peterman family had been in eastern Pennsylvania for generations. Issachar's father and grandfather were both carpenters. Issachar used those skills plus talent as an upholsterer to become a mattress maker.

William was educated at Clara Barton Elementary before graduating from Olney High School. The blue-eyed blond became quite the athlete. "Like any kid, I played on the lots and dreamed of the big leagues," he said.[4] He grew to be 6-feet-2-inches tall and weighed 185 pounds. He threw and batted right-handed. Earning the title of "Most Athletic" for his class, he played soccer, basketball, and baseball at Olney.

Olney has sent six ballplayers on to the majors. In addition to Peterman they are Elmer Burkart, Del Ennis, Jack Crimian, Al Spangler, and Lee Elia.[5] The area newspapers provided good coverage of high-school sports during Peterman's time. He was captain of his soccer team in 1939 and most likely played forward or midfield. In basketball he began his career as a guard and was moved to center his final season, when he served as captain. He must have graduated in January (not uncommon, the team lost three players the previous year at semester) because he played in several recreation leagues starting in February. Before leaving the high-school team, he was third in the area in scoring.

In baseball, Peterman played with multiple teams during the summers he was in high school. In 1939 he played with one of the strongest area squads – Stonehurst Hills. He was spotted by a scout for the Boston Red Sox and signed late in the summer.[6]

The Red Sox sent Bill to the Centreville (Maryland) Red Sox in the Class-D Eastern Shore League in 1940. There he joined catcher Stephen DeCubellis. The team started the season poorly and many roster moves were made ,including jettisoning both catchers before either had played 10 games. According to box scores in the *Daily Times* of Salisbury, Maryland, Peterman made eight appearances and batted .308 (4-for-13).

Peterman was released by the Red Sox and joined the Phillies organization with the Ottawa-Ogdensburg team in the Class-C Canadian-American League. An injury had sidelined the number-one catcher and the team needed a partner for 20-year old Dixie Howell. The 19-year-old Peterman debuted on July 2 and went 4-for-4 with two doubles. "He seemed right at home behind the plate and exhibited a strong throw to second base," an Ogdensburg sportswriter observed.[7]

The Senators, also known as the Double-O's, had a unique schedule, playing their home games in two countries. The roster was loaded with talent that would

ONE-HIT WONDERS

go on to the majors, including pitchers Paul Masterson and John Podgajny. The Senators made a shamble of the pennant race, finishing with an 84-39 record, only to collapse in the first round of playoffs and be eliminated.

Besides catching, Peterman was used at second base and third base when injuries and illness sidelined the regular. In one doubleheader while playing at second he turned three double plays and had three hits.[8] He batted .253 in 46 games but delivered only seven extra-base hits.

The Phillies placed Peterman with Allentown the next year; in turn Allentown sent him to join the Wausau (Wisconsin) Timberjacks in the Class-C Northern League. The Timberjacks' roster was loaded with bats and arms. Outfielder Chet Cichosz was second in the league in batting at .356 and his 31 home runs outhomered both Winnipeg (28 homers) and Fargo-Morehead (24). Peterman was sixth in the league at .336 as Wausau batted .291 as a team. Pitcher Hugh Orphan led the league with 21 wins and 261 strikeouts.[9]

Peterman took an immediate liking to the pitching in the league, and at the beginning of June his batting average was over .400.[10] Wausau surged to the top of the standings and stayed there for the season. The Timberjacks took on the league all-stars on July 21 and, while they won 11-7, it nearly proved disastrous. Peterman was hit while at bat and it was feared he had fractured two fingers. After going 2-for-3, he was forced from the game. His counterpart on the all-stars, Wes Westrum, was also injured in the game.[11]

Peterman was back in action quickly as the injury provide to be not as bad as initially feared. Wausau took the title and faced Duluth in the first round of the playoffs. The Timberjacks entered the postseason in "injury ridden" condition.[12] Peterman went 9-for-21 in the first round, but his teammates struggled. Duluth defeated the Timberjacks four games to one. The Phillies were impressed with Peterman's bat and his league-leading 139 assists. They added him to their roster with orders to report to Florida in the spring of 1942.[13]

Peterman was anxious for his chance at the majors and was in the first group that left Philadelphia on February 27 headed to Miami Beach. The club had appointed veteran Hans Lobert as manager with hopes of finishing higher than the cellar, where they'd been the last four seasons. Peterman was joined in camp by holdover catchers Mickey Livingston and Bennie Warren.

Warren, a better hitter than Livingston, got more work than expected when Peterman split a finger the same day that Livingston pulled a muscle in his leg. Livingston and Peterman were back in action within 10 days. Warren opened the season as the regular catcher, Livingston was the backup and Peterman worked in the bullpen.

On April 27 Peterman was sent to the Williamsport Grays in the Class-A Eastern League. He was paired with Gus Hixson as the catching corps. Bill batted .205 in 200 at-bats. Showing little power again, he had a slugging percentage of .245. In August his draft board changed his status from 3-A to 1-A and told him to report for induction.

Peterman entered the Army on September 9, 1942. He was assigned to the 1301st Service Unit, headquartered at the New Cumberland Reception Center near Harrisburg, Pennsylvania. The facility fielded a powerful baseball squad the next summer with Pat Mullin, Harry Marnie, Bob "Ducky" Detweiler, Paul Minner, and Tommy Hughes among the players. Their only losses were to the Phillies, Senators, Buffalo (International League), and the Homestead Grays.[14]

The team defeated every Army unit it faced and hoped for a late-season series versus the Great Lakes Naval base team. That series never materialized. Joe Lawlor, who had some collegiate coaching experience, was the baseball manager and also coached the Center basketball team. Peterman played basketball in the winter, joined by newly enlisted Elmer Valo. The next year the teams added Ron Northey.

Peterman remained at the Center until January 1945, when he was transferred to service in the China-Burma-India Theater.[15] He returned a year later and was mustered out on January 15, 1946. A month later he signed his Phillies contract and prepared to join 71 other candidates in spring training.[16] One writer noted, "Nobody knows everybody else on the Phillies."[17] Thirteen of Peterman's teammates were returning from military service.

Andy Seminick, who like Bill was 25 years old, and Hal Spindel were the returning catchers. Former catchers Cy Perkins and Benny Bengough were in camp to offer instruction to the receivers.[18] Ben Chapman was the manager and he ran a looser camp than Peterman experienced in 1942 under disciplinarian Lobert. The catchers even put together a calypso singing group that wrote a song about how Bengough lost his hair.[19]

Early in camp, "Bill Peterman, a big brawny rookie prospect[,]" split time with Seminick. Spindel played poorly in camp and management went looking for

ONE-HIT WONDERS

a veteran receiver.[20] On March 25 Rollie Hemsley was purchased from the Yankees. A few days later, Peterman was sent to the minor-league camp. On April 22 he was sent outright to the Utica Blue Sox of the Eastern League.[21]

Peterman opened the season for Eddie Sawyer's team going 2-for 4 with two RBIs in a 5-4 win over Binghamton.[22] The year would prove to be Bill's second most productive offensively as he batted .260 with a .311 slugging percentage for the seventh-place Jays.

Peterman was married to Grace Marie Haber on March 6, 1947. Grace was an Olney graduate (a year behind Bill) and had served as a WAVE during the war. Her brother Bill had played baseball with Peterman in high school.

They left for training camp three days later as Bill joined a Philadelphia Athletics farm club, the Birmingham Barons of the Double-A Southern Association, for 1947. In the preseason it was thought that Peterman and Ed Murtyn would give the team a powerful catching staff.[23] Instead they each lasted less than a month. Peterman was optioned to Lincoln after only 10 games and 27 at-bats.

The Lincoln (Nebraska) A's were in the Class-A Western League and destined for last place. Peterman started hot for the A's but on May 22 he suffered a broken thumb and was sidelined nearly a month. The woeful A's would spend the summer feeling the wrath of their fans. One day Peterman became their target after a bad throw. Later in the game he delivered a single and acknowledged the fans by "doffing his cap as he ambled to first base."[24] It was one of the few times Peterman showed his feelings toward the fans on the diamond.

In December it was announced that Peterman's contract was sold to Montgomery in the Class-B Southeastern League.[25] The Rebels were managed by Frank Skaff and had won the playoffs the previous season. Peterman went to spring training where he split time with John Sosh. Once the season began, Peterman got a couple of starts and went 2-for-9 before his contract was sold to the Augusta Tigers in the Class-A Sally League.

Peterman spent only about 10 days with the Tigers. He went 6-for-19.[26] His last game with the Tigers came on May 7. Three days later he debuted with the Savannah Indians in the same league. There he found himself paired up with Ed Mutryn again. Mutryn played first base and outfield on days that Peterman caught.

Peterman's season ended in late June when he was hit near the left eye by a pitched ball. Grace recalled that it was the "most horrible thing I have seen in my life."[27] It was feared that the injury was so severe he might not play again. "Physicians expressed only faint hopes of saving the eye."[28] As often happens, the fears were exaggerated; he returned to the game the following year.

Peterman was offered the position of player-manager with Moultrie (Georgia) A's in the Class-D Georgia-Florida League. He replaced another former Phillies catcher, Joe Antolick. One sportswriter suggested that the Philadelphia Athletics were requiring minor-league managers to have a Phillies background.[29] To prepare, he and Grace played catch by the hours to improve his eyesight and coordination. Peterman played 31 games with the A's before he removed himself from the active list and concentrated on managing.[30] He had little talent to work with and the team finished 40 games out of first.

The franchise was moved to Cordele, Georgia. For the 1950 season with Peterman again at the helm. He was joined again by second baseman Skeeter Kell, who batted .353. Kell was the only player on Peterman's squads to eventually make it to the majors. Cordele also had a young pitcher named Mike Deitch, who lived only a few miles from Peterman in the offseason. The A's finished in seventh place and Peterman's managing career came to an end when ownership hired former Army teammate Detweiler for the 1951 season.

Bill left baseball after that and went to work as a delivery truck driver, often for grocery chains. He was no longer playing baseball but his love for the game never wavered. He became a steadfast member of the Philadelphia Hot Stove League, which began in 1952. The group held yearly banquets in the winter to get fans and players together to talk baseball and keep the spirit alive.[31]

Living in the Philadelphia area and being a former player gave Peterman opportunities to participate in events with the Phillies like the 100th anniversary. One of his last appearances came in 1998 when he joined former Army teammate Harry Marnie and others at an Alumni Night at the ballpark.

Peterman died on March 13, 1999, just short of his 78th birthday. He had suffered for about a year from prostate cancer. He was buried at the Hillside Cemetery in Roslyn, Pennsylvania. During his life he was often asked about the 1.000 batting average. He once told a reporter, "I get a little embarrassed when my friends talk about that hit. Heck, there are so

ONE-HIT WONDERS

many guys who have played a thousand games, had a thousand times at bat. I only had one."[32]

ACKNOWLEDGMENTS

Minor-league records/standings are courtesy of the *The Encyclopedia of Minor League Baseball*, First edition. Unless noted otherwise, statistics come from Baseball-Reference.com.

NOTES

1. Ralph Bernstein, "Phils Plan Birthday Celebrations; Will Peterman Deliver?" *Daily American* (Somerset, Pennsylvania), February 10, 1983: 16. Peterman would have thrown out the first pitch if Enzmann had been unavailable.
2. "Phils to Celebrate 100th Season," *Daily Item* (Sunbury, Pennsylvania), February 10, 1983: 31.
3. "Phils to Celebrate 100th Season."
4. Bernstein.
5. Ted Silary, "Carillo's Performance Leads to Semi-Sweet Win," *Philadelphia Daily News*, May 30, 1997: 124.
6. "Stonehurst to Meet Villagers in Scribes Play," *Delaware County Daily Times* (Chester, Pennsylvania), September 21, 1939: 23.
7. "Double-O's Win, Oswego Stays for Winter Park Today," *Ogdensburg* (New York) *Advance News*, July 3, 1940: 9.
8. "Double-O's Rout Roman in Double-Header Games at Ottawa Park Yesterday," *Ogdensburg Advance News*, July 17, 1940: 13.
9. *Sporting News Official Baseball Record Book* (St. Louis: The Sporting News, 1942), 351-356.
10. "Bears Rightfielder Second in Northern League Batting Race," *Leader-Telegram* (Eau Claire, Wisconsin): 10.
11. "Wausau Whips All-Star Team, 11-7," *Leader-Telegram*, July 22, 1941: 6.
12. How They're Batting in the Playoffs," *Leader-Telegram*, September 17, 1941: 10.
13. "Phils Recall Farm Players," *Winnipeg Tribune*, August 23, 1941: 19.
14. William G. Smock, "Tom Hughes' Team Claims Service crown," *Times Leader, The Evening News* (Wilkes-Barre, Pennsylvania), August 12, 1943: 15.
15. Mel Antonen, "The Time of Their Lives," *USA Today*, December 29, 1999. Located in Peterman's Hall of Fame file.
16. "Phils Sign Hodkey," *Times-Tribune* (Scranton, Pennsylvania), February 20, 1946: 16.
17. Harry Grayson, "Nobody Knows Everybody Else on the Phillies," *Trenton Evening Times*, March 10, 1946: 15.
18. Grayson.
19. Art Morrow, "Vaudeville Back (Phillies Version)," *Philadelphia Inquirer*, March 24, 1946: 34.
20. John McMullan, "Phils Seek Lamano or Lakeman of the Reds," *Miami News*, March 5, 1946: 9.
21. From Peterman's file at the Baseball Hall of Fame.
22. "6,000 See Trips Lose Opener, 5-4, Despite 2 Homers," *Press-Sun Bulletin* (Binghamton, New York), May 2, 1946: 22.
23. Leroy Simms, "Barons Plead for More Help," *Montgomery* (Alabama) *Advertiser*, April 3, 1947: 12.
24. Walt Dobbins, "I Could Be Wrong," *Lincoln* (Nebraska) *Journal Star*, July 10, 1947: 10.
25. *Sioux City* (Iowa) *Journal*, December 5, 1947: 19.
26. "Tiger Averages," *Augusta* (Georgia) *Chronicle*, May 11, 1948: 5.
27. Antonen.
28. *Lincoln Journal Star*, July 6, 1948: 10.
29. Fred Pettijohn, "In the Pressbox," *Tallahassee Democrat*, January 25, 1949: 6.
30. Fred Pettijohn, "In the Pressbox," *Tallahassee Democrat*, June 17, 1949: 11.
31. Edgar Williams, "The Scene," *Philadelphia Inquirer*, January 8, 1994: 14.
32. Bernstein.

DAN PLESAC

By Paul Hofmann

A three-time All-Star with the Milwaukee Brewers, Dan Plesac was a left-handed pitcher with a mid-90s fastball and a biting slider who became one of the game's dominant closers during the late 1980s. In addition to the time spent with the Brewers, Plesac's 18-year major-league career included stints with the Chicago Cubs, Pittsburgh Pirates, Toronto Blue Jays, Arizona Diamondbacks, and Philadelphia Phillies.

Daniel Thomas Plesac was born on February 4, 1962, in Gary, Indiana. He was the second of three sons of Joseph and Gloria Plesac. Joseph was a veteran of the US Navy and a steelworker at the Inland Steel Company.[1] He passionately enjoyed racing and training standardbred harness horses, and was a lifetime member of the Illinois Harness Racing Association.[2] Joseph's love for horses was later shared by Dan. Gloria was a hairdresser who later owned a salon in Crown Point, Indiana. Dan's brother Joe, who was a year older, was also a baseball player. Joe had a younger brother named Ronald.

Joe was recruited to play baseball at North Carolina State University. A right-handed pitcher, he was a two-time first-team All-ACC selection (1980 and 1981) who was drafted in the second round of the June 1982 amateur draft by the San Diego Padres. He advanced as far as Double-A. He finished his professional career in 1987 with a career record of 19-31 and a 6.18 ERA. Joe's son, and Dan's nephew, is Zach Plesac, a right-handed starting pitcher who broke into the majors with the Cleveland Indians in 2019. Dan started playing baseball with Gary's East Glen Park Little League.[3] He attended Andrean High School in Merrillville, a Gary suburb, for two years. After his sophomore year, the family moved to Crown Point, a city 17 miles south of Gary. He attended Crown Point High School for his final two years and graduated in 1980.

Plesac was an all-around athlete in high school. He played baseball, football, and basketball, and ran track. However, baseball was not his first love. According to Plesac, "I certainly didn't think my life was headed toward baseball. Basketball was my sport, and baseball was something I did in the spring to get busy."[4] In fact, he signed a national letter of intent to play basketball for North Carolina State. All this changed when Crown Point baseball coach Dick Webb asked Dan if he would be willing to pitch.

Plesac spent his junior and senior baseball seasons primarily patrolling the outfield and playing first base for the Crown Point Bulldogs when Webb approached him about pitching. "He said, 'Listen, we have a pretty good team but don't have any pitching, would you want to pitch?'" Plesac recalled. "I said alright, but I had no training and no idea what I was doing. Then one game turned into 15 strikeouts, then another game, and the next thing you know I'm the 41st player taken

ONE-HIT WONDERS

in the 1980 draft, by the St. Louis Cardinals."[5] The Cardinals selected Plesac in the second round.

Perhaps surprisingly to some, he did not sign with the Cardinals and decided to attend North Carolina State, with one small change – his scholarship was transferred to baseball. Reflecting back on the decision, Plesac said, "It wasn't as difficult a decision as you might think, because I just didn't have any idea what I was doing in baseball. Kids today are so far advanced compared to where I was in terms of mechanics. I really hadn't pitched that much, I felt like I needed to go to college to learn more about pitching. I don't think I'd have reached the big leagues if I'd signed with the Cardinals."[6]

While at North Carolina State, Plesac earned Second Team All-ACC honors during his freshman year (1981). After his junior year, 1983, he was selected in the first round (26th overall) by the Milwaukee Brewers and started his professional career with the Paintsville (Kentucky) Brewers of the Rookie Appalachian League. In 14 starts, he went 9-1 with a 3.50 ERA and struck out 85 in 82⅓ innings pitched. His nine victories led all hurlers in the circuit.

On July 28 Plesac came within one out of throwing a seven-inning no-hitter against the Pikesville (Kentucky) Cubs. Pikesville outfielder John Turner ended the no-hit bid with an RBI single as the Brewers beat the Cubs, 4-1, on a pair of two-run home runs, one of them hit by future major leaguer Glenn Braggs.[7]

Plesac started 1984 with the Stockton Ports of the Class-A California League. He made 16 starts for the Ports and was 6-6 with a 3.32 ERA before being promoted to the El Paso Diablos of the Double-A Texas League. Plesac made seven starts for the Diablos and finished 2-2 with a 3.46 ERA. He returned to El Paso in 1985 and in 25 games (24 as a starter) he went 12-5 with a 4.97 ERA.

Plesac made the Brewers roster out of spring training in 1986 and made his major-league debut on April 11, 1986, at Yankee Stadium, when he relieved starter Bill Wegman with two outs in the bottom of the sixth inning. With runners on first and second, he struck out the first batter he faced, Mike Pagliarulo, who had hit a two-run home run off Wegman in the bottom of the fourth. Plesac pitched 2⅓ innings of scoreless baseball and gave up only a harmless single in the Brewers' 3-2 loss.

One week later Plesac earned his first major-league victory, at County Stadium in Milwaukee. Entering the game in relief of Wegman with the Brewers trailing the Yankees, 5-2, Plesac pitched four innings of no-hit baseball as the Brewers rallied for three runs in the seventh and one in the eighth to win, 6-5.

Plesac finished his rookie season with a career-high 10 victories to go along with a 2.97 ERA. His 14 saves were two fewer than the 16 recorded by Brewers closer Mark Clear. He did not garner a single vote for American League Rookie of the Year, but was named to the *Baseball Digest* 1986 Rookie All-Star Team, and the future looked very bright for the 24-year-old.

It was during his rookie year that Plesac received sage life advice from a Brewers teammate. "Robin Yount, a teammate of mine my rookie year who's now in the National Hall of Fame, said something to me one day in the outfield that really resonated with me. He said, 'You know Dan, it's nice to be important, but it's more important to be nice.'"[8] It was advice he said he took to heart.

After Plesac's rookie year, he began dating Leslie Caufield, a friend back at Crown Point High School. On January 9, 1988, they were married. They had two daughters, Madeline and Natalie. In 2005, after nearly 18 years of marriage, the Plesacs divorced. According to Leslie, it simply became too difficult to balance the needs of her family with the demands of her husband's professional baseball career. "I tried to hang on to me, but it was tough to do in the fast-paced life that required Dan to be gone nine months a year."[9]

The Brewers and Plesac got off to a hot start in 1987. The team won its first 13 games, tying the major-league record for consecutive wins to the start the season.[10] Plesac, who by this time had moved into the closer role, earned his fifth save in the record-tying victory and saved seven in all during the month of April. By the end of June, Plesac was 4-0 with 16 saves and a minuscule 1.29 ERA. His performance during the first half of the season earned him a spot on the American League All-Star team.

Plesac made his All-Star Game debut on July 14 at the Oakland-Alameda County Coliseum when he pitched the top of the eighth inning. He tossed a one-two-three inning, retiring Bo Díaz on a fly to right, getting Dale Murphy on a pop foul, and striking out Hubie Brooks. The National League All-Stars went on to win the game 2-0 in 13 innings.

After the All-Star break, Plesac, who never suffered a major injury or spent time on the disabled list, went 1-4 with five saves, a 3.72 ERA, and eight blown saves. The fall-off, in part, was attributed to a sore left elbow he injured on August 19 when he ran into the outfield wall while shagging fly balls.[11] He finished the season with a record of 5-6, 23 saves, and a 2.61 ERA. After the Brewers' hot start, they finished in third place in the American League East with a record of 91-71.

Plesac's 1988 season followed a similar pattern as the previous year. He was 1-1 with 22 saves and a 2.08 ERA at the All-Star break, earning his second consecutive spot on the American League squad. With two outs in the top of the eighth, he was brought on to face Darryl Strawberry, who stuck out to end the inning. The American League hung on for a 2-1 victory at Cincinnati's Riverfront Stadium.

Plesac appeared to be on pace to break the franchise's record for saves in a season – 31 by Ken Sanders in 1971 – when tendinitis in his left shoulder limited him to eight appearances over the last two months of the season. He finished the year with a record of 1-2, 30 saves, and a 2.41 ERA.

In 1989 Plesac did break the record, recording a career-high 33 saves to go along with a 3-4 record and a career-best 2.35 ERA. His record-setting 32nd save came against the Toronto Blue Jays on September 23 at County Stadium. Coming on in relief of Chuck Crim with two out in the bottom of the ninth, he retired Fred McGriff on a fly ball to left to end the game.

Plesac made his third and final All-Star Game appearance on July 11 at Anaheim Stadium. With runners on first and second and two down in the top of the eighth inning, manager Tony LaRussa called on him to relieve Texas Rangers right-hander Jeff Russell. Left-handed-hitting Von Hayes greeted Pleasc with a single to left to drive in Alvin Davis and cut the American League's lead to 5-3. Doug Jones relieved Plesac to record the last out of the inning, on his way to a four-out save.

After his three consecutive All-Star seasons, Plesac's productivity as a closer began to diminish during the 1990 season. That year he blew 10 of 34 save opportunities, his record slipped to 3-7, and his ERA ballooned to 4.43, nearly two runs higher than his career ERA coming into the season.

He did little better in 1991, finishing with a record of 2-7 and a 4.29 ERA while converting only eight saves in 12 opportunities. Closing games requires a pitcher to throw often and by the end of the season, Plesac admitted that his arm wasn't bouncing back from one outing to the next as it had earlier in his career.[12] After 311 consecutive relief appearances, Plesac attempted to reinvent himself as a starting pitcher. He made 10 starts to close out the season and went 2-3 with a 4.69 ERA.

On September 14, in the sixth of these starts, he found himself on the wrong side of history. The Tigers and Brewers were scoreless at the end of three innings when Cecil Fielder, who was on his way to hitting 44 home runs after hitting 51 the year before, led off the top of the fourth against Plesac. Swinging at the first pitch, Fielder drove the ball over the left-field bleachers, completely out of the ballpark. The home run was estimated to have carried 520 feet and was the only one to completely leave County Stadium in left.[13] Years later Plesac laughed about it saying, "It was an absolute bomb."[14]

Entering the final year of his contract with the Brewers, Plesac came to spring training in 1992 hoping to contend for the fourth spot in the starting rotation. But he struggled with his mechanics throughout the spring, and spent most of the season in the bullpen. In 44 games, 4 as a starter, he finished with a record of 5-4 and a 2.96 ERA. On September 4 he nailed down a 6-3 victory over the Detroit Tigers for his final save with the Brewers. As of 2021 his 133 saves remained the franchise record.

No longer a dominant closer, Plesac found a new home as a member of the Chicago Cubs bullpen when on December 8, 1992, he signed a two-year, $3.2 million contract. The situation seemed ideal for Plesac because it allowed him to pitch close to home. "The perfect scenario would have been for me to come here and play in Chicago, and it's come true. It almost seems too good to be true," the 30-year-old said.[15]

According to agent Tom Selakovich, both the Texas Rangers and Pittsburgh Pirates showed interest in signing Plesac. However, once the Cubs made an offer, talks with the other two suitors came to an end. Acknowledging that he might have sacrificed more lucrative offers, Plesac rationalized his decision by stating, "This is where I want to be."[16]

Plesac's two-year tenure with the Cubs did not live up to expectations. In 1993 he appeared in 57 games and went 2-1 with a 4.74 ERA. He followed that up with a 2-3 record and 4.61 ERA during the strike-shortened 1994 season. He recorded his only save with the Cubs on July 20, 1994, when he relieved José Bautista in the bottom of the ninth with the Cubs clinging to a 9-8 lead. With runners on first and third and two down, Plesac struck out pinch-hitter Vinny Castilla to end the game.

After not being offered arbitration, Plesac rejected a one-year offer by the Cubs and signed a two-year, $1.8 million contract with the Pittsburgh Pirates. The Pirates felt Plesac would provide stability to a young and often erratic bullpen that lacked a proven veteran arm.[17]

ONE-HIT WONDERS

Plesac was primarily used as a set-up man and situational left-hander with the Pirates. In 1995 he pitched in 58 games and finished with a record of 4-4 with three saves and a 3.58 ERA. This was also the season that he joined the unique "One-Hit Wonders" club.

Plesac's lone major-league hit came on August 12 in a wild game against Los Angeles at Dodger Stadium in which the two teams combined for 39 hits. The 6-foot-5-inch Plesac came on in relief of Esteban Loaiza with runners on first and second and one out in the bottom of the sixth and the Pirates ahead 7-4. Plesac quickly got out of the inning by striking out pinch-hitter Billy Ashley and center fielder Mitch Webster. Rather than lift Plesac for a pinch-hitter with one out in the top of the seventh, Pirates manager Jim Leyland allowed the left-handed-hitting pitcher to bat. Using a bat he borrowed from backup rookie first baseman Mark Johnson and swinging on the first pitch, Plesac sliced a single down the left-field line off left-hander John Cummings. The Dodgers rallied from three down in the bottom of the 10th, after tying the game in the bottom of the ninth, and beat the Pirates 11-10 in 11 innings. Plesac finished his career 1-for-15 at plate (.067).

In 1996 Plesac had an expanded role with the Pirates. He appeared in 73 games and went 6-5 with a 4.09 ERA and 11 saves, as he split the closer duties with rookie right-hander Francisco Cordova. It was the last year Plesac recorded double-digit saves.

After the season Plesac was traded with infielder Carlos Garcia and outfielder-first baseman Orlando Merced to the Toronto Blue Jays for Craig Wilson, Abraham Núñez, José Silva, and three minor leaguers. The nine-player deal was the Pirates' biggest since the 10-player deal that sent future Hall of Famer Ralph Kiner to the Chicago Cubs in June of 1953.[18] While the Pirates were able to shed payroll in a much-needed cost-cutting move, the Blue Jays didn't get much out of the trade. Only Plesac was with the team beyond 1997.

The Blue Jays used Plesac exclusively as a left-handed specialist – a role he occupied during the remainder of his career – frequently called upon to retire one hitter or to finish an inning. In 1997 he went 2-4 with a 3.58 ERA and one save. In 1998 Plesac appeared in a career-high (and franchise record for left-handed pitchers) 78 games. He finished with record of 4-3, a 3.78 ERA, and four saves.

Plesac got off to a rocky start in 1999 and never seemed to get on track. His record was 0-3 with an 8.34 ERA – despite holding left-handed hitters to a .186 average – when on June 12, the Blue Jays traded him to the Arizona Diamondbacks for infielder Tony Batista and right-handed pitcher John Frascatore.[19] The Diamondbacks were in need of a second left-hander in the bullpen and just like that, Plesac went from a third-place team, 10 games out of first place in the AL East, to a first-place team with a two-game lead in the NL West. In 34 games with the Diamondbacks, Plesac went 2-1 with a 3.32 ERA and one save to help the team win the division title with a record of 100-62.

Plesac had his first and only taste of postseason baseball when the Diamondbacks faced the New York Mets in the National League Division Series. Plesac made one appearance in the series. The Diamondbacks were trailing 4-2 in Game Three with one out and the bases loaded in the bottom of sixth when Plesac came on in relief of right-hander Darren Holmes to face left-handed-hitting John Olerud. Olerud singled to right, scoring Bobby Bonilla and Rickey Henderson. Roger Cedeño followed with a single to left, driving in Edgardo Alfonzo as Olerud took third. Cedeño stole second and both runners held when Robin Ventura grounded out to second. Darryl Hamilton then singled to center to score Olerud and Cedeno, prompting Diamondbacks manager Buck Showalter to remove Plesac. In what seemed like a heartbeat, the Mets' lead increased to 9-2. Plesac never appeared in another postseason game.

Plesac returned to the Diamondbacks in 2000 and enjoyed a solid season. In 62 games he went 5-1 with a 3.15 ERA as the team finished in third place in the NL West. After the season he signed a two-year, $4.4 million contact with the Blue Jays and returned to Toronto.

Plesac went 4-5 with a 3.57 ERA and one save for a Blue Jays team that was, at best, mediocre in 2001. In 2002 he was 1-2 with a 3.38 ERA when he was traded once again. This time the Blue Jays sent him to the Philadelphia Phillies in exchange for right-handed pitcher Cliff Politte. In 41 games with the Phillies, Plesac was 2-1 with a 4.70 ERA.

For Plesac, the highlight of that season may have come at Veterans Stadium in a game against the Montreal Expos on August 28. That night he became just the seventh major-league pitcher to pitch in 1,000 games. After the game Plesac thanked Phillies manager Larry Bowa for allowing him to reach the milestone. "I appreciate Larry giving me the opportunity to get there," a grateful Plesac said. "With the possible work stoppage and rain forecast for [Thursday], this was a unique situation and he wanted to make sure I had the opportunity. I can't thank him enough."[20] The only thing that spoiled the evening was that the Expos beat the Phillies, 6-3.

As it turned out, 2002 was not Plesac's final season. Now 41 years old, he returned for one more season with the Phillies. In 58 appearances, he was 2-1 with a 2.70 ERA and two saves. On September 28, in the final game of the season, Plesac stuck out Ryan Langerhans to record the last out in the top of the ninth of the Phillies' 5-2 loss to the Atlanta Braves. In doing so, Plesac became the last Phillies pitcher to pitch at Veterans Stadium. At the end of the season, he retired as a player.

In 2009 Plesac reflected on his decision to retire and the time he spent in Philadelphia. "When I put the glove and bat down for the last time, I knew it was time to walk away," he said. "I will always have special ties to the Phillies. Part of me wishes I'd played all my 18 seasons in Philadelphia. It's a tough place, but they are the most passionate, loyal sports fans in America. That was part of what I liked so much about playing there. You knew you were accountable for what you did on the field."[21]

Pleasc finished his career with 1,064 games pitched, seventh-most all time as of 2021, a record of 65-71, 158 saves, and a 3.64 ERA. His longevity and durability were hallmarks of his career.

After retiring, Plesac returned to a passion he inherited from his father and became a trainer of standardbred harness horses. In 2009 he estimated that he had owned all or part of 150 horses since 1982.[22]

Plesac began a broadcasting career in 2005. He said the transition to broadcasting was a natural one for him. He worked as a news telecaster for Comcast Sportsnet Chicago, co-hosting the Chicago Cubs and pregame and postgame shows from 2005 until the end of the 2008 season. Plesac joined the MLB Network as an analyst in January 2009. He also worked as a broadcaster for the *MLB: The Show* video game franchise.

SOURCES

In addition to the sources cited in the Notes, the author relied on Baseball-reference.com and Retrosheet.org.

NOTES

1. Joseph F. Plesac. Retrieved from legacy.com/obituaries/post-tribune/obituary.aspx?n=joseph-f-plesac&pid=117526256&fhid=4991.

2. Joseph F. Plesac.

3. Curtis Hankins, "A Northwest Indiana Life in the Spotlight: Dan Plesac," *NWI Life* (Munster, Indiana), March 11, 2020. Retrieved from nwi.life/article/a-northwest-indiana-life-in-the-spotlight-dan-plesac/.

4. Paul Trambacki, "Plesac Pleased to Be Back at Crown Point," *NWI Times* (Munster, Indiana), May 15, 2004. Reitrved from nwitimes.com/sports/plesac-pleased-to-be-back-at-crown-point/article_9e0ef28f-9cb4-5cac-925c-1c7c2fdf3bed.html.

5. Hankins.

6. Hankins.

7. Turner ended a no-hit bid by Bristol's Joe Perrotte with a lead-off single in the bottom of the seventh inning of the opener that evening, a 7-1 victory by Bristol over Pikesville.

8. Hankins.

9. Leslie Plesac, "About Me," retrieved from leslieplesac.com.

10. The 1982 Atlanta Braves were the first team to open a season with 13 consecutive wins.

11. Rick Gano, "Plesac's Aching Elbow Keeps Him on Sidelines," *Fond Du Lac* (Wisconsin) *Commonwealth Reporter*, September 9, 1987: 17.

12. Rick Gano, "Plesac Hoping to Land Fourth Spot in the Rotation," *Daily Citizen* (Beaver Creek, Wisconsin), March 28, 1992: 13.

13. Chip Greene, "September 14, 1991: When Cecil Fielder's Home Run Left the Park," in G. Wolf (Ed.), *From Braves to Brewers: Great Games and Exciting History at Milwaukee's County Stadium* (Phoenix: Society for American Baseball Research, 2015), 228.

14. Mike Heller, "WATCH: Cecil Fielders Home Run Out of County Stadium in 1991." Retrieved from foxsports1070.iheart.com/featured/the-mike-heller-show/content/2017-05-26-watch-cecil-fielders-home-run-out-of-county-stadium-in-1991/.

15. Alan Solomon, "Cubs Staff Bolstered by Plesac," *Chicago Tribune*, December 9, 1992: 67.

16. Solomon.

17. "The Press Box: Plesac Goes to Pirates," *Chicago Tribune*, November 90, 1994: 60.

18. Paul Meyer, "Payroll Savings Plan," *Pittsburgh Post-Gazette*, November 15, 1996: 40.

19. Jack Magruder, "Diamondbacks Trade for Plesac," *Arizona Daily Star* (Tucson), June 13, 1999: 31.

20. Sam Carchidi, "A Long Night Ends with a Defeat," *Philadelphia Inquirer*, August 29, 2002: E01.

21. Nicole Kraft, "Ex-Phillies Reliever's Greatest Save," *Philadelphia Inquirer*, November 28, 2009. Retrieved from inquirer.com/philly/sports/phillies/20091128_Ex-Phillies_reliever_s_greatest_save.html.

22. Kraft.

BOB POSER

By Henry Berman, MD

Fewer than 30 major-league players have gone on to be physicians; half of those were pitchers. Several had noteworthy accomplishments. John Lee Richmond pitched the first perfect game in professional baseball history, in 1880; and Hub Pruett faced Babe Ruth on 30 occasions between 1922 and 1924, striking him out 11 or 12 times.[1]

Richmond had an unusual career. He graduated from Brown University four days after his perfect game and finished his first year with a won-lost record of 32-32 and an ERA of 2.15. [He was the first left-hander to win 30 games.] In both 1881 and 1882 he pitched over 400 innings. In 1883 he experienced arm problems and was primarily an outfielder. He then retired. Pruett, on the other hand, seems to have struggled except when he faced Ruth. He won 29 and lost 48 with an ERA of 4.63.

The careers of most of the pitchers who became physicians were similar to that of Pruett – 75 percent had losing records. The best of them is Doc Medich; he won 124 and lost 105 with an ERA of 3.78 and a WAR of 19.6 At the other end of the spectrum is Bob Poser. Poser pitched two-thirds of an inning in 1932 (with an ERA of 27.00) and another 13⅔ innings in 1935 (with an ERA of 9.22).

Baseball proved to be a very small part of Poser's life.

John Falk "Bob" Poser was born in Columbus, Wisconsin, on March 16, 1910. His father, Eduard, originally a pharmacist, had graduated from Rush Medical School in 1895. He then moved to Columbus to establish the Poser Clinic. Bob's mother, Adele, daughter of a pharmacist, had four boys on her hands – three future doctors, and one future lawyer.

In 1932, after graduating from the University of Wisconsin, where he had led his team to the Big Ten championship with a league-leading .432 batting average, Bob made his debut with the Chicago White Sox. He had negotiated with both the owner of the White Sox, Charles Comiskey, and his finance officer, Harry Grabiner, for a signing bonus of $1,500 and a salary of $500 per month.[2] Luke Appling, a future Hall of Famer, was his roommate on the road.

Poser's White Sox pitching career consisted of only two-thirds of an inning, in 1932; he gave up two runs on three hits and two walks. The commentary accompanying the box score noted, "In the eighth, Poser and (Archie) McKain were reached for seven hits and as many runs as 13 Indians went to the plate."[3] Poser also played one inning in the outfield and pinch-hit four times, with three outs and one walk. In one of the games he pinch-hit for future Hall of Fame pitcher Red Faber. His minimal appearances are likely secondary to his suffering a severe hamstring injury in spring training that interfered with his hitting, leading to him switching to pitching.

Bob Poser.

Courtesy of Ann Poser.

ONE-HIT WONDERS

Bob then spent several years in the minor leagues. He went from the White Sox to Double-A Toronto, in the International League, where he was in 23 games, with 11 hits in 64 at-bats, for a .172 average, with four RBIs. He pitched in five of those games – two of them complete games. In 23 innings, he gave up 19 runs on 31 hits and eight walks. Poser finished the year at Double-A[4] Minneapolis, in the American Association, where he had three at-bats with no hits.

Bob began the 1933 season at Minneapolis, where had no hits in six at-bats. As a pitcher he appeared in four games, throwing nine innings and giving up 12 runs, all earned, on 18 hits and two walks. He struck out one batter. He was interviewed about his 1933 teammate, Joe Hauser, in *Voices from the Pastime*.[5] His interviewer said: "Joseph John Hauser hit more than 60 home runs in two minor-league seasons with the Minneapolis Millers. His best season was in 1933 when he hit 69 home runs, drove in 182 runs, and batted .332. Prior to that phenomenal feat he hit 63 round-trippers in 1930. Bob Poser (AL pitcher, 1932 and 1935) remembers Hauser from their days playing in the minor leagues. 'He was one of the first power hitters I had ever seen who used a lightweight bat,' he said. 'Joe used a 31 oz. bat, which was unusual back then. Just as a reference, Babe Ruth used [a] 52 oz. bat before August, then switched to a 49 oz. bat late in the season.'"[6]

Poser then played for Des Moines of the Class-A Western League, where he hit in 12 games, going 13-for-28, for a batting average of .464. In a 1996 interview with Rick Bradley of the SABR Oral History Committee, he said, "I hit a double my first time up. I hadn't played ball, and hadn't run bases, and I got my feet mixed up and didn't touch first base or I would have hit .500 – 14 for 28."[7] He was 3-1 as a pitcher there, with an RA9 (runs average per 9 innings; no ERA is listed in Baseball Reference) of 4.06. Poser also spent 1934 with Des Moines, playing in 54 games with a batting of .289 and a 3-5 record as a pitcher, with an RA9 of 5.74.

In 1934 Poser left baseball and returned to the University of Wisconsin Medical School, joining his brother, Chub (whose given name was Rolf. He was a chubby baby and got stuck with that name); while in school Bob coached the university's baseball team. In August of 1935 Poser learned that Rogers Hornsby, the manager of the St. Louis Browns, was looking for a relief pitcher. Hornsby signed him for $1,650. While with the Browns, he pitched right-handed (and batted left-handed).[8]

Poser's record with the Browns consisted of pitching in four games, a total of 13⅔ innings, giving up 15 runs (14 earned) on 26 hits and four walks (and just one strikeout) for an ERA of 9.22. His six plate appearances garnered one walk, one sacrifice, one strikeout, and only one base hit, a single in the first game of an August 27 doubleheader against the visiting Washington Senators. Combining both the White Sox and Browns, his career ERA was 10.05 with a batting average of .143.

A post in the *Pecan Park Eagle* read, "In these 52 annual attendance figures from Baseball Almanac, pay special notice to how bad things got during the Great Depression years. 1935 was their worst year. The Browns drew only 80,922 fans for the season in 1935. To say the least, their per game average of 1,044 fans was both abysmal and unsustainable by today's financial needs. The Browns' fans had little to cheer in the 1930s."[9]

This chart shows why:

Year	Wins	Losses
1930	64	90
1931	63	91
1932	63	91
1933	55	96
1934	67	85
1935	65	87
1936	57	95
1937	46	108
1938	55	97
1939	43	111

The *New York Times* obituary (February 28, 2017) of Ned Garver – one of the best pitchers in the history of the Browns franchise – included Garver's famous comment: "The crowd didn't dare boo us," Garver once said of his nearly five seasons with the lowly Browns before sparse crowds at Sportsman's Park, which they shared with the popular Cardinals. "The players had them outnumbered."

Sam Poser, Bob's nephew, noted that his uncle's only starting-pitcher assignment came on August 20, 1935, in the second game of a doubleheader against the Boston Red Sox.[10] His fellow pitchers noticed that Boston was starting Lefty Grove – considered by most the best lefty in history.[11] Bob's teammates were kind enough to suggest to Hornsby that it would be best to start the rookie, Bob Poser, against one of best pitchers of all time, and he did. Bob got the 7-3 loss, his only loss in the majors. He pitched two innings, giving up four runs, all earned, on six hits. The commentary accompanying the box score for the game states: "Hornsby started his recruit, Bob Poser, in the second game against Grove, but erratic support handicapped the youngster, and he was driven out in the third."[12]

All in all, Bob Poser played *with* three future Hall of Famers, and *against* teams with another 12.[13] He also had a brief interchange with another future Hall of Famer: Babe Ruth. "I had been writing to Babe Ruth since I was 10 years old. He never answered me because he probably got 1,000 letters a day. But I said I'll meet him, and the Sox always had a dozen or two baseballs the players could take and give for autographs. I took one out and Babe Ruth came in and there was a seat next to him and I sat down next to him and I said, 'Babe, would you please autograph this ball for me?' And he said, 'Sure, kid.' (I was just a kid to him. I was 22.) So he did. I had my own pen – as I remember I had green ink in one of these fountain pens. He talked to me; I shook hands with him; I brought the ball home. It was sitting in a vase on my mantel from 1932 to at least 1945. When I came back out of the Army it was gone."[14]

Bob Poser's father, Eduard, had been a standout second baseman for his medical school team – he was given a tryout by the Chicago Cubs in 1892. In 1895, after completing medical school at Rush Medical School, he moved to Columbus, Wisconsin (population 2,350 at the time, now 5,000) to open a practice – the Poser Clinic. His office was on the second floor, above the Sharrow drugstore. After more than 50 years his sons, Bob and Chub, built the present Poser Clinic.

In the 1996 interview with Rick Bradley for the SABR oral history project, Bob explained why he was named John, but was always called Bob. His mother loved curly hair (the way Shirley Temple's hair looked 18 years later). So she did not cut his hair for two or three years. When Bob ran – he always ran – his hair bobbed, earning him the nickname Bobby.[15]

Bob's wife, Libby, said that he was fearless. His first day of kindergarten he said to his teacher, "I'm not afraid of tigers, I'm not afraid of lions, and I'm not afraid of you."[16]

In a 1999 interview with a local journalist, Poser stated: "I started getting interested in baseball ... (and) at age ten or eleven, I started writing different ballplayers ... I still have the letters that they wrote back to me."[17] Some of the players did more than write back, some even visited Columbus to see the young fan who had written them. "Gabby Hartnett was the catcher for the Cubs. He was the best catcher in baseball without a doubt, at that time at least, and he called me up one night after I had written him," Poser explained. "I thought it was my brother Pody at first because he was interning there in Chicago at the time. I remember Gabby said, in a loud voice, 'Hi, yeah I'm Gabby, want me to come up to Columbus to visit?' I was a bit tongue-tied, but I said 'yes.'

"They had a night train at 11:00 P.M. and I went down to the station to meet him. The train eased to a stop. I could not believe it when he actually got off the train – he stayed with us for a couple of days." Years later, Gabby returned and the two of them played golf at Maple Bluff Country Club in Madison. Poser remembered, "When we got done with our game, everybody swarmed around him, even Oscar Mayer."[18]

Poser and Hartnett developed a close relationship over the years. In August of 1924, Hartnett responded to a letter he had received from Poser by telling him that if he came to Chicago, he would like to meet him – an admirer. A year or two later Hartnett responded to another letter from Poser that promised him (whom he now addressed as Bobby) that he had sent him a baseball autographed by all the Cubs players – and in the future he would send him "all the baseballs he would want."[19]

Later, Hartnett gave Poser inspiration and winning advice. "Gabby told me that I was a pretty good ballplayer for a kid and he gave me some pointers like putting the thumb underneath the fingers in the catcher's mitt and keeping the throwing hand near the catching hand. Gabby was real good. He had a powerful arm so they had trouble hanging on to the ball when he threw it."

In 1935, when Poser was playing for the Browns, he went through Chicago and spent some time in Hartnett's apartment. "Gabby talked about when he was playing the Yankees in the 1932 World Series and the Yankees beat the Cubs. That was when Babe Ruth was supposed to have 'pointed' a home run. He didn't. He was pointing at Root, who was pitching. What he meant was, 'Two strikes, Root. I can hit one yet.' And the crowd wanted to say he was pointing to the center field bleachers.

"Gabby told me he didn't. (He) was sitting there. 'No, he didn't (point to the bleachers).' He was just saying I got two strikes, but nobody can ever believe it because people want to say he pointed for a home run. Babe Ruth never denied it, but he couldn't really. It's a good story. He didn't say he did though, either. But Gabby did tell me and I told some people – a statistician, and they said we know that, too, but you can't change the public's mind. One of the photographers who gave me a lot of pictures of my big-league life was sitting from here to the door to take pictures. He was sort of in the batter's box and he said, 'I didn't hear Babe Ruth say that and I heard him talking.'"[20]

Hartnett followed Poser's career closely. Poser later said, "I was proud of the fact that I was a good hitter. We beat Northwestern once there. A big score and I got four hits and four runs at four times at bat and I was tickled because I knew Gabby Hartnett would see the score and, sure enough, I called him that day (we were pretty good friends) and he said, 'Pretty good day, huh?'"[21]

When Bob was a junior in medical school, he became the University of Wisconsin baseball coach. "I was head coach at UW while in med school, for $1,000 a year. We would have won the Big Ten but we went to Peoria and I wanted three pitchers to pitch. My brother was a junior, and he had been pitching, but he quit because he said he had a sore arm. He didn't really because he went to play softball instead. I think he didn't like me coaching him."[22]

After finishing school and his stint with the Browns, Poser attended St Luke's Hospital in Chicago as an intern, went back to the University of Wisconsin for two years of general surgery, and then transferred to Chicago's Cook County Hospital to finish general surgery. When he could, he pitched batting practice for both the White Sox and the Cubs – where Gabby Hartnett was the manager. "Gabby later became manager of the Cubs, and when I was interning at St. Luke's in Chicago, I had every fourth afternoon off; if the Cubs were in town I'd pitch batting practice for them. I'd put on a Cubs suit; same thing for the Sox. And all those Cubs and Sox players were my friends. That was quite a way to grow up. I think I could have gone back with the Sox after internship, pitching, but I didn't. I went home and practiced medicine."[23]

With 1½ years left in his surgical program at Cook County, he was drafted into the Army as a captain and was sent to Carlisle, Pennsylvania, for basic training during World War II. Although he expected to be sent to Europe, by the time he finished his training the military had concluded that the war in Europe would be won soon, and there was a greater need for physicians to treat wounded veterans who had returned from the war. Poser was assigned to Kellogg Hospital, in Battle Creek, Michigan, treating vets with peripheral nerve injuries; he was subsequently transferred to Atlanta to care for vets with paraplegia.

Poser explained, "In Atlanta, I was stationed at Lawson General Hospital. … They had 3,000 patients; I had 60 of them to take care of. And Luke Appling, my best friend – along with Ted Lyons – when I was with the White Sox, was my sergeant in charge of those 60 patients. Luke and I played ball – they had a good ballclub down there. They knew I played ball and asked if I'd come out, so Luke and I played on the same Army team. I hit .384 and Luke hit 392. I used to kid him about how I could outhit him, but he wrote me, "Here are the averages," and said, "Bob, I can out hit YOU!"[24]

When he was a resident, Bob met his future wife, Ibby, on a blind date – she was a junior at the University of Wisconsin. She said she really fell for him, so much so that she even adopted the nickname Libby. Bob had misunderstood her real name, Ibby, but she didn't want to correct him. They were married in 1945.

After the war ended, Poser returned to Cook County to complete his surgical training, and, with Libby pregnant, then moved to her Edgerton, Wisconsin, home with a doctor father who delivered their son, John. After finishing at Cook County in 1946, Bob and Libby moved to Bob's hometown of Columbus to join his father, along with his older brother, Eduard ("Pody"), an ear, eye, nose, and throat doctor, and his younger brother, Chub, an internist at the Poser Clinic. There Bob cared for a wide range of patients, doing everything from setting broken bones to delivering babies. He would invite a University of Wisconsin doctor to Columbus for more difficult cases. Poser saw a number of patients who were injured while riding motorcycles; he would take his children with him when he was called in to see an injured rider so that they themselves would never ride a motorcycle.

Ann Poser recalled, "When I was 8 or 10 years old, Dad wanted me to work at the hospital. He wanted me to wash bloody surgical gloves for ten cents a pair. (There were, of course, no disposable gloves then.) I remember being all alone in a sterile-looking room after one of the nuns who ran the hospital (St. Mary's) showed me what to do. I lasted one day.

"Also, he loved sports so much that even during our Thanksgiving dinners he would turn the big heavy TV toward the dining room so that he could watch the game while we ate."

ONE-HIT WONDERS

Bob's wife and daughter agreed that "[h]e never got irritated with patients. The strongest word he would say was 'Christmas.'"

Bob Poser practiced medicine at the Poser Clinic for 45 years.

Interviews with his wife and daughter create a picture of a man who was both fearless and engaging: "In 1936, he and a friend traveled to Berlin, for the Olympics. As Hitler drove by, the crowd, including his friend, saluted him. Bob did not.

"He enjoyed talking with everyone. One time, while we were in Atlanta, he learned that Jimmy Dorsey (brother of Tommy Dorsey, and a big-band leader in his own right), was staying in a nearby hotel. He called Dorsey up. Jimmy invited him to his room, where they talked for hours. Bob then invited Jimmy for breakfast, promising that his wife would serve him her special oatmeal. Dorsey said it was the best oatmeal he had ever had." The two women agreed about another characteristic of Bob's: "He loved baseball; he could talk about stats all night."[25]

While attending Wisconsin, Bob had also played basketball, guarding John Wooden (later Hall of Fame coach of UCLA). John Poser said, "As I got older as a resident in surgery, my phone would ring and it would be Johnny Wooden, who would say, 'Your dad said I should call you to see how you're doing.' Following these conversations with Johnny, now in recent years, I would fly out to see him with my good friend Ted Kellner whom I played basketball with in Wisconsin, [and who in 2020 is a billionaire and part-owner of the Milwaukee Bucks] and then on another trip out to Las Vegas we stopped to see Johnny in his apartment. We became good friends."[26]

Bob's son John tells the following anecdote: "While I was living in Gainesville, Florida, Johnny came to the University of Florida when the president, an intern at UCLA under Johnny, invited him out for a talk. I sat in front of his daughter and she turned around and said, 'He wants to see you.' So, I jumped up on stage and went backstage and I walked up behind him and I heard him say, 'Do you know where Dr. John [Bob's birth name] Poser is?' to my great surprise, reflecting the fact of what a good friend he was with my dad and myself."[27]

Bob also got to know Green Bay Packers coach Vince Lombardi. Tom Poser (Bob's youngest son) wrote, "I did see a newspaper column about Dad playing [golf] with Lombardi. Dad sank a very long putt and Lombardi said 'What a competitor, what a competitor (in his Brooklyn accent).' When I was about 10, Dad took my friend, Bob Sullivan, and me to a Packers pregame in Milwaukee. Dad asked if we wanted to go into the locker before the game. [I'm sure Dad dropped Vince's name]. ... My football hero was Jim Taylor. Sure enough, we all went in and there was Lombardi talking to Taylor while Jim was getting taped up for the game.

"Unbelievable! Bob and I were so gobsmacked, absolutely nothing came out of our mouths. I believe Marie Lombardi would come down from Green Bay to go to the Poser Clinic. I think she saw Chub (Bob's brother) and not Dad."[28]

In Bob's later years he was interviewed by Eddie Poser, Pody's son. Their discussion provides some valuable information and perspective.

"Who was inspirational in your life?"

"Well, a couple of doctors have been great. You do the best you can, and go as far as you can in medicine. But I had to inspire myself. Since I was a kid I wanted to be a big-league ballplayer. I thought I was going to be. I never doubted it. And while I had some good years as a college boy, I had even better years as a kid. I was good and I gotta brag about it. Batting practice would only be twice a week maybe. I'd get some kids to pitch to me out at the park. I kept hitting but I should have turned and hit *both* ways. I didn't know at the time you could. I hit left-handed but I threw right-handed. A lot of guys did."

"So how did you start hitting left-handed?"

"It's the way you pick up the bat and want to do it. I felt probably stronger with this arm. This was a pusher and that's the way it felt good, I suppose, since I was 3 years old. A lot of guys can hit left-handed but they have to learn how to hit the other way. I think my right eye was stronger, but they were both 20/10. You know I had such good vision: I could read the spin on a curveball – I could read which way it was spinning; I could tell if it was a curve or a fastball the minute it left the pitcher's hand. By the time it got out of the pitcher's hand, of course, it was a tenth of a second. By the time the ball left the pitcher's hand I could see the spin on the ball."

"It looks like today's pitchers are a lot better, don't you think?"

"They have more *big* pitchers. The guys didn't grow as big [in the old days]. You know what made them grow? World War II. You know why? People started eating more fresh fruit. When I was a kid, if we saw an orange, it was something. They didn't even sell them in grocery stores. You'd get a pack of them from your aunt who was wintering in Florida. They'd

ONE-HIT WONDERS

send up a box of oranges, and so there was a vitamin shortage until World War II."

"Baseball has been a big piece of your life ..."

"It taught me a lot. I knew when I was in it that wasn't my future because $5,000 a year isn't much to live on. As you get older as a ballplayer, there are a lot of ballplayers running gas stations and so forth – and a lot of them do pretty well."

"What value do you have that you want to pass on to your kids?"

"I won't give up on anything. If I don't think I'm gonna do it, I wouldn't start it."

Bob and Libby lived in same house for 54 years. He was a member of the American College of Surgeons and a highly regarded member of the Columbus community. Bob served as city health officer for 34 years. In that role, he signed birth and death certificates, reporting cases of communicable diseases and "reports of nuisances," from 1953 to 1987.

Bob Poser died on May 21, 2002, in Columbus, of a heart attack.

In summary, his son, John, wrote, "My dad was a specialist in fulfilling the doctor's dream in the movie *Field of Dreams*. He was a true professional, a doctor, and a friend's best friend, with characteristics much like his good friend, Johnny Wooden, and later good friend, Vince Lombardi who, after a golf game, called Bob 'a great competitor.' He loved life, family, people, patients, and sports, and was kind and giving to all."

SOURCES

In addition to the sources cited in the Notes, the author relied on Baseball-Reference.com and baseballalmanac.com. He interviewed Bob Poser's wife, Libby; his daughter, Ann; his sons, John and Tom; and his nephews, Sam and Eddie.

NOTES

1. The questionable strikeout may, or may not, have occurred on July 8, 1923.
2. According to the contract card that had been filed with the AL president's office, Poser was promised an additional $500 bonus if the team finished in third place or better. (They did not.)
3. May 1, 1932, at Cleveland. The Indians won the game, 11-1.
4. Double A then was the equivalent of Triple A today.
5. Nick Wilson, *Voices from the Pastime. Oral Histories of Surviving Major Leaguers, Negro Leaguers, Cuban Leaguers and Writers*. 1920-1934 (Jefferson, North Carolina: McFarland, 2000), 186. Hauser had a number of good seasons in the majors from 1922 to 1929, the highlight being 1924, with 27 home runs and 115 RBIs. He then played minor-league baseball for the rest of his career – hitting more than 60 home runs in two of the seasons.
6. Wilson.
7. Interview with Bob Poser conducted by Rick Bradley, September 28, 1996, for the SABR Oral History Committee.
8. Sam Poser, communication with author, September 2018.
9. bill37mccurdy.com/tag/game-attendance.
10. Sam Poser, communication with author, September 2018.
11. There has been little disagreement that the best lefties in baseball history (not including active pitchers) are Grove, Randy Johnson, and Sandy Koufax. Modern analytics all measure Grove as the best. A number of years ago, Bill James wrote that the two best lefties of all time were Grove and Koufax. He concluded with, "There's not a dime's worth of difference between them, but I put my nickel on Grove." cybermetric.blogspot.com/2010/01/lefty-grove-vs-sandy-koufax-randy.html.
12. A copy of the box score of the game, played at St. Louis on August 20, 1935, includes this commentary. See *The Sporting News*, August 22, 1935: 6.
13. Poser played *with* Ted Lyons, Luke Appling, and Red Faber. He played *against* teams that included Charlie Gehringer, Earl Averill, Rick Ferrell, Earle Combs, Bill Dickey, Lou Gehrig, Tony Lazzeri, Red Ruffing, Jimmie Foxx, Lefty Grove, and Joe Cronin.
14. Taped interview by Eddie Poser, Bob's nephew, circa 1990.
15. Sam Poser interview, September 2018.
16. Telephone interview, July 17, 2018.
17. J.J. Rafield-Edgar, "Local Retired Surgeon and Baseball Great Shares Fond Memories of Columbus Blues," *Columbus* (Wisconsin) *Journal Republican*, May 8, 1999.
18. Bob's son, John, in a written communication with the author in the summer of 2018, described the visit with Hartnett much differently: "Young Bobby noticed that Gabby had a hand injury and invited him to take the train from Chicago to Columbus to see his dad. Gabby got on the train and had his consult, and hit fly balls to Bobby."
19. Letters supplied by John Poser, May 12, 2019.
20. From taped interview by Eddie Poser, circa 1990.
21. Interview by Eddie Poser.
22. Interview by Eddie Poser.
23. Sam Poser interview, September 2018.
24. Email from son John, May 20, 2019: "Luke would call often to the house and my dad would order me to go to the phone and order Luke Appling to tell me who was the best hitter that Luke Appling had ever seen and he would go 'You, Bob, you were the best hitter, you, Bob.'"
25. Telephone interview with author on July 17, 2018.
26. John Poser interview, September 2018.
27. John provided another story about John Wooden. "In 1976 the Final Four, famous sportswriter for *Milwaukee Journal*, Earl Gillespie, was pounding on the door but no one would let him in. My dad walks through with his camera, knocks on the door, the policeman opens the door and he said, "This is Dr. Bob, tell Johnny," next the door reopens, and we go in and there's Gail Goodrich and Lew Alcindor putting on their shoes as my dad talks to Johnny Wooden." Email communication with the author, May 20, 2019.
28. Written material submitted to author, May 12, 2019.

AL RAFFO

By Brian C. Engelhardt

On April 26, 1969, pitcher Al Raffo of the Triple-A Eugene Emeralds received the good news from his manager, Frank Lucchesi, that he was moving up to the parent Philadelphia Phillies. In his eighth season and eighth team in the Phillies organization, Raffo was asked shortly before he was called up if he thought he was ready for the big leagues, to which he replied, "If I'm not ready, I'm very close. I know it has to be soon because I'm 27."[1] Raffo was eager to breathe the rarefied air of the major leagues.

Explaining how he maintained his perspective during the seven-year odyssey through the Phillies farm system before finally moving to the major leagues, Raffo said, "I was always very conscious of the fact that a lot of other people who wanted to play the game were never getting the chance that I was having. I really appreciated this when I finally got to the major leagues."[2]

With the Phillies in 1969 Raffo appeared in 45 games – all in relief. While modestly describing his role in the bullpen that season as "mop-up work," Raffo emphasized its importance to the team, adding, "It's my job to get the rally stopped."[3] In a game against the Pittsburgh Pirates at Forbes Field on July 2 that Raffo referred to as "the highlight of my season," he took "mop-up work" to its highest level in the course of earning what amounted to a career trifecta with his performance that night both on the mound as well at bat.

"Long, lean and articulate Al Raffo"[4] entered the game with two outs in the bottom of the first inning in relief of starting pitcher Billy Champion with the Phillies down 2-0 and the bases loaded. After getting Pirates shortstop Fred Patek to ground out, Raffo held the Pirates to two runs over the next 5⅔ innings. Relieved by John Boozer in the seventh inning of the 14-4 Phillies win, Raffo earned his only major-league pitching victory – the first leg of the career trifecta.

In the top of the second inning the Phillies had already rallied for two runs when Raffo came to bat with Mike Ryan on third base and Ron Stone on second. Raffo got his bat on what he described as a "big roundhouse curve" thrown by future Hall of Famer Jim Bunning,[5] driving in both runners when the ball glanced off the glove of another future Hall of Famer, first baseman Willie Stargell, then rolled to the outfield grass. Although Raffo was thrown out at second base by catcher Manny Sanguillen when he tried to advance on Stargell's throw to the plate, he still had given the Phillies a 4-2 lead with his only major-league base hit – the second leg of the trifecta. On returning to the dugout, Raffo said to manager Bob Skinner, "Hey Skip. How about that?" Skinner, described by Raffo as being sparse with compliments, replied, "Your butt was all the way in the dugout when you hit that."

ONE-HIT WONDERS

In the sixth inning Raffo's suicide squeeze bunt drove Ryan in from third base to give the Phillies a 7-3 lead.[6] This and the two runs Raffo drove in with his single were his only major-league RBIs, completing the trifecta.

Born on November 27, 1941, in San Francisco, Albert Martin Raffo was the only child of Angelo and Mathylia (Draper) Raffo. When Raffo was 5 his parents divorced and he moved with his mother to Laguna Beach, California, then again moved with her to Los Angeles when he was 13.

Graduating from Los Angeles High School in 1959, Raffo in his senior year was named the third baseman on the Los Angeles High School All-City Team, with his .451 batting average the highest on the team.[7] He played at Los Angeles City College, which he attended for two years.

While playing in a Los Angeles winter league, Raffo was prompted by his coach to try pitching – not only because of his strong arm, but also because he didn't hit with the power usually expected from corner infielders. Raffo's pitching drew the attention of Phillies scout Paul Owens and he signed for a $1,500 bonus, most of which went to pay for much-needed dental work for his mother.

Assigned to the Miami Marlins in the Class-D Florida State League, Raffo immediately learned the meaning of "hard luck": In nine starts and one relief appearance he was 0-9 despite a 2.81 ERA. Sympathetic about Raffo's losses (his last a 1-0 complete-game loss to St. Petersburg in which he surrendered only three hits), Marlins manager Andy Seminick[8] noted that the team had not scored a run over the last 34 innings he had pitched and declared, "Raffo's not that bad a pitcher."[9]

Despite the 0-9 record, on June 23 Raffo was promoted to the Bakersfield Bears of the Class-C California League, which he described as "not really a move up but more like a move across the country to save expenses when they would release me." Although happy to be closer to home, Raffo was unhappy with his role at Bakersfield, which he described as being "limited to pitching in relief in games that were lopsided by the time I got in." Appearing in only six games with nine innings pitched, Raffo posted a record of 1-0 and an ERA of 4.00.

Raffo's biggest problem at that level was with his pivoting in his pitching delivery, which resulted in his surrendering walks at a rate of 5.5 per nine innings. Describing Bakersfield manager Bob Wellman as being "very supportive" in trying to address the problem, Raffo even received a visit from Paul Owens to try to work with him. The problem was resolved in the offseason when Wally Kincaid, then the baseball coach at Cerritos Community College in Norwalk, California, showed him a pivot technique that as Raffo related, "stopped me from sliding around on the rubber" and "really changed my game." At Bakersfield, Raffo developed a friendship with Mike Marshall, the team's starting shortstop who later converted to a relief pitcher. The two roomed together on the road that year as well in later seasons when they were teammates.

In 1963 the Phillies assigned Raffo to the Magic Valley (Twin Falls, Idaho) Cowboys of the Class-A Pioneer League. Managed by Wilber "Moose" Johnson, the Cowboys won the regular season pennant.[10] A highlight of the season for Raffo was pitching a 7-2 complete-game victory against Boise on August 1 while slashing out four hits himself.[11] In 22 starts Raffo posted a record of 11-7, with an ERA of 3.84. Referring to his teammates as "a cast of characters," Raffo indicated that the chemistry of the group combined with the colorful personality of Johnson made that season the most memorable in off-field antics in his career. Raffo's favorite story concerned a breakdown of the team bus in the middle of Yosemite National Park while traveling to Montana. With the team stranded for the night until a substitute bus arrived, outfielder Alex Johnson would periodically shout, "I'm going to shoot a moose."

In 1964 Raffo was assigned to the Eugene (Oregon) Emeralds of the Class-A Northwest League. Again managed by Bob Wellman. As a starter, he was 14-10 with an ERA of 3.67.

Pitching for the Chattanooga Lookouts of the Double-A Southern League and manager Andy Seminick in 1965, Raffo posted a 5-14 record with an ERA of 4.67.[12] With the 60-80 Lookouts' attendance a league-low 25,767, the franchise moved to Macon, Georgia, for 1966. Over the offseason a Chattanooga sportswriter sought Raffo out for an interview. Raffo recalled with a chuckle, "The article he wrote had a headline that I helped kill baseball in Chattanooga. I felt kind of guilty."

Although the 1965 season lacked many on-field highlights for Raffo, an off-the-field highlight was meeting Nancy Holloway on a double date arranged by a teammate, Phil Krous. They dated throughout the summer and were married on March 5, 1966.

The next season Raffo played for Macon, again under Seminick, Raffo had a brand-new role, pitching

ONE-HIT WONDERS

in 41 games in relief and posting an 8-5 record and a 2.44 ERA.[13]

In 1967 Raffo joined the Reading (Pennsylvania) Phillies of the Eastern League, the Phillies' new Double-A affiliate. Under manager Frank Lucchesi, he returned to a starting role after a few relief appearances. On June 30 Raffo pitched a 5-4 complete-game win over the Pittsfield Red Sox in which he led a charmed life, surrendering 14 hits and walking six, but stranding 14 runners.[14] After posting a record of 5-1 in August, during which he threw three consecutive shutouts Raffo was named Reading's August Player of the Month.

The final shutout of Raffo's streak, a 2-0 victory in 11 innings over the Waterbury Giants on August 19, involved a near-brawl after Raffo argued over an umpire's call. The batter, Giants catcher Jose Morales, called out to Raffo to "stop complaining and pitch." This, according to Raffo, "broke an unwritten rule of baseball that you don't talk to the pitcher from the batter's box."

When the next pitch grazed Morales' cheek, he charged the mound with bat in hand.[15] Raffo did not retreat, recalling, "I didn't want to give (Morales) the satisfaction." Quickly tackled by Raffo's teammates, Morales was ejected from the game. (Eastern League President Rankin Johnson, who was at the game, did not issue any punishments.)[16]

Finishing the season with a 12-6 record and a career-best 2.22 ERA, Raffo was named Reading's Most Valuable Player.

Among Raffo's teammates in Reading was future Hall of Famer Robin Roberts, who at age 40 had signed a minor-league contract with Philadelphia. Under a self-imposed deadline, Roberts retired on June 15 when no major-league team expressed interest in him.[17] Calling Roberts a positive influence with the other pitchers, Raffo said, "He never looked down on you just because you were young." Raffo said Roberts initiated a daily routine in which the pitching staff would sit on the grass in a circle and "just talk baseball, where Roberts would make suggestions not just about mechanics but also the mental parts of pitching."[18]

Promoted to the San Diego Padres of the Pacific Coast League in 1968, Raffo started 22 games and relieved in 12, posting a record of 11-7 and an ERA of 2.68. He threw two one-hitters, a 2-1 win over the Tulsa Oilers on May 10,[19] with relief help from Bill Wilson, and a 1-0 victory over the Denver Bears on June 26.[20] As happy as Raffo may have been on August 31 after picking up his 10th victory in a 1-0 win over the Phoenix Giants,[21] it did not compare to the joy he experienced the next day, when Nancy Raffo gave birth to their son, Gregory.

Assigned to the Phillies' new Pacific Coast League affiliate, the Eugene Emeralds, to begin the 1969 season, Raffo pitched twice in relief before his April 26, 1969, promotion to the Phillies. Raffo brought a very simple pitching arsenal to the Phillies, his primary pitch being a fastball that he described as "almost like a slider" because of the way he gripped the ball to avoid developing blisters on his right middle finger. Raffo also occasionally threw what he described as "a big curveball" which, he added with a laugh, "was often kind of a hanging curve." Although he tried to develop a changeup, he had little success, and said, "We didn't have a lot of coaching. You had to work on things yourself. Occasionally there would be a roving minor-league coach who would make a visit, but that was about it."

Raffo made his major-league debut on April 29 in a 10-0 loss to the Chicago Cubs at Philadelphia's Connie Mack Stadium. Entering the game in the top of the sixth inning with the Phillies trailing 8-0, Raffo allowed four hits and one run in three innings. Next he pitched in a May 5 exhibition game in Philadelphia against the defending World Series champion Detroit Tigers. Before Raffo entered the game, veteran Phillies reliever Turk Farrell asked him if he was scared. Raffo replied, "I have been working for a long time to get here and I've worked too hard to be scared." He pitched scoreless eighth and ninth innings; Phillies manager Skinner commented that Raffo's "fastball was moving real well."[22]

On May 30 in a 13-6 Phillies victory over the Los Angeles Dodgers in Philadelphia, Raffo earned his only major-league save, pitching 3⅔ innings of one-hit relief. Of Raffo's performance, Skinner said, "We need somebody down there who gives himself a chance, who challenges hitters the way Raffo challenged them tonight."[23]

At the end of June, communication issues between Dick Allen, the team's best player, and Skinner led to Allen being suspended for 26 days.[24] Raffo found Allen to be "a supportive and considerate teammate," as Allen tried to help him further develop his slider. Allen's absence, juxtaposed with an injury to right fielder John Callison, eliminated two of the team's primary offensive contributors for the first weeks of July. Still, during that period the Phillies put together a nine-game winning streak that turned out to be the high point of their season.

The streak began with a 6-5 victory in 10 innings over the New York Mets at Shea Stadium on June 25 in which Raffo contributed when he entered the game in the fifth inning in relief of starting pitcher Lowell Palmer with one out and the Mets leading 5-0. Raffo got two groundballs to end the inning with no further damage – "doing his job to stop the rally."[25] Raffo then pitched a hitless, scoreless sixth inning as the Phillies came back from the five-run deficit for the win.

Raffo's career trifecta came in the ninth victory of the streak, which temporarily vaulted the Phillies into fourth place, a game ahead of the St. Louis Cardinals. The streak ended with an 8-5 home loss to the Montreal Expos on July 4.[26] All of the wins came on the road, tying a team record (since eclipsed) for consecutive road wins.[27]

In a July 12 game against the Cubs in Wrigley Field, Raffo entered the game with the Phillies behind 6-2 in the bottom of the fourth inning in front of 26,732 fans and an *NBC Game of the Week* audience. As he entered the game on what he remembered as "a beautiful Saturday afternoon," Cubs fans were yelling, "Raffo, sit down, you can't get our Cubbies out." Calling the total scene, "a real baseball day in a real baseball environment," Raffo contrasted it to the Phillies home park in the dilapidated Connie Mack Stadium (tactfully described by Raffo as "a stadium that needed to be replaced") before crowds that frequently numbered less than 5,000.[28] Raffo pitched three innings, surrendering three hits and one run in the 7-4 loss. "I got a lot of good big-league hitters out," he observed.

Appearing in 13 games in June with 18⅔ innings pitched, 14 games in July with 29⅔ innings pitched, and in three games during the first week of August, Raffo was carrying a team-best 2.77 ERA. It was at this point that, as he succinctly put it, "My arm went dead." Working with the trainer provided no solution; at one point the trainer questioned his motivation, using the phrase "Jake out." Raffo told him he didn't work to come this far after seven years to "jake out." He even contacted former teammate and kinesiology student Mike Marshall, whose long-distance diagnosis was that the constant use and constant warming up, even on days that he would not go into games, was causing nerve damage resulting in the "dead arm" sensation.

Raffo's arm problems were apparent in consecutive games at Cincinnati when, on August 8, he gave up five runs in 1⅓ innings in a 12-5 loss, including a home run to Pete Rose, then the next night gave up another home run to Rose that drove in the winning runs in a 12 inning 4-2 loss. After being limited in action for two weeks, Raffo gave up five runs in two innings in a 13-4 loss to the San Francisco Giants at Candlestick Park on August 26. Aggravating the situation was that a group of Raffo's friends and relatives were in the stands that day. After finishing the season with 45 appearances in relief and posting a 1-3 record with one save, and an ERA of 4.11, Raffo was assigned to Eugene.[29]

Starting the 1970 season with Eugene, Raffo pitched in 15 games in relief, then went on the disabled list on May 22 with a rib injury. He asked to be assigned to Double-A Reading in July when he was able to return because he preferred the role of starter and Reading needed one. Raffo's second time around with the Reading Phillies began favorably; he won his first start 10-4 over the Pawtucket Red Sox on July 12.[30] This was followed by a string of difficult defeats, none worse than a 3-2 loss at Waterbury on August 9 that went 12 innings in which both Raffo and future Pittsburgh Pirates stalwart Bruce Kison went the distance. Despite the loss, which dropped Raffo's record to 1-5, the *Reading Eagle* described him that night as "tougher than tooled steel; tougher than he's been since his demotion from Triple-A."[31] In 12 starts at Reading, Raffo finished with a record of 3-8 and a 5.31 ERA.

Again assigned to Reading in 1971, Raffo pitched exclusively in relief under manager Nolan Campbell. For a second time at Reading, he had as a teammate a future Hall of Famer, Mike Schmidt. Raffo remembered Schmidt as "a good teammate who kept to himself … (and) was very focused on things on which he worked to try to improve – one being hitting the slider."

On July 12 Raffo posted his first win of the season, a 7-3 home victory over Pawtucket; he pitched scoreless eighth and ninth innings, and Reading staged a five-run late-inning rally keyed by a bases-loaded double by Schmidt, who earlier in the game hit his first official home run[32] as a professional.[33] In 29 relief appearances at Reading, Raffo finished the season with a record of 2-0 and a 2.31 ERA.

Although his 1971 ERA was close to a career best, Raffo saw, as he put it, "the writing on the wall" and retired to obtain his degree in Spanish. His daughter Angela was born in 1972. In 1973 Raffo began a career in education, teaching Spanish and coaching baseball at South Pittsburg (Tennessee) High School. Three years later he accepted a similar position at Marion County High School in Jasper, Tennessee. Over the next several years, he earned a master's degree in education at Middle Tennessee State University.

Known to the students at Marion County High School as "Señor," Raffo earned numerous professional honors during his teaching tenure, including Marion County Teacher of the Year in 1990.[34] Teams coached by Raffo earned multiple district championships and state playoff berths, with the 1990 team being runner-up for the state championship. A 10-time recipient of the District Coach of the Year Award, Raffo was named Region Coach of the Year five times. In 2001 the Marion County High School baseball field was renamed Raffo Field.[35] Special to Raffo was the 1990 team, which lost in the finals for the state championship. With a record of 17-13, Raffo recalled, "When other teams looked at our record, everyone wanted to play us. We surprised people."

After retiring from coaching, in 2004 Raffo was named the high-school principal, and served in that position until he retired in 2006.

Evidence that the Raffo family has baseball in its blood is that his son Greg, after playing at Middle Tennessee State University, pitched for three years in the Detroit Tigers minor-league system while Raffo's granddaughter, Ansley Blevins, accepted a softball scholarship at Middle Tennessee State University in Murfreesboro.

On the life that he and Nancy have led since settling in Jasper, Raffo declared, "I have … a lot of positive things to say about my experience here in a small town where I was able to raise my children and do what I needed to do. We've had a good life." Asked about Raffo, Logan Carmichael, publisher of the Marion County Messenger.com, volunteered, "You won't find anyone here in Jasper who has anything but good things to say about Al Raffo."[36]

SOURCES

In addition to the sources cited in the Notes, the author consulted Baseball-Reference.com, Retrosheet.org, the Al Raffo player file at the National Baseball Hall of Fame Library, and the following:

Johnson, Lloyd, and Miles Wolff, eds. *Encyclopedia of Minor League Baseball, Third Edition*, (Durham, North Carolina: Baseball America, 2007).

NOTES

1. Allen Lewis, "Phillies Rip Reds, 6-1, With 11 Hit Attack," *Philadelphia Inquirer*, March 11, 1969: 32.
2. Unless otherwise attributed, all quotations by Al Raffo are from interviews with the author on May 27, 2019, and August 5, 2020.
3. D. Byron Yake, "Raffo:'Mop Up Man.'" *Pottsville (Pennsylvania) Republican*, July 3, 1969: 10.
4. Bill Conlin, "It's a Mistake to Switch Off Phillies," *Philadelphia Daily News*, July 3, 1969: 54.
5. Bunning was also the ace of the Phillies staff from the 1964 through the 1967 seasons.
6. Ryan also scored from third base in the ninth inning; it was the only time in his 636-game 11-year major-league career that he scored three runs in one game.
7. Jerry Weiner, "Bluestone, Raffo Cop All City Nods," *Los Angeles Evening Citizen News*, June 13, 1959: 4.
8. Seminick also managed Raffo at Chattanooga in 1965, Macon in 1966, and Reading in 1970.
9. Rick Pezdirtz, "37,428 Fans Make Prophet of Durney," *Miami (Florida) News*, June 24, 1962: 80.
10. The Cowboys featured several league leaders: Future major leaguer Jeff James tied for the lead in wins (16) and led in strikeouts (218); the league batting champion was Gene Kerns (.349); and the home-run and RBI champion was future major leaguer Alex Johnson (35 HRs, 128 RBIs).
11. "Timely Hits," *Billings Gazette*, August 2, 1963: 12.
12. This was even more losses than the last time Raffo played for Seminick, but at least with five victories this time.
13. Raffo's 2.44 ERA was ninth-best in the league. Ranked right ahead of him, in eighth place with a 2.33 ERA, was his former roommate Mike Marshall, now of the Montgomery Rebels, the Detroit Tigers Double-A affiliate. ("Southern Association," *The Sporting News*, September 24, 1966: 36). According to Raffo, after Marshall began to pitch full time at Chattanooga, Rebels manager Wayne Blackburn liked what he saw and persuaded the Tigers to purchase Marshall's contract from the Phillies. Statistics on saves were not available for Raffo's various minor-league teams.
14. "Rested Perkins Brings Joy to Pressbox," *Reading Eagle*, July 1, 1967: 6.
15. Batting .382 with 15 RBIs and three home runs against Reading so far that season, Morales was no doubt already in a bad mood when he stepped into the batter's box, having been dusted off by close pitches twice the previous night.
16. "Phillies Win, 2-0, in 11th Behind Raffo," *Reading Eagle*, August 20, 1967: 53.
17. See C. Paul Rogers III's SABR biography of Roberts at sabr.org/bioproj/person/robin-roberts/.
18. Raffo had the distinction that year or playing either for or with three future managers of the Philadelphia Phillies. His manager, Frank Lucchesi, managed Philadelphia beginning in 1970 until midway through the 1972 season. Reading's shortstop that season was Larry Bowa, remembered by Raffo as being "full of fire and not satisfied with mediocrity," who managed the Phillies from 2001 to 2004. Dallas Green, a player-coach with Reading, managed Philadelphia from 1979 to 1981, and became a piece of Phillies history when he managed the team to its first World Series championship in 1980.
19. "Coast Roundup," *The Sporting News*, May 25, 1968: 34.
20. "Coast Roundup," *The Sporting News*, July 13, 1968: 41.
21. "Coast Roundup," *The Sporting News*, September 11, 1968: 30.
22. Bill Conlin, "Lab Tests Find Relief Remedy," *Philadelphia Daily News*, May 6, 1969: 66.
23. Bill Conlin, "Allen's Homer Sparks Phillies 13-6 Victory, *Philadelphia Daily News*, May 31, 1969: 29.
24. See Rich D'Ambrosio, "Dick Allen," SABR biography, sabr.org/bioproj/person/dick-allen/#sdendnote27sym.

ONE-HIT WONDERS

25 Although Raffo got Art Shamsky and Ed Kranepool to each to hit groundballs to second base that otherwise have been considered routine, the fact that third baseman Rick Joseph had just been moved to second base to replace Cookie Rojas, who had been ejected, added some excitement to each play. Joseph removed the excitement by capably handling each.

26 The Phillies lingered in fourth place until a third straight home loss to Montreal on July 5 banished them to fifth place for the rest of the season – taking little consolation over finishing ahead of the expansion Expos, managed by their former skipper, Gene Mauch.

27 Alan Lewis, "Phillies Pound Pirates for 9th in Row: Raffo Victor," *Philadelphia Inquirer*, July 3, 1969: 28. See "McCubed Net, Philadelphia Phillies Winning and Losing Streaks," mcubed.net/mlb/phi/astrkawr.shtml. The 1954 Phillies also won nine road games in a row, but the wins were not consecutive; the streak was interrupted by several home losses. Although the 1969 Phillies lost their next game after the July 2 victory over the Pirates, they won their next road game, 7-5 over the Cubs in Chicago on July 11. A loss to the Cubs the next day ended the road win streak at 10. The 1976 Phillies won 13 consecutive road games between an 18-16 victory over the Cubs in Chicago on April 17 and a 4-1 win over the Cardinals in St. Louis on June 2.

28 The Phillies continued to play in Connie Mack Stadium until Opening Day of the 1971 season, when they moved to Veterans Stadium.

29 Allen Lewis," Phillies Get Money, No Players in Draft, Lose Hurling Prospect to White Sox," *Philadelphia Inquirer*, December 2, 1969: 30.

30 "Phils Memorable Game," *The Sporting News*, August 1, 1970: 43.

31 "4 Runs, 4 Losses for Reading," *Reading Eagle*, August 10, 1970: 26. The 1969 streak remains special: During neither the 1954 nor the 1976 road win streaks did the Phillies win nine consecutive games.

32 Schmidt hit his first home run as a professional in a June 17, 1971, exhibition game against the Reading Phillies in Reading. Schmidt's home run was the winning blow. See Brian C. Engelhardt, *Reading's Big League Exhibition Games* (Charleston, South Carolina: Arcadia Publishing, 2015), 96.

33 Duke DeLuca, "Schmidt Powers Phillies; Hitting Woes May Be Over," *Reading Eagle*, July 13, 1971: 25.

34 Tennessee House Resolution, No.192 of 2003, filed on May 22, 2003. legislature.state.tn.us/bills/103/Bill/HR0192.pdf.

35 Tennessee House Resolution, No.192 of 2003.

36 Interview with Logan Carmichael, May 16, 2019.

LARRY RAY

By Mike Cooney

Larry Dale Ray was born at King's Daughter's Hospital in Madison, Indiana, on March 11, 1958. The youngest of nine children, he was raised with a farming family near Vevay, Indiana. Ray's parents, William and Dorothy Ray, had a dairy farm and grew tobacco. Larry worked the family fields as well as those of other tobacco farmers.[1]

Reflecting on his early years, Ray said, "My spare time was spent hunting and fishing with my older brothers. I also played ball – we called it ball then, not baseball – with my friends.

"I started to dream of playing baseball early on but work always came first – then ball. My dad liked baseball so that made it a little easier when I decided to try out for little league and later to play baseball in school.

"As I grew older, my success on the baseball field began to be recognized, but it was the work in those tobacco fields that helped me maintain a strong work ethic and helped me become physically strong. That work ethic and physical strength allowed me to play four years of high school baseball under Coach Bernie Burke."

Despite never going to practice because he had to work on the farm,[2] Ray was instrumental in his Switzerland County High School team's winning the Ohio River Conference championship with a 14-0 record in his senior year, 1976. In the two games that clinched the title, Ray hit three home runs and, though he was primarily an outfielder, was the starting and winning pitcher for the second game. Ray was the conference batting champion (.558) and was Most Valuable Player.[3]

After graduation, Ray led the Madison American Legion team in hitting[4] before heading to Roane State College (Harriman, Tennessee) on an athletic scholarship.[5] After one year, Ray moved to Kentucky Wesleyan College. In his first season, 1977, he was the leading hitter for Kentucky Wesleyan with a .365 batting average.[6] In 1978 Ray batted .335[7] while setting school records with 8 home runs and 36 walks.[8]

By his third season, 1979, Ray was looking for the opportunity to become a professional. He told **(a)** sportswriter, "I'd rather do that than be in school next year. ... I don't like school." Ray felt, at 21, "It's getting late. ... I'm about as old as I can get for them to take me. If I don't make it this year, I'm not going to make it."[9]

Ray batted .413 in his third season with Kentucky Wesleyan. After watching Ray play during the season, Houston Astros scout Ray Holton graded him 46 of a possible 50 (major-league ready), which meant that "with just a little polish and experience he will be ready for the major leagues."[10]

After his third season at Kentucky Wesleyan, Ray held school records for games played (117), hits (122), home runs (16), RBIs (83), and stolen bases (22).[11] The

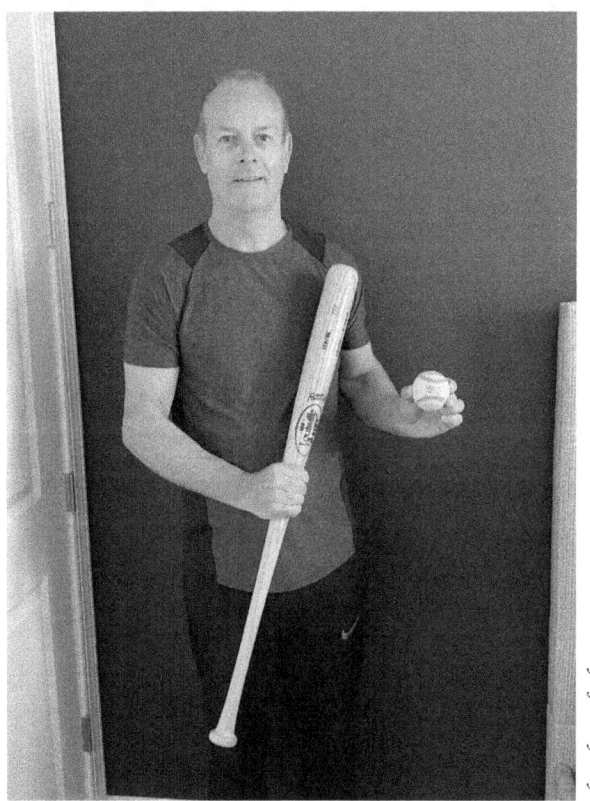

Larry Ray, with the bat and baseball from his base hit.

Courtesy of Larry Ray.

ONE-HIT WONDERS

season over, he went home to Vevay, Indiana, to wait for the 1979 major-league amateur draft. He had been contacted by numerous teams in both leagues.[12]

Ray "was just lying around the house" when the phone call he was hoping for came. It was the Astros' Walt Matthews telling him the club had drafted him in the fourth round.[13] He later learned from his college baseball coach, Corky Withrow, that "Montreal meant to pick him in the third round, and, in fact, thought they had." According to Withrow, "Montreal picked him, but their choice wasn't recorded properly or acknowledged, so he was still available in the fourth round."[14]

Ray signed an Astros contract that included a $15,000 signing bonus with a $650 monthly salary, then headed for the Astros' minor-league facilities in Sarasota, Florida. Before beginning his trip, Ray told the hometown *Vevay Reveille-Enterprise* he thought "it will probably take him two years to make the (Astros)."[15]

Ray remembered: "Four days after the draft, I drove 17 hours from Vevay to Sarasota, stopping only for gas. Once in Sarasota, I stayed the night in a motel before reporting to rookie ball the next morning. We practiced for 10 days before starting actual games in the Rookie League. We would practice from 8:00 A.M. until 11:00 A.M. and have lunch. Then, at 12 noon, we would play a game against rookies from other teams."

"On the day the first 'real' Rookie League game was scheduled, Julio Linares, the Astros Rookie league manager, called me in his office and said: 'Ray, you are going to the Astros Daytona Beach A ball team.'"

Ray played 62 games for Daytona Beach in 1979, batting .256 with three home runs. His manager, Carlos Alfonso, called his performance "not all that impressive." Alfonso added, "He was a raw individual when he reported last summer. ... He was so raw that players like him usually aren't even drafted. ... He's got a lot of tools. Right now, the question is developing those tools. ... Some kids are born with bats in their hands. Ray was born with a plow in his."[16]

Six weeks into the 1980 season, Ray was being touted by a sportswriter as "possibly the finest all-around hitter in the Class A Florida State League." At the time, he was leading the league with 26 RBIs while his four home runs were second and his .327 batting average was fourth.[17]

At the same time, not all was great. After a late May game in which he Ray, struck out three times before being lifted for a pinch-hitter, *Orlando Sentinel* sportswriter Tim Povtak wrote: "The Stinger got stung bad the other night – real bad. ... Larry Ray may be a fast learner, but he's still got some homework to do. ... Ray was grossly overmatched Monday night."[18]

Ray's response to being overmatched: "I may be a little behind because of my background. In fact, I had never even seen a slider before I came here. But I figure, if I have the talent, it'll come together quick enough. If not, I might go back and farm."[19]

He didn't have to go back to the farm. Instead, he was "among the hitting leaders all season." The week of July 20 he was named the league's Player of the Week after going 9-for-20 with six RBIs.[20] He was named Player of the Week again[21] and was named the most valuable player of the league's Northern Division.[22] (The author found it interesting that his manager did not pick him as the team MVP while he was picked the division's MVP)

After the season Ray played winter-league baseball in Barranquilla, Colombia. "The first month in Barranquilla was difficult," he recalled. "The accommodations they had for us had wooden beds, no mattresses. I was accustomed to working long hard days in the tobacco and hay fields back home, but when I laid my head down at night, I had a comfortable bed. The sleeping conditions in Barranquilla were not so nice. The guys on the team got together and made it clear that either we got new accommodations, or we would be leaving. Someone must have listened – the next place was better.

"Communication was a challenge, to say the least. In the beginning the only place we went was from the hotel to the ballpark. Eating was another challenge. I lost 30 pounds in the four months I was there.

"We would travel to Cartagena, where we played against other teams. When we left the games, the opposing team's fans would often throw rocks at our bus. We had several windows broken. It was scary at times. But since we won the Colombian league that year, maybe that explains the rocks."

The 1981 season started with a promotion to the Double-A Southern League Columbus Astros. Playing for manager Matt Galante, Ray saw his batting average slide to .253 but he hit 21 home runs with 107 RBIs and was selected to the league all-star team.[23] In the offseason he was added to the Houston Astros' 40-man roster[24] and was invited to spring training with the Astros.

Of his first spring-training day, Ray said, "It was pretty cool walking into that major-league clubhouse for the first time. Looking around the room I

ONE-HIT WONDERS

recognized all the great players that were on that team and it was a great feeling to think that I was getting close to joining them. My number was 37 – it was a great number to have! Just next to my locker, there was number 34 Nolan Ryan, number 36 Joe Niekro, number 37, Larry Ray (me!), number 38 Tim Tolman, and number 50 J.R. Richard."

Two of his favorite memories of the 1982 spring training involved Richard and Ryan.

In a split-squad game, after Richard had walked the first two batters he faced, Ray came to the plate. The first two pitches were called balls. Ray said, "I had never seen a baseball thrown that hard. I was thinking, here we go. If I hit it hard in this situation, I could really help myself. I dug in knowing that I was about to see a 100-mph fastball coming my way. My guess was right, but the location wasn't – JR drilled me in the back."

As for Nolan Ryan, Ray said, "The first time I met Nolan Ryan, our manager, Bill Virdon, made everyone stand up and introduce themselves, saying where they were from and where they played. Virdon told Nolan to introduce himself but he wouldn't. Virdon told him again so Nolan started standing (at that moment it seemed like it took him forever to stand up). When he was standing, he tugged at his pants and what he said sounded something like this ... 'I am Nolan Ryan and I own the state of Texas!'"

With seven spring training days left, Ray was sent to the Tucson Toros of the Triple-A Pacific Coast League. At the start, it took time for Toros center fielder Scott Loucks and Ray, playing right field, to get comfortable with each other's range, speed, and ability.[25]

On May 13 Salt Lake Gulls pitcher Bob Stoddard had a no-hitter going into the eighth inning against the Toros. Ray broke up the no-hitter with a leadoff single.[26] Shortly thereafter, he suffered a hand injury that caused him to miss 15 games.[27]

Once he returned to action, Ray continued to hit PCL pitching until an August 10 game against the Phoenix Giants. He suffered strained ligaments in his left ankle when he jammed his foot into the right-field fence going for a fly ball.[28] Ray did not return to the field until August 28. After two innings he was replaced after noticeably limping. In those two innings, Ray hit his 15th home run which, despite his missing 32 games[29] with injuries, led the team.[30]

Though his leg injury limited his play in August, Ray was called up by the Astros when rosters expanded on September 1.[31]

Toros manager Jimmy Johnson played a little joke on Ray, calling him into the office to discuss the need for the Toros to finish strong in their last four games. When Ray started to leave the office, Johnson, using his nickname, said: "LRay, wait a minute. You are not going to play the last four games this season. You are going to Houston – as soon as you get your bags packed."

Ray said, "I went to my apartment, loaded my Ford Bronco, and headed to Houston. I got out my Texas map and started the 20-hour trip. I arrived in Houston at 4:00 A.M. and before 6:00 A.M. my Ford Bronco had been stolen.

"Just seeing the Astrodome for the first time was awesome. But, walking into the locker room and seeing my own personal locker with my name on it was AMAZING! I remember looking around and seeing all the names … Ryan, Sutton, Niekro and (José) Cruz. I knew I was in the big leagues. The most exciting part, however, was getting dressed and walking down the tunnel and then onto the field. It was priceless."

Then came Friday, September 10, 1982. Facing right-hander Tom Niedenfuer, Ray pinch-hit for Nolan Ryan. It was his first major-league at-bat and he was admittedly nervous in front of all the Houston fans. He struck out. "I didn't get a hit – but at 24, I became an official major-league baseball player that day."

His first and only major-league hit came the next time he faced Niedenfuer, on September 17 at Dodger Stadium. The Astros were losing 9-2, and it was the top of the ninth. With a runner on first and one out, he was sent in to pinch-hit for Randy Moffitt. He singled to left field. "Steve Garvey, the Dodgers first baseman, asked me if that was my first hit and I told him, 'Yes, sir, it was.' He called time, gave me the ball, shook my hand, and said congratulations and that he hoped I got a bunch more, just not against the Dodgers!"

Ray got his first and only major-league start on October 2, against the Cincinnati Reds. In the sixth inning, he capped off a four-run rally with a sacrifice fly for his only major-league RBI.[32]

After appearing in five games to finish out the 1982 season with the Astros, Ray returned to the Tucson Toros for the start of the 1983 season. Manager Matt Galante called Ray one of the team's "only legitimate power hitters."[33]

Having played right field throughout his professional career, Ray was moved to left field for the 1983 season. Asked if he thought the reason for the shift to left field might be that the Astros' left fielder was

ONE-HIT WONDERS

36-year-old José Cruz, Ray said: "I hope that's what they're trying to do, I'd love to be up there. I think it is (my position)."[34]

Ray hit a walk-off home run on May 29 against Salt Lake City Gulls, but by late July he had missed several games with tendinitis in his right shoulder[35] and several more with a tender right (throwing) elbow,[36] which for a time kept him from throwing or swinging a bat.[37]

Despite his injuries, by the end of July, Ray continued to show power, hitting .296 with 11 home runs, 21 doubles and 69 RBIs.[38] Before his elbow injury, he had thrown out nine baserunners.[39]

From that point on, Ray was "relegated to be a designated hitter and pinch-hitter."[40] He said his arm bothered him most of the season, but that the tendinitis wasn't diagnosed until July. He told a sportswriter: "I just got it from throwing. I could field ... but why take a chance this late in the season is the way they feel about it ... and they're right. But I don't like not playing the field."[41]

A designated hitter the last month, Ray, with his team-leading .308 average, was named the Toros' MVP.[42] When the Astros expanded their 1983 roster, he was not on the call-up list.[43] The Astros decision was perhaps because the Astros were in the National League in 1983 and Ray had finished the year restricted to being a designated hitter.

As the 1984 season rolled around, Ray was once again assigned to the Toros.[44] Hoping for a big year, he got off to a poor start, hitting just .059 with one home run and four RBIs through his first 34 at-bats.[45] A week later, after a three-hit game, he had raised his batting average to .125.

He said, "I feel a lot better. I'm back to my old self, I think."[46] The reason for his slump: "I've been tentative at the plate. I've been on my front foot, leaning forward. Plus, I've been pressing too much."[47]

But after 21 games, Ray had only raised his average to .174. Still, he told Jim Elsleger of the *Arizona Daily Star*, "(My) ticket to the major leagues definitely will be earned at the plate." He also told Elsleger "he considered himself to be an above-average fielder."[48]

Elsleger disagreed, writing, "he'll probably never be put in a game for defensive purposes."[49]

By mid-June, Ray's batting average had improved to .233 when, to open a roster spot for the Toros, he was loaned to the Philadelphia Phillies affiliate Portland Beavers.[50] Ray was to "remain in Portland until after the season, when he will either be reclaimed, traded, or bought outright."[51]

The baseball Larry Ray hit.

A week after reporting to Portland, Ray seemed to have regained his power as he hit two home runs and had a game-winning RBI against the Las Vegas Stars.[52] By the end of the season, he had 12 home runs and 63 RBIs.

When the Astros announced the 1985 Toros roster, Ray was included.[53] However, instead of the Toros, Ray played for the Mexico City Diablos Rojos in the Mexican League.[54]

Playing for the Diablos Rojos (Red Devils), Ray remembered bad roads, buses, and hotels without air-conditioning, and a Mexican League championship. Three days after he left Mexico City, the city suffered an 8.0 magnitude earthquake that killed over 10,000 people.[55]

After three years without another call-up to the major leagues, Ray considered retirement. That thought changed when Bill Wood, the Astros' minor-league coordinator, asked him if he would be interested in playing and helping the young players on the Double-A Columbus Astros in 1986. Columbus had many good players, the most recognizable being Ken Caminiti. Even with Caminiti, Columbus was 24-48 when manager Dave Cripe was replaced by

ONE-HIT WONDERS

Gary Tuck. Columbus went on to make the playoffs and win the Southern League championship.

Jeff Datz, who debuted with the Detroit Tigers in 1989 and was with Columbus in 1986, said Ray and Tuck were responsible for the team's turn-around. Datz said, "LRay was respected by all. He was a quiet leader – when he spoke, we listened. When he came to Double-A Columbus he had already been in the major leagues and had had three or four successful Triple-A seasons. He could have snubbed the younger players – but he never did. Instead, he took Columbus from worst to first. He was the reason I have a championship ring from that season."[56]

"Larry treated everyone the same both on and off the field. He took me under his wing and worked with me day after day. He is the type of guy who back in the day would give the shirt off his back – and he still will today"[57]

Datz said his favorite memory of Ray happened on June 30, 1986, the day Bo Jackson made his professional baseball debut against Columbus. "ABC cut into the game to see Bo's first at-bat. I was catching and was asked to go to the mound and stall a minute so ABC could be ready. Besides ABC, many journalists were at the game to watch Bo. That night, LRay stole the show by hitting two home runs. Larry was interviewed after the game but didn't want the fanfare. He never did. He was always a quiet leader who mentored and supported his teammates. He was never about himself."[58]

Ray finished the season with 24 home runs and 108 RBIs and was named to the Southern League All-Star team.[59] He was not recalled by Houston.

By 1987, Ray was 29 years old and back in Triple A with the Pacific Coast League Vancouver Canadians, a Pittsburgh Pirates affiliate. He says he was loaned there. After 16 games, 19 official at-bats, and a .053 batting average, he retired from professional baseball.

After retiring from baseball, Ray began working in automotive equipment sales. He and his wife, Robin, have five children between them. Ray has three sons – Dylan, Tanner, and Logan. Robin's children are Amanda and Michael. Larry Ray went to Little Rock after he retired from baseball. He continues to work in the same field, but now in Nashville, Tennessee.

On October 29, 2015, Ray was inducted into the inaugural class of the Switzerland County (Indiana) Athletic Hall of Fame.[60]

SOURCES

In addition to the sources cited in the Notes, the author consulted Baseball-Reference.com

NOTES

1. All biographical information not directly attributed to a specific source comes from several phone, email, and face-to-face interviews/conversations with Larry Ray between July 1, 2015, and October 1, 2015.
2. Tim Povtak, "Stinger," *Orlando Sentinel*, May 22, 1980, 100.
3. "The Pacers: Baseballers win ORVC title," *Vevay (Indiana) Reveille-Enterprise*, May 27, 1976: 7.
4. "Larry Ray," *Vevay Reveille-Enterprise*, August 19, 1976: 10.
5. "College-Bound!" *Vevay Reveille-Enterprise*, September 9, 1976: 4.
6. "Baseball," *Owensboro (Kentucky) Messenger-Inquirer*, September 9, 1977: 11.
7. "Pro Prospect Wesleyan's Ray Isn't Amused by 10-6 Laugher in Home Opener," *Owensboro Messenger-Inquirer*, March 30, 1979: 14.
8. "Leave it to Seaver," *Owensboro Messenger-Inquirer*, May 12, 1978: 12.
9. "Pro Prospect Wesleyan's Ray Isn't amused."
10. "For Whom the Bell Tolls," *Owensboro Messenger-Inquirer*, June 7, 1979: 13.
11. "Astros Call Up KWC grad," *Owensboro Messenger-Inquirer*, September 1, 1982: 15.
12. "Astros Draft Larry Ray," *Vevay Reveille-Enterprise*, June 7, 1979: 2.
13. "For Whom the Bell Tolls."
14. "For Whom the Bell Tolls."
15. "Larry Ray Signs with the Houston Astros," *Vevay Reveille-Enterprise*, June 14, 1979: 1.
16. Povtak.
17. Povtak.
18. Povtak.
19. Povtak.
20. "Score Board," *Fort Myers (Florida) News-Press*, July 27, 1980: 50.
21. "Astros' Strucher Captures FSL," *Orlando Sentinel*, September 21, 1980: 393.
22. "Astronotes," *Orlando Sentinel*, August 22, 1980: 57.
23. "Post-season All-Star Teams," milb.com. See milb.com/southern/history/postseason-all-star-teams Accessed April 27, 2021.
24. "Who's Who for the Toros," *Arizona Daily Star* (Tucson), April 9, 1982: 74.
25. Jack Magruder, "Canadians, Toros Lack Precision; Toros Lack Victory," *Arizona Daily Star*, April 18, 1982.
26. "Salt Lake Tops Toros on 4-hitter," *Arizona Daily Star*, May 14, 1982: 63.
27. "Toros Notes," *Arizona Daily Star*, June 6, 1982: 25.
28. "Toros Notes," *Arizona Daily Star*, August 13, 1982: 30.
29. "Injuries Depleted Team," *Arizona Daily Star*, September 2, 1982: 29.
30. "Toros Notes," *Arizona Daily Star*, August 30, 1982: 14.
31. "Deals," *Owensboro Messenger-Inquirer*, August 31, 1982: 9.
32. "Big Inning Boosts Astros Over Reds," *Marion (Ohio) Star*, October 3, 1982: 21.
33. "Here's How Toros Line Up," *Arizona Daily Star*, April 8, 1983: 74.

ONE-HIT WONDERS

34 "Toros Notebook," *Arizona Daily Star*, July 31, 1983: 36.

35 "Galante Calls Shot."

36 "Toros Lose to Las Vegas," *Arizona Daily Star*, July 30, 1983: 56.

37 "Toros Lose in 9th," *Tucson Citizen*, August 2, 1983: 16.

38 Toros Lose in 9th."

39 "Toros Notebook," *Arizona Daily Star*, July 31, 1983: 36.

40 Jim Elsleger, "Toros Beat Giants, 6-2, as Ray Sits," *Arizona Daily Star*, August 26, 1983: 59.

41 "Tucson Triumphs over Phoenix, 6-2," *Arizona Daily Star*, August 26, 1983: 62.

42 "Toros Notes," *Arizona Daily Star*, August 29, 1983: 4. At the time, the newspaper reported his average as .307.

43 Mike Chesnick, "Astros Call Up 5 from Toros," *Tucson Citizen*, August 27, 1983: 12.

44 "Many '83 Toros Return," *Arizona Daily Star*, April 15, 1984: 46.

45 Mark Emmons, "Ray Hits in Ninth," *Tucson Citizen*, April 23, 1984: 32.

46 "Toros Take Southern Division Lead," *Arizona Daily Star*, April 27, 1984: 13.

47 Jim Elsleger, "Ray's Hopes Still High Despite Slump," *Arizona Daily Star*, May 7, 1984: 21.

48 "Ray's Hopes Still High Despite Slump."

49 "Ray's Hopes Still High Despite Slump."

50 "Notable," *Tucson Citizen*, June 23, 1984: 22.

51 "Toros Notes," *Arizona Daily Star*, June 24, 1984: 12.

52 "Bevos Win, 6-5," *Statesman Journal* (Salem, Oregon), June 29, 1984: 12.

53 "Sports Writers' Notebook," *Arizona Daily Star*, November 18, 1984: 40.

54 "1985 Mexico City Diablos Rojos Roster," Statscrew.com, statscrew.com/minorbaseball/roster/t-mr12961/y-1985. Accessed April 23, 2021.

55 "Mexico City Earthquake, of 1985," briatannica.com. See britannica.com/event/Mexico-City-earthquake-of-1985 Accessed April 27, 2021.

56 Author interview with Jeff Datz on October 24, 2015.

57 Jeff Datz interview.

58 Jeff Datz interview.

59 "League honors Glavine, Steinbach," *Greenville* (South Carolina) *News,* September 2, 1986: 5.

60 "First Hall of Fame Class is Announced," VevayNewspapers.com, September 24, 2015. vevaynewspapers.com/first-hall-of-fame-class-is-announced Accessed April 27, 2015.

ARTHUR RHODES

By Ryan Brecker

Arthur Rhodes forged a 20-year major-league career by establishing himself as a reliable left-handed reliever for nine franchises. He is the career leader (as of 2020) in holds since it became an official statistic in 1999, with a total of 231. Rhodes overcame family tragedy to become one of the oldest first-time All-Stars at the age of 40, and capped his career with a World Series victory with the St. Louis Cardinals in 2011.

Arthur Lee Rhodes was born on October 24, 1969, in Waco, Texas. One of four children, he followed his older brother, Ricky, who was drafted by the Yankees in the 35th round of the 1987 draft, into pro baseball. Ricky Rhodes never advanced past Class-A ball in the Yankees system and went on to a second career as the women's basketball coach at McLennan Community College, where as of 2020 he has been head coach since 1999.

Growing up, Ricky and Arthur, who were just under 17 months apart in age, pushed each other on the diamond. Ricky noted that they would challenge each other to see who could throw the hardest, "We played a game called burnout. We'd pitch to each other and let it go. Who won just depended on the day. We both loved the game and tried to make each other better."[1]

Arthur Rhodes started playing in the Southern Little League in Waco and became a star for the La Vega High School Pirates. In his senior season, Rhodes pitched to a 17-0 record in 1988 and set a Texas Class 3A record with 16 strikeouts in the playoff semifinals.[2] La Vega fell to Stinton in the championship game, with Rhodes throwing 4⅔ innings of relief.

It was during this run to the championship game that Rhodes was selected by the Baltimore Orioles in the second round, 34th overall, of the 1988 draft. Rhodes noted, "I felt like a little kid in a candy store. I just wanted to play pro ball. After I pitched in the state championship game, I signed with the Orioles."[3] After being signed by Orioles scout Ray Crone, Rhodes advanced quickly through the Orioles system, reaching Double A in 1990 and rising up prospect lists, being recognized by *Baseball America* as the number 6 overall prospect entering the 1991 season.

Rhodes pitched up to this potential, in 1991 being named the Orioles Minor League Player of the Month in July and the Eastern League pitcher of the year for the Double-A Hagerstown Suns. This strong performance earned Rhodes his first taste of the major leagues, where he debuted against the Texas Rangers on August 21, 1991. He went four innings and took a no-decision in his first start, noting, "My family was there and I was nervous, I always got butterflies before I pitched, but I had a good game."[4] He made eight starts down the stretch in 1991, but pitched to an 8.00 ERA.

Despite these initial major-league hiccups, the potential was still evident and *Baseball America* ranked

Arthur Rhodes on the mound.

Courtesy of the Baltimore Orioles.

ONE-HIT WONDERS

Rhodes as the number 5 overall prospect heading into the 1992 season, which he split between Triple-A Rochester and the Orioles while refining his arsenal that featured a fastball, slider, and changeup. He married his first wife, Kerry Garrett, on October 24, 1992.

Rhodes remained on the shuttle between Rochester and the Orioles for the 1993 and 1994 seasons, pitching exclusively as a starter. He appeared to be turning a corner with consecutive shutouts against Minnesota and Milwaukee to earn AL Player of the Week honors in early August of 1994. This run was halted by the 1994 strike.

Rhodes was unable to continue his Player of the Week success as a starter in either the 1995 or 1996 season, and found himself moved to the bullpen. He noted, "When I struggled as a starter, they had to move me somewhere else. My career went up from there. I really didn't change my approach. I just had to prepare myself to get loose and ready to go into the games."[5] He thrived in this relief role, pitching middle relief with a 9-1 record in 1996 and a 10-3 record in 1997. He earned down-ballot MVP votes in 1997, finishing in 20th place with 5 points.

The 1998 season saw Rhodes get his only major-league base hit, on June 8 with a groundball single off Phillies reliever Jerry Spradlin in the seventh inning. This was one of only six plate appearances Rhodes had in his career, and the only one that did not result in a strikeout.

Rhodes reached free agency after the 1999 season, and signed a four-year, $13 million contract with the Seattle Mariners. He was a bullpen mainstay for his four seasons in Seattle, appearing in at least 66 games each season. The 2001 season was particularly noteworthy as he finished with an 8-0 record supported by a 1.72 ERA for the American League record-setting 116-win Mariners.

On August 25, 2001, Rhodes was involved in one of the more unusual ejections in major-league history during an afternoon game in Seattle against the Cleveland Indians. He was summoned from the bullpen with two outs in the ninth inning of the 2-2 game and an Indian at first base. Omar Vizquel complained to home-plate umpire Ed Rapuano about sunlight reflecting off the diamond earring that Rhodes was wearing. Rhodes refused to remove the earring and was ejected from the game, resulting in a bench-clearing brawl. The Mariners did prevail in 11 innings, winning 3-2. Indians bench coach Grady Little noted, "It may be the first and last time you see that. But he wears those big earrings, and with the sun where it was, there

Arthur Rhodes.

Courtesy of the Baltimore Orioles.

was a lot of glare coming from those and it was one of those things where most of the time no one says anything about it. But today it was bothering Omar, so he said something about it."[6]

Rhodes was also brought into pitch the next evening against the Indians. Umpire crew chief Tim McClelland, who had ejected Rhodes, insisted that he remove his earrings, "I didn't know, but I figured that (Cleveland) would ask that the earrings be removed. I just didn't want to go through again what went on yesterday. So I asked him to remove the earrings and he said, 'Why?' I told him I didn't want a repeat."[7] Rhodes reluctantly complied, noting "(McClelland) told me I wasn't going to pitch if I didn't take them off. Once the umpire stopped me, I knew what I had to do. Stay calm. Stay cool. Stay in the game."[8] Rhodes wore earrings throughout his career, and these are the only reported instances of their causing a problem.

Rhodes was a free agent after the 2003 season; and signed a three-year, $9.2 million contract with the Oakland Athletics. The team planned to use him as a closer, hoping his success as a set-up man would translate. The deal did not work out as planned, with Rhodes struggling to find his footing as a closer, demoted to middle relief by mid-June, and on the disabled list with an upper back sprain before the end of the month.[9] Oakland acquired Octavio Dotel to be the closer, and after the season Rhodes found himself traded for the first time. He commented, "I knew they were going to trade me, the whole year was very frustrating."[10]

Rhodes was on the move not once, but twice that offseason. His first trade was from the Athletics to the Pittsburgh Pirates along with Mark Redman and cash for Jason Kendall and cash. About two weeks after that, Rhodes was flipped to Cleveland in a trade for Matt Lawton. In Cleveland, Rhodes re-established himself as a dominant set-up reliever, appearing in 47 games with a 2.08 ERA; despite appearing in only three games after August 2 due to an at the time undisclosed family illness.[11]

Cleveland traded Rhodes to Philadelphia in January of 2006 for outfielder Jason Michaels. Rhodes struggled in his first season in the National League, going 0-5 with a 5.32 ERA, and missing time down the stretch with a sore elbow. Seeking to recapture his success with the Mariners, Rhodes signed a minor-league contract with them for the 2007 season. However, he missed the entire season after being found in spring training to have a torn ulnar collateral ligament – the cause of his elbow pain in 2006 – requiring Tommy John surgery.

Rhodes entered the 2008 season on another minor-league contract with the Mariners and while he did not make the Opening Day roster, he was added after a single minor-league appearance on April 14. Rhodes found his form and at age 38 pitched to a 2.86 ERA over 36 games with Seattle. He was a trade-deadline acquisition by the Marlins, for pitching prospect Gaby Hernandez. His second go-around in the National League was much improved, with a minuscule 0.68 ERA over 25 games for the Marlins down the stretch.

The offseason of 2008 brought great tragedy for Rhodes: His 5-year-old son, Jordan, died in December. The intensely private Rhodes didn't speak publicly of this for over 18 months – disclosing only when a reporter asked in 2010 what he scratched in the mound when he pitched. Rhodes had started scratching "JR" in the mound after his son's death. He said, "I feel like he's right behind the rubber, watching me pitch."[12]

It was young Jordan's illness that had led to Rhodes' absence at the end of the 2005 season. While Rhodes didn't speak publicly about the details of Jordan's illness, his daughter Jade has been more open, noting that Jordan died of brain and spinal cancer.[13] Regarding the effect this tragedy had on her father, Jade Rhodes said, "It's hard, it really is. He kind of lost everything; he couldn't really talk."[14] Jade Rhodes went on to become an All American Softball Player at Auburn, appearing in the College Softball World Series, and played professionally in the National Pro Fastpitch league, winning the Rawlings Gold Glove Award as the league's top fielder.[15]

Jordan's death led Rhodes to contemplate retirement, but he instead decided to keep pitching in Jordan's memory and signed a two-year, $4 million contract with the Cincinnati Reds. Rhodes had a late-career renaissance with Cincinnati, pitching in 135 games with a 2.41 ERA over the 2009 and 2010 seasons. During the 2010 season, Rhodes tied a then major-league single-season record with 33 consecutive scoreless appearances,[16] spanning 30 innings.[17] After the streak ended at the end of June, Rhodes said, "I was thinking about it when I was running in. Now it's over. I have to move on and try to start another streak."[18]

This streak led to Rhodes' selection by National League manager Charlie Manuel to his first All-Star team at the age of 40, becoming only the fifth player to make his first All-Star roster after the age of 40.[19] Reds manager Dusty Baker had the honor of telling Rhodes he was selected for the 2010 All-Star Game, but pranked the reliever first by telling him he'd been traded to the New York Mets, before revealing the real reason for the meeting.[20] Recalling the meeting, Rhodes remarked, "I just got silent and quiet and couldn't say a word. I just said, 'Thank you very much.'"[21]

It was during the All-Star festivities that Rhodes first spoke about his son's death publicly. He left tickets in Jordan's name[22] and noted, "I knew he'd have liked to be at the All-Star Game, like the rest of the other kids running around. But he's my little idol, and he's up there. He'll be there with me and he'll be watching me pitch."[23] Rhodes did not appear in the game, but teammate Brandon Phillips summed up Rhodes' demeanor and status as an elder statesman, "He's like Benjamin Button – he's getting better with age. But he's always been good, and he's always approached the game the same way. Everybody says they've never seen him smile, but hey, that's just how his personality is. When he's on the mound, he's all about business."[24]

Rhodes returned to his Texas roots and signed with the Rangers for the 2011 season. Happy to return home at the age of 41, Rhodes said, "I like playing at home.

ONE-HIT WONDERS

My family gets to come to the games and I can enjoy myself. I'm still having fun. I just take it year by year and do whatever I can for the team."[25]

He was released in early August, and signed quickly with the St. Louis Cardinals. As luck had it for Rhodes, he made his first World Series appearance as the Cardinals advanced and defeated his prior team, the Rangers, in the World Series. Rhodes pitched in three games in the Series, retiring the lone batter he faced in each appearance. Rhodes was only the third player to play in the World Series against a team he had played for earlier in the season, following Lonnie Smith and Bengie Molina. Rhodes commented on the Cardinals' World Series win, "Winning the World Series made me feel like a little kid again. It takes you back to when you were a little boy, playing baseball for the first time. I really wanted to do it for my son, Jordan. That's kind of why I hung around that long."[26]

Rhodes did not sign a contract for the 2012 season and never pitched professionally again, although it wasn't until 2015 that he officially retired.[27] He explained, "I wasn't thinking about retirement back in 2011. I had just won the World Series, and it was a dream come true. Then you get into the offseason and start facing the work that has to be done to stay in shape. … I wasn't really looking to come back, but after three years away I just said, 'It's time to retire.'"[28]

Rhodes' post-baseball career has included coaching youth baseball programs in and around Waco,[29] as well as appearing at Mariners fantasy camps.[30]

SOURCES

In addition to the sources cited in the Notes, the author consulted Baseball-Reference.com and the Arthur Rhodes player file at the National Baseball Hall of Fame.

NOTES

1. John Werner, "Ageless Former La Vega Star Still Pitching in Major Leagues," *Waco Tribune Herald*, June 26, 2011. Accessed November 13, 2019. wacotrib.com/sports/high_schools/ageless-former-la-vega-star-still-pitching-in-major-leagues/article_a2a60a5a-b523-586e-8bf5-98efa0ce51c8.html.
2. "Cooper Captures Crown," *Victoria* (Texas) *Advocate*, June 11, 1988.
3. Werner.
4. Werner.
5. Werner.
6. Patrick Dorsey, "Yearbook, Aug 25: The Earring Ejection," ESPN.com, August 25, 2010. espn.com/blog/playbook/visuals/post/_/id/7749/yearbook-aug-25-the-earring-ejection. Accessed November 13, 2019.
7. John Hickey, "Rhodes, Forced to Remove Diamond Earrings, Blows Save," *Seattle Post-Intelligencer Reporter*, August 26, 2001. seattlepi.com/sports/baseball/article/Rhodes-forced-to-remove-diamond-earrings-blows-1063868.php.
8. Hickey.
9. Burt Graeff, "As Closer, Rhodes Was Set Up to Fail," *Cleveland Plain Dealer*, March 26, 2003.
10. Graeff.
11. "Indians Rhodes Ends Year," *Albany* (New York) *Times Union*, September 14, 2005.
12. Tyler Kepner, "For the Reds' Rhodes, Pitching Becomes a Tribute," *New York Times*, July 6, 2010. nytimes.com/2010/07/07/sports/baseball/07kepner.html.
13. James Crepea, "The Rhodes Unknown: Auburn Softball Slugger Defined by Loss of Brother, Estrangement with Former Major League Father," AL.com, June 2, 2016, updated March 7, 2019. al.com/sports/2016/06/the_jade_rhodes_unknown_auburn_softball_loss_brother_estranged_father.html.
14. Crepea.
15. Doug Fernandes, "Column: Rhodes Gloves Fold for MPF Softball Comets," *Sarasota* (Florida) *Herald Tribune*, August 26, 2018. heraldtribune.com/sports/20180826/column-rhodes-gloves-gold-for-npf-softball-comets.
16. Mark Guthrie had 33 consecutive scoreless appearances in 2002 and Mike Myers had 33 consecutive scoreless appearances in 2000
17. Mark Sheldon, "Rhodes' Scoreless Streak Ends in Reds' Loss," June 29, 2010. Mlb.com (paper copy in files at the National Baseball Hall of Fame).
18. Sheldon.
19. Satchel Paige, Connie Marrero, Jamie Moyer, and Tim Wakefield are the other players to make their first All Star Game after turning 40.
20. "At 40, Reds' Arthur Rhodes Is an All-Star at Last," Foxsports.com, July 13, 2010. foxsports.com/stories/mlb/at-40-reds-arthur-rhodes-is-an-all-star-at-last.
21. "At 40, Reds' Arthur Rhodes Is an All-Star at Last."
22. Werner.
23. Kepner.
24. Kepner.
25. Brice Cherry, "Arthur Rhodes' Legacy Continues Past Mound," *Waco Tribune-Herald*, January 23, 2015. wacotrib.com/sports/brice-cherry-arthur-rhodes-legacy-continues-past-mound/article_ac9affa1-d81d-5542-a93a-767e4c108100.html.
26. Cherry.
27. Bill Baer, "Arthur Rhodes Officially Retires," mlb.nbcsports.com, January 16, 2015. mlb.nbcsports.com/2015/01/16/arthur-rhodes-officially-retires/.
28. Cherry.
29. Cherry.
30. "Mariners Announce Coaching Staff for 2020 Fantasy Camp," MLB.com, August 15, 2019. mlb.com/press-release/press-release-mariners-announce-coaching-staff-for-2020-fantasy-camp.

EDDY RODRIGUEZ

By Gerard Kwilecki

Cincinnati Reds right-handed pitcher Johnny Cueto started his windup, his hips twisting to allow his chest to face second base. He delivered a slider to San Diego Padres rookie catcher Eddy Rodriguez. Rodriguez had just been called up to the majors after six years in the minors (including two years in independent ball) with two different organizations. Rodriguez was facing the team that drafted him in the 20th round of the 2006 major-league draft from the University of Miami. He had spent three seasons in the Reds' minor-league system before being released before the 2009 season. Rodriguez was batting eighth in the lineup and stepping in the batter's box for his first major-league at-bat. It was a sunny afternoon in Cincinnati on Thursday, August 2, 2012.

Eddy Rodriguez.

Photograph by Scott Wachter, courtesy of San Diego Padres.

Cueto hung a slider on a 1-and-2 pitch. Rodriguez swung and drove the ball to deep left-center field. Rodriguez told the author eight years later, "I knew I had it out for a home run."[1] There was no doubt this ball was headed in the stands. Rodriguez sprinted around the bases with a celebratory jog. "Celebrate like you will never get to do it again," he said.[2] It was a "culmination of emotions, shock, numbness, and meant a lot just to have the opportunity."[3] He and his family had made sacrifices to get to this point. He was wearing number 1 on the back of his jersey. As he rounded third, he shook the third-base coach's hand and crossed the plate for the Reds' first run of the game. A fan had been gracious enough to return the ball to the field and the ball was thrown into the dugout as Rodriguez reached it. His teammates congratulated him and high fives were being made all around. Rodriguez thought this was the start of a long career in the majors. He didn't know that this would be the only hit of his career.

Rodriguez was just lucky to be alive. He was born on December 1, 1985, in Villa Clara, Cuba, to Edilio and Ylya Rodriguez. He was 8 years old when he thought his parents were taking him fishing, along with his older sister, Yanisbet, and his cousin, Carlos. Unbeknownst to Eddy, they were leaving Cuba and attempting to defect to the United States. They left Cuba in a small boat on August 29, 1993. They spent four days on the boat, dealing with starvation and storms to reach Miami. Edilio and Ylya did not know if they would survive to give Eddy and his sister a chance at the American dream. "The third day was the worst. There was a storm that made the sea turn black, said a tearful Ylya."[4] One particularly bad storm nearly capsized the boat and drowned the family. Eddy said he could remember everything that happened and was still haunted by the experience. The Coast Guard rescued the family and took them to Miami. Eddy was in the right city to pursue his baseball dreams. However, the most important thing to Eddy was … life.

ONE-HIT WONDERS

After reaching the United States, the Rodriguez family had to start over. The family farmed when they lived in Cuba, but left that work behind. Ylya cleaned houses and Edilio worked for a construction company to support the family. But they were grateful to be in the United States.

Eddy fell in love with the University of Miami Hurricanes and with baseball, which he had played in Cuba "with a stick and a taped-up rock."[5] He told his mother he was going to play for the Hurricanes when he was old enough to attend college. His mother said, "Eddy, you know I can't afford to send you to this university. We just came from Cuba."[6] He told his mother not to worry about paying for it: "Don't worry. I'll make it happen."[7] His promise at an early age came true in his sophomore high-school season when he was offered a scholarship with the Hurricanes.

Eddy's parents signed him up for Little League. Then he starred at Coral Gables High School in Miami. Coral Gables boasts many players who have played professionally, among them major leaguers Yonder Alonso, Mike Fuentes, Mike Lowell, and Eli Marrero. He earned all-Dade County selections during his sophomore, junior, and senior seasons. He also earned gold glove awards for his defensive skills at catcher. He was team captain his senior year, hitting .250 with 6 home runs, and 25 RBIs. Rodriguez attended a Perfect Game top prospect showcase in 2002. The scouting report after the showcase said, "Rodriguez might be our pick as the best defensive catcher in high school baseball. Plus arm strength and accurate! Outstanding quickness and agility behind the plate. Looks every bit a major league catcher. He has a pretty nice swing, but we would like to see him be a little more aggressive and attack the ball. He has a very good strong body, quick hands and great balance. Those attributes need to be transferred into his swing. If he hits, he will be a first-round catcher. If he don't [sic] hit, he will be a top three round catcher."[8]

The University of Miami baseball program is one of the most storied programs in NCAA history. As of Rodriguez's freshman season in 2004, the Hurricanes had won four national championships since 1982 and had 21 College World Series appearances since 1974. They were coming off a 45-17-1 record in 2003 and a trip to the College World Series, in which they were eliminated by national runner-up Texas.

Rodriguez provided depth at catcher in 2004, his freshman year, appearing in 23 games, starting five, hitting .241 to help guide the team to a 50-13 record and a return trip to the College World Series. He was a much-improved player as a sophomore. He started all 55 games, 52 at catcher and three as designated hitter. He hit .320 with 8 home runs and 33 RBIs. He earned all-region honors at catcher and was the Atlantic Coast Conference player of the week during the season. He led the Hurricanes to a 41-19-1 record and a NCAA tournament appearance.

The 2006 season, his junior year, was Rodriguez's year to get noticed. He hit .318 with 9 home runs and 34 RBIs. He was named a finalist for the Johnny Bench Award, given annually to the best collegiate catcher. Rodriguez had a .987 fielding percentage while throwing out 39 percent of would-be basestealers. He led the Hurricanes to a 42-24 record and another appearance in the College World Series. After defeating Oregon State in the first game, they lost to Rice and eventual national champion Oregon State. The Cincinnati Reds selected Rodriguez in the 20th round of the 2006 draft. Rodriguez decided to forgo his senior season and turn pro. He signed with the Reds and reported to their Gulf Coast League affiliate in Sarasota, Florida. The young boy who barely survived escaping Cuba was now a professional baseball player.

Rodriguez played in seven games for the GCL Reds, and for 2007 the Reds assigned him to Dayton of the low Class-A Midwest League. Rodriguez played in 83 games, hitting .236 with 6 home runs and 33 RBIs.

Rodriguez started the 2008 season with the Sarasota Reds in the advanced Class-A Florida State League. In 70 games he batted .201 with 5 home runs and 20 RBIs. He finished the season with the Chattanooga Lookouts of the Double-A Southern League, batting .240 in 28 plate appearances. He went to major-league spring training in 2009 but was released by the organization on April 3. As best he could tell, the club simply felt they had better options.[9] No other organization signed him, so Rodriguez spent the next two seasons in the independent leagues. In 2020 he called his release at an early age "the best thing that ever happened to me."[10] He went to the independent leagues and improved on his defensive catching skills. He said the talent level in independent ball is just as good as the majors, that the players are "humble and busting their tails"[11] to get back to Organized Baseball. He had a great second year in the American Association (.259, 13 home runs, 55 RBIs in 80 games with Sioux Falls in 2010). He had made up his mind that he was not going back to the American Association for a third year. If a major-league team did not sign him, he would retire and return to Florida to teach and fish. The San Diego Padres scouted him and liked what they saw, so they

ONE-HIT WONDERS

signed the 25-year-old catcher on February 15, 2011. He said of his time in the American Association, "I am eternally grateful for the opportunity they gave me."[12]

Rodriguez spent the 2011 season playing with three Padres minor-league teams, from A ball to six games with Triple-A Tucson. He played in a combined 70 games hitting .246 with 10 home runs and 30 RBIs.

Rodriguez's 2012 season was a special one for him. He began the season with the Advanced-A Lake Elsinore Storm. On July 31 the Padres' rookie catcher Yasmani Grandal was placed on the disabled list. Rodriguez was watching the game when Grandal was hurt. (It was an offday for him.) He thought he might get called up to Double A to replace the catcher who might get promoted. He never thought he himself would get promoted to the majors. But his manager, Shawn Wooten, called him and said, "Eddy, you aren't going to Double A, you are going to the majors."[13] It was one of the best days of his life and he said he was "grateful to the Padres for giving him the opportunity."[14]

It was 86 degrees on Thursday, August 2, 2012. The Padres were playing at the Great American Ballpark in Cincinnati. The Padres entered the game with a record of 44-62. Rodriguez was in the starting lineup, the catcher, batting eighth. His major-league debut was against the team that had drafted him six years earlier. Ross Ohlendorf was the starting pitcher for the Padres and Johnny Cueto was on the mound for the Reds. Cueto and Rodriguez were batterymates in the Reds organization. Cueto had not given up a home run since May 25, when Colorado Rockies first baseman Todd Helton hit a two-run shot off him. Rodriguez said later, "We still talk and when we see each other, he gives me a smirk, knowing it was his first home run given up since May."[15]

Rodriguez finished the game 1-for-3 with the home run and a walk in a 9-4 loss to the Reds. (He was the second Padre to hit a home run in his first major-league at-bat.) He started another game on August 6. He went 0-for-2 with a walk and two strikeouts in a Padres win over the Chicago Cubs. Three days later Rodriguez was optioned to Triple-A Tucson.

Rodriguez finished the season with Tucson, but immediately after the Toros' season the Padres designated him for assignment, removing him from the 40-man roster. Rodriguez attended the Padres' 2013 spring training as a nonroster invitee. He spent the entire season between Triple-A Tucson and Double-A San Antonio. At the end of the season, he was not offered a contract, and became a free agent.

Rodriguez signed with the Tampa Bay Rays for the 2014 season. He played in only 13 games for the Triple-A Durham Bulls before being released on May 5. He signed with the Boston Red Sox on May 22 but spent much of the season as a minor-league coach, thinking his playing career was over. He was in Puerto Rico when the New York Yankees called with another shot.

Rodriguez spent the 2015 season with Triple-A Scranton/Wilkes-Barre and Double-A Trenton, and all of 2016 with Scranton/Wilkes-Barre. He signed with the Minnesota Twins organization in December 2016 but was released at the end of spring training. He re-signed with the Yankees in April 2017 and spent the season with Scranton/Wilkes-Barre.

Rodriguez was out of baseball in 2018 but in 2019 was the Los Angeles Angels' minor-league catching coordinator. It was his first coaching position. He was named a catching coach with the Miami Marlins for the 2020 season with a two-year contract. The young Marlins made the expanded playoffs as a wild-card team with 31-29 record during a pandemic-shortened season. The pandemic-shortened season could have easily been a disaster for the Marlins, who numerous COVID-19 cases, with up to 18 or 19 players gone at one point. Rodriguez said, "The credit goes to the players. They could have used every excuse to fold their cards in July but they overcame the adversity and busted their tails to have a playoff season."[16]

A resident of Melbourne, Florida, with his wife and two children, Rodriguez worked with young players in the offseason. He became involved with youth baseball camps, hosting catching lessons virtually under the name Gold Glove Catching. He was also the technology integration and catching director with the TNXL Academy in Ocoee, Florida.

SOURCES

In addition to the sources cited in the Notes, the author consulted Baseball-Reference.com and the following:

Charity, Kevin. "Who the Heck is Eddy Rodriguez?" *Fansided*, August 1, 2012, friarsonbase.com/2012/08/01/who-the-heck-is-eddy-rodriguez/.

Jenkins, Drew. "Eddy Rodriguez Brings Feel Good Story to the Tampa Bay Rays," *Fansided*, January 14, 2014. rayscoloredglasses.com/2014/01/14/eddy-rodriguez-brings-feel-good-story-tampa-bay-rays/.

Katz, Marc. "Daring Escape Brought Dragons Catcher to America/Cuban-Born Eddy Rodriguez and His Family Crossed Stormy Seas on a Small Fishing Boat in 1993," *Dayton Daily News*, June 5, 2007. web.archive.org/web/20140611111240/http://www.highbeam.com/doc/1P2-11996982.html.

Kerasotis, Peter. "For the Yankees' Other Rodriguez, Little Fanfare but Big Adventures," *New York Times*, March 15, 2015. nytimes.com/2015/03/16/sports/baseball/for-the-yankees-other-rodriguez-little-fanfare-but-big-adventures.html.

ONE-HIT WONDERS

Miami Hurricanes baseball web page, miamihurricanes.com/roster/eddy-rodriguez/.

2020 Miami Marlins Media Guide, 33.

Rodriguez, Ken. "After Escaping Cuba as a boy, Eddy Rodriguez Living His Dream," *Sports Illustrated*, July 24, 2013. si.com/mlb/2013/07/24/eddy-rodriguez.

2013 San Diego Padres Media Guide, 146, 196.

Snyder, Matt. "Thursday's Feel-Good Moment: Eddy Rodriguez Homers in First Big-League At-Bat," CBS Sports, August 2, 2012. cbssports.com/mlb/news/thursdays-feel-good-moment-eddy-rodriguez-homers-in-first-big-league-at-bat/.

TXNL Academy, Ocoee, Florida. tnxlacademy.com.

NOTES

1. Eddy Rodriguez, telephone interview with Gerard Kwilecki, October 19, 2020.
2. Rodriguez interview.
3. Rodriguez interview.
4. Omar Kelly, "Living American Dream," *South Florida Sun Sentinel*, June 9, 2006. sun-sentinel.com/news/fl-xpm-2006-06-09-0606081598-story.html.
5. Kelly.
6. Kelly.
7. Kelly.
8. Perfect Game Showcase, June 14, 2002. perfectgame.org/Players/PlayerProfile.aspx?ID=108647.
9. Eddy Rodriguez e-mail to author, October 26, 2020.
10. Rodriguez interview.
11. Rodriguez interview.
12. Rodriguez interview.
13. Rodriguez interview.
14. Rodriguez interview.
15. Rodriguez interview.
16. Rodriguez interview.

ROBERTO RODRIGUEZ

(A/K/A ROBERTO MUÑOZ)

By Tony S. Oliver

When danger arose and duty called, mild-mannered reporter Clark Kent would duck into a telephone booth to change into Superman. The typically phlegmatic Dr. Bruce Banner, if sufficiently provoked, would struggle not to unleash his alter ego, the Incredible Hulk. The metamorphosis of Venezuelan pitcher Roberto Muñoz was far less dramatic and indefinitely less colorful; crossing the United States border would change him into Roberto Rodríguez. Hispanic culture anoints children with the surnames of both parents; in his case, Muñoz was his paternal last name and Rodríguez his mother's. Much like Puerto Rican star Víctor Pellot Pove (a/k/a Vic Power) and Dominican legend Felipe Rojas Alou, generations of fans would know the Venezuelan pitcher by a truncated name. (This biography uses the anglicized version, *Roberto Rodríguez*, since it was one used in major-league baseball.)

Roberto was born on February 5, 1941, in the capital city of Caracas to Juan Muñoz, who would work for 44 years at the local brewing company Cervecería Caracas, and Julia Rodríguez, who stayed at home with the children. They were of humble socioeconomic status; Roberto shined shoes and delivered newspapers to aid the family budget and liked to play baseball whenever he could. His uncles, both semiprofessional players, infected him with the bug.

Former minor leaguer Tony Pacheco discovered him as a catcher. Signed by the Kansas City Athletics one day shy of his 22nd birthday, Rodríguez reported to the Florida State League in the spring of 1963. He appeared in 38 games for Class-A Daytona Beach and fielded well (241 chances, 218 putouts, 19 assists, four errors, three double plays, and 11 passed balls), but his offensive contribution was anemic (20 singles and three extra-base hits in 133 at-bats).

His demeanor was chipper: "I was always in good spirits, so when I wasn't catching the game, I could throw batting practice."[1] A Kansas City scout, Bill Posedel, saw something in the young right-hander and asked Rodríguez to come early the next day for an experiment. "First, I threw four fastballs and then a slider. … They told me there was no reason to keep throwing, and from that moment they ordered me to switch the mitt for the pitcher's glove."[2] He would spend the rest of the season working on his pitching.

Assigned to the Class-A Midwest League in 1964, Rodríguez pitched in 24 games, earning 11 victories against eight defeats on the strength of a 3.35 ERA for the Burlington Bees. He also appeared in four contests in the Class-A Northwest League, tossing four innings and allowing five earned runs for the Lewiston Broncs. He returned to Lewiston in 1965 and delivered a robust 3.97 ERA over 136 innings (13-4, two saves) to earn a promotion to the top farm club, Vancouver of the Triple-A Pacific Coast League. His 1966 record (seven wins, seven losses) belied strong fundamentals, including only nine home runs allowed and a 2.55 ERA over 148 innings. He was even more impressive in 1967, improving to 12-4 while lowering his WHIP to 1.047 and receiving the much-desired call-up.

Rodríguez broke into the American League with the Athletics, who were subjecting Kansas City to one last losing season before departing for Oakland. A pair of 21-year-old prospects would blossom into Hall of Famers, as Reggie Jackson and Catfish Hunter would be the nucleus of the early 1970s three-peating Athletics, but their early exploits were inconsistent. Rodríguez became the third Venezuelan-born player to pitch in the majors after Alex Carrasquel and Ramón Monzant, upon his debut on May 13 at Minnesota, hurling 1⅓ innings without allowing a run to earn a hold.[3]

The A's lost his next three appearances, with Rodríguez allowing four runs to close out May with a 5.14 ERA. The team sent him back to the minors before recalling him for the stretch run. He was stingy

ONE-HIT WONDERS

in August, pitching 14⅔ innings and allowing only two runs; he picked up his first save on August 19 as the Athletics beat the Senators, and his second one a few days later in Baltimore. To close the month, the franchise gave Rodríguez the opportunity to start, and he took full advantage of it, scattering four hits over 6⅓ innings to beat Detroit. Future Hall of Famers Eddie Mathews and Al Kaline failed to get a hit in six at-bats, though the latter reached base on a fielder's choice. Rodríguez's fortunes turned in September, as 12 men crossed the plate against him in 18⅔ innings, including his first loss, also at Minnesota. As the season ended and the franchise packed its bags for California, Rodríguez could be forgiven for thinking he would follow suit, but the front office returned him to Vancouver for more development. Topps was also fooled, giving him card number 199 (alongside Darrell Osteen, "Athletics Rookie Stars") in the 1968 set, fully expecting him to be part of the Athletics' season.

Back in the minors and given 28 starts, Rodríguez generated 23 decisions (12 wins, 11 losses) but his peripherals worsened; his ERA jumped to 4.20 and his WHIP to 1.356 as the Mounties finished last in the league in 1968. That season was a turning point for the PCL; it would shrink from 12 franchises to eight after San Diego and Seattle were granted expansion major-league franchises to begin playing in 1969, making minor-league ball in those cities financially challenging. In preparation, Oakland moved its affiliation to the American Association, resurrected after a seven-year hiatus. The Iowa Oaks were consistent; they finished fourth in the standings, fourth in runs per game scored, and third in most runs allowed in the 1969 season. Rodríguez struggled, tossing 130 innings between the starting rotation and the relief corps; he ended the season with five wins, eight losses, and four saves on a 4.92 ERA and 1.608 WHIP.

Rodríguez began the 1970 season with Iowa but appeared in only two games (three innings, two hits, three strikeouts) before making his way back to the majors, rejoining his Athletics teammates. He was not frequently used, appearing in only six of the team's first 35 games. He provided a solid 2.92 ERA in 12⅓ relief innings, as Hunter, Blue Moon Odom, and Vida Blue led a strong, yet still young, starting rotation. The franchise sold his contract to San Diego but he played in only 10 games with the Padres before being sent to the Chicago Cubs for cash considerations. Going from an expansion team to one of the National League's oldest franchises was a new experience. Rodríguez's third team in one year – all in different divisions – gave him meaningful contests late in the season and he shared the clubhouse with four eventual Cooperstown legends (Ron Santo, Billy Williams, Ernie Banks, and Fergie Jenkins). Through his last 26 major-league games, Rodríguez enjoyed successes (three wins, two saves) and tasted bitter defeats (two losses, one blown save). After the historical collapse of the 1969 Cubs, the 1970 edition led their division through the summer but yielded the crown to the Pirates, finishing in second place with an 84-78 record.

Rodríguez's three most memorable games in a Chicago uniform involved Bill Hands. The Venezuelan proved his mettle by inheriting a bases-loaded situation from Hands in the top of the ninth inning with no outs against Montréal on July 6. He struck out John Bateman and Coco Laboy before getting Bob Bailey to ground out to shortstop to finish the game and earn the save. On July 26 the Cubs hosted a doubleheader against Atlanta. They fell behind early in the opener, as starter Hands was manhandled by Orlando Cepeda (three home runs in as many at-bats, including a grand slam) to bring Rodríguez into the game. Chicago manager Leo Durocher would have preferred to wait until the fifth inning to change his hurler, as the pitcher's spot was up first in the next frame, but his starter's

ONE-HIT WONDERS

struggles left him no choice. Having inherited runner Tony González, Rodríguez walked Mike Lum before retiring Clete Boyer.

Rodríguez had barely taken off his glove before he was summoned to the plate. Perhaps he was in a hurry to return to the dugout to discuss how to approach the next few hitters; maybe he just saw a pitch he liked and did what any hitter seeks to do. The throw from Pat Jarvis disappeared not just over the fence, but out of the park, as Rodríguez attained his first and only career hit with a four-bagger. Through the 2019 season, 1,306 retired players have enjoyed only one hit in the majors.[4] Of those, only 19 (1.45 percent) have done so with a round-tripper, making it a remarkable accomplishment.[5] Rodríguez had never hit a home run in the minor leagues or during Venezuelan competition. In a television interview, he was humble about the accomplishment: "That was by chance. Jarvis was not bad, he had won 16 games in a season. Maybe he thought, 'This is the pitcher, I'll just throw something by him.' I thought, 'The first one I like, I'll swing.' I think it took me half an hour to circle the bases!"[6]

Rodríguez remained on the mound and stopped the bleeding by keeping all 10 hitters he faced from crossing the plate; however, the team needed more runs so Durocher lifted him for Al Spangler in the seventh inning. The Cubs lost the contest, 8-3, but won the second half of the doubleheader, with Rodríguez picking up his fifth save. He won a pair of games and lost another, with his last major-league appearance occurring on September 26. Chicago dropped its 157th game to Philadelphia, 7-1, with Hands once again getting an early hook (six runs in 1⅔ innings). Juan Pizarro provided 2⅓ scoreless frames before turning over the ball to Rodríguez, who faced 10 batters, striking out one, walking another, and allowing two hits; a double play and a runner caught stealing kept the Phillies from scoring again during his three innings.

In 1971 Rodríguez returned to the PCL as a member of the Tacoma Cubs, providing a veteran presence, starting 26 games (completing 11), relieving in five others, and posting a 4.01 ERA in a career-high 204 innings. Chicago switched its Triple-A affiliation in 1972, to Wichita. Rodríguez would play three full seasons (1972-1974) in with the American Association's Aeros, tossing 308 total innings for a 19-15 record with 16 saves.

Rodríguez's major-league numbers (4.81 ERA, four wins, three losses, seven saves in 57 games, five of which were starts) have long been eclipsed by his fellow Venezuelan pitchers. His sole hit was memorable, though he also reached base one other time in his career, in 1967 against Baltimore on an error, later scoring on a Bert Campaneris triple. He started the game but did not get the decision as he was lifted after 4⅓ innings.

Though his major-league career was brief, Rodríguez's foray in the Venezuelan winter league was legendary. Appearing in the box score as Roberto Muñoz, he played for multiple franchises from 1961 through 1979 (except for 1962-1963). He won the championship with the Tigres in 1971-1972, 1974-1975, and 1975-1976 (though he did not take the mound in the championship series). He won the finals MVP award in 1971-1972, appearing in six games, winning two and saving one and yielding only three runs in 16⅔ frames. He appeared in four other championship series: with the Valencia Industriales (1965-1966 and 1967-1968), the Tiburones (Sharks) of La Guaira (1966-1967), and the Navegantes (Navigators) of Magallanes (1968-1969).

Rodríguez was the first hurler to record 50 career victories and an equal number of saves in the Venezuelan league. Throughout this career, he led the league in ERA, strikeouts, innings pitched, complete games, and saves on various occasions.[7] With Aragua he earned the "Iron Horse" nickname as he was seemingly always relieving the team's starters. His 64-49 record, with 59 saves and a 3.04 ERA, was amassed in 267 relief appearances (second place all-time) and 1,228⅔ innings (fifth place all-time). He also ranks fifth in strikeouts with 734. During the semifinals (first round of postseason) he forged a 3-3 tally with four saves in 60⅓ frames, with an additional 7-6 mark and one save in the finals.

Rodríguez's contemporary, Nelson Castellanos, gave him the sobriquet "Pluto," though years afterward, Rodríguez was vague as to why: "Maybe because he thought I was aloof, though I picked off a lot of men on base. … Maybe because I'd walk around the pitcher's mound before throwing to home plate."[8] He cherished a friendly rivalry with Isaías "El Látigo" (The Whip) Chávez, whose career was cut tragically short in a 1969 plane crash that claimed all 84 passengers and 70 people on the ground.[9] They faced off twice in 1967-1968, each one winning a contest by the slimmest of margins, 1-0.[10]

In one of his best anecdotes, Rodríguez recalled swinging wildly at a pitch while Adolfo Phillips stole home; Caracas pitcher Diego Seguí retaliated by hitting him in the elbow, causing him to be taken out. Caracas then rallied to win the game and the

ONE-HIT WONDERS

Venezuelan title. "Later that year, while playing minor-league ball, Seguí and I faced each other. I drilled him in the head, and then visited him in the hospital. He told me, 'Venezuelan, as soon as I get out of here I'm going to get even.' I answered, 'Cuban, you beaned me there, I got you back here. Now we're even.'"[11] The two would be teammates in the minors (Vancouver, 1967), the majors (Kansas City, 1967, Oakland, 1970), and the Venezuelan league (Caracas, 1978-1979).

Rodríguez's post-playing career was bittersweet. He worked at a car dealership and at a Maracay baseball academy owned by former big leaguer Carlos Guillén. A falling-out with the Aragua ownership strained ties with the ballclub. Although the franchise was in other hands, he confessed in a television interview not to have attended a game in many years, though he would "be proud to throw a first pitch" if he were invited.[12] He had sued Aragua for 190,000 bolívares and won the lawsuit; as a result, he felt he was blackballed not just from a job in the winter league, but also from the Venezuelan Baseball Hall of Fame. The slight originated from the 1972 Caribbean Series, when Rodríguez felt the players were ill-treated by management. He was particularly incensed at the suggestion of a club official that players' wives should pay for their own travel. "I said, 'Well, then you put on the uniform, pick up the glove, and go pitch, because I won't.'"[13] Ownership acquiesced, claiming it was a misunderstanding, and Rodríguez played in the series (in the Dominican Republic), "but the damage was done."[14] Team Puerto Rico won the series but was handed its only defeat by Venezuela. Rodríguez appeared in five games, saving three, and being named to the all-tournament team.[15] He struggled in the 1975 edition, dropping two games against the Dominican Republic.

Married to Carmen since 1963, Rodríguez had three sons, the eldest of whom died in 1995 from cardiac arrest. His nephew, Nelson Torres, followed his footsteps to the pitching mound. In a dozen years in the Venezuelan league, he appeared in 104 games, going 10-10 while picking up six saves.[16]

In addition to his 368 Venezuelan winter league games, Rodríguez also appeared in one season in the Mexican league (14 games, 2-4, two saves).[17] He was elected to the Venezuelan Baseball Hall of Fame on September 13, 2011, with his plaque dedicated the following year.[18] "I wasn't expecting to be elected. … This has great meaning for me. To be considered and to go in with such stars is a great honor."[19] He died of a heart attack on September 23, 2012, in Maracay and is buried in the Cementerio Metropolitano de Aragua. His uniform number was belatedly retired by Aragua in 2015 during a pregame ceremony attended by his widow, two surviving children, and grandchildren.[20]

SOURCES

In addition to the sources cited in the Notes, the author consulted game information on Baseball-Reference.com and Retrosheet.org.

NOTES

1. "Los Venezolanos en las Grandes Ligas," May 20, 2012. grandesligasve.blogspot.com/.
2. "Los Venezolanos en las Grandes Ligas."
3. Though the "hold" statistic was not official until the 1980s, they have been retroactively awarded to pitchers. For more information, consult MLB.com's glossary: m.mlb.com/glossary/standard-stats/hold.
4. Baseball-Reference search query: one career hit, retired players as of September 7, 2019. baseball-reference.com/tiny/oI6pI.
5. Baseball-Reference search query: one career hit, one career home run, retired players as of September 7, 2019. baseball-reference.com/tiny/bdsWo.
6. *La Voz del Fanático* television show, hosted by Ramón Corro. Meridiano Televisa, 2007 original broadcast. youtube.com/watch?v=z9BYzrbUorw.
7. pelotabinaria.com.ve/beisbol/mostrar.php?ID=munorob001.
8. Alfonso L. Tusa, "Pluto y el Caballo de Hierro," Magallaneando Blog, September 24, 2012. magallanenando.blogspot.com/2012/09/pluto-y-el-caballo-de-hierro-los.html.
9. Kevin Czerwinski, "El Latigo Left Legacy in a Career Cut Short," MiLB.com, March 26, 2008. milb.com/milb/news/el-latigo-left-legacy-in-a-career-cut-short/c-365649.
10. Tusa.
11. Tusa.
12. *"La Voz del Fanático."*
13. *"La Voz del Fanático."*
14. *"La Voz del Fanático."*
15. Miguel Dupoy Gómez, "Béisbol Inmortal: Roberto Muñoz, el 'Caballo de Hierro' Venezolano," September 1, 2016. beisbolinmortal.blogspot.com/2016/09/roberto-munoz-el-caballo-de-hierro.html.
16. pelotabinaria.com.ve/beisbol/mostrar.php?ID=torrne1001.
17. "Wilson Alvárez, Luis Salazar, Oswaldo Guillén y Roberto Muñoz exaltados al Salón de la Fama 2011," September 13, 2011. valenciainforma.obolog.es/wilson-alvarez-luis-salazar-oswaldo-guillen-roberto-munoz-exaltados-al-salon-fama-2011-13-9-2011-1274738.
18. museodebeisbol.com./salon_fama_venezolano/get/2011.
19. Ignacio Serrano, "Se fué un inmortal, el gran Roberto Muñoz," *El Emergente*, September 24, 2012, elemergente.com/2012/09/se-fue-un-inmortal-el-gran-roberto-munoz.html.
20. "Retiran el número 20 con que jugó; Roberto 'Pluto' Muñoz será homenajeado este domingo en Aragua," *Correo del Orinoco*, December 13, 2015. correodelorinoco.gob.ve/roberto-pluto-munoz-sera-homenajeado-este-domingo-aragua/.

FRANK SAUCIER

By Jim Ball

At age 25, after becoming the best hitter in three different minor leagues – preceded by two-years' service as an officer in the US Navy – Frank Saucier was the St. Louis Browns' most sought-after and anticipated post-World War II rookie since the club signed future 20-game-winning pitcher Ned Garver and slugger Roy Sievers, the American League's first Rookie of the Year, in 1949.[1]

On August 19, 1951, against the visiting Detroit Tigers, the left-hand-hitting Saucier, starting in right field, was headed to home plate in the bottom of the first inning in the second game of a doubleheader in Sportsman's Park, when his and baseball's world came to a shocking standstill. Why? The phenom outfielder, suffering from an injured shoulder and severely blistered hands, had suddenly been removed from the game by the public-address announcer, making the 6-foot-1, 180-pound Saucier the most famous major-league leadoff batter never to step into the batter's box for one unprecedented reason: his replacement was 3-foot-7, 26-year-old showman Eddie Gaedel, the most famous and shortest-lived Brownie rookie never to swing a bat.[2]

Their walks of fame past each other became one of the most storied strolls ever in a big-league game. The result for Saucier was a laughable few minutes from the bench, and for Gaedel, a statuesque squat in the right-hand batter's box that led to an unforgettable photograph and zany free pass to first base. Only Little Eddie's boss-for-a-day, Browns owner Bill Veeck, could conjure the wacky scheme he needed to excite the Sunday afternoon crowd of 20,299 (18,369 paid), the largest of the year.[3] No ballpark gag was ever too extreme for Veeck, baseball's sideshow impresario, whose Browns were wading through another lackluster season, buried in the American League basement and on their way to losing 102 games. Veeck's bit of "dog days" theatrics was a dandy, despite his Browns losing both games, 5-2 and 6-2.[4]

Gaedel's one official plate appearance was more a speed bump than a milestone along baseball's endless highway of significant events. Veeck's circus act in the second game is one of the twentieth century's most laughable sports comedic moments, eventually resulting in a major-league rules change prohibiting midgets, contract or no.[5] Years later, an online story in bleacherreport.com listed Gaedel's official at-bat as number 98 in its list of 200 events that "defined, shaped and changed major-league baseball." Saucier's reaction: "Maybe, or maybe not. It might have cost me a time at bat," Saucier recalled in his memoir, "but Eddie's antic remains the funniest thing I ever saw, in or out of baseball."

Crouching in front of Detroit catcher Bob Swift to further shrink his strike zone, Gaedel drew a walk on four straight pitches from amused and confused right-handed pitcher Bob Cain.[6] Hard as he tried, Cain never sniffed the strike zone, becoming part

Frank Saucier.

Courtesy of Jim Ball.

ONE-HIT WONDERS

of an asterisk incident never to be repeated in a major-league game. Gaedel made it to first base, gave way to pinch-runner Jim Delsing and tipped his hat to the crowd. When the laughter died, so did Veeck's last-ditch effort to elevate the Browns to any level of respectability. American and National League club owners, both league presidents and the commissioner's office railed at Veeck's production that afternoon, banning Gaedel from the game and warning Veeck never again to make a mockery of professional baseball.[7]

Unknown to Veeck, his stunt meant the beginning of the end of the St. Louis Browns. American League owners began to apply every pressure possible to get Veeck out of baseball. They succeeded. Under duress, Veeck sold the club, and after the 1953 season, the Browns moved to Baltimore and became the Orioles. The Veeck-Gaedel "Midget Caper" was, however, neither the beginning nor end of Francis Field "Frank" Saucier, born on May 28, 1926, on a 160-acre farm outside Leslie, Missouri, 60 miles southwest of St. Louis. Much more defines his professional baseball, business, and private lives than one crazy afternoon in the westernmost (at the time) major-league ballpark that, like its owners, no longer exists.

Frank was the last-born child of Alexander Von Steuben Saucier and Margaret Isabel (McGee) Saucier, a family with roots reaching back to French pioneers who had been in North America since 1660. A youthful Frank studied the rudiments of baseball by watching his four brothers and sister play the game. Living near to St. Louis later brought both National League Cardinals and American League Browns games on radio into the Sauciers' farmhouse. They were the only big-league clubs at the time to play all home games in the same ballpark, obviously on different days.

When Frank was 5, the Sauciers moved 15 miles north to own and work a larger farm near the Missouri River town of Washington. There, his much older brother Clay taught him to throw, catch, and hit a ball, immediately becoming his full-time mentor and longtime adviser. "Clay treated me like I was his boy long after my adolescent years," Saucier recalled. "He was a superb tutor and cared for me greatly. As a teenager, Frank became an accomplished sandlot catcher and all-positions fielder, playing with grown men for several town baseball and softball teams. "When Adolf Hitler marched into Poland on September 1, 1939, I marched into Washington High School, knowing that before I graduated, America would likely be drawn into war," Saucier wrote in his memoirs.

Washington High had no baseball team, so Saucier became a basketball star. His play and academic accomplishments fetched the attention of Westminster College in Fulton, Missouri, where he accepted a partial scholarship. Without sufficient funds for a full ride, Saucier entered Westminster in 1943 via a different route – the US Navy's V-12 officer training program. Completing the Navy's accelerated study and training curriculum, he was able to forgo the college's undergraduate math and physics curriculum and was commissioned an ensign as World War II in the Pacific wound down. Saucier became a star varsity basketball player and a catcher-outfielder on Westminster's baseball team. Before leaving campus for his final V-12 program semesters at Notre Dame University in 1944, he batted .519, a Missouri College Athletic Union record. Long after Saucier's half-season with the Browns, Westminster renamed its ballfield Saucier Field.

After leaving Notre Dame only weeks before his 19th birthday, Saucier volunteered to join Scouts and Rangers, a combat duty group that was a forerunner to the Navy Seals. He sought command and was assigned to train and lead a beach party that would land on Japanese soil. In August 1945, halfway to the Philippines, the group learned that Army Air Force bombers had dropped two atomic bombs on Japan, effectively ending the war. There was still duty to perform. After an uncontested landing on Wakayama Beach, a few miles south of Hiroshima, Saucier made his way there to view the devastation created by the first A-bomb blast on August 6, 1945. He recalled, "I could hardly believe what I saw as my Jeep driver and I approached the bridge leading into the ashes of a city that would become powerfully engrained in history." Saucier's postwar duty ended in China as a lieutenant (j.g.) aboard the USS *Mount Olympus*, an amphibious force command ship. After four months' service, he returned to America, eager to resume his senior year at Westminster and enjoy a final baseball season. He also hoped for a tryout in Sportsman's Park, owned by the Browns and leased to the Cardinals. As did Ted Williams and thousands of veterans, Saucier left the Navy with a reserve officer obligation for six years, plus a new and powerful credential: The GI Bill of Rights. Passed by Congress and signed by another Missourian, President Harry S. Truman, the legislation among other things guaranteed veterans funding to pursue a college education; Frank could now complete, tuition-fee, a degree in physics and math.

ONE-HIT WONDERS

Years before entering Westminster, Saucier had a business career goal to play professional baseball and accumulate enough capital to become an oil wildcatter somewhere in America's Southwest. He firmly believed that baseball would be a stepping stone to successful drilling ventures. A construction job supplemented his meager savings, but a roommate's father, a successful oilman, offered counsel about what it took to find and produce oil at a profit. Until he could make a buck, the aspiring entrepreneur banked the advice. In the spring of 1948, Saucier finished his collegiate baseball season batting .500. Scouts from the Philadelphia Athletics and Browns had been watching, and began calling. St. Louis sent chief scout and management confidant Jack Fournier to arrange a visit, talk about a contract and deliver Frank to Sportsman's Park and a tryout for Browns manager Zack Taylor and club owners, brothers Bill and Charlie DeWitt. An impressive workout led to a contract offer, which Saucier turned down, explaining that his degree came first, but that he would consider signing after graduating.

Diploma in hand a few weeks later, Saucier agreed to DeWitt's contract terms to catch for the Belleville Stags of the Class-D Illinois State League. As he returned home to sign his contract, the car in which he was a passenger ran off the road, injuring both the driver and Frank, whose right knee banged into the dashboard. His pal suffered severe facial cuts from broken glass, Shaken, but undeterred, the pair finished the slow trip home to Washington without further incident. Saucier did not tell Charlie DeWitt about the crash and his deep bruise.

After convalescing for several days, the Browns' newest phenom took a bus to St. Louis with his clothes, spikes, catcher's mitt, and outfielder's glove stuffed into one suitcase. Signed and ready for delivery to Belleville by Jack Fournier, they crossed the Mississippi River. En route, Saucier learned that a new young batterymate would soon arrive. Charlie DeWitt had also snagged a 17-year-old local high school phenom for $600 – a flamethrowing righty named Bob Turley.

The five-year age difference between Saucier and Turley benefited both rookies. Turley had never worked with a collegiate catcher, and Frank now had a willing student. At 6-feet-2 and 200 pounds, Turley was raw and wild, according to Saucier, but went the distance in his first start. As the Stags advanced toward the playoffs. Saucier had become the league's top hitter, aided by 20/10 vision and a reliable swing. He was batting .357 with fewer than 20 regular-season games left and catching righty Mike Blyzka when a foul tip broke his right thumb: Season over.[8]

"Too bad for Frank, a terrific hitter," recalled another Illinois State League rookie, scrappy 17-year-old second baseman Earl Weaver, signed by the St. Louis Cardinals to play for the West Frankfort (Illinois) Cardinals. The future Hall of Fame manager would later give Bill Veeck's extant club the stature Bill so sorely wanted. "(Frank) was hittin' the hell out of everything and leading the league in batting when he got injured. Broken thumb, I believe."[9] What a memory, without being prompted during an interview nearly 60 years later. Saucier's thumb healed over the winter to the obvious delight of the DeWitts, who sent him to Florida for spring training as a catcher with its Triple-A Baltimore Orioles club, where he would start the 1949 International League season. Saucier didn't like early spring East Coast weather and demanded to play in Texas, where the Browns had two teams, the Double-A San Antonio Missions and the Class-B Wichita Falls Spudders. He insisted that his Baltimore salary of some $6,000 also travel to the Lone Star State. The DeWitts agreed to pay the sum, which was far above the organization's average and $1,000 more than the major-league minimum at the time. With veteran catcher and second-year manager Gus Mancuso already in place at San Antonio, the Missions' roster was full, so Frank reported to Wichita Falls, close to the oil patches of his dreams.

At Wichita Falls, Saucier dazzled his teammates, winning the Big State League batting title with a .446 average, then the highest-ever mark in the history of Organized Baseball. He had 141 hits in 316-at bats, earning him the Hillerich & Bradsby Silver Slugger Award as the minor leagues' top hitter. Saucier's astonishing season landed him at Double-A San Antonio as a full-time left fielder in 1950, despite the DeWitts' pleas to come to St. Louis. Saucier's three-part response to their urging in early September settled the issue: San Antonio had a shot at the Dixie Series, the Texas League offered more lucrative contacts with owners in the oil business, and it had better hotels than where the Browns stayed. Frank's biggest advocates promoting his status quo were Charlie DeWitt and Frank's skipper, former Browns infielder Don Heffner, "the best manager I ever had."

Throughout the 1950 season, Saucier was locked in a three-way race for the batting title, finishing with a league-leading .343 average, edging out Fort Worth's future Hall of Famer Dick Williams and Beaumont's Gil McDougald, a Yankees farm phenom and

ONE-HIT WONDERS

soon-to-be American League Rookie of the Year. San Antonio won the Texas League Shaughnessy Playoffs, first sweeping Rogers Hornsby's Beaumont club in the best-of-seven first round and defeating Tulsa four games to two, earning the right to face Nashville in the Dixie Series.[11] Saucier led his team to that seven-game championship, was named MVP and promptly drove to Niagara Falls, New York, for a honeymoon vacation with Virginia Pullen, whom he'd met while playing in Wichita Falls. Now married, the Sauciers were satisfied through the winter that baseball was in their rear-view mirror, especially when their Oklahoma oil wells were producing high quality crude worth a steady $2.38 a barrel.

Oil and baseball aside in 2020 at age 94, Saucier greatly praised Charlie DeWitt and defended both owner-brothers with regard to spending money where and when they needed it most. "The DeWitts were not cheapskates, as many during my career wrongly described them. They were shrewd, honest business operators, just not with the wealth of the Yankees, Red Sox, and other perennial first division teams. Charlie changed a lot of little things during and after the 1950 season and often traveled with us. We used to carry our own bags from trains and hotels, and Charlie put a stop to that. He didn't have to, but thought it only right, even when the club was losing money and going South." By Christmas 1950, still under contract to the Browns, Saucier voluntarily retired from baseball. A week later, he read that *The Sporting News* had named him Minor League Player of the Year; front-page coverage with his illustrated likeness along that of the Major League Player of the Year, Yankees shortstop Phil Rizzuto. Three weeks later, the Associated Press wrote of Frank, "Saucier, pronounced Sow-Shay, is like a figure in a dime novel. His batting feats during his three years of organized baseball are truly amazing. If he can come anywhere near his minor league marks with the Browns, they may come up with the greatest individual drawing card they've had since George Sisler."[10]

Despite the notoriety and press focus on the Browns, Saucier declined the DeWitts' pleas for him to reconsider retirement and report to Browns' spring training in California. His oil wells were running smoothly and the price per barrel rising. A frustrated Bill DeWitt said that because Saucier would neither renew his contract nor report to camp, he would ask the American League to place him on the ineligible player list.

Saucier explained, "I told Harry Mitauer of the (St. Louis) *Globe-Democrat* that I'd mortgaged everything I owned and had borrowed considerable money to buy an interest in a wildcat oil well. I'm getting a tidy sum now," he wrote on April 15, and added that the well was producing about 150 barrels a day. Two days later, Commissioner Happy Chandler wired Saucier that he was ineligible to play for St. Louis. Two months later, North Korea invaded South Korea, beginning a two-year-long war that would take Saucier from spring training into active service in the Navy through 1954.

The route to Saucier's eventual end as a major leaguer began in July 1951, two days after Bill Veeck bought the club from the DeWitt brothers and a handful of other shareholders. "Shirtsleeve Bill," so labeled by baseball writers, was desperate to resurrect his fast-fading enterprise. The day before he took over the Browns ownership, St. Louis had dropped an Independence Day doubleheader to the Yankees, leaving baseball's most flamboyant operator with a fire-sale acquisition, a 21-49 won-lost record and sole possession of the American League basement. Veeck never doubted that Saucier wouldn't remedy his team's biggest problem: lack of hitters.

Through much pleading, and knowing that Saucier had missed spring training, Veeck made a wild midnight dash from St. Louis to Washington, Missouri, to persuade him to sign a contract his new boss admitted he couldn't afford. Saucier waited a day to unretire, agreeing to bring a sorely needed spark to the Browns' impotent offense. Veeck's price to accommodate them both was $10,000 and two IOUs, the latter a handsome reserve amount for Saucier while his oil interest continued to flourish. Pitcher Ned Garver, third baseman-outfielder Roy Sievers, and right-handed pitching legend Leroy "Satchel" Paige were the only Browns to earn more money that season.

With the Browns on a road trip, Saucier reported to Sportsman's Park bringing a badly-injured right shoulder, hurt the previous season in San Antonio. Veeck and manager Zack Taylor rushed him into catch-up batting practice regimes that produced constantly bleeding and scabbed hand blisters. "After the first week in pain, and unable to swing the bat that had brought me back-to-back batting titles, I was never really the same. Having 20/10 vision simply wasn't enough." On July 21 he appeared in his first game at home, against the Yankees. After a few more games mainly as a pinch-hitter and pinch-runner, Saucier was in right field on August 19, unaware that he was a half-inning away from his most extraordinary

ONE-HIT WONDERS

appearance as a professional. His only action afield occurred in the opening frame, when he snagged a chest-high line drive roped by Detroit right fielder Vic Wertz. Then came the Gaedel star appearance. Amid the clamor of such opening-frame antics, not even a well-orchestrated comedy could save the Browns, who lost, 6-2.

Saucier's hands and right shoulder never healed. He played in eight more games, starting one, and having spot roles in others. His lone big-league hit, a long pinch-hit double in Cleveland's cavernous Municipal Stadium off Mike Garcia, came on August 7. After his last outfield start, on August 26, 1951, Saucier watched 33 more games from his own and three visitors' dugouts, a brief but historic time as a Brownie: 18 games, three starts, one hit, four runs scored, one RBI, two pinch-hit walks, one HBP, four strikeouts, and two errors made in the first game he started against the Yankees. Nonetheless, Frank Saucier had accomplished an aspiration to be a major leaguer.

When the New York Yankees and Giants squared off in the World Series, Saucier's and Veeck's sights were already on the 1952 season under new manager and St. Louis favorite, Hall of Famer Rogers Hornsby. Frank was familiar with the Beaumont and Texas League All-Star game manager, after a celebratory 1951 season as pilot of the Pacific Coast League champion Seattle Rainiers. The great right-hand hitter, and the last National Leaguer to bat over .400, telephoned Saucier after New Year's Day and asked him to report early to spring camp in El Centro, California. Hornsby knew Saucier's batting skills, telling him three days later, "You're my left fielder." As Veeck later told Saucier, "If a professional baseball player couldn't hit at least .300, Rogers – who'd compiled a .358 average over 23 years – wasn't all that interested in him. I knew that after that first week, he was salivating to begin the season with you in the daily lineup."

The Browns moved to Burbank to finish preseason work with Saucier and newly acquired slugger Jim Rivera already composing two-thirds of Hornsby's outfield. Rivera had been Hornsby's all-everything star at Seattle and hands-down Pacific Coast League MVP and batting champ (.352, 231 hits, 135 runs scored). Hornsby especially needed Saucier and Rivera to carry the Browns offense after former AL Rookie of the Year and Veeck's only other legitimate .300 hitter, Roy Sievers, went down in El Centro with a shoulder injury, his second since batting .306 in his rookie season, and was never well enough to regain his third-base position. Frank remained confident that he would be in Hornsby's starting lineup if one looming cloud of doubt was removed: the prospect that as a former active-duty Navy officer with a reserve-duty obligation, he could be recalled at any time during the lengthening and grueling Korean War.

At Burbank and St. Louis in 1951, Saucier unknowingly had been sent orders to report to active duty a month before his 27th birthday. It wasn't his first notice from Uncle Sam. A locker-room attendant handed him a second telegram from the Navy, forcing Veeck to reveal that he had received and destroyed Saucier's first recall orders. Frank's future was cast, and pro baseball would become a thing of the past. When Saucier cleaned out his locker to leave Burbank, Veeck stopped by to explain his peculiar action to hide the Navy's quest to locate their reservist. Saucier told Veeck, a Marine disabled by accident during World War II service in the Pacific, that his misconduct could have been a prosecutable federal crime. To cover his transgression and without blinking, Veeck told Frank, "I needed you more than the Navy. I needed to protect my investment, especially after Roy's injury."

Saucier said goodbye to an embarrassed Veeck, a dejected Hornsby, and his locker mate from the '51 season, Satchel Paige. He reported to Pensacola Naval Air Station, and for the next two years was put in charge of all preflight administration protocols at Base Headquarters Cadet Battalion. He also played left field for the preflight Goslings, leading them to the Sixth Naval District championship and batting over .500. His final game at Memphis Naval Air Station was also his last ever in flannels. Three months later, as a newly promoted lieutenant, Frank had a visit from Veeck, who in midseason had shed himself of Hornsby, choosing another St. Louis favorite, Marty Marion, to manage the club to the finish line. Veeck came to Pensacola for one reason: to make a hat-in-hand appeal to Navy brass to release Saucier – still his official American League contract player – from active duty to play in 1953.

Saucier said he was shocked at Veeck's brazen suggestion, reminding him that the Sauciers belonged to the Navy, and halfway through their hitch were still celebrating the birth of their first child, Sara. Again, Frank declared that his baseball career was over. Veeck resisted, saying that if Saucier wouldn't reconsider going to spring training, he would fly to Washington to meet with Saucier's "fellow" Missourian, President Harry S. Truman. "Bill was adamant, saying he would stop at nothing to ask the soon retiring commander-in-chief to have me discharged in order to

ONE-HIT WONDERS

'protect my interest.' I laughed and told Bill that his effort would be wasted time. Truman had six weeks left in office before former five-star General Dwight D. Eisenhower was inaugurated as the 34th president.

"I suggested to Veeck that Truman probably had other things on his mind," Saucier later wrote. "I thanked Bill, told him I appreciated everything he had done for me and handed him back the two IOUs that he gave me in July of 1951. Bill was surprised, but we both knew he needed the money a lot more than I did. If he ever made good on his effort to see President Truman, I never knew about it. I could only hope that he didn't."

Saucier and Veeck never met again. Saucier was released from active duty in April 1954 and, with family in tow, left Pensacola for Texas. The next 38 years were spent in the oil, gas, and chemical industries in Tyler, where son John was born; Pampa; and Amarillo. Virginia died in 2009. She remains the answer to decades-long inquiries about Frank's greatest thrill in baseball. "Meeting Virginia Pullen in 1949 in Wichita Falls," he responded unhesitatingly about his baseball, business, and life partner. "The night she said 'yes' was the biggest thrill of my life."

On his 94th birthday, May 26, 2020, Frank Saucier was the lone surviving player in Bill Veeck's 1951 "Midget Caper." When the 2019 World Series ended in Houston on October 30, Saucier was one of only 26 living former major leaguers to have served in World War II.[14] Still in Amarillo as of August 2020, he said he looked forward to signing autographs from fans of all ages. Regrets? "None," he said. "I got to be a major leaguer and invested my Browns money, which fueled my business future. I'm always proud to credit the DeWitt brothers, whose generosity and faith in me led to a good baseball and business life, shared with a wonderful wife, two loving and educated children, and always peace of mind. My cap is always off to those men, the St. Louis Browns, little Eddie Gaedel and of course Bill Veeck, who gave me a second chance to become a big leaguer."

SOURCES

All direct quotes not otherwise attributed are from interviews with Frank Saucier by the author and from Saucier's memoirs. In addition to the sources cited in the Notes, the author also consulted Baseball-Reference.com and the following:

Saucier, Frank. *My Story* (60-page memoir typed in 1997, containing personal recollections, photos and press clippings (many publication datelines and page numbers missing) from the *Dallas Times-Herald, Fort Worth Star-Telegram, San Antonio Express-News, Fort Worth Press, St. Louis Post-Dispatch, The Sporting News, Waco Tribune, Wichita Falls Record-News,* and *Washington Missourian*, April 1948-March 1952).

O'Neal, Bill. *The Texas League* (Austin, Texas: Eakin Press, 1987).

Rapoport, Ron. *Let's Play Two* (New York: Hachette Books, 2019).

INTERVIEWS

Garver, Ned, October 8, 2009, St. Louis.

Saucier, Frank, multiple from 2006 to 2020.

Sievers, Roy, October 8, 2009, St. Louis.

Weaver, Earl. November 9, 2007, Fort Worth, Texas.

Broeg, Bob, July 28, 2007, St. Louis (SABR 37).

NOTES

1. Miles Wolff, ed., *The Baseball Encyclopedia*, 9th ed. (New York: Macmillan Publishing Co., 1993).
2. Frank Saucier, *My Story*, memoir, 1997. See also Frank Saucier and Jim Ball, *It Wasn't All About Eddie* (unpublished manuscript, 2020).
3. Author interview with Bob Broeg, July 28, 2007.
4. *St. Louis Globe-Democrat*, August 20, 1951: C3.
5. Bob Broeg, *Bob Broeg: Memories of a Hall of Fame Sportswriter* (Champaign, Illinois: Sagamore Publishing, 1995).
6. *St. Louis Globe-Democrat*, August 20, 1951: C3.
7. Bill Rogers, ed., *Pop Flies: The Official Magazine of the St. Louis Browns Historical Society*, St. Louis, issues from 2009-2015.
8. *News-Democrat* (Belleville, Illinois), August 4, 1948. At season's end, he finished second in batting average to Richie Martz's .361.
9. Earl Weaver interview, Fort Worth, Texas, November 9, 2007.
10. Associated Press, "Browns Have Another Sisler on Way Up from Texas League in Francis Saucier," *Washington Post*, January 25, 1951: 18.

SCOTT SERVICE

By Len Pasculli

Pitcher Scott Service had a long and workmanlike professional career. He appeared in 338 major-league games from his debut on September 5, 1988, until his final game on September 26, 2004. With his minor-league games included, Service's professional career spanned 905 games over 19 seasons from ages 19 through 37 (1986-2004), including the one game he pitched in the Japan Central League in 1991.

Scott David Service, born in Cincinnati on February 26, 1967, was the youngest child of John and Ruth Service. He had four older sisters. His mother listened to Reds broadcasters Marty Brennaman and Joe Nuxhall all the time. She told everybody that her boy was going to be a Reds player one day.[1]

Service played baseball and football (punter and backup quarterback) at Aiken High School and graduated in 1985. He said he was not outstanding in high school. However, he is the only Aiken High School alumnus to play in the major leagues.[2] The 6-foot-6 right-hander worked at developing both his body and his fastball in his senior year. He played summer league baseball and pitched for the West All-Stars who defeated the East All-Stars 10-9 on May 27, 1985. Service struck out four batters in two innings, was the winning pitcher, and was voted the West's Most Valuable Player.[3]

Service was scouted by the Expos, Blue Jays, Yankees, and Phillies. At a tryout in August 1985, he impressed Phillies scout Tony Lucadello with his 90-mph fastball. Lucadello signed him on the spot as an undrafted free agent.[4]

Service honed his craft in the Philadelphia Phillies farm system from 1986 through August 1988, both as a starter and a reliever. He toiled for three Class-A clubs in 1986 (Spartanburg, Utica, and Clearwater). In 1987 he bounced from Clearwater to Double-A Reading (Eastern League).

Service made nine starts for Reading when the 1988 season began. He made 18 starts for Triple-A Maine (Old Orchard Beach) and led the team in wins (8) and ERA among the starters (3.67). When his manager George Culver beckoned Service to tell him he was going to "The Show," Service had won six of his last eight games.[5]

As one might expect from such a long professional career, Service experienced many colorful and memorable baseball moments, starting with his arrival in Philadelphia's Veterans Stadium on September 1, 1988. The first player to meet Service at his locker was Mike Schmidt. It was not long after Service stammered through his greeting that he learned that Schmidt had been asked by Lucadello, who had signed the future Hall of Famer in 1971, to take Service under his wing.[6]

Service was scheduled to make his major-league debut as the Phillies' starter in the second game of a Labor Day doubleheader against the Chicago Cubs at Wrigley Field on September 5.[7] However, the game on Sunday was rained out and Sunday's scheduled starter Shane Rawley started the Labor Day nightcap instead.

As it turned out, Service got the ball for the first time in the sixth inning of the opener that day with the Phillies trailing 10-3. The first batter he faced was Shawon Dunston, who singled to left but then was erased in a double play. Service faced the minimum six batters in his two innings, including strikeouts of Ryan Sandberg and Rafael Palmeiro in the seventh. He was the most effective of the six Phillies who pitched in that game, which the Phillies lost 14-3. During his maiden September call-up, Service made five relief appearances, and allowed only one run in 5⅓ innings pitched.

Still young, Service returned to the minors in 1989 for more seasoning. He spent his age 22 campaign first with Reading and then with Scranton/Wilkes-Barre, the Phillies' new Triple-A team. At Scranton, he got six saves and three wins, with a 2.16 ERA in 23 relief appearances. In 1990 he made 45 appearances, including nine starts, for Scranton, with five wins, two saves, and 8.8 strikeouts per nine innings. He began utilizing his big sweeping slider to complement his fastball. Later in his career, probably helping to protract his career in fact, Service also developed a forkball. But

ONE-HIT WONDERS

it was that slider that paid the bills. And it was that slider that Service's buddy Bronson Arroyo wanted to learn when they both played for the Nashville Sounds, the Pirates' Triple-A team, in 2002 (and which Service believed improved the trajectory of Arroyo's career).[8]

After spending five years in the Phillies farm system, Service was granted free agency in October 1990 and was signed by the Montreal Expos in November. In 1991 he pitched well for the Triple-A Indianapolis Indians: 2.97 ERA, with a 1.005 WHIP. Yet, rather than giving Service a call-up, the Expos sold his contract in July 1991 to the Chunichi Dragons of the Japan Central League. He was surprised but excited to go.

In 1981-1993, the Japanese league allowed only two non-native players on the active roster, three in the organization. The Dragons were looking for insurance in case Scott Anderson, who had been released by the Expos and signed by the Dragons eight months before Service was signed, went down with an injury.[9] In the 2½ months he was in Japan (July-September 1991), Service played mostly on Chunichi's taxi squad, made up of players who were not on the active 25-man roster. Anderson stayed healthy and appeared in 54 games (46 starts) over two seasons before catching on with the Florida Marlins organization in 1993. Service, on the other hand, faced five batters in a mere one inning of work for the Dragons. (He allowed one run on three hits.)

Service returned to Indianapolis when the Expos signed him as a free agent after the 1991 season. The Expos told him that with his fastball-slider repertoire, he would be a good reliever. It appears they were right. At Indianapolis he made 13 relief appearances and chalked up a 2-0 record with a stellar 0.74 ERA and 0.863 WHIP. He struck out 25 batters in 24⅓ innings. However, he did not perform nearly as well when he was called up by the Expos (15 hits, 11 earned runs in 7 innings).

Service was released by Montreal on June 8, signed with the Reds the next day, and joined their Triple-A affiliate, the Nashville Sounds. In 39 games (two starts), his ERA was 2.29. He struck out 87 batters in 70⅔ innings. In a Sounds loss to the Buffalo Bisons on August 18, Service struck out all nine batters he faced in three innings of relief. After he struck out the eighth batter, Bison Jeff Richardson popped up into foul territory near the Sounds dugout. Pitching coach Frank Funk yelled to first baseman Russ Morman, "Don't catch it!" Service looked into the dugout quizzically, and asked Funk, "Why'd you do that?" Funk replied, "Just strike him out." And Service did. In the next moment, he was rushed by his coaches and teammates, slapping him on the back as if he had just won a playoff game.[10] That's when he learned that his nine consecutive strikeouts set a new American Association record.[11]

Soon after the trip to Japan, Service married Tonya Hahn, his high-school sweetheart. She enjoyed traveling with him to Japan and to Venezuela (for winter league while Service was with the San Francisco Giants). "All the years were fun," she said. Throughout his career, he shuttled between the majors and the minors quite a bit. "We were excellent packers," said Tonya.[12]

Looking at it now, Service's hot and cold career – so customary for a middle reliever – had just enough spice to counteract the ice and to keep him in the majors for 12 more years after 1992. He got his first real taste of the major leagues in 1993. He appeared in five games with the Expos in 1992 and three with the Colorado Rockies in 1993 before he was selected off waivers by the Cincinnati Reds. From July 10 through the end of the season, he appeared in 26 big-league games for the Reds.

On July 10, 1993, Service relieved Tim Belcher in the sixth inning with the Reds trailing the Pittsburgh Pirates, 7-6. Service pitched three perfect innings while his teammates scored four runs. Rob Dibble pitched a perfect bottom of the ninth, and saved Service's first major-league win.

On August 5, in a road game against the Los Angeles Dodgers, Reds staff ace Jose Rijo was coasting with an 11-1 lead after seven innings. Then came a moment that Service did not see coming.

Manager Davey Johnson had already used three pinch-hitters and one pinch-runner, and another position player, Barry Larkin, was out with a sprained

ONE-HIT WONDERS

thumb. So, when Rijo's batting turn came up in the bottom of the seventh, Johnson looked down the row of players in the dugout, at their feet.

"Serv," he hollered. "You have your spikes on? Grab a bat." Up to that point, Service had five major-league at-bats — "all forward K's or backward K's." But he strolled to the plate to pinch-hit. "I just stuck out my bat," Service said, and grounded out to second. "I shoulda never put my spikes on," he said with a touch of rue.[13]

Then came the game that put Service in the "one-hit wonder" category. By August 7 he had come to bat in the big leagues six times, twice in 1992 and four up to this point in 1993. Five of those at-bats had produced strikeouts, plus the groundout two days earlier.

In the August 7 game against Orel Hershiser and the Los Angeles Dodgers, Service surprised everyone, including himself. Reds second-year pitcher Tim Pugh got into trouble early against the Dodgers, allowing five hits and two walks. Los Angeles scored three runs in the third, and Pugh was lifted with two outs. Service came in from the bullpen and struck out Cory Snyder to end the rally.

Leading off the top of the fourth against Hershiser, Jeff Branson singled to center. After Hal Morris grounded out, Kevin Mitchell and Chris Sabo both singled, and Reggie Sanders tripled to right field. The score was now tied, 3-3. Joe Oliver worked out a walk. Hershiser intentionally passed Juan Samuel in order to bring Service to the plate. That walk was the only time in Service's major-league career – 12 years, 17 at-bats – that the opposing pitcher intentionally walked the batter immediately ahead of Service in order to pitch to him. But on this day, the Dodgers strategy failed. Service hit a line drive to left field to score Sanders and give the Reds a 4-3 lead. Service did have 11 hits (out of 93 at-bats) in the minor leagues. However, that RBI single in Dodger Stadium was the only hit he got in the big leagues, and the only time that he hit the ball out of the infield. The Dodgers got a run off Service in the bottom of the fifth and tied the game; however, the Reds eventually won 9-6 on three unearned runs in the eighth and ninth innings.

On September 4 the Reds hosted the Phillies. Cincinnati was leading 6-1 when closer Rob Dibble came on in the ninth and allowed three runs on four walks and two hits while getting only one out. The bases were loaded when Davey Johnson called on Service to put out the fire. Service got Milt Thompson to ground into a force play at second, allowing one of Dibble's runners to score. But when Kevin Stocker grounded out, the Reds came away with the 6-5 victory, and Service earned his first major-league save.

Although the next stretch of professional service time for Service was certainly stamped by solid stints with major-league clubs, those years were best marked by his run with a minor-league team. From 1991 to 1997, before he was traded to the Kansas City Royals on July 15, 1997, Service pitched in 106 games in the major leagues for the Expos, the Rockies, the Reds, and the Giants. During that same time span, he pitched in 196 games for the Indianapolis Indians. The Indians were the Triple-A affiliate of the Expos when Service played there in 1991 and 1992, and when he played there from 1993 to 1997, they had become an affiliate of the Reds.

The 196 games Service pitched for Indianapolis were the most games he pitched for any major- or minor-league team. He was the Indians' closer in his last four years with the team, which he helped finish in first place twice (1994 and 1995) and second place in the East Division in 1996 and 1997. In those four years, Service racked up 13, 18, 15, and 15 saves, respectively, to go along with the four he got for the club in 1992-1993, for a total of 65 saves, making him the career leader in saves for the Indianapolis Indians.

On July 21, 1995, the Reds were in first place but needed help in their rotation. Service and pitchers John Roper and Ricky Pickett, infielder Dave McCarty, and outfielder Deion Sanders were traded to the San Francisco Giants for pitchers Dave Burba and Mark Portugal, and outfielder Darren Lewis. This was noteworthy because the Reds finished in first place in the NL Central that year but Service was not there for the postseason. He was in first place with the Reds in 1994 but that was the year the players went on strike, and there were no playoffs or World Series. Service was also with the Oakland Athletics in 2000 when they went to the American League Division Series, but he was not on the postseason roster. Thus, he came close three times but never pitched in a major-league postseason game.

Service pitched well with the Giants in 1995, achieving a personal-best 3.19 ERA. He had three wins, seven holds, and allowed only 18 hits in 31 innings over 28 relief appearances. Yet, he was released after his one season with the Giants. He went back to the Reds as a free agent and played two more seasons with them. In 1996 he regained the success he had with the Reds back in 1993. In 34 games he struck out 8.6 batters per nine innings (8.7 in 1993; 8.9 over his entire major-league career) and held opponents to

ONE-HIT WONDERS

3.94 earned runs per nine innings (3.70 in 1993; 4.99 for his career).

As if getting one hit in a 12-season major-league career was not momentous enough, Service topped it. In 338 appearances, he was the starting pitcher in only one contest. He was a starter in over 100 minor-league appearances. So, what happened? "I just never considered myself a starter in the big leagues," he said.[14]

The game Service did start took place on July 22, 1996. He had been called up in early July. Coming out of the All-Star break, the team had already played on 11 consecutive days and was now scheduled to play a doubleheader against the Phillies. Manager Ray Knight gave the ball to Service in the nightcap, his first major-league start after 81 relief appearances. He gave up eight hits and left the game after five innings with his team trailing 3-0. He came away with a no-decision when his teammates scored five runs in the last four innings to win the game, 5-3.

Service has another out-of-the-ordinary story. From time to time, a major-league pitcher will have the same name as a position player. Broadcasters and writers seem to enjoy taking note of those occasions when they face each other in a game. In 1991 a catcher and future major-league manager by the name of Scott Servais (pronounced SER-vis) made his major-league debut with the Houston Astros. Over the next five years, the catcher Servais came to bat against the pitcher Service eight times. True to form, a YouTube video[15] and newspaper articles[16] chronicled several of those instances. In all, Scott Servais went 2-for-6 (single and double) with two strikeouts, a popup, a fly out, a walk, and a sacrifice when batting against Scott Service.

When two players have similar names, sometimes the press does not get it right. On September 3, 1999, Scott Servais the catcher hit a pinch-hit home run while with the San Francisco Giants. However, the Associated Press wrote: "Scott Service batted for Estes in the ninth and hit his first career pinch-home run."[17] The writer and the editor swung and missed on that one.

By definition, one never knows when luck with all its fickleness will strike. For Service, it was in March 1997. Twice in the same week, at a gas station in Dunedin, Florida, near Plant City Stadium, the Reds' spring-training site, he purchased five computer-generated lottery tickets for $5. The first time he won $34,500 and the second time he collected $21,900 for a total of $56,400. That two-day haul was equal to about 30 percent of his salary from the Reds that year.[18]

The Indianapolis chapter of Service's life story actually ended with a dose of melancholy. He opened the season with Cincinnati in 1997 but was sent down to Indianapolis in April. His mother, who had gotten sick with cancer, said, "Don't worry, I'll wait for you to come back to Cincinnati." In July Ruth Service took a turn for the worse. Scott jumped in his Corvette and made the 110-mile trip to Cincinnati in under 50 minutes. Ruth did wait for Scott; however, she died on July 10.[19] Five days later, Service was traded to the Kansas City Royals.[20]

After the trade, Service was assigned to the Triple-A Omaha Royals to be seasoned as a late-inning reliever. He appeared in 16 games without allowing a run, picking up nine saves in the process. When he was promoted to the Royals on August 30, he stuck with the parent club for the remainder of that season plus the next two (1998-1999).

The 2½ years with the Royals were Service's most productive major-league years. His 175 innings pitched and 23 decisions fall short of the Baseball-reference.com minimums (500 innings or 50 decisions) in its lists of team pitching leaders. However, his 9.36 strikeouts per nine innings as a Royal place him above Ian Kennedy, the team's current career leader with 8.36 strikeouts per nine innings.[21]

Service achieved personal bests in 1998 by appearing in 73 games, pitching 82⅔ innings and earning six wins. His 3.48 ERA was second only to the 3.19 he achieved with the Giants. His rate statistics in the three categories that analytics measure pitchers by today were very good: 10.34 strikeouts per nine innings, 3.7 walks per nine innings, and 0.76 home runs per nine innings. He was a late-inning specialist with 18 holds in 1998 and seven in 1999. His four saves in 1998 and eight in 1999 were second best on the team each year to the franchise's all-time saves leader, Jeff Montgomery. Over a two-week stretch in July 1999, while Montgomery was on the disabled list, Service picked up a win plus five consecutive saves. These two seasons were as close as Service would get to an all-star season.

However, a shakeup was inevitable; the Royals led all of baseball in 1999 with 30 blown saves. After the 1999 campaign, Montgomery retired and Service was released.[22] Yet, Service continued to be a sought-after commodity. Between 2000 and 2004 he was signed by the Oakland Athletics (2000), Los Angeles Dodgers (signed but released after spinal bone spur surgery before the 2001 season began), Cincinnati Reds (2001), Pittsburgh Pirates (2002), Arizona Diamondbacks

ONE-HIT WONDERS

(2003), Toronto Blue Jays (2003), Cincinnati Reds again (2003), and the Arizona Diamondbacks again (2004). That he played in 141 minor-league games and 215 major-league games as a quality late-inning reliever *after* age 30 is testament both to his perceived value to the organizations that signed him and to his physical conditioning and mental pluckiness.

Service played his last game on September 26, 2004, for the Diamondbacks. He was released on November 3, 2004, but received no calls. It appeared that he had reached the end of his run. He was 37 years old. He suffered with degenerative disks. And he was missing his kids growing up, Kyle (b. 1998) and Krystal (b. 2000). He decided to retire.[23]

As of 2021 Service lived in Cincinnati. He has worked as a pitching instructor and various other jobs for different companies since retiring from baseball. He is divorced; his daughter Krystal in 2021 was a nursing student at The Christ Hospital in Cincinnati and his son Kyle was a pitching prospect in his junior year at Northern Kentucky University. Scott worked with his son on his pitching.

Asked in 2020 what he would like to do next, Service quickly replied: "I would really like to get back into baseball. I'm only 53 and there are a lot of coaches older than that. And a lot of guys I never heard of. I think I have something to offer."[24]

SOURCES

In addition to the sources cited in the notes, the author used SABR.org, retrosheet.org, Baseball-Reference.com, Baseball-Almanac.com, statscrew.com, tcdb.com [*Trading Card Data Base*], and NewspaperArchive.com.

The author wishes to acknowledge, with thanks, the contribution of information from Alain Usereau, fellow SABR member, sports broadcaster, and author of The Expos in Their Prime: The Short-Lived Glory of Montreal's Team, 1977-1984 (Jefferson, North Carolina: McFarland & Co., 2012).

NOTES

1. Information obtained directly from Scott Service for this article (edited by the author for clarity) was provided to the author in phone conversations on October 22 and October 28, 2020, and in several follow-up e-communications (collectively referred to as "Service interview").
2. baseball-reference.com/schools/index.cgi?key_school=295f38bb.
3. Greg Hoard, "Reds Notebook: Oester Returns, but Shoulder Still Aching," *Cincinnati Enquirer*, May 28, 1985: D-4. The game was played at Riverfront Stadium prior to the Reds-Cubs game that night.
4. Service interview.
5. Service interview; see also Mark Winegardner, *Prophet of the Sandlots* (New York: Prentice Hall Press, 1990), 260-262.
6. Service interview.
7. Chic Riebel, "Padres Fatten Up on Sagging Phils," *Delaware County Sunday Times* (Upper Darby Township, Pennsylvania), September 4, 1988: 70.
8. Service interview.
9. Service interview.
10. Service interview.
11. Larry Taft, "Service's Strikeout Record Can't Save Sounds," *Tennessean* (Nashville), August 19, 1992: 1C.
12. Tonya Hahn, telephone interview, October 18, 2020.
13. Service interview.
14. Service interview.
15. YouTube, Service takes on Servais in epic face-off. Retrieved on October 16, 2020. (Reds pitcher Service struck out Cubs catcher Servais on July 7, 1996. In the video, the broadcasters erroneously report that Servais singled off Service the day before. Indeed, on July 6, 1996, Servais had three singles; however, both baseball-reference.com and retrosheet.com indicate that when Servais faced Service in the bottom of the seventh inning, he walked, not singled.)
16. Sprout and Baggot, "Commentary: Montana Can't Leave Too Fast," *Wisconsin State Journal* (Madison), August 3, 1993: 2D. Retrieved on October 16, 2020, from newspapers.com/image/406348993. (The article references Astros catcher Servais singling off Expos pitcher Service on May 25, 1992 and Astros catcher Servais popping out off Reds pitcher Service on July 27, 1993.)
17. Associated Press, "Kent, Burks Help Giants Top Bucs," *Altoona* (Pennsylvania) *Mirror*, September 4, 1999: B2.
18. Associated Press, "Lucky Service," *Panama City* (Florida) *News Herald*, March 13, 1997: 6C; Jeff Miller, "Easy Second Income," *South Florida Sun Sentinel* (Fort Lauderdale). Retrieved on October 23, 2020, from sun-sentinel.com/news/fl-xpm-1997-03-16-9703150163-story.html. The winning lottery numbers were 9, 10, 15, 17, and 18.
19. Service interview.
20. Service and pitcher Hector Carrasco were traded to the Kansas City Royals for infielder-outfielder Chris Stynes and outfielder Jon Nunnally. Service was assigned to the Royals' Triple-A affiliate in Omaha.
21. Retrieved on October 27, 2020, from baseball-reference.com/teams/KCR/leaders_pitch.shtml.
22. Montgomery and Service each had seven blown saves in 1999.
23. Service interview.
24. Service interview.

ROE SKIDMORE

By Rory Costello

"In my mind's eye, I can still see Joe Torre – he was playing third base for the Cardinals – jumping and the ball going over his glove. Jerry Reuss was pitching. He threw me a slow curve. It was a clean hit. A single down the left-field line. When you get only one hit, you don't forget."[1]

That was Roe Skidmore in 1986, sharing a laugh with Jerome Holtzman of the *Chicago Tribune* as he recalled his only plate appearance in the majors. It was September 17, 1970, and the Chicago Cubs were playing St. Louis on a rainy afternoon at Wrigley Field. The Cardinals had knocked Bill Hands out of the box in the third inning, and they were leading 8-1 when Skidmore came up as a pinch-hitter with two out in the seventh inning.

The next batter, Don Kessinger, hit into a force play. Skidmore then came out of the game for a new pitcher. The Cubs had 14 games left to play that season, but he did not get into any of them. He deserved another shot – in fact, he earned it several times over. Yet he never was recalled to the majors in a pro career that lasted five more years in five different organizations. "I always had good years in Triple A, good enough to get traded and to get an invitation to spring training," he said.[2] Yet while tinges of regret remained about what might have been, there was not a hint of bitterness.

Robert Roe Skidmore was born in Decatur, Illinois, on October 30, 1945. From birth, he went by his middle name, which came from his father. "My kindergarten teacher called me Bobby," Skidmore recalled, "and I told her in no uncertain terms to call me 'Roe' like my dad!"[3] Mike Downey, also of the *Chicago Tribune*, wrote, "Roe Skidmore – now there's a name. A beauty. So good it sounds made up, like something out of a John R. Tunis children's book. Or a Damon Runyon fable. A real made-for-the-game name."[4]

Father Roe C. Skidmore was a salesman at Raupp's Shoes, a Decatur institution.[5] His wife, Mary (maiden name Austin) never worked outside the home. Roe was the younger of their two children, coming after his sister Sharon.

"I grew up in a house about two blocks from a public park," said Skidmore. "When I was six or seven years old, my mom would let me go to the park and watch high school games, summer league baseball, and softball games. From first thing in the morning until after dark at night, all I wanted to do was play ball. When I was old enough to realize Decatur had a professional team, that sealed the deal."[6]

From 1901 through 1974, Decatur was a minor-league baseball town. When Skidmore was a boy, his father would often take him to the Commodores games at Fans Field after dinner. "A back exit from the dugout and a short path underneath the bleachers led to the players' clubhouse. In about the eighth inning, Roe would stake out a choice spot to collect autographs from the players."[7]

The field manager and general manager of the Commodores from 1955 through 1957 was Al Unser, who had played in the major leagues from 1942 through 1945. Unser was an instrumental figure in Decatur baseball and in Skidmore's career. "Indeed, he was the first scout to sign me and was one of the nicest men I met during my baseball days," said Skidmore. "I used to shag balls in the outfield when I was 8-10 years old for the Commodores along with several of Al's sons, one of whom was Delbert Unser. Del and I have been friends all these years and remain good friends today. Del and I both signed in 1966 from our respective college teams and Del went on to have a great big league career."

"Al was well known for his generosity and love for the game. I spent many hours with Al watching me and Del in the batting cage which Al constructed in his backyard in Decatur. Then later, we spent time together during the winter at 'Hot Stove League' gatherings in the Decatur area."[8]

"As a kid growing up, I always played shortstop," Skidmore remembered. "Third base in high school."[9] He went to Eisenhower High School in Decatur. One of the physical education teachers there, as well as the track coach, was Pete Innis, whose son Jeff pitched

ONE-HIT WONDERS

for the New York Mets from 1987 through 1993. Roe's friend Del Unser became a high-school rival because Del attended St. Teresa, a Catholic high school in Decatur. In Skidmore's junior year, 1962, Eisenhower won the Illinois state high school baseball championship.[10] He told blogger Tom Owens in 2013 that as luck would have it, his high school coach (a man named Clete Hinton) was at Wrigley Field to see his one hit in the majors.[11]

Skidmore stayed in Decatur to get his college education, going to Millikin University. "I played basketball in high school and one of the reasons I went to Millikin (small school) was so I could play basketball as well as baseball. I played at Millikin for two years before I was drafted, averaging 19+ points my second year in the CCIW conference."[12]

Playing shortstop once again, Skidmore was captain of Millikin's baseball team in both 1965 and 1966. The physical education major (who earned his degree in 1968) was selected by the Atlanta Braves in the 47th round of the amateur draft in June 1966. Al Unser, who had become a scout in 1963, got him for a bonus of $2,500.[13] "Al was very supportive and encouraging to me even after I left the Braves organization and throughout my career," Skidmore said.[14]

Skidmore was actually drafted as a catcher. "I was only catching," he said, "because the two regulars were hurt."[15] When he signed, Skidmore was slated to be the number-one catcher for Rapid City of South Dakota's Basin League.[16] This high-quality regional circuit, which boosted the careers of many collegiate and minor-league prospects, was in existence from 1953 through 1973. There was another good option much closer to home, the Central Illinois Collegiate League, but "I never played in the CICL and did not make it to the Basin League."[17]

Skidmore's first professional experience came with the Yakima (Washington) Braves of the Northwest League. He hit just .193 with no homers and 14 RBIs in 47 games. He started the 1967 season with West Palm Beach in the Florida State League, but played just nine games there.

A bad break then turned into a good break. As Mike Downey put it, "A broken ankle in Florida and a glut of catchers caused the Braves to let Roe go. On a long drive back to Decatur, with a pregnant wife and no prospects, his career appeared over before it really began. But up stepped a Giants scout, Swede Thompson, who signed him."[18] Gene Thompson, also known as "Junior" during his days as a big-league pitcher (1939-47), was the first big-leaguer from Decatur to play in the World Series. He scouted for the Giants for 41 years. He went on to scout for three other clubs before retiring at the age of 89.[19]

"I owe Swede Thompson a lot!" said Skidmore. "He picked me up when I was down and gave me another chance. When Atlanta released me, I felt like my world had ended. But, thanks to Swede, two days after arriving back in Decatur, I was in a Commodores uniform playing first base in a doubleheader against the Quincy Cubs. I went 6-for-7 in that doubleheader, including two long balls out in the street in left field – I was suddenly back on top!"[20]

As it happened, the Decatur Commodores were then a farm club of the Giants in the Midwest League (Single-A). Playing in front of a hometown crowd, Skidmore maintained his power stroke, hitting 14 homers in 362 at-bats and batting .276. He followed with 27 more homers in 1968, although his average slipped to .246. "It was great playing in my hometown on the nights I hit a home run, however on my 'two strikeout' nights – no fun. Too many people were watching who knew me – ha!"[21]

"I never caught for the Giants," said Skidmore. "Swede Thompson, who had scouted me at Millikin, always thought that first would be my position. So I played there from the git-go with the Giants."[22] Though he was a righty, he proved to be a skillful glove man at first.

In December 1968, the Cubs selected Skidmore from San Francisco in the minor league draft. He jumped to Triple-A Tacoma for the 1969 season and held his own (.261-16-84 in 140 games) – in fact, he was named to the Pacific Coast League's All-Star team. "No way Roe Skidmore didn't deserve a full shot in the big leagues after his '69 season," said his friend, outfielder Mike Floyd. "That field [Tacoma's Cheney Stadium] was cold and damp and the ball didn't travel. "I used to wear plastic zip-lock bags inside my shoes because the outfield was like a marsh and would soak your feet to the bone."[23]

On August 18, Skidmore took part in an in-season exhibition game between the Cubs and their rival from the South Side of Chicago, the White Sox. The annual Boys Benefit game took place at Comiskey Park before a good crowd of 33,333. The *Tribune* showed a pregame picture of Ernie Banks demonstrating his batting grip to Skidmore, who later came in to replace "Mr. Cub" at first base.[24]

Tacoma won the PCL playoffs, and the team got championship rings. They were rather modest pieces, but Skidmore treasures his. "I have it on my ring finger

ONE-HIT WONDERS

next to my wedding band right now," he said in 2016. "I have worn it every day since we all received it, and I never take it off...even when I work out!"[25]

He had to wait until after that victory, but Skidmore actually got his first call-up to the majors in September 1969, while the Cubs were in the process of losing the National League East to the New York Mets. He did not get into a game, though. "Mainly we just sat there and waited. [Manager] Leo [Durocher] wouldn't play us [the call-ups]. He didn't deviate from his regular lineup."[26] Skidmore left before the season ended to play in the Arizona Instructional League.[27]

According to Cubs general manager John Holland, "He's so quiet, Leo said that when he reported, he said 'Hello' and that's the last word he heard from him in the two weeks he was up. But, in his own way, he's a determined, hard-nosed kid."[28] In retrospect, Skidmore thought that being quiet may have contributed to his lack of opportunity with the Cubs. As David Margolick of the *New York Times* wrote in 1999, "He thinks Durocher had it right about nice guys finishing last. 'I didn't whine,' said Skidmore."[29]

In Arizona, Roe followed up with a very strong showing (.305-11-35 in 41 games). That December John Holland said, "We're very high on Skidmore. After seeing him in the Instructional League, Leo is planning on keeping him with us all season. . .With Leo just breaking him in easy, there will be no pressure on him and we feel that he'll make steady progress."[30]

During camp in March, Durocher said of Skidmore, "He has the greatest opportunity in the world. He can hit the ball out of any park in the world. If he can play, I can rest Ernie [Banks] for a couple of days."[31] This echoed Holland's earlier remarks about how Banks had gotten little rest because his backups were not viewed as good fielders. The GM's described Skidmore on defense this way: "very smooth around the bag, has a strong, accurate arm and makes the reverse double play as well as any righthander ever did."[32]

As the 1970 season developed, however, the Cubs used Jim Hickman at first base more than Banks, who missed time with an arthritic left knee. Willie Smith picked up most of the playing time that was left over, and Joe Pepitone was around after late July too. Durocher's view on young players was ambivalent. Over his career, he backed certain rookies, notably Willie Mays. Yet looking back, Cubs reliever Phil Regan said, "Leo didn't like young guys."[33]

Skidmore minced no words when it came to The Lip. "Leo Durocher was the most intimidating, foul-mouthed, nastiest, arrogant man I have ever met. Just being honest. He was your typical 'old school' tobacco-chewing hard-nosed baseball man. He didn't like the young players and he let us know it by totally ignoring us. On the other hand, my two Cubs minor-league managers were two fine gentlemen – Whitey Lockman and Jim Marshall. Very knowledgeable about the game, but also respectful, quality individuals."[34]

Skidmore went back to Tacoma to start the 1970 season, and he went into an early 0-for-31 slump.[35] He hit .207-11-37 in 78 games and so went down to Double-A San Antonio. There he rebounded (.316-6-39 in 52 games). It was enough to warrant another call-up when the big-league rosters expanded that September. Again it was a tight race in the NL East, this time a three-way battle with the Pittsburgh Pirates as well as the Mets.

When the opportunity to play came at last, it was not a pressure situation, but "I remember my knees were shaking," Skidmore told Jerome Holtzman. In his 2003 chat with Mike Downey, he gave even more detail. "'I remember going to the bat rack, being so nervous. I grabbed J.C. Martin's bat because I couldn't find one of mine. I had faced Jerry Reuss in the minors. I knew he had this big overhand curve ball. Well, his first pitch was a fastball down the middle. I swung about an hour late. Fouled it to the first-base side.' He took the next pitch, a ball. 'The third pitch, he threw me that overhand curve. He did me a favor.'"[36]

Skidmore told Holtzman that as he was trotting back to the bench after being forced out, first-base coach Joe Amalfitano ran beside him and handed him the ball. 'Here,' Amalfitano said, 'it's your first hit. Save the ball.'"[37] It went up on his mantelpiece, inscribed by his wife, "1st Big League hit," – as David Margolick put it, "not knowing she could have written 'last' or 'only' too.[38]

"I thought that was the beginning," Skidmore told Holtzman. "It never occurred to me it was the end."[39] Downey's story added that Roe thought he was going to get a chance to play a couple of innings in the field against Montreal the next day. Another coach, Peanuts Lowrey, had told him to warm up. "The inning ends, I run from the bullpen, almost get to the infield, look up...and here comes Willie Smith [the box score shows it was Pepitone]. He got sent in by Leo to play first. I don't know why. Nobody said a word. I just went back to my seat."[40]

Still, despite his lack of game opportunity in Chicago, Skidmore attracted media attention because of his roots in the state. As he said to Tom Owens,

271

ONE-HIT WONDERS

"Jerome Holtzman and Rick Talley were newspaper writers at that time, and they did several articles on me being from Illinois. Jack Brickhouse, Lou Boudreau and Vince Lloyd also had me on the radio pre-game show several times."[41] In 2014, he added, "My dad is a staunch Cubs fan and he indoctrinated me early. To get to play for them was beyond my wildest dreams."[42]

At the end of November 1970, the Cubs traded Skidmore, along with pitchers Pat Jacquez and Dave Lemonds, across town to the Chicago White Sox in exchange for José Ortiz and Ossie Blanco. Blanco was also a first baseman, but the Cubs viewed Ortiz, a speedy center fielder, as the key player in the deal from their point of view.[43]

Tucson, the top farm club of the White Sox, used Skidmore as an outfielder for part of 1971 because the team was shorthanded. That August, the *Tucson Daily Citizen* quoted Toros manager Gordon Maltzberger: "'They never complained no matter where I wanted to put them,' said Gordy, and he singled out Roe Skidmore as the prime example of a player who went into the outfield when called although he doesn't like that position. He's a first baseman, period. 'Skidmore is a wonderful fellow to have on the ball club,' Maltzberger said. 'His attitude is just great.'"[44]

Roe also produced well with the bat in 1971 (.299-20-77 in 125 games). His future as a first baseman with the White Sox became very cloudy, though, when the team traded for Dick Allen that December. On April 28, 1972, Skidmore went to the Cincinnati Reds organization to complete the deal in which Tucson had acquired Tony Muser and Buddy Bradford.[45] He had started slowly with the Toros but picked up with Indianapolis, the Triple-A farm club of the Reds. Overall, between Tucson and Indianapolis, he hit .284-13-90. He was named the Indians' Most Valuable Player.

During the winter of 1972-73, Skidmore played winter ball in Venezuela with Cardenales de Lara. He got into 20 games and hit .280-1-12 in 75 at-bats. "My experience in Venezuela was very positive," he said. "I played there only one full winter season, but I got to be in the lineup with Luis Aparicio, Buddy Hunter, Dwight Evans, Johnny Lowenstein, Al Cowens, Bill Lee, and Lew Krausse. It was a great experience for me and my family."[46]

Skidmore had another good year at Indianapolis in 1973 (.281-19-79 in 125 games), but Tony Pérez was in his prime as Cincinnati's first baseman. On the rare occasions when Pérez was not in the lineup, the primary backup was rookie Dan Driessen, who was playing out of position at third base that year.

After the minor-league season was over, on September 30, 1973, Skidmore went to the Cardinals as the player to be named later in the July trade that had sent Ed Crosby and Gene Dusan to Cincinnati Reds in exchange for Ed Sprague. He started the 1974 season with Tulsa, the top affiliate of the Cardinals, but his contract was sold to the Houston Astros that May. He was assigned to Denver, also in the American Association.

Skidmore was known for his love of country music, as he recalled along with Mike Floyd, who became his teammate in Denver. Skidmore said, "He and I used to sit around and listen to country all the time – everyone else was into the Beatles, etc. We both wore our cowboy boots and were pretty weird for doing so." Even in 2016, Skidmore noted, "I still wear boots every day."[47]

Floyd added, "He was a quiet, funny guy who enjoyed my humor and we used to talk about the lyrics and laugh. One morning about 6 AM in Tulsa, our phone rang. When I picked it up, a voice said, 'Turn on Channel 10' and I went over and cut the TV on. It was a local access channel with some crazy-looking country band dressed like Bill Monroe with straw cowboy hats creased like butterflies and singing 'Truck Drivin' Man'. It was hilarious."[48]

Between Tulsa and Denver, Skidmore put up another pretty good year (.286-13-80 in 119 games). Yet again, however, he was traded that December, going to the Boston Red Sox in exchange for Bob Didier. Mike Floyd observed, "Roe and one of his peers, Adrian 'Smokey' Garrett, were always discards wherever they went and I never could see why. Once you got branded as a Triple-A player, it was hard to shake that monkey."[49]

In 1976, Skidmore played in just 12 games for Pawtucket, the top Red Sox farm club. The starter at first base was a prospect named Jack Baker, who made it to the majors for 14 games with Boston in 1976 and 1977. Skidmore was "unhappy about being a benchwarmer for the first time. 'I can't hit very well sitting here with my legs crossed,'" he said.[50]

"I was new to Boston's organization and felt very much out of place," he recalled. "I felt like no one knew if I could hit or not. This was the first time I hadn't been an everyday player in 10 years. I called Joe Sparks, manager for Houston's Triple-A team in Des Moines, and asked him to please see what he could do to get me out of Pawtucket! Joe pulled some strings and my contract was sold to Des Moines, where I played first base every day the rest of that year."[51] Overall, he hit .265-14-52 in 123 games.

At that point, however, Skidmore had had enough. He was 29 years old. "The last year I played, my children were in four different schools from January to June – Decatur, Winter Haven (Florida spring training), Pawtucket, and Des Moines. My only other alternative was to leave my family in Decatur until school was out. No thanks! I missed my kids too much. So I decided to stop putting my family through the struggles any more.

"To this day I have regretted that decision. I wish I would have stayed around as a manager and coach as my career choice. What's done is done and I have no complaints. I have had a good life right here in Decatur."[52]

In 1976, California Angels beat writer Dick Miller asked the Angels which ballplayers they most admired as a professional. Catcher Ed Herrmann, who knew Roe from their days with the White Sox, gave Skidmore's name, saying "He had good year after good year in the minors and kept trying."[53]

"I married Jan Hoffman in spring 1993, the second marriage for both of us," said Skidmore. "Our five children are a blended family: Suzi, Roe Jr., Ryan, Natalie, and Brent." After retiring from baseball, Roe went into the insurance business back at home in Decatur. He spent 32 years as an agent with AXA Advisors, becoming a Chartered Life Underwriter, a member of the Centurion Club, and earning lifetime honors as part of the Million Dollar Round Table (MDRT) and the AXA Equitable Hall of Fame. He remained in the business as a senior consultant with New Horizons Insurance Marketing, brokering Medicare Supplement contracts to agents around the country. At age 70, he said, "Just can't sit still!"[54] As of 2018, however, he turned his financial business over to his son-in-law.[55]

In 1999, Skidmore admitted to David Margolick that "every spring training, a certain hollow feeling [grabbed] his gut. 'I'll go two or three weeks where I don't even want to pick up the paper,' he said. 'I just kind of ignore the fact that it's starting.'"[56] Nonetheless, he remained involved with baseball. In 2005, he became a scout for the Philadelphia Phillies. Though some reports give him credit for the signings of Ryan Howard and Jayson Werth, Skidmore said, "I don't know where that came from. They are both from my area, and I watched both guys play, but that is incorrect."[57]

In 2011, Skidmore joined the New York Mets organization as a scout. He then moved to the Baltimore Orioles in 2013. As of 2016, he was back with the Phillies, helping his friend Scott Trcka, the team's scouting supervisor for the Midwest. He could work just when he wanted to, cross-checking.[58] In 2018, however, Skidmore gave up scouting too because he didn't want to be away from his wife. "My life is much more peaceful and less stressful now," he said. "I still communicate frequently with many of my old ballplayer pals and keep up with the game through autograph signings and old-timers get-togethers." His father, who was still living in Decatur too until his death in November 2020 at the remarkable age of 104."[59]

From 1901 through 2019, some 91 players had a career batting average of 1.000 in the majors. Yet perhaps no other man besides Roe Skidmore has attracted as much attention for the feat. "I feel very blessed and privileged to have gotten the opportunity to wear a big-league uniform," he said, "and even more fortunate to have played for all those years."

"Baseball has dominated my thinking my whole life. Not a day goes by that I don't have thoughts of hitting and fielding in the various parks I played in. Bottom line – there is no greater or more fulfilling feeling than hitting a breaking ball high over the left-field scoreboard and running around the bases wishing and hoping that the feeling will never end."[60]

Grateful acknowledgment to Roe Skidmore for his memories (letters received on March 8 and April 7, 2014, plus subsequent e-mails). Thanks also to Mike Floyd.

SOURCES

Internet resources

www.baseball-reference.com

www.retrosheet.org

www.newhorizonsmktg.com/team/roe-skidmore

http://www.ihsa.org/SportsActivities/BoysBaseball/RecordsHistory.aspx

athletics.millikin.edu

NOTES

1. Jerome Holtzman, "Still Batting 1.000 On Memory Lane," *Chicago Tribune*, February 20, 1986.
2. Holtzman, "Still Batting 1.000 On Memory Lane."
3. Letter from Roe Skidmore to Rory Costello, received April 7, 2014.
4. Mike Downey, "In a way, his short baseball career perfect," *Chicago Tribune*, July 13, 2003.

ONE-HIT WONDERS

5. Bob Fallstrom, "Skidmore recalls the good old days of downtown Decatur," *Decatur Herald-Review*, August 27, 2013. The family-owned business marked its 100th anniversary at the same downtown location in 2009. It was still in business as of 2020.
6. Letter from Roe Skidmore to Rory Costello, received April 7, 2014.
7. Shawn Touney, "Going Home: Digging up the story of the Kane County Cougars' ancestors," Kane County Cougars blog, August 7, 2012 (http://kccougars.wordpress.com/2012/08/07/digging-up-our-past/)
8. Letter from Roe Skidmore to Rory Costello, received March 8, 2014.
9. Letter from Roe Skidmore to Rory Costello, received April 7, 2014.
10. Bob Fallstrom, "Eisenhower baseball champs of 1962 reminisce at reunion," *Decatur Herald-Review*, October 9, 2012.
11. Tom Owens, "The Heart-warming History of Cub Roe Skidmore," Baseball by the Letters blog, October 3, 2013 (http://baseballbytheletters.blogspot.com/2013/10/the-heart-warming-history-of-cub-roe.html)
12. Letter from Roe Skidmore to Rory Costello, received April 7, 2014.
13. W.C. Madden, *Baseball's First-Year Player Draft*, Jefferson, North Carolina: McFarland & Co., 2001, 148.
14. Letter from Roe Skidmore to Rory Costello, received March 8, 2014.
15. Letter from Roe Skidmore to Rory Costello, received April 7, 2014.
16. Don Lindner, "'65 Ace Hilts Whiffs 14 in Opening Win," *The Sporting News*, June 25, 1966, 24.
17. Letter from Roe Skidmore to Rory Costello, received April 7, 2014.
18. Downey, "In a way, his short baseball career perfect."
19. Thompson was born in the nearby town of Latham but grew up in Decatur. Bob Fallstrom, "Decatur's 'Swede' Thompson traveled nationwide contributing his baseball talents," *Decatur Herald-Review*, June 9, 2012.
20. Letter from Roe Skidmore to Rory Costello, received April 7, 2014.
21. Letter from Roe Skidmore to Rory Costello, received April 7, 2014.
22. Letter from Roe Skidmore to Rory Costello, received April 7, 2014.
23. E-mail from Mike Floyd to Rory Costello, January 22, 2016. Floyd played in the PCL in 1971 and 1973.
24. For discussion of this game and Skidmore's appearance, see "Roe Skidmore and Ernie Banks," Can't Have Too Many Cards blog, February 16, 2012 (http://canthavetoomanycards.blogspot.com/2012/02/roe-skidmore-and-ernie-banks.html)
25. E-mail from Roe Skidmore to Rory Costello, January 22, 2016.
26. Downey, "In a way, his short baseball career perfect."
27. Edgar Munzel, "Leo Plans to Curb Cubs' Outside Interests," *The Sporting News*, October 18, 1969, 16.
28. Edgar Munzel, "Skidmore a Slick Backup Man for Banks," *The Sporting News*, January 3, 1970, 43.
29. David Margolick, "New Season for Stars and One-Game Wonders," *New York Times*, April 4, 1999.
30. Munzel, "Skidmore a Slick Backup Man for Banks."
31. "Balance, Callison Give Cubs Chance," Associated Press, March 21, 1970.
32. Munzel, "Skidmore a Slick Backup Man for Banks."
33. Neil Hayes, "Fast rise, fast to exit for former Cub pitcher." *Chicago Sun-Times*, May 15, 2008. Subject: pitcher Darcy Fast.
34. Letter from Roe Skidmore to Rory Costello, received April 7, 2014.
35. "Skidmore snaps slump to bring Cubs win," United Press International, April 30, 1970.
36. Downey, "In a way, his short baseball career perfect."
37. Holtzman, "Still Batting 1.000 On Memory Lane."
38. Margolick, "New Season for Stars and One-Game Wonders."
39. Holtzman, "Still Batting 1.000 On Memory Lane."
40. Downey, "In a way, his short baseball career perfect."
41. Tom Owens, "Cub Roe Skidmore Reflects On Illinois Roots," Baseball by the Letters blog, October 10, 2013 (http://baseballbytheletters.blogspot.com/2013/10/cub-roe-skidmore-reflects-on-illinois.html)
42. Letter from Roe Skidmore to Rory Costello, received April 7, 2014.
43. Jerome Holtzman, "Cubs Are High on Speedster Ortiz," *The Sporting News*, January 16, 1971: 54.
44. *Tucson Daily Citizen*, August 25, 1971: 40.
45. *The Sporting News*, May 20, 1972: 34.
46. Letter from Roe Skidmore to Rory Costello, received April 7, 2014.
47. E-mail from Roe Skidmore to Rory Costello, January 22, 2016.
48. E-mail from Mike Floyd to Rory Costello, January 22, 2016.
49. E-mail from Mike Floyd to Rory Costello, January 22, 2016. Floyd himself never got past Triple-A.
50. *The Sporting News*, May 10, 1975, 34.
51. Letter from Roe Skidmore to Rory Costello, received April 7, 2014.
52. Letter from Roe Skidmore to Rory Costello, received April 7, 2014.
53. Dick Miller, "Angels Also Have Idols, Poll Shows," *The Sporting News*, May 29, 1976, 12.
54. E-mail from Roe Skidmore to Rory Costello, January 25, 2016.
55. E-mail from Roe Skidmore to Rory Costello, July 5, 2020.
56. Margolick, "New Season for Stars and One-Game Wonders."
57. Letter from Roe Skidmore to Rory Costello, received April 7, 2014.
58. E-mail from Roe Skidmore to Rory Costello, January 25, 2016.
59. Roe C. Skidmore obituary, Decatur Herald-Review, November 5, 2020.
60. Letter from Roe Skidmore to Rory Costello, received April 7, 2014.

CHARLIE SNOW

By Mike Cooney

Charlie Snow had a perfect major-league batting average and a perfectly imperfect fielding average. He was probably the most unlikely player to get a hit in his first major-league at-bat and yet, perhaps, the most likely player to never get a second at-bat.

Charles M. Snow was born on August 3, 1849, in Lowell, Massachusetts, to Benjamin Snow, a laborer, and Laura G. Snow.[1] In the 1850 federal census, Benjamin Snow was listed as a "manufacturer."[2]

Charles had two younger sisters, Ida and Ella. Benjamin is no longer shown as part of the family unit starting with the 1860 census. His mother, Laura, shows as a housekeeper.[3] Snow's youngest sister, Ella, no longer shows in the family unit beginning with the 1865 Massachusetts State census. At 16, Snow was listed as a clerk.[4]

By 1870, the family had moved to Suffolk County, Massachusetts (Boston). Then 21, Snow claimed he had no occupation.[5] It is safe to assume Snow joined one of the three main Boston amateur baseball teams, probably the Boston Atlantics,[6] during the early 1870s.

Beginning with the 1874 season, the Boston Atlantics changed their name to the Boston Amateurs.[7] Snow was a member of the Amateurs on October 1 when the major-league Boston Red Stockings played the Brooklyn Atlantics in what would result in a 29-0 Boston victory.[8]

In their game the day before, Atlantics catcher Henry Kessler broke his thumb in the third inning. The Atlantics had to play the rest of the game with eight players.[9]

With Kessler injured, Brooklyn had to telegraph catcher Jake Knowdell to report to Boston for the October 1 game.[10] With Knowdell's arrival, the Atlantics were able to put nine men on the field. However, in the fifth inning, Knowdell broke the second finger of his right hand. Knowdell's injury again left the Atlantics with just eight players.[11]

SABR member and nineteenth century baseball historian David Nemec speculates that the Atlantics, in order to continue the game with nine players, looked to the fans for a replacement. Snow was at the game and either volunteered or was recommended by a Boston player who knew him.[12] Snow joined the Atlantics for the final three innings.

Since Snow replaced catcher Knowdell, most baseball data sites show him as a catcher who had three fielding chances and made three errors for an unparalleled fielding percentage of .000 for a player with more than two chances.[13]

A blogger who calls himself The Flagrant Fan, in his *A Charlie Snow Day*, wrote: "According to Charlie Snow's player page, in that one game behind the plate, most likely catching Tommy Bond, Snow had three chances in the field and botched them all."[14]

However, Charlie Snow did not play catcher for the Atlantics. Brooklyn third baseman Bob Ferguson went behind the plate, shortstop Dickey Pearce moved to third base, and center fielder Pat McGee moved to shortstop. Charlie Snow replaced McGee in center field.[15]

As for Snow's fielding, the *Boston Post* box score for the game shows Snow had three chances and made three of the 30 errors made by the Atlantics,[16] while the *Boston Globe* box score shows he had four chances and made four of the 36 Atlantics errors.[17]

The *Boston Globe*, in commenting on the 29-0 game it called "the funniest game of the season," wrote: "The chief cause of the disaster lay in the loose play of (Al) Martin, Ferguson, Knowdell and his substitute Snow."[18]

It is difficult to understand why the two major Boston newspapers differed in the total Atlantics team errors as well as the number of errors made by Snow. Regardless, whether Charlie Snow made three errors or four, it was as a center fielder.[19]

What is not in question is Snow's hitting prowess. In a game where Boston's future Hall of Fame pitcher Al Spalding gave up only four hits, 25-year-old Charlie Snow singled in what was his only major-league at-bat.[20]

ONE-HIT WONDERS

It is easy to speculate that Spalding "eased up" when pitching to Snow, thus allowing him to get a hit. However, David Nemec commented that, based on Spalding's reputation, he would not ease up on anyone, let alone an amateur fill-in.[21] In other words, Snow's hit was probably well earned.

After the game, Snow went home with a 1.000 major-league batting average and a .000 fielding average. At the time he was the only major-league player to finish his career with a 1.000 batting average.[22]

He would never get another at-bat in the majors. In fact, there is no evidence that Snow played baseball at any level after that October 1 game.

It does appear that Snow moved to Brooklyn, New York, shortly after the game. In the 1880 US Census, he is shown as living in Brooklyn and working as a ticket agent.[23] Snow continued to live in Brooklyn, at some point moving from his ticket-agent job to that of a stationery salesman.[24]

A review of federal census reports would indicate Snow never married.

Snow was 80 years old when he died on August 27, 1929. He is buried at Green-Wood Cemetery in Brooklyn.[25]

Charlie Snow seemingly lived an anonymous life except for one October day in 1874 – the day he made major-league history that can never be bettered (or worsened in the case of his fielding): one game, one at-bat, one hit, 1.000 batting average; three or four chances, three or four errors, .000 fielding percentage.

SOURCES

In addition to the sources cited in the Notes, the author also consulted Baseball-Reference.com.

Special thanks to David Nemec for sharing his insight and his research on Charlie Snow.

NOTES

1. Massachusetts, Town and Vital Records, 1620-1988 for Charles M. Snow (Ancestry.com).
2. 1850 United States Federal Census (Ancestry.com).
3. 1860 United States Federal Census (Ancestry.com).
4. Massachusetts, State Census, 1865 (Ancestry.com).
5. 1870 United States Federal Census (Ancestry.com).
6. "Base-Ball," *Boston Globe,* May 9, 1874: 3.
7. "Local News," *Boston Post,* May 16, 1874.
8. "Base Ball," *Boston Post,* October 2, 1874.
9. "Base Ball," *Boston Post,* October 2, 1874.
10. "Base Ball," *Boston Post,* October 2, 1874.
11. "Base Ball," *Boston Post,* October 2, 1874.
12. Author interview with David Nemec, November 12, 2019.
13. Tom Ruane of Retrosheet ran a query and found the following players who committed errors in both of their only two chances: Bob Allen, Jodie Beeler, Harry Fuller, Pete Hasney, Rontrez Johnson, James Morris, John Rudderham, Lefty Schegg, Brian Slocum, Tom Thobe, and Mauro Zarate. Emmanuel Clase of the 2019 Texas Rangers falls in this category as of the beginning of 2020. There are 73 players who made an error in their one and only chance. Tom Ruane email to Bill Nowlin, December 2, 2019.
14. passion4baseball.blogspot.com/2014/02/a-charlie-snow-day.html.
15. "Base Ball," *Boston Post,* October 2, 1874.
16. "Base Ball," *Boston Post,* October 2, 1874.
17. "Out-Door Sports – Base Ball," *Boston Globe,* October 2, 1874: 5.
18. "Out-Door Sports – Base Ball," *Boston Globe,* October 2, 1874: 5.
19. Retrosheet.org in fact lists Snow as a center fielder. Baseball-Reference.com says he was the catcher. Both say he made three errors.
20. David Nemec, *The Rank and File of 19th Century Major League Baseball. Biographies of 1084 Players, Owners, Managers and Umpires* (Jefferson, North Carolina: McFarland & Company, Inc., 2012), 267-268.
21. David Nemec interview.
22. David Nemec interview.
23. 1880 United States Federal Census for Charles Snow (Ancestry.com).
24. 1920 United States Federal Census for Charles Snow (Ancestry.com).
25. findagrave.com/memorial/57680032.

JOE STAPLES

By Bill Staples Jr.

On page 1,444 of the fourth edition of *The Baseball Encyclopedia* published in 1979, Joe Staples nestles in obscurity between journeyman outfielder Leroy Stanton and Hall of Famer Willie Stargell.[1]

The scant entry is the reflection of a rather unremarkable career. He appeared in seven games with the 1885 Buffalo Bisons, recorded just one hit in 22 at-bats, and finished with a microscopic career batting average of .045. For decades, baseball historians knew little about Joe Staples. And as of 2020, it now appears that what little we did know was mostly inaccurate.

The most notable correction to Joe Staples' career record is not in his stats, but his name. "Joe Staples" was born Joseph F. Stabell on August 4, 1864, in Buffalo, New York.[2] His father, Frank Stabell – surname also spelled Staebell and Staebel – immigrated to America from France. At 18 young Franz Staebel departed the port of Havre, France, on the passenger ship *Palestine* for New York, arriving on October 5, 1846.[3]

The Stabell homeland of Alsace, France, is in a historical region in the northeastern area of the country located on the Rhine River, bordering Germany and Switzerland. It has alternated between German and French control over the centuries and reflects a blend of those cultures.[4] Given that both of Joe's parents, Frank and Martha, were born in France and spoke French, it is quite possible that this "one-hit wonder" spoke with a French accent. While just conjecture, this might be a plausible explanation as to why English speakers could have incorrectly heard the pronunciation of his surname as "Stay-pulz."[5]

The Stabell family included six children, three girls and three boys – Martha, Eliz, Jacob, Abbie, Joseph, and George.[6] Two of Joseph's siblings died young. In 1877 sister Martha died at 16, and in 1880 the oldest brother, Jacob, died at 22.[7] By the time he was 16, Joseph was no longer a student and was now working in a liquor store. His younger brother George, 14, attended "School 18" in Buffalo's public-school system.[8] Over the course of the next four years, Joe remained in the spirits industry and eventually took a job in a distillery with his father as a distiller, Frank's profession for the last decade.[9]

On October 20, 1884, the *Buffalo Commercial* reported, "The Buffalos and Clippers, of Hamilton, Ont., played an exhibition game at Hamilton, Saturday [Oct 18], the former winning by a score of 9 to 7. The Buffalo battery consisted of Galvin and Staples, the latter an amateur of this city."[10] This game recap represents the first documentation of Joe Staples playing baseball – catching future Hall of Fame pitcher James Francis "Pud" Galvin, nonetheless.

The first amateur baseball league of Buffalo was organized the summer of 1879 when young Joe was 15.[11] The popularity of the local game grew over the years

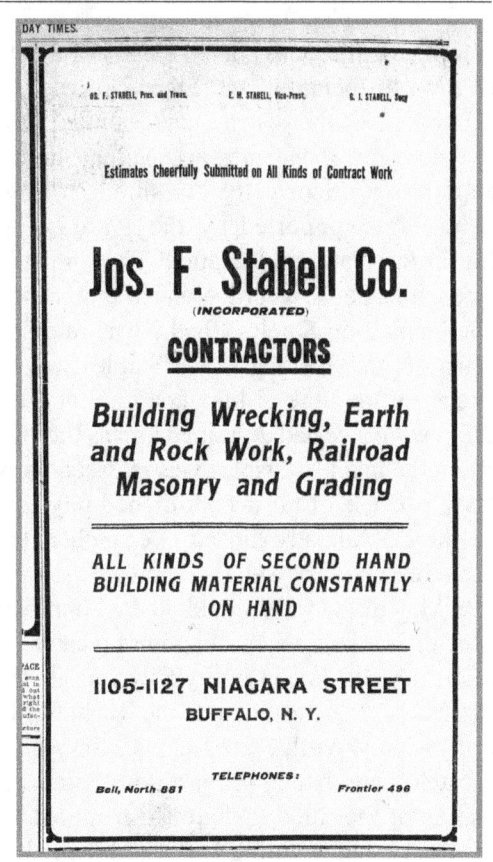

Advertisement for Joe Stabell's business.

and by 1884 the Amateur Base-Ball League of Buffalo consisted of five teams, the Perrys, the Travelers, the Alerts, the Comets, and the Stars.[12] The name of the team Joe Staples played for between 1880 and 1884 (age 16 to 20) has yet to surface, but we do know that, based on his brief appearance with the Buffalo Bisons in late 1884, he did indeed compete with one of those five ballclubs.

Someone in attendance at that Buffalo-Hamilton exhibition game may have seen a glimmer of potential in the young player, because four months later Staples signed his first professional contract. On February 19, 1885, President Nicholas E. Young announced the list of men signed by the eight teams of the National League of Professional Base Ball Players: Boston, Buffalo, Chicago, Detroit, Providence, New York, Philadelphia, and St. Louis.[13]

The newcomers to Henry V. Lucas's St. Louis Maroons for the 1885 season included William O'Donnell, George F. Baker, Joseph Quinn, Fleury P. Sullivan, Frank W. Bandle, William H. Colgan, Frederick Lewis, and Joseph Staples. Notable players signing with other clubs that same season include Buck Ewing and Mickey Welch in New York, Pud Galvin and Dan Brouthers in Buffalo, and Mike "King" Kelly and Cap Anson in Chicago.[14]

The St. Louis Maroons played the previous season in the Union Association, and after that league collapsed, Lucas made the switch to the National League. Sabermetrics guru Bill James argues that the Union Association was incorrectly classified as a major league, a claim supported by the Maroons' poor showing in the National League.[15] They finished in last place with a 36-72 record. None of that ineptitude could be blamed on Staples, for he was released by Lucas just before Opening Day.[16] Staples was listed as a catcher at the time of his departure, and weeks before, *Sporting Life* had described him as the "heaviest man on the team."[17] Staples was released on April 29. Was it because of his deconditioned physique or because the club already carried five catchers on the roster? No reason was given in the press.

In late May of 1885, Staples signed with the Jersey City Skeeters in the Eastern League as a catcher and center fielder.[18] His time in Jersey City was also brief. A few weeks later he moved on to the Rochester Flour Cities of the New York State League, for whom he played catcher and batted primarily in the number 7 and 8 spots of the lineup.[19] Staples struggled at the plate in Rochester, securing just one hit in 11 plate appearances. His first documented hit occurred on July 11 against pitcher George Chapman of the Albany Senators in a 7-4 loss.[20]

With Rochester located roughly 75 miles east of Buffalo, it was convenient for Joe to return home on offdays. On August 3, 1885, Staples, then 22, is documented playing shortstop with a local ballclub, the Plymouths in a weekend contest.[21]

Perhaps the recent local play caught the attention of officials with Buffalo of the National League, or maybe it was his prior pickup with the team in 1884. Whatever the case, Staples was suited up, playing right field, and batting ninth in the lineup with the major-league Buffalo Bisons on September 18, 1885. According to the box score in the *Buffalo Times*, he went 2-for-5 at the plate in a 14-12 victory over Rochester, his old ballclub.[22] The two hits off pitcher-outfielder Tom Mansell would not count toward his major-league statistics because Rochester was a member of the NYSL, and not the National League.

It is not known if Staples was right- or left-handed. According to the historical record, he was said to be 5-feet-10. No weight is given in that same source, but according to reports from his time in St. Louis as "the heaviest man on the team," we can deduce that he weighed more than 194 pounds, the weight of teammate Frederick Lewis, the heaviest recorded for players with St. Louis in 1885.[23]

A week later, Staples faced his first major-league-caliber pitcher in New York's future Hall of Fame pitcher Tim Keefe. Staples was hitless in three at-bats in the 4-1 loss at the Polo Grounds.[24] On September 20 Buffalo manager Jack Chapman experimented by moving Staples to second against the Philadelphia Quakers. Facing Charlie Ferguson, the ace of the club, Staples went 0-for-3 in the 12-2 loss.[25]

After the failed infield experiment, Chapman moved Staples back to his more familiar spot in the outfield. On September 21 Staples and his Bisons teammates faced Keefe again. The curveball specialist pitched a shutout, winning 10-0, and allowing five scattered hits. One of those five hits belonged to Staples.[26]

Buffalo finished out its major-league schedule with five games against New York and a season finale against Boston. The Bisons lost all four games against New York — twice against Keefe, and the others against Mickey Welch and Larry Corcoran.[27] In the final contest, against the Boston Beaneaters, about 100 fans showed up to watch Buffalo lose, 13-2.[28] Staples went 0-for-4 at the plate against Charlie Buffinton, a righty who finished the season with a 22-27 record.[29]

ONE-HIT WONDERS

It is worth pointing out that Staples' one major-league hit came while he played under Buffalo manager Jack Chapman, a man who played a noteworthy role in the history of baseball's color line. Chapman continued to manage the Bisons the following three seasons and, with Frank Grant at second base, his 1886 club was one of several integrated teams in the International League.

When the color line was drawn in 1887, Chapman was vocal in his disappointment with the decision, and his support for Frank Grant. "Grant, (George) Stovey, (William) Renfroe and (Robert) Higgins are the leading colored players now in the International League. … It is really a pity that the league should draw the color line, for it is a treat to see Grant play second base," said Chapman.[30] The Bisons manager said he valued Grant at $5,000, which at this time rivaled the highest paid players in the majors, Fred Dunlap of the Detroit Wolverines and Charles "Old Hoss" Radbourne of the Boston Beaneaters, who both earned $4,500 (the equivalent of $125,000 in 2020).[31]

By 1886, Staples was out of major-league baseball, but at just 22 he continued his playing career in local leagues. On May 3 the *Buffalo Times* reported that "Big Joe Staples, with St. Louis and Buffalo last season[,]" was now playing with a local team called the Exiles. Holding down the hot corner, he went 3-for-6 against the Perry club in a high-scoring contest that ended 14-12 in favor of the Exiles.[32] When Staples wasn't competing as a player on the field, he kept the peace as an umpire in the same league.[33] Off the field, he and brother George buried their father Frank, a decorated Union veteran, who died in June 1886 at 58.[34] Their mother, Martha, died four years later at 61.[35]

In mid-August of 1887, the *Buffalo Times* reported that the grocers and butchers of Buffalo held their first annual picnic at Germania Park, a festive event that included a baseball game and track and field events. The Stabell brothers are documented competing in the track and field events for the Butchers. George placed second in the 100-yard dash, while Joe and George were among the top three athletes in the hop, step, and jump; running long jump; and standing long jump. Although no ballplayers were mentioned by name, most likely the brothers also competed in the baseball game that was played earlier in the day when the Diamond Kings baseball club defeated the Stars 13-12.[36]

In 1888 Joe and George teamed up again on the diamond as members of the Niagaras of Buffalo's West Side Baseball League. Other clubs in the league included the North Buffaloes, Queen Citys, and West Ends.[37] George batted leadoff and played third base, while Joseph hit in the two spot and caught.[38]

By the 1890 season, the brothers had changed clubs again. On July 21 the West Ends of the Buffalo Baseball League announced the signing of Joe and George, emphasizing that they were much-needed additions to a team that was losing players to a popular crosstown rival, the Casinos.[39] Lady luck was not with the West Enders again. By the end of the month, the brothers joined the exodus and left the West Ends for manager Jac Horn's Casinos.[40]

Weeks later the Casinos defeated the Elks, 13-4. Roughly 500 fans were on hand for the contest in which the "Staples" brothers guarded the middle infield – George starting at shortstop and Joe at second base. The box score reveals the surprising athletic ability of the girthy Joe – he turned an unassisted 4-3 double play, and recorded three putouts and four assists. Offensively, he and George both hit doubles.[41]

"Big Joe" continued his playing career with the East Buffalo club during the 1891 season. Seven years after being documented as the batterymate of Pud Galvin with the Bisons in late 1884, the press still identified him as "Staples." In a contest at Buffalo's Champion League Grounds on June 15, Joe started at first base and batted ninth in the lineup. He performed well that day despite the team's 15-4 loss to the Casinos. Staples participated in three double plays on defense and was 3-for-4 against William Schellerman, one of the best professional pitchers in Buffalo.[42]

About 900 were in attendance to see the Casinos' pickup pitcher Schellerman strike out 15 East Buffalo batters. At the time of this game with the amateur Casinos, Schellerman was at the peak of his professional career. Between 1890 and 1893, he played with the Buffalo/Montreal Bisons and the Grand Rapids Shamrocks of the International Association, and the Providence Clamdiggers of the Eastern Association.[43]

In 1892 the Stabell brothers shifted their focus away from athletics to politics.[44] In anticipation of former President Grover Cleveland making a second run for the White House after losing to William Henry Harrison in 1888, George Stabell became president of the Cleveland and Stevenson Democratic Club for Buffalo's 23rd Ward.[45]

As the President of the Democratic Club for their neighborhood ward, George also advocated for his brother Joseph, who was running for city council alderman. The *Buffalo Courier* called the former professional baseball player an "an excellent candidate," and shared the following brief biographical sketch with potential voters:

> "Joseph F. Stabell, Democratic candidate for Alderman in the 23rd Ward, was born in that ward (the old 11th) August 4, 1864, and has lived there all his life. He received his education in the public schools. Mr. Stabell is General Manager of the Ferrolothic Paving Company, and prominent member of the Foresters, Court Frontier No. 7688. He has always been a Democrat, and one of the hardest and most loyal workers in the party. Mr. Stabell never sought office before but is making a great run."[46]

While Grover Cleveland managed to win a second bid for the presidency, Stabell was not as fortunate. He lost to Republican candidate William K. Williams, who secured the victory with 704 votes. Stabell's final vote count was not reported in the press.[47]

Stabell dusted himself off after his political defeat and returned to the construction industry, and baseball. In September 1893, he played in a charity baseball game played at Buffalo's Olympic Park between the members of the Real Estate Exchange and the Builders Exchange. Proceeds from the game benefited the nonprofit Fresh Air Fund, founded to help disadvantaged city children enjoy a free summer in the country.[48] According to the *Buffalo Courier,* many of the players participating in the game were "old-time ball tossers," including Stabell, first baseman for the Builders.[49]

In 1894 Joseph Stabell partnered with Thomas Brown to form Brown & Stabell, a contracting firm initially promoted for cellar and sewer building services. The firm quickly expanded its offerings and by July was bidding on city contracts for the collection and removal of garbage.[50] By the end of 1895, Stabell was viewed as a leading excavation expert in Buffalo and was asked occasionally to testify in court on related legal matters.[51]

With his ballplaying days clearly behind him, Stabell, now 33, settled down and married Eva Marie Krumholz in January 1896.[52] Forever the sportsman, though, he found his competitive outlet in bowling as a member of the Genesees team in Buffalo's West Side Bowling League.[53]

Stabell maintained a high profile in Buffalo, as his name was still in the papers in 1897 as a potential Democratic Party nominee for 23rd Ward alderman.[54] His prominence in the community may have helped him and his expanded company – Brown, Stabell, & Griffiths – win the contract to construct the canal system at the Pan-American Exposition grounds. Stabell and his business partners hired 1,000 men to remove 2,500 cubic yards of dirt a day in preparation for the 1901 World's Fair hosted by Buffalo.[55] Stabell's pride in his work and the global spotlight placed on his hometown is reflected by his enthusiastic decision to rename his bowling team the Pan-Ams.[56]

The Pan-American Exposition was held in Buffalo from May 1 through November 2, 1901. Today it is remembered as the site of President William McKinley's assassination on September 6, 1901. The day before being shot by an assassin's gun, McKinley addressed an audience of 50,000 Expo attendees, which included business leaders of the Buffalo community. At the time of this writing, there are no known photos of Joseph Stabell; however, because of his position as a respected business leader in the Buffalo community, it is possible that he is a face in the crowd in the photo of McKinley delivering his final public speech.[57]

Compared with his paltry major-league career, Joe Stabell was a big-league champion when it came to the construction industry. His success as a respected business owner allowed him and his wife to travel the world and to build a "handsome residence" in Buffalo's Central Park area. The house was noted for its lofty value of $25,000 in 1916 (the equivalent of $623,000 in 2020).[58] In 1921, at age 57, he remained active in local politics, serving on the Democratic County Committee for Buffalo's 19th Ward.[59]

Stabell's positive impact on the community could be found in the hundreds of state and local construction projects worked on by his company, the last of which he operated with his brother George as the Stabell Brothers. He also gave back to his community, supporting a variety of charities including the St. Vincent Orphan Asylum.[60]

Despite his apparent success as a community and business leader, he did face notable challenges, such as:

- In 1914, the stables that housed his team of 100 horses used for construction hauling during jobs burned down, causing $3,000 worth of damage (the equivalent of $78,000 in 2020).[61]
- In 1918, during World War I and a time of rationing, he was charged with hoarding sugar and other commodities. The inspector who visited Stabell's house "found in the attic 161 pounds of sugar, 30 boxes containing 2,500 cakes of soap, and in the cellar a half-box of grapefruit, a third of a box of lemons and a half a box of oranges"[62] (Given Stabell's early career in the spirits industry, it is quite possible that these were ingredients

– minus the soap – for a homemade distillery in anticipation of the proposed Wartime Prohibition Act, which passed in November 1918.[63])

- In 1922 Stabell's outstanding business debts caused his creditors to request involuntary bankruptcy in federal courts.[64]

Joe Stabell died on July 10, 1923, a few weeks shy of his 59th birthday. He was 58, the same age as his father when he died. His passing that morning occurred early enough for it to make the evening edition of the *Buffalo Commercial*. "Contractor Dies," the headline read. There was no mention of his early career as a baseball player. The article summarized his better-known profession: "Mr. Stabell had been in the contracting business with offices in Niagara street for the past forty years. ... He was survived by his wife Martha and three daughters, Mrs. Arthur I. Yeager, Mrs. Robert J. Felhousen and Victoria E. Stabell."[65] Not mentioned in the obituary was the fact that his business partner, former baseball teammate, and brother, George Stabell, also resided at the family home on 1127 Niagara Street.[66]

Services were held at Holy Angels Roman Catholic Church.

Despite not locating Joe Stabell's photograph, we now have a better picture of his life and baseball career to make his entry on Baseball-Reference.com – now the de facto replacement of *The Baseball Encyclopedia* – more complete.[67]

And best of all, "Big Joe" is now a candidate—and the only one for now until other candidates might be discovered—for a new and interesting baseball trivia question: Which "one-hit wonder" recorded his only major-league hit off of a Hall of Fame pitcher? The answer: Joe Staples, 1885 Buffalo, off New York pitcher Tim Keefe (elected to Cooperstown in 1964).

NOTES

1. The author first learned about "Joe Staples" at age 10 (1979) and for decades wondered if he was a distant relative. The research for this SABR biography answered that question – no relation.
2. "Excellent Candidate," *Buffalo Courier*, November 5, 1892: 5.
3. Franz Staebel in the New York, Passenger and Immigration Lists, 1820-1850, Ancestry.com.
4. Alsace, France, *Encyclopedia Britannica*, britannica.com/place/Alsace.
5. Another possibility for Joe Stabell playing ball under the name Joe Staples is that, at the time, baseball was not considered a reputable profession. Thus, maybe Staples was his identity on the field to keep it separate from his professional/business identity.
6. Frank Staebell in the 1870 United States Federal Census, Ancestry.com.
7. Deaths, *Buffalo Courier*, November 8, 1880: 2.
8. Frank Stabell in the 1880 United States Federal Census, Ancestry.com. See also "Regents Examination," *Buffalo Commercial*, June 23, 1882: 3.
9. Joseph Stabell, 1884 Buffalo City Directory, 841.
10. "Miscellany," *Buffalo Commercial*, October 20, 1884: 3.
11. "Base-Ball," *Buffalo Commercial*, June 23, 1879: 3.
12. "Sporting," *Buffalo Commercial*, March 20, 1884: 3.
13. "The League Players Under Contract," *St. Louis Globe-Democrat*, March 1, 1885: 9.
14. "The League Players Under Contract."
15. Bill James, *The Bill James Historical Baseball Abstract* (New York: Villard, 1985).
16. "Fitch and Staples Released," *Sporting Life*, April 29, 1885: 7.
17. "Staples the New Catcher," *Sporting Life*, April 15, 1885: 7.
18. "Lancaster vs. Jersey City," *Sporting Life*, May 27, 1885: 5.
19. "Forging to the Front," *Democrat and Chronicle* (Rochester, New York), June 9, 1885: 6.
20. "The Wind Blew Right," *Democrat and Chronicle*, July 11, 1885: 7.
21. "Sporting News," *Buffalo Times*, August 3, 1885: 1.
22. "Anything to Beat Rochester," *Buffalo Times*, September 19, 1885: 1.
23. Frederick Lewis entry, Baseball-Reference.com, https://www.baseball-reference.com/players/l/lewisfr01.shtml.
24. "New York, 4; Buffalo, 1," *Boston Globe*, September 27, 1885: 6.
25. "Baseball Notes," *Buffalo Sunday Morning News*, September 20, 1885: 4.
26. "The New Yorks Whitewash the Buffalos," *Boston Globe*, September 22, 1885: 5.
27. "Popular Autumn Sports," *Buffalo Morning Express and Illustrated Buffalo Express*, September 26, 1885: 2.
28. "Boston Defeats Buffalo," *Buffalo Times*, September 30, 1885: 1.
29. Charlie Buffinton entry, Baseball-Reference.com, baseball-reference.com/players/b/buffich01.shtml.
30. "Around the Bases," *Democrat and Chronicle*, July 26, 1887: 7.
31. "MLB's annual salary leaders since 1874," by Michael Haupert, Society for American Baseball Research, sabr.org/research/article/mlbs-annual-salary-leaders-since-1874/.
32. "The Sports on Sunday," *Buffalo Times*, May 3, 1886: 1.
33. "Great Day for Sport," *Buffalo Times*, May 31, 1886: 5.
34. "Died," *Buffalo Evening News*, June 10, 1886: 1.
35. New York, Wills and Probate Records, 1659-1999 for Martha Stabell, Ancestry.com.
36. "Their Day Off," *Buffalo Times*, August 18, 1887: 1.
37. "West Side League," *International Gazette* (Black Rock, New York), May 4, 1888: 4.
38. "West Ends vs. Niagaras," *International Gazette*, May 19, 1888: 5.
39. "Sporting Notes," *Buffalo Times*, July 21, 1890: 1.
40. "Amateur Baseball," *Buffalo Courier*, July 31, 1890: 8.
41. "Elks Extinguished," *Buffalo Courier*, August 4, 1890: 8.
42. "The Casinos' Easy Victory," *Buffalo Morning Express and Illustrated Buffalo Express*, June 15, 1891: 6.
43. William Schellerman entry, Baseball-Reference.com, baseball-reference.com/register/player.fcgi?id=schell002wil.

ONE-HIT WONDERS

44   It is worth noting that at this stage of Stabell's career, the press did not refer to him as Joe Staples when off the diamond, suggesting that "Staples" might have been Joe's "Americanized baseball identity" much like "Connie Mack" for Cornelius McGillicuddy, or "Willie Keeler" for William Henry O'Kelleher Jr.

45   "Ward Clubs," *Buffalo Courier,* July 13, 1892: 5.

46   "An Excellent Candidate," *Buffalo Courier,* November 5, 1892: 5.

47   "Official Figures," *Buffalo Enquirer,* November 18, 1892: 5.

48   "The Fresh Air Fund, Learn About Us," freshair.org/learn-about-us/.

49   "Real Estates and Builders," *Buffalo Courier,* September 30, 1893: 8.

50   "Some Interesting Figures," *Buffalo Courier,* July 24, 1894: 7.

51   "Excavating Expert," *Buffalo Courier,* October 30, 1895: 6.

52   "Engagements," *Buffalo Courier,* January 12, 1896: 12.

53   "Fillmores vs. Genesees," *Buffalo Courier,* April 15, 1896: 11.

54   "Other Candidates," *Buffalo Courier,* April 14, 1897: 6.

55   "Are Excavating," *Buffalo Courier,* December 27, 1899: 8.

56   "Queen Cities Win Out," *Buffalo Courier,* Nov 2, 1901, 9.

57   The unsuccessful search for a photo of Joe Stabell has included all known baseball archives, newspaper archives, historical societies associated with Buffalo and the Pan-Am Expo, and outreach to known relatives identified through Ancestry.com.

58   "Mr. Stabell Will Build New Home in Central Park," *Buffalo Evening News,* August 27, 1910: 46.

59   "Member of County Committee, Democratic, Nineteenth Ward," *Buffalo Courier,* September 21, 1921: 12.

60   "St. Vincent's Orphan Asylum," *Buffalo Courier,* December 12, 1900: 5.

61   "One Hundred Horses Saved from Stable Fire," *Buffalo Commercial,* March 11, 1914: 6.

62   "Baker Hoarded Sugar/Must Quit Business," *Buffalo Evening News,* June 21, 1918: 13.

63   Michael A. Lerner, "Going Dry: The Coming of Prohibition," National Endowment for the Humanities, HUMANITIES, September/October 2011, neh.gov/humanities/2011/septemberoctober/feature/going-dry.

64   "New York State News Briefs," *Evening Leader* (Corning, New York), March 2, 1922: 3.

65   "Contractor Dies," *Buffalo Commercial,* July 10, 1923: 3.

66   US City Directories, 1822-1995 for George J. Stabell.

67   Joe Stabell entry, Baseball-Reference.com, baseball-reference.com/players/s/stapljo01.shtml (as of 11/15/2020).

TOM SULLIVAN

By Mike Mattsey

Reaching the major leagues is the pinnacle of a baseball player's rise through the professional ranks. A player whose uniform says "Philadelphia" rather than "Scranton" knows without being told that he is competing against the greatest players the game has to offer. For some, a long and fruitful career is in the offing. But for others, a major-league career is painfully short. It is in the latter category that one finds Tom Sullivan, left-handed pitcher for the 1922 Philadelphia Phillies. Sullivan's career in the big leagues encompassed a scant three games, but he had the opportunity to pit his talents against some of the game's all-time greats. He recorded only one hit for his career, but it was one to remember.

Thomas Augustin Sullivan was born in Boston on October 18, 1895, one of seven children born to James and Mary (Donovan) Sullivan. James was born in Massachusetts and Mary was an immigrant from Ireland. They met, married, and had all seven of their children in Boston. James worked as a house painter and Mary was employed as a seamstress. Tom was a good student, and after high school he attended nearby Boston College, though he did not play on the Eagles' baseball team.[1] He did feature for teams in the Blackstone Valley League during the summer months. This league, a semipro summer industrial league, was recognized as "playing the best brand of ball" of any of the Boston area summer leagues.[2] Tom was no doubt trying to get noticed by scouts in order to be signed by a professional baseball team but was instead called up by another organization, the United States Army.

Sullivan enlisted in the Army in May 1917, after the United States declared war on Germany in World War I, and was placed in the 101st Infantry Regiment of the 26th (Yankee) Division. Sullivan's unit was sent to France to join the Allied forces. The 101st participated in some of the worst fighting in the war, front-line trench warfare. Sullivan fared better than many; his assignment to the Yankee Division's supply company offered a break from the trenches and the brutal hand-to-hand fighting that was standard fare for a World War I infantryman. However, Sullivan's position with the supply company was not without its dangers. He was wounded in action and was awarded the Purple Heart.[3] Sullivan was honorably discharged in May 1919 after returning to Massachusetts. He married Bostonian Mary Flaherty and together they raised three children, Eleanor, Irene, and Thomas Jr. It was also at this time that Sullivan's professional baseball career began.

The 1921 season marks Sullivan's first appearances in a professional box score. He signed to be the third starter in manager Joe Birmingham's rotation for the Class-A Eastern League's Albany Senators. Sullivan's first appearance for Albany marked him as a young prospect to watch. He allowed only two hits to the Hartford Senators in a 2-1 triumph. In the effort, Sullivan fanned nine Hartford batters.[4] Sullivan had an up-and-down season for Albany, but occasionally he showed flashes of brilliance. On August 14 he was tabbed to start the second game of a doubleheader against the Worcester Boosters. Sullivan started slowly, allowing three first-inning runs, but recovered to shut down the Boosters the rest of the way. He finished the game with a seven-hit complete-game, 9-3 victory with eight strikeouts.[5] For the season, Sullivan finished with a 6-10 record covering 19 mound appearances with a 4.27 ERA and 72 strikeouts in 135 innings of work. As a pitcher, he fared well at the plate, batting .208 with two home runs. For his debut season, the 25-year-old rookie held his own. Bigger things were in store.

Sullivan attracted the notice of the Philadelphia Phillies organization and his contract was purchased from Albany before the 1922 season. He went to spring training in Leesburg, Florida, with an opportunity to win a berth in manager Kaiser Wilhelm's pitching staff. The opportunity was nearly lost before it got started. In early March, Sullivan reported to camp with what he thought was a bad cold. He was worried that reporting it to the Phillies' brass would jeopardize his

ONE-HIT WONDERS

chances to make the team, so he kept it to himself. The cold worsened to the point where doctors were called in and they noted that Sullivan's illness was a "hop skip and jump" from pneumonia.[6] The doctors were able to prevent pneumonia, and he was soon back on the mound.

On March 14 the Phillies played the Leesburg town team. As expected, the major leaguers pounded the amateur side, 17-2. However, this was a noteworthy game for Sullivan in his quest to win a job with Philadelphia. The game was out of hand in the sixth inning when he was sent in to pitch for Leesburg, and he performed admirably against his would-be teammates. His "southpaw shoots" limited the Phillies to four hits over the final three frames.[7] Shutting down the Phillies may have been the perfect way to impress the Phillies management. When Philadelphia broke camp, Sullivan had made the Opening Day roster as a member of a team trying to improve on the prior season's last-place finish.[8] After just one season in the minors, Tom Sullivan was going to the bright lights of the National League.

Sullivan began the season on the bench for Philadelphia as the team opened the season with a game at Sportsman's Park against Branch Rickey's St. Louis Cardinals. Manager Wilhelm sent out pitcher Bill Hubbell to start the game, and he got shelled early. Hubbell retired only one batter and allowed four runs on five hits before being yanked in favor of Huck Betts. Betts fared only slightly better, lasting one full inning and giving up four more runs. When Wilhelm went to the mound to replace Betts, his signal was for the rookie left-hander. It was time for Sullivan to make his first appearance in the big leagues.

Sullivan entered the game with runners on first and second and one out. Jack Fournier was the first man he faced, and the first baseman fouled out. Sullivan was one out away from stranding the runners he had inherited, but Austin McHenry had other ideas. The left fielder slashed a line drive to right for a two-run double. Pinch-hitter Les Mann lined out to left, and Sullivan had weathered his first storm. The Cardinals struck for four more runs in the third on run-scoring hits by Milt Stock, Rogers Hornsby, and Fournier. The next hitter, McHenry, hit a foul ball near the St. Louis bench. Phillies third baseman Goldie Rapp, oblivious to the 12-0 deficit, made an attempt at a circus catch but injured himself badly as he crash-landed into the Cardinals dugout. Rapp was forced to leave the game and was taken to St. John's hospital with two fractured ribs and a sprained ankle.[9] The injuries were enough to shelve the Phillies third sacker for nearly a month.

On the mound, Sullivan fared little better than Rapp. Wilhelm left the rookie in the game until the end on a day when the Cardinals' bats were on fire. Over the final 6⅔ innings, St. Louis scored 14 runs off Sullivan on 15 hits and two walks. It was Sullivan's work with the ash that left the southpaw with his moment in the sun. Sullivan had four at-bats for the game. In his first, in the third inning, he tapped back to the box for an easy groundout. His second appearance came with two out in the fifth. With runners on first and second, Cardinals starter Bill Doak caught Sullivan looking at a called third strike to end the frame. The next at-bat was one to remember.

In the seventh inning, with the score no longer in doubt, Rickey inserted relief pitcher Clyde Barfoot into the game to finish things off. The Phillies' first batter of the inning, Frank Withrow, greeted Barfoot with a single to center field. As Sullivan stepped to the plate, he was probably more than a little angry. He had waited a month on the bench before being given a chance to pitch, and the day couldn't have been going worse for him. Whatever the situation, Barfoot delivered a "fast one" that caught too much of the plate and Sullivan slammed it into the right-field bleachers for a two-run home run.[10] It was the only hit of Sullivan's major-league career. He had taken one for the team on the mound, and the home run proved to be his only reward. His final appearance at the plate resulted in a groundout to the first baseman. The remainder of the game was uneventful, ending in a 19-7 triumph for the Cardinals.

After the shelling by St. Louis, it was more than two weeks before Sullivan was again called upon to pitch. On May 30 the first-place New York Giants were the visitors for a doubleheader at Philadelphia's Baker Bowl. Sullivan appeared briefly in relief in both games. In the opener, Wilhelm inserted Sullivan into another sticky situation, though the score at 3-2 was much closer than it had been in St. Louis. Sullivan was brought into the game in the fourth inning to relieve starter George Smith with the bases loaded and one out with future Hall of Fame second baseman Frankie Frisch at bat. The young left-hander received a huge break when Phillies catcher Butch Henline picked off the runner at first for the inning's second out. However, Sullivan walked Frisch to load the bases again for Heinie Groh. Groh's famed bottle bat never left his shoulder as Sullivan walked his second

ONE-HIT WONDERS

consecutive hitter to force in a run, making the score 4-2. Wilhelm pulled Sullivan in favor of Lerton Pinto who retired the side after allowing another run-scoring walk. Though Sullivan did little to help the cause, the Phillies did rally late and won the game in extra innings. Sullivan also featured in the second game of the twin bill. This time, he replaced Pinto in the ninth inning of a 16-7 rout. Sullivan was far more effective in this outing; he pitched a scoreless inning to close out the Philadelphia loss. Unfortunately for Sullivan, fate stepped in and he never got the chance to build on this success.

On June 5 the Phillies were hosting the Pittsburgh Pirates at Baker Bowl on a rainy Monday afternoon. Before the game, Sullivan was pitching batting practice when a vicious line drive struck him on the leg. He was taken to Stetson Hospital and initial reports suggested that he had suffered a broken leg. More promising later reports said he had "an ugly bruise but will be able to do 'bull pen' duty within a few days."[11] Some blamed Sullivan's "badly injured leg" on "the lively ball" that was resulting in higher-scoring games.[12] The injury was the death knell of Sullivan's major-league career. In July, the Phillies sent him down to the Eastern League to finish out the season with Waterbury.[13] Never again did he appear in the major leagues.

Sullivan was back in the Eastern League in 1923, though his stay was a brief one. He signed with the Waterbury Brasscos but in late May was "fined $50 for alleged indifferent work."[14] He returned back home to pitch in the Boston Twilight League until late June when he was "turned over" to Macon in the South Atlantic League by Waterbury.[15] He did not appear in box scores for Macon, and likely never reported to Georgia. Sullivan jumped the Eastern League for the next two seasons and remained in the Twilight League as a pitcher for the 1923 and 1924 seasons. After two years on the fringes, Sullivan applied for reinstatement in March of 1925 to the Eastern Leagues and his petition was granted.[16] He was back in Organized Baseball.

Sullivan opened the 1925 season with the Hartford Senators of the Eastern League. He was ineffective and in August was dealt to the Pittsfield Hillies. Sullivan had two more big-time performances remaining in his left arm. Now called "Lefty" in the papers, Sullivan was called upon to start both games of an August 23 doubleheader against the club that had let him go, Hartford. The first game did not go well for Sullivan. Hartford scored five times in the first inning and chased Sullivan to the bench. The second game went much better for Sullivan and the Hillies. In the second game he held Hartford to a 4-4 tie for eight innings. He led off the top of the ninth with a single and went to third base when the right fielder let the ball get by him. He scored one out later and held off the Senators in the bottom of the ninth to preserve a 5-4 victory.[17] His last hurrah as a player came in September in a game against the Worcester Panthers at Pittsfield's Wahconah Park. Worcester player-manager Casey Stengel's team was helpless that day as Sullivan threw a five-hit shutout to send the home fans home happy. It was the last game Sullivan won as a professional pitcher. Sullivan was back with Pittsfield before the 1926 season, but by the summer he was back in Boston pitching in the industrial leagues as the "mound mainstay" for the Boston Typos.[18] It was after this season that Sullivan stopped appearing in box scores and his playing days came to a close.

After his baseball career ended, Sullivan returned to the trade he learned in his Army supply company. He worked as a freight handler and worked his way up to a labor foreman at a Boston-area Army depot. He and his wife remained in Boston their entire lives, raising their three children. The couple's youngest child, nicknamed Tommy Joe, inherited some of his father's athletic prowess and put it on display as a freshman halfback on Boston College's 1951 football team. The season's final game pitted BC against their arch-rivals, nationally-ranked Holy Cross, in a game at Braves Field before a crowd of 40,000. With seconds remaining in the game and BC losing by two points, Tommy Joe, the "fastest footer on the B.C. squad," hauled in a 56-yard pass to set up the winning touchdown as the Eagles knocked off the Crusaders 19-14.[19]

Sullivan died on September 23, 1962, at the age of 62. He was survived by his wife and their children. His career as a major-league pitcher was a brief one, but he had one thing about his stay he could always remember with fondness. He may have only had one hit for the Phillies, but he knocked it out of the park.

SOURCES

In addition to the works cited in the Notes, the author utilized Baseball-Reference.com for statistical data and game notes and Fold3.com for information relating to the 101st Infantry.

NOTES

1. Ernest J. Lanigan, *New Major Leaguers*, 1922. Document on file with the National Baseball Hall of Fame.

ONE-HIT WONDERS

2   Albert J. Woodlock, "Baseball Shifts Soon From Shore and Mountain," *Boston Globe*, August 23, 1926: 9.

3   US Headstone Applications For Military Veterans, ancestry.com/imageviewer/collections/2375/images/40050_649063_0425-00233?tree-id=&personid=&hintid=&usePUB=true&usePUBJs=true&_ga=2.31075255.904082447.1601661829-890328165.1572627534&pId=420775.

4   Lanigan.

5   "Lawmakers and Boosters Divide Twinbill," *Bridgeport* (Connecticut) *Telegram*, August 15, 1921: 5.

6   "Phillies Southpaw Escapes Pneumonia," *Philadelphia Inquirer*, March 9, 1922: 16.

7   "Phillies Surprised by Lees," *Philadelphia Inquirer*, March 15, 1922: 16.

8   "Philadelphia Nationals Roster for 1922," *Brooklyn Standard Union*, April 5, 1922: 14.

9   John J. Sheridan, "Game Sidelights," *St. Louis Daily Globe-Democrat*, May 16, 1922.

10 Sheridan.

11 "Phils Ahead When Rain Stops Game," *Philadelphia Inquirer*, June 6, 1922: 18.

12 "Sport Summary," *Lancaster* (Pennsylvania) *New Era*, June 6, 1922: 10.

13 "Eastern League Notes," *Berkshire County Eagle* (Pittsfield, Massachusetts), July 22, 1922: 8.

14 "Eastern League Notes," *Berkshire County Eagle,* May 23, 1923: 10.

15 "Eastern League Notes," *Berkshire County Eagle,* June 22, 1923: 19.

16 "Eastern League Notes," *Berkshire County Eagle,* March 20, 1925: 26.

17 "Locals Get Gift in First Contest," *Hartford Courant*, August 24, 1925: 7.

18 "Boston Typos To Meet Neponset Nine Sunday." *Boston Globe*, August 13, 1926: 10.

19 "B.C. upsets Holy Cross, 19-14." *Boston Globe*, December 2, 1951: 1.

CLAY TOUCHSTONE

By Joe Schuster

Although right-handed, side-armed pitcher Clayland Maffitt "Clay" Touchstone Jr. has a sparse major-league resume – no decisions in 12 games spread over parts of three seasons, including a 16-year gap between appearances at one point – he nonetheless had a long, often successful career in the minor leagues, winning 272 games, making multiple all-star teams, and having sufficient fame that car dealers and appliance stores used his name and photo to sell radios, refrigerators, and automobiles.

Described in newspaper accounts as blond and burly, right-handed-hitting Touchstone (listed at 5-feet-9, 170 pounds) was born on January 24, 1903, in Prospect Park, Pennsylvania, as the sixth of seven children of Clayland M. Touchstone Sr. and Ada B. (Strout) Touchstone. There is evidence that he tried throughout his career to shave two years off his age. Although the 1910 census has his date of birth as 1903, a 1945 player questionnaire lists it as 1905.[1] Likewise, several 1925 articles reporting his signing his first professional contract, with Waterbury of the Eastern League, give his age that year as 20, as do several articles from early 1926 when the Cubs invited him to spring training.[2] Articles announcing his signing a contract with the Chicago White Sox in 1945 also reduce his age by those two years.[3]

During Touchstone's childhood, his father worked in various capacities in the railroad industry, while census records describe his mother as not being employed outside the home. Touchstone appears to have gotten only as far as the eighth grade in his education, at Prospect Park's Lincoln Avenue School; by the time of the 1920 census, when he was 17, his occupation was listed as messenger boy for a steam railroad.[4] He grew up in something of a baseball family, as his oldest brother, Vernon Touchstone, spent two seasons, 1907 and 1909, in the minor leagues. Touchstone credited Vernon with helping him develop as a pitcher.[5] In 1928 several newspapers reported that a second brother, Fred Touchstone, was a member of the Providence Grays, although neither Baseball-Reference nor Retrosheet shows any statistics for him.[6] Another article from that year describes Fred as briefly a bullpen catcher for the Boston Braves.[7]

Starting in 1922, Touchstone spent three seasons playing semipro ball in the Philadelphia area, primarily as a pitcher but also in the outfield and infield on days he wasn't on the mound, acquiring a reputation for his "powerful right arm" and a "trusty bat."[8] With Salem in the Salem County League in 1922, he went 18-6.[9] The next year, he moved to a team sponsored by Lit Brothers Department Store in the Philadelphia Baseball Association, finishing the season 21-7.[10] In September that year, Lit Brothers played an exhibition against a rival, Ascension Catholic Church, which featured Babe Ruth at first base, participating as a favor

Clay Touchstone.

ONE-HIT WONDERS

for the church's pastor, Father William Casey, to help raise money to pay off the parish debt for its athletic field.[11] (Lit Brothers won 2-1, as its pitcher, Howard Gransbach, held Ruth to one hit in three at-bats.[12]) The next season, Touchstone was once again back with Lit Brothers, then in the Penn-Jersey League, reportedly going 15-8.[13]

In August of 1925, after he threw a one-hitter in a game against Ascension that ended in a 0-0 tie, the Detroit Tigers invited Touchstone to a tryout, although it appears they did not offer him a contract, since going into the 1925 season Touchstone was preparing to play for another Penn-Jersey League semipro team, Camden.[14] However, instead he got an offer from Waterbury of the Eastern League when Billy Whitman, manager of the Penn-Jersey team in Chester, who also doubled as a scout for the Chicago Cubs, recommended him to Waterbury manager Kitty Bransfield.[15]

Touchstone made his professional debut on April 24, 1925, in relief in a 5-4 loss to the Springfield Ponies in Springfield; the box score shows he pitched in the eighth inning, likely facing a single batter, as his line was zero innings, no hits, no strikeouts, one walk.[16] He got his first professional start the next day, also in Springfield, going nine innings in a game that ended a 2-2 tie when the umpires stopped it on account of darkness. Touchstone allowed five hits, walked three and struck out seven, while collecting his first professional hit, a double.

Throughout the season, in which Waterbury won the championship, Touchstone alternated between starting and relieving; once in a while, his name shows up in a box score playing the outfield or as a pinch-hitter. In all, he appeared in 65 games, 46 as a hurler, ranking second among Waterbury pitchers for appearances, after Jim Bishop's 51. Touchstone's final record was 10-11, with a 3.73 ERA, 89 strikeouts, and 95 walks.

Touchstone crowned his season in an odd fashion. On September 17 the Hartford Senators came to Waterbury for a doubleheader, with Waterbury leading Hartford by two-tenths of a percent atop the standings with four days remaining. Waterbury took the opener, 6-5 in 12 innings. Then, as the second game began, controversy arose when umpires ran out of the official league-sanctioned baseball. According to the *Berkshire Eagle* account, umpires procured a supply manufactured by a different company and league President Dan O'Neill, who was in attendance, gave his approval to use them. Hartford manager Paddy O'Connor immediately announced he was playing under protest. After Waterbury took a 3-0 lead in the third, the Senators scored in each of the next four, taking an 8-3 lead in the top of the seventh when they plated four off reliever Moose Fuller, prompting Bransfield to bring on Touchstone with two outs. He retired the only man he faced, ending the inning. Waterbury answered by scoring five in the bottom of the inning, the last two coming in on a long drive to right by catcher Tommy McCarthy, who tried to stretch the hit into a triple, but was apparently cut down, as the umpire ruled him out, but then reversed himself, saying the Hartford third baseman had dropped the ball. The ensuing argument emptied both benches as the "diamond took on the aspect of a riot scene." After calm returned, the umpires ordered play to resume, but O'Connor kept his team off the field, and the umpires awarded the game to Waterbury in a forfeit. As Touchstone was the pitcher of record, he got credit for the victory.[17] Waterbury never relinquished its lead in the standings and, after league owners voted to reject O'Connor's protest, Waterbury nailed down its second consecutive Eastern League championship, the first team to win back-to-back pennants in the league's short history to then.[18]

The Chicago Cubs invited Touchstone to spring training in 1926, and he was among the earliest players to report to camp.[19] His progress was slowed in the second week, when he took a line drive off a shin and the injury become infected.[20] However, he did have his bright moments; for example, he earned a positive notice in the *Chicago Tribune* for his performance in a March 9 intrasquad game when he threw four scoreless innings after the opposing squad had pummeled starter Tony Kaufman for 11 runs in the first five frames.[21] Despite that, the team assigned him to Waterbury once again, as the final player cut before Opening Day.[22] However, Touchstone refused to report, and instead went home and spent the season playing in the Camden County semipro league, under an assumed name, Johnny Carr.[23]

Before the 1927 season, Waterbury sold Touchstone to another Eastern League team, the Providence Grays, and he turned in solid work there over the next two years. In 1927 he went 17-17 with a 3.73 ERA, 99 strikeouts, and a league-high 128 walks for a team that finished last, at 61-91. In 1928 he made his first minor-league all-star team when he went 16-13 with a 3.27 ERA and finished third in the league in WHIP among pitchers with at least 150 innings, 1.264. He also recorded 100 strikeouts against 77 walks.

ONE-HIT WONDERS

That September, the Boston Braves recalled Touchstone and he made his major-league debut in the second game of a doubleheader against Brooklyn on September 4, coming on in the top of the eighth with Boston trailing 5-2 and playing as if they were "in a trance on the field."[24] Babe Herman greeted him with a bunt single down the third-base line, and the second batter reached as well when Braves first baseman George Sisler made a wild throw after fielding a groundball, putting runners on second and third. Touchstone induced the next batter to ground to short, the runners holding, but then Rube Bressler's single plated both runners. With two outs, Touchstone walked a man and gave up a two-run triple to Watty Clark, before closing out the ugly inning on a lineout to center. He managed to get through the ninth with no further damage – allowing only a single – giving him a final line of two innings, four runs, all unearned, four hits, one walk, no strikeouts.

In all, Touchstone saw action in five games that month, as the Braves finished out a miserable season, ending up 50-103, in seventh place. Touchstone recorded no decisions in throwing eight innings, finishing with a 4.50 ERA, allowing eight runs, four earned, on 15 hits and two walks, while registering one strikeout, which came in his final appearance that year, on September 25, when he fanned the Pirates' Mack Hillis. That last game saw Touchstone's longest outing of the season with Boston: He went four innings, garnering his first strong notices from the Boston press. He came on to begin the top of the fourth with the Braves down 8-1 and steadied the ship enough to allow Boston to creep back into the game, allowing single runs in the fifth and sixth, while Boston was scoring seven. While Boston ended up on the short side of the eventual 13-8 score, Touchstone earned praise from two Boston daily newspapers. The *Globe* said, "Touchstone was the only Boston pitcher who could hold the visitors."[25] The *Herald* was even more enthusiastic, saying he was "easily the best of the four Boston pitchers," and adding that after he entered the game, "Boston looked better, because the Pirates could not take liberties with his stuff."[26]

Boston returned Touchstone to Providence for 1929 and he had his best year in professional ball to that point, going 22-12, leading the league in innings (292) and strikeouts (132), and finishing second in victories. His ERA of 3.39 ranked second among hurlers with at least 150 innings, as did his WHIP of 1.301. He also gained his second consecutive selection to the Eastern League all-star team. His success earned him a second trip to the major leagues, when Boston called him up in September. This time Touchstone saw action in only a single game, 2⅔ innings in relief against the Pirates on September 20. He came on with one out and a runner on second in the bottom of the sixth and suffered what would turn out to be the worst stint in his brief major-league tenure, allowing five consecutive hits, three for extra bases, capped by a three-run home run by Lloyd Waner, increasing the Braves' 4-2 deficit to 10-2. He managed to go the rest of the distance without allowing another run, giving up only one more single. His line for the game (and that major-league season): 2⅔ innings, five runs (all earned), six hits, no walks, one strikeout (of Bill Windle, in his second and final major-league plate appearance).

Although his game on the mound was abysmal, Touchstone did have one career highlight that day, his first and, as it turned out, only major-league hit, a one-out single to left in the eighth inning, off Jesse Petty. While Touchstone advanced to second with two outs, on a single by Freddie Maguire, that was as far as he got on the basepaths, as the next hitter, Sisler, grounded out, ending the inning.

In nearly every other era of baseball history, that likely would have been the end of Touchstone's major-league career, such as it was. However, he did have one more shot at the big leagues – only he had to wait 16 years.

Boston assigned Touchstone to Newark of the International League for 1930. In May, with his record 1-2, Boston sold his contract to the Southern Association Birmingham Barons.[27] There, he became a bona fide star. Even before he arrived, the local press was lauding him. Describing him as a "burly righthander" and, because of his 1929 workload, "a real life iron man," the *Birmingham News* said, "Touchstone is a hurler of proven Class A ability (who) should cop a lot of games in the Southern, provided the climate agrees with him. ... (He is) a curve ball pitcher, although he has a fast one, a knuckler and one or two other varieties in his repertoire."[28] He made a positive impression nearly immediately, starting his first game as a Baron in Atlanta on May 26 and going the distance in an 11-inning, 3-2 victory, again earning effusive praise: "In addition to showing (Atlanta) a world of stuff, Clay Touchstone showed that he had courage ... to keep right on pitching in the face of adversity and blasted chances for runs. Few Baronial hurlers have broken in with the goods the former Boston Brave put on display for 11 innings. ... Touchstone's hurling should serve as a great tonic for the Barons."[29]

ONE-HIT WONDERS

Touchstone went 15-6 with the Barons, giving him a combined record for the year of 16-8. His 15 victories with the Barons ranked second on the team, despite his joining it in late May and also missing the final week when he returned to Pennsylvania because his mother had fallen ill, dying on September 9.[30] His performance earned him his third selection to a minor-league all-star team, and helped establish him as enough of a name in the city that a local car dealer ran a photo of him and two of his teammates buying Buicks to promote the dealership, and a local appliance store hired him to sell radios and refrigerators during the offseason, using Touchstone's photograph and name, and those of several other professional ballplayers, in its advertising.[31]

Although 1931 turned out to be a bit of a down year for Touchstone – he posted his worst minor-league ERA to that point, 4.76, highest among all Barons hurlers that year, although he did win 15 games (against 11 losses). He did have one significant positive moment. After the Barons won the Southern Association in a bit of a walk, finishing 10½ games ahead of second-place Little Rock, they met Texas League champ Houston in the annual best-of-seven Dixie Series. Houston was led that year by two future Hall of Famers: Dizzy Dean, who'd been spectacular, leading the Texas League in wins (26) and strikeouts (303), while posting a 1.53 ERA, and Joe Medwick, who'd led the league in home runs (19) and RBIs (126). The first four games were pitchers' duels, all shutouts, as Birmingham took the opener, defeating Dean 1-0, and Houston took the next three by scores of 3-0, 1-0, 2-0, pushing the Barons to the brink of losing the series. To start the win-or-go-home game five, Barons manager Clyde Milan tapped Touchstone, his first action in the series, and he responded by "going the route in never-wavering fashion, speeding down the last five innings like a midnight express passing through a tank town," scattering seven hits in nailing down a 3-1 victory that kept Birmingham alive.[32] The Barons won the last two, bringing home the championship, their second in three years.

Touchstone spent two more seasons in Birmingham. He struggled again in 1932, posting a league-high ERA among pitchers with at least 150 innings, 5.56, although he did manage to go 16-15, for a fifth-place Barons team that finished 68-83. The next season, however, was far better. Touchstone began working out in earnest in January, prompting Milan to predict he would win 20 games.[33] He got the ball as Opening Day starter; while he allowed 10 hits, he "flashed an amazing curve" and went the distance in the victory.[34] He went on to win six in a row in all, finally losing his first of the season on May 11. By the end of the June, he was 12-5 and pitching so well that the Barons staged a "Touchstone Day" at the ballpark during a July 2 doubleheader, at which Touchstone hosted semipro pitchers in a skills competition in between the two games, and fans presented him with a Gladstone bag. Then he had his worst day of the season to that point, losing 8-7 when he allowed two runs with two outs in the top of the ninth.[35] He finished the season 21-13 (his 21 wins tied for tops in the Association), and ranked third both in innings pitched (283) and ERA among hurlers with at least 150 innings (3.21). His performance landed him his fourth all-star selection, in both the Associated Press and United Press polls.[36]

Despite his success on the field, and the postseason recognition, Touchstone ended 1933 on an unfortunate note: On December 30, he and shortstop Jess Cortazzo were arrested for possession of alcoholic beverages and operating a game of chance; Touchstone pled guilty in early January 1934, paying a fine of $40, and his plea led the court to drop the charges against Cortazzo.[37] Roughly three weeks later, the Barons traded Touchstone to Memphis for a career minor-league southpaw, Clarence Griffin. Some reports suggested the arrest might have been a factor in the deal: "In Touchstone's case there must have been some motive other than a desire for southpaw strength, as the portly curve-baller found his best stride ... last year. ... Perhaps the idea of 'cleaning house' balanced the ledger. ... Again the difficulties Clay found himself in when officers discovered beer at his lunch stand bore some influence."[38]

Touchstone spent three seasons in Memphis, with uneven success. The team acquired him hoping to build on the prior two seasons when they had finished with the best overall record in the Southern Association. It was not to be, as Memphis never repeated during Touchstone's tenure there. In 1934 he experienced his first sub-.500 season since his initial year in professional baseball, finishing 16-18, although his 2.78 ERA ranked second among league hurlers with at least 150 innings, and his 275 innings also ranked second.

The next season Touchstone again was in the 20-win club, going 22-11 (his victories ranked fourth in the league), and he also ranked fourth in innings, 283, although his numbers may have been better than that if he had not suffered bad cuts to his hands when a water faucet snapped off when he was bathing.[39] It later turned out that the injury may have cost him

ONE-HIT WONDERS

another shot at the major leagues, as shortly before Touchstone sliced his hands, Clark Griffith, owner of the Washington Senators, had considered picking him up but was dissuaded when it was not clear how the injury would affect his pitching.[40] Nonetheless, his season landed him yet again on the all-star team, his fifth such selection.

Touchstone's final year with Memphis was an abysmal one, for both Memphis and him. He began it by holding out in a salary dispute, not signing until mid-March.[41] He didn't make his first start of the season until April 20, the Chicks' ninth game of the season, against New Orleans, and although he allowed only six hits and a walk in eight innings he ended up losing because he hit five batters, three of whom scored.[42] He finished with his worst record to that point in his professional career, 12-18, the first time since his initial professional season that he did not reach at least 15 victories. His ERA, 4.57, was the third worst among pitchers with at least 150 innings. As far as the Chicks fortunes went, they finished last, 60-90, the first time since 1920 that they ended the season below .500 and in the second division.

After the close of the season, Memphis traded Touchstone to Oklahoma City for career minor-league pitcher Ed Marleau, and Touchstone spent two years there, performing well in each season, though not without significant challenges in the latter year.

In the first of those, 1937, he went 19-11 with a 2.53 ERA and a career-high 181 strikeouts in 277 innings, earning selection to yet another all-star team. Interestingly, he was only the second-best hurler for Oklahoma City, which went 101-58: even better was career minor leaguer Harold "Ash" Hillin, who went 31-10, with a 2.34 ERA in 302 innings; Hillin took league MVP honors.

In the offseason, Touchstone began feeling ill and when he consulted a doctor, he was diagnosed with diabetes and anemia, conditions that caused him to lose a considerable amount of weight and weakened him to the point that doctors suggested that if he were to pitch at all in 1938, it might not be until June 1.[43] He did come back sooner, beginning his season in mid-April by working strictly in relief. A sportswriter from the *Daily Oklahoman* described one such appearance (in the nightcap of an April 24 doubleheader against Fort Worth):

"The Tribal invalid, skinny Clay Touchstone, staggered into the picture (with one out) in the second inning. ... Everyone felt sorry for poor Clay, but he made his way to the pitching mound without assistance. He couldn't stand up out there. But he got two men out. ... Then, in the Indian half, his fragile wasted form presented a sorry picture at the plate. The bases were loaded. Two were out. The ghost swung and the result was a clean single into left for two tying runs."[44]

Despite his slow start, Touchstone nonetheless pitched well for most of the season, ending up 16-11 with a 2.42 ERA; his victory total tied for 10th in the league, while his ERA stood eighth among pitchers with at least 150 innings, and his WHIP (0.996) was second. For his work, he earned another selection to a Texas League all-star team. Nonetheless, when the season ended, declaring they were pitching-rich and hitting-poor, Oklahoma City traded him to Dallas, for career minor-league outfielder Tony Governor, and cash.[45]

Perhaps mindful of his slow start in 1938, Touchstone returned his signed contract to Dallas quickly after receiving it, enclosing a note saying the was confident he was fully healthy and "rearing to go."[46] However, he suffered a leg injury in a preseason game that delayed his first regular-season appearance until the eighth game, on April 22, but his performance that day made plain that he was, indeed, "rearing" to go, as he shut out Tulsa 8-0, allowing six hits and two walks, fanning eight.[47] In all that year, he threw seven shutouts, posting a record of 20-12, with a 2.70 ERA in 253 innings, and earning yet another spot on the Texas League North all-star team.[48]

As it turned out, that was the last truly outstanding season of Touchstone's career, as he never again finished a year with a winning record: In 1940, still with Dallas, he went 11-14, with a 3.67 ERA in 218 innings, although he was still enough of a fan favorite that he earned a berth on the North all-star team.

Before the 1941 season, Dallas sent Touchstone back to Oklahoma City, in exchange for right-handed pitcher Otho Nitcholas. There, he ended up 13-18, with a 2.99 ERA, highest among Oklahoma City pitchers with at least 150 innings. However, in October, Touchstone was invited to participate in an exhibition game in Oklahoma City, pitting a team of "All Stars" headed by Bob Feller against the Kansas City Monarchs, whose major draw was hurler Satchel Paige.[49] Paige was a no-show, as he was unable to get timely transportation from Kansas City; despite that, the Monarchs prevailed 3-2, scoring one run off Feller in his three innings of work and the other two off Ed Marleau, who took the loss. Touchstone pitched the final two frames, setting down all six he faced.[50]

ONE-HIT WONDERS

Standing in for Paige was Booker T. McDaniels, later the first African-American pitcher in the PCL when he joined the Los Angeles Angels in 1949.[51]

The next year, 1942, was Touchstone's last in the minor leagues. He was again back with Oklahoma City, which had an even worse season than the team had in 1941, finishing 58-95. In fact, the team was so awful it went through four managers, beginning with Homer Peel, who was fired on June 12 with the team 24-35, followed by scout Jimmy Payton, who served as acting manager until June 17, when the team turned to second baseman John Kroner, who resigned on August 3 after the team went 18-32 during his brief tenure. To replace Kroner, the team turned to Touchstone, who took over with the team in a challenging spot: not only was it in seventh place, but in good part because of the World War II draft, it had an active roster of only 13.[52] Under Touchstone, the team ran out the string, going 14-24. As for his individual numbers, Touchstone ended up 10-17 with a 3.11 ERA.

When the season ended, the Texas League suspended operations for the duration of the war, and Oklahoma City sold Touchstone's contract to the Baltimore Orioles of the International League.[53] However, in March 1943, the 40-year-old pitcher announced that he had no interest in playing, retiring instead to run a tavern he owned in Beaumont, Texas, Service Amusement Club.[54] His career minor-league totals: 272 wins, 230 losses, 1,766 strikeouts, 1,196 walks, and a 3.51 ERA.

As it turned out, Touchstone was not entirely finished with baseball. In 1945, with major-league rosters depleted by the demands of the war, the Chicago White Sox approached him about joining the team as a relief pitcher, and Touchstone agreed, telling *The Sporting News* that although he not thrown a pitch in more than two years, he "suddenly got the hankering to try it again and figured with manpower conditions being what they are, now would be a good time for a whirl in the majors."[55]

The 42-year-old Touchstone did not see much action. Although on the roster the entire season, he pitched in only 10 innings over six games, all in relief. He recorded no decisions, put up an ERA of 5.40 on 14 hits and six walks, while striking out four. His final appearance came on September 8 against the Athletics in Philadelphia, when he came on to begin the bottom of the fifth, relieving Eddie Lopat with the White Sox losing 5-0. In an echo of his first major-league game, he was hurt by a key error, when third baseman Ray Schalk made a wild throw after fielding a groundball, eventually leading to three unearned runs. Touchstone allowed another in the seventh, on a home run by Hal Peck, which closed out the scoring in the 9-0 A's victory. In the game, Touchstone recorded his sixth and final major-league strikeout, of pitcher Jesse Flores leading off the bottom of the seventh. The final major-league batter Touchstone faced was George Kell, who grounded back to Touchstone for a 1-3 putout.

When the season ended, with the regulars returning with the end of the war, the White Sox released Touchstone, assigning him to Little Rock, but he elected not to report, giving up the professional game once and for all. He returned to Beaumont to run his amusement club, until his death on April 28, 1949, of pulmonary thrombosis.[56] He left a wife, Elsie (Crowel) Touchstone, whom he'd married in 1928, as well as three sons. Touchstone is buried in Forest Lawn Memorial Park in Beaumont, Texas.

SOURCES

In addition to the sources cited in the notes, the author referred to *The Encyclopedia of Minor League Baseball*, Lloyd Johnson and Miles Wolff, editors; *The Minor League Register*, Lloyd Johnson, editor; *Minor League All Star Teams 1922-1962*, by James Selko; as well as Baseball-Reference.com and Retrosheet.org. He also consulted SABR's BioProject.

NOTES

1   1910 Census; The National Archives in St. Louis, Missouri; St. Louis, Missouri; *WWII Draft Registration Cards for Oklahoma, 10/16/1940-03/31/1947*; Record Group: *Records of the Selective Service System, 147*; Box: *511*;

2   "Eastern League Notes," *Berkshire Eagle* (Pittsfield, Massachusetts), March 9, 1925: 13; "Prospect Park Hurler Signs," *Delaware County Times* (Chester, Pennsylvania), March 5, 1925: 11; "Cubs Line Up 14 Pitchers for Trip," *San Antonio Light*, January 31, 1926: 37.

3   "Game in Touchstone's Blood," *The Sporting News*, March 29, 1945: 16.

4   "Prospect Park Hurler Signs," *Delaware County Daily Times*, March 5, 1925: 11; "Eastern League Notes," *Berkshire Eagle*, March 9, 1925: 13.

5   "Prospect Park Hurler Signs."

6   "Have a Brother Battery," *News Herald* (Franklin, Pennsylvania), August 3, 1928: 13.

7   "Eastern League Notes," *Berkshire Eagle*, August 13, 1928: 13.

8   "Lit Brothers Defeat Camden in Fast Game," *Morning Post* (Camden, New Jersey), August 15, 1928: 4.

9   "Prospect Park Hurler Signs."

10 "Prospect Park Hurler Signs."

11 "Ruth in Sandlot Game," *Washington Evening Star*, September 5, 1923: 24.

12 "Pitching Battle Draws Interest," *Lancaster* (Pennsylvania) *New Era*, September 6, 1923: 12. Gransbach later spent five years in the New York-Penn League, pitching for four different teams. The writer was not able to determine whether Touchstone appeared in the game; there do not appear to be any extant box scores.

13 "Eastern League Notes," *Berkshire Eagle*, March 9, 1925, 13.

ONE-HIT WONDERS

14 "Lits and Ascension in Scoreless Deadlock," *Courier-Post* (Camden, New Jersey), August 1, 1924: 19; Unheadlined note about Touchstone, *Courier-Post*, August 4, 1924L 19; "Swigler Will Not Play for Camden," *Courier-Post*, February 21, 1925: 12.

15 "Prospect Park Hurler Signs."

16 "Ponies Win in Initial Game on Home Field, 5-4," *Bridgeport (Connecticut) Telegram*, April 25, 1925: 24.

17 "Ponies Win in Initial Game on Home Field, 5-4."

18 "Only One Game in Brass City Today," *Hartford Courant*, September 20, 1925: 37.

19 John Hoffman, "Several Rookies Join Bruins for Drive to Pennant," *Chicago Daily News*, February 10, 1926: Two-1.

20 "Caught on the First Hop," *Camden Courier-Post*, March 4, 1926: 24.

21 Irving Vaughan, "Cub Subs Drub Cubs Regulars," *Chicago Tribune*, March 10, 1926: 23.

22 William H. Becker, "Cubs Are Ready," *Chicago Daily News*, April 12, 1926: Two-1; "Touchstone Released, Will Join Waterbury," *Camden Courier-Post*, September 29, 1926: 20.

23 "Demoe, Touchstone sold to Providence Nine," *Boston Globe*, December 1, 1926: 13; "Circuit Also Approves Deighan and Spaulding" *Camden Courier-Post*, September 3, 1926: 30.

24 James C. O'Leary, "Three Home Runs in Braves Double Loss," *Boston Globe*, September 5, 1928: 12.

25 James C. O'Leary, "Pirates Get Very Busy and Beat Braves, 13-8," *Boston Globe*, September 26, 1928: 13.

26 Burt Whitman, "Pirates Swamp Braves, 13-8," *Boston Herald*, September 26, 1928: 22.

27 "Providence Fails to Land Pitchers from Newark Club," *Scranton Republican*, May 16, 1930: 16.

28 James L. Conners, "Barons Obtain Iron Man in Touchstone," *Birmingham News*, May 20, 1930: 18.

29 Zipp Newman, "Dusting 'Em Off," *Birmingham News*, May 27, 1930: 17.

30 "Former Baron Blanks Milans with One Hit," *Birmingham News*, September 9, 1930: 16.

31 "Three Members of Baron Team Buy Buick Automobiles from Drennen Motor Car Co.," *Birmingham News*, September 14, 1930: 40; display ad for West End Radio Co., *Birmingham News*, October 5, 1930: 17.

32 Zipp Newman, "Clay Touchstone Gives Barons Second Victory, 3-1," *Birmingham News*, September 22, 1931: 10.

33 Zipp Newman, "Dusting 'Em Off," *Birmingham News*, January 20, 1933: 9; Zipp Newman, "Dusting 'Em Off," *Birmingham News*, March 10, 1933: 16.

34 Zipp Newman, "Manager Milan Chased by Ump in First Inning," *Birmingham News*, April 12, 1933: 8.

35 Zipp Newman, "Bill Hughes Blanks Vols in Nightcap," *Birmingham News*, July 3, 1933: 5. According to the *Birmingham News* account, a pitcher named Lewis Reynolds won the skills competition.

36 "New Orleans Pels Land Three Stars on All-Loop Team," *Birmingham News*, September 11, 1933: 8; "Managers Pick Lee Head," *Knoxville Journal*, September 12, 1933: 7.

37 "Barons Arrested," *Birmingham News*, December 31, 1933: 1; "Touchstone Fined," *Birmingham News*, January 4, 1934: 4.

38 Bob Murphy, "Tommy Keeps Modesty; 'Revenge' Game Starts Tough for Mr. Mack," *Knoxville News Sentinel*, February 16, 1934: 12.

39 "Touchstone Injured," *Knoxville Journal*, September 8, 1935: 16.

40 Don Whitehead, "Clay Touchstone Hopes to Shake Off Injury Jinx This Year," *New Orleans State*, May 13, 1936: 8.

41 "Memphis Pitcher Is Not Satisfied with Terms," *Tampa Tribune*, February 14, 1936: 19; "Rain Halts Chick's Drill, Clay Touchstone Signed," *Tennessean* (Nashville), March 17, 1936: 17.

42 "Memphis Star Plunks Five Pels in Ribs," *Tennessean*, April 21, 1936: 9.

43 Jim Hopkins, "Touch Says He'll Be Ready," *Oklahoma News* (Oklahoma City), March 29, 1938: 10.

44 Charles Saulsberry, "Hillin Gains Shutout, 6-0, Draws Second Victory, 6-5," *Daily Oklahoman* (Oklahoma City), April 25, 1938: 8.

45 Charles Saulsberry, "Governor Is Obtained in Indian Swap," *Daily Oklahoman*, November 15, 1938: 16.

46 "Touchstone Signs Dallas Contract," *Fort Worth Star-Telegram*, January 20, 1939: 20.

47 "Tulsa Drops Game to Indians, Dallas Gets New Nickname," *Monitor* (McAllen, Texas), April 10, 1939: 5; "Rebels Drub Tulsans, 8-0," *Fort Worth Star-Telegram*, April 23, 1939: 12.

48 Tony Governor, the player that Oklahoma City got in exchange for Touchstone in their search for a bat, ended up not providing much help: he appeared in only five games with them, going 3-for-19, and then temporarily retired from professional baseball, only returning five years later, when the minor leagues were in search of bodies to fill rosters that had been depleted by the military draft.

49 John Cronley, "Satchel Paige Opposes Bob," *Daily Oklahoman*, October 5, 1941: 39.

50 John Cronley, "Monarchs Are the Best After Feller Leaves," *Daily Oklahoman*, October 9, 1941:18.

51 Prescott Sullivan, "The Low Down," *San Francisco Examiner*, June 15, 1949: 27.

52 "Touchstone Takes Over as Okla. City Manager," *The Sporting News*, August 6, 1942: 1.

53 C.M. Gibbs, "Gibberish," *Baltimore Sun*, February 25, 1043: 18.

54 "Jones Signs Pact, Touchstone Quits," *Baltimore Sun*, March 20, 1943: 8.

55 "Game in Touchstone's Blood."

56 Clay Touchstone death certificate, on file in the National Baseball Hall of Fame Archives.

MATT TUPMAN

By Bill Nowlin

An article in the *Concord* (New Hampshire) *Monitor* said of catcher Matt Tupman, "He once played with a roaring fire inside, fueled by a hardboiled youth that created a chip on his shoulder the size of second base. That fire made for hustle on the field, but led him to challenge authority off it."[1]

The young catcher was born to Lesa Tupman and Billie H. Tupman Jr. in Concord on November 25, 1979. Both parents were Massachusetts natives and met while both were living in Gloucester. In 1978 Billie Tupman took a position at the New Hampshire State Prison for Men and worked for eight years as a corrections officer. "We both loved New Hampshire and wanted to move here," Lesa Tupman said from Concord in 2019.[2] They raised three children – Matt, Stephen, and Garrett. A year or so after Matt was born, Lesa Tupman began working in medical offices. Billie Tupman began work as a background investigator for the Human Resources department of Fidelity Investments, commuting to Boston for about a dozen years from Concord.

"When I was younger," Tupman said in a November 2019 interview, "my parents just kind of had me play. My dad always loved baseball. My dad was not an athlete, but he always loved baseball. Had he been alive when sabermetrics were coming out, he probably would have loved that. He was a statistical person. He used to tell me the stats of all the old players. He was born in 1949, so the Seventies and Eighties … He was a Yankees fan. He loved all those guys."[3]

Tupman threw right-handed and batted from the left side. "My dad claimed he taught me. He said I picked up the bat right-handed and he taught me to hit left-handed. Even though he was a Yankees fan, he still wanted me to swing the bat like the Splendid Splinter. That's what he liked to say."

"I never tried to hit righty. I really couldn't hit live pitching righty."

During his high-school years, Matt's father battled alcoholism and it led to a broken relationship between them. After Matt had been drafted and entered the Kansas City Royals' minor-league system, though, his father spent considerable time in Spokane in 2002 and Burlington, Iowa, in 2003. "We had patched things up by then," Matt said. "I learned a lot about him, that he was sick. But once I got drafted, he was so proud."[4] Unfortunately, his father was also a heavy smoker and he suffered a seizure from a brain tumor in Burlington, a metastatis from lung cancer. He returned to New Hampshire, dying on October 1, 2003. Lesa recalled with fondness a moment near the end of her husband's life. "When I was told by the medical staff Billie was almost out of time I called Matt home and when he walked into the hospital room his father looked at me then back at Matt and said, 'Oh shit. I must be sicker than I thought. You're not supposed to be home from

Matt Tupman. Courtesy of Lesa Tupman.

ONE-HIT WONDERS

baseball yet!' He always had a sense of humor, right to the very end."[5]

Recommended by scout Steve Connelly, Matt was drafted by the Royals in the ninth round of the June 2002 amateur draft, the 258th pick overall in that year's draft.[6] After his 2001 season with UMass Lowell, *Baseball America* named Tupman "the ninth best pro prospect in the New England Collegiate League."[7] Scouts had their eyes on him. A *Lowell Sun* story in mid-April reported 16 major-league scouts at the April 17 game.[8] The UML River Hawks won the Northeast-10 championship. On May 10, hitting .350 with five homers and 39 RBIs, he was named first team All Northeast 10 Conference, along with fellow UML players Dave Williamson and Allen Mottram.[9] He went to the College World Series both in 2001 and 2002.

Looking back on it, Lowell coach Jim Stone was amused to remember that he had tried to dissuade Tupman from transferring to UML from Plymouth State. He'd been all-conference there, but "I wanted to play in a better program," Tupman said. "We were happy with our catching situation," Stone said. "That's why when Matt came here, he didn't get the starting job right away."[10] In 2002 he was named to the Division Two All-American second team. The River Hawks played in the NCAA Division Two World Series.

If Matt was selected in a high-enough round during the June draft, he was prepared to forgo his senior year and go professional. As noted, he was picked in the ninth round. Dave Williamson was selected in the seventh round by the St. Louis Cardinals.

Once signed, Matt left on June 13 for Spokane to play for the Spokane Indians in the low-A short-season Northwest League. "They've indicated that I'll be the No. 1 catcher, that it will be my spot to lose," he said, admitting, "Coming out of Concord, I would have signed for just a plane ticket. They gave me more than I ever dreamed of. I'm living a dream right now."[11]

In 51 games and 201 plate appearances, Tupman drove in 23 runs while hitting for a .271 average and a very good .364 on-base percentage. He was charged with only three errors in 348 chances.

His 2003 season was spent in Iowa, playing for the Class-A Midwest League's Burlington Bees. In 81 games, he struggled more at the plate, hitting .223 (.288 OBP) with 38 RBIs. His fielding was down a bit, too, but he still finished a .984 fielding percentage.

Matt enjoyed a very supportive family. His mother, Lesa, noted that he was the first-born son on both sides of the family. His aunts Suzan and Marylou and his uncle Dickie traveled as a group to Delaware to watch him play with the Burlington Bees. Suzan and Dickie, and Marylou and her husband, Gussie, and a couple of cousins traveled to Las Vegas. "I went to almost every spring training. We all traveled all over hell to watch him play."[12]

After joining the Royals early in spring training in 2004, Tupman moved one more rung up the ladder, to high Class A, catching for Carolina League's Wilmington Blue Rocks in Delaware. He played in 108 games. His fielding percentage went back up to .990, and he hit an even .300 (.361 OBP) with 35 RBIs. In 2004 *Baseball America* named him the best defensive catcher in the Royals organization.[13]

In 2005 Tupman was promoted to Double A. He was based in Kansas and played in 109 games for the Wichita Wranglers (Texas League). He hit .263 (.355 OBP) with 32 RBIs. He was invited to join the major-league team after Wichita's season was done, but was never actually added to the roster. "I was brought up in 2005 as the third catcher and traveled with the team the entire month of September. But Allard Baird didn't want to activate me." Not adding him to the roster extended the time the Royals could keep him under team control.

That fall, he played in the Arizona Fall League.

In 2006 Tupman, now age 26, enjoyed spring training with the big-league club but started the season with the Wranglers once more, playing in 73 games through July 11. He played in the Texas League All-Star Game, coming to the plate twice, with a base on balls and a double to show for it.[14] He hit .305 that year with a very strong .425 on-base percentage, and earned himself another promotion, this time to the Triple-A Omaha Royals of the Pacific Coast League. He got into 21 games and hit .247 (.321 OBP), his first Triple-A hit breaking up a no-hitter in the sixth inning.[15] He drove in four runs for Omaha.

In August 2006 Tupman was named to the USA Baseball roster for the Olympic Qualifying Team.[16] The Royals gave him the time off to play for coach Davey Johnson, and the team won the gold medal in Havana, qualifying to play in the Summer Olympics in Beijing in 2008. Kurt Suzuki and Jarrod Saltalamacchia were the two other catchers on Team USA; Suzuki was his roommate. Tupman appeared in three games, and was 1-for-3 with a single against the Dominican Republic. Early in the 2008 season, he was with the Kansas City Royals; he did not go to Beijing.

ONE-HIT WONDERS

Tupman established himself as a solid Triple-A ballplayer in 2007, spending the whole season with Omaha. Appearing in 86 games, he hit .281 (.361 OBP) with 32 RBIs.

That winter, he played baseball in the Dominican Republic for the Tigres del Licey. He saw action in 36 games and hit .293 (.322 OBP). He played in the Caribbean Series and hit .364 in the six games, collecting two hits in the final championship game when Licey beat Aguilas, 8-2. Playing in the Dominican Winter League had paid off in terms of catching the eye of Royals GM Dayton Moore. After the season, Moore had talked about Tupman: "I think any time a player commits to go to winter ball and especially stays there the whole time it shows an intense desire to get better. ... It's certainly enhanced Matt Tupman's value as a baseball player to our organization."[17]

For his part, Tupman said that people play winter ball for a number of reasons. "This would have been my sixth (full) year, so I would have been a (minor-league) free agent. I'm not a big name, so I needed to market myself. As it turned out, I got noticed by the team I was playing for all along."[18] He added, about having been added to the major-league roster, "How can I not be excited? This is a lifelong dream. This is everything I've ever wanted. This is why I was in the weight room every day at UMass Lowell."

In December 2007, he married Addie Vega, his high-school sweetheart. They had two children, Gwendolyn and Pippa. They later divorced.

In 2008 Tupman opened the season on the Royals' major-league roster, serving as backup catcher to John Buck, while regular backup Miguel Olivo served a four-game suspension for his part in a late 2007 brawl with the New York Mets. "If that happens, so be it," he said. "That will be cool if I make it. It is my dream to make it here. I feel like I've been on the cusp for maybe a year or two now."[19]

Though on the roster and with the team, Tupman saw no game action. After Olivo served his suspension, Tupman was optioned to Omaha again near the end of the first week of April.

He was called back to the big leagues after John Buck's wife gave birth to twin boys on May 15, some 12 weeks prematurely, and Buck was given emergency leave to join her. This time he got into a game, on Sunday afternoon, May 18, at Dolphin Stadium in Miami. Zack Greinke was pitching for the Royals and Burke Badenhop for the Marlins. At the end of eight innings, both pitchers were gone. The score stood 9-3 in favor of Kansas City. Kevin Gregg was the sixth pitcher of the day for the Marlins; he was asked to work the ninth.

First up was Mark Teahen, who worked the count to 3-and-2, then popped up to the shortstop. Royals manager Trey Hillman then asked Tupman to pinch-hit for pitcher Jimmy Gobble. Tupman took the first pitch for a ball, then swung at the second and lined it into short right field for a clean single. The next batter was catcher Miguel Olivo, who hit into a double play; he lined a 1-and-1 pitch to the second baseman, Dan Uggla, who threw the ball to first; Tupman couldn't get back to the bag in time and was out.

Tupman replaced Olivo as catcher in the bottom of the ninth. Working for the Royals in the ninth was right-handed reliever Yasuhiko Yabuta. A groundout to second, a walk, and a 6-4-3 double play brought the game to an end.

The very next day, Buck was reactivated and Tupman was optioned back to Omaha, but not before the Royals had traveled from Miami to Boston, where the Red Sox were due to host Kansas City. His wife, daughter, and a family friend had all been given tickets to the game, hopefully to see Matt play. Learning that he had been optioned, with Buck back on the team, he sat in the seats at Fenway – and watched Red Sox lefty Jon Lester no-hit the team he'd played with just the day before.

Tupman might never have had that one at-bat had it not been for Jose Guillen. The Royals left fielder knew that Tupman was about to be optioned and interceded with manager Hillman to try to get his friend Matt at least one at-bat before he was sent back to Triple A. Tupman told Sam Gardner of Fox Sports, "Jose was one of the team leaders at that point in time, and he knew that I should have gotten an at-bat, but in all honesty, for some reason, the manager didn't like me." (Tupman had previously clashed with Double-A manager Frank White, as well.) "I was called up in a time of necessity, so he was reluctant to really, actually, play me."

"But Jose, knowing I could play and knowing what I did all winter long, knowing it was the right thing to do – we were blowing them out – he had Miguel, who was the starting catcher that day, basically go to Hillman and say, 'Look man, I feel sick, it's a hot day in Miami,' and he basically took himself out of the game so that I could get one at-bat."[20]

Arguably, Tupman should perhaps have started the May 18 game. Zack Greinke was pitching and the two knew each other well. They had both spent much of the 2006 season together as batterymates in Wichita.

ONE-HIT WONDERS

"I played with Zach in 2002 when we were drafted together. I knew Zach well. He was pitching – he's easy to catch, too, the guy hits every spot. But it ended up, I'm not catching that day. It was just one of those things."

It was fortunate that Guillen spoke up. Though one couldn't know it at the time, as it happens, Tupman's major-league career was over. He had seen two pitches and had himself a 1.000 career batting average.[21]

"Everybody has a story," Tupman said in 2019, "but statistically if you look at the time period when I was in the Royals' minor leagues, I was one of the better catchers. I knew I was a backup catcher. I wasn't the starting catcher at the major-league level. I didn't hit for enough power. I easily could have hit .250 in the major leagues. Easily. But I had no power, so I was a backup guy. I was the best defensive catcher in the organization from like '04 to '09. I wasn't too bad with the bat, either. I didn't hit for power, but I walked more than I struck out. I was a good hitter. I just didn't crush the ball."[22] He admitted to still feeling a sense of bitterness – fading in time – that he didn't get more of a chance.

"The manager of the Royals at that time [Trey Hillman], he did not like me. I don't really know what happened." They were like polar opposites, Hillman "a God-fearing Texas guy" and Tupman from New England. Tupman recalled a time in spring training. "I was in the bullpen in and John Buck was at bat. I didn't sprint from the bullpen to the dugout. I was kind of walking along the warning track, watching John hit. I came into the dugout and put my helmet on – if he got on, I was going to go pinch-run. Later, they called me into the office and were telling me that I didn't hustle – 'This is just wrong. ….' I'm looking at them, and I'm thinking, 'Do you know how the f--- I *got* to spring training in major-league camp? It's because I *am* Mr. Hustle.' He just didn't like me."

"I never saw right with him. The previous manager, Buddy Bell? Loved him. Buddy was my kind of guy. Hard-nosed, didn't-mess-with-him kind of guy. And the previous manager before that – Tony Peña. I loved Tony. I went to the Dominican Republic for three straight offseasons. Tony was the manager with the Aguilas. I played for Licey. They go crazy down there for baseball. It's awesome. I fell in love with their culture. And Tony Peña would make it a point to come over to the other dugout and say hi to me. And then I meet Trey Hillman, and it was pretty much the end after Trey."

With Omaha, he hit four home runs – not being a power hitter, those four homers constituted a career high.

After the 2008 season, his contract was assigned outright to Omaha.

Tupman got to play 59 games in 2009, 21 with Omaha (.261, 7 RBIs) but was released by the Royals. His last game with Omaha was June 17. A few weeks later, he signed on with the Arizona Diamondbacks and played 38 more games in 2009, starting on July 6 playing Double-A ball for the Southern League's Mobile BayBears (.254, 19 RBIs).

He returned to the Dominican Republic to play winter ball once more, but this time he hit only .229 in 38 games.

In December 2009 Major League Baseball announced that four players had been suspended: Jefferson Segundo (St. Louis Cardinals), Joel Tamares (Florida Marlins), Daniel Vasquez (Arizona Diamondbacks), and free agent Matt Tupman. Each was given a 50-game suspension "after each violated the Minor League Drug Prevention and Treatment Program."[23]

"We were down there partying," Tupman said. "I really don't have an excuse for it." His young daughter, Gwen, was in art class, shown a copy of a newspaper story talking about her father. Matt had to explain. Ray Duckler wrote, "The rugged catcher with the chip on his shoulder who had always followed his own path, who had gone toe-to-toe with Frank White, who had never allowed anyone to see his vulnerable side, was humbled by a little girl."

"His little girl."

"'I cried,' Tupman said. 'It was harder than telling anyone here.'"[24]

He was under contact to the Mets, but the Mets voided the contract and Tupman sat out the entire 2010 season. He lost more than 50 games. "Obviously I messed up," Tupman said, but due to a technicality – if you are not on an active roster, you cannot serve your suspension. He lost the whole year, and went into independent-league baseball before the commissioner's office responded to his appeal midway through the 2011 season and granted him active status again. But no team called.

In 2011 Tupman played independent baseball in Pennsylvania for the Atlantic League's Lancaster Barnstormers. He hit .268 with four home runs over the course of 57 games. He committed only one error in 317 chances.

ONE-HIT WONDERS

He was, however, only making about $250 per week, not enough to support a growing family. At age 32, he stopped playing baseball.

He had started to find other work in 2010, beginning work at the Concord Sports Center, where his mother, Lesa, was office manager.

He coached the Concord Cannons that year; they put up a 30-7 record. They were a young team, mostly 11 years old. Another team he coached – Concord's Post 21 American Legion team – won the 2013 state title in Legion ball.

"It's what I live for," he told the *Concord Monitor* at the time. "I'm so excited for this. I love coaching baseball now. It has come full circle."[25]

He coached Legion ball from 2013 to 2015. He was giving baseball lessons, working seven evenings a week, and on weekends, too, while his wife worked days. He stayed home to provide day care for their kids, and then the two switched off. This understandably left him burned out.

He took a job for a stretch installing glass for Portland Glass Company, mostly auto glass. "I did that for a while, with the personal training and the baseball lessons. Then I decided to just do the personal training full time."

He worked some at Concord Sports Center, but, as he explained, "I'm a full-time personal trainer. I'm a smaller guy, so lifting weights and all that stuff was something that I did my whole career. I'm employed by a company called Forty-three Degrees North. They're new. They've only been around for about 18 months."[26]

"Everyone has their tale," he added of his perfect career batting average. "A fan might see 1-for-1, 1.000, but there's so much more that goes into it. It was 28 years of hard work put into that single."[27]

On the brink of turning 40, Tupman said, "I think the bitterness has left now. I just kind of used that word to describe how I left back then. It's less now than it was. It's just frustrating. It's a hard thing to sit there and be passed up constantly. You do well, and your management is saying, 'We love what you do. Don't change a thing' – for six or seven or eight years straight. And then nothing. It just got mentally frustrating."

"But looking back at it, I absolutely loved it. I wouldn't trade it for anything. The friends I made, the memories I have, the cities that I visited, the food that I got to eat. It's culture. Like going to Louisiana. Louisiana is the polar opposite of New Hampshire. You get to see all the different cultures. You get to meet foreign people. If I hadn't played baseball, I wouldn't have gotten to maybe 97 percent of the places I've been to. I've been to 45 of the 50 states. Cuba. The Caribbean. When I was younger I played on a travel team that went to Australia. All because of baseball."[28]

SOURCES

In addition to the sources cited in the Notes, the author consulted Baseball-Reference.com and Retrosheet.org.

NOTES

1 Ray Duckler, "After Long Journey, Tupman Has Come Full Circle," *Concord* (New Hampshire) *Monitor*, July 29, 2013.

2 Lesa Tupman email to author on November 12, 2019.

3 Author interview with Matt Tupman on November 11, 2019. Unless otherwise indicated, all direct quotations come from this interview.

4 Ray Duckler.

5 Lesa Tupman emails November 11 and 15, 2019.

6 His mother, Lesa, said, "I was working the day Matt was drafted, I left work and went to his apartment and he greeted me at the door all smiles as I yelled, 'Matt, we got drafted!'" Lesa Tupman email, November 15, 2019.

7 "Outlook Sunny for UML Baseball Club," *Lowell* (Massachusetts) *Sun*, March 19, 2002: 16.

8 Chaz Scoggins, "To Guns Again," *Lowell Sun*, April 18, 2002: 17.

9 "UML Trio Headline Star Team," *Lowell Sun*, May 13, 2002: 16.

10 David Pevear, "Nice Catch(er) for UMass Lowell Baseball Program," *Lowell Sun*, May 23, 2002: 19.

11 "Tupman Latest to Sign Pro Contract," *Lowell Sun*, June 12, 2002: 11.

12 Lesa Tupman email November 15, 2019.

13 Chaz Scoggins, "Tupman Gets Around," *Lowell Sun*, September 21, 2006: 14.

14 Susan Denk, "Old-Timers Event Will Keep Going," *The Hawk Eye* (Burlington, Iowa), June 25, 2006: 58.

15 "Down on the Farm," *Nashua* (New Hampshire) *Telegraph*, July 16, 2006: C3.

16 Susan Denk, "Hochevar Has Big Goals," *The Hawk Eye*, August 21, 2006: 3B.

17 Associated Press, "Suspension Gives Tupman Chance with Royals," *Hays* (Kansas) *Daily News*, February 17, 2008: 16; Associated Press, "Olivo's Suspension Opens Door for Tupman," *Joplin* (Missouri) *Globe*, February 17, 2008: 7D.

18 Dave Pevear, "Royalty: Tupman Close to a Major Accomplishment," *Lowell Sun*, March 28, 2008: 17.

19 Associated Press, "Olivo's Suspension Opens Door for Tupman."

20 Sam Gardner, "One & Done: Matt Tupman's Hit Made Him Feel Like a Royal Success," FoxSports, July 28, 2015, at foxsports.com/mlb/story/kansas-city-royals-matt-tupman-s-hit-made-him-feel-like-a-royal-success-072815.

21 Tupman's base hit can be seen at youtube.com/watch?v=e4Dsouc2ovI.

22 Author interview. Through 2007, Tupman had relatively similar numbers in walks (222) and strikeouts (259).

23 "Transactions," *San Francisco Chronicle*, December 5, 2009: 19.

24 Ray Duckler.

25 Ray Duckler.

26 Author interview. Tupman is listed as Trainer and Group Exercise Instructor. See 43northnh.com/.

27 Sam Gardner.

28 Author interview.

FRED WATERS

By Jeff English

Fred Warren Waters was born to Wyatt and Mattie Waters on February 2, 1927, in Benton, Mississippi, an unincorporated community in Yazoo County. One of 12 children, young Fred shared duties with his nine brothers (Wyatt, Wilton, Melvin, Jack, Louis, David, Herbert, Leslie, Luby) and two sisters (Fredene, Betty Ann), around the family farm located near Highway 433, which runs straight through the county. When Fred was 11 years old, his mother Mattie, 43 years old but in ill health, died just hours after giving birth to Luby. His father, Wyatt, instilled in his children a strong work ethic and an expectation that a fair day's work deserves a fair day's pay. While he excelled at sports as a youth, teenager Fred's education largely focused on a future career in farming. At 14 he was selected as one of 18 candidates for the Green Hand degree, the first degree in Vocational Farming sponsored by the Benton Chapter of Future Farmers of America. Three years later, he was chosen chapter president.

Fred graduated from Benton High School in 1945 after lettering for four years in baseball and basketball. He enrolled at Holmes Junior College, in Goodman, Mississippi. He joined the football team and quickly became the team's best "scatback," known more for his speed and elusiveness than for his relatively slight frame.

The following year he and brothers Melvin and Jack, both veterans of World War II, enrolled at Southern Mississippi in Hattiesburg. Fred joined the basketball and football teams and his hard work drew the notice of his coaches and teammates. On January 25, 1946, Waters scored 16 points, including the game-winner, against a team from nearby Camp Shelby, in a game so marred by fighting that Southern Mississippi coach Reed Green decided to cancel the remainder of his team's schedule.[1] Fred's all-out effort at halfback in team scrimmages garnered plenty of praise. But where he really made his mark was on the diamond.

Southern Mississippi played only 13 games in 1947. The team finished the season with nine wins, including all seven played at home. The team featured three Waters brothers, with Jack a pitcher and Melvin often found behind the plate or at first base. Fred played center field and proved one of the team's best hitters, posting an average over .400 while finishing among the leaders in home runs and runs batted in. At the constant urging of friend and teammate Johnny LeGros, the left-handed Waters finally decided to take a try on the mound. On April 22, against the Spring Hill Badgers, Southern Mississippi starting pitcher Doc Cranford was struck by a batted ball at the end of the third inning, necessitating a replacement. Waters took over to start the fourth inning. Pitching six innings,

Fred Waters.

ONE-HIT WONDERS

he struck out nine and walked 12 strikeouts against a dozen walks, while allowing only two hits and a lone run. For good measure, he secured the 6-5 victory with an inside-the-park home run in the bottom of the ninth.

As the 1947 college season wound down, Waters joined the small-town Purvis semipro team, where he continued to hone his skills on the mound. Purvis finished the first half of the season in second place in the six-team league, at 8-6, and Waters hitting and pitching figured prominently in the club's success. In the season's second half, Waters settled into a groove. On July 9 he tossed a 10-inning complete-game victory over Lumberton, allowing five hits and striking out nine. Four days later he struck out 15 in a 5-1 victory over the Yellow Cabs. On July 17, pitching in the Mississippi State semipro tournament, he struck out seven while blanking the Laurel Jaycees over eight innings in a game called on an eight-run mercy rule. Waters' play drew the attention of the Philadelphia Phillies, who signed his Southern Mississippi teammate, Johnny LeGros in July. Waters also received an offer but rejected it "unless the ante (was) raised considerably."[2]

In 1948 Southern Mississippi's baseball team finished the season with a 12-11 record. Waters batted a team-high .400, but it was his performance on the mound that made the biggest impression. On March 19, against Spring Hill in the season's first game, Waters allowed a lone hit while striking out nine, including eight in a row, over four innings in a 10-5 victory. He contributed three hits, including two doubles, in five trips to the plate. Six days later he took the mound against the University of Mississippi Rebels and held them to three hits with 11 strikeouts before getting lifted for a reliever who promptly allowed a game-winning home run to the second batter he faced. On April 16 Waters fanned 17 in a complete-game victory over Millsaps College. On April 24 he suffered his first loss of the season, a tough 5-4 decision to Loyola, despite striking out a dozen batters and going 3-for-4 at the plate. His 16-strikeout, 8-1 victory against the Mississippi College Choctaws on April 28 snapped his club's three-game losing streak. His second hard-luck loss of the season, a two-hit pitching performance, came against Spring Hill College on May 8, by a score of 2-1. On May 11 Waters turned in one of the most remarkable pitching performances in school history. On only two full days' rest, he faced 56 batters and struck out 19 in a 14-inning rematch with Loyola. Despite not allowing an earned run while issuing only one walk, he suffered the loss when a two-run error at shortstop spoiled his effort in the bottom of the 14th inning.

As the college baseball season came to a close, Waters and three of his Southern Mississippi teammates (Bubber Phillips, Mel Didier, and Cliff Coggins) joined the local semipro Laurel Jaycees. Their combined presence on the club made it one of the stronger teams in the league. In June Waters, Phillips, and Didier were invited to Detroit for a tryout before Tigers manager Steve O'Neill and the team's top scouts. On June 30, 1948, Southern Mississippi coach Reed Green announced that Phillips and Didier had signed contracts with Detroit. Waters was offered a contract as well. According to Tigers scout Howard Camp, "Waters looked good in the outfield but didn't seem to loosen up pitching. He was offered a contract as an outfielder but wants to pitch and is going to try to get his arm in top shape. I'll keep looking at him."[3] Waters returned to Hattiesburg and the semipro Jaycees, He helped the team reach the Mississippi all-state semipro title game, where it was defeated 4-1 by the Cleveland (Mississippi) Indians. Waters contributed an eighth-inning triple at the plate, but was thrown out trying to stretch it into a round-tripper. His efforts garnered him a selection on the all-state semipro tournament team as selected by umpires and scorekeepers.

On February 25, 1949, Fred married Dorothy Jean Bethea of Hattiesburg, a few days before it was announced that scout Wid Matthews had signed him to a contract with the Brooklyn Dodgers' Fort Worth club. After reporting to Brooklyn's spring camp, he was optioned to Greenwood, Mississippi, a Dodgers affiliate in the Class-C Cotton States League. On April 20, 1949, Waters made his professional debut on the mound against the Greenville Bucks, tossing a complete-game shutout with nine strikeouts in a 5-0 victory. He followed up that performance five days later by shutting out the Pine Bluff Cardinals, a St. Louis Browns affiliate, 9-0. In his first 18 innings on the mound as a professional, Waters recorded 22 strikeouts while allowing only five hits and no runs. His performance drew raves from Dodgers President Branch Rickey, who said, "The boy can't miss."[4] He finished the season with 18 wins and six losses, tossing a league-high six shutouts and earning a first-team selection on the 1949 league's all-star team.[5]

For a host of reasons, the 1950 season proved to be one of the most trying of Waters' career. His performance the previous season brought high expectations. In camp, Branch Rickey and coach George Sisler spent many hours helping Waters develop a slower curveball

ONE-HIT WONDERS

to complement his lively fastball. They also urged him to vary his pace on the mound in order to disrupt the batters' timing. Initially, Waters struggled with the new instruction. In one spring start, he hit a batter in the first inning, issued five straight walks in the second inning before striking out the side, and balked home two runs in the fourth.[6]

Pitching for the Elmira Pioneers of the Class-A Eastern League, he eventually settled down and a month into the 1950 season emerged as the club's most reliable relief option. After earning an April win out of the bullpen, on May 7 he carried a no-hit starting effort into the seventh inning of the second game of a doubleheader against Utica. But two infield mistakes in the final inning resulted in a 2-1 loss. On May 12 Waters lost a 4-2 decision to the Binghamton Triplets despite surrendering only six hits and fanning 10 batters in nine innings. On June 5 his record dropped to 1-5 when he allowed eight singles in as many innings while striking out seven in a 6-3 loss to the Wilkes-Barre Indians. His wasted efforts from a lack of support became a running theme in the local press, who took to calling him Hard Luck Fred.[7]

On June 13 Waters tossed 6⅔ innings of hitless ball before surrendering four hits with six strikeouts in a 4-1 victory against the Albany Senators. It was his second recorded win against five losses. The next day Waters left the team for Benton, Mississippi, to be with his ailing father, who died shortly after Fred's arrival. He returned to the mound against the Utica Blue Sox on June 22 and won his third game, with ample support, 20-3. His next several appearances were undone by wildness, and his overall record fell to 5-9. In late July, citing a sore arm, Waters left the team and returned to Mississippi. On July 30 he took the hill in relief for the Hub City Comets against the Jackson Senators in an exhibition game back home. After a discussion with Dodgers minor-league supervisor Fresco Thompson, Waters was reinstated and on August 1 he reported to Fort Worth of the Double-A Texas League, as a roster replacement for a player promoted to Triple-A St. Paul. Waters was widely regarded as one of the Brooklyn organization's brightest prospects.

In 1951 Waters played a lot of baseball. After missing spring training at Vero Beach, he was scheduled to begin the year at Fort Worth. But an offseason, high school teaching job in Mississippi forced the club to place him on the voluntarily retired list until the end of the school term.[8] He belatedly began the year with the Newport News Dodgers in the Class-B Piedmont League. After just three appearances, he was sent to the Asheville Tourists in the Class-B Tri-State League on June 1. He made two starts, including a six-hit, 6-3 win in his debut with the club. He also continued to periodically star as a pitcher-outfielder for the Hattiesburg Comets in the Mississippi Semipro league well into June, having joined the team after failing to report to Fort Worth.

On July 2 Comets manager Noel Boland announced that Waters would no longer be available to the club, having been asked to report back to Greenwood in the Cotton States League. When he arrived, he quickly rattled off half a dozen wins before yielding six runs for a no-decision verdict in what ended as an 11-8 loss to Pine Bluff on July 29. He suffered a loss on August 8, a 2-1 verdict at the hands of the Monroe Sports. He went on to win five more games to finish the season with a 11-1 record in less than two full months of work.

Despite not joining the league until July, Waters was selected to the Cotton States League all-star team. He recorded seven strikeouts to earn a 5-4 win against Pine Bluff in the opening round of the league playoffs. But in a rematch on September 6, he allowed five hits and seven strikeouts in a tough 1-0 loss. Two days later, Pine Bluff eliminated Greenwood, 6-3, despite 7⅓ innings of relief work from Waters, who allowed only one run. The Monroe Sports eventually claimed the league's title, and with the season ended, Waters returned to Hattiesburg, where he continued to find places to play.

Waters reported to camp at Vero Beach in the first week of March 1952 and was assigned to the Mobile Bears in the Double-A Southern Association.[9] He made his first exhibition start on April 6 against the Nashville Volunteers, and allowed a lone run on five hits in six innings of work. On April 15 he began his regular season with a four-inning stint against the Memphis Chicks in which he recorded five walks, four hits, two strikeouts, and two wild pitches. He earned his first victory with four innings of relief work against the New Orleans Pelicans on April 22. As the season progressed, Waters was reduced to mostly relief work as he struggled to control his fastball and keep runners off base. He did not win his second game until July 31, an 8-6 effort against Chattanooga in which he walked five and struck out eight. His record sat at 2-5. In an August 15 start against Chattanooga, he failed to get out of the first inning. His uneven performance continued, and by season's end his record was an underwhelming four wins and eight losses. The following April, Brooklyn sold him to the Milwaukee

ONE-HIT WONDERS

Fred Waters.

Braves-affiliated Atlanta Crackers in the Southern Association. He was 10-10 in 32 appearances, mostly with the Lincoln Chiefs in the Western League, where he arrived May 19.

On December 26, 1953, Milwaukee traded Waters, now 26, and fellow pitchers Larry Lasalle, Curt Raydon, and Max Surkont, outfielders Sid Gordon, Sam Jethroe, and $100,000 to the Pittsburgh Pirates for third baseman Danny O'Connell. It remains the only six-for-one player trade in major-league history. When Waters arrived at the Pirates camp in Fort Pierce, Florida, in February 1954, he was met with an expectation from general manager Branch Rickey that he be converted into a left-handed catcher. Waters told *The Sporting News*, "I caught maybe 10 games in high school and semipro ball. I simply like to play ball and if this will give me an opportunity, let's go."[10] Fortunately for Waters, the experiment did not last long, and he went on to post a 13-4 record in 23 appearances with Class-B Waco and Class-A Denver.

Waters began the 1955 season with a 4-1 record at Waco before being sent in June to the Mexico City Tigers. His impact was immediate, as he pitched the Mexican League's first shutout of the year on June 4 against Veracruz, 5-0.[11] Waters dominated Mexican League hitters to the tune of a league-high 18 wins and only three losses. He collected a triple crown of sorts by pacing the league with 126 strikeouts and a sparkling 2.06 ERA.[12] He was rewarded for his efforts with a call-up to the Pirates on September 11.

Waters made his major-league debut on September 20, 1956, with a four-inning relief appearance in which he yielded six hits and two earned runs in an 11-1 loss to the New York Giants. He added a scoreless inning the following day in his only other appearance of the season. Fred Waters could now call himself a "big-league" pitcher. He returned to Hattiesburg and took up duty coaching high-school football and basketball.

Waters reported to camp the following spring in Fort Myers and, for the first time, was able to bring Dorothy and their three young daughters (Mary Frances, Claire, and Dollie) along for the experience.[13] He performed unevenly throughout spring camp and found himself optioned to the Hollywood Stars of the Pacific Coast League to begin the season. In June Branch Rickey traveled to California for a 10-day scouting trip in search of immediate help for the Pirates roster. He was expected to pass judgment on Fred Waters and teammate, Joe Trimble.[14]

On July 6 Waters and teammates Cholly Naranjo and Bill Mazeroski were called up to the Pirates from Hollywood. After seven relief appearances between July 14 and 23, Waters earned a 4-0 win in his first major-league start with seven shutout innings against the Cubs on the 26th. After being lifted for reliever Howie Pollet, he said, "I would have given $100 to finish but he had to take me out. I was tired. I had good stuff but I was forcing a little. That was the longest I've pitched in over a month."[15] He continued to pitch well in relief in mostly losing efforts until he received his second starting opportunity, in the second game of a doubleheader against the Giants at the Polo Grounds on August 12. In a battle of left-handers, he bested Giants starter Windy McCall in an 11-3 win. Waters allowed two earned runs in $5\frac{1}{3}$ innings before giving way to reliever Roy Face. He aided his own cause by breaking the game open with a bases-loaded triple into right-center off McCall in the fourth inning, the first and only base hit of his major-league career. He made seven more appearances during the season, including a losing start against the St. Louis Cardinals on August 24. Although Waters finished the season with a 2-2 record and a respectable 2.82 ERA, he also issued 30 walks against just 14 strikeouts. Nearing his 30th birthday, he never played another game in the major leagues.

ONE-HIT WONDERS

Waters bounced around the minor leagues for a few more seasons, back at Hollywood for 11 starts in 1957, and then with the Washington Senators-affiliated Chattanooga Lookouts after being purchased in May 1958. His stay with the Lookouts was brief, however, and he finished the season by rejoining the Mexico City Tigers. He pitched in Mexico again in 1959.

On August 8, 1960, Waters became the head baseball coach at Pensacola (Florida) High School after spending the previous two years at nearby Gonzalez Tate High School where he also coached football. At the time of his hiring, he boasted a 12-6 pitching record for the Pensacola Angels of the Class-D Alabama-Florida League.[16] He spent the next two seasons as Pensacola's ace lefty, going a combined 27-6, including numerous high-strikeout performances that dazzled the locals. In 1962 he led all of the minor leagues with an impressive 1.42 ERA. His manager in 1962, Wayne Terwilliger, described him as "a lefty who still knew how to get 'em out with a little of this and a little of that."[17]

Waters' brilliance for Pensacola in 1962 marked the end of his dedicated playing career, and while he continued to coach high-school sports, he applied for the head coaching job at Florida State University in September 1963. His résumé included a 101-25 coaching record in five seasons at the high-school level. He commented to a sportswriter, "I was told the job was wide open."[18] But Florida State ultimately hired Fred Hatfield so Fred Waters, never one to sit still, accepted a job in 1964 as manager of the Minnesota Twins-affiliated club in the Florida Rookie League.

As a high-school coach, Waters garnered a well-deserved reputation for stressing fundamentals. As head coach of the Escambia High Gators, he built one of the most dominant baseball programs in Florida. His 1971 pitching staff featured two future major leaguers: senior starter Dennis Lewallyn, and junior starter Preston Hanna. In 1972 his club, bolstered by staff ace Hanna, won Florida's Class 4A title, defeating Tampa Robinson in the state tournament. Two years later, they won the Class 4A title again, defeating Miami Beach High 7-2. Senior pitcher Kevin Saucier led the 1974 team with a 13-2 record and a 1.32 ERA.[19] In 1976, when freshman shortstop Jim Presley joined the team, Escambia remained the team to beat in Northwest Florida.

In May 1981, after 18 years, Waters retired from coaching high-school baseball. The 54-year-old confessed, "I'm getting a little age on me, and working until after dark every night starts to wear you down."[20]

He continued to stay on at the school as an administrative dean. During his tenure as a high-school coach, he sent over a dozen of his players into the professional ranks.

Waters was not done entirely with baseball. He continued to manage the Elizabethton Twins in the rookie-level Appalachian League, a post he had held since 1975. He managed the team for 12 seasons, winning 443 games, second most all-time in franchise history, and capturing two league championships (1978 and 1984). He was chosen Appalachian League Manager of the Year three times (1978, 1981, and 1984).[21] Among the players he helped guide as young professionals were Jim Eisenreich, Steve Lombardozzi, Kirby Puckett, and Gene Larkin. After persuading the Twins to draft Pensacola high-school shortstop Jay Bell in the first round of the 1984 major-league June amateur draft, he managed Bell to an Appalachian League title that very summer.

After the 1986 season Waters stepped down from managing and retired to Pensacola. His influence on baseball in Northwest Florida indelible, local coaches continued to seek his advice and guidance.

Fred Waters.

Courtesy of the Pittsburgh Pirates.

ONE-HIT WONDERS

Fred Waters died at the age of 62 on August 28, 1989, after a lengthy illness. He was buried at Roseland Park Cemetery in Hattiesburg, Mississippi. At the time of his death, he was survived by his wife and three children.

Waters' loss was felt deeply throughout the Northwest Florida baseball community. Before long, a number of his former players got together and organized the annual Fred Waters Memorial Baseball Clinic. Of the camp and its organizers, Fred's wife, Dorothy said, "I think they're wonderful to give their time and do this. Nothing would please Fred Waters more than to see his boys out on the baseball field."[22]

The first clinic was held at the University of West Florida in January 1990 and offered free instruction in baseball fundamentals to players from little league to high school. Over the years, numerous current and former major leaguers have volunteered to participate, including Dennis Lewallyn, Preston Hanna, Kevin Saucier, Jim Presley, Greg Litton, Hosken Powell, Will Clark, Greg Luzinski, Jay Bell, Travis Fryman, and Mark Whiten.

SOURCES

In addition to the sources cited in the Notes, the author consulted Baseball-Reference.com and the following:

Brown, Scott. *Baseball in Pensacola: America's Pastime & the City of Five Flags.* United States: History Press, 2013.

newspapers.com/

Pittsburgh Press

2020 Appalachian League Media Guide

Pensacola Magazine, Nov/Dec 2012

southernmiss.com/documents/2018/7/25/1544_genrel_2012_13_misc_non_event__fred-waters.pdf

NOTES

1. "Southern May Cancel Remainder of Cage Schedule," *Hattiesburg American*, January 26, 1946: 6.
2. "Southern Loses John LeGros to Phillies," *Hattiesburg American*, July 21, 1947: 4.
3. "Bubber Phillips, Mel Didier Sign with Detroit Tigers," *Hattiesburg American*, July 1, 1948: 1.
4. Pat Robinson, 'Stan Musial Opposed to 'Cheap' Homers," *Pittsburgh Sun-Telegraph*, May 10, 1949: 26.
5. "Two Dodgers on All-Star Team," *Greenwood Commonwealth*, December 3, 1949: 6.
6. "Pioneers Win 3rd Straight; Mobile Outfielder Joins Club," *Star Gazette* (Elmira, New York), April 8, 1950: 6.
7. *Elmira Advertiser* June 6, 1950: 11.; *Star-Gazette*, June 8, 1950: 37; *Star-Gazette*, June 26, 1950: 12.
8. "Narleski Wins Third Shutout," *The Sporting News*, May 16, 1951: 27.
9. "Sports from a Ringside Seat," *Hattiesburg American* April 3, 1952: 11.
10. "Another Southpaw Catcher for the Bucs," *The Sporting News*, March 10, 1954: 7.
11. Lou Hernandez, *The Rise of the Latin American Baseball Leagues, 1947-1961* (Jefferson, North Carolina: McFarland & Company, 2011), 20.
12. Hernandez, 22.
13. Mary Irene Moffitt, "Pirates Wives Enjoy Florida Sunshine, Too," *Pittsburgh Post-Gazette*, March 10, 1956: 21.
14. "Rickey Back After Scouting West for Quick Aid to Bucs," *The Sporting News*, July 4, 1956: 25.
15. "Quiet Man Waters Once Quit Baseball," *Pittsburgh Sun-Telegraph*, July 27, 1956: 12.
16. "Waters Joins Staff at PHS," *Pensacola* (Florida) *Journal,* August 9, 1960: 1B.
17. Wayne Terwilliger with Nancy Peterson and Peter Boehm, *Terwilliger Bunts One* (Guilford, Connecticut: Insiders' Guide, 2006), 151.
18. "Waters Shoots for FSU Post," *Pensacola News,* September 10, 1963: 9.
19. "Phils Sign Kevin Saucier," *Pensacola News Journal*, June 9, 1974: 7C.
20. "Waters Calls It Quits," *Pensacola News Journal*, May 20, 1981: 11.
21. Allen LaMountain, *Appalachian League Baseball: Where Rookies Rise* (United States: Xlibris, 2014), 79.
22. "Giants' Clark Headlines Waters Baseball Clinic," *Pensacola News Journal*, January 13, 1990: 21.

DANA WILLIAMS

By Tony S. Oliver

Though their demanding fans may disagree, the 1980s Red Sox were successful by most measures. While they lost a heartbreaking World Series in 1986 and suffered a League Championship Series sweep two years later, the team enjoyed eight winning seasons against only two losing ones. Their hitters outscored their opponents by an average of 42 runs per season and the ancient turnstiles welcomed more than 19.5 million fans to their beloved Fenway Park. The farm system produced its finest pitcher (Roger Clemens) and third baseman (Wade Boggs). Compared with the fortunes of long-suffering franchises like the Mariners or the Indians, the Red Sox had few gripes.

As the decade began, the outfield was the club's strength, set in stone by a homegrown trio. Jim Rice had won the MVP in 1978, accumulating 406 total bases, the highest tally since Stan Musial in 1948. Fred Lynn had won both the MVP and the Rookie of the Year awards in 1975 and added the 1979 statistical triple crown with a .333/.423/.637 slash line. Dwight Evans, at 28 the eldest statesman of the group, had picked up three Golden Gloves for his magnificent command of Fenway's irregularly shaped right field.

But developing players is part art and part science. Boggs supplanted Carney Lansford, who was traded after winning a batting title because his heir apparent was ready. Rich Gedman, while a solid backstop, could not fill the enormous void left by Carlton Fisk, who left for the White Sox. The past-his-prime Tony Pérez, the underpowered Dave Stapleton, and the solid yet unspectacular Bill Buckner manned first base; the franchise was unable to develop any prospects for typically the easiest position to fill in a roster. Red Sox fans were shocked when Lynn, mired in a contract dispute with the club, was traded with Steve Renko to the Angels before the 1981 season. While the Red Sox picked up Joe Rudi, Frank Tanana, and Jim Dorsey, the sudden departure of a young building block was a harbinger of a frustrating, strike-interrupted season. Slugger Tony Armas filled the center-field void in 1983, but the farm system was busy generating other outfielders: Mike Greenwell, Ellis Burks, Todd Benzinger, Kevin Romine, and Dana Williams.

Williams was born on March 20, 1963, in Weirton, West Virginia. His father, Nathaniel, worked in the Weirton Steel Mill but died when Dana was 6 years old. Growing up, Dana and his brothers loved to play the sport: "that's all I ever did … started at six years old, fell in love with it and never lost the passion. I still have the passion. My dad would tell all of our neighbors to 'watch my son slide!'"[1] His mother, Barbara, remarried and moved the family to Alabama, where Dana grew up. She and her new husband, Joseph Garlington, pursued a religious calling as pastors; in 2019 they led the Covenant Church of Pittsburgh.

ONE-HIT WONDERS

In Alabama, Williams continued to turn heads with his athletic abilities. Through the end of the 2019 season, the state had produced 1.7 percent of all men to appear in the major leagues, but its quality surpassed its quantity. Nine Hall of Famers (Hank Aaron, Monte Irvin, Heinie Manush, Willie McCovey, Satchel Paige, Ozzie Smith, Don Sutton, Billy Williams, Early Wynn) hailed from the Yellowhammer State, almost 2.7 percent of the Cooperstown immortals.[2]

On the high-school diamond, Williams split time between shortstop and the pitching mound. Cincinnati chose him in the 34th round of the 1981 draft, but he opted not to sign and enrolled at Enterprise-Ozark Community College. Baseball celebrated a winter draft to supplement the summer one, and Detroit picked him with the 24th choice in early 1982, but "the money wasn't right ... the true money was in the June draft."[3] Williams returned to school before agreeing to terms with Boston as an amateur free agent on May 17, 1983, for a reported $40,000. Alabama legend Ed Scott, who had discovered Aaron for the Indianapolis Clowns, nudged the Red Sox to offer Williams a contract. This connection to baseball royalty triggered an immense source of joy for Williams: "I'm so proud Ed Scott signed me; he signed Aaron and also Tommie Agee."

His first professional campaign (1983) saw him split time between Elmira of the short-season Class-A New York-Pennsylvania League and Winston-Salem of the Class-A Carolina League. His bat spoke volumes – he hit .335 in 210 plate appearances – but his defense stuttered: 14 errors in 165 chances at second base, shortstop, and the outfield.

The following year, the Red Sox brass wanted to move Williams to second but "I wasn't able to do it, so on the last day of spring training they moved me to left field. I ended up leading the league in hits and little by little the errors went down while my hitting improved." Now patrolling the Winter Haven outfield, he paced the 1984 Florida State League with 167 hits and a .327 batting average, outperforming fellow prospect Burks. In 1985 the organization promoted him to New Britain of the Double-A Eastern League and he responded with a .309 batting average, sixth in the circuit and tops on the team. However, Sam Horn captured the attention of the Red Sox front office, as he projected to be a better power hitter; Burks, while more strikeout-prone, was regarded as a speedier outfielder.

In 1986 there was another promotion, this time to Triple-A Pawtucket. The top farm club is only 46 miles from Boston, but for Williams it may as well have been a world away. Though he appeared in 101 games and garnered 400 plate appearances, his performance was overshadowed by soon-to-be big leaguers Greenwell, Romine, and Jody Reed. The logjam of talent frustrated Williams: "Rice and Evans, they were on their way out; I had no chance. But Burks, Greenwell, Brady (Anderson) ... they all jumped over me. (Boston) just didn't have a place for me." Power was often cited as the main drawback, but "they put me on the roster I so knew someone wanted me, but they wouldn't trade me."

He began 1987 back in Double A but proved he was beyond the competition, producing a .335 average with an .800 OPS in 78 games before returning to Pawtucket. Greenwell was now in Boston and Williams's .317 average trailed only Benzinger and Horn among farmhands with more than 100 plate appearances. It was a tough year: "I did good; I put the numbers. Why would I quit? I only thought about it when in Triple A behind Greenwell, I hit .270. Greenwell went to the majors and I thought it was my turn, but they sent me to Double A. That was the only time I thought about quitting. But I ended up doing better; I made my second Double-A All-Star team." Frustrated with Boston's obsession with round-trippers, he aimed for the fences in 1988, hitting a career-high 10 home runs. But his batting average suffered, dipping to .253.

Meanwhile, the 1989 Red Sox took several steps backward. While their 83-79 record was only six games behind the 1988 pace, the Blue Jays (89-73) and the Orioles (87-75) produced better years. Greenwell delivered solid numbers (123 OPS+ in 145 games) but not as spectacular as his breakthrough 1988 statistics (second in MVP voting, .946 OPS, 160 OPS+). Burks, on the ascend, hit over .300; Evans, on his way out, contributed 20 home runs and 100 RBIs. Boggs turned in his customary numbers (.330 with a .430 OBP) and Clemens garnered 17 wins on a 132 ERA+. Heralded prospect Horn struggled mightily, much to the chagrin of the Red Sox faithful; a washed-up Rice played only 56 games and slashed a career-low .234/.276/.344. In hindsight, the summer was successful because the amateur draft yielded Mo Vaughn, who would win the 1995 MVP Award with the Red Sox, and Jeff Bagwell, who would enter Cooperstown, although as an Astro after Boston flipped him for Larry Andersen in 1990.

After playing 104 games with Pawtucket, Williams was called up to the Red Sox. He entered the June 19 game as a pinch-hitter as Boston trailed the Chicago White Sox 8-2. Manager John McNamara lifted

ONE-HIT WONDERS

center fielder Randy Kutcher in the ninth inning to call upon his rookie. Like thousands of others before him, Williams grabbed his bat and headed to the plate, dreaming of a hit. While he could not win the game in a single swing, he could ignite a rally by reaching base. Though the cult of OBP was not yet in vogue, players would still take a walk if needed; though not as glorious as making contact, it nevertheless got the job done. Chicago pitcher Donn Pall, working on his third inning, hit Williams with the first pitch. "Bob Stanley told me sometimes pitchers will hit hitters because they don't want you to get their first hit off them. I don't know if that was the case or not," said Williams of the incident. Ninth-place hitter Ed Romero, who would be released on August 5, popped his first offering to right field. Iván Calderón, who played 755 career games in the outfield thanks to a strong arm, dropped the ball, making Williams an easy out at second on the force play; Williams lamented "there was nothing I could do about it" as he headed to the dugout.

As the month progressed, Williams pinch-ran on June 20, played two innings a day later (one at-bat, a strikeout), and enjoyed one plate appearance on June 24. A day later, he found his name on the starting lineup against the Twins. While not a household name, Minnesota starter Allan Anderson spent six years in the majors, enjoying a brief cameo for the 1987 underdog World Series winners (12⅓ innings pitched) and a mediocre 29 games (5-11, 4.96 ERA) for the 1991 last-to-first edition. Between those two campaigns, he shockingly led the league in ERA in 1988 (2.45) and won a career-high 17 games in 1989. Williams, hitting ninth, came to bat in the third inning; he drove an Anderson offering to center field but the ball was caught by John Moses, starting for fan-favorite and eventual batting champion Kirby Puckett's day off. Though Anderson was not overpowering the hitters (he would not record a strikeout in the game), his mix of pitches kept the Red Sox off-balance and off the scoreboard. Two innings later, with his former minor-league teammate Romine on first, Williams sought the counsel of hitting coach Richie Hebner, who "told me, 'He's getting a lot of guys out on fastballs, take a hack.' I stayed behind on a changeup, missed a home run by about two inches." The famous Green Monster, bane of many a pitcher, had taken away a round-tripper, but given Williams a two-bagger. Left field at Fenway Park is irregularly sized; hitters are seduced by the wall's enticing presence. The 37-foot-high wall ensures that home runs are not cheap but also buoys the doubles totals for hitters.[4] Until 1996, a scant 315 feet separated home from the foul pole; its distance to left-center increased to 379 feet via an almost 90-degree angle. The ballpark's asymmetrical nature has baffled visitors; Red Sox legends bolster their bona fides by learning how to play its caroms and quirks. In his brief career, Williams enjoyed only one defensive chance while guarding the Monster; he adroitly gunned down Geno Petralli on June 21 when the Rangers catcher attempted to take second on his sharply hit line drive to left-center.

After sprinting 180 feet but disappointed at not having circled the bases, Williams did not score as Reed lined to second and Luis Rivera popped to the catcher. The Red Sox stranded what would be their best scoring opportunity in the game. In the seventh inning, Williams hit a weak grounder to Greg Gagne, who tossed the ball to Gene Larkin at first. Williams was on the on-deck circle when the game ended; Danny Heep, pinch-hitting for Romine, flied out to short right field as Jeff Reardon closed the 7-0 Twins victory.

Williams pinch-ran in a 5-4 loss to Milwaukee on June 27 and a 3-1 win over the Blue Jays on June 30. He scored the tying run in the latter game on Kutcher's sacrifice fly off Jimmy Key, and appeared in his final game on July 2, running for Rick Cerone in the ninth inning of a 4-1 Boston victory over Toronto. He was sent back to Pawtucket in July then was traded to the Chicago White Sox on August 2 for Ray Chadwick, who had enjoyed a brief call-up with the California Angels in 1986. A right-handed pitcher, Chadwick tossed 38 frames for Pawtucket before finishing his career with the 1990 Omaha Royals. Williams appeared in four games for Triple-A Vancouver, going 5-for-15 before powering the Canadians to the circuit title over the Albuquerque Dukes.

Williams had a tough 1990 season, splitting time between the Canadians and the Double-A Charlotte Knights. He hit .258 for the year in 82 games, though he was by now an old soul, a few years older than his teammates. The Fleer baseball card company was emboldened by his minor-league accolades, picturing him as number 648 of its 1990 regular-season set. Sharing the cardboard with Rich Monteleone of the Angels, Williams appears relaxed with a shot of Fenway Park's outfield behind him.

After taking two years off from baseball, Williams suited up for the independent Northern League Duluth-Superior Dukes in 1993. Though the team finished last in the league, he hit .297, a solid 26 points above the average batter. By then, it seemed his baseball peers had surpassed him. Younger, faster, stronger players were in the league; Frank Thomas, the AL MVP, was five years younger than Williams, while Barry Bonds, the NL's best player, was 15 months his junior.

Players often dream of turning back the clock; for Williams, freezing time almost became a reality as he attempted to make the Pittsburgh Pirates' 1995 roster. The devastating 1994-1995 strike wiped out one World Series and the opportunity for records to be broken; it frustrated fans everywhere who voiced their discontent through the media and their wallet. The national pastime had survived two world wars and a global depression, but it could not withstand the greed of millionaires and billionaires aloof to public opinion. For some, it represented a golden opportunity to reach the upper echelon of their profession. A few had previously tasted the glory; others had not yet quenched their thirst. While fans, owners, and striking players all espoused different opinions on the morality of their actions, no one doubted the replacement players' love for the game. More than two decades later, the fans' scars may have healed, but the perceived transgressions still evoke long-held passions. For every Doug Cinnella, who argued that "the Major League Baseball Players Association did nothing for minor-league players," there was a Will Clark, who stated, "You can't replace the top echelon of a business with the lower echelon."[5] A few of the picket-crossers, such as Rick Reed and Kevin Millar, would enjoy lasting major-league success. Others, like Williams, saw their last chance for big-league glory slip by when players and management were ordered back to the bargaining table by future Supreme Court Justice Sonia Sotomayor. Like Cinderella, their glass slippers and golden carriages turned into pumpkins. Unlike the fairy tale, their bubble was burst without warning, rather than at a much-forewarned midnight strike of the clock.

Impartial observers would be hard-pressed to fault Williams. The Red Sox could have promoted him to the majors at a younger age; they could have traded him to other clubs to address other roster needs. The Pirates were not a franchise booming with success. After enjoying three consecutive NL East crowns (1990-1992), the club had fallen in hard times. By early 1995 Bonds had departed for San Francisco; Bobby Bonilla for New York; Doug Drabek for Houston. Prospects like Orlando Merced and Al Martin did not live up to the hype; second-bananas Jeff King and Jay Bell were not able to sustain their production; Denny Neagle, while promising, was too raw. Andy Van Slyke, the sole member of the nucleus management had retained, failed to age well. Williams "did well but sat around waiting to come to Pittsburgh." Shortly after the union and the owners agreed to a deal, he laconically told the *Pittsburgh Post-Gazette* "nothing has come in the way of me and my dream. My dream was to play in the major leagues. I accomplished that [eight games with the Boston Red Sox in 1989]. But I wanted to play longer."[6] Despite the disappointment of the prior spring, Williams was not yet ready to hang up his spikes. He returned to the independent Northern League, this time patrolling the outfield for the 1996 Sioux City Explorers. After hitting .254 through 30 games, he decided to call it a career.

The term "Four-A player" has been used in a pejorative sense for those hitters who cannot succeed at the major-league level but are above the highest ranking of the minors. Williams fits the criteria; while he hit .291 in the minors, he was not successful in the majors. However, he was barely in the major leagues, with only five at-bats to his credit. Other players suffer through the shuttle of round-trips between the majors and the minors, frustrating fans and front offices alike.

After his playing career, Williams found success in the dugout. "A friend in Mobile worked as the field coordinator for the Seattle Mariners; through him, I became a coach in the organization." He began with the Lancaster JetHawks of the California League in 1997 as the hitting coach, a role he would hold through 2000. The team made the postseason in three of those campaigns but switched its affiliation to the Diamondbacks in 2001, so Williams, the players, and the coaching staff relocated to San Bernardino.

The Mariners organization promoted Williams to the Midwest League before the 2002 campaign, where the coached the Class-A Wisconsin Timber Rattlers hitters, including Adam Jones and Shin-Soo Choo, who would soon taste major-league stardom. Williams was phlegmatic about this role: "Either you can hit or you cannot. Jones could hit; leave him alone. With Choo, the power came, they kept telling him to pull the ball." He spent the 2002, 2003, and 2004 campaigns with the team before returning in 2007. Confidence, above all, was often the missing ingredient: "I feel that my job is trying to build the confidence in the players. In baseball you try to look day-by-day. I like to look at it at-bat by at-bat. I know these guys can hit, they wouldn't be at this level if they couldn't."[7]

Williams managed the Rookie League's Arizona Mariners in 2005 and 2006, having tested the desert in 1998 as an assistant coach. He recalled that his biggest

ONE-HIT WONDERS

contribution was telling the Mariners "to put Rafael Soriano on the mound; he was a right fielder but could not hit." He moved to the Frontier League in 2010 as the hitting coach for the Washington Wild Things. As of 2019 Williams coached high-school baseball with Penn-Trafford, near Pittsburgh, after managing East Allegheny for three years. He said he enjoyed grooming the next generation of players and regaling them with stories of his career; his charges mention "his experiences with traveling and all the unique characters he encountered along the way are great. He has a lot of funny stories about the bus rides and other experiences. It's pretty cool to hear stories about some of the big leaguers and people you've heard of before."[8]

ACKNOWLEDGMENTS

Dana Williams for graciously agreeing to an interview with the author.

Kerry Sean Hetrick, athletic director of Penn-Trafford High School, and Dan Miller, baseball head coach of Penn-Trafford High School, for connecting the author to Dana Williams.

SOURCES

In addition to the sources cited in the Notes, the author relied extensively on Baseball-Reference.com.

NOTES

1. Author interview with Dana Williams on September 5, 2019. Unless otherwise specified, all quotations come from this interview.
2. Major League Baseball player figures at the conclusion of 2019 (baseball-reference.com/leagues/) and place of birth (baseball-reference.com/bio/).
3. 1982 Draft Results, January Secondary Draft, mlb.mlb.com/mlb/history/draft/draft.jsp#season=1982&player_name=&draft_type=NS&draft_team=&draft_round=&page=1&sort_order=&sorted_by=.
4. Left-center field at Fenway Park was listed as 315 feet from home plate from 1936 through 1995 but has been listed as 310 feet since 1995. mlb.com/redsox/ballpark/facts-figures; https://www.baseball-almanac.com/stadium/fenway_park.shtml.
5. Steven Marcus, "Twenty years ago, replacement players almost opened baseball season," *Newsday*, March 28, 2015. newsday.com/sports/baseball/twenty-years-ago-replacement-players-almost-opened-baseball-season-1.10142935.
6. Chuck Finder, "Back to Reality," *Pittsburgh Post-Gazette*, April 27, 1995: E-13, E-14.
7. The Minor Leaguers of 1990: Greatest 21 Days, greatest21days.com/2012/10/dana-williams-higher-level-651.html.
8. Joe Sager, "Penn Trafford Baseball Gets Boost from Former Pro Dana Williams," TribLive High School Sports Network, May 27, 2019. tribhssn.triblive.com/penn-trafford-baseball-gets-boost-from-former-pro-dana-williams/.

LES WILLIS

By Joel Rippel

At the age of 39, Lester Willis got his first invitation to a major-league spring-training camp.

In February 1947 in Tucson, Arizona, Willis, a left-handed pitcher who had spent 13 seasons in the minor leagues, caught the attention of Cleveland Indians manager Lou Boudreau immediately.

According to one newspaper account, Boudreau, on the first day of workouts, "did a double take as his eye caught the last man out (onto the practice field). He was a roly poly fellow with an overhanging ledge of flesh."[1]

The Indians had acquired the 5-foot-9, 195-pound Willis during the offseason through the Rule 5 draft, but Boudreau was getting his first glimpse of Willis.

"Who is that guy," Boudreau inquired incredulously, "one of the new stockholders?"[2]

Les Willis.

Courtesy of Cary Smith.

Willis, who had won at least 20 games three times and 18 games twice in the minor leagues, made himself known.

On the second day of camp, Willis suffered a leg injury. Boudreau suggested he take a few days off to recuperate.

"Not me," said Willis. "I've been waiting for 15 years for a chance to make it to the big leagues, and no pulled muscle is going to interfere. I'll be out there."[3]

Willis was called the pitching standout of the first intrasquad game of camp, on March 5. A newspaper report said, the "unstreamlined southpaw pitched four perfect innings."[4]

The account said Willis "throws a very good screwball, the pitch that breaks away from right-handed hitters and in to left-handers. He throws a curve that starts from somewhere around first base. His fast ball will not make you think of Bob Feller, but it isn't drifting tumbleweed, either."[5]

Willis made Cleveland's Opening Day roster.

Willis was born to E. and Daisy Willis on January 17, 1908, in Nacogdoches, Texas. His father, a native of Missouri, worked as a filer at a sawmill. Lester had four older brothers, Roy, Louis, Aubrey, and George.

After graduating from Smithville (Texas) High School, Willis attended the College of Marshall in Marshall, Texas (now East Texas Baptist College). He was a three-sport star, playing football, basketball, and baseball. When he wasn't pitching for the baseball team, he played in the outfield. In 68 games for Marshall, he batted .343.

His former coach, Clarence Hamel, reminisced about Willis's career at Marshall.

"In three years with the College of Marshall, he lost only one game," Hamel told a Shreveport, Louisiana, sportswriter. "That was to the Stephen F. Austin Teachers at Nacogdoches. It was a 13-inning affair, and the contest was decided, 13-12, when a batted ball went through a hole under the fence for a home run."[6]

Hamel went on to say that Willis "won honors as an 'iron man.'" He added, "I remember one afternoon

ONE-HIT WONDERS

at Ruston one of our hurlers took sick before a game with Louisiana Polytech and Willis asked permission to work both games. He won them, 6 to 4 and 6 to 2. He went to bat four times in one game and hit a home, a triple and two doubles."[7]

Willis made his professional debut in 1931 with McAllen of the Rio Grande Valley League, which was in its first year of existence.

The four-team Class-D league did not complete its season, but Willis had a good rookie season, despite missing several games in May after suffering a head injury when he ran into a fence. McAllen finished with the best record (55-37) in the league before it disbanded on July 29.

According to the Louisiana sportswriter, Willis won 16 games and lost 6 "and played a major part in his team winning the championship."[8]

Willis was the winning pitcher in two of the three games of the league's championship series with La Feria. The series, originally scheduled for a best-of-seven, was called off after three games, likely because of poor attendance.

In the opener, Willis pitched a three-hitter with 15 strikeouts in a 5-2 victory. In the second game he went 2-for-5 while playing left field in McAllen's 9-2 victory. In the deciding game, he entered the game in relief in the seventh inning and was the winning pitcher in McAllen's 14-13 victory.

Willis began the 1932 season with Shreveport of the Texas League. The season got off to a noteworthy start when Willis pitched seven scoreless innings in an exhibition game against the Chicago White Sox in Shreveport. He gave up three runs in the eighth inning in the Sports' 9-3 victory.

The team's stay in Shreveport was short-lived. After the Sports ballpark was destroyed by a fire on May 4, the Sports (9-21 at the time) played one game in Longview, Texas, before finishing the season in Tyler, Texas. For the season, Willis was 0-6 with a 4.06 ERA in 27 appearances for the Sports, who were 57-93.

Willis went to spring training with Tulsa of the Class-A Texas League in 1933, but in late April the club released him. He split the 1933 season between Baton Rouge and Jackson of the Class-C Dixie League. He went 2-10. In 1934 he split the season between two Class-C teams, El Dorado of the East Dixie League and Joplin of the Western Association. He was 0-2 with Joplin and 5-11 with El Dorado.

After going 7-29 the previous three seasons, Willis had a breakthrough season in 1935. He went 20-7 with a 3.22 ERA to help El Dorado win the East Dixie League title. He completed 23 of 24 starts and was named to the league's all-star team. The Fort Worth Cats of the Texas League, who had a working agreement with El Dorado, recalled Willis in late August and he went 0-1 in three appearances with the Cats.

In 1936 he went 20-8 with a 3.25 ERA for Pine Bluff of the Class-C Cotton States League despite missing two weeks in August when he fractured a fractured thumb on his pitching hand in a play at the plate. He tied for the league lead in victories as Pine Bluff finished third with a 77-62 record.

Willis returned to Pine Bluff in 1937 and put together the best season of his career. He went 22-8 with a 2.79 ERA and a league-leading 200 strikeouts (in 274 innings) to lead the Judges to the Cotton States League title. The Judges (87-51) finished 10 games ahead of second-place El Dorado.

After that season, Willis was purchased by Memphis, a St. Louis Cardinals farm team. In March 1938, he was one of 74 Cardinals minor leaguers declared free agents by Commissioner Kenesaw Mountain Landis, who declared that the Cardinals were covering up players by controlling farm teams in the same leagues.

In April 1938 Willis signed with Louisville of the American Association. He went 9-21 while pitching a team-high 239 innings for the Colonels, who were 53-100. He spent the 1939 season with Milwaukee of the American Association, going 6-8 for the Brewers.

In April 1940 Milwaukee sold Willis to Memphis of the Southern Association. He spent the next three seasons with the Chickasaws. In 1940 he went 18-14 for the Chicks (79-72), who lost to Atlanta in the first round of the Southern Association playoffs.

Willis and the Chicks slumped in 1941. Willis was 14-15 as Memphis finished 69-85. He was 8-9 in 1942.

Willis missed the next three seasons while he worked a defense job at a laundry in his hometown of Jasper, Texas. He rejoined Memphis for the 1946 season and put together an outstanding season. He went 18-7 with nine shutouts and a 2.37 ERA for the Chickasaws. In one stretch he threw four consecutive shutouts and 37⅓ consecutive scoreless innings.

In late August Willis pitched a 3-0 no-hitter against league-leading Atlanta in Memphis. He retired the first 25 hitters he faced before an error with one out in the ninth kept him from recording the first perfect game in the Southern Association in 29 years.

"I knew I was right about the third inning," Willis said. "I just wheeled 'em in there and took the consequences."[9] After the error, Willis retired the final two hitters to complete the no-hitter.

Willis, who struck out seven, said, "I didn't worry about a no-hitter. Ralph McNair (the catcher) knew what to ask for and I had it to give this time."[10]

Despite winning 28 of 32 games in one stretch and finishing with 90 victories, the Chickasaws (90-63) finished 5½ games behind Atlanta.

In the first round of the Southern Association playoffs, Willis pitched Memphis to victories in Games One and Four over Chattanooga to help Memphis take a 3-1 lead in the series. In a 6-0 victory in the series opener, Willis tossed a five-hit shutout and contributed a solo homer and three RBIs. In Game Four, he pitched a complete game in a 5-3 victory. Memphis won the series 4-2 (with one tie).

In the finals, Atlanta outlasted Memphis, winning the series in seven games.

On November 1, 1946, Willis was selected by the Cleveland Indians in the Rule 5 draft.

He made his major-league debut against the Detroit Tigers on April 28 – the ninth game of the season for the Indians – in Cleveland. He entered the game in the top of the ninth inning in relief of starter Red Embree with the Tigers leading 3-0.

Willis struck out Dick Wakefield, who had two hits in his first three at-bats, for the first out before Hoot Evers doubled. The next hitter, Eddie Mayo, reached on an error by second baseman Joe Gordon. Evers tried to score on the play but was thrown out at the plate by Gordon. Pat Mullin grounded out for the third out of the inning.

After pitching 3⅓ innings without allowing a run in his four appearances, Willis pitched three scoreless innings – his first save by today's save rule – in the Indians' 8-4 victory in the first game of a doubleheader against the White Sox on May 30 in Chicago. He also got his first major-league at-bat, grounding out in the eighth inning against Joe Haynes.

Two days later, against the New York Yankees in Cleveland, Willis retired two hitters for his seventh consecutive scoreless appearance.

That streak ended on June 3, when Willis gave up a solo home run to Jerry Priddy in the top of the ninth inning and was the losing pitcher in the Indians' 6-5 loss to the Washington Senators. His first major-league decision was highlighted by his only major-league hit.

With two outs in the bottom of the eighth, in his second major-league at-bat, Willis singled to center off Senators starter Bobo Newsom.

Willis did not allow a run in his next four appearances. After 11 relief appearances, in which he allowed just one run in 12⅔ innings, Willis made back-to-back starts. They were his only two starts of the season.

On July 6, in the first game of a doubleheader at Chicago, he allowed three runs – one earned – in six innings in the Indians' 3-2 loss to the White Sox.

In his second start, in the second game of a home doubleheader against the Philadelphia A's, Willis allowed four earned runs and eight hits in 4⅔ innings. He did not get a decision in the Indians' 5-4 victory.

In back-to-back relief appearances against the Yankees on July 15-16 in Cleveland, Willis was roughed up for five runs in four innings.

He regrouped over his next five appearances – allowing just one earned run in eight innings – before being victimized again by the Yankees, who were en route to a pennant-winning 97-victory season.

On August 21 Willis allowed two runs in two innings in a 9-3 loss to the Yankees in Cleveland. Two days later, he entered the game in the second inning. With the Yankees leading 5-0, he retired the first hitter he faced – Joe DiMaggio – before allowing 14 hits and six runs (three earned) in 6⅔ innings in the Yankees' 13-6 victory. His longest outing of the season would turn out to be his final major-league appearance.

In early September, the Indians sold his contract to Memphis. But Willis, nursing a sore shoulder, did not make any appearances for Memphis.

In 22 appearances for the Indians, Willis was 0-2 with a 3.48 ERA. He allowed 58 hits in 44 innings. In five appearances against the Yankees, he allowed 10 earned runs and 26 hits in 13⅓ innings. As a hitter, Willis was 1-for-11.

In the spring of 1948, there were reports that Memphis was counting on Willis to join the team. A wire service report in late March said he was one of six players "still missing from spring training camp."[11]

Two weeks later, another report said Willis was one of a "quartet of experienced hands who may yet report."[12]

In late April, an update said the status of Willis "was still unchanged."[13]

No formal announcement was made, but Willis had retired. He remained in Jasper, Texas, the rest of his life, running his laundry and cleaning business. He got involved in local government, serving on the Jasper City Council and as Jasper's mayor. Jasper, a town of about 4,000 in the first half of the twentieth century, is the birthplace of another former Cleveland Indian, Max Alvis.

Willis died on January 22, 1982, five days after his 74th birthday, in Jasper.

ONE-HIT WONDERS

SOURCES

In addition to the sources cited in the Notes, the author consulted Baseball-Reference.com, familysearch.com, Newspapers.com, Retrosheet.org, and statscrew.com.

NOTES

1 Frank Gibbons, "Les Willis Catches On with Tribe," *Dayton* (Ohio) *Herald*, March 6, 1947: 36.
2 Gibbons.
3 Gibbons.
4 Gibbons.
5 Gibbons.
6 Joe R. Carter, "Raspberries and Cream," *Shreveport Times*, April 4, 1932: 9.
7 Carter.
8 Carter. Note: *The Encyclopedia of Minor League Baseball*, 2nd Edition, lists Adrian Johnson of Harlingen as the league leader in wins (14). Willis' bio on baseball-reference.com does not mention his 1931 season with McAllen.
9 "Wimpy Willis Knew He Was Pitching No-Hit, Run Game," *Knoxville News-Sentinel*, August 28, 1946: 14. The story mentioned that it was the third no-hitter of Willis's career, saying he had thrown one in 1936 and one in 1937. But neither no-hitter is mentioned in *The Encyclopedia of Minor League Baseball*, 2nd edition.
10 "Wimpy Willis Knew He Was Pitching No-Hit, Run Game."
11 United Press, "Too Many Missing," *Nashville Tennessean*, March 24, 1948: 22.
12 *Birmingham News*, April 7, 1948: 28.
13 Associated Press, "Birmingham and Little Rock Set Southern Mark for Left on Bases," *Nashville Banner*, April 24, 1948: 6.

KID WILLSON

By Bob Webster

Frank Hoxie "Kid" Willson was born on November 3, 1895, in Bloomington, Nebraska, to Frank Warren and Isabella A. (Hoxie) Willson. He grew up working on his family's truck farm along with his two younger sisters, Ida Mae and Veda A., and his younger brother, Edward. The elder Frank also worked as a hotel clerk, stenographer, and bookkeeper.[1]

The Willson family moved to Siloam Springs, Arkansas, in 1911 and to Sumner, Washington, in 1912. Frank played on the Sumner High School football team that won the 1912 state football championship.[2]

At Sumner High School Frank also met his future wife, Adeline Mertice Huff, the granddaughter of William Moore Kincaid, a founding father of Sumner. Frank and Adeline were married on October 27, 1914, in Sumner after she finished high school and the couple was blessed with eight children; Frank, Robert, Richard, William, Joseph, Marta, Margaret, and Stephen.[3]

The Willsons were the parents of two children by the time Frank embarked on his professional baseball career in 1918 at the age of 22. Their first child, Frank Hartley Willson, was born on March 29, 1916, and Robert was born on August 1, 1917.[4]

The 1918 Pacific Coast International League (PCIL) season kicked off on April 30 as the Tacoma Tigers took on the Spokane Indians at Athletic Field in Tacoma with Kid Willson making his minor-league debut in right field for the Tigers. In the first inning with the Tigers ahead by one run with the bases loaded, Willson singled to left, left fielder Art Bourg let the ball get past him, and by the time the play was over, all three baserunners as well as Willson scored on the play to make the score 5-0.[5] Nice start for the young man's career.

With World War I taking many of the resources – human, product, and monetary – baseball was one of the industries that suffered. For lack of fans and revenue, the Tacoma club folded on May 26, 1918, and Willson was sold to the Vancouver (British Columbia) Beavers of the PCIL.[6] On June 22, it was reported in a Vancouver newspaper that Willson had been sold to the Chicago White Sox. The article said: "There is no man in the league, or probably on the Pacific Coast, that can cover the ground and run bases with the speed that Willson can."[7] The plan was for Willson to remain with Vancouver until the end of the season, but when the team folded on June 26, Willson left for Chicago.

With Tacoma and Vancouver, Willson collected 68 hits in 47 games. He was leading the league in triples and was batting .347 with 20 stolen bases when he left for Chicago.[8]

The 1917 World Series champion White Sox had a tough go of repeating early in the 1918 season. They had lost some players to the war effort and their star center fielder, Happy Felsch, missed some spring training because of illness. Due to foul weather in Chicago, the White Sox were only able to play two homestands in Chicago during the months of April and May. The team finished the month of May with a 17-16 record, in fifth place, five games out of first.

May was especially hard on the White Sox outfielders. Felsch left the team for 12 days after the May 8 game to tend to his brother, who had been trampled by a horse at a Texas Army camp.[9] On May 12 Joe Jackson, who was granted a deferment by his draft board in Greenville, South Carolina, because he was married, was told that the decision had been reversed and that he was draft-eligible. He left the team.[10]

The White Sox progressed through June hovering around the .500 mark. Felsch was hitting above .300 into the second week of the month, but was involved in a contract dispute with team owner Charles Comiskey and by July 1, Felsch was hitting .252 and had left the team.[11]

After Secretary of War Newton D. Baker issued a "Work or Fight" order on July 1,[12] the White Sox were at risk of losing even more players. The White Sox needed an outfielder and Willson was given a chance with the team. The military tried to avoid taking married men with families. Since Willson had a wife and

ONE-HIT WONDERS

two children, his baseball career looked safe from war or related activities.

Willson arrived in Chicago and made his major-league debut on July 2 against the Detroit Tigers in the second game of a doubleheader at Comiskey Park. Pinch-hitting for Chick Gandil in the ninth inning, he drew a walk from Tigers pitcher Rudy Kallio. He went to third on a hit by Shano Collins and scored on a fly ball by Swede Risberg. The Tigers won the game, 11-8.[13]

Willson pinch-hit the next day, too. In the eighth inning, with the White Sox leading 6-5 and bases loaded with nobody out, Willson batted for relief pitcher Joe Benz. It was the perfect opportunity for Willson to blow the game wide open and chalk up his first major-league hit, but he struck out. The White Sox eventually won 9-5.[14]

On July 4 the White Sox and Tigers played their second doubleheader in three days. The first game was a wild affair in which Ty Cobb went 5-for-6 as the White Sox won in 12 innings, 7-6. The Tigers scored two runs in the top of the ninth to take a 6-5 lead. In the bottom of the ninth, Ray Schalk was hit by a pitch and Willson ran for him. Risberg sacrificed Willson to second, and singles by Murphy and Nemo Leibold scored Willson to tie the score at 6-6. The White Sox won it with a run in the bottom of the 12th.[15]

Willson's only other appearance with the White Sox in 1918 was on July 11, against the Boston Red Sox at Fenway Park. Down 4-0 entering the ninth, the White Sox rallied. Murphy started the inning by grounding to second baseman Dave Shean. Murphy hustled down to first and appeared to beat the throw to first baseman Babe Ruth, but umpire George Hildebrand called him out. Liebold and Eddie Collins both singled and Chick Gandil was hit by a pitch to load the bases. Willson came in to run for Gandil as Shano Collins stepped to the plate with the bases loaded and one out. He sent a low line drive toward first and Willson, who had a bit of a lead, stopped to see if right fielder Babe Ruth was going to catch the ball. It looked catchable to Willson, so he tried to get back to first. Ruth saw this and knocked the ball down, then grabbed it with Willson right in front of him. Ruth tagged Willson and stepped on the bag for the game-ending double play.[16]

Willson was released by the White Sox three days later. Since he had played only 47 minor-league games before joining the White Sox, it was determined that he needed more time in the minor leagues. He boarded the train in Boston for the long train ride to Tacoma.[17]

Kid Willson.

Willson hit .233 with the Regina Senators of the Class-C Western Canada League in 1919.

Willson was back with the Vancouver Beavers for the 1920 and 1921 seasons. He batted .305 with seven home runs in 1920 and an astonishing .360 in 1921 with 162 hits for the season.

In 1922 Willson split time between the Beavers and the Greenville Spinners of the Class-B South Atlantic League. He was hitting .307 with the Beavers of the Western International League (formerly the Pacific Coast International League) before going to Greenville, where his batting average dipped to .237. The Western International League folded in June 1922 and Willson was sold to Greenville. Willson was with Greenville in 1923 where he hit .430 in 79 at-bats.

In 1924 Willson played with the Hutchinson Wheat Shockers of the Class-C Western Association, where the 28-year-old kept up his torrid hitting with a .391 batting average in 100 games.

The Waco Cubs of the Texas League were Willson's team for 1925, 1926, and most of the 1927 season. His batting averages for the three seasons were .351, .400, and .440.

ONE-HIT WONDERS

Kid Willson on the field.

In late May, White Sox center fielder Johnny Mostil was placed on the voluntarily retired list, paving Willson's way back to the majors. Willson had been out of the majors for nine years. He finally got his first major-league hit on May 20, a single to left field off Sam Gray of the Philadelphia Athletics in the bottom of the ninth inning. The White Sox lost the game, 12-5.

Edward Burns of the *Chicago Tribune* wrote: "The fans got their first look at Willson, the new slugging outfielder from the Texas League, when he batted for (Sarge) Connally in the third inning and then relieved (Bibb) Falk in left field. He was up four times, made a run and a hit, and each time took a healthy cut at the ball."[18] While joining the White Sox, Willson was reunited with player-manager Ray Schalk. The two had been teammates when Willson played with the White Sox in 1918.

Willson pinch-hit in the ninth inning of a 7-1 loss to the Tigers on May 28. On June 3 he replaced leadoff hitter Alex Metzler in center field in the fourth inning and recorded four putouts against the Red Sox in Boston. The following day, Willson popped out to short, pinch-hitting for pitcher Ted Blankenship.

On June 7, playing the Yankees at Yankee Stadium, Willson pinch-hit for pitcher Tommy Thomas. The left-handed hitter stepped into the batter's box to face future Hall of Famer Waite Hoyt. One can imagine him digging in, preparing to take his swing. If the magnitude of the moment didn't strike him at the time, for years afterward he could recall the time he had Hoyt on the mound, Lou Gehrig playing first base and, behind Gehrig, Babe Ruth in right field. They were all ready to make a play on the ball that Willson was planning to hit. Willson became one of Hoyt's 1,206 strikeout victims.

He appeared as a pinch-hitter and a pinch-runner in two more games before being sent back to Waco.

In 1928 Willson split time between the Shreveport Sports and the Dallas Steers, both of the Texas League.

Willson did not play in 1929, but in 1930 he returned to the Dallas Steers and also made a stop with the Toledo Mud Hens of the Double-A American Association. He hit .344 for Toledo under manager Casey Stengel.

Willson played his final professional baseball season in 1931 at age 35 with the Seattle Indians of the Double-A Pacific Coast League.

After retiring from baseball, Willson spent the rest of his life in the State of Washington. He lived in Vancouver in the late '30s and worked at the Bonneville Dam on the Columbia River during World War II. He also served as town marshal of Bonneville, a company town of the dam owners. He was later a weighmaster with the State of Washington and worked for Boeing, the airplane builder, before retiring.[19]

The generations of family members that followed Willson have been heavily involved in sports. Willson's son Joe was a boxer. Another son, Bill, played high-school football. Bill's son Larry was a pole vaulter, while Bill's two daughters could both run well. Suzanne threw the javelin very well for her high-school track and field team. The track coach had the boys race Suzanne and if they could beat her, they made the team. Suzanne's sister Molly was also a track star. Molly went to the Junior Olympic Trials in Portland and ran 73 yards of the 75-yard dash before falling just before reaching the finish line. She anchored her junior high's district champion 440-yard relay and broke the record for the 50-yard dash. She also excelled in the shot put.[20]

Another daughter, Marta Willson Mayes, was the mother of some fine athletes. Her son Bob Mayes led Hudson's Bay High School of Vancouver, Washington, in track and in football, and broke the national high school hurdles record at the Olympic Indoor Track Invitational. At Oregon State University, Bob was a member of the school's 440-relay team that broke the world record in the first heat of the 1967 Fresno

ONE-HIT WONDERS

Relays. Bob was also a member of the 1967 Oregon State University "Giant Killers" football team that beat number-2 Purdue on the road, 22-14, tied number-2 UCLA, 16-16, also on the road, and beat number-1 Southern Cal, 3-0.[21]

Bob's older brother, Gary, was voted "Best Athlete" at Hudson's Bay High School in 1961. He earned the maximum number of varsity letters in football, basketball, baseball, and track. At Humboldt State University he played four years of football and two years of baseball. He played rugby, baseball, and soccer in adult leagues in the Bay Area into his mid-50s when knee injuries forced him to quit.[22]

Gary and his wife, Lynn, had three sons that Gary coached as youngsters. Their youngest son, Ryan, had aspirations to play college soccer, but serious knee injuries kept him from doing that. He did however, rehab his knees and went on to become one of the outstanding high-school track athletes in the Bay Area. He went on to compete for the University of Oregon track team.[23]

Beginning with Kid Willson, there have been five generations of superb athletes in the Willson family. Lynn Mayes said, "I think the greatest legacy passed down by Grandpa Willson was the drive, determination, and positive work ethic instilled in each succeeding generation. The power of a never-give-up attitude."[24]

Frank Hoxie "Kid" Willson died on April 17, 1964 in Union Gap, Washington, and is buried at Sumner Cemetery in Sumner, Washington. The inscription on his gravestone reads, "He marks not that if you won or lost, but how you played the game. Grantland Rice."

SOURCES

In preparing this biography, the author used Retrosheet.org and Baseball-Reference.com for stats and game information, as well as a telephone interviews and multiple emails with Molly Willson-Perry, Lynn Mayes, Larry Willson, and Bob Mayes, all family members of Kid Willson.

NOTES

1. Lynn Mayes and Bob Mayes, email correspondence, April/May 2020.
2. Lynn Mayes (family historian), email correspondence, April/May 2020.
3. Lynn Mayes.
4. Bob Mayes.
5. "Bengals Snow Indians Under," *Tacoma Times*, May 1, 1918: 6.
6. "Interest Is in War Work, Tigers and Indians Quit," *Tacoma Times*, May 27, 1918: 6.
7. "Chicago White Sox Secure Ike Wolter and Frank Wilson," *Vancouver* (British Columbia) *Daily World*, June 22, 1918: 14.
8. "Chicago White Sox Secure Ike Wolter and Frank Wilson."
9. "Eddie Collins Ready for Sox Infield Again," *Chicago Tribune*, May 10, 1918: 13.
10. I.E. Sanborn, "Jackson Notified He's Due for Early Call in the Draft," *Chicago Tribune*, May 13, 1918: 13.
11. Jim Nitz, "Happy Felsch," SABR BioProject, sabr.org/bioproj/person/cd61b579.
12. Matt Kelly, "On Account of War," baseballhall.org/discover-more/stories/short-stops/1918-world-war-i-baseball, Retrieved May 10, 2020.
13. James Crusinberry, "White Sox Win While Sun Shines, but Lose Twilight Go," *Chicago Tribune*, July 3, 1918: 13.
14. James Crusinberry, "Tigers Ring Up Fifteen Hits but Lose Battle to Sox, 9-5," *Chicago Tribune*, July 4, 1918: 13.
15. James Crusinberry, "Ardor of 1776 Fills Sox; Repulse Savage Tigers Twice," *Chicago Tribune*, July 5, 1918: 9.
16. James Crusinberry, "Helpless Sox Make 4 to 0 Victory Easy for Boston," *Chicago Tribune*, July 12, 1918: 8.
17. James Crusinberry, "Sox Drop Willson, Rookie Who Cost Wads in Rail Fares," *Chicago Tribune*, July 15, 1918: 11.
18. Edward Burns, "Sox Hurlers Fall Beneath Macks' Attack," *Chicago Tribune*, May 21, 1927: 15.
19. Larry Willson, telephone interview, April 2020.
20. Molly-Willson-Perry, email correspondence, May 9, 2020.
21. Lynn Mayes and Bob Mayes, email correspondence, April/May 2020.
22. Lynn Mayes.
23. Lynn Mayes.
24. Lynn Mayes.

GEORGE YANTZ

By Tim Hagerty

George Webb Yantz was a bricklayer, journeyman catcher, and tough negotiator who reached the major leagues for one game and retired with a 1.000 career batting average.

Yantz was born on July 27, 1886, in Louisville, Kentucky, the second oldest of five children born to Josephine and Charles Yantz. Charles worked as a bricklayer and contractor, while Josephine was a homemaker. The year before George began his professional baseball career, his older brother, William, was killed when he fell 40 feet while working at the Schaefer-Meyer Brewing Company's building in 1906.[1]

George Yantz with the 1912 Birmingham Barons.

By the time he was 21, George Yantz had established himself as one of the top ballplayers in Louisville. He starred for the Fetters amateur team in 1907, winning a Best Batter gold medal at a postseason banquet honoring 44 local players.[2]

He made his professional debut with the Class-B Grand Rapids Wolverines in 1907. It was a local connection that sent Yantz to Grand Rapids; Louisville native Phil Arnold owned the Wolverines and knew of Yantz. After a month with Grand Rapids, Yantz returned to Louisville and played for the Fetters team.

Yantz broke a finger in an indoor game on March 6, 1908. The Fetters and the Sutcliffes, another local amateur team, played in Louisville's armory in front of a "small but enthusiastic" crowd.[3] Yantz was playing first base when he broke his pinky finger and had to leave the contest. His finger healed in time for the 1908 regular season.

Yantz stayed close to home in the Kentucky-based Blue Grass League over the next two seasons. He suited up for Lawrenceburg in 1908 and hit what is believed to be the first home run of his professional career on August 13 of that year against the Frankfort Statesmen. On May 5, 1909, Yantz married Eleanor Grass in Louisville and then played in a game two days later. He also made a second commitment, this one less permanent than marriage, signing a nonreserve contract with Frankfort.

Or at least Yantz thought it was a nonreserve contract when he signed to play for the Texas League's San Antonio Bronchos in 1910.[4] Officials of the Frankfort team had other ideas, claiming they still held Yantz's rights. The *Louisville Courier-Journal* wrote that "Yantz has never been released by Frankfort and will not be, it is believed, without a substantial consideration. He was one of the very best catchers in the Bluegrass (League) last season and is a valuable man in any place. It is said that he claims he understood the agreement between him and the Frankfort team was that he was to have his release at the end of the season, but no one was given authority to make any such agreement."⁵

All parties must have come to a resolution, because Yantz packed up and left for San Antonio in 1910. While reporting on the local guy Yantz's departure, the *Courier-Journal* said he "is expected to make good," calling him "a youngster" with a "promising future" and describing him as "a tireless worker, a fine thrower and a good hitter."⁶

Most of Yantz's defensive career was spent behind the plate, but he occasionally lined up as an infielder or outfielder, leading one reporter to say of Yantz: "Probably no backstop ever plugged an infield hole with more zeal or brilliance than the Texas Leaguer."⁷ He brought that zeal for versatility to San Antonio in 1910 and used it in a 23-inning 1-1 tie against Waco on July 5.

Yantz started in right field that day and batted ninth, going 2-for-7 with a double. (It's not often a team's ninth batter gets seven at-bats.) Yantz probably felt sympathy for his teammate Louis Schan, who caught all 23 innings in San Antonio's summer heat. The 23-inning marathon set the record for the longest game in Texas League history, a record that stood until San Antonio and Rio Grande Valley played 24 innings 50 years later on April 29, 1960.⁸

In 1911 Yantz joined the Southern Association's Birmingham Barons and appeared in 121 of the club's 138 games. A memorable day from that season came when Yantz was served with nine police warrants (one per inning) for playing on a Sunday in Nashville, where Sunday baseball was banned. The Barons' president and manager had to pay fines, while the players were all found innocent in court the next day.⁹

The Barons invited Yantz back for the following year but the 1911-1912 offseason brought him more contract chaos. Yantz held out for more money, refusing to report to the team unless it agreed to pay him an extra $100 per month.¹⁰ The Barons were offering an extra $25 per month, but that didn't cut it for Yantz.¹¹ The 1912 season was approaching but Yantz was holding his ground and telling anyone who would listen that he was ready to work on a farm instead of reporting to Birmingham.

Finally, in late March 1912, Yantz ended his personal strike, leading the *Birmingham News* to exclaim, "George Yantz, the hold-out Baron backstop, has reported!"¹² It's unclear if his financial demands were met. When Yantz arrived, Birmingham manager Carlton Molesworth felt that the Yantz "salary thing is settled"¹³ and he didn't elaborate to the press. It was

George Yantz with Cleveland.

neither the first nor the last time George Yantz was part of a transaction with twists and turns.

It proved to be a good career choice when Yantz picked baseball over farming in 1912. He excelled for the Barons that year, batting 20 points higher than the previous season while continuing his robust defense behind the plate, helping Birmingham win the Southern Association title and earning him serious consideration from major-league teams.

September 1912 was a transitory month for Yantz. First he was drafted by the St. Louis Browns in mid-September,¹⁴ but he never played a game for the team. The draft rules in those days allowed major-league teams to return minor leaguers within five days after drafting them,¹⁵ and that's what the Browns did with Yantz, citing an excess of new talent as their reason.¹⁶

The Chicago Cubs had also "put in a bid for" Yantz and were able to scoop him up as soon as the Browns cut him loose.¹⁷ The Cubs originally drafted Lena Blackburne from the American Association's Milwaukee Brewers, but Cubs owner Charles Murphy became concerned that Blackburne had an injured leg, so he surrendered Blackburne back to Milwaukee, opening up space on the Cubs' depth chart for Yantz.[18] The Cubs immediately added Yantz to their major-league roster and his first and only major-league stint was underway.

It was partly because of another player's injury that Yantz was acquired by the Cubs and it was another player's injury that got Yantz into his lone major-league game. Cubs starting catcher Jimmy Archer played the first seven innings on September 30, 1912, in the last week of the season, before a foul tip to his knee forced him out of the game. Acting manager Joe Tinker summoned Yantz from the bench to catch the final two innings against Pittsburgh, receiving the pitches of reliever Bill Powell in both frames.[19]

Sportswriters took notice of the height disparity between the 6-foot-2 Powell and the 5-foot-6 Yantz. "They immediately acquired the soubriquet 'the long and short battery,' for Powell belong [sic] to the tall and rangy class, while Yantz is as short as his name, and just as full of pepper as it sounds," the *Davenport (Iowa) Daily Times* quipped.[20] Yantz was listed at 168 pounds, and batted and threw right-handed.

Yantz's two-inning visit to the majors included one at-bat. He stepped into the batter's box against Pirates righty Claude Hendrix on a dry day in Chicago with temperatures in the 60s[21] and struck a single. Or was it a double? Baseball stories can get distorted as years pass by, and the story of Yantz's base hit certainly was. Obituaries decades later stated that Yantz "hit a double off the Pirate pitcher in his only batting appearance," but all reliable box scores list his hit as a single.[22] The Cubs lost the game, 9-3.

Had it not been for Archer's knee injury, George Yantz might not have ever entered a major-league box score. His name wouldn't have been immortalized in baseball encyclopedias; instead it would've been mythically floating with other "phantom major leaguers," a dubious list of players who reached the major leagues but never appeared in a game.

Yantz believed he would have played in more than one game in the big leagues had the Browns kept him in the fall of 1912. "The Browns could have used me," he recalled in 1964. "The Cubs said I was too small and let me go."[23] None of the three Browns catchers who appeared in 40 or more games in 1913 batted higher than .208. Perhaps the last-place Browns would've been an ideal spot for an up-and-coming catcher like Yantz to get more major-league experience.

As it turned out, Yantz never got a second major-league game, but it wasn't for lack of effort. He roamed through the minor leagues for four more seasons, beginning with the Southern Association's New Orleans Pelicans in 1913.

Moving Yantz to The Big Easy wasn't easy. The Cubs sold his contract to New Orleans in December 1912, but the National Association of Professional Baseball Clubs flagged the deal because Murphy forgot about a new rule requiring major-league players to pass through waivers before being sent to a minor-league club.[24] The waiver wildness was sorted out and Yantz officially joined New Orleans in early March of 1913. While the incident didn't spawn media mentions of an unofficial "George Yantz Rule," the Cubs' misstep was a reminder to other organizations that they had to follow the new waiver policy.

Yantz overcame his personal hesitation about joining the Pelicans; he was originally reluctant to go, claiming that every time he played in New Orleans for Birmingham he got "a touch of malaria."[25] (The New Orleans catching corps also included Louisville native Leo Angermeier, who played sandlot ball with Yantz as a kid.[26])

Malaria didn't end Yantz's 1913 season, but a broken leg did. The injury happened in the second inning of a home game against Chattanooga on May 15 when Yantz stumbled while running to second base and broke a bone above his left ankle.[27] This limited Yantz to just 44 games in 1913.

He regained his health and was ready to play again in 1914. New Orleans sold Yantz's contract to the American Association's Toledo Mud Hens in January.[28] By May of 1914 he had been acquired by the Pacific Coast League's Portland Beavers, in a move that took extra time to execute because the Beavers thought Yantz might jump to the Federal League.[29] Yantz kept his pledge to Portland and played in 65 games for the PCL champion Beavers.

On September 20, 1914, Yantz was behind the plate for a baseball rarity – a no-hitter loss. Portland lefty Johnny Lush threw nine hitless innings against the Venice Tigers, but the Beavers lost 1-0. The only run came in when a low pitch snuck past Yantz with a runner at third.[30] It was the second time in PCL history that a pitcher had tossed a no-hitter but lost the game.[31]

Portland traded Yantz to Venice on October 27, 1914,[32] but Yantz never played for the Tigers, who released him outright shortly before the 1915 season.[33] It left Yantz looking for work until he signed with another group of Tigers, the Western League's Lincoln Tigers, in May. Lincoln's pitching staff included Bill Powell, the same pitcher Yantz caught in his only major-league

ONE-HIT WONDERS

game. Yantz played 90 games for Lincoln in his next to last season in professional baseball.

Yantz signed with the Central League's Evansville Evas early in the 1916 season. Late in the year, he was popped in the head by an opponent's knee and his doctor advised him not to play again that season.[34] Yantz didn't play in any future seasons either, retiring in 1917, ending a 10-year professional baseball career with one major-league stretch in 1912.[35]

After his professional playing career, Yantz worked full-time as a bricklayer, a job he held until his late 60s. He continued to play or manage amateur games in Indiana and Kentucky until his mid-50s, hanging up his catcher's mitt for good at age 54 when he determined his eyesight was worsening.[36] Yantz also stayed connected to baseball as a part-time scout; he is credited with discovering six-time major-league All-Star Paul Derringer when Derringer was a high-school pitcher in Springfield, Kentucky.[37]

Yantz's wife, Eleanor, died in 1942 at age 53.[38] They had one child, a daughter, Jacqueline, who occasionally performed with her accordion before Louisville minor-league games.[39]

Yantz's record-tying big-league batting average had a legacy of its own in Louisville. In an 80th-birthday tribute in 1966, the *Courier-Journal* wrote that Yantz "is the only man in the all-time record books with a major-league batting average of 1.000."[40] That wasn't true, and it still isn't true, but the newspaper's description illustrates the lore that Yantz's hit carried in Louisville decades after it occurred.

Yantz rooted for Louisville's minor-league clubs and watched major-league games on television in his later years.[41] He was honored on the field between games of a Mets-Reds doubleheader on September 25, 1966, at Crosley Field's Former Major Leaguers Day, recognizing anyone in the Cincinnati area who played at least one game in the majors. It was likely the final time George Yantz stepped foot on a professional baseball field. He died at Louisville's St. Joseph Infirmary on February 26, 1967, at age 80, leaving behind his second wife, Mabel, daughter Jacqueline, two grandchildren, and a perfect major-league batting average.

SOURCES

In addition to the sources cited in the Notes, the author used Baseball-Reference.com, Retrosheet.org, FamilySearch.org, and the subject's player file from the National Baseball Hall of Fame Library.

NOTES

1. "Falls to Death," *Kentucky Irish American*, November 10, 1906.
2. "Medals for Best Players," *Louisville Courier-Journal*, November 17, 1907.
3. "Fetters Win Indoor Game," *Louisville Courier-Journal*, March 7, 1908.
4. "League Gossip," *Louisville Courier-Journal*, February 15, 1910.
5. "League Gossip."
6. "Louisville Ballplayers Who Will Play in Professional Company Next Year," *Louisville Courier-Journal*, December 26, 1909.
7. "Molesworth Hits Again," *Birmingham News*, June 14, 1911.
8. "Marathon Games," baseball-reference.com/bullpen/Marathon_Games.
9. Johnny Carrico, "1.000 at Bat in Big Leagues," *Louisville Times*, October 6, 1963.
10. "George Yantz, Baron Backstop, a Holdout," *Birmingham News*, February 19, 1912.
11. "George Yantz Holds Out for More Money," *Montgomery Times*, February 19, 1912.
12. "'Hold-Out' G. Yantz Reports to Moley," *Birmingham News*, March 29, 1912.
13. "'Hold-Out' G. Yantz Reports to Moley."
14. "Sport Conversation," *Birmingham News*, September 18, 1912.
15. "Mayor Gives Up Keys of City," *Baltimore Sun*, September 24, 1912.
16. "36 Candidates After Jobs on West Side Club," *Chicago Inter Ocean*, December 22, 1912.
17. "36 Candidates."
18. "Chicago Cubs Take Heckinger," *Racine* (Wisconsin) *Journal Times*, September 23, 1912.
19. "Pittsburgh Again Outclasses Cubs," *Davenport* (Iowa) *Daily Times*, October 1, 1912.
20. Pittsburgh Again Outclasses Cubs."
21. AccuWeather, email correspondence with senior meteorologist Tom Kines, December 31, 2019.
22. "George Yantz, Ex-Baseball Player, Dies." *Louisville Courier-Journal*, February 27, 1967.
23. "1.000 at Bat in Big Leagues."
24. "Cubs Recall George Yantz," *Chattanooga Times*, January 22, 1913.
25. "Whole Team Must Have Had Malaria," *Birmingham News*, February 26, 1913.
26. "Pel Catchers Are Old Pals," *Nashville Banner*, January 14, 1913.
27. "Pels Blank Lookouts, Who Get But One Hit," *New Orleans Times-Democrat*, May 16, 1913.
28. "Yantz Is Sold," *New Orleans Times-Democrat*, January 28, 1914.
29. "May Come to Beavers and Then Again He May Not," *Oregon Daily Journal* (Portland), May 7, 1914.
30. "Bricklayer and Ex-Ballplayer Gets 50-Year Union Card," *Louisville Courier-Journal*, May 4, 1956.
31. Pacific Coast League, *2019 PCL Sketch & Record Book* (Round Rock, Texas: Pacific Coast League, 2019), 176.
32. "Coast League Cuts Salary Limit and 1 Umpire Is Ordered," *Oregon Daily Journal*, October 28, 1914.
33. "Four Beavers Are Coming to Rest for Game," *Oregon Daily Journal*, April 7, 1915.
34. "Sport Dope," *Evansville Press*, September 2, 1916.
35. R.A. Cronin, "Byron Houck Seems to Have Arrived at End of Usefulness," *Oregon City* (Oregon) *Journal*, May 15, 1917.
36. "1.000 at Bat in Big Leagues."
37. Earl Ruby, "Ruby's Report," *Louisville Courier-Journal*, July 24, 1966.
38. "Deaths and Funerals," *Louisville Courier-Journal*, December 20, 1942.

ONE-HIT WONDERS

39 Tommy Fitzgerald, "Colonels Get 2 Hits, Lose 4th Place," *Louisville Courier-Journal*, July 15, 1939.

40 Ruby.

41 Tommy Fitzgerald, "Critics with Washboard See No Need to Rub It In," *Louisville Courier-Journal*, May 1, 1939.

JOE ZAPUSTAS

By Mike Mattsey

To the layman, the life of a professional baseball player is nothing but glitz and glamour. Large salaries, first-class travel and accommodations, and the adoration of millions are considered the norm for athletes who play at the highest levels. While that may be true for a Mike Trout or a Mickey Mantle, it is definitely not the case for the lion's share of baseball players. For every player who earned the lower berth in a Pullman car while traveling between Philadelphia and Pittsburgh, there were hundreds more who slept on rickety, overcrowded buses on an overnight trek from Pensacola to Valdosta. Even those players lucky enough to win a berth in the majors weren't guaranteed a lengthy stay. The term "cup of coffee" was invented by baseball writers who noted that for many players the duration of their stay in the majors amounted to little more than the time needed to slug down a cup of coffee before heading off to start the day. It was in this category that one finds Joe Zapustas, a late-season call-up for the 1933 Philadelphia Athletics. Despite the fact that Zapustas's two-game career in the big leagues was unremarkable, he was able to parlay that brief stint into a lifelong career in sports for which he was celebrated as a referee, coach, and mentor to young athletes.

Zapustas was born in 1907 in Liepaja, a port city that was then part of the Russian Empire but is now a part of Latvia.[1] He was the eldest child of Joseph and Antonia (Rusteiko) Zapustas. In 1912, the family left Latvia and sailed to America to begin life in the New World. By 1920 the family had settled in Boston where Zapustas's father worked as a machinist.[2] The young Zapustas's academic and athletic prowess at South Boston High School were strong enough to win him a berth on both the baseball and football teams at Fordham University, where his athletic career began in earnest.

By the 1931 football season, Zapustas had won the starting fullback spot in the Rams' wishbone-style offense as the team roared to a 6-1-2 record for the season.[3] Joe quickly emerged into a dominant force for Fordham on both the diamond and the gridiron. His final year at Fordham, the 1932-33 school year, saw him named All-American in baseball as an outfielder and selected to the East-West Shrine Game as an end in football.[4] That level of collegiate success was sure to attract the attention of professional scouts and, after Zapustas's graduation in 1933, two professional leagues came calling. Rather than pick between the two, Zapustas tried his hand at both.

In the summer of 1933, Connie Mack's Philadelphia Athletics were chasing the American League pennant. Always looking for top talent, Mack's scout Ira Thomas arranged a tryout for Zapustas before the A's legendary skipper. Mack liked what he saw, and the A's inked Zapustas to a contract.[5] Later that season with Philadelphia Zapustas's major-league career began and ended in the span of two games during the course of a long weekend. In late September, with a third-place finish locked in, Mack gave the Fordham star a crack at big-league competition.

Zapustas debuted for the Athletics on September 28, 1933, against the Red Sox at Philadelphia's Shibe Park in a 4-3 loss for the home side. Zapustas's lone at-bat was limited to a ninth-inning appearance against Boston starter Lloyd Brown. Zapustas hit a popup to first baseman Joe Judge for the second out

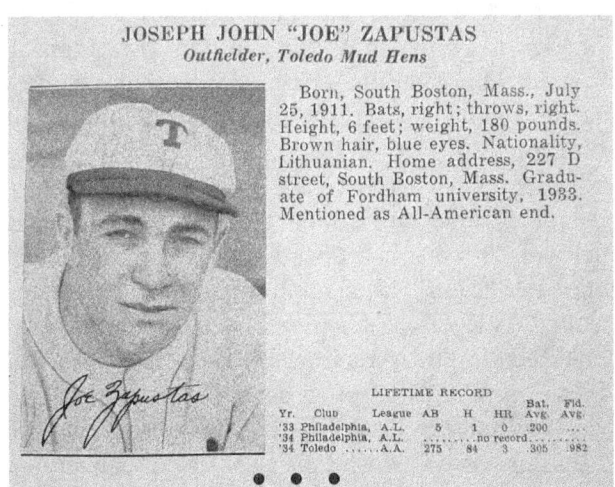

Joe Zapustas, 1935 photo.

ONE-HIT WONDERS

of the inning. One batter later, Brown retired the side and Zapustas's initial sojourn in the major leagues was over moments after it began. Two days later, on September 30, Zapustas was given another shot against the Red Sox. This time he was in the starting lineup.

The A's and Red Sox were playing a doubleheader. Boston won the first game 2-1 and for game two Mack decided to give left fielder Bob Johnson the rest of the day off. His replacement was Zapustas, who was tabbed to bat third, just ahead of slugger Jimmie Foxx, who was having a brilliant season for Philadelphia and would be voted the league's Most Valuable Player. Zapustas's first at-bat came with two outs in the first inning against Red Sox hurler Ivy Andrews. Zapustas duplicated his efforts of two days prior, again popping up to Joe Judge. His next at-bat was the one he would remember for the rest of his life.

Zapustas's next at-bat came with two outs in the fourth inning with Boston leading 9-0. Not only was the game out of reach, but Andrews, having set down all 11 Philadelphia batters he had faced thus far, was perfect for the day. Zapustas put an end to that in short order. He hit a groundball in the direction of second baseman Freddie Muller and reached safely ahead of the throw with the first and only hit of his major-league career. Zapustas batted twice more in the game, both times against Andrews. Leading off the bottom of the seventh, he popped up to the catcher, Lou Legett. Then with two out in the eighth, Zapustas grounded to Muller, forcing Dib Williams at second base. Zapustas was never again to appear in the major leagues … at least not in baseball.

Zapustas's gridiron career at Fordham had not gone unnoticed. After the A's season was over, he signed with the New York Giants of the National Football League for the 1933 season. The Giants, under coach Steve Owen, enjoyed a fine campaign in 1933, going 11-4 to capture the Eastern Conference title before losing the league championship game to the Chicago Bears. As with his experience in Philadelphia, Zapustas's contribution to the team was minimal. In two game appearances, Zapustas was credited with one reception from his position at end for a gain of 26 yards. As with his brief career with the Athletics, Zapustas's NFL tenure ended with the end of the season. One base hit, one reception. But though he never again sniffed the rarefied air of major-league baseball or the NFL, Zapustas's involvement in sports was far from over. The two-sport athlete's career continued, but at the minor-league level.

Zapustas spent the 1934 and 1935 baseball seasons bouncing around the minor leagues. Though he batted a respectable .305 for the Double-A Toledo Mud Hens in 1934, he never again caught the notice of Mack or any other major-league manager in his quest to return to the big time. His brief stint with Toledo in 1935 saw his average dip to a paltry .204 mark, and after that year he never again appeared in Organized Baseball. But he had football to fall back on. He spent the 1935 through 1939 seasons with the Boston Shamrocks of the American Football League.[6] The 1935 squad posted an 8-3 record and won the AFL championship.[7] After the Shamrocks' 1939 season, Zapustas never again competed in a professional arena. However, he was far from finished with athletics as a profession. In fact, Zapustas kept his hand in professional and amateur sports throughout his adult life.

Zapustas became an educator and coach. He taught for 30 years at Stetson High School in Randolph, Massachusetts, and coached the school's basketball, football, and baseball teams.[8] In 1941, Zapustas married Barbara Dugan and the couple raised three sons, Joseph Jr., Robert, and Richard. He also stayed in the limelight of professional sports as a referee. Beginning in 1945, Zapustas moonlighted as a boxing referee for more than 20 years, mainly for preliminary level bouts. But as was the case with his playing career, Zapustas officiated bouts of some of the biggest names in the game. On July 10, 1950, Zapustas, "a former South Boston athlete of some renown," worked the main event at Braves Field which featured heavyweight contender Rocky Marciano against Gino Buonvino.[9] Zapustas stopped the fight in the 10th round, giving the future champion Marciano a convincing TKO victory and preserving his unblemished record at 28-0. Marciano was not the only boxing legend to share a ring with Zapustas. Former champions Ezzard Charles, Kid Gavilan, Willie Pep, and Jose Torres all squared off in Zapustas's ring.[10] Zapustas also worked amateur bouts such as the 1965 Harvard Interhouse Championships.[11]

After his stint as coach at Stetson, Zapustas took on the role of athletic director at the school, a position he held for 25 years.[12] He also was the director of recreation for the city of Randolph from 1951 to 1991. They named its ice arena for him.[13] In 1972 Zapustas was inducted into the Massachusetts High School Hall of Fame.[14] And in 1979 he was enshrined in the Fordham Hall of Fame for his football and baseball exploits.[15] Zapustas passed away at the age of 93 on January 14,

ONE-HIT WONDERS

2001 in Randolph, survived by Barbara, their three sons, and a large extended family.[16]

Joe Zapustas may not be remembered in Cooperstown or Canton, but he was able to parlay his athletic prowess into a lifelong career in sports in the Massachusetts area. To some, he is best remembered as the first native Latvian to play in the major leagues, but his enduring legacy lies in the countless young athletes he helped nurture as a coach and administrator in his adopted hometown of Randolph, Massachusetts.

SOURCES

In addition to the works cited in the Notes, the author utilized Baseball-Reference.com and Pro-Football-Reference.com for statistical data and game notes.

NOTES

1. ancestry.com/family-tree/person/tree/114912740/person/260140206387/facts.
2. ancestry.com/interactive/6061/4311558-00833/68338664?backurl=https://www.ancestry.com/family-tree/person/tree/114912740/person/260140206387/facts/citation/820352585459/edit/record.
3. Fordham University vs. College of the Holy Cross Football Program, October 17, 1931: 4. Fordham University Libraries Digital Collections (accessed December 1, 2019 at digital.library.fordham.edu/digital/collection/p17265coll9/id/138.
4. George Rose, *One Hit Wonders: Baseball Stories* (Bloomington, Indiana: iUniverse, Inc., 2004), 6.
5. Rose, 6.
6. Rose, 7.
7. "Football at Fenway: Boston Shamrocks," fenwayparkdiaries.com/football/boston%20shamrocks.htm.
8. Rose, 7.
9. Bill Nowlin and Bob Brady, eds., *Braves Field: Memorable Moments at Boston's Lost Diamond* (Phoenix: SABR, 2015).
10. boxrec.com/en/referee/402184?offset=0 (Accessed December 28, 2019).
11. Steven L. Cotler, "Quincy Wins Interhouse Boxing," *Harvard Crimson*, March 12, 1965.
12. Rose, 7.
13. Rose, 7.
14. mhsfca.net/hall-of-fame-members.html (Accessed December 1, 2019).
15. fordhamsports.com/hof.aspx?hof=367 (Accessed December 28, 2019).
16. Obituaries, *Boston Globe*, January 27, 2001.

ED ZMICH

By Gregory H. Wolf

Stout left-hander Ed Zmich won only one big-league game, but for a few weeks in the summer of 1910, the Class-D hurler caught the attention of the baseball world, resulting in an unusually fierce bidding war.

Edward Albert Zmich was born on October 1, 1884, in Cleveland. His father, Max, emigrated from Germany in 1873 and married that same year Rosa Kronenbitter, herself a first-generation German-American, and together they raised seven children, five daughters and two sons, born between 1874 and 1890. Two other children died in childbirth; Edward was the fourth-oldest.[1] The elder's job as carpenter enabled the family to live modestly in their own home in the Brookside neighborhood of west Cleveland. According to US Census reports, young Ed completed six years of formal schooling.

A robust and rugged youth, Ed began playing baseball on the sandlots and lakefront diamonds in the rapidly expanding industrial city on Lake Erie. By the age of 20, the 6-foot, 185-pound southpaw had a reputation as a hard-throwing moundsman. He graduated to the competitive semipro league, and hurled for Cohen's Cutters in 1907 when he caught a break. According to one story, Jimmy Austin, third baseman for the Dayton Veterans of the Class-B Central League, who resided in Cleveland in the offseason and who knew Zmich, introduced the hurler to Angus Grant, player-manager of the South Bend Greens in the same league.[2] Green offered Zmich a tryout in 1908, and thus commenced the southpaw's career in Organized Baseball.[3] Suffering from bouts of wildness, his career-long bugaboo, Zmich lasted less than a month with the club before he was farmed out to the Danville Speakers in the Class-D Eastern Illinois League.[4] His statistics are unknown in a league racked by financial difficulties that caused it to disband on August 20 with the Speakers (themselves forced to relocate to Staunton in mid-July) declared the champions.[5]

In the offseason, the Grand Rapids Wolverines of the Class-B Central League acquired Zmich.[6] The left-hander's lack of control led to his trade after a brief look-see to the Marion Diggers of the Class-D Ohio State League for catcher Charles Lushing.[7] Zmich emerged as a workhorse, leading the circuit with 21 victories (15 defeats).

The turning point in Zmich's baseball career was 1910. Back with the Diggers, Zmich proved to be the league's best pitcher, and according to the sportswriter S.E. Gooden of *Marion Daily Mirror*, "had been followed constantly" by big-league scouts beginning in mid-June.[8] Included were scouts from the Cincinnati Reds and Dick Padden of the Washington Senators, as well as Heinie Peitz of the Louisville Colonels of the Double-A American Association; however, the St. Louis Browns and their scout Billy Doyle seemed to have an inside track. "Zmich is just what the major league clubs are looking for," opined the *Portsmouth Daily Times*, "a big southpaw with the goods. He has control, speed, good curves and above all a good head. His batting is also a valuable asset."[9]

Zmich responded to the additional pressure, tossing a no-hitter in the second game of a doubleheader against the Newark Newks on July 4, winning 6-2, seemingly unperturbed by his teammates' five errors leading to the pair of unearned runs, and also drove in three runs himself.[10] That performance drew even more scouts to the small Ohio towns to watch the league's pitching sensation.

Diggers skipper Joe Lewis decided to deliver the knockout blow and summoned all interested parties to Lancaster, where Zmich would be on display on Sunday afternoon, July 17, and announced that the club would finally accept an offer for its prized twirler. The scene in the small town of about 13,000 residents, 30 miles south of Columbus, must have been a who's who of bigwigs in baseball. Among those eyeballing Zmich were Hughie Jennings, skipper of the Detroit Tigers, and Pittsburgh Pirates scout Howard Earl. Browns owner Robert Hedges joined Doyle and scouts from at least four other teams.[11] A new entry in the Zmich sweepstakes was the St. Louis Cardinals, who sent player-skipper Roger Bresnahan into the fray. In a

ONE-HIT WONDERS

Ed Zmich, with the 1911 St. Louis Cardinals.

fairy-tale performance, Zmich blanked the Lanks, 3-0, fanning nine and driving in two runs,[12] leading to an old-fashioned bidding war that took place that evening at the Neil House Hotel in Columbus. One can imagine the cigar-smoke-filled room, where bidders dropped out one by one. Finally there were two left standing, and when Hedges bowed to Bresnahan, the Cardinals emerged as the unlikely victor with an offer of $4,000, considered then to be the highest bid for a player in league history.[13]

Zmich reported immediately to the Cardinals, a floundering franchise that had posted just two winning seasons since joining the NL in 1892 and had never finished higher than fourth (and had reached that just once). Team owner Stanley Robison cautioned fans not to expect much from either Zmich or pitcher Earl Hennis of the Central League Terre Haute Stags, whom the club had also acquired on Bresnahan's two-day scouting spree. "The signing of young players is a lottery," quipped Robison. "It doesn't appear to make any difference what price is paid for the players. If they make it, you're lucky."[14]

Not a ringing endorsement from your boss, but then again, Zmich was attempting a monumental jump from Class D to the big leagues. Six days after his acquisition, Zmich took the mound for the Cardinals on July 23 at Robison Field, the rickety wooden ballpark located at the intersection of Vandeventer and Natural Bridge Avenues on the north side of the Gateway City. According to the *St. Louis Post-Dispatch*, Zmich's debut "proved anything but a howling success," as the southpaw surrendered five runs on four hits, issued four walks, threw a wild pitch and balked in just three innings to be collared with the 9-2 loss against Christy Mathewson and the New York Giants.[15]

Zmich's season didn't get much better for the Redbirds who ultimately finished in seventh place with a pitching staff that ranked last in the majors in team ERA (3.78). After hurling five innings of one-run relief in the Redbirds' 9-4 loss to the Giants at the Polo Grounds, where he collected what proved to be his first and only big-league hit (a single off Hooks Wiltse), Zmich earned his third start of the season and tossed his maiden complete game in the second game of a twin bill against the Boston Doves at the South End Grounds in the Hub City on August 15. "Zmich suffered a terrific bombardment," opined the *St. Louis Star and Times,* adding, "Bresnahan evidently felt disposed to let Zmich get a good hard bumping."[16] The Doves clobbered Zmich for 14 hits; the hurler also uncorked three wild pitches and hit a batter, resulting

ONE-HIT WONDERS

in an 8-1 drubbing. Zmich saved his "best game" for his final appearance of the season, wrote the *Star and Times*, yielding just five hits, though he walked seven in a complete game in the second contest of a doubleheader against the Giants at the Polo Grounds on September 20.[17]

Zmich had the misfortune to be matched up against skipper John McGraw's ace, "Big Six" Mathewson, who punched out 10 and emerged victorious, 3-2. Zmich caused a minor brouhaha when he publicly alleged that the pitcher's mound at the Polo Grounds was doctored and saturated with oil (a claim that others had made before); and that Bresnahan, himself a former Giant, knew that, and therefore had threatened to levy a $10 fine on any Redbird hurler who tried to rub the ball in the dirt to get a better grip on the ball. Furthermore, Zmich claimed that the Giants hurlers were unaffected because they carried rosin.[18] With or without oil, Zmich lost all five of his decisions, posted a 6.25 ERA, and walked almost as many batters (29) as innings pitched (36).

When the Cardinals arrived in New Baden, Indiana, in February 1911 to immerse themselves in the hot mineral springs and prepare themselves for spring training there, skipper Bresnahan still believed that Zmich could develop into a starter.[19] Lumped together with three other southpaw recruits (Bunny Hearn, Lou Lowdermilk, and Earl Hennis), Zmich vied to replace the top left-handed starter, 14-game winner Johnny Lush, who had abruptly retired from baseball even though he was just 24 years old. In the end, none in that trio broke through. On April 25 Zmich made his season's debut, hurling three-hit ball over seven innings of mop-up duty, yielding three runs against the Pittsburgh Pirates at Robison Field. Despite the relatively effective outing, Zmich pitched only one more time before appearing in both games of a doubleheader on June 1 against the Cincinnati Reds in St. Louis. With the Cardinals trailing 5-0 after eight innings, Zmich pitched a scoreless ninth, though he hit a batter, in what appeared to be another mop-up outing, but the Redbirds stormed back to score six runs to win, giving Zmich his first big-league victory. He hurled the final 3⅔ innings, yielding two runs in the second game, a 6-4 loss. Two days later, the Cardinals released Zmich to the Louisville Colonels with the expectation that he'd be recalled.[20]

Zmich's tenure in the American Association lasted only three weeks before the club turned him over to the Chillicothe Infants of the Class-D Ohio State League, where he went 10-7.

Zmich's future in baseball was in doubt as spring training began in 1912. He did not report to the Infants, leading one sportswriter to wonder if he was "still on the docks in Cleveland."[21] Still the property of the Cardinals, Zmich was sold to the Chicago White Sox in April and assigned to the Springfield (Illinois) Senators. Zmich's stint in the Class-B Three-I League lasted about two months, during which he posted a 2-2 slate and logged 57 innings before he was released in late June.[22]

At the age of 27, Zmich's career in professional baseball was over just as his brother George's career seemed to commence. In 1913 George, a shortstop, was signed by Mike O'Neill, skipper of the Utica Utes of the Class-B New York-Penn League.[23] [It does not appear that George ever played a game in the minors.]

Ed Zmich was a lifelong resident of the west Cleveland neighborhood and never married. He held down various jobs, including dock worker, cook, and bartender. According to the 1940 Census, he lived with three of his siblings (also unmarried) at 2118 West 59th Street, which appears to be the same address where he was born. [He was born at 41 Purdy Street; in 1906 that street was renamed 59th Street].

Zmich died at the age of 65 on August 20, 1950. The cause was coronary thrombosis. He was buried at St. Mary's Cemetery, where his parents had also been interred.

SOURCES

In addition to the sources cited in the Notes, the author accessed Retrosheet.org, Baseball-Reference.com, the SABR Minor Leagues Database, accessed online at Baseball-Reference.com, SABR.org, *The Sporting News* archive via Paper of Record, the player's Hall of Fame file, newspapers via Newspaper.com, and Ancestry.com.

NOTES

1. According to the 1900 US Census.
2. "Austin Says that he Discovered Zmich," *Portsmouth (Ohio) Daily Times*, March 10, 1911: 11.
3. "Ed Zmich Cleveland Southpaw," *Akron Beacon Journal*, February 12, 1908: 2.
4. "Notes for the Fans," *Fort Wayne (Indiana) News*, April 27, 1908: 3.
5. Lloyd Johnson and Miles Wolff, eds., *The Encyclopedia of Minor League Baseball* (Durham, North Carolina: Baseball America, 1997), 160.
6. "Zmich Lands in Local Fold," *Marion (Ohio) Daily Mirror*, April 26, 1909: 6.
7. "Grand Rapids Club Trades for Lushing," *Marion Star*, April 26, 1908: 6.
8. S.E. Gooden, "Offer Big Money for Eddie Zmich," *Marion Daily Mirror*," July 2, 1910: 6.
9. "St. Louis After Big Ed Zmich," *Portsmouth Daily Times*, July 1, 1910: 13.

ONE-HIT WONDERS

10 "Marion and Newark Split Even Monday," *Marion Star*, July 5, 1910: 6.

11 "Scouts to Gather at Lancaster," *Chillicothe* (Ohio) *Gazette*, July 16, 1910: 3.

12 "Zmich Won His Own Game by Hitting Ball," *Marion Star*, July 18, 1910: 6.

13 "St. Louis National Get Pitcher Zmich," *Marion Star*, July 18, 1910: 6.

14 "Buying Talent Like Lottery, Says Robison," *St. Louis Post-Dispatch*, July 20, 1910: 9.

15 "Giants Worry Zmich in Bow as a Cardinal," *St. Louis Post-Dispatch*, July 24, 1910: 23.

16 "Doves Win Two from Cards," *St. Louis Star and Times*, August 16, 1910: 8.

17 "Giants Steal Ten Bases on J. Bliss," *St. Louis Star and Times*, September 21, 1910:8.

18 "Polo Pitching Box 'Doctored,'" *St. Louis Star and Times*, March 2, 1911: 7,

19 "Roger to Take Players South, if It Is Cold," *St. Louis Post-Dispatch*, January 18, 1911: 7.

20 "Cardinals Release Hearn and Zmich," *St. Louis Post-Dispatch*, June 4, 1911: 27.

21 "Where Is Zmich?" *Portsmouth Daily Times*, April 6, 1912: 10.

22 "Quincy Winner in Ten Innings," *Decatur* (Illinois) *Herald*, June 25, 1912: 4.

23 "State League Notes," *Wilkes-Barre* (Pennsylvania) *Record*, March 24, 1913: 4.

CONTRIBUTORS

Niall Adler is a longtime sports publicist with work at Long Beach State, Stanford, and with USA and Australian Baseball. He comes from a long line of writers and editors, dating back to his great-great-grandfather, Bill Cuddy, who was the editor of the *Oregonian*, along with a great-grandmother and both grandmothers who published works as well. He currently is the marketing and communications director at Mission College in Silicon Valley.

Malcolm Allen, a Baltimore-born Orioles fan, earned his journalism degree from the University of Maryland. He resides in Brooklyn, New York, with his wife, Sara, and daughters, Ruth and Martina. He enjoys pre-1980s Jamaican music and misses Memorial Stadium.

Jim Ball is a baseball fan of 70-plus years, first addicted via post-World War II radio broadcasts featuring the Texas League's Fort Worth Cats and Dallas Eagles. He joined SABR in 1994, during its 24th convention in his hometown of Arlington, Texas, which heightened his awareness of SABR's mission to capture and report all aspects of baseball's rich history. Jim enjoyed a 40-year-long journalism and public relations career, 30 as an executive of then Dr Pepper-Seven-Up Cos., Inc. For Frank Saucier's biography, Ernie Banks-Bobby Bragan DFW Chapter president and author, C. Paul Rogers, III, inspired Jim to research Saucier's brief career as a St. Louis Browns outfielder, minor-league phenom, and Silver Slugger winner. Coincidentally, Jim saw Frank play twice in 1950 as a San Antonio Mission in Fort Worth's long-gone LaGrave Field, and still has the scorecards. Because of the BioProject, he maintains a close relationship with his subject, who turned 95 in May 2021. They are completing their manuscript for a book revealing Frank's take on Browns owner Bill Veeck and his renowned stunt on August 19, 1951, when Frank was pulled for pinch-hitter, 3-feet-7, Eddie Gaedel. Jim roots for the Texas Rangers and Los Angeles Dodgers.

Dr. Henry Berman was a pediatrician who moved from New York to Spokane in 1981, where he became president of Group Health Northwest five years later, building the HMO into the largest in the Inland Northwest. He moved to Seattle in 2006 and practiced in adolescent medicine at Children's Hospital. Author of four books, he served on several national boards such as the American Board of Preventive Medicine. When he announced his retirement in 1998, he said, "It's not a coincidence that baseball season starts on my last day. I already have tickets to a Mariners game soon after that." An earlier SABR publication was in the 1989 *Baseball Research Journal*, the article co-authored with Jeremy Giller, "Hall of Fame Teams: Study in Paradox." Henry Berman died in February 2020.

Charlie Bevis is the author of seven books on baseball history, most recently *Red Sox vs. Braves in Boston: The Battle for Fans' Hearts, 1901-1952*. A member of SABR since 1984, he has contributed more than five dozen biographies to SABR's BioProject as well as several to SABR books, including *The 1967 Impossible Dream Red Sox* and *The Glorious Beaneaters of the 1890s*. He writes baseball from his home in Chelmsford, Massachusetts.

Richard Bogovich is the author of *Kid Nichols: A Biography of the Hall of Fame Pitcher* and *The Who: A Who's Who*, both published by McFarland & Co. He has contributed to such SABR books as *Pride of Smoketown: The 1935 Pittsburgh Crawfords* and *Bittersweet Goodbye: The Black Barons, the Grays, and the 1948 Negro League World Series*. He works for the Wendland Utz law firm in Rochester, Minnesota.

Ryan Brecker has been a SABR member since 2004 and is chair of the Luke Easter SABR Chapter. An emergency medicine physician by night; he lives in Penfield, New York, with his wife, Stephanie, and two daughters, Cadence and Quinn.

Alan Cohen has been a SABR member since 2010. He serves as vice president-treasurer of the Connecticut Smoky Joe Wood Chapter, is datacaster (MiLB First Pitch stringer) for the Hartford Yard Goats, the Double-A affiliate of the Colorado Rockies, and has been serving as head of SABR's fact-checking committee since December 13, 2020. His biographies, game stories, and essays have appeared in more

ONE-HIT WONDERS

than 50 SABR publications. Since his first *Baseball Research Journal* article appeared in 2013, Alan has continued to expand his research into the Hearst Sandlot Classic (1946-1965), from which 88 players advanced to the major leagues. Stan Johnson, a "one-hit wonder," appeared in the *San Francisco Examiner* games in 1953 and 1954 but was not selected to go to the Hearst Game in New York. Alan has four children and eight grandchildren and resides in Connecticut with his wife, Frances, their cats, Morty, Ava, and Zoe, and their dog, Buddy.

Mike Cooney: While I have never had the opportunity to swing a bat in a major league park, my baseball claim to fame came with my first base hit as a high school freshman. The opposing pitcher was a senior named Eddie Watt. My first two times at bat I struck out on three pitches – at least that is what the umpire said. I didn't see them. On my third at-bat, I tried to time Watt's first pitch from windup to called strike. On the second pitch I started to swing as Watt was in his windup. It worked. I was still late but was able to pop the ball over the first baseman's head for a single. Watt went on to pitch 10 years in the majors. I went on to get a master's degree in journalism. I retired from the Automotive industry after 40 years and from Ivy Tech Community College (Indiana) where I was an adjunct professor teaching English composition for 10 years. As a hobby, I have written over 500 *A Stones Throw* columns for our local newspaper. Now retired for the fourth time, my wife Jade, our two rescue German Shepherds, and I, live on a bluff overlooking the Ohio River.

Rory Costello has been a Mets fan since 1969 – which has meant enduring some lean periods, such as the early '90's, when one of his subjects in this volume appeared. Rory lives in Brooklyn, New York, with his wife, Noriko, and son, Kai.

Richard Cuicchi joined SABR in 1983 and is an active member of the Schott-Pelican Chapter. Since his retirement as an information technology executive, Richard authored *Family Ties: A Comprehensive Collection of Facts and Trivia about Baseball's Relatives*. He has contributed to numerous SABR BioProject and Games publications. He does freelance writing and blogging about a variety of baseball topics on his website, TheTenthInning.com. Richard lives in New Orleans with his wife, Mary.

Tim Deale is chairman of the Larry Doby Chapter of SABR. A native of Deale, Maryland, now residing in South Carolina, Tim is a contributor to BioProject and the Nineteenth Century Research Committee. A former sports talk show host in Annapolis, Maryland, he is currently writing books about baseball. Among the things he enjoys are researching statistics, old-time baseball, and making lists of the top players and pitchers in various categories. He learned about baseball at an early age listening to Baltimore Orioles games on the radio with his grandmother, and now wants to help preserve baseball history and pass it on to other generations. He would like to write/make a baseball documentary.

Max Effgen is a lifelong baseball fan born and raised in Chicago and currently living in Seattle. He is a graduate of the University of Michigan and the University of Washington. Max joined SABR after researching photos of Lefty Grove left to him from his grandfather. A consultant and entrepreneur by trade, he has also served baseball as a local Little League president, board director, and coach.

Brian Engelhardt is a native of Reading, Pennsylvania, where he resides with his wife, Suzanne, a good sport about any number of things. The author of *Reading's Big League Exhibition Games*, he has written several SABR biographies together with articles appearing in other SABR publications. He is also a regular contributor to *The Historical Review of Berks County* with his subjects covering various local matters of historical note, including baseball.
The collapse of the 1964 Phillies along with his mother throwing out his baseball cards about that time resulted in his emotional growth being stunted at age 13. Although he and Suzanne raised their three daughters as Phillies fans, his daughter living in Pittsburgh with her husband and two sons seems to also favor the Pirates (as evidenced by the picture of Bill Mazeroski in their family room). This has resulted in Brian, being a loving father and grandfather, developing a warm spot for the Buccos as well as the Phils.

Jeff English lives in Tallahassee, Florida, with his wife, Allison, two sons, Elliott and Oscar, and four cats. A graduate of Florida State University, he counts the Seminoles and the Chicago Cubs among his lifelong passions. He has contributed to multiple SABR projects.

ONE-HIT WONDERS

Brian Flaspohler is a retired manufacturing engineer. His baseball interests focus on ball players born in Missouri and any baseball history related to St. Louis. When not doing baseball research you can find him running the trails and byways around St. Louis.

Steve Friedman has been a SABR member since 1990. He has recently contributed articles for SABR publications and BioProject. He has resided in the Pacific Northwest since 1985 and has been a season-ticket holder of the Seattle Mariners since 1995. His youth was spent in the San Francisco Bay Area, where he followed his beloved Giants. Steve is currently retired after a career of over 35 years as an owner and operator of cable television systems.

Darren Gibson spent his Little League, Colt League, and high-school years in Lakewood, California, playing alongside multiple athletes who eventually made "The Show," but his baseball highlight was actually getting a "call-back" during walk-on tryouts at UCLA in the fall of 1988. Darren has been an avid baseball simulation player for decades, coached baseball and softball for his four children, and he still "bleeds Dodger blue." He has written over 20 SABR player biographies, and is currently a high-school math teacher and coach in San Juan Capistrano, California.

Tim Hagerty is the broadcaster for the Triple-A El Paso Chihuahuas and has called professional baseball games since 2004. He has broadcast two major-league games and has been heard nationally covering various sports for Fox Sports Radio and Westwood One. He's the author of one baseball book and of freelance articles for *The Sporting News*, *The Hardball Times*, and other publications. He resides in El Paso, Texas, with his wife, Heather, and son, Carson.

Tom Hawthorn is a writer who lives in Victoria, British Columbia. He wishes he'd had even one hit in the major leagues.

John Heeg received his degree in sociology/anthropology with a minor in secondary education in 2000 from Dowling College. he has a master's degree from Touro College in special education and a postgraduate certificate in school administration from Stony Brook University. Heeg contributed to *Scandal on the Southside: The 1919 Chicago White Sox* and has also contributed articles to historical and educational sites such as The Councilor for Social Studies, University of Kansas Medical Center, and simplek12. He lives on Long Island with his wife and son.

Paul Hofmann, a SABR member since 2002, is the associate vice president for international affairs at Sacramento State University and a frequent contributor to SABR publications. Paul is a native of Detroit and a lifelong Tigers fan. He currently resides in Folsom, California.

Mike Huber, a professor of mathematics at Muhlenberg College, joined SABR in 1996. That same year, he taught his first course in Sabermetrics at West Point. As an officer representative with the Army baseball team, over the next 10 years he often accompanied the team on its annual spring-break trip to Tampa, Florida. The team played on many fields in the Tampa Bay area, perhaps even at some of the same venues that third-string catcher and One-Hit Wonder Curly Onis played on.

Tara Krieger recalls the thrill of being close to a one-hit wonder herself, when she hit her only home run (a grand slam!) for her high-school softball team. After that, she realized she was better writing about sports than playing them. She has previously been on staff as a sportswriter at *Newsday* and as an editorial producer for MLB Advanced media. She currently works as an attorney for the City of New York and has been a member of SABR since 2005.

Gerard Kwilecki and his family reside near Mobile, Alabama, birthplace of five members of the National Baseball Hall of Fame. He is a native of Bainbridge, Georgia, and graduated from Valdosta State University. He is employed with the University of South Alabama and is a member of the Jaguar Dugout Club. He has been a member of SABR since 2015 and is a lifelong Atlanta Braves fan, his favorite player being Bob Horner.

Bob LeMoine is a librarian and adjunct professor in New Hampshire. A lifelong Red Sox fan, Bob has contributed to several SABR projects and was co-editor of two SABR books: *Boston's First Nine: the 1871-75 Boston Red Stockings*, and *The Glorious Beaneaters of the 1890s*.

Len Levin is a longtime newspaper editor in New England, now retired. He lives in Providence with his wife, Linda, and an overachieving orange cat. He now

ONE-HIT WONDERS

(Len, not the cat) is the grammarian for the Rhode Island Supreme Court and edits its decisions. He also copyedits many SABR books, including this one. He is just down the interstate from Fenway Park, where he has spent many happy hours.

Mitch Lutzke is a high-school teacher and track and field coach at Williamston (Michigan) High School. He has written for other SABR projects in addition to pieces in *Michigan History* magazine. His 2018 book, *The Page Fence Giants, A History of Black Baseball's Pioneering Champions,* won a Michigan Notable Book Award and a SABR Jerry Malloy Committee Robert Peterson Book Award. His baseball interests include Black baseball, 1800s-era baseball, the minor leagues, and all things Detroit Tigers. He is on the leadership board of the Southern Michigan SABR group. Mitch is also the president of the local Williamston museum and was recently inducted into his state's high-school Track and Field Coaches Hall of Fame. He is married with three children and resides in Williamston.

Mike Mattsey lives in Sacramento, California with his wife, Maia, and his son, Otis. He has a bachelor's degree from Indiana University and a master's from Indiana State University. He enjoys reading and writing about baseball's glorious history and has contributed to several SABR works. He enjoys collecting baseball cards and memorabilia, particularly pieces featuring his beloved Chicago Cubs. His favorite baseball moments include Game Seven of the 2016 World Series, bringing his father and son to Wrigley Field to watch the World Series flag being raised over the field the following spring, and managing his son's Little League team to the 2018 championship.

Chad Moody is a nearly lifelong Detroit-area resident, where he has been a fan of the Detroit Tigers from birth. An alumnus of the University of Michigan and Michigan State University, he has spent 30 years working in the automotive industry. From his humble beginning of having a letter published in *Baseball Digest* as a teenager, Chad has since contributed to numerous SABR and Professional Football Researchers Association projects. He and his wife, Lisa, live in Northville, Michigan, with their dog, Daisy.

Jack V. Morris is the head of a large pharmaceutical company's research library. He lives in suburban Philadelphia with his wife and is the father of two adult daughters. His baseball biographies have appeared in numerous books including *The Team That Forever Changed Baseball and America* (1947 Brooklyn Dodgers) and *Scandal on the Southside* (1919 Chicago White Sox). He is not the Jack Morris of World Series fame but, every once in a great while, wishes he was.

Bill Nowlin only ever had one base hit in a major-league ballpark. At a charity baseball game at Fenway Park in 2002, he popped up to the shortstop, then shot a couple of foul balls into the seats in left but popped up to third base. His third time up, he lined a clean single between short and third and into left field. Apparently any scouts at the park lost his contact information so he continued his work at Rounder Records and, to fill the void as his playing career stalled out, started writing for SABR after that year's SABR convention in Boston with *The Fenway Project*, co-edited with Cecilia Tan.

Tony S. Oliver is a native of Puerto Rico currently living in Sacramento, California, with his wife and daughter. While he works as a Six Sigma professional, his true love is baseball and he cheers for both the Red Sox and whoever happens to be playing the Yankees. He is fascinated by baseball cards and is currently researching the evolution of baseball tickets. He believes there is no prettier color than the vibrant green of a freshly mown grass on a baseball field.

Len Pasculli is a retired lawyer and adjunct college professor born in one of baseball's alleged birthplaces, Hoboken, New Jersey. He has been a member of SABR since 2001. He played at Mets Dream Camp (Port St. Lucie, Florida) in 2001 and Yankees Fantasy Camp (Tampa, Florida) in 2013, and now he plays over-60 Senior Softball. Besides writing for SABR's BioProject, playing pickleball, and pulling out his remaining curly hair while managing his Rotisserie League baseball teams, Len enjoys cooking and traveling with his wife Jan — whom he met at Penn State and married in 1977 — and spending time with their children and grandchildren.

A productive and energetic member of SABR, **Chris Rainey** passed away in 2020. He was introduced to the world of baseball research by former SABR President Eugene Murdoch around 1976. He was active in BioProject as an author and also head of the fact-checking team. An avid Cleveland Indians fan,

ONE-HIT WONDERS

he had pictures of all but 12 of the teams from 1901 to 2019.

Alan Raylesberg is an attorney in New York City. He is a lifelong baseball fan who enjoys baseball history and roots for the Yankees and the Mets. Alan also has a strong interest in baseball analytics and is a devotee of baseball simulation games, participating in both draft leagues and historical replays. Alan has written a number of articles for SABR, including other biographies. Before going to law school, Alan was the sports director of his college radio station and dreamed of a career in sports broadcasting or journalism. Now, after many years practicing law, he is grateful for the opportunity that SABR has provided to allow him to realize at least some of that dream from many years ago.

Carl Riechers retired from United Parcel Service in 2012 after 35 years of service. With more free time, he became a SABR member that same year. Born and raised in the suburbs of St. Louis, he became a big fan of the Cardinals. He and his wife, Janet, have three children and he is the proud grandpa of two.

Joel Rippel, a Minnesota native and a graduate of the University of Minnesota, is the author or co-author of 10 books on Minnesota sports history and has contributed as a writer or editor to several SABR publications.

Benjamin Sabin is a writer for Last Word On Baseball, editor-in-chief of Cheap Seats Press, and a baseball card artist. He enjoys keeping score at ballgames and prefers sauerkraut on his dogs. He is a proud SABR member since 2017.

Dan Schoenholz is community development director for the City of Fremont, California; in that role, he oversees the city department in which Emil Mailho worked as a building inspector in the 1960s. While this is Dan's first contribution to a SABR book, his baseball-themed fiction has appeared in *Aethlon, the Journal of Sport Literature*; he has written accounts of baseball road trips for the *San Jose Mercury News* travel section; and his crossword puzzles, often peppered with baseball-related entries, are published regularly in the *New York Times* and *Los Angeles Times*.

Joe Schuster is the author of the baseball novel *The Might Have Been* (Ballantine) and two baseball-related titles in Gemma Media's series of books for adult literacy programs, *One Season in the Sun*, and *Jackie Robinson*. He has contributed to numerous SABR books, including *20-Game Winners*, *Bridging Two Dynasties*, *Sweet 60*, and *Drama and Pride in the Gateway City,* among others. A lifelong St. Louis Cardinals fan, he is married, the father of five, and the grandfather to three, all of whom share his passion for the Redbirds.

Peter Seidel has been a member of SABR since 2014. A lifelong Yankee fan, Pete grew up in southern Westchester County a short ride from the Stadium. After earning a master's degree from Harvard University, Pete relocated to the Dallas-Fort Worth area with his two children for his day job as business development executive for AT&T. Pete has contributed to several SABR books starting with the Mike Sandlock book in 2016 as well as many articles to the SABR Baseball Games Project. Aside from being a diehard Yankee fan, Pete enjoys spending time with his teenage kids, bicycling, hiking, kayaking, and playing guitar in whatever spare time he has.

Bill Staples Jr. of Chandler, Arizona, has a passion for researching and telling the untold stories of the "international pastime." A SABR member since 2006, he includes among his areas of expertise Japanese American and Negro Leagues baseball history as a context for exploring the themes of civil rights, cross-cultural relations, and globalization. He is the author of *Kenichi Zenimura, Japanese American Baseball Pioneer* (McFarland, 2011), and co-author with Kazuo Sayama of *Gentle Black Giants: A History of Negro Leaguers in Japan (*NBRP Press, 2019). His other works are listed on his blog at zenimura.com. Staples is also a one-hit-wonder himself. In 2003, he went 1-for-3 against former major-league pitcher Bill "Spaceman" Lee in a baseball camp at Dodgertown, in Vero Beach, Florida.

Clayton Trutor holds a Ph.D. in US history from Boston College and teaches at Norwich University. He is the state chairman of SABR Vermont and is the author of *Loserville: How Professional Sports Remade Atlanta – and How Atlanta Remade Professional Sports* (University of Nebraska Press, 2021). He'd love to hear from you on Twitter: @ClaytonTrutor

Eric Vickrey is a lifelong baseball fan and frequent contributor to SABR's BioProject. He is an emergency medicine physician assistant and lives in Seattle,

ONE-HIT WONDERS

Washington, with his wife, Gina. As a Cardinals fan since childhood, attending Game Six of the 2011 World Series is his favorite baseball memory, and he looks forward to the day the Mariners finally bring a championship to the Pacific Northwest.

Bob Webster grew up in northwestern Indiana and has been a Cubs fan since 1963. After relocating in 1980 to Portland, Oregon, Bob spends his time working on baseball research and writing and is a contributor to quite a few SABR projects. He worked as a stats stringer on the MLB Gameday app for three years, is a member of the Pacific Northwest Chapter of SABR, and is on the board of directors of the Old-Timers Baseball Association of Portland.

Phil Williams, of Oreland, Pennsylvania, sometimes wonders if he ever could have managed just one hit off major-league pitching. Then he recalls his Little League career and such whimsy quickly fades. Thankfully, he finds solace in studying the Deadball Era, focusing upon Philadelphia-based teams.

Gregory H. Wolf was born in Pittsburgh, but now resides in the Chicagoland area with his wife, Margaret, and daughter, Gabriela. A professor of German studies and holder of the Dennis and Jean Bauman Endowed Chair in the Humanities at North Central College in Naperville, Illinois, he has edited more than a dozen books for SABR. He is currently working on projects about Shibe Park in Philadelphia and Ebbets Field in Brooklyn. Since January 2017 he has been co-director of SABR's BioProject, which you can follow on Facebook and Twitter.

Jack Zerby has always enjoyed researching and writing about the unsung accomplishments of ballplayers who, for one reason or another, had obscure careers in the majors. The story of Roger McKee is a perfect example and working with his family to develop details was a true pleasure. Jack joined SABR in 1994, but it wasn't until the Baseball Biography Project was formed in 2002 that he found a perfect niche for his research and writing interests. Now retired from a career as an attorney and trusts/estates administrator, Jack and SABR colleague Mel Poplock co-founded the Seymour-Mills chapter in southwest Florida. Jack and his wife, Diana, live in Brevard, North Carolina, close enough to historic McCormick Field in Asheville to enjoy a Tourists game now and then.

Don Zminda has been a White Sox fan since attending his first game at Old Comiskey in August of 1954. As director of publications for STATS, Inc. (now STATS Perform) from 1988 to 2000, he co-authored or edited a dozen annual sports publications. Don's book *The Legendary Harry Caray: Baseball's Greatest Salesman* was a 2019 CASEY Award nominee; his latest offering, *Double Plays and Double Crosses: The Black Sox and Baseball in 1920*, was published by Rowman & Littlefield in March 2021. A SABR member since 1979, he is retired and has lived in Los Angeles with his wife, Sharon, since 2000.

SABR Books on the Negro Leagues and Black Baseball

From Rube to Robinson: SABR's Best Articles on Black Baseball

From Rube to Robinson brings together the best Negro League baseball scholarship that the Society of American Baseball Research (SABR) has ever produced, culled from its journals, Biography Project, and award-winning essays. The book includes a star-studded list of scholars and historians, from the late Jerry Malloy and Jules Tygiel, to award winners Larry Lester, Geri Strecker, and Jeremy Beer, and a host of other talented writers. The essays cover topics ranging over nearly a century, from 1866 and the earliest known Black baseball championship, to 1962 and the end of the Negro American League.

Edited by John Graf; Associate Editors Duke Goldman and Larry Lester
$24.95 paperback (ISBN 978-1-970159-41-7)
$9.99 ebook (ISBN 978-1-970159-40-0)
8.5"X11", 220 pages

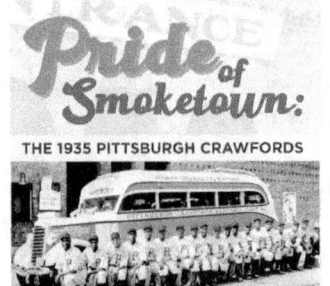

Pride of Smoketown: The 1935 Pittsburgh Crawfords

The 1935 Pittsburgh Crawfords team, one of the dominant teams in Negro League history, is often compared to the legendary 1927 "Murderer's Row" New York Yankees. The squad from "Smoketown"—a nickname that the *Pittsburgh Courier* often applied to the metropolis better-known as "Steel City"—boasted four Hall-of-Fame players in outfielder James "Cool Papa" Bell, first baseman/manager Oscar Charleston, catcher Josh Gibson, and third baseman William "Judy" Johnson. This volume contains exhaustively-researched articles about the players, front office personnel, Greenlee Field, and the exciting games and history of the team that were written and edited by 25 SABR members. The inclusion of historical photos about every subject in the book helps to shine a spotlight on the 1935 Pittsburgh Crawfords, who truly were the Pride of Smoketown.

Edited by Frederick C. Bush and Bill Nowlin
$29.95 paperback (ISBN 978-1-970159-25-7)
$9.99 ebook (ISBN 978-1-970159-24-0)
8.5"X11", 340 pages, over 60 photos

The Newark Eagles Take Flight: The Story of the 1946 Negro League Champions

The Newark Eagles won only one Negro National League pennant during the franchise's 15-year tenure in the Garden State, but the 1946 squad that ran away with the NNL and then triumphed over the Kansas City Monarchs in a seven-game World Series was a team for the ages. The returning WWII veterans composed a veritable "Who's Who in the Negro Leagues" and included Leon Day, Larry Doby, Monte Irvin, and Max Manning, as well as numerous role players. Four of the Eagles' stars—Day, Doby, Irvin, and player/manager Raleigh "Biz" Mackey, as well as co-owner Effa Manley—have been enshrined in the National Baseball Hall of Fame in Cooperstown. In addition to biographies of the players, co-owners, and P.A. announcer, there are also articles about Newark's Ruppert Stadium, Leon Day's Opening Day no-hitter, a sensational midseason game, the season's two East-West All-Star Games, and the 1946 Negro League World Series between the Eagles and the renowned Kansas City Monarchs.

Edited by Frederick C. Bush and Bill Nowlin
$24.95 paperback (ISBN 978-1-970159-07-3)
$9.99 ebook (ISBN 978-1-970159-06-6)
8.5"X11", 228 pages, over 60 photos

Bittersweet Goodbye: The Black Barons, The Grays, and the 1948 Negro League World Series

This book was inspired by the last Negro League World Series ever played and presents biographies of the players on the two contending teams in 1948—the Birmingham Black Barons and the Homestead Grays—as well as the managers, the owners, and articles on the ballparks the teams called home. Also included are articles that recap the season's two East-West All-Star Games, the Negro National League and Negro American League playoff series, and the World Series itself. Additional context is provided in essays about the effects of baseball's integration on the Negro Leagues, the exodus of Negro League players to Canada, and the signing away of top Negro League players, specifically Willie Mays. Many of the players' lives and careers have been presented to a much greater extent than previously possible.

Edited by Frederick C. Bush and Bill Nowlin
$21.95 paperback (ISBN 978-1-943816-55-2)
$9.99 ebook (ISBN 978-1-943816-54-5)
8.5"X11", 442 pages, over 100 photos and images

Friends of SABR

You can become a Friend of SABR by giving as little as $10 per month or by making a one-time gift of $1,000 or more. When you do so, you will be inducted into a community of passionate baseball fans dedicated to supporting SABR's work.

Friends of SABR receive the following benefits:
- ✓ Annual Friends of SABR Commemorative Lapel Pin
- ✓ Recognition in This Week in SABR, SABR.org, and the SABR Annual Report
- ✓ Access to the SABR Annual Convention VIP donor event
- ✓ Invitations to exclusive Friends of SABR events

SABR On-Deck Circle - $10/month, $30/month, $50/month

Get in the SABR On-Deck Circle, and help SABR become the essential community for the world of baseball. Your support will build capacity around all things SABR, including publications, website content, podcast development, and community growth.

A monthly gift is deducted from your bank account or charged to a credit card until you tell us to stop. No more email, mail, or phone reminders.

  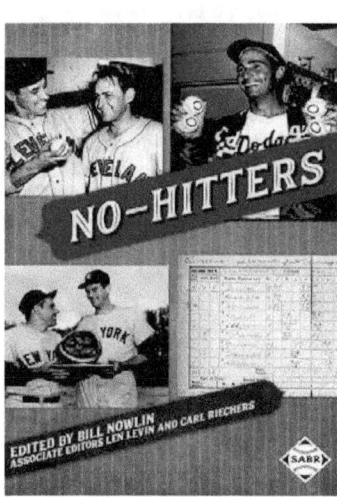

Join the SABR On-Deck Circle

Payment Info: _____ Visa _____ Mastercard

Name on Card: _____

Card #: _____

Exp. Date: _____ Security Code: _____

Signature: _____

○ $10/month

○ $30/month

○ $50/month

○ Other amount _____

Go to sabr.org/donate to make your gift online

Society for American Baseball Research
Cronkite School at ASU
555 N. Central Ave. #416, Phoenix, AZ 85004
602.496.1460 (phone)
SABR.org

Become a SABR member today!

If you're interested in baseball — writing about it, reading about it, talking about it — there's a place for you in the Society for American Baseball Research.

SABR memberships are available on annual, multi-year, or monthly subscription basis. Annual and monthly subscription memberships auto-renew for your convenience. Young Professional memberships are for ages 30 and under. Senior memberships are for ages 65 and older. Student memberships are available to currently enrolled middle/high school or full-time college/university students. Monthly subscription members receive SABR publications electronically and are eligible for SABR event discounts after 12 months.

Here's a list of some of the key benefits you'll receive as a SABR member:

- Receive two editions (spring and fall) of the *Baseball Research Journal*, our flagship publication
- Receive expanded e-book edition of *The National Pastime*, our annual convention journal
- 8-10 new e-books published by the SABR Digital Library, all FREE to members
- "This Week in SABR" e-newsletter, sent to members every Friday
- Join dozens of research committees, from Statistical Analysis to Women in Baseball.
- Join one of 70+ regional chapters in the U.S., Canada, Latin America, and abroad
- Participate in online discussion groups
- Ask and answer baseball research questions on the SABR-L e-mail listserv
- Complete archives of *The Sporting News* dating back to 1886 and other research resources
- Promote your research in "This Week in SABR"
- Diamond Dollars Case Competition
- Yoseloff Scholarships

- Discounts on SABR national conferences, including the SABR National Convention, the SABR Analytics Conference, Jerry Malloy Negro League Conference, Frederick Ivor-Campbell 19th Century Conference, and the Arizona Fall League Experience
- Publish your research in peer-reviewed SABR journals
- Collaborate with SABR researchers and experts
- Contribute to Baseball Biography Project or the SABR Games Project
- List your new book in the SABR Bookshelf
- Lead a SABR research committee or chapter
- Networking opportunities at SABR Analytics Conference
- Meet baseball authors and historians at SABR events and chapter meetings
- 50% discounts on paperback versions of SABR e-books
- Discounts with other partners in the baseball community
- SABR research awards

We hope you'll join the most passionate international community of baseball fans at SABR! Check us out online at SABR.org/join.

SABR MEMBERSHIP FORM

	Standard	Senior	Young Pro.	Student
Annual:	❏ $65	❏ $45	❏ $45	❏ $25
3 Year:	❏ $175	❏ $129	❏ $129	
5 Year:	❏ $249			
Monthly:	❏ $6.95	❏ $4.95	❏ $4.95	

(International members wishing to be mailed the Baseball Research Journal should add $10/yr for Canada/Mexico or $19/yr for overseas locations.)

Participate in Our Donor Program!
Support the preservation of baseball research. Designate your gift toward:
❏ General Fund   ❏ Endowment Fund   ❏ Research Resources   ❏ _____
❏ I want to maximize the impact of my gift; do not send any donor premiums
❏ I would like this gift to remain anonymous.
Note: Any donation not designated will be placed in the General Fund.
SABR is a 501 (c) (3) not-for-profit organization & donations are tax-deductible to the extent allowed by law.

Name _____

E-mail* _____

Address _____

City _____ ST _____ ZIP _____

Phone _____ Birthday _____

Your e-mail address on file ensures you will receive the most recent SABR news.

Dues $ _____
Donation $ _____
Amount Enclosed $ _____

Do you work for a matching grant corporation? Call (602) 496-1460 for details.

If you wish to pay by credit card, please contact the SABR office at (602) 496-1460 or sign up securely online at SABR.org/join. We accept Visa, Mastercard & Discover.

Do you wish to receive the *Baseball Research Journal* electronically? ❏ Yes   ❏ No
Our e-books are available in PDF, Kindle, or EPUB (iBooks, iPad, Nook) formats.

Mail to: SABR, Cronkite School at ASU, 555 N. Central Ave. #416, Phoenix, AZ 85004

www.ingramcontent.com/pod-product-compliance
Lightning Source LLC
Chambersburg PA
CBHW081343070526
44578CB00005B/703